KNOWING WOMAN

the text of this book is pri
on 100% recycled

KNOWING WOMAN

A Feminine Psychology

by

Irene Claremont de Castillejo

HARPER COLOPHON BOOKS

HARPER & ROW, PUBLISHERS

New York · Evanston · San Francisco · London

ACKNOWLEDGEMENTS

Some of the sections of this book have been published in pamphlet form by The Guild of Pastoral Psychology, and others have appeared in Harvest, the annual publication of the Jungian Analytical Psychology Club, London, with whose kind permission they are reprinted here.

Robert Frost's poem 'Escapist - Never' is quoted from The Poetry of Robert Frost *edited by Edward Connery Lathem by permission of Jonathan Cape Ltd and Holt, Rinehart and Winston, Inc. Copyright © 1962 by Robert Frost. Copyright © 1969 by Holt, Rinehart and Winston, Inc. The extract from Christopher Fry's play* The Dark is Light Enough *is quoted by permission of the Oxford University Press.*

A hardcover edition was originally published by
G. P. Putnam's Sons in 1973. It is here reprinted by
arrangement.

First HARPER COLOPHON edition published 1974.

STANDARD BOOK NUMBER: 06–090349–x

PREFACE

I describe here what I have learned of woman's present psychology. Perhaps I am only describing myself. But in twenty years as a Jungian analyst I have been concerned by the break-up of marriages, by misunderstandings between man and man, and between men and women. I have tried to follow the psychology of different kinds of women and their effects on men, and I have wondered about our personal as well as our collective responsibility for the state of society around us.

Women are today face to face with some unforeseen consequences of their new equality with men.

May 1967   I. C. de C.

CONTENTS

I

Meeting

THE OTHER DAY a friend asked me a question which set me thinking. 'Is it exhausting to listen and talk to people all day?' I answered as anyone else might have done. 'Sometimes very exhausting, sometimes not at all.'

Then I began to wonder on what this question of fatigue depended. Certainly not on the amount I personally put out. It almost seemed at first sight as though it were an inverse ratio. One is often less tired when one contributes a lot to a conversation than if one is a passive listener.

As I considered actual conversations with other persons, not only those in working hours, I began to realize that the question was not one of fatigue or lack of fatigue, but rather of fatigue or refreshment.

And suddenly it was so clear and obvious that I could not imagine why I had not seen it before. We are only exhausted when talking to other people if we do not meet them, when one or both of us are hiding behind screens.

On the rare occasions when we are fortunate enough to meet someone, there is no question of fatigue. Both are refreshed, for something has happened. It is as though a door had opened, and life suddenly takes on new meaning.

Why is it then that we meet so seldom? The curious thing is that we spend our lives not meeting people. All day we mix with others, in the bus, in shops, at work or play; but it may be that not once in the course of days or weeks or months do we meet any one of these people in such a way that a vibration is set up between the two. Nothing happens.

After the business of the day we go home and join our families, where it is quite easy for the various members to rub alongside one another without meeting each other at all, and without anybody noticing the fact.

Meetings are of course on various levels. There are meetings of the body and meetings of the mind; meetings in realms of the intellect and during the companionship of daily living or working together. Meetings can be of every conceivable degree of closeness or duration, on one level only or on all at once. There can be meetings of mystical spiritual intensity. But on no level does mere physical proximity or mutual exchange of ideas necessarily constitute a meeting. Frequently husbands and wives have the closest physical intimacy for years and yet have no real meeting. Each is wrapped away in an isolation of his own.

For there to be a meeting, it seems as though a third, a something else, is always present. You may call it Love, or the Holy Spirit. Jungians would say that it is the presence of the Self. If this 'Other' is present, there cannot have failed to be a meeting.

Duration has nothing to do with it. Nor have common interests. The touch of a hand may suffice. I can recall some conversations with total strangers which have never lost their flavour because in some inexplicable way there had for a little while been a real meeting.

I have never forgotten the smile of a bus conductor as I alighted from a bus at the age of twenty. It was a smile shared. We never saw one another again, nor needed to, but for a few seconds we really met. I have written a little poem about it:

> A million footprints
> On solitary sand
>   Are washed away,
> Yet the fragrance of a smile
> Between a bus conductor
> And a girl alighting
> Has lingered in the air
> Full forty years.

Even in as brief a meeting as that, some infinitesimal but indestructible thing has been added to the whole atmosphere.

This something which springs into being at every real meeting is not identical with sympathy. Sympathy can be resented, it can even be harmful, tearing down the banner of courage held high. But a meeting can never harm. It adds another banner to that already flying.

This something which springs into being is more than thoughts shared. (It can be devastating to be asked what one is thinking.) Sharing is on a different level altogether. It brings people together and helps them to grow in the same direction. Some sharing is required for any lasting relationship; but sharing is not in itself what I am talking about, nor is relationship. I am talking of the capacity to meet and to be met. Such meetings, from time to time, are the essential growing points in any live relationship, but they may also happen where the term relationship could hardly be used.

It is possible, I am sure, for more than two people to meet at the same time. The happening of a presence may occur between three, or perhaps even four. 'When two or three are gathered together in My Name, there shall I be.' This is probably the same Presence, as in meetings between two, of which I have already spoken.

The modern emphasis on relationships between only two people can sometimes degenerate into mere exclusiveness and a self-conscious sharing which, valuable though it is, may become an infringement of privacy, or an abuse of intimacy. Deliberate sharing is sometimes as dangerous as sympathy. New ideas which are forming in the depths of the mind can actually be destroyed or crippled by being shared too soon. It is like dragging a baby from the womb before it is ready to be born, or digging up a bulb to watch the sprouting of the roots. Respect for another person's privacy is as important as sharing thoughts. The deepest communication will in any case take place in moments of silence.

Sometimes I wonder if it is wise to work directly at relationship. What matters is to be centred oneself, willing and ready, always ready for the moments or hours of meeting when they come. Then the relationship can be trusted to take care of itself.

Every time, I think, it is one's own attitude, not the relationship, on which one needs to work. It is a fact that in any partnership, if one of the partners becomes quite clear *in himself* what it is that the situation requires, the chances are it will not even be necessary to voice it; the other will somehow pick up the point and comply, with no words said. Internal clarity anywhere seems to have the effect of an invisible guiding force which can be trusted to affect not only personal relationships, but outer situations. For the person who has achieved inner clarity, new paths appear and doors open without the need to knock.

I think unwillingness to be met is the element which is so often left out in our thinking. Women in particular, who know that relationship is primarily their concern, try to bring everything out into the open. But if a man is unwilling to be met he feels a victim. So does a woman when she is urged to express what she cannot formulate, even if she would. Such attempts at forcible sharing effect no magic.

In the analytical hour one has an unusual opportunity of noticing this phenomenon of meeting. Analyst and patient do not always meet. If the analyst is exhausted after an hour he may be quite sure that he has failed to meet his patient. He may have been too active, pouring himself out when it was not required. He may have been too passive, feeling the vitality sucked out of him against his will. In neither case will there have been that dynamic meeting which engenders healing.

Willingness to be met on the part of the analyst, no less than on that of the patient, is essential. Sometimes the analyst is unwilling to dive deep enough to meet the submerged patient, the refusal being a sound instinct for self-preservation. Sometimes he may be unduly afraid to follow into the obscure and diverse paths to which a patient beckons him. But in either case there is no meeting, and no healing. It is only the moments of true meeting which open the door to an illumination that heals, and refreshes both patient and analyst alike.

Exactly the same kind of situation exists in daily life. How is it then that we fail to meet so often?

There seem to be three main reasons. The first is that we are often living on a different level of awareness from the other person. The second is that one of us at least is often playing a role, or is somehow possessed. And the third is that we fail to listen to each other. I will deal with these three barriers in this order.

I think it helps us to understand the problem of meeting if we realize that all the time, whether we are men or women, we are living on several distinct levels of awareness. In particular there is a very clear difference between the focused consciousness of mankind, and a diffuse awareness which has not been fully appreciated.

Focused consciousness has emerged over thousands of years from the unconscious, and is still emerging. All our education is an attempt to produce and sharpen it in order to give us power to look at things and analyse them into their component parts, in order to give us the ability to formulate ideas, and the capacity to change, invent, create. It is this focused consciousness which we are all using in the everyday world all the time. Without it there would have been no culture and no scientific discoveries.

It is however not the only kind of consciousness. Most children are born with and many women retain, a diffuse awareness of the wholeness of nature, where everything is linked with everything else and they feel themselves to be part of an individual whole. It is from this layer of the psyche which is not yet broken into parts that come the wise utterances of children. Here lies the wisdom of artists, and the words and parables of prophets, spoken obliquely so that only those who have ears to hear can hear and the less mature will not be shattered.

If we realize that on the whole the basic masculine attitude to life is that of focus, division and change; and the feminine (in either sex) is more nearly an attitude of acceptance, an awareness of the unity of all life and a readiness for relationship, then we can accept a rough division of the psyche into masculine and feminine. But today, when masculine and feminine characteristics are so interwoven in people of both sexes, it may be clearer to speak of 'focused consciousness' on the one hand and 'diffuse awareness' on the other, knowing that these qualities belong to both men and women in varying degrees.

It is important to remember, however, that diffuse awareness more commonly pertains to women. From early life the small girl tends to delight in everything that concerns life and living while the small boy shows passionate interest in what makes the wheels go round, or why the kettle steams when it boils. Wheels and possible uses of steam usually leave little girls cold. Similarly most women feel akin to trees and running water, and have a sense of belonging under a night sky, and all of them are linked with the rhythm of the moon. It is men who want to go there and explore its extinct volcanoes. However, the man in love will have been temporarily inspired by the realm of diffuse awareness and may perhaps voice it later in a poem. The woman who looks through the telescope will for the time being have her mind clearly focused and may even write a scientific treatise.

Unfortunately, while we are standing on one level, the other seems such nonsense that we tend to repudiate it wholly. It is a real dilemma. I offend my head or I offend my heart. And always it is one's heart which finds itself in the greater dilemma, as this is the sphere which ordinarily has no voice. This problem of different levels is not confined to communication between different people.

There is a constant lack of harmony within the mind of the same person. How often one argues with oneself, because the two inner voices cannot meet. What, for instance, should I do when a beggar comes to my door? 'Give help,' says one voice. 'Don't be a fool,' says the other. 'I can't possibly slam the door in his face,' says the first voice. 'You are only encouraging vagrancy,' says the second. The two truths do not coincide. They often do not even impinge on one another.

Those who are able to stand firmly on the basis of rational common sense will shut the door in the beggar's face, more or less politely, convinced that the slight, just discernible twinges of guilt at their own lack of charity are signs of childish sentiment which they should have outgrown long ago. This is the attitude of our masculine culture, the fruit of our focused consciousness: a fruit we have won at the cost of hardening our hearts. But for those who are aware that all life is one, and that what is done to any is done to all, it is inconceivable to refuse the beggar.

This diffuse level is where children live, until we educate them out of it, educate them to be more sensible. However, any adult who lives solely on this diffuse level comes near to being like the Idiot in Dostoievsky's novel. The Idiot returning, as a young man, to normal society after years of insanity, sees life with the simplicity of a child, and in every situation reacts with a direct and frank naïveté which shows up the edifice that society has built in its stark hypocrisy. Dostoievsky's Idiot faithfully portrays the feminine sphere of acceptance without any masculine discrimination whatsoever. With the innocence of a child he knows no boundaries for love and sees no sense in hiding truth. He leaps over wire fences, heedless of their warning barbs. His willingness to meet and to be met is unconditional. The havoc he causes brings his world crashing about his ears, and his only hope is to take refuge in insanity once more.

Focused consciousness and diffuse awareness are not only impotent to convince one another, they can even become mutually destructive. Over awareness of diffuse feminine values may paralyse us and make action impossible in the outer world. On the other hand a too focused consciousness may render the wisdom from the feminine layer of our psyche invisible, and burn it up with too bright a flame. As I write, a beautiful many-coloured butterfly has alighted upon my reading lamp, fallen and died. This is what happens to diffuse awareness.

Unfortunately education does not help us. The sensitive boy, aware of things beneath the surface, finds from the moment he goes to school, that his innate wisdom is not honoured. He will hide it away first from his fellows to avoid their scoffing, and finally from himself.

The girl, often taught by women who have more interest in ideas than experience of living, has hard work to keep hold of her innate femininity. Success at school depends on devoting her time and energy to masculine pursuits; a good job may demand a university degree. It is a path which she gladly treads because it has been denied her so long. But the feminine layer of diffuse awareness can very easily be submerged, and if it is lost, the ability to meet and allow herself to be met in later life is rendered much more difficult.

How can a woman live out her masculine side and at the same time be her own feminine self?

I know one young married woman who was sufficiently alive to this problem to detect that the irritation between herself and her husband, after her long day's work in an office, was not due to fatigue alone. She arranged to get home from work a good hour before her husband so that she had a breathing space in which to throw off her masculine side, and collect her more feminine self before he came in. When it was not possible to get home early she asked her husband to delay his own return. He then spent the hour in a pub reading the paper. I am not advocating this as a solution, but the effect of this odd arrangement was miraculous. Irritable evenings vanished.

The whole question of being there to be met, of being really present, is extraordinarily subtle. The trouble begins when two people are trying to communicate, unaware that they are speaking from different levels. They may, for instance, be discussing the use of nuclear weapons. The one who is on the level of focused consciousness will argue quite rationally about the possibility of agreement between Russia and the West, and the futility of consenting to the suspension of tests or disarmament without control. While the one who is at that moment on the level of diffuse awareness will be in despair. 'Can't you see the criminal stupidity of the whole thing? Who cares whether Russia or China may play us false? The lives of posterity are at stake — we should refuse to have anything to do with nuclear arms here and now, whatever anyone else does. Can't you see?'

No, he can't. He will begin arguing about the possibility of making 'clean bombs', and may add that: 'In any case the percentage of children affected in the future is so infinitesimally small when you compare it with the population of the world. The important thing is to preserve the freedom of the individual and this is why we can take no risks.'

And by this time the other party is mentally, or actually, wringing her hands with frustration and wanting to scream. (I have assumed for the moment she was a woman, though it is often the other way round.) These two can go on arguing forever, but neither will have the slightest effect on the other because they are speaking from different levels which, like parallel lines, never meet.

I had a clear example the other day of meeting, and failing to meet, the same girl in the space of half an hour. I knew her well. She came to see me and talked at length about her mother. I got more and more bored until I became convinced that this was not what she had come to say. So I asked her, 'What did you really come to tell me?' She was very annoyed and said this was exactly what she had come about and it wasn't her fault if I was bored, which I obviously was. I apologized. Then she said she was all muddled now and didn't know any longer what she had come for. I apologized some more for having confused her. Finally, she burst into tears and began to tell me all the things she had already told me about her mother. But this time we met because it was *she* who was talking. The things she said were the same things that I had already heard, but a different person was speaking.

It transpired that while travelling to me in the underground a poem had been forming in her mind. She was no doubt on the level of diffuse awareness and was groping for formulation. When she arrived at my door she was still on this level with her poem. But it was in fact her mother she had come to talk about, so she had handed the matter over to her masculine spokesman, the animus, who lives on the level of focused consciousness, and instructed him to carry on. He did so, telling me all the things she wanted me to know, but just because it was not herself speaking, I could not meet her, I could not even listen.

The interesting thing is that in order to meet this girl I did not have to go to the level of the poem. She was not wanting to talk about the poem. It was she who came to the level of focused consciousness and met me there, but this time co-operating with her masculine spokesman on that level instead of just handing over to him and absenting herself as she had at the beginning. Please note that she and I had to be on the same level before it was possible for us to meet at all.

Now this uncertainty as to where we stand brings me to my second topic, the barrier of not being truly *present* in order to be met. One of the main reasons why we so often fail to meet other people is that we are so seldom really there.

To begin with we are so often identified with our roles in society, and no one can meet a role. I cannot meet a doctor, a civil servant, a hospital nurse, or a shop girl unless these throw off their disguise and look me in the eye – any more than I can meet an acted Hamlet, though I might conceivably meet a real one. Similarly to be met I must be myself.

This facile but mistaken belief that we are identical with the role we act is common to everybody. But the fact that we are not always ourselves is recognized in common speech. 'So and so is not himself today' we say, or 'Tom was beside himself' (an odd place to be). Or 'He was like one possessed' we say. Possession by some part of the psyche for which we do not take full responsibility is a more common situation then we like to realize — though we often notice it in others. Sometimes we can actually hear ourselves saying things which we know we do not mean, or things we had made up our minds not to mention; and we are sometimes horrified at the knowledge that it is our tongue and lips which are being used. It is as though we were listening to another person speaking.

Most women have had this sort of shattering experience, all the more disturbing because both the hearer and she herself are left shaken and wondering if these strange words spoken might not be the truth. They sometimes are; an idea uttered has been given tangible life and can never be unspoken, no matter how often it is denied.

So we are brought straight up against the question: Who am I? What is this mysterious thing that calls itself 'I'? It is of course the 'I' which says yes or no, it is the 'I' which chooses. And one of the choices before us at any time is on which level, the focused or the diffuse, I take my stand.

Mixing of the levels inadvertently can cause diabolical confusion and one sees it occurring every day. For example, the wife who asks her husband which is more important to him, she or his work, is standing on her feminine truth of relationship where love is what matters. If the husband has a glimmering of understanding he will meet her on her level and reply, 'Why you, of course.' But when she follows this up with a plea that, in that case, he should put her first and give his work less time and energy — she has jumped without noticing it on to the plane of everyday where man's work needs first place. He feels he has been tricked, as indeed he has unintentionally, by an innocent confusion of levels.

The worst kind of confusion, absence, or hiding behind a screen, occurs when a woman unconsciously hands over to the spokesman of the level of masculine focused consciousness which Jung named the animus and — as in the case I have shown — remains hidden herself in the background. She then allows him to pronounce all sorts of collective opinions which are not quite relevant to the situation, and are not what she herself thinks or feels.

This is called 'animus possession' and I shall deal with this phenomenon in another chapter. We can almost always detect his presence by his irrelevance. However, it is not the fault of the animus if what he says is beside the point. Whenever a woman hears this sort of thing inside her own head, she should call for help. The voice is always false.

Tears, spontaneous, genuine tears will, without fail, dispel any form of animus possession. (It was when the girl wept that I was able to meet her.) Tears in a woman should be welcomed, not repressed. They wash away all falsity, and leave her naked, truly herself, and ready to be met.

A man can also be possessed when, unbeknown to himself, the unconscious feminine — or anima — has taken over (a state of possession expressed more by moods than words, as the feminine is seldom vocal). The moods may range from caprice to irresponsibility, from sulks to vanity, from sentimentality to sheer bad temper. He has stumbled inadvertently into the sphere which he does not at all understand, and wonders why he is so ill at ease.

On the other hand, a man who knowingly enters the feminine level of diffuse awareness will be able to use his natural gift for formulation to express the wisdom that he finds there.

In this kind of achievement artists are supremely important. A creative artist is a person who, in spite of the pressure of education and the need to adapt to a society based on focused consciousness, succeeds in never losing his contact with the field of diffuse awareness where the unbroken connection of all growing things still reigns. This explains the artist's state of continual conflict, and his often strange behaviour. His art is not the result of a one-sided development, as has often been suggested, but of a greater capacity to live the whole of his personality; and whether his art sees the light of day or not, he has done something of immense significance, not only for himself but for society as a whole.[1]

It is not only our uncertainty as to who we are or where we are standing which makes us hide behind a screen; it is also our fear of being led along dangerous paths if we embark upon the business of meeting someone else: the fear of being taken advantage of, and the terror of possible involvement which we had never intended. But usually a clear knowledge of where we stand, and the ability to change our stance, allays these fears.

The problem of the beggar is a case in point. A beggar came to my door one day. He had only one arm and a heavy basket. I was in a feminine mood. I did not want his goods, but he put the basket down, looked me in the eyes and said, 'I am so tired, could you give me a cup of tea?' Across the kitchen table while I fed him, the beggar and I talked and really met. As he was about to leave he shook me by the hand, tried to draw me to him for a kiss and whispered, 'When is your husband out?' I did not allow the kiss, but I retained his hand for I did not want to hurt him. I shook my head and answered, 'You must not come again. Next time I shall not be here.' He never came again. He was not meaning to take advantage. He was merely caught on the level of diffuse awareness where we had both met.

It was of course my ability to change from that level to one of common sense which had enabled me to talk to him so freely.

Meeting is of course always something of a miracle, and cannot be planned nor explained. Mercifully, real, vibrant meetings which always entail the presence of the mysterious 'third', are vouchsafed us from time to time whether we are conscious or not.

[1] I owe this observation about artists to Neumann, who first defined the difference between focused and diffuse awareness. Neumann says that this fact applies to the creative artist in men, as that of women is more complicated.

They befall us as a grace, and stand out like beacons, and no forceful removal of barriers will, of its own accord, bring them about. But I should like to conclude this chapter by discussing what I have called the third great barrier to true, genuine meeting.

This barrier is the failure of communication: that we very often do not say what we really mean, and those who are at the receiving end equally often fail to listen.

Communication often fails to take place because we do not know ourselves well enough to be clear what we want to say. This is particularly true of many social groups. The worker, for example, who demands higher wages may not have recognized that boredom in our technological age is a more fundamental cause of his unrest than his pay cheque. But he will talk about his pay cheque, and the real cause will remain unmentioned.

Even highly conscious groups such as doctors are not necessarily conscious enough to voice their real complaint. G.P.s for instance, have been vociferous about their unjust remuneration and inferior status in the medical hierarchy, but I have never heard them mention what is much more likely to be the fundamental nature of their unhappiness: that the *archetype of healer* which has sustained and nourished them throughout the centuries has fallen from their shoulders leaving them as little cogs in the great machine of modern medical practice. It is not a greater share of the world's wealth they lack, but 'mana'.

The dwindling congregations in our churches is another example. Men have not ceased to be spiritually hungry, but the people to whom the priest, or minister, or rabbi addresses his words have changed, and no longer understand his language.

However, I do not propose to deal with any particular problem of communication here. I wish to deal with a much more curious failing: the difficulty of listening.

I remember when I was at school, attending a small class of advanced mathematics for the sixth form, where the teacher one day carefully explained some new theory. Did we all understand? I admitted I did not. The teacher explained again. Was it clear now? I shook my head. 'I am sorry, I still don't quite see.' Once more with infinite patience the teacher went through the whole thing. Again I shook my head. Then suddenly the light dawned. 'The truth is,' I said brightly, with delight at the discovery, 'I haven't been listening.' That is the point, we do not listen.

Miss Whetnall has written a very interesting book on deaf children and has pointed out that deafness in children, with resulting dumbness, is by no means always due to a faulty hearing mechanism. It may be due to the failure on the part of the child in the interpretation of the meaning of a sound. Sometimes, she tells us, the parents of a child who appears to be deaf stop talking to it so that it gets no practice in attaching meaning to a sound. Miss Whetnall has discovered that patiently talking to the child individually, not teaching him to lip read, but talking to him audibly, can sometimes rectify this. The child begins to apprehend and will spontaneously begin to talk. The value of residual hearing has apparently been overlooked hitherto in teaching so called deaf and dumb children to speak.

Miss Whetnall has also realized that correct testing of deafness in a child depends not only on the loudness of a sound, but on its relevance. A deaf child may not flicker an eyelid at a loud bang behind him, for it is only one more meaningless sound, yet it may turn round to investigate if a teaspoon is tinkled in a cup.

This book on deaf children seems to throw light on the whole problem of listening in adult life. It seems that we can only give attention to a topic when we can give meaning to it — otherwise we turn away or think of something else.

Certainly, as we mature, we make more and more conscious choices of the fields of ideas we will cultivate. And it may be that man is helped to specialize by an actual increase in deafness or 'screening out' fields other than his own – as though the openness of the child to *all* impressions has to give way to canalization for some and deafness towards others. He has, as it were, to produce a sieve which will let through only relevant sounds.

The growing deafness, or rather inability to listen, of the adult in the course of specialization, certainly meets us at every turn. People who are materially oriented are unable often to hear words that were meaningful to them as children. As an extreme example, many children seem capable of hearing overtones in the word God which will be wholly repudiated by them at a later age. So much so that if anyone talks to them as adults about God they cease to listen. Others continue to hear overtones of increasing richness in the word God. Communication between these two groups then becomes impossible.

There is an inner listening as well as an outer which can be learned or ignored. When only one of these hearing skills is acquired it becomes well nigh impossible for the exponents of either the inner or outer process to communicate their experience to the other.

Mercifully most of us have experience of both worlds. But we do not always know which we are standing in at any particular time and this is one reason why communication often breaks down. The frustration caused by vain attempts to communicate between inner and outer often arouses anger and contempt on both sides.

However, this impatience of one with the other, which precludes either from attempting to listen to what the other is saying is largely a defence reaction. For in point of fact each attitude does dangerously menace the other. We do not generally recognize the extent to which, nor how easily, we can undermine the whole groundwork upon which another individual has built his life. Often a woman will provoke emotion and leave her man floundering in it while she goes off singing. She does this when she can't stand his cool reasonableness any longer, but although emotion clears the air for her, to the man it can be disruptive, prevent him from thinking, and make work impossible. Conversely the very clarity of a man's thought can be destructive. A valuable idea which is pushing its way up through the dark in a woman's mind, may be utterly withered and destroyed if an arc lamp of focused consciousness is thrown upon it. A woman who is simply trying to hold on to her diffuse awareness may feel as though she is being punched in the solar plexus by a battering ram if a man hurls a mass of logic at her.

In either case the very foundations of our whole attitude to life are threatened. So we shut our ears to one another, and vociferously try to shout the other down.

In the same way, in international matters, the East and the West often do not listen to one another because they have already decided that their opponent cannot be trusted. And even in government, where one would hope for a reasonable exchange of views prior to legislation, discussion often degenerates into a clever scoring of points, and listening plays little part.

In less extreme cases the exposition of another point of view may even be felt as menacing when there is nothing intrinsically wrong with it. It is the disturbance of emotion and thought which terrifies us and makes us put up our defence of not listening to whatever produces this alarmingly uncomfortable state. We all recognize this feeling, which can vary in degree from merely getting hot under the collar to positive panic, whenever the validity of our own attitude towards life seems threatened. Yet the first step towards any synthesis of the two half truths known and expressed by our opposing kinds of consciousness, lies in their learning to *listen* to one another.

Of course the technique of listening is different for each group. The exponents of diffuse awareness have to learn to focus. This is their weakest point, as their insight has always been dependent on a vision which is blurred just because it is so wide. On the other hand the people who have always trusted their ability to draw logical deductions from proven facts, need to listen by reading between the lines, as it were. It is no use their taking the words at their face value and then proving they make no sense.

Even in actual reading this is so. One can examine a book sentence by sentence to discover what each sentence actually means. Or one can blur one's focus and read the work as a whole without analysis. This is a reading between the lines. The effect of this method is completely different. One may find it difficult or impossible to make a precis afterwards of what the author has said, but one often receives a staggering impact which, paradoxically, can never be forgotten. I remember reading Maurice Nicoll's *Living Time* in this way. The book made a lasting impression on me though I have never been able to tell anyone else what the book was about.

Unfortunately, although the spoken or written word is our greatest tool of communication it is deceptively blunt. Even an unemotional word like 'society' means one thing to the labour leader, another to the social worker, and something even more different to the debutante. Still more troublesome are words which have emotional overtones, like love or God. These convey meanings which are worlds apart to different people. The old man with a white beard in the sky would hardly recognize himself in the abstract guise in which he is clothed today. Similarly the word love can be stretched from a simple sex encounter to the most sublime mystical union. When using these words we may be approximately near one another's meaning, but in my analytical work I am constantly reminded how very approximate it is, and that the use of words can build a wall between people as easily as it opens a road of communication.

In effect we have to live a paradox. To close our ears to the irrelevant is a cultural necessity for the preservation of our own individualities. When we have found our true individual road we have to keep to it. To follow every bypath in outer life gets us nowhere. To follow the call of every voice in the inner world leads to disorientation.

This ability to select is one of man's greatest gifts. But the ability to meet other men is another great quality, and this involves opening those ears which we have been so busily closing in order to select.

As we begin to achieve this we start to lower one of the great barriers to meeting.

II

Responsibility and Shadow

TODAY THE WORLD'S problems are too technical and too vast for ordinary individuals to feel they have the power to influence them. Our educational institutions still pay lip service to the importance of training our children to think and take responsibility. But once outside school or college we plunge them into a society where independent thought ceases to be an asset. The government employee (and more and more of us are working for the government) knows that he can never take final responsibility. The last word rests with the bureaucracy.

So most of us shrug our shoulders, turn our backs on the monstrous problems of our civilization, and enjoy life as best we can. Our sense of responsibility for the outer world has left us.

Curiously enough there are two forces at work aggravating this situation. The first is the obsession for conformity which has overtaken us. We buy the same things, see the same television programmes, read the same newspapers, and more and more of us go to the same type of schools. We conform to the opinion of our set, a union, a church, a business company, an undefined company of so-called free thinkers, or a particular psychological school.

The second force at work is, curiously enough, modern psychology itself, which is making the great mistake of urging people to turn inwards, and deal with their problems inside themselves, rather than dealing with them in external life. Psychologists are so often taught to regard their sole contribution to society as lying within the sphere of self-knowledge, that they tend to evade the outer aspect of a man's responsibility towards the world at large. Psychological theory claims that we tend to project our own bad qualities on the outside world, and if we withdraw our projections and deal with them inside ourselves all will be well. However, I have grave misgivings that the psychologists' insistence on this need to withdraw projections may be having the wrong results. A readiness to protest externally is an essential part of a living democracy. If we fail to voice our feelings of pleasure or horror we deprive our leaders of one of the essential factors on which their judgment rests. The psychologists' method of making individuals deal with the shadow solely *within* themselves, is making many intelligent citizens turn their backs on the problems of the outside world.

Discouragement of natural rebels is no service to a democracy. But psychologists are so scared of allowing anyone to foster anything resembling a saviour complex, that the dynamism which goes with a reforming zeal is being damped down and lost to the world. Great deeds can only be achieved when we are more than our little selves. When we are lent wings we should not reject them.

Today the normal appears to be the modern goal. The normal? Could anything be more uninspiring? If a man can be got back into the labour market, able to carry out some dull little job, be some insignificant cog in the great anonymous machine of industry or Civil Service, the psychiatrist considers he has ably done his job; though he plunges the man back into the very society and the very work which had made him ill.

We tend too much to level down. Christ would have fared badly had he lived today. He might so easily, in his agony, have found his way to a mental hospital and been rendered fit to keep a normal job. The Romans did better when they crucified his body. They did not diminish, they enhanced his spiritual power.

Pscyhologists have inadvertently side-slipped into this dreary passion for normality. But I am not so sure that to be balanced is necessarily a virtue. Some urgent inner problem or some imbalance may actually provide the impetus for dealing with outer wrongs. The rebel who is stirred to action by injustice or cruelty to others may well have himself suffered from an inner tyrant which bullies him.

Most geniuses in whatever field are, to ordinary eyes, more than a little mad. The heavy price some artists have to pay for their unusual insight may be lack of balance. The world would have been a poorer place without Van Gogh.

The trouble is that psychologists believe they can see and explain the patterns of behaviour. On certain levels maybe they can, but let us never forget the unique unknowableness of every individual soul. Psychological thinking has seeped through into ordinary life, and it is so easy to explain a situation by some psychological slogan — yet the inner meaning may lie in a very different place.

Parents, too, tend to see the defects and to believe they know the complexes of their children; but if they are wise they will remember that they do *not* know the innermost truth of their children's souls. We do *not* know the destiny to which another has been born. We do not know where he is to rebel, which mistakes he is to make. Perhaps some idiosyncracy or some failure to fit into society may be that child's particular contribution to the world, which should not be cured but fostered.

We may see the mistakes of the young but if we are wise we must also learn to be blind; to know and yet *not* to know is one of the paradoxical secrets of relationships.

Some course of action which seems so clearly to be leading to disaster may contain a twist of fate which lifts it to success. That accident whose cause was so apparent may have had an inner meaning we cannot see. That sudden death which we think could have been so easily avoided with greater consciousness may not have been the tragedy it appears. The man who died may have been needed elsewhere. We simply do not know. Scientists discover and theologians affirm; but faced with the mystery of life and death we know almost nothing. We can learn from the experts, but our experience may not fit their theories and it is our experience and our experience alone that we should trust.

I have criticized the trend of modern psychology towards conformity, but on a deeper level it is paradoxically psychology which is trying to help people move away from conformity by teaching them to take internal and individual responsibility for their own shadow.

The shadow is that part of the psyche which could and should become conscious, yet of which we are unaware. It consists of those characteristics we do not recognize in ourselves. Unfortunately people tend to believe that 'the shadow' means our bad qualities. But the shadow can be bright and good as well as dark and bad. A real virtue is often hidden away in the unconscious. For instance, a timid and shy person may show courage in an emergency which surprises himself as much as his friends. Or an habitually mean man may have fits of unexpected generosity which he finds a positive embarrassment. The generosity and courage could both be styled 'shadow qualities' because they are unknown to their owner, but the shadow here would be bright. It is the habitual unconsciousness of a quality that makes it a shadow, not its badness.

Whether our shadow qualities are bad or good, we need to know their presence, in order that we can begin to take responsibility for their effect on others and on ourselves.

Having made this clear, I am now going to talk principally about the dark shadow qualities, as they are the most actively dangerous.

It is common knowledge that we project qualities upon other people and dislike, or positively hate, the other person for some characteristic which we unconsciously share ourselves. So long as we only see black shadows on someone else, we can take no responsibility for them in ourselves. We merely hate the other fellow.

A good way of learning to detect one's shadow is to notice what qualities in others make us angry or irritated. We should allow ourselves to feel irritated or angry with other people to the full. And then when we have calmed down, if we turn our thoughts inward and enquire whether we have some similar quality in our own nature, on some level or another, we can generally find it. If we can succeed in doing so, the projections we had made on the other person will be automatically withdrawn because it is only qualities of which we are *un*conscious that we project.

The removal of our projections may actually make other people nicer. Our effect on others is far greater than we suppose, and it is difficult not to be as disagreeable as is expected of one. This is what 'carrying a projection' means. But even if the other person remains unpleasant — in fact he may *be* unpleasant — the removal of our projection will enable us to see him as he is, without the anger or irritation we felt before.

The bright shadow qualities, on the other hand, of which we are unaware, we envy in other people. I doubt if we ever envy qualities which do not intrinsically belong to us.

An integrated individual is one who carries his own dark shadow of undesirable qualities, frees those around him from his projections, and by so doing actually transforms a fraction of the evil in the world. When he carries his own bright shadow he takes up his courage, his strength, and his dignity, and his own imaginative insight, and refuses to be bowed down by burdens which others are unknowingly projecting on to him.

Now the three shadows which we should perhaps take special note of today are the national shadow, our own personal shadow, and, darkest of all, woman's shadow.

Unconscious projection — and projection is always unconscious — is probably at the root of most wars. We project our national shadow on to other countries. Let us look first at this, since it concerns us all.

Today we spend a lot of energy rabidly hating the Russians or the Chinese for their disregard of individual life and individual liberty. We are so busy inveighing against these things in Russia and China that we do not even notice what has happened here.

On the rare occasions when I get caught in the rush hour, I see a swarm of sad tired people, with unsatisfied faces, all pushing one another for the right to stand up for an hour, jammed tightly together in a fetid atmosphere. And when I recall that these people are obliged to do this twice daily, and during the intervening hours most of them work, or evade working, at something which interests them little and often bores them excruciatingly, I wonder where is the respect for individual life of which we boast? Where is our vaunted freedom? Our thoughts are dictated by a narrow daily Press, our values are decided by advertisements and television. Our activities are curtailed by regulations and orders without number, and even our representatives in the government no longer speak from the depth of their consciences, but obey the command of the party machines.

We see these tyrannies in Russia or China and hate them with all our souls, but because we have not noticed that we are no longer free ourselves, we vent our hatred on the Chinese or Russians, instead of on the tyranny.

If only we would realize that it is here in our own country that capacity and brains and willingness to work are no longer usable unless first wrapped in a parcel of paper qualifications. It is here, in this country, that the law meddles with the private morality of individuals. It is true we can still say what we like in public, but already the tapping of private telephones is the thin end of a very ugly wedge.

This is part of our national shadow, and if we can see our

own serious defects at home we shall be able to recognize that despotism, the inevitable shadow of over-rational planning, is not a speciality of the Chinese, it is the same virus the world over.

To see this tyrannical shadow only outside in other countries leads straight to war, but to know and deal with despotism at home is to take responsibility for our share of this monster. It does not exonerate us from protesting at barbarism elsewhere, but it does give us the possibility of fighting the evil on our own ground, instead of forever thinking it is someone else's business.

So much for our national shadow. Now let us look at our personal shadow.

To take full responsibility for our own personal shadow involves having some knowledge of our inferior function, about which there seems to be some confusion in people's minds.

Let me explain this matter in psychological terms. Jung has described four ways of mental functioning: *Thinking, Feeling, Sensation,* and *Intuition. Thinking* and *feeling* he calls rational, in that when either of them are being used we are making judgments. *Thinking* analyses, *feeling* is the function which evaluates worth, whether a thing is good or bad.

The other two functions, *sensation* and *intuition* do not judge in any way; they are ways of perceiving. With our sensation we perceive how things are, whether within or without; with our intuition we have hunches of how they might be, or we perceive inner meaning and significance.

This is of course a gross over-simplification, and only intended as a reminder. In actual fact there are innumerable complexities, varieties and combinations.

A person of high intelligence will never be characterized by only one function. It is well known, however, that we tend to use one function more than the others, though we can gradually develop the use of the others also.

It is the function which is least well developed in any particular person which is called the inferior function. It could as well be called the fourth function and perhaps with less confusion.

Even those of us who are fairly all round people tend to have a fourth function which is decidedly elusive. We all know the thinkers whose feeling is so bad that they can unwittingly trample underfoot by their logic what to someone else is precious. We know the women who are so sure of their feeling judgment that they will tell one that something is 'so right' or 'so wrong' without seeing the slightest need for logical proof. We know the sensation types who (especially if they are extraverts) only trust their own senses, and gape in amazement at the intuitive's capacity to see round corners or beneath the surface. Thomas the doubting Apostle must have been one of these. And we certainly know the people who are always running off on to some new track, forever at the mercy of a new idea, who are incapable of dealing with ordinary facts like catching trains or managing their money. These are the intuitives, and sensation or a sense of reality is their weakest point.

It is often easier to determine which is a person's fourth undifferentiated function than which is his best. Our weakest points are the ones which stand out. But if we can see the fourth, the first can be arrived at by inference.

For instance, the man whose shocking lack of tact (which means poor feeling) is his besetting sin, is likely to be predominantly a thinking type. Or the one quite incapable of logical thought is likely to function predominantly with feeling. The man who gets stuck in a situation and can conceive of no possible way out is probably a sensation type, whereas an intuitive is beset on all sides by so many different possibilities that he has the greatest difficulty in remaining in any situation at all.

The other day, for example, I watched with amazement an intelligent original boy of fourteen trying to work out how many exercise books of different colours he needed for the various subjects he was about to study at a new school. Blue for this subject, green for that, and so on. But he was in difficulties. 'Can't you see,' he said, 'that colours and numbers have no connection with one another? They just don't add up.' This was an extreme case of almost total lack of sensation function. There were so many possibilities, permutations and combinations between the colours and the various subjects that it was well nigh impossible for the boy to fix them. This boy is capable of clear thought. His feelings are warm and reliable. So we can infer that his first function is intuition. This in fact accounts for his originality. Most original thinkers are intuitives.

Now the only way of developing our lesser functions is to give less energy to the first. This is no easy task, but we can learn to do so. Certainly an analysis can help to the extent of developing the second and third functions; but probably only the hard knocks of life itself can induce us to give up our best developed conscious function to the point of having enough available energy to dive down and reach our fourth.

Jung's theory of different psychological types is an invaluable aid because it helps us out of our habitual assumption that other people's minds work in the same way as our own. It was, I believe, an attempt to explain his own difference with Freud which set Jung off on this particular investigation.

In the degree to which a person is able consciously to use *all* his functions of thinking, feeling, sensation and intuition, he is liberated from the tyranny of any one of them and is able to use such function at any particular time as the situation demands — a far distant ideal which by no means appeals to all of us.

But knowing one's own type has another significance of enormous importance. It is through the inferior or fourth function that evil creeps in unawares. So if one knows which is one's inferior function one can more easily be on guard to see that it does not lead one wildly astray.

Our fourth function, being the one which is least within our conscious power to handle, is inevitably lit or touched in some way by the unconscious. When suddenly it comes to our aid it brings as it were the magic or mystical quality of the collective unconscious in its train. I am an intuitive, and I remember Jung once explained to me that I must not expect my fourth function, sensation, to be like the sensation of a sensation type. On the contrary, it would always appear to have a numinous quality. This is true. I have always despaired of mastering everyday reality with the same efficiency as other people I admire. At the same time matter, things, seem to behave much more oddly around me than they do with many of my friends. You see, to the intuitive it is the things of the senses which are magical not his intuitions which he takes as a matter of course.

On the other hand to the sensation type a sudden intuition appearing as it will out of the blue, lit by a glow from the unconscious, will seem heaven-sent. It may even be heaven-sent.

Similarly, if a feeling type, to whom thinking is of the utmost difficulty, is suddenly able to think something out, the result will appear with a luminous clarity; while the thinker whose feeling is touched will be overwhelmed by the force of his unexpected emotion. (Please remember that emotion is not identical with feeling or any other of the functions. Emotion always has its roots in the unconscious and manifests itself in the body.) The emotion of the thinker whose sympathy is aroused is likely to be far more overwhelming than that of the feeling type.

The case of Goebbels has been cited as a man whose feeling function was so faulty that he could connive at the extermination of millions of Jews, yet when his canary died he wept. Such sentimentality is not lack of feeling, but negative inferior feeling arising from the unconscious.

This brings me directly to the connection between evil and the fourth function. Goebbels had no adequate feeling function in consciousness with which to evaluate his monstrous deeds. Nor presumably had Hitler, nor any of his close collaborators. They knew what they were doing. Their thinking function enabled them to plan the crimes which served their ends. But they could not evaluate them consciously and correctly. The unconscious overwhelmed them through their inferior feeling and provided the terrific dynamism which enabled them to carry out their evil schemes.

Hitler prided himself on being guided solely by intuition. He treated his intuitions like commands of God. It is of course a fact that we all tend to treat our first function as though it had the authority of God. But Hitler was a house painter, and therefore probably a sensation type. If this is so then his intuition would be his fourth function which would explain its terrific force.

No intuition as a first conscious function could possibly have had the dynamism of Hitler's. His intuitions arose from the depths of the collective unconscious, alight with the flames of Hell. Hitler was a man possessed.

It was through his inferior or fourth undifferentiated function that evil did not creep but burst upon the world.

Baynes has pointed out that there may be such a thing as a national psychological type, and different nations tend to use one of their functions more consciously than the others.

He has pointed out that Germany is probably a thinking nation, and this is perhaps why the flames of Hitler's regime were able to spread throughout Germany. Lack of sound feeling opened the door to Germany's possession, and prevented the Germans from evaluating their deeds in all their horror. Germany is certainly a nation of philosophers, and has habitually been guided by philosophical principles. But, as thinkers, the feeling function of the Germans probably tends to be not a sound valuing of human life, but a combination of sentimentality and callous brutality.

The English, according to Baynes, are largely sensation types. Throughout history they have been the great colonizers because they knew how to handle facts. The areas they conquered were won neither in accordance with a principle nor out of any passionate love of country, but because they liked adventure and overcoming material obstacles. The British Empire was accumulated by accident.

Moreover England's diplomatic relations with other countries have continued to be a series of handling facts. That is why we are called perfidious Albion. We so often betray what other countries think must be our principles. In reality we have almost no principles to betray, so if one set of solutions does not work we simply try another.

Baynes has also pointed out that there is a very strong introverted feeling side to the English character, and this appears in the legend of King Arthur and the Knights of the Round Table. All clans tend to hold together by force of kinship, but the Arthurian Knights widened kinship to embrace humanity. Any man, woman or child in distress was their concern and could call upon them for succour. The spirit of the Arthurian legend has filtered down through the centuries, and appears daily in the Anglo-Saxon ideal of fair play. Fair play is not a rigid principle, it is not inexorable like justice: it is an essentially human feeling and is only concerned with essentially human values. British Common Law has been built up by past judges purely in the spirit of fair play. Fair play is a sign of a good feeling function.

But as recently as 1962, the British Government landed itself in an awkward dilemma. The Home Office granted the use of the platform of Trafalgar Square to the neo-Fascists, and refused it to the Campaign for Nuclear Disarmament.

In psychological terms what does this mean? Moseley, like Hitler, seemed to be lacking a feeling function. Racial injustice is repugnant to anyone capable of making a sound feeling judgment. It is anathema to our Arthurian traditional ideal of making all humanity our kin. Moreover, like Hitler, the Mosleyites seemed also to be possessed by inferior intuition. 'The blacks', they said, 'will completely override the whites. Send them back to

Africa. Let us keep England white. The Jews are the financiers of the world, they own all the armament factories, they thrive on and foster war. Down with the Jews!' — and so on. This is negative intuition, charged with fear arising from the unconscious through the inferior function, and it lies at the root of the neo-Fascist movement.

This ill-developed fourth function is the gateway through which evil might once more try to explode its way. We have here a problem with no easy solution. To refuse a platform to the neo-Fascists could drive them underground where they would be still more dangerous. And yet officially to permit the public preaching of race hatred seems as irresponsible as allowing a dangerous drug to be put on the market. On the other hand it may be a risk we have to take.

The case of the Campaign for Nuclear Disarmament is almost the opposite. The scientist's two supreme functions are brilliant intuition combined with thought. To give his ideas tangible shape the scientist also needs to use his sensation. But feeling, the judgment and appraisal of human values, can easily be dispensed with. It would appear to be through the ill-developed feeling function that the world is threatened by Russia and China and even the United States. Indeed, lack of feeling function seems to be a general malady. England, too, is apparently throwing over her native feeling and guiding herself more and more by her inferior thinking — and therefore throwing overboard her ability to act as a brake in the suicidal arms race.

Those who campaign for Nuclear Disarmament are fully aware of man's danger and are public-spirited enough to concern themselves with fighting for man's survival. We may or may not agree with them, but there is no question of psychic contagion as there is with the neo-Fascists. To ban the bomb at the moment may be impracticable. It may even be unwise, but this is a matter of opinion. It is possible that the feeling of these campaigners, which puts the survival of humanity before all else, may be misled by poor thinking, so that they may in fact bring war nearer by misleading the Russians or Chinese into a false belief that we will never fight. But Bertrand Russell could hardly be accused of poor thinking.

How can we decide to which protagonist we should lend our weight? I can see neither principle nor psychological validity underlying the refusal of Trafalgar Square to the Nuclear

Disarmers. Their rejection was of course a matter of expedience — the sensation function at work on the part of the British Government and the Police: a tactic to delay the impact of their protest.

These movements which I have described in Trafalgar Square, are of course in the outer world generally. They are probably outer manifestations of an inner movement which we can understand if we look at the Archetype of the Eternal Youth.[1]

Puer Aeternus is the name given to those many young men today who seem overly endowed and inspired as youths, yet do not grow into what is normally considered responsible adult citizens. They remain at heart, and often in behaviour, eternally young. They may be artists, poets, airmen, scientists or 'angry young men'. Their main characteristic is that one feels that they are permeated with and activated by some spirit of an outstanding quality. We have all met them and easily recognize them in our midst. They have their counterpart among young women also.

Hitherto psychologists have tended to regard these young people as immature Peter Pans who cannot grow up, men and women with mother complexes. Treat them and they will with any luck take up the responsibilities of life in a normal way. Very often they do so but not uncommonly at the price of losing their spiritual gifts. They may even swing to the opposite extreme of utter banality.

The apparent increasing number of these young men and women today is evidence of an inner happening. Organized religion has become fossilized, which inhibits the spiritual transformation necessary to keep pace with man's development. The fossilization of religion goes hand in hand with the police state. The archetype of spiritual renewal is finding its way not within the churches but through the individual young men and women of whom I am speaking. They are the channels along which a new spiritual awareness is trying to break through. They are in fact activated and possessed by the archetype of spiritual renewal. Their danger is that they do not always know what has got into them and may identify with the archetype itself. They then think

[1] I owe this to a brilliant lecture by Marie Louise Van Franz addressed to the Congress of the International Association of Analytical Psychology on 'The Archetype of the Puer Aeternus'.

they have the monopoly of this new spiritual awareness, often believing themselves to be prophets or saviours.

To be identified with an archetype is one of man's most common but most acute perils, and it is not unusual for these inspired youths to break down and land in mental hospitals. In these cases evil has crept in through the fourth function. Not through its dynamism, as with the neo-Fascists, but through its almost total lack. Reality sense is absent.

If only these people could understand that they are being used by the archetype of renewal, as we all are in any moment of inspiration, but that it is essential to avoid identifying with it, many personal catastrophes might be avoided. Indeed holding fast to their own individual intuitive gifts, at the same time as they keep their feet on the ground of reality, is a spiritual achievement of unique service to mankind. By so doing within themselves the new spiritual awakening has a chance of filtering through to mankind as a whole.

On the whole the menace to civilization today seems to come from man's over-developed thinking, and the consequent unadaptedness of his fourth function, feeling, which thereby lets in the evil. His feeling brings with it all the dynamic forces of the unconscious, good and bad — its courage and inspiration, but also its terror — which makes us pile armament upon armament, hydrogen bomb on hydrogen bomb.

This terror 'gets us all in the night', and the weakest of us fly for succour to the doctors. Unfortunately their remedy is often to calm anxiety at all costs. Even the ordinary discomforts of pregnancy must be relieved. On the face of it, to relieve anxiety with tranquillizers so that people can carry on with their ordinary business may seem to be a boon to the suffering individual. A tranquillizer in a moment of crisis may be essential. But what happens to the anxiety thus suppressed? Is it not mounting up in the unconscious with ever increasing magnitude and momentum till one day it will be forced to explode?

It is not when we are feeling cheerful and complacent, but when we are in the throes of distress that we pray. Similarly it is not our lightness of heart but our distress which gives us the impetus to seek our inmost truth. Too much medical tranquillizing may actually cheat the more sensitive among us from becoming whole.

Jung maintains that our only hope of holding the blind, hysterical masses in check is for enough people to contain the opposites within themselves instead of either swinging violently from the one extreme to the other, or projecting the undesirable opposite upon an outer enemy. We do not yet know the extent to which a relatively few integrated individuals can break the force of a rising storm; but their impetus is not that of numerical superiority, nor in the field of action, their healing effect is in the unconscious which we all share.

To have the use of all four functions means to have an ego which is in no danger of being submerged by the unconscious through an ill-developed fourth function, or a possession by some partial aspect of ourselves. It means rather to be in touch with that vital centre of ourselves, which Jung calls the Self. It is this centre, not our active little egos, which effects the healing.

To accept one's own personal shadow means to accept responsibility for its behaviour, not necessarily the licence to live and put in practice all we find within — this is a common fallacy. It demands not only self-knowledge but the utmost vigilance to see it does not break out unawares. And if it should, to call it back and make amends and admit very humbly that this unruly shadow is a bit of me.

What one does, one is. Not what one says nor thinks one is, but what one does. Doing may be a concern of an inner invisible process which we call being, but it is still what in fact one does; though, of course, the quality of our being will depend on the value of our actions or our influence.

It may sometimes be wisdom to use one's shadow deliberately. Anger is a shadow quality in our well-behaved society, but consciously directed it can move mountains. I once saw a small boy aged four rush angrily up to a Spanish mule-driver shouting, 'I won't have you beat the mules like that.' The man stopped, utterly taken aback, and turning to the couple of men behind him, ordered sheepishly, 'Master Johnny says we are not to beat the mules.' On that occasion at least the mules carried out their heavy work free from blows owing to the anger on the part of a small child, spontaneously but correctly used.

Christ vented his anger on the moneylenders in the temple. He knew what he was doing. We also need to know what we are doing, as it is only when our shadow comes up unbeknown that it causes mischief.

Hardness of heart is another shadow quality, and the people who are hard in life without knowing and without intention may cause much misery for others and themselves. Yet there are moments when use of one's hard, unyielding shadow is the one thing necessary to save the situation. We need at times to use our shadow, but never to be its victim.

It is only if we are truly centred that we can be trusted to use our shadow qualities spontaneously in the right time and place. 'When the wrong man does the right thing it will turn out wrong' says the Chinese saying, 'and when the right man does the wrong thing it will turn out right.' To be the right man requires more than consciousness. It requires to be centred.

Life insists on being lived, and anything that belongs to one's life which is allowed to lie dormant has to be lived by someone else. If we do not accept our shadow we force our children to carry the burden of our undeveloped capacities. They may become mediocre scientists or artists because we denied our own talents. They may become doctors, which they are not suited to be, because we failed to use our innate capacity for healing, or inept politicians to fulfil our unlived ambitions.

Our interconnection does not end with the family. We all meet in the unconscious. How many men have been hanged for murder merely because they were the weak recipients of the murderous shadow of the whole race? There would be fewer murders if we could all acknowledge within ourselves how easy it would be for anyone of us to kill. In wartime we explain our brutality some other way. In peacetime we forget and some man or woman slightly weaker than the rest is hanged virtually for us.

I will write at greater length of woman's bright shadow in another chapter, but I cannot close this one without speaking of woman's direst and most destructive shadow. The witch is chiefly woman's responsibility. All women who have not totally lost contact with the unconscious are in touch with power. Power is not necessarily bad. Its direction is what makes it good or bad.

The life force which surges up through women is a tremendous power, whether employed biologically or in some other way. We have heard a great deal about woman's suffocating quality. She pours out energy on those for whom she cares and does not know she suffocates. Giving feels like love, but giving without measure and without discrimination stifles.

It is when a woman actually uses the power with which the feminine is in contact for her own personal ends that she becomes truly a witch. This is real evil which needs all our resourcefulness to fight. I suspect there are few women who will not find a witch lurking somewhere within themselves if only they dig deep enough.

But I think that a woman will also turn witch today for other reasons than personal power. The deeply buried feminine in us whose concern is the unbroken connection of all growing things is in passionate revolt against the stultifying, life-destroying, anonymous machine of the civilization we have built. She is consumed by an inner rage which is buried in a layer of the unconscious often too deep for us to recognize. She becomes destructive of anything and everything, sometimes violently but often by subtle passive obstruction.

I believe it is often this inner protest which breaks out in neurotic illness, in sensitive men as well as in women; or turns destructive in places where it was not intended. With more consciousness, feminine anger could be harnessed to a creative end.

I have touched on three levels of responsibility. In the outer world it is imperative, for the sake of peace, that we see our own dark shadow and admit that it is ours, instead of projecting it on to other countries.

But ultimately our most far-reaching contribution lies on a deeper level in the carrying of our own individual shadows, dark and bright. Dark shadows, once conscious, can to some extent at least be curbed from causing mischief, and their dynamism can be redirected. Our bright shadows of dormant potentialities are obviously also needed both for ourselves and for the welfare of the whole.

Deepest of all lies the feminine shadow. Above all, I appeal to women to find the shadow within themselves, not only the destructive power-demon witch, but also their own peculiarly feminine spiritual quality of which we seem equally unaware. This exists today also in men, but wherever it may dwell it needs a voice.

Our personal responsibility for the outer world may seem infinitesimal — indeed it is. But taking individual responsibility for our own personal shadow, dark and bright, is a small attainable achievement, though it demands a lifetime's determination and a lifetime's courage. And as we are all connected beneath the surface, our little individual pebbles of consciousness may send ripples to the furthest shore.

III

Man the Hero

TWO YEARS AGO a couple of boys who live on opposite sides of my road rigged up a private telephone between the two houses. Even their parents were thrilled when the toy catapult actually carried their wire from roof to roof. This phone, quite illegal of course, has been in constant use ever since, saving the parents, incidentally, quite a lot in telephone bills.

One day the two boys, by then about fourteen, came home from a jaunt in town in a state of great jubilation. 'We have been doing a swop with the telephone company,' they said, and proudly showed a new telephone mouthpiece. 'How do you mean "swapped"?' inquired the parents. 'Well, we've got this in exchange for our old one which wasn't working very well.' Parents began to look anxious. 'But who gave it to you?' 'Oh, no one *gave* it to us,' they replied with scorn, 'we took this mouthpiece from a public telephone box and fitted up ours instead. It works allright,' they added, 'we tried, to make sure. You see the public telephones work with a stronger current than ours so they can afford to have a weak apparatus. It won't make any difference to them but it will make a lot of difference to us.'

The parents were by that time in the constant quandary of parents: how to show disapproval without being so damping that they will never hear of future exploits. They managed with skill and adroitness.

To me this incident was a godsend. I suddenly realized how fine is the line between heroism and delinquency. These boys had carried out a skilled operation in full view of the public. The thrill of danger far outweighed in their minds any sense of moral disapproval. I had to admit that I should have enjoyed the exploit myself. These boys clearly had it in them to become delinquents — or heroes, and which it would be, depended very largely on the kind of challenges life offered. These boys' cultural future is adequate to turn them into heroes. But boys who are kept throughout their adolescent years seated at school desks in a state of boredom, trying to evade learning matters in which they have no interest, are thwarted of any challenge whatsoever. By the time they leave school the desire to achieve has been stifled in most of them.

However, the stronger and more imaginative ones will still be impelled to some form of audacious action. Heroes they *must* be. Without some form of heroism a man hardly feels himself to be a man. It is the hero in man which makes him really male.

Our delinquents, of whom society complains so bitterly and so complacently, are the failed heroes — the ones who tried and couldn't find the right channel. Better rob a train than be a nobody. Better prove one's prowess in a gang war than remain an anonymous fool. Even rapes and murders surely have their original impulse in the need to be a hero.

This hero impulse in man needs to be better understood, if we are not to make serious mistakes. This was demonstrated, remember, in an alleged spy trial in 1963, where heroism was mistaken for delinquency. An Italian atomic physicist was arrested and tried for preparing to give secrets to the Russians. He was not in secret work and had no secrets to give. But as the story unfolded at the trial it became obvious that here was a man who was fascinated by danger. He had been in the Italian Resistance during the war, and so had been trained to act alone on his own initiative against the enormous odds of an organized army. The accused explained at the trial that he had hoped by going along with the Russians, accepting their information of how to pass them secrets, and their gadgets which would enable him to do so, that he might in the end uncover the intricacies of their spy ring for the benefit of the British Government. The prosecutor and the judge poured scorn on the likelihood of so intelligent a man being such a fool as to think he could fight the Russians single-handed. This man's life hung in the balance for a fortnight on the court's understanding or failure to understand the significance of the hero archetype. Mercifully the jury showed some insight, and in face of the clearest possible direction by the judge to convict, had the courage to acquit the accused on every count.

Now in what lies the significance of the hero archetype in man? It is probably at the root of his emergence from the level of the animal kingdom. It is his particular instinctual drive which has enabled him to overcome the obstacles of nature, enlarge his knowledge and utilize Nature's energies and secrets for his own purposes. Every new mastery over the resources of the earth, every new penetration, whether into outer space or into the mysteries of the atom, is an achievement of heroes. This impulse to overcome danger and difficulties is built into the structure of man's psyche, and evidence of the pattern is clear enough even in little details.

But heroism is not limited to man's prowess against external odds. Going hand in hand with these has been man's heroic fight for consciousness. It is this struggle which is depicted over and over again in mythology. The hero with a thousand faces is always the same hero-consciousness. The struggle for consciousness is the perennial struggle of the son to break free from the Great Mother. The degree of our consciousness and our conscious control over our lives is illusory. Man's ego, which he has evolved with such labour over the ages, is far less strong than we like to think it. And the drive towards consciousness demands all man's heroic qualities. It is one long wrestle, already lasting for millennia — and still going on — a wrestle whose outcome is by no means assured.

I have seen even children training themselves to face danger. On the dark landing at the top of my stairs in Spain, my children used to imagine a lion lurking under a settee, and I watched the genuine terror on their faces as they ran downstairs to the lighted hall. But no sooner had they reached safety than they crept upstairs to taunt the lion all over again. They needed to face fear.

This was a tiny repetition of a constant psychic pattern. You may recall the legend of Theseus who insisted, against all the wishes and contrivances of the king his father, on being one of the twelve men and maidens who were chosen to face the Minotaur. His destiny demanded that he should be a hero and slay the dreaded monster.

The spirit of David the shepherd-boy who single-handed slew Goliath, still lurks beneath man's skin. The history of man is one long procession of heroes overthrowing tyrants, even old divinities, stretching from Prometheus who stole fire from the Gods, to such civilized protests against tradition as the Bishop of Woolwich's best-seller, *Honest to God*.

We have come some way since the days when men had to summon their energies to hunt or go to war by means of ritual dance. We have learned to focus our energies so that we can pursue an outer goal or a line of thought with some continuity, and without sinking back into lethargy. But lethargy is always just round the corner, and politicians still have to beat their drums in modern journalistic fashion to make us go to war.

However, man has unquestionably emerged from a state of tribal consciousness to that of the responsible individual. But the process is so precarious that it appears to be in danger of tipping over into its opposite of a new form of collectivity.

Man has climbed up from the Great Mother of the collective unconscious, but he is falling inadvertently into the Great Mother of the affluent society whose nurse is the welfare state. He has become little more than a number. His skill is required less and less as the machines take over. His personal responsibility is diminished the greater our organizations grow. He has been sucked back into a different kind of collectivity and is in the same peril as the child who had begun to emerge as an individual personality but has withdrawn. He is in danger of becoming an idiot, an idiot disguised as a well-dressed efficient automaton.

To meet this danger a new kind of hero is needed. We do not lack the heroism which makes men risk their lives encircling the earth or facing journeys to the moon. Our daily press is full of outer heroism. Not long ago, no fewer than seven men offered to go down a narrow tube two hundred feet below the surface of the earth to help rescue miners trapped in a flooded mine. Even a child will risk its life to save another. But in our extraverted modern world we have become so oriented outwards that the inner world with its living images, its treasures and its terrors, has for the most part been forgotten. We have repressed our natural fears of the inner world and in so doing we have projected our fear on to some outer political enemy: or some sinister figure of our acquaintance.

We no longer have a Medicine Man who will probe the secrets of the unconscious for us and protect us with his ritual magic. The Churches which shielded us in the past have lost their power to do so. The danger from the unconscious, by which we are in fact threatened all the time, has been reasoned out of existence, with the result that paranoia has become a common complaint (almost as rife as the common cold).

My subject is 'Man the Hero'. Now does this mean man as distinct from woman or does it mean mankind? I think it means man. It unquestionably is the male of the human race who is the active partner and has explored the greatness of the earth and the heavens and the smallness of invisible particles. It is also he who became conscious first and has, as a result, been the architect of modern culture.

The consciousness of woman is a very recent acquisition:

> While Eve lay sleeping
> Man awoke
> And clambered on her breasts
>
> Poised on their towering
> Domes he reached
> Beyond the Night
>
> From her lifted knees
> Far leaping
> Grasped the light
> While Eve lay sleeping.

Today woman is sleeping no longer, with the uneasy results we see all around us. Gender seems to be confused. One is no longer quite sure whether women are feminine, nor how far men are male.

But the emancipation of women came about through their finding a hero within themselves. It was this which overcame all obstacles in their path: the law, tradition, the obscurantism of their own as well as of the other sex.

The change in woman's attitude towards the hero in the last fifty years is very marked. Before the First World War it was men's business to be heroes. Women had assumed that men fought while women wept. The harridans who presented men in mufti with white feathers were only an extreme expression of woman's general unconscious assumption that man was of course a hero, and if he was not, there must be something wrong with him. Women in fact projected on to men their own unconscious cowardice as well as their own latent heroism.

In the interval between the two Great Wars, however, women won a great part of their battle for equality. In doing so they found that they too could stand up against outer odds and were quite capable of being heroes themselves, and by the time the Second World War broke out women were prepared to take their part alongside the men.

From then on there is no doubt about it that the new generations of women have also shared with the men a new leap forward of consciousness. The young people today of both sexes seem to have started off on a level of awareness to which their parents had only painfully and pantingly arrived.

None the less, although woman no longer projects her own latent hero on to her men folk, which of course in the past did actually help the men to be heroes, she does not appear to have outgrown her old expectation that a hero is what he ought to be.

So the poor man suffers doubly. No longer boosted by the women on the one hand, and actually competed with by them on the other, he feels depotentiated and unable to rise to the heights expected of him. All this at the same time as he is rightfully developing his own more sensitive feminine side.

One constantly meets the gentle understanding man, without an ounce of hero in him, the source of quite unreasonable exasperation on the part of his wife who has not yet realized that modern men for the most part just are not heroes, and have no more reason or aptitude for heroism than she. She has to learn that if it is a hero she wants she had better find him within herself.

In his essay on 'Modern Women in Europe' Jung says that man can go no further in the pursuit of consciousness until woman catches up with him. This was written before the Second World War, and since then she has been very busy catching up. But her task is a double one since she has to develop her own masculine ability to focus, before she is able to throw her new found light on to her own mysterious nature and make this conscious also.

The first part of this task is similar to that of the mythological masculine hero who has to free himself from the Great Mother by achieving an ego, a will of his own. This step woman has already partially taken but she now finds herself in new danger of blindly accepting man's values as though they were her own.

A new act of heroism is needed before she can delve into her own feminine nature and salvage her own feminine values. Even in those cases (comparatively rare) where she has done this and knows what her true values are, she still has before her the enormous task of holding to her true self with firmness so that her values begin to permeate society and check or alter the disastrous course of materialistic progress and over-population on which we are hurling ourselves pell mell.

The heroism of men is still turned to outer space. All honour to their imagination, their skill in wresting the secrets from nature, and above all to their incredible courage. But one cannot help wondering if man's pursuit of the physical moon is not the outer counterpart of his paramount need, of which he is not yet fully aware, to explore the cold unpredictable half-light of his own feminine nature.

Modern education is not conducive to the emergence of heroes in any field other than that of scientific discovery and the conquest of outer space.

We need a new kind of hero. We have always had reformers who would fight against the evils of society, but, with the general collective depersonalization of society, our reformers have become impersonal associations such as the 'Association for the Abolition of this, that or the other.' There is not much room for personal heroism here. We rely on the static weight of numbers rather than on the far more dynamic hero archetype.

But the sphere where the hero archetype can still have full play is within the individual himself. It requires all the qualities of a hero to turn from the pleasant harmless 'persona' mask which one has so carefully cultivated, and which one really believed one was, to find the elements of cruelty within oneself of which one had no idea. One may even find a full-blown sadistic tyrant, such as could have been a very efficient governor of a concentration camp had circumstances placed one in Hitler's Germany.

Or one may discover beneath the most well meant and generous gestures, a witch who is busy plotting in the shadows to achieve her own power-inspired ends. Here, within, is where evil can be adequately met.

There are inner heroes too. One can recognize the hero in modern young men and women of a particular indefinable spiritual quality. They are the visionaries who refuse to lose their vision and yet do manage to live in the materialistic world in which they find themselves, holding the opposites together within them rather than going out as preachers or reformers.

This is an enormously difficult task today, the opposites are so far apart. These incipient heroes often fail. Again and again we see a young man, or woman, with a light in the eyes which illumines as well as sees. Yet again and again as the exigencies of life crowd in on them the light fades and they settle down to the rat race of competing with the Joneses, indistinguishable from all the other rats.

More tragic, and no less a loss, are the visionaries who have been overwhelmed, whether by the incandescence of the vision or the suffocating menace of society. These break down. Their vision is treated as an illness, neither valued nor understood. There is no attempt to canalize its energy. It is regarded as an illness to be cured.

Only a few achieve the colossal task of holding together, without being split asunder, the clarity of their vision alongside an ability to take their place in a materialistic world.

These are the modern heroes. All the more are they heroes for not being recognized as such. Some are invisible, the struggle fought unobserved. Some openly shrug their shoulders at the disapproval of their fellows, refusing to deviate one hair's breadth from their standpoint, though the invisibility of their goal makes them victims of misunderstanding and taunts of being escapists.

Among the ranks of these are the artists, poets, musicians, painters. Artists have at least a form within which they can hold their own conflicting opposites together. But there are some who have no recognized artistic form to serve this purpose. They are artists of living. To my mind these last are the supreme heroes in our soulless society.

Robert Frost describes such a one in a poem entitled:

Escapist — Never

He is no fugitive — escaped, escaping,
No one has seen him stumble looking back,
His fear is not behind him but beside him
On either hand to make his course perhaps
A crooked straightness yet no less a straightness.
He runs face forward. He is a pursuer,
He seeks a seeker who in his turn seeks
Another still, lost far into the distance.
Any who seek him seek in him the seeker.
His life is a pursuit of a pursuit forever.
It is the future that creates his present,
He is an interminable chain of longing.

IV

Roles of Women—Woman as Mediator

THE HERO ARCHETYPE pertains specially to masculine psychology. Being a woman myself I am particularly interested in the psychology of women and am constantly wondering how far they have legitimately different roles to play in life from that of men.

Many of my contemporaries maintain that there is little difference between the working of a man's or woman's mind and that it is only in their biological function that they play different roles. Simone de Beauvoir is one of these. To her it is only their education and the assumptions of their parents which creates an illusory distinction.

My own view is just the opposite. It is based not on theory but on personal observation. Moreover the many years I have lived in Spain, which, in many respects, is still a matriarchal country, have perhaps given me more direct contact with the unconscious of woman than I could easily have had in England.

We are certainly living in an age in which it is increasingly difficult to speak of the different characteristics of man and woman. Women are fast developing their masculine side and more and more men are in touch with the feminine in themselves. None the less, women are still basically feminine and men basically masculine, so I shall speak of man and woman and ask you to remember that what I say may not necessarily fit any particular case. I can only speak of conditions in the West and more particularly of the conditions prevailing in England.

At the close of the period of rationalism which led up to the First World War many of us, shocked at the Armageddon which appeared to have been the result of a masculine culture, really believed that if women took their place in the control of affairs the world would *ipso facto* become a pleasanter place, and that their influence would stop wars and make civilization more humane.

Forty years later we look around with dismay. Women have penetrated every field of society, but the world in which we live is more, not less, tormented.

Men's often heard criticism that though women are successfully vying with them in every field, they lack creative imagination is, I believe, on the whole a fair one. They lack the spirit of adventure, the generous willingness to sacrifice self for a cause, which has always been such a notable characteristic of the male. Have women, I wonder, carried into the world at large their feminine limitation of outlook which has concerned itself from time immemorial with the individual relationships of a woman to her man and to her children? *Her* children and *her* man. Women do not readily bother about Vietnamese children or the horror of concentration camps unless they actually *see* them.

The greatest lovers of humanity have nearly all been men — Christ, St. Francis, Gandhi. With few exceptions the great women of history — Joan of Arc, St. Teresa, Florence Nightingale, Elizabeth Fry, Nurse Cavell — have been blessed with a good proportion of masculinity. They could not possibly have done what they did without.

Women have permeated man's world, but, instead of regenerating it, they seem to have contaminated it with their own pettiness of outlook, with the sublime indifference of a tree which is concerned with its own growth, and its own acorns, caring nothing, for it knows nothing, of the forest as a whole.

At the same time the greater preponderance of the feminine in man's psyche today no doubt also contributes to this state of affairs. Just as the masculinity in women is apt to be less creative than that of men, so also the femininity in man is less concerned with the values of life and relationship than the femininity of woman. He tends to adopt her softness rather than her strength, her vanity rather than her capacity to give.

The tendency in both men and women to take over the less vital characteristics of the other sex and, in so doing, to lose touch with their own fundamental truth is, I believe, a transitional one, but in the meantime it has a disastrous effect. Many women have forgotten, in the modern emphasis on a career and economic independence, that woman has a role to play towards man which is inherent in her nature, a role which is not a sharing of his intellectual interests nor the providing of his meals; not becoming the mother of his children nor being his sexual partner; but over and beyond all these, her role is still, as it always has been, to be a mediator to man of his own creative inspirations, a channel whereby the riches of the unconscious can flow to him more easily than if she were not there.

At present it is the young men who appear most unsure of themselves, not the young women. Men feel threatened in their masculine role because women are now competing, but do not yet know what is the next step in their own evolution.

The young women, on the other hand, are still buoyed up by the exhilaration of their newly found status. They continue to be wives and mothers, yet are successful in man's world as well. But in so doing they often fail to realize how precarious men feel, and how much the particular man needs his woman to believe in him and to welcome his vision with as much warmth and tenderness as she accepts his child.

He looks to her for recognition of his unique personalness. He does not want to be merely the man about the house, the husband whose duty it is to earn money, and wash up after supper. Perhaps man's need is to be trusted even more than to be understood. He needs to be believed in, and his work, whether she understands it or not, to be given full value.

But he needs her also to *express* herself. Herself. It is her own deepest self that he must know, not her opinions which she has picked up from parents, schools and the daily press, but her *deepest* self. How many women can give him that?

To be a true mediator to the masculine, whether it be an actual man or the masculine in herself, requires not speech but consciousness on the part of the woman. Over and over again one sees the increased consciousness of a woman influencing her man, with no words said. Language can falsify by its very precision. Clever conversation does not make a relationship. True communion happens in the silence.

Yet to be fully conscious *herself*, a woman needs to be able to make some formulation in words. One does not really completely know what one cannot express at all, and most women are incredibly inarticulate about the things which matter to them most; though, curiously enough, the more educated they are the less they seem to be aware of this fact.

Unfortunately, most women do not realize how little they express their true selves. They talk in slogans, adopt man's principles without his flexibility, and fight man's causes without man's charity. There is nothing so ruthless as a woman with a cause between her teeth.

It looks to me as though we are caught in a dichotomy. On the one hand women are educated to accept man's values blindly. Schools and colleges have grown up throughout the centuries to meet the needs of growings boys, and girls have fitted themselves into what was already there. They have accepted without question the masculine over-valuation of a thinking function and of physical prowess. Girls have adopted the ability to do mathematics as the test of intelligence and a capacity for games as the criterion of bodily perfection. Many an inferiority complex stems from these mistakes.

On the other hand, women on the whole are more biologically minded than they care to recognize, which undermines their modern education.

The vast majority of women are still willy-nilly housewives and mothers, and for the sake of the children born and yet unborn they want security and material comfort and the status quo. With her new found power, woman has become the hub around which society revolves. It is not her vote but her purchasing power which counts. The advertizing agencies know and exploit this fact. It is she who pushes up the material standards of living, seeking ever-new gadgets to ease her burden of overwork, not noticing that in doing so she is binding her husband's feet more firmly to the crippling treadmill he detests in order to meet time payments and the monthly bills. Her panacea is always more gadgets, not more simplicity.

Over-worked she certainly is, but how often she has failed to understand the nature of man's malaise or to see how heavy is the burden she loads on him. She is blissfully unaware of her failure to give him what he needs. Her achievement of becoming a creative being in her own right and a factor of importance in the economic world, is of little avail if she deprives man of her fundamental role of helping him to find himself. To do this she must never lose her natural contact with the living springs in the unconscious. This is her direct responsibility.

The parable of the wise virgins who kept oil ready in their lamps for the coming of the bridegroom expresses, I believe, the basis of feminine spirituality.

One must have lived near the Mediterranean to feel the deep significance of oil. It is pressed with hard labour from the bitter inedible olive, fruit of a wild tree which has been drastically pruned. It is plunged into deep water to be purified, and when it rises to the surface clear and greenish-gold it becomes a staple food and fuel for light. It is not for nothing that kings are anointed with oil, for it is a symbol of spiritual transformation. This is the oil that women need to keep ever ready in their lamps.

To do so is an attitude of mind. It is the readiness for relationship in whatever field, whether it be with God, another human being, a work of art, a blackbird's song, or with one's own inner masculine counterpart. It is a readiness of the feminine soul for the meeting with another, though that other may be her own creative spirit.

Her task is two-fold. If she fails to have oil always ready in her lamp for the actual man, she fails him in the essential role he asks of her. But it is more than this. The oil is her feminine spirituality in the totality of her own psyche. It expresses an attitude of spiritual waiting, and tending, and readiness for the meeting with its opposite which is a prerequisite for inner wholeness.

Without this she becomes a prey to the masculine within herself, a raging spirit of intellectual or physical activity to which no man can be related, and to which she can in no way relate herself. She is a woman possessed.

But if she can hold the oil ready within the lamp, then, when the masculine spark comes, there burns a flame which is alive, and lights our human world.

This flame is Love. Love is wholly beyond us. It alights upon us and illumines our lives *only* when the opposites meet. Love may be born of the meeting between living creatures, or it may shine from within any human being, born of his or her own inner wholeness. It is equally in man or woman where the masculine and feminine meet, but the inner wholeness of men would, I believe, become less difficult if we women could remember to play our part.

It is primarily women who need to keep in contact with the springs of life, with the inseparable connection of all growing things and their eternal continuity: spring, summer, autumn and winter, followed eternally by another spring.

On every level death is the forerunner of life renewed. There is no birth without a prior death. The acorn dies for the emergence of the oak. At the birth of the baby the maiden dies to become a mother. In regions of the mind every new idea rings the death knell of ideas out-worn. In the life of the spirit, only through death can there be immortality.

In the book Jung wrote with Kerenyi[1] he points out the essential awareness of continuity between mothers and daughters:

> We could say that every mother contains her daughter in herself and every daughter her mother, and every woman extends backwards into her mother and forwards into her daughter. This participation and inter-mingling give rise to that particular uncertainty as regards time; a woman lives earlier as a mother, later as a daughter. The conscious experience of these ties produces the feeling that her life is spread out over generations. The first step towards the immediate experience and conviction of being outside time, brings with it a feeling of immortality.

I suspect that when women lose their contact with this underlying feeling of immortality they undermine the sense of purpose and worth-whileness of life for men as well. Man in his rationality may have relied on women to retain their hold on the irrational until he could find it for himself. What, oh what, have we done in blindly following him into the strictly rational?

The tragedy of today is that civilization in the West has gone too far in the direction of masculine separation and the masculine urge to discover and create for its own sake and the accompanying danger that women are throwing over their sense of cosmic awareness and the connection of all growing things in order to adopt men's values in their stead. That only serves to upset the necessary balance between the opposite poles. It is now imperative for men and women alike to stretch from pole to pole in order to achieve the paradox of holding both attitudes at once.

I have tried to describe in a little poem the contribution of the feminine side when woman's own conscious masculine discrimination has freed it from being a stifling jungle or a submerging sea. It is the contribution that the spiritual feminine has to offer to the masculine world, and the individual woman to the individual man.

[1] C. G. Jung and C. Kerenyi, *Essays on a Science of Mythology*, Princeton University Press.

The Water She Brings

Water, dancing to break the light
Into a million colours.
Water mirroring the flight
Of circling birds.
A pool, guarded by tall trees,
Waiting for him to dive and salve
The drowning stars.
Water for parched lips, unfailing
And water for the moon to trace the path
Of his last sailing.

Now do all women play this mediating role? And what really does it mean to be a mediator?

To mediate is to be a connecting link between two things. To begin with, what are the two things or states between which woman is supposed to stand, holding out a hand to each as it were, helping them to come to terms? We can think of mediators in any field. Let us begin at the circumference of our lives and work inwards, seeing at which levels women do in fact play this mediator's role.

On the world stage mediation between conflicting powers or opposing ideologies is often called for. I have not noticed that women take any particular part. In such spheres as these, women as yet seldom play any role at all, for in the realm of ideas and power politics women as women have not learned to function. There are occasional exceptions but on the whole they join the ranks of men adding their moral weight to his through numbers, not through any different quality of being.

The same is true within our nation states. Industrial disputes, the quarrels of political parties, dissension between rival churches, show no sign of any woman's mediation to soften their bitterness. There are associations of women's groups but I doubt if they do more than exacerbate the situation.

The first glimmer of any such thing as real mediation appears within the schools, and that but sparsely. The child who finds a teacher that can actually help him pass from childhood into the adult world is fortunate, for teachers who have the gift of standing halfway between a child's mind and that of an adult are rare, and they are just as likely to be men as women, perhaps

even more likely. The ones I happen to have known have all
been men.

Drawing our circle closer we come to the family, and here at
last we arrive at the fundamental, archetypal pattern in which we
are all nurtured, where father is Father and mother, Mother.

What does this mean? In actual fact it is often all mixed up and
mother's animus frequently plays the role of Father, wielding the
stick of authority over children and husband alike; while the children run, not to her, when they are hurt, but to father.

None the less it is here, within the family, that woman has, in
outer life, her first real opportunity to play her role of mediator.

When father is in fact Father he stands for law and order and
authority, and the big world outside. He can lead the children to
respect and obey its forms, and finally to take their place in adult
society.

But the world is harsh and wholly unpredictable to the child
who has only half emerged from the mists and timelessness of the
great unconscious. Fiery dragons are far easier to deal with than
irate grown-ups. In the boundless realm of fantasy one can take a
sword and kill the smoking monster, emerging as the hero. Even if
the giant enemy is too strong, or has a hide too thick for one's small
sword to penetrate, one can always render oneself invisible, or
spread one's wings and fly over his head with a mocking laugh and
sail away to the next adventure.

In the prosaic world of everyday a mocking laugh is more likely
to produce a scolding. How bewildering a child's life must be. He
is assailed on both sides by two completely different sets of
values.

When already in my forties I had a dream which most aptly
described the predicament of my own childhood, or that of any
other small child caught between these opposing worlds: *In the
dream I was a shy little girl aged six* (I was in fact a shy little girl)
*who went to visit the House of Lords. I opened the door and crept
in. There they all were in a large square hall, dressed in black and
all jabbering at once in Latin. I was much too small for them to
notice me so I slipped round the edge of the hall and up the great
wide stairs to an imposing gallery where sat still more rows of
black clothed men. I looked round carefully. Yes, there he was, the
man I was looking for, the Archbishop of Canterbury. I ran
towards him and flung myself upon his neck weeping with a cry of
protest: 'But the Queen doesn't believe in God!'*

Indeed she could not believe in the God of these black clothed Latin-mumbling men, for the picture of the queen, full-sized before my eyes, was not that of the reigning Queen Victoria, nor of my own mother, but a glowing colourful Queen of Hearts.

Heart and intellect had different gods even at the age of six, and the child was in tears in her bewilderment. I woke from that dream in actual tears.

Heart and intellect, love and thought, the poetry of mystical insight and prosaic reality, No. 1 and No. 2 personalities, were all opposites, hardly on speaking terms.

How badly the child needs a mediator, someone who can understand both worlds and help to bring them a little closer together. This can be and often is, the role of woman, for women, more easily than men, can stand with one foot in either world, and can ease the child's heartbreaking predicament.

But not only the child's for it is man's predicament as well. Woman as mediator can restore to him a world he has lost, a world that he needs if he is not to become as mechanical as the machines of his own invention, and as dessicated as the synthetic foods with which he is vainly trying to nourish himself.

It is, as I have said before in an earlier chapter, to Neumann, more than to anyone else, that we owe the realization that the consciousness which has been so hardly won by man over the centuries, liberating his mind from the primal unity of all things, is not the only kind of consciousness. There is also a more diffuse awareness which is yet far removed from a state of unconscious mist, and cannot be called *un*consciousness. Neumann calls this 'matriarchal consciousness' as distinct from the patriarchal consciousness of man's world.

I should like to quote from Neumann's Essay 'On the Moon and Matriarchal Consciousness':

For matriarchal consciousness, understanding is not an act of the intellect, functioning as an organ for swift registration, development and organization; rather it has the meaning of a 'conception'. Whatever has to be understood must first 'enter' matriarchal consciousness in the full, sexual, symbolic meaning of a fructification. This means that the conceiving and understanding have brought about a personality change. The new content has stirred the whole being, whereas in patriarchal consciousness it would too often only have been filed in one intellectual pigeon-hole or another. Just as a patriarchal consciousness finds it difficult to realize fully, and not merely meet with 'superb' understanding, so a matriarchal consciousness finds it difficult to understand without first 'realizing' and here to realize means to 'bear' to bring to birth: it means submitting to a mutual relation and interaction like that of the mother and embryo in pregnancy.

The comparative passivity of matriarchal consciousness is not due to any incapacity for action, but rather to an awareness of subjection to a process in which it can 'do' nothing, but can only 'let happen'. In all decisive life situations, the feminine, in a far greater degree than the nothing-but-masculine, is subjected to the numinous elements in nature or still better, has them 'brought home' to it. Therefore, its relation to nature and to God is more familiar and intimate, and its tie to an anonymous Transpersonal allegiance forms earlier and goes deeper than its personal tie to a man.[2]

You will have noticed that Neumann speaks of this feminine matriarchal consciousness as 'it'. He is indeed most emphatic that this type of consciousness, which I prefer to call diffuse awareness, can also be found in men. It is not a question of sex at all, but rather of a masculine or feminine attitude of mind, the possibilities of both being latent in every individual. Artists and poets of necessity have both.

None the less, woman tends to be more naturally guided by an inborn diffuse awareness than is man, and although she is seldom able to formulate the things of which she is aware, her very presence in a close relationship with a man will open the door, as it were, to the wealth of the collective unconscious in the man himself. So he also, in contact with his own diffuse awareness, finds the unity of all growing things.

I cannot stress too strongly that matriarchal consciousness or diffuse awareness is *not* identical with the formless chaos of the unconscious. It is emphatically *not* *un*consciousness. Its difference in quality from masculine focused consciousness with which we are all familiar, lies in its whole unbroken state which defies scientific analysis and logical deduction, and is therefore not possible to formulate in clear unambiguous terms.

[2] *Spring*, 1954, Analytical Psychology Club of New York.

Woman's supreme role as mediator is here: between a man's clear-cut intellect, and the awareness of wisdom and wholeness lying latent within himself.

How woman achieves this mediation is a mystery. She certainly will not succeed by attempting to explain. At best her words will only hamper, at worst they will sound ridiculous. Inability to formulate the unformulatable is a hurdle she cannot jump. But nature has its own unerring ways. The seed sprouts in the dark and ideas are germinated in the silence:

> When Eve uncovers on the salt sea bed a pearl,
> She does not claim her ownership
> Nor break it up to find the speck of sand within,
> Spoiling its opaque loveliness,
> But softly lets it fall in man's quiescent mind
> In deep forgetfulness;
> And when some day it comes to light unsought,
> She is the pearly iridescence of his thought.

When a woman knows that this is what she does, that it was she who brought the pearl up from the depths of the uncon-scious, will depend upon the quality of her own *focused* con-sciousness. It takes a high degree of focused consciousness in a woman before she can be able to observe what she is in fact doing instinctively.

But please note that Eve in the poem has not opened the door to cheating, she has handed her man the bare ingredients of a grain of sand and an oyster shell.

The pearl has been created, rounded and perfected. She did not make it, but it was she who found it because it is she who is at home in the sea of the unconscious and can dive more easily without being drowned. She brings up this symbol of wholeness, unbroken and still opaque. Such pearls are her jewels of aware-ness, her values which are utterly destroyed by man's dissection. A dissected pearl has ceased to be.

Now do all women behave like this? I suspect some of my readers will shake their heads with lack of recognition. Some will be angry at the very idea. No, I am convinced that only a par-ticular kind of woman plays this role of mediator to man of the mysteries of his own psyche.

It was Toni Wolff who made a study of personality types in

women.[3] She was one of Dr. Jung's first and most important collaborators, both in confronting the mysteries, beauty and terror of the collective unconscious, and also as a brilliant analyst.

During many years of analysis of all kinds of men and women she observed that, quite apart from Jung's four psychological functions of Thinking, Feeling, Intuition and Sensation, woman can also be characterized by one or more of four distinct types of personality. She emphasized that the younger generation tends to combine at least two of these main types in contrast to older generations who seem more often to have been limited to one. And she contended that the process of individuation in woman demands a gradual assimilation of all four characteristic attitudes.

She calls these four basic feminine types, maternal, hetaira, amazon and mediumistic and describes their respective relationship to man.

The maternal type is the most obvious, but I find it illuminating that in her view this type not only cherishes all that is young and tender and growing, but relates to the man principally as father to her children. One can, I think, see this also in the intellectual realm where a wife looks to the husband as the source of her ideas, and readily accepts his notions on politics, religion or whatever it may be, with the same blind wholehearted acceptance with which she accepts his child. The 'mothering' which tends to become smothering and which we so deprecatingly attribute to mothers is, if I understand right, the negative side of the maternal which cherishes where cherishing is no longer needed, and more likely to arise from the unconscious in women who are actually not mother-types.

There is a good parallel here to the functions. Bad thinking is not the sin of thinking types. Nor is bad possessive mothering likely to be the sin of real differentiated mother types. The compulsive mothers are those whose maternal instinct comes rushing up from the *un*conscious in a most *un*differentiated way. It is then that the mother archetype takes charge and the woman feels like killing anyone who touches or criticizes her offspring, and is quite unable to distinguish between mothering and smothering.

It seems doubtful whether the maternal type as such acts as mediator between a man and his unconscious though she may

3 Toni Wolff, *Structural Forms of the Feminine Psyche*, Zürich, Students Association, C. G. Jung Institute, 1956.

mediate between father and children. She does however care for and protect whatever is new and growing in the man, if it enhances his position or influence in *outer* life, as such things are important in his role of husband and father to the children.

On the other hand any aspect of his personal development which is outside the family boundary, or does not accrue to the family's benefit, is frowned upon as a dangerous menace to the family's welfare. The poor man's danger from a wife who is such an extreme maternal type is that he feels spiritually imprisoned, and only valued as a financial provider or a useful piece of furniture.

The extreme opposite and furthest away from the maternal type is, according to Miss Wolff, the hetaira or companion. This type relates to man for his own sake, not as father to her children. She can be a companion on any level, intellectually, spiritually or sexually or all three at once, but not necessarily all three. She may in extreme cases be a 'femme inspiratrice'. One frequently meets her in marriages where the children are only of secondary importance. And outside marriage she constantly fills the gap which a maternally oriented wife may leave in a husband's psyche, giving him value in himself, not only as husband and father.

To the hetaira the personal relationship with the man is all important. It is the only thing in life which matters. Everything else can be swept aside as irrelevant. She does indeed give value to the man but she also reflects his personal anima, with all its inspiration and its flattery, to such a degree that she may lapse into the role of seductress. If so, she may lure him away from his real destiny, or the practical necessities of outer life, in favour of some illusory anima ambition, and so ultimately ruin him.

It is of the utmost importance that a woman should know her hetaira potentialities both in their positive and dangerous aspects, for if they are repressed she may turn her sons into secret lovers and her daughters into close girl friends thus hampering their ability to make their own relationships.

Though readily carrying a man's anima it is to his *personal* unconscious that the hetaira type relates and so it is his personal unconscious which she can be said to mediate to him.

The hetaira is not an easy role for a woman to play as it does not fit into accepted patterns of society. Nor do the women of this type always realize that they have a definite role to play; so they continually try to change their status of mistress to that of wife, mistakenly believing that marriage is the inevitable desired goal. To quote once more from Toni Wolff:

> Everything in life must be learned, also human relationship; and it is therefore only natural that the hetaira cannot begin with it on the more differentiated levels. But once she has learned it, she will carefully observe the laws of individual relationship, she will notice what belongs to it and what not, and she will if necessary know when a relationship has become fulfilled and complete.

The hetaira woman who breaks other people's marriages in order to become the wife herself has not yet learned what belongs to her particular form of relationship.

The third type, the amazon, is one we are seeing more and more frequently today. She is independent and self-contained. She is primarily concerned with her own achievement. She claims equality with men. Although she may have love affairs or even marry and have children she is not dependent on the man for fulfilment, as are both the maternal and hetaira types. She meets man on a conscious level and in no way acts as mediator for him. She frequently lives her love life like a man, sometimes even misusing her relationships to further her own career.

The suffragette was of course the unadulterated amazon whose emergence filled men with horror. But today she has ceased to be the hard masculinized woman of yesterday and, having found her own level, no longer behaves as a menacing rival to man. Consciously he accepts her as a comrade, a pleasant work mate and a worthwhile challenge which stirs his own endeavours. None the less, I am pretty sure that in the unconscious of men, the appearance of the amazon is still both feared and hated. I can find no other explanation for the persistence of the inner voice in every woman I have ever met which dins into her ears the words, 'You are no good.' I believe this is her negative animus picking up man's collective unconscious fear of woman's rivalry, and his passionate desire to keep her in her place. If men could become more conscious of their inner disdain, women might become less aggressive in self-defence against this insidious unconscious corrosion.

The relationship of the amazon type to man is like that of brother and sister. They understand one another, participate in similar activities and act as mutual challengers and rivals. There seems no place here for the amazon type to play a mediator role.

Toni Wolff's fourth personality type is what she calls the mediumistic woman and here we have par excellence the woman whose principal role is that of mediator.

She is permeated by the unconscious of another person and makes it visible by living it. She may pick up what is going on beneath the surface of the group or society in which she lives, and voice it. I have known women who were working in a group to dream dreams which seemed unmistakably to be messages to the group as a whole. She may become permeated by a religious creed and put herself at its service. She may express in her own person the spirit of an epoch. Joan of Arc was such a one. Her voices from the collective unconscious speaking to her with the lips of saints, impelled her to live in her own person, and almost to bring into being, the spirit of nationhood which was trying to emerge in France. To quote Toni Wolff, 'The mediumistic type is rather like a passive vessel for contents which lie outside it, and which are either being simply lived or else are being formed.' In this sense she is immensely valuable in giving shape to what is still invisible. Women like Florence Nightingale or Elizabeth Fry were instrumental in bring to consciousness a humanitarian spirit which had been lying latent. Toni Wolff suggests that women writers sometimes have a flair for mediating to their own time some wholly other epoch. Mary Renault is surely one of these. *The King Must Die* and other novels by her seem quite miraculously evocative of the spirit of Ancient Greece.

On a more personal level I know one woman who dreamed a whole series of dreams pertaining not only to the man with whom she was in intimate contact but to his whole family. When she recounted them they were so dramatically relevant to his family situation that the man's attitude was changed and he was enabled to undertake a difficult task with his father which, before he was told the dreams, would have seemed utterly impossible.

I know other women who seem able to help men to die as their time approaches. These women may be aware that they do this. Sometimes the man in question also knows that the woman is fulfilling this strange role for him. But it is not always necessary to have an intimate relationship for such a thing to happen, and the emergence of such a mediator role may be as complete a surprise to the woman as to the man. I have met this in my own experience.

On one occasion I visited a man in hospital whom I did not know at all well, but who was a member of a society to which I belonged and with whom I had always felt some affinity. I visited him again when he was sent home to his wife to die. To my surprise he told me intimate things of his life which he had never before mentioned to anyone. I said almost nothing but when I rose to leave I kissed him lightly on the forehead. To my bewilderment he burst into tears. Without knowing at all what I was doing I had freed him from the dry prison of his intellect in which he had been immured and put him in touch with his own unconscious feeling, with its promise for the future. Next day his wife told me I was the only person he wanted to see. I sat by his bed and listened to his delirium. But it was no longer guilt-ridden. He had already embarked on a journey. He died that night.

Such a mediatory role was entirely unconscious and unforeseen. But I have known other women who appear to realize what they are doing. One of these was the wife of a modern high-ranking scientist, newly working in one of the old universities, and finding it difficult to adapt. She told me one day that she was haunted by a male figure in black medieval clothes who appeared every night in her dreams: *He wore a high pointed hat from the apex of which poured a cascade of fine black lace falling to the ground. Black lace covered his face and it was her business to encircle with small white feathers the point of his hat from where the black lace fell. He held in one hand a money box raised to the level of his head.*

As she woke each morning she clearly saw him standing by the bed. She was used to dreams but the insistence of this figure troubled her. I could not tell from what she told me whether he was a part of her psyche, which she needed to contact, or if she was picking up some unknown figure in the unconscious of her husband of which he was unaware. I suggested she should draw him. She did so and showed the picture to her husband. He had learned to respect her imagery. He looked carefully at the drawing. 'Yes,' he said, 'that belongs to me.' The dreams and the hallucination ceased. She had been the means of giving her husband an image from the collective psyche which concerned him and which he had needed to contact before he could feel at home in the medieval setting in which he actually found himself.

The mediumistic woman is, as Toni Wolff makes clear, not easy to discover, as she seldom appears in public and is not publicly recognized as having a definite role to play; yet it is she more than

*A voice said, 'Your dog will do your chicks no harm. Look in
the backyard for the marauder.' And there she saw an owl feeding
with the hens, no one noticing that he is the enemy of little birds
and eggs.*

The dreamer digested this as best she could but some years later
had another far more frightening dream: *She saw an immense
hollow tree, an entrance near the base. Outside the entrance was
again an image of small animals, but this time they were kittens
lying peacefully in a kind of nest.*

*She peered inside the hollow tree and saw to her surprise all
sorts of animals big and little. As she looked a lioness strolled out
and walked among her own children outside the tree. The lioness
moved among them easily without the shadow of a menace and it
was clear that the children neither did nor had need to fear her.
Then the dreamer looked higher within the hollow trunk and at
the top of it she saw fiery luminous snakes reach out from the walls
of the tree, their heads meeting together in the centre. It was the
light they emitted which made the contents of the whole tree
visible. Alarmed at their dangerous proximity to the children she
stepped back. 'That tree must be smoked out immediately,' she
said.*

Whether she was right that the tree should be smoked out seems
highly doubtful. These fiery snakes, which being at the top of the
tree presumably stand for spiritual insight, do appear to be shown
as the dangerous element in contrast to the harmless lioness. To
smoke them out would, for the woman, have been to lapse into a
state of semi-consciousness and forego the fruits of years of
analysis. The dream was perhaps telling her to close the door of
the tree so that the snakes could neither emerge, nor the children
wander inside inadvertently.

Although woman's role as mediator lies in her capacity to mediate the unconscious to man, not all women do this. The hetaira
type will reflect for him the attitudes of his personal anima, but in
order to mediate the contents of the collective unconscious to him,
a woman needs to have an ingredient of the medium type in her
make-up.

Moreover if she is to be a good mediator and not just open the
door to that very chaos man has left behind him, woman needs to
have, along with her own diffuse feminine awareness, enough
masculine ego consciousness to be able to discriminate between
these two forms of consciousness. She needs to know which world

she is in at any given moment, never confusing one with the other. She needs to know that one world cannot be expressed in the language of the other, but that the more she herself is aware of who she is and where she stands the more likely will she be to hand man, not the chaos of the collective unconscious, but pearls, opaque yet formed, from the realm of diffuse awareness.

Editor's note: This chapter has been concerned with a woman's roles in her relationship with men. But the author wanted to add a further section about relationships between women, which she felt to be of great importance, and different in kind.

She was pondering these additional pages during the last days of her life, but did not write her thoughts down.

V

The Animus—Friend or Foe?

IN MY EARLIER chapters I have tried to distinguish between the feminine and masculine way of functioning within the same person whether man or woman and, following Jung, I have referred to the masculine in a woman as the animus. The following is an attempt to clarify what is meant by this obscure term.

Most men recognize that their women folk are not always their feminine selves but constantly behave or talk more as didactic men do, or get emotional about some matter which does not call for emotion, all of which they find irritating and disconcerting. Occasionally the woman notices it herself. It is as though a man suddenly obtruded into a woman's psyche from time to time and made remarks on his own. Sometimes he even seems to be in total possession, overshadowing the woman herself until she can hardly be seen. This masculine appearance in a woman's psyche we call the animus, and as he is most noticeable when he is being objectionable he has earned a bad name for himself.

My purpose is to show that the animus, who is indeed like a woman's male partner, is not only irritating and destructive but is of the utmost value, and is essential for any creativeness on her part.

The first thing to stress is the collective nature of this figure. Like the anima of a man he is the personification of a function which belongs in the psyche of all women and is not a personal idiosyncrasy.

To be possessed by the animus may be a misfortune but it is not a personal disgrace. Unfortunately, our habit of talking about Mrs. Smith's animus or Mr. Brown's anima causes confusion, making one forget that the personal guise worn by these images is only a cloak covering the eternal collective figures which animate them.

Where emotions are rising quite unnecessarily in any discussion and people are getting hot under the collar, it is an enormous help if we can learn to stop saying, as we point an accusing finger, 'You said so-and-so,' which only makes it worse, and instead call a halt and say, 'Oh damn! the devil has got into this, we shall have to start afresh.' Not your devil, nor my devil, but *the* devil.

The following remarks are based entirely on personal experience, my own and that of the women who have come my way. I do not want to draw conclusions, but to throw out a few ideas which have occurred to me for further study, and to hand over to you a few practical tips which I have found useful in dealing with this difficult partner of ours.

When I speak of woman I mean *basic woman* — which of course none of us are. Similarly, I am using the word man to mean basic male, which no actual man is either.

Some years ago (I was already working as a psychotherapist) I had the following dream: '*I was walking peacefully along a country lane when I met a band of men, a dozen or so, going in the opposite direction, accompanied by a sort of wireless apparatus. I knew in the dream that, though they looked harmless enough, they were a menace to me, and I felt extremely frightened. But I was told that I could pass them in safety if I saluted each one in turn, saying the words,* 'palabra de honor'. *This is Spanish for* 'word of honour', *but in Spain honour is more sacrosanct than here. Honour is the value for which one would give one's very life. So* 'palabra de honor' *is the most sincere and dramatic password a Spaniard could devise.* (I must explain that my husband was a Spaniard and that I lived in Spain for many years, but the stress on honour in the dream will also tell you that I personally speak from the opposite standpoint of extreme femininity. What follows may not fit other types of women.) *This ritual I solemnly carried out, saluting each man in turn and repeating to each the password,* 'palabra de honor'.

There was a great deal more to the dream but I want to use this as my opening scene, for I have come back to it again and again during the succeeding years, each time with a little more understanding that this is the key, the magic password which will turn the animus from foe to friend.

First of all note that there are a number of men and each one in turn has to be placated. We know that the animus often appears as a group, a committee, a jury, etc. This group of men in my dream, however, was not a homogeneous group which could be dealt with as a whole. Each man had to be saluted separately. I believe this to be fundamental. In trying to contact the animus we tend to think of him as one person, although we know he has a multitude of shapes. He can appear as an old man or as a little boy, a learned scholar or an aviator, a god or a devil, a romantic lover or the prosaic figure who styles himself one's husband.

To any of these we can talk, but we can no more talk to the animus with a capital A than we can talk to man with a capital M. Nor is it enough to remember that the animus is dual, both positive and negative. For instance, if an evil-looking man appears at my door in a dream it is no use my recalling that though this may be a dark side of the animus he also has a light aspect, because then I am powerless to deal with him. How can I grapple with a robber if I am thinking 'After all, if only I could see his other side he might by my guardian angel.' This paralyses one from a true reaction. I believe one needs to act in as single-minded a way to each facet of the animus as one would to a real man. I should not in actual life wait to be robbed or raped. I should ask an intruder what he wanted. If I did not like his answer I should request him to go away. I should be quite indifferent to this man's possible good intentions. One reacts directly to the aspect of man which presents itself. So also to the animus.

Now, if only we can succeed in splitting the animus up into distinct and separate persons we can deal with him. Then I can kneel and ask a blessing of the priest, befriend the feeble-minded boy, face firmly, but with due respect, the devil and order the mealy-mouthed sycophant out of my house. But woe betide me if I lump them all together, call it the animus, and try to deal with that.

I know one woman who has a great deal of active imagination and talks to some twenty different aspects of her animus under different names. She will say: 'I had a refreshing talk with Jim, the cowboy, yesterday,' or 'My learned friend Andrew told me so-and-so.' But one day, in a rash, adventurous moment, she collected them all together in one room, and was surprised to find her knees shaking with terror at the assembled power she had conjured up. She dealt with the situation by very humbly addressing her grandfather, who was one of the company, and beseeching his help and protection.

Note, please, that every aspect of the animus is personified separately and, if one is to have a true relationship with the whole, each of these separate persons must be dealt with separately, in all sincerity of feeling, from the depth of one's being. There can be no half measures, no false sentiments, no rationalized devaluation of one's feeling towards any one of them. There must be no mere lip service to the priest, no cringing to the bully, no idle blustering to the devil:

> To thine own self be true,
> And it must follow, as the night the day,
> Thou canst not then be false to any man.

This is as valid for a woman's relationship to her animus as to any human being. *Palabra de honor.* Utter sincerity is the password. My life depends on my acceptance of this most masculine conception, honour.

To be sincere with one's own animus! That is the key to this relationship as to every other. How simple, and how difficult! For to be sincere to one's own true feelings, to stand for one's own inner knowledge, demands that one should know what one's feelings are and what one's inner knowledge is. To see clearly enough to know something quite definitely, so solidly that one can express it and say 'This is my truth, here I take my stand,' one needs the help of the animus himself.

I personally like to think of my helpful animus as a torchbearer: the figure of a man holding aloft his torch to light my way, throwing its beams into dark corners and penetrating the mists which shield the world of half-hidden mystery where, as a woman, I am so very much at home.

In a woman's world of shadows and cosmic truths he makes a pool of light as a focus for her eyes, and as she looks she may say, 'Ah yes, that's what I mean,' or 'Oh no, that's not my truth at all.' It is with the help of this torch also that she learns to give form to her ideas. He throws light on the jumble of words hovering beneath the surface of her mind so that she can choose the ones she wants, separates light into the colours of the rainbow for her selection, enables her to see the parts of which her whole is made, to discriminate between this and that. In a word, he enables her to focus.

To me it seems that the power to focus is the essential quality which makes man the creative creature that he is. Sparkling ideas or images of incredible loveliness may float through the mind of almost anyone; float through and out again, unused, unavailing and unhoused. But he who has the ability to focus, see and hold the idea as it emerges, can create something with it. He can build a temple or a philosophy. He can build an atom bomb.

Ability to focus is not the same as ability to think, although a strange confusion seems to have arisen here in many women's minds. I have constantly heard the thinking function of a woman equated with animus, but this is a misunderstanding. Thinking is a function, a fundamental way of approaching life like any other function.

The ability to focus applies irrespective of function. Focusing is not the same as thought, though, certainly, there can be no creative thinking without the power to focus. But neither can feeling be creative without the power to hold the nameless joy or pain, and out of it give birth. Intuitions, glinting with iridescent colours, are of no more value than a pest of flies buzzing round one's head, if there is no power to focus on one of them and give it life. Sensation, reality, can be a prison if there is no power to focus on some aspect of it and change its shape.

The power to focus is man's greatest gift but not man's prerogative; the animus plays this role for a woman. He is the same in kind as the spirit which imbues man and makes him a creative being, but different in quality for, dwelling in the unconscious as he does, woman contacts him indirectly, as it were. But there he is functioning more or less well whenever she focuses on anything in order to see what it really is, whenever she analyses, discriminates, selects, formulates, creates.

Please do not misunderstand me. By focusing I do not mean consciousness. Woman (remember I mean basic woman) has a consciousness of her own, a 'diffused awareness'. Everything is accepted, enjoyed or hated as a whole. She feels herself equally at one with the stars or a drop of dew, a rose or a blade of grass. She does not analyse them nor want to do anything about them. She is simply aware. For man, and again I refer to the extreme male, the scent of the rose is not enough. He must learn all he can about it, prune and graft the plant to obtain even better roses. No woman, as woman, does such things. They would not occur to her.

Yet woman is not just earth. To be told, as she often is told by psychologists, that man represents the spirit and she the earth, is one of those disconcerting things a woman tries hard to believe, knowing all the time that they are not true; knowing that the pattern provided does not fit, however hard she tries to squeeze herself into it. She is not merely blind nature and life force. She has a spiritual awareness of her own which has little to do with the masculine culture in which we live, and nothing to do with philosophy and cosmologies. If she has succeeded — and not all women succeed — in holding on to her true feminine soul in spite of the weight on her shoulders of the masculine education she is asked to carry, she will dimly recognize her own direct spiritual awareness, which she is nonetheless wholly unable to express and almost unable even to admit. Her innermost feminine soul is as dumb and as shy as is any man's anima. But her awareness is there, diffuse and all-pervading. She can walk in the dark and place her feet as delicately as a cat without any light from her animus's torch.

It is only when she needs a focused kind of consciousness that the help of the animus is needed, and today she needs this most of the time. And there he is, always at hand, with his torch ready lit. The trouble is that he does not always shine it on the right things. At the slightest beckon of her finger he appears, throws his light in answer to her question on what seems to be the formula she seeks, and out she comes with a slogan, correct enough probably as a general truth, or in its rightful context, but just irrelevant to the matter in hand, or the particular case. When he is wide of the mark he is not so dangerous because his bad aim is apparent. Often, however, he is only a hair's breadth away from the truth and then sounds so plausible that, unperceived, in a few minutes the woman, and not infrequently her hearers, have been subtly led far astray from the matter in hand. Friend has turned foe.

This sudden insidious turn of face is a phenomenon we all know only too well. It may happen in a discussion between two people and it inevitably leads to irritation. But it also happens when a woman is talking to herself, the animus being one of the persons taking part in the conversation. Then, indeed, he becomes her most deadly foe for, without seeing where or how, she is flung or, worse, gently led right out of her own path into a morass of conventional ideas where she may flounder helplessly for weeks or months until she suddenly realizes who is at the bottom of the trouble. If only she can catch him at it she is saved. She can then face her adversary and, with a stamp of the foot, order him to get out of her way. Instantaneously, she will find herself on safe ground, again on her own pathway, the fog cleared — until next time. (Let it be a real stamp of the foot and the command 'get out' given in a loud voice; unless she is a woman used to commanding in real life, in which case she may need to learn the opposite technique of an appeal for help or a bewitching smile.)

Now why does this occur? It almost looks like deliberate evil intent on the part of the animus. It is certainly this behaviour which gives him such a bad name and enables us to hurl the word 'animus-y' at our neighbour with such opprobrium. But is it really his fault? And is it really his particular delight to be so destructive?

Barbara Hannah,[1] in a paper on the animus, quoted his answer to this question. He told her that he understood nothing of her world, but that he could not bear a vacuum, so he always slipped in when a vacuum occurred. He told her that he needed to know about our world as much as we needed to know about his, and that it is a woman's business to enlighten him. In my own talks with the animus on this point he has expressed a similar idea, using the particular imagery in which he has shown himself to me. He has explained that he, the torchbearer, is an autonomous spirit whose sole concern is shedding light, focused light, light for its own sake. He has no feelings towards us, neither good nor ill, he has no feelings of any kind. Feeling is a human prerogative. He has no interest in us one way or another except, and this is vitally important, that he needs us for his very existence, for it is only in the human mind that he can dwell. He needs a human being to see the light he sheds. But shed his focusing light he must. To me, this is who he is.

In this sense, and in this sense only, has he any concern in our becoming conscious, for the more conscious we are the more we use his torch; and the more he is an essential part of us, a comrade and a partner, the nearer we approach that impossible goal of individuation.

So, it would appear that he sheds his light on whatever he thinks we will look at. If we appeal to him as a friend and ask him to throw his light on different aspects of the problem in hand he will surely do so. If our aim is the pursuit of some particular study he will readily put his torch at our disposal. Intellectual and professional women have all gained his friendship, sometimes, it is true, handing over the rein to him and allowing him to run their lives, carry through their careers or write their books for them. In these cases the animus may or may not be the dominant partner in the concern, but he is being creative. A woman who, with his aid,

[1] Analyst and lecturer of the C. G. Jung Institute, Zürich.

has made herself a student on, say, medieval churches or the treatment of cancer, no matter what, even though it be to the exclusion of a domestic life, may be called an animus woman, but will probably not be 'animus-y', for her animus is purposefully used and directed.

It is the woman who is not using the animus creatively who is at his mercy for he *must* throw his light somewhere. So he attracts her attention by throwing his light on one formula or slogan after another quite regardless of their exact relevance. She falls into the trap and accepts what he shows her as gospel truth.

A metallic note in a woman's voice or some physical rigidity will announce his presence; it may be a stiffening of the shoulders; a slight twist of the lips or rigidity of the whole body. Words are powerless to remove him. Only action can do so — an affectionate gesture, a playful shake or even a cup of tea!

Irrelevance is, I believe, the unmistakable hallmark of a negative animus statement. If looked at in isolation, animus generalizations are mostly sound remarks in themselves, for they are the fruit of experience garnered through the ages and they express the moral code of the place and time in history in which we live. But they may happen to be irrelevant to the living moment.

So we come to this: the animus is a woman's greatest friend when he shines his light on what is relevant, and turns foe the moment he lapses into irrelevance. A woman once dreamed that she saw four people spitting into the open mouth of a frog who in his turn croaked forth their spittle. On painting the dream, she realized that three of the spitters were the three analysts with whom she had worked at different times and the fourth was her own helpful animus. Everything that these four had said to her of meaning and significance at one time or another had been swallowed by this cold-blooded, amphibious creature, who later disgorged their remarks, out of their context, at inappropriate moments, causing her infinite distress. This frog is a perfect example of an animus figure whose destructiveness was solely due to the irrelevance of his croaking.

The reader may have noticed that I have myself fallen into the unhelpful way of talking of the animus as if he were one and undivided. I have deliberately left this lapse as an illustration of how easily this mistake can be made. When in moments of forgetfulness I accuse the helpful animus of going round and round me in sickening circles, he pulls me up at once. He says that was not he but his fool of a brother, to whom he hands his torch when I won't look at what he is trying to show me.

How can a woman detect the difference? For such discrimination needs the help of the animus himself, the very fellow who appears to be causing the trouble. There is only one way that I know of grappling with this difficulty. The woman must use every endeavour to give him all the data she can find. Animus opinions are based on insufficient knowledge of facts: 'the majority is always right,' 'where there is a will there is a way,' 'psychology is not to be trusted,' or any other half truth. So also, in an inner dialogue, what the animus tells her will be a valueless generalization unless she gives him all the facts; above all, the facts of her feelings, their intensity, their object.

How often a woman will listen to her animus telling her that her children should be pushed out of the nest or, if he shifts his torch a little, that a home should be provided for them until they are ready to fly. Either might be wrong in a particular case. How often he will tell her that her love affair is a shallow business, bound to end soon because love affairs always do: or that she must not trust the man because men are always fickle; and she omits, simply omits, to tell the animus the depth of her own feeling, the nature of the particular man or the significance of the affair. Having no feelings himself, he does not know these relevant facts, and she, as likely as not, is too shy, too lacking in confidence, even of her own image of the animus and above all too unaware of his power and his prevalence, to tell him the truth.

Yet her honesty would have got her past a menacing animus in safety; it would even have turned the foe to friend, for he is as willing to throw his light upon what is relevant for her to see, as to destroy her by showing her inappropriate generalities. The password is on her lips if she will but say: 'My feeling is this. These are the things which matter to me. Here I take my stand.'

But how seldom we do this. Today women have become so immersed in a masculine world of ideas and principles that they forget their own basic truth. For instance, any educated woman can understand the principles of freedom and democracy for which we fight our wars. With her trained masculine mind she may agree that wars are inevitable — nay, praiseworthy; but if she is true to the basic woman in herself she must never forget for one moment that the death of every single man slain by a machine for a principle is an outrage far greater than a murder committed in anger; that torture and enslaving on the altar of ideology is to her the vilest of human crimes.

To a woman who is true to her basic self, *un*relatedness is the touchstone of abomination. She must never forget that *un*related sexual intercourse much as she may enjoy it, festers in her belly; and that spiritual and intellectual achievements which are destructive of life cause the air which she breathes to stink. These are the things she must remember and of which she must constantly tell the animus, if he is to guide her aright through the maze of a masculine culture whose walls are lined with precepts. It is only if he knows her truest feelings, feelings upon which she takes her irrevocable stand, that he can be relied upon to throw his light on what is relevant to *her*, relevant to the situation, relevant to the living moment.

Maurice Nicoll in *The New Man*[2] speaks of the different *levels* of meaning in Christ's parables and of how the disciples often accepted the shallow meaning instead of the deeper one. The Devil, says Nicoll, is the creature who mixes up the levels, and this seems to me a description par excellence of the animus at his most satanic.

Mixing of the levels is the most diabolical form of irrelevance. But if you can still bear to follow my imagery you will see that it is the same thing. The focusing torch of the animus is destructive whenever it fails to hit the mark exactly, whether it be beside the point, too high or too low.

Talking on different levels without being quite aware of the fact is, as I have described in the chapter on 'Meeting', one of the most common and disastrous causes of misunderstanding between a man and a woman.

Our need is to keep the balance between masculine focused consciousness and woman's diffuse awareness — or, if you prefer, between the creative spirit which uses man as its vehicle and the life force which uses woman. Both these great impersonal forces are equally ruthless. They meet in the human mind, and I believe it is the task of every individual man and woman to help humanize them both. It seems today as though we have lost this vital balance.

The so-called emancipation of woman has resulted in women invading what was hitherto man's world in every branch. In other words they are living the life of the animus. There would be nothing wrong in that if it were not that in going over to man's

[2] Maurice Nicoll, *The New Man*, Stuart and Richards, London, 1968.

world, woman's essential values so often get thrown overboard. Even when biologically a woman is fulfilling her role, getting married and having a family, there is still a tendency for her life energy or libido to be elsewhere: sending her child to a crèche while she takes a job, reading a book while she is breast-feeding her baby.

Hovering over this now familiar situation I see an enormous menacing question mark: has woman's libido gone so far over to the masculine world of ideas and mechanics that the feminine passionate concern with life is actually denuded of the libido which it needs in order to hold the balance between the opposites? Is this imbalance perhaps one of the deep-rooted causes of the most devastating wars the world has ever known?

On the other hand, even among apparently domesticated women there are many today fighting to be allowed to live something other than the hitherto accepted biological pattern. Their masculine aspirations are sincere attempts to fulfil themselves. The battle for these women is a hard one for they do not know who they are nor on what to take their stand. A traditional inner voice still tells them that, not being career women, their only duty is to be wives and mothers, and this voice is picked up by the animus and shouted at them through a megaphone at every opportune and inopportune moment, or dropped like poison into their ears when they are relaxed.

Woe betide such a woman who falls into the hands of a psychologist who believes it is the feminine side which needs to be fostered. For then the animus voices are strengthened a hundredfold and the poor woman feels caught in a vicious circle. Every blow in self-defence is hurled back at her as unwarrantable animus aggression, and the familiar little imp who tells her she is no good grows fat and laughs and crows over her more than ever. In attacking the aggressive animus we actually feed this other animus figure who is a far greater menace to the woman herself. (I will return to this little imp presently.)

Her only way out of the impasse is to salute in all solemnity her most helpful animus and to tell him that on her word of honour she is not pining to have a baby and that her most sincere aspiration is creation in another field, intellectual, artistic, or maybe that most precious of all creations for a woman: conscious, human relationship. Then the taunting voices cease and the chains drop away. She can sigh with relief and accept herself as she really is: a human being with spiritual aspirations who, though born a woman, was not born to procreate. If she can accept this, then her energy is freed and she can develop along the lines of her own destiny.

Whether she makes a relationship to a real man or to her own creative animus she will have fulfilled her woman's need and lived her woman's role. Relationship with an actual man is of course the easiest way of learning to relate to her own creative animus; but merely the affirmation that she has to go her individual way and not the way of biology will turn her animus, hitherto her enemy because he knew no better, into her friend and ally, helping her to attain the very goal which before he slandered. You see, he does not care which way it is. Relationship, tenderness and cherishing are no concern of his. He is an archetype, with no human qualities whatever.

But note that it is not knowledge which the animus provides. If the knowledge needed is to be found in books, he enables a woman to gain it by throwing his light on the page so that she can read the words. Whether or not she understands the words she reads will depend upon her education and her power to think as well as on her ability to focus. This is a question of type, not of animus. If the knowledge to be gained is within, waiting to be drawn out from the storehouse of the collective unconscious, here also the role of the animus is, I believe, principally one of focusing and collecting.

If I am not mistaken it is through his anima that a man receives his inspirations. She is the fountain from which he drinks. She holds the treasures in her lap and offers them when he is ready to receive her gifts. But, having received them, it is his masculine, discriminating mind which gives form to the elusive riches she offers. She is the *femme inspiratrice*. It rests with him to mould the inspiration.

But the animus is not a woman's inspiration. He holds no treasures. Woman is vaguely aware of being herself in direct touch with the mysterious source, but her awareness is so diffuse that she can seldom even speak of it. She needs, passionately needs, the animus's torch to light up for her the things which she already innately knows, so that she can know she knows them. He brings no treasures, but he can throw the light of his torch on to one of the myriad jewels nestling darkly in her lap so that she can pick it up and, holding one glistening gem in the hollow of her hand, can say, 'Look what I have found.' Without his help she cannot braid her mermaid's hair, nor weave into a poem her wordless songs. Without his help she cannot catch the coloured fragrance of her world and show it clearly even to herself.

I have here a picture which I drew some years ago to illustrate what I have just been saying.

The huge figure behind is the Source. You may call her the Great Mother or you may call her the Nature Self which thrusts its children out into the everyday world to seek their own little ego-consciousness before they can find her again, at long last, as the Self of Becoming. But whatever you call her she is the Source from which the little girl, unlike the boy, is never separated. The woman standing between her giant knees is in direct intimate contact with her. The woman is drawing and in order to do so she uses the animus in the shape of her phallic pencil. He is the torch which throws light on her canvas, on herself and on the great figure behind; and note that by the aid of his light she can see that the Source is also winged, also a spiritual figure. The animus is the woman's measuring rod, her light and actually the pencil she uses, but her inspiration is gathered from her direct contact with the Source itself.

A woman today lives in perpetual conflict. She cannot slay the dragon of the unconscious without severing her own essential contact with it; without in fact destroying her feminine strength and becoming a mere pseudo-man. Her task is a peculiarly difficult one. She needs the focused consciousness her animus alone can give her, yet she must not forsake her woman's role of mediator to man. Through a woman, man finds his soul. She must never forget this. Through a woman, not through a pseudo-man. Through man, woman finds the animus who can *express* the soul she has never lost. Her burning need is to trust her own diffuse awareness, to *know* what she knows and to learn to speak of it, for until it is expressed she does not wholly know it.

How can a woman tell whether what her animus shows her with his light harmonizes with her own basic truth, or is some deceptive slogan? There is, I believe, only one criterion: quite simply whether or not it clicks. As we all know, an analyst may interpret a dream in such a way that we shake our heads and say, 'That is not right.' Or he may give an interpretation that makes our hearts beat faster or tears come to our eyes. Then we know that what he said has clicked. The same applies in conversations with our own helpful animus.

He may throw the light of his torch upon all sorts of things which do not click. Then it is important to tell him, 'No, I don't think that is the point. Please try again.' If not, one may be in danger of accepting the dictates of one animus figure with the help of another who likes to hear what he has heard before, or who tells us that we *ought* to accept whatever is told us by the unconscious. But if we are stirred, if we weep, there is no doubt that what the animus is telling us truly belongs, for a woman's tears accompany her deepest truth. An emotional response is usually a woman's surest guide to what belongs to her. But even when she discovers what belongs to her, she still has the greatest difficulty in telling her animus what she means, not only because she cannot focus enough to give form to her ideas, but because she does not seem to have adequate language at her disposal.

A woman uses the only language she has learned, yet in her own mind makes it fit her conception of the ideas, quite oblivious that her husband means something very different.

Two words that shine out in this connection are *Love* and *Spirit*.

I speak more of love in another setting but the word *Spirit* must be dealt with here for it is a great cause of confusion, both between actual men and women and between a woman and her animus.

To a woman, spirituality, or a life of the Spirit, implies relationship in its very essence: relationship to God in those intangible fleeting moments when she is aware of a presence, whether it be in the sudden impact of a white cherry tree in blossom, or the rhythmical furrows of a ploughed field; whether it be in a moment of unforgettable union with another human being or alone in the stillness of her own silence. Wherever it may happen there is for her always relationship. But the word 'spiritual' is not, I think, generally used in this sense. In the minds of many women the word Spirit evokes a memory of some direct experience very near to an awareness of the Holy Ghost.

If only she would voice her difficulty all would be well. But more often than not she is too bewildered by this difference in the use of words even to speak of her bewilderment. She neither tells her man of her failure to understand what he is saying, nor tells her own helpful animus and inner guide of her distress. If an analyst uses the expression 'spiritual animus' to convey the idea of something bad which is taking her away from life, then her bewilderment reaches its climax. That there is an animus who takes her away from life we all know very well. He may be the animus of collective ideas, of what is 'done'; he may be an intellectual recluse, a puritanical prig, or a pseudo-mystic. Any of these can seduce a woman away from life, but for the sake of mutual understanding let us not call him spiritual; for that word, to a woman, touches the highest that she knows and is imbued with a sacred relatedness which can never be destructive, for it is the giver of meaning to life.

Indeed, the expression 'spiritual animus' is, to a woman, a contradiction in terms. The animus is by his very nature an *in*human spirit and is therefore in his essence *un*related. Whereas to be spiritual is to her the very essence of relationship. It would be a help if the animus were only called spiritual when a woman has really succeeded in making a vivid relationship with him and he can be relied upon to co-operate as a friend.

If a woman will only be honest and stand her ground in a conversation with her own animus whenever there is something wrong, he will cease reiterating, parrot-wise, the same old saws. He may perhaps show her where she has not understood the meaning of what she has been told. He may even enable her to see, in a sudden flash from his illuminating torch, that the giving she had thought was love was little more than nature's flow of sap, the surging forth of life which uses her; and that to love, really to love, she needs the full co-operation of her partner, the animus, to direct her giving to the measure of the need. It is not love to choke one's children with more milk than they can swallow. Nor, if a man asks for a sip of water, is it love to drown him in a waterfall.

And in her turn she may make the animus understand — perhaps she may even make some man understand who had not known it before — that the essence to her of a spiritual life is one of relatedness.

I should like to say a little more about the animus that is woman's worst bugbear. He is the one who tells her she is no good. This voice is particularly dangerous because it only speaks to the woman herself and she is so cast down by it that, as likely as not, she dare not tell anyone about it and ask for help. In fact, it seldom occurs to her to do so. On the contrary, without knowing it, the analyst or anybody else, in any criticism, no matter how kindly made, is always in danger of actually feeding this destructive little imp, more particularly if a woman's aggression is really expressing her powerlessness to get across what she means, her defence of the half-glimpsed treasures which she knows are there but for which she can find no words. Then anyone's attack upon the aggressive animus will so bolster up this demon who shouts or whispers, 'You see, I was right, you *are* no good,' that the woman can be almost crushed by it.

And yet even this little wretch can also become an asset if only one will face him and say, 'Why do you tell me I'm no good, when in fact I have done so and so and achieved such and such, have lived through this and that crisis without wavering?' Gradually one amasses one's good qualities and one's achievements until his 'You're no good' looks silly. In other words this poisonous little voice forces one in sheer self-defence to be conscious of who one really is. His poison, like many another poison, brings healing.

Once the animus has become a friend upon whom one can rely, I believe a still further achievement with him can be reached. I speak of this with much diffidence, for, although I have it on his own authority, it may not sound convincing. But I pass on his message to me, to take or leave as you will. *He can and should be changed*. That he does change is obvious enough when one recalls that the moral precepts he voices at any one time and place in history differ from the moral precepts of some other time and place.

But what of our individual responsibility to change him? I believe if only women will hold true to their values as women and constantly tell the animus: 'Here I take my stand,' to an infinitesimal degree they may change the words he utters, not only to themselves, but also to other women. If we will tell our helpful animus, and continually repeat, that to the basic woman in us the slaughter of our sons and the crippling or enslaving of life anywhere is monstrous and unforgivable, then we may do the inestimable service of helping to keep in balance the two ruthless forces between which we are impaled, crude nature and relentless mind.

Moreover, in any close man–woman relationship, if the woman takes her stand on her own deepest truth and feelings, she not only makes a relationship of sincerity to her own animus, but the man's attitude will, sometimes without any word or explanation, change too. One constantly sees this happen in marriage-problem cases when only the wife is having an analysis.

How does this come about? For one thing, when a woman ceases to project her own aspect of the negative animus on to her man, he becomes free to function unhampered by this incubus. But perhaps also, on a deeper level, when a woman turns the animus from foe to friend and keeps him faithfully informed of her deepest feelings, these may seep through the ground and fruitfully water the thoughts and ideas of man himself.

VI

The Second Apple[1]

WHEN ADAM ATE the apple offered him by Eve he was thrown out of Paradise. He had ceased to be an innocent follower of instinctive nature for he had stolen a fragment of God's creativeness. He had stolen the power to choose.

Man had gained the power to obey nature or defy her. Man had sinned. No animal can sin as it has no choice. It can only obey the laws of its being. Man alone can sin.

And ever since that unfortunate incident of the apple men have felt guilty, and have done their best to make women feel guilty too.

Still, in the twentieth century, after the birth of a baby, our Christian Churches demand that a woman shall be ritually 'cleansed' by the priest, implying that she has sinned. Yet if there is ever a moment in a woman's life when she does not feel sinful it is when she has given birth. If she is truly in touch with her *own* feelings I cannot conceive that anything will ever make her believe that the act which led to the conception of her child could possibly have been a sin.

The woman with a newborn baby by a man she loves is as nearly in tune with nature as she can ever be, and when we are in tune with nature we feel ourselves to be in a state of grace, not sin.

I believe the sense of sin surrounding the sexual act is not indigenous to feminine psychology, but has been superimposed upon her by man and fostered quite especially by the Church. All the nonsense talked about the sacredness of woman's virginity, 'more precious than life itself,' is, I believe, far more a relic of man's claim to ownership than anything else. On the contrary in my limited experience, deep in the unconscious of most women lurks a primitive desire to be raped. This does not square with a passion for virginity, though one can certainly say that a desire to be raped in

[1] The image of 'The Second Apple' was given to me by my daughter Jacinta Castillejo de Nadal.

the unconscious is to be expected where there is an overvaluation of virginity in the conscious mind. But 'virginity' used not to mean lack of sexual experience. The 'Virgin' Goddesses were those who were sufficient unto themselves, under the dominion of no one. This did not preclude them from using males for purposes of fertility.

That woman fears sex is undeniable. She has reason to do so. Her whole life may be changed by a sexual encounter in a way that a man's is not. In the words of the Abyssinian woman quoted by Kerenyi:

> ... the day when a woman enjoys her first love cuts her in two. She becomes another woman on that day. The man is the same after his first love as he was before. The woman is from the day of her first love another. That continues so all through her life ... She must always be as her nature is. She must always be maiden and always be mother. Before every love she is maiden, after every love she is a mother.[2]

I believe these words are basically true in the psyche of most women, but in modern society the fear is increased by the slur and the ostracism which, though certainly less than before, is still put upon illegitimacy. Since the advent of Freud, man's whole attitude towards sexuality has begun to change. It seems that he has more or less digested the apple from the tree of knowledge of good and evil given him by Eve, and, stretching out his hand to the same tree, he has plucked a second apple and this time it is he who has offered it to her. He has discovered the contraceptive.

By so doing he has opened to mankind a vast new world of consciousness. By its means men and women alike are enabled to plumb greater depths of degradation than ever before, but also to touch spiritual heights which had hitherto been reserved for the fortunate few.

It was Eve who freed Adam from the blindness of nature. Now Adam has freed Eve from the inexorability of its rhythmical wheel. Like the first apple, the second has opened vistas more far-reaching than a changed attitude towards sex.

Eve has been avid in her eating of this newest stolen fruit. Her energy, once locked (not necessarily unhappily) in an endless chain of bearing and rearing children, has been freed for pursuits

[2] Jung and Kerenyi, *Essays on a Science of Mythology.*

of every kind. She has both soared, and elbowed, her way through thick and thin, filling her lungs with her new found freedom till Adam, and sometimes Eve herself, must have wondered if he had been wise to let her taste that second apple.

But once tasted there is no going back, and now it is woman's turn to shoulder a genuine sense of guilt. The contraceptive is for her a sin against nature in a way that simple sexuality never was. It is in line with the whole modern search for an illusive ideal of security. Our effete society is riddled, it is rotted, with the idea of playing safe. We insure against every risk. Even our love is pressed into the same ignoble pattern. 'Use Durex and be safe.'

To a deep layer of the feminine psyche this is abhorrent. The fact that medicine has made childbirth relatively free from danger does not liberate woman from her innate willingness to risk her life. Love which does not risk all is sadly lessened. And if risking all entails pregnancy, the basic woman is ready to risk her life again in birth, or if need be, in abortion. To 'play safe' is the one thing that those women who are in touch with their feminine nature cannot do, without leaving some trace of guilt in their psyche, however buried in the unconscious this may be.

But the apple has been eaten and there is no going back. Now she also is burdened with the sin entailed in choice. Hitherto, unless she eschewed nature altogether to become a nun, she had virtually no choice. Biology and racial needs had held her firmly in Nature's grip.

This is not quite true. There was always a narrow door of escape for the most daring from a continual round of procreation, through abortion. I cannot prove this but I suspect that abortion must have been practised from time immemorial. Literature abounds with references to the old woman down the side alley to whom girls resorted when in trouble. And presumably these old women were descendants of witches who carried out abortions behind the back of the Church and overstrict husbands in the same spirit as they administered love potions.

Curiously enough I believe that abortion is far less obnoxious to women than to men, provided of course that it is the woman herself who rejects the child and that she is not being forced to rid herself of a baby she really longs to have.

To the Church and to civilized man the destruction of a life that has already begun seems to be more heinous than to prevent conception. But I am not at all sure that this is true of woman's basic instincts. Doubtless men resent the casting out of 'their' seed by a woman. But to her the sacredness of the man's seed only applies if she loves him. The deeper her love, the more total is her acceptance of the new life. But where there is no love she is singularly un-sentimental about life. For a great many women a foetus of only a week or two holds no emotional appeal. Death in any case is part of life. Woman, who is so intimately and profoundly concerned with life, takes death in her stride. For her, to rid herself of an unwanted foetus is almost as much in accord with nature as for a cat to refuse its milk to a weakling kitten.

It is man who has evolved principles about the sacredness of life (which he very imperfectly lives up to) and women have passion-ately adopted them as their own. But principles are abstract ideas which are not, I believe, inherent in feminine psychology. Woman's basic instinct is not concerned with the *idea* of life as such, but with the *fact* of life. The ruthlessness of nature which discards unwanted life is deeply engrained in her make-up.

Modern woman is of course far removed, in her image of herself, from ruthless nature. Civilization depends upon overcoming nature. If Eve had never tempted Adam with that first apple there would have been no civilization. But tempt him she did, and woman also became civilized. I have, however, been struck by the spontaneous reaction of many women and young girls to the thal-idomide tragedies. So often I have heard them exclaim with ab-solute conviction, 'Of course they should be aborted! It is criminal to make a woman carry a child which she believes may be de-formed.' They have gone further and declared, when once their attention was drawn to the problem. 'It is monstrous that man should decide whether a woman should or should not have her own baby.'

This is not Christian morality. It is a spontaneous expression of Nature's law, which has its own morality. Although Nature may often have to be overcome, we ignore it at our peril.

Now what is the effect of an abortion upon a modern civilized mother? For years I have been much concerned at noticing the disturbances caused by past abortions upon the minds of my women patients. I had thought that this was due to the abortion itself which I had assumed was contrary to women's psychological make-up. But recently I have become overwhelmingly convinced that the bad and lasting effect upon the woman is not the fact of the abortion itself but is artificially induced by abortion laws. If

my contention is correct that abortion has from time immemorial
been part of women's lore, its possibility must be inherent in the
deep layers of a woman's psyche.

Abortion was doubtless made illegal in an honest attempt to
safeguard the lives of women who suffered at the hands of
abortionists with insufficient skill and no hygiene, as well as to
satisfy the moral qualms of the Church.

Women today however are less in need of protection than of
help. More and more they are becoming conscious individuals, no
longer content to be solely occupied with procreation. They are
conditioned and educated to play their part in society as a whole;
and within their marriages tend to be as much concerned with
being their husband's companion as mother of his children.

Family planning has come to their aid. It is recognized and
respected in all walks of life. Even Roman Catholics, who are not
allowed to use mechanical contraceptives, plan their families in so
far as possible by use of the so-called rhythm method. Yet the
moment, through some miscalculation, pregnancy actually occurs,
a woman finds herself suddenly trapped in an impossible
emotional situation by our antiquated abortion laws.

But there is many a woman of the highest calibre, physically
strong and mentally balanced, who feels that a child is undesirable. She may be unmarried and consider it actually wrong to
bring a fatherless child into the world. She may be already the
mother of several children, and for the sake of the other children
feels that another baby is more than she can cope with. It may be
for the sake of the husband who also deserves attention yet gets
very little in these servantless days when the wife is constantly
tending a young baby. Love itself may sometimes demand the
denial of nature. But whatever the reason, such a woman on becoming pregnant feels completely trapped.

Although abortion laws are being relaxed, there are still many
areas in which the law does not allow her the common-sense solution of speedily terminating an unwanted pregnancy unless to
continue it will endanger her life or health. This includes mental
health. Provided a woman shows signs of mental breakdown the
termination is legal.

The doctors cannot help her. No matter how sympathetic they
may be their hands are tied by the law. Two things can, and do
happen; if she is determined enough the woman may risk her life
or health at the hands of some illegal abortionist and face the

possibility of prison if it is discovered. Or she may go from doctor
to doctor all of whom may agree that she is being perfectly reasonable, but are only able to pass her on to someone else, until the
suspense has reduced her to a nervous wreck. Not until this has
happened will she legally qualify to have the termination of pregnancy for which she has pleaded. Once she is officially in danger of
a mental breakdown she can get an abortion legally.

And what, I ask, is the final result of such a course upon her
marriage? The effect of this struggle is not being adequately faced
by men. A woman's need is for mind and body to work in harmony together. In a gladly accepted pregnancy this happens.

A woman on the other hand who is determining *not* to carry an
unwanted child is split in two, her mind refusing to follow the
dictates of her body. Every day's delay accentuates this split. The
obstacles put in her way permeate her with a guilt which is not
basically hers, but is projected upon her by society. On the other
hand every day the foetus which she could have aborted lightly
with no harm to herself and without offending her nature, is
nearer becoming a child who claims her love. Less and less is she
clear what path is right. Society says to abort is a crime — while, to
her, to bring into the world a child, of which in her heart and
mind she has tried to be rid, is just as immoral.

The split and confusion widens until she either breaks down
mentally and is granted a legal abortion or, as a last resort, she
obtains one illegally. In either case she has ceased to be the normal
balanced woman she was before the struggle began.

I am convinced that from this artificially induced split many a
woman never recovers. When in later life it is seen that she has
become frigid, or some other marital disharmony has appeared,
the blame is put upon the termination of pregnancy itself. I emphatically refute this. The blame should be laid squarely where it
belongs, on antiquated abortion laws with all their consequences;
and it should be fully recognized that husbands eventually suffer
as deeply as their wives. If only for the sake of her marriage a
woman must be allowed to decide herself whether or not she will
carry a child. It is an insult to her that a man-made society should
make this decision for her.

In a society where women are given equality of education and
of status, and where they are expected to take responsibility for
earning their own living and to share in civic duties, it is wholly
incompatible that in the realm of childbirth, which is so par-

ticularly and intimately woman's concern, she is still subject to laws which abrogate her personal responsibility. This is an indignity which she should no longer be asked to suffer.

So far I have spoken of the effects upon women of our abortion laws. But what of the unwanted child the less determined woman is forced to bear? It has become an accepted fact that unwanted children are the seed bed from which delinquency and much unhappy neurosis springs. Yet every year the state insists on the birth of thousands of unwanted children and sees no discrepancy between these two facts.

I am told that many women who would have gladly relieved themselves of an undesired pregnancy if it had been easy to do so, become devoted mothers in the end and are glad that they went through with it. I know this is true but I find it quite irrelevant as an argument for denying abortion.

I personally should like to see the responsibility for bearing children put upon the women themselves. Undoubtedly many women, married and unmarried alike, would decide to terminate their pregnancies and might, in later years, weep bitter tears of regret. We only learn from our mistakes. To me it is emphatically not the business of the law to save a portion of our less wise women from making their own mistakes.

I look for the day when women may both carry and keep the illegitimate babies they may have wanted without social stigma, and also take full responsibility for *not* bearing unwanted children.

I am not suggesting that abortions should be carried out lightly but only after learning from the doctor and the psychologist or the priest all the pros and cons. Our doctors are in fact in as much need as the women to be freed from laws which over and over again oblige them to act (or refrain from acting) in opposition to what they recognize would be best for a particular woman or a particular marriage. If the laws were changed the doctor could warn husband and wife of all the dangers, both physical and psychological, which may be incurred by an abortion and offer his advice, yet leave the responsibility of final choice to the woman herself. I do not underrate the importance of the father's wishes, but it is the woman who carries the child in her body and it is *her* attitude during pregnancy which will affect the child throughout its whole life. So the ultimate decision should, in my view, rest with her.

With the freedom to choose her own sexual life the burden of sin is already fully woman's own. She must be allowed to carry her choice through to the end. This is paradoxically her psychic pregnancy from which there is no escape: that she shall become a conscious and fully responsible being. Adam has already given Eve the second apple. Once tasted it can never be taken back.

VII

Bridges

FEW DAYS PASS in which I am not concerned in some way or other with the man-woman relationship; and every day I become less sure of the answers. The only certainty I have is that since no two people are alike, relationships between them are bound to be dissimilar.

With the rapid growth of consciousness of today, while women have developed their masculine creative side and entered man's outer world whether of action or of thought, men have become more receptive and sensitive to a sphere beneath the surface where women had hitherto been apt to dwell alone, albeit silently and only half aware. Only artists have hitherto been in touch with the feminine world.

This penetration by each sex of the other's realm has progressed so far that to speak of a man-woman relationship as though it were something definite is beyond me. As I once heard it half humourously put, there are no longer two sexes, but six. There are men, women, homosexuals and lesbians, and there are also bisexuals and neuters. These physical and psychological anomalies and divergencies must never be forgotten for they are much more common than would appear on the surface. I must needs talk about the norm but I have never met it.

I have called this chapter Bridges because my contention is that a free relationship demands some degree of separation between individuals.

When people fall in love with one another they are so completely entangled that to tear them apart is like tearing a living creature asunder. Together they are a whole, separate they are two bleeding, mutilated halves. This vision of shared wholeness is known to us all but few of us are allowed to keep it for very long. This is not what I mean by a free relationship.

Relationship is a cold word. It has no vibrancy like, for instance, kinship, which immediately stirs something in one's blood, or like love with its infinity of overtones. It may mean great things or almost nothing. Every encounter with a member of the other sex can become some sort of man-woman relationship, and I am here going to treat the man-woman relationship very broadly to cover, for instance, my own friendly relationship with my gardener, pleasantly and mildly coloured by the fact that he is a man and I a woman, as well as the most intimate relationships between the sexes.

I am not equating relationship with love. I am not going to talk about love. Love is, I believe, something quite different. One can build a bridge of relationship but one cannot build love. In the richest relationships it will certainly be present but even when it vanishes temporarily or permanently, a valuable relationship may still exist. Love is greater than any bridge. I talk about love later in another chapter.

In considering the bridges between two separate people I ask myself how we can prevent ourselves from undermining the bridges we have so painstakingly built. I am hoping you will forgive me if I talk more about the woman's end of the bridge than the man's. I prefer to talk of things I know directly.

About the original difference between a man and a woman there is one inalienable fact which we cannot escape: the girl baby emerges from a being which is like herself. Being born, traumatic as that must be for any baby, is for a girl nonetheless a continuation of her identification with mother. Physical separateness goes along with a psychological identification which lasts for years. Mother lives again in the daughter and the little girl lives mother's life and shares her activities from the moment she can act at all. They are even in love with the same man.

The small boy on the other hand emerges from a being who is different from himself. The first person he recognizes is also mother, but from the very beginning of awareness he is clearly different from her and his interests are different too.

Simone de Beauvoir's contention that the difference in psychological attitude of boys and girls is due solely to difference of upbringing and expectations of the parents, seems to me, in part at least, to be belied by these elementary facts. The difference in attitude of boys and girls is visible almost from the outset.

I have seen a baby girl aged three months quiver with excitement as she lay beneath an apple tree in blossom, while her brothers of the same age were already fascinated by moving wheels which left her comparatively indifferent. I knew one little girl, who, at the age of two and a half, was so aware of her feminine role that when one day a man came to the house who did not respond to her flirtatious glances, she remarked to her mother on going to bed, 'Funny man. *Looks* like a man!'

This original difference of being different from or similar to mother, probably implants in the minds of men and women a pattern which appears in later life as an unconscious assumption of what relationship should be.

Women tend to seek identification with the person whom they love. A woman likes to follow her man and will even change her political ideas or her religion in her attempt to achieve once more that sense of union with another that was hers in the beginning. Even the modern woman who consciously admits a man's right to live his life without accounting for every moment of his day and expects to do the same herself, still wants to share his inmost thoughts and feelings, for that to her is the essence of true relationship.

Not so man. For him, separation is inevitable, and it is from his island of separateness that he tries to relate. For him the woman's attempts to probe the inmost recesses of his mind feels, consciously or unconsciously, like a threat to engulf him. He often feels her to be a siren from the deep luring him within her coils, or a gigantic white-crested wave which may submerge him. A woman finds it difficult to understand why he feels threatened. She herself rides the wave so easily. She has never been wholly separated from the water in which she floated at ease within her mother's womb.

Man has pulled himself out of the unconscious matrix with the effort of thousands of years. But his rational supremacy is somewhat precarious and he rightly fears to be submerged again. So, as often as not, he avoids emotion and teaches his womenfolk to do likewise. A man does not understand that a show of emotion on the part of a woman does not have the devastating effect on her that it has on him.

Women are most at home when ankle-deep in the unconscious. They can handle emotions. For them a burst of anger clears the air, and a flood of tears is the storm which releases thunderous tension and leaves them calm. The woman, who, in her desire for identification with her man, represses emotions as he has done, deprives not only herself but him as well.

Again and again I am surprised at the determination with which some intellectual men try to educate their wives to be as rationally minded as themselves, only to turn on them when they have succeeded. Such a man, and I am constantly meeting them, is really trying to turn his wife into another man. It may be that he is not yet mature enough to be able to relate to his opposite so he seeks in his wife the easy companionship which people of similar tastes and ways of thought can share. It is not till he has achieved this happy condition that he realizes that something is missing and blames his wife for his own mistake. A woman who has lost all her native contact with the irrational has ceased to be herself and is no longer the woman who originally met his need. The opposite situation where a wife drags her husband into her own emotional sphere, though luckily less frequent, is even more disastrous, for the man is brought to the verge of breakdown.

There are other men, on the contrary, who have such a large ingredient of the feminine in their own make-up that they seek a woman with a well-developed masculine side in order to encounter their opposite; but this, unlike the case where the man tries to make the woman like himself, may be one of those modern reversals of role between the man and the woman which are inevitable in this generation. It is not necessarily a sign of immaturity.

Now about the bridges. Any interest which two people share clearly forms a bridge on which they can meet. This is so obvious that we tend to put the cart before the horse by substituting all sorts of interests shared for the emotional bonds which are lacking. It is not uncommon, for example, for women to watch football Sunday after Sunday though it bores them to death. But such frail bridges easily totter. Men on the other hand seem less willing to suffer boredom for the sake of relationship and perhaps rightly so.

Ultimately of course communication in some form or other is the fundamental foundation for any kind of stable bridge. But communication does not necessarily mean talking things over. Spontaneous reactions are more likely to be valuable than studied words. Curiously enough talking is often one of our greatest stumbling blocks to mutual understanding. It sounds so simple, so easy to be frank and say what one means, but we so often omit to notice who in fact we are talking to. I would go further and say we are not always aware who is doing the talking. Neither party in a relationship is always him or herself, as everyone knows, but frequently forgets.

Endless confusion arises until one understands that there is no such thing as a simple relationship between one man and one woman. It is as though there were at least four personalities always involved, the man and his feminine side; the woman and her masculine side. (The unconscious of any ordinary masculine man is feminine in character and can be personified by the figure of a woman. Similarly the unconscious of an ordinary feminine woman is masculine in character and is personified by the figure of a man or a group of men.)

Though we do not usually think in these terms most people are very well aware of the phenomenon especially when things are not going right. For instance, when a man becomes moody and irritable, without giving one any idea of what is the matter, it will be because the feminine in his unconscious has for the time being taken charge of his personality. He is at that moment as incapable of expressing his real feelings as any shy girl; although it is also from the feminine in himself that a man gets his inspiration, he, the man, providing the form in which the inspiration will be expressed.

Inability to find words is one of the outstanding characteristics of the feminine. Some women have the greatest difficulty in expressing verbally their deepest thoughts and feelings. This may sound nonsense for women are proverbial talkers. But the loquacious woman, whether intellectual or not, is in reality as possessed by her masculine side as the moody man is by his feminine.

So long as this masculine, discriminating side is actively and fully employed by a woman all is well. She will be efficient and creative. It is when purpose is lacking that the masculine in a woman becomes negative. If then he turns his attention outwards she will make those sweeping generalizations that ruin general discussion, or throw out remarks which sound all right but which are actually just beside the point, causing unwitting havoc in the thinking of all around her. This constantly happens when the real inner woman is secretly concerned with some other matter much nearer her heart, when she should have known that she was really bothered inside about something quite different from the words her lips are uttering, and have remained silent; or have admitted to herself that the matter in hand was something about which she knew very little and that her contribution could be nothing more than opinions she had picked up from newspapers, or mere reiterations of what her parents used to say. If she would learn to listen to herself she would be surprised to find how often her observations are no more than this.

When a woman hands herself over to her masculine spokesman, while the real woman in her retires into her own inner sanctuary, cliché after cliché may even come rolling out in a voice vibrant with emotion and then her husband or lover will probably end by walking away and slamming the door.

On the contrary when the real inner woman is present in the situation, her masculine side can express what she, as woman, really means. This is not nearly as easy as it sounds, for women are so educated to think and behave like men today that they are in constant danger of losing touch with their own real inner truth. It is very serious when woman's negative masculine side has no external outlet at all for his energy. Then he will turn on the woman herself. He will convince her that she is useless, and that her life past, present and future, is utterly devoid of meaning.

Other misunderstandings between men and women are apt to occur when one of the four personalities of which I have spoken is absent. A man who tries to communicate with a woman without the aid of his feminine feeling to make the bridge and enable him to meet her on her own ground, is likely to produce a dry intellectual dissertation which either paralyses her or makes her angry, according to temperament. Similarly, the woman who assumes that her man will know what she is feeling without her telling him, because to her it is quite obvious, has omitted to utilize her own inner masculine clarity to convey the message, and leaves her actual man bewildered and in the dark.

I have often wondered why women are more tolerant of a man's moods than he of her irrelevant vocal outbursts. Perhaps it is because a woman at heart tends to think of men as little boys, and after all one can be tolerant of little boys. Moreover she understands irrational moods and caprices. They are qualities she not only recognizes in herself, she deliberately uses them to her advantage when it suits her to do so. She is so familiar with their fickle transitoriness that she can afford to greet them in her man with a shrug of the shoulders, and wait for the mood to pass.

The man on the other hand is really put out by her clichés. They shatter his clarity of thought because they lead him astray by their very nearness to the truth. And perhaps, I suggest this with all temerity, perhaps men are unaware how often they too are just off the mark themselves. It is the things we are unaware of in ourselves which make us so very angry when we see them in other people.

As I have already said, in our present transitional stage no one quite knows his or her role. A man no longer knows what part in life he is supposed to take. Young men today constantly feel quite shattered by this uncertainty for both at home and in the outside world the roles of man and woman have been made to overlap. On the other hand I constantly meet the wife who has become ousted from her own kitchen, or is so organized by her husband within her own realm that she feels completely depotentiated as a woman. Her life becomes deprived of purpose, and without purpose she can no more live than can a man. Her only refuge is to join the ranks of her career sisters, a solution which is as likely to aggravate the problems between husband and wife as heal them.

In casting her net in wider waters modern woman has caught not only the fish she sought but a devouring monster as well which is busy destroying the more feminine among her number. Woman's invasion of man's sphere has, I believe, aroused in man's unconscious the determination to maintain his former superiority at all costs, even among those who consciously believe in and are most vociferously in favour of equality between the sexes. Consciously men welcome woman's emancipation but in the unconscious they despise her and are determined to keep her in her place. As one young woman I know puts it, 'Men like us to be creative because that is what makes us interesting, but they hate us to create as that's trespassing on their preserves.'

It is the *un*consciousness of this resentment which shatters the woman for it is picked up by her in her *un*conscious where it fortifies her own doubts of her own powers. It appears as a masculine voice which reiterates over and over again in a half-caught whisper or a resounding shout, 'You cannot do it, you are no good.' I have yet to meet the woman who is not familiar with this voice. A woman can in her own obscure way counter a man's open opposition. It puts her on her mettle. As my old mother used to say, 'One can't knock one's husband down but one has got to get round him somehow.' But antagonism when hidden can neither be circumvented nor dissolved. It reinforces all women's internal doubts and is, I am convinced, responsible for endless frustration and even breakdown on the part of women. This is the devouring monster she has caught unwittingly in her emancipated net. It silently destroys every bridge that men and women try to build.

However this may be, for any real deep communication to take place between two people of the opposite sex, all four personalities, two in the conscious and two in the unconscious, must always be present at the same time. This is true whatever admixture of masculine and feminine there may be in each individual.

The most powerful bridge of all, is of course sexuality, but it is not always such a firm safe structure as it would appear to be. It is a common enough experience for a man and woman each to step upon it from his or her own side of the river only to find that it breaks in the middle throwing both partners into a stream turbulent with frustration and resentment.

One partner may dash too quickly across the bridge to find that the other has disappeared. The woman perhaps was not really in her body at the time after all, or her body was not ready, so there was no encounter; or a premature ejaculation overtakes a man, breaking the bridge before it could be crossed. Each will return sadly to his or her own domain whenever either party is for some reason unable to meet the other spiritually as well as physically. I am sure this is true of both men and women.

I am speaking of course of a real relationship. There is no bridge and no relationship in shallow experimental physical encounters.

But in this field we are up against faulty education. Women tend to believe quite erroneously that a man only wants her body. Early warnings, newspaper reading and novels all help to inculcate this mistaken idea which is picked up by an inner voice and whispered into a woman's ear at the most inappropriate moments, turning her suddenly into a baffling icicle when all her warmth had actually been needed. On the one hand she is taught from infancy that man is a dangerous animal creature who is to be trusted at her peril, inculcating fear on the physical level from the start. On the other hand she is *not* taught that he is in fact dangerous because his truth and hers do not necessarily coincide, so, unprotected and unwarned, many a woman allows herself to be raped intellectually and spiritually over and over again.

I use the word rape deliberately for completely helpless children are impregnated by immature adults with false ideas. On those girls who have not been specially gifted with independence of mind this crime is perpetrated over and over again. Unknowingly they nurture such false ideas with their life's blood and finally bring forth monsters. As an example of what I mean: the educated women today who are so strenuous in their advocacy of physical punishment for juvenile offenders have obviously been raped in their childhood with the idea that vengeance is synonymous with justice, an idea which has ousted their innate protectiveness of the young wherever found. Any girl who grows to womanhood without knowing that love is her supreme value has been spiritually raped. Justice is one of our noblest concepts, yet the woman who would deliver up her husband, lover or son for the sake of justice, no matter what crime he had committed, would, to me, be a woman only in name. And I am sure that most women would agree with me.

The sensitive boy and man no doubt suffers, just as acutely. His struggle to retain his hold on his own truth may be even harder, because the expectations of society that material success should be his inevitable goal and physical sport the route to attain it, weighs upon him even more heavily than upon a girl. Nonetheless his innate power of discrimination is more likely to save him from the dire consequences of mistaken education. He may suffer outrage but he is less likely unknowingly to nurture monsters. Though admittedly he sometimes does so.

However this may be, a girl needs to be warned of her two-fold danger: one that the fear of physical rape is so deeply inculcated that it may lurk beneath the surface long after she has rationally dismissed it; and two that her real danger is in that most unsuspected place, her mind and her very soul.

As a rule a man has no conception of the basis of woman's fears nor of the inner voice that repeats them to her. For him sexual intercourse will in itself restore any broken harmony. He has no idea that for a woman a bridge of spiritual attunement must first be built before she is able, not willing, but able to trust herself to cross the bridge of sex.

Another aspect of woman's confusion is brought about by her modern education. Men's modern problem is apparently the separation of spirit and body. To what extent the Church has inculcated this split in man's psyche I cannot judge but it is unquestionably there as every analyst can testify.

The fact is that modern women have been brought up in this same school of thought where things of the mind and spirit are honoured and the functions of the body are debased, while our supreme gift of physical creativity is relegated to shady stories and lavatory jokes. Even the natural process of menstruation is called 'the curse'.

This divorce of mind from body pertains in girls' school nearly as much as in boys' so that women also tend to put the mind on a pedestal and at best their own bodies on the same level as that of cows or rabbits. Only the very feminine girl escapes this innuendo underlying her education. For most women very considerable experience of life is needed to grasp the truth for which they had been completely unprepared: that for the whole woman there is no possible cleavage between spirit and body, for it is in her body that her spirit dwells.

This discovery can come upon her like a revelation, and once understood, her inhibiting fear that man only wants her body vanishes into thin air. She can abandon herself as never before in the physical encounter for she knows that if he can meet her in her body he cannot fail also to find her spirit.

But neither partner must ever take the other for granted. The bridge may be strongly built, but leave to cross has to be asked and granted anew each time. This applies throughout all the sphere of the man-woman relationship, not only in matters of sex. Nothing is so disheartening as being taken for granted, day after day and year after year, whether it be the woman who takes for granted that her man will provide the money or he that she will cook the supper. Taking for granted is of course more likely to happen in marriage than in other relationships, but wherever it happens, it stultifies the imagination and turns the relationship into a suffocating prison.

For thousands of people marriage has become a prison, and I want to look a little closer at this phenomenon to see if we can understand what has happened.

The determining factor is what goes on in the *un*conscious, for the unconscious is the source of dynamism, whether for building or destruction, not our conscious rational intentions.

What in fact is the unconscious of both man and woman doing to marriage? Some force is certainly very busy breaking marriages up. Jung has suggested that the numerical preponderance of women in the modern Western world is partly responsible. He suggests that the thousands of women for whom no husband is available, try in the unconscious to devalue the marriages of their envied sisters with the secret aim of annexing their husbands for themselves. Jung maintains that the undermining process is so widespread beneath the surface that even wives are affected by it, till they too weaken the marriage bond in their lurking doubt whether after all marriage is worth the bondage.

But this explanation was written before the last war and it hardly seems adequate today, when the preponderance of women over men is rapidly righting itself. More deep-seated is, I believe, the growing desire to be free.

Women, still dazzled by the glitter of what they thought would be freedom promised by their emancipation, find themselves either pressed into the new unexpected moulds of our commercialized society or swamped by domesticity with no outlet for the talents modern education has fostered in them.

In either case they chafe and fret and, with their feminine subtlety of indirect attack and their capacity to close their eyes to what they do not want to see, break the prison that is nearest them and within their ability to break: the marriage of their neighbour or their own.

Jung's greatest plea for women is to learn to know their goal. What today is woman's goal? I believe few women have any idea towards what end they are striving. The unmarried certainly would not admit that they are trying to break the marriage institution, nor do wives admit that it is they who undermine the marriage walls. Yet marriage after marriage totters and becomes a shambles.

Doubtless another reason for this collapse is the decline of religion. The highest values of mankind today are without a home. The channel for man's mystical aspirations and his need to worship something greater than himself was hithero provided by the Church. Today man finds himself with no definite spiritual goal. The energy thus freed has been poured by men into the advance of science, or material progress or the State. But these gods are too impersonal for a woman to worship. If there is no God at least there is a man to love. So all her displaced energy flows into a man-woman relationship. There surely she will find her deepest values. This tenuous human relationship becomes her all. She fills it with her idealism, her expectations and her love. There is no limit to the value it is asked to hold.

Moreover contraceptives have freed immense energy which would otherwise have been used in bearing and rearing children. So the surplus energy of women is doubly great. When it all goes into the marriage relationship (which seems to many a woman to be the only place of value which is left to her) by the very frailty of its humanness the marriage bursts asunder and leaves her desolate. Maybe this tottering institution of marriage has, in its present rigid form, outworn its usefulness and we shall have to find new more flexible forms for those unions which also embrace a family.

Another mistaken orientation from which modern woman suffers is, I believe, the adoption of man's goal of independence. She thinks she *has* to leave home and lead a life of her own like a man. There is of course nothing against a woman living on her own if she wants to do so, and for some it is imperative, but the number of girls who pine in solitary studio apartments or furnished rooms, for no better reason than the assumption that this is what is expected of them, is tragic. More devastating than this chilly form of abode is the belief that it is essential for them to free themselves entirely from any inner psychological tie with their parents. This may be right for a man, but I am sure that there are many cases where it is quite unsound for a woman.

Women of one generation and the next overlap. It is as though there were a continuous rope of posterity running down through the women. And for a young woman to think she can opt out and deliberately cut herself off from this is often to belie her nature and enslave herself in an abstract theory. One modern very independent-minded young professional woman, who had been much preoccupied with what seemed to her a too close tie with her mother, said to me one day, 'You can't think what a relief it is to know I do not need to break with my mother, to know that it is through her that I am a link in a chain back into the past and forward into the future. For the first time I feel free.'

I have an uneasy feeling that the trend of today wherein women so largely live their masculine side in careers and jobs, and men have become correspondingly more sensitive and receptive, is hiding extreme danger under a deceptive appearance of greater wholeness in the individual.

There can be little doubt that with rare exceptions the masculine of woman is inferior in quality to that of a man. It is apt to be less original and less flexible. She tends to be impressed by organization and theories which she frequently carries to excess because her masculine power to focus runs away with her. She then becomes hidebound by regulations and obsessed by detail. She is much less likely to be willing to make exceptions than a man, as the masculine side which runs away with her is wholly impersonal and disregards the human need of any particular man or woman.

But the same sort of thing applies to the feminine within man. It is less vital and dynamic than that of woman. The feminine in women is not solely passive and receptive. It is also ruthless in its service of life, or rather of those particular lives which personally concern her. She is as ruthless as nature. There are no lengths to which a woman will not go to foster the welfare of her immediate family or those she loves. The feminine of man on the other hand is soft and gentle, lacking this ruthless service of life every bit as much as the masculine of woman lacks originality and flexibility.

Man's way of cherishing is to build a welfare state which will care for all: an admirable civilized institution but so depersonalized that in spite of the excellency of its aim, it appears to be in danger of sapping the will and sense of responsibility of the individual man and woman.

Like that of woman, the man's contrasexual side is always wholly impersonal. This is the thing to be remembered: the forces in the unconscious, whether in man or woman, hold the dynamism but are inhuman and impersonal.

Our task is to allow these dynamic forces to work through us (for without them we are impotent) yet to avoid being mercilessly enslaved by them; only so can we reduce their force to human proportions. To be human is our greatest need, and also the thing we find most difficult.

Take another quality: ambition. Without ambition it is doubtful if anyone would have the necessary drive to achieve any great work. Ambition is indispensable. It is one of the qualities of mankind which has helped to achieve our civilization. Ambition is, I should say, a masculine attribute whether found in man or woman. Nature is ruthless but in no sense ambitious. The apparently feminine woman who ceaselessly eggs on her man to greater achievement regardless of his own desires, is in fact unconsciously possessed by an ambitious masculine devil within her, which has got completely out of hand. It is when ambition is harnessed in the service of life that it furthers the development of mankind. Our enormous advances in medicine are notable examples.

Similarly, if men, without knowing it, are taken over by their negative feminine side in the form of vanity, they also become victims of inhuman impersonality. They are spurred on to ever greater and greater heights, and the needs of life are forgotten in the fascination of their own powers of creation. No matter that a quarter of our globe is starving and millions of refugees pine in camps; no matter that spiritual anaemia is rife throughout the world, the moon is conquered and mankind has won the power to commit racial suicide.

This state of affairs is probably the product of each sex being *invaded* by the characteristics belonging to the other rather than by being consciously and positively related to the opposite in themselves. Perhaps men are in the greatest danger here, for the age of enlightenment set reason on a throne. The resulting devaluation of the irrational feminine within man himself thus turned it into an enemy to be repressed rather than honoured as the essential other side of life. It is the repression of a dynamic force which renders it explosive.

Women on the other hand, have not in the past repressed their masculinity. It existed only as a potential. But, when unrelated to, it can also be a menace, though it has not the same terrifying disruptive lunatic force that the feminine has in man's psyche when it breaks its boundaries, as happened in the two great wars which were due mainly to the eruption of the repressed and dishonoured irrational feminine, gone mad throughout the world.

The prevalent unconscious contrasexual invasion within individuals is in a sense a set-back rather than an advance in maturity; though I have no doubt that it is a temporary and necessary stage which will be followed, if we survive, by an enormously enlarged awareness. It is, I hope, a case of *reculer pour mieux sauter*. The place to which we shall finally have to jump is a state of mind wherein the masculine and feminine are consciously experienced and related to one another *within* each individual rather than between two individuals of the opposite sex. At present this ideal is only the ultimate goal of a long life fully lived; if aimed at too soon the young may cheat themselves of an essential stage of their lives.

I have called this chapter Bridges. As man and woman have, throughout the ages, walked on either side of the river of life there have always been some bridges which have enabled them to meet. Mutual understanding may have been at a minimum but we have always been able to trust that devotion, passion and sexuality would throw bridges across the stream over and over again.

Mutual responsibilities with joys and sorrows shared have strengthened the foundations and built, stone by stone, bridges which could withstand storms and rushing torrents. But in the past each partner still dwelt on his or her own bank of the river.

Today it is as though the banks were crumbling, narrowing the river bed until it can be jumped across. Already I see in my mind's eye the sands from either side mingling and mounting slowly till they form a terra-firma on which anyone can walk in easy companionship.

But if this should happen, the dynamic river would have ceased to flow, dammed up by the mingling sands. How long, I wonder, would it be before the imprisoned accumulating weight of water crashed over us, drowning our endeavours towards equality in a gigantic bid for freedom to flow once more between two banks.

I believe we have it in our power to avert such a dread calamity if we will only learn that the opposites must always be separate if they are to be related.

Paradox is the essence of living. Perhaps the greatest paradox in man's psyche is our longing for union, for peace, for solutions, though experience has taught us that it is our conflicts and our failures which are in fact our points of growth.

We can throw bridges of understanding across the abyss between our hate and our love, our doubt and our faith and every other pair of opposites. And the mystic can doubtless at moments hold them all together, but to do so continuously is the finality of death.

Separation is the keynote of relating the opposites in life. It is the keynote of a free relationship between man and woman. But the separation of the past with a clearcut distinction between the two sexes, who were nonetheless joined compulsively to form one whole, is over. The present is a confused intermingling of male and female in both sexes which befogs relationships. Yet the future may hold some clarity where men and women may each relate to the opposite within themselves without women being swallowed by their masculine or men by their feminine characteristics.

I believe that ultimately we shall have to find wholeness within ourselves in order that we may walk along the river of life on either bank making relationships with individuals on the other side of like wholeness to ourselves. These meetings of whole people will surely take place on bridges which span the stream of life flowing between two separate banks.

VIII

What Do We Mean By Love?

My DAYS ARE spent listening while people tell me their troubles, and as they all inevitably speak from time to time of love I have had much occasion to be astonished at the different meanings with which they endow the word. Men and women often see it from bewilderingly different angles, each speaking of love with complete assurance, unaware that it means something else to their partners.

I am not referring to the forms of love's expression. We are all familiar with its endless variations from the lowest to the highest. The confusion lies in what people think is the nature of love itself. Of this I have made no special study, except for my ordinary woman's preoccupation with love. I am merely feeling my way around the periphery of this great ball of light which seems to be at the centre of our lives, and voicing some of my musings.

I do not know what love is. When I was a girl of eighteen I had no doubts. I scorned books on love with impatience. It all seemed so simple. Words could do nothing but confuse and blur our innate clarity of direct vision. Words could do no more than provide a golden cage for a bird whose wings had been clipped, drooping in its gilded prison. I was very healthily aware of the danger of practising as Aldous Huxley puts it: 'Alchemy in reverse – we touch gold and it turns into lead; touch the pure lyrics of experience, and they turn into the verbal equivalents of tripe and hogwash.' That was at eighteen. But the further I have travelled, following as all natural women do the voice of love, the less sure have I become that I know anything about it at all.

Please notice that I am not writing about 'relationship' here, nor about 'sex', nor any other particular form or expression, but about love itself in whatever place or form it happens to alight on us.

Love is known by everyone, yet the direct experience becomes so hedged around with assumptions that we get confused. And then, when life disproves these assumptions, we begin to wonder if the essence we thought we knew had only been a mere trick of the light. Perhaps these assumptions are the gilded bars of the cage.

The first of these popular beliefs, which is very soon and most disconcertingly proved false, is that love is permanent. We assume that the love between parents and children should persist, that the love of wives and husbands should last their lives, that lovers should be true unto death. Yet the permanence of love's presence is an ideal which bears little resemblance to the facts. How many children love their parents when they no longer need their care? One has but to scratch the filial surface to find emotions very akin to hate or a far more poisonous indifference. How many married couples, at best, retain more for one another than tolerance, kindliness and sympathy? The divorce courts tell the tale of the worst. How few of us are capable of being Tristans and Isoldes!

It is a pathetic disillusionment when we stare these facts squarely in the face. It seemed for a while that psychology was coming to our aid when it said, 'Ah, those people you speak of never loved at all. It was all a delusion, a mirage. Those cases were only projections. The little child projects the unconscious in all its power for good and evil on its mother. It projects the wisdom of the ages on its father, and they in turn project their future, their ambition and their immortality on their child. Men project their inner image of woman on wives and mothers, and women the spirit of culture and authority on their men.' 'Withdraw your projections,' we were told, 'only then can you learn to love.'

Learn to love? Was not that only another assumption? Another bar of the gilded cage? Has anyone ever learned to love? We can withdraw our projection certainly, and by so doing we can learn to understand one another. But I do not believe anyone ever learned to love.

Love happens. It is a miracle that happens by grace. We have no control over it. It happens. It comes, it lights our lives, and very often it departs. We can never make it happen nor make it stay.

In Christopher Fry's play *The Dark is Light Enough*, the Countess in the last scene denies to Gethner that she had ever loved him. He is incredulous, in view of all she has done for him, but supposes her to mean that he never deserved her love.

She replies in these words:

> It never came about.
> There we have no free will.
> At the one place of experience
> Where we are most at mercy, and where
> The decision will alter us to the end of our days,
> Our destination is fixed;
> We are elected into love.

We can perhaps learn to prepare for love. We can welcome its coming, we can learn to treasure and cherish it when it comes, but we cannot make it happen. We are elected into love.

This is, I believe, equally true of every kind and degree of love, from the love that shines in a baby's eyes when it first really sees its mother and gives her a smile of recognition, through the whole gamut of intimate human relationships, both spiritual and physical, to the furthest extreme of impersonal love which we call Agape; of this the life of Christ is the supreme example.

Even this impersonal, healing love, some measure of which is attained by a few great spirits, is utterly beyond anyone's power to learn or to control. It also happens. No man can make love shine through his life at will, no matter how he strives. The striving may prepare the ground, but he can take no credit for the love. To that he was elected. It happened. To some it may come simply without apparent torment, and I would dare hazard that those through whom love shines most brightly are supremely unaware of it. Impersonal love is like humility. Those who have it do not think about it, much less talk about it. But in no case is there any choice, it comes by grace.

The young man does not choose the moment which transforms his life by love, nor can he choose the woman who evokes the transformation. The baby does not choose its mother and cannot withhold the love which is between them. Love simply happens.

Yet we take this miracle so for granted that when it has occurred we think it should be ours forever. May it not have been an attempt to soften our disillusionment at love's passing which made the psychologist in the past deny that it had ever been there when the young fall out of love? 'It was only an anima-animus projection,' they told us. But were they not themselves caught in the false assumption that love is permanent?

The miracle of being in love is too overwhelming an experience ever to be dismissed as a projection. I do not believe for one moment that a projection can in itself light up the whole world. It is the love which goes with it that lights the world.

I do not deny the projections, nor the need for them to be withdrawn, but if we do not honour love itself as also present during that brief time, I think we are wilfully blind and we belittle our human stature. When we allow this to occur we have entered the realm of the debunkers and handed our psychological tools to the devil.

Please remember that I am not attempting to make a distinction between different kinds of love: physical or spiritual love, Eros and Agape or any other classification. To me love is always the same wherever it appears. The differences lie in our capacity. Where love is, it is as though some presence had alighted, a third, a something else, a something greater than the little persons who are involved.

I find it easier to think of love as being present than to talk of loving. It fits better with my belief that love happens and cannot be taught or learned. It is a monstrous conceit to think we can teach a little child how to love. He knows. He knows far better than we disillusioned grown-ups. Even in the transient trustful smile a baby will give a stranger, something lights up and the stranger will go on his way feeling more vital and more at ease with himself. Was that not love? I think perhaps it was. But it didn't stay. The stranger and the baby met for a moment and parted. They had no further concern with one another.

In the home the presence of a child will normally bring love with it. There is no question of learning here, and I do not doubt the genuineness of the love. Yet this is the very place where we find one of the biggest and falsest of the assumptions which surround our common usage of the word love. The immense flow of libido of a mother towards her child occurs at the same time as real love, and in the mother's mind the two are synonymous.

But are they the same? Is a mother's instinctive care of her child necessarily love, or may it not sometimes be a flow of nature's milk of which she must rid herself as urgently as of an overcharged breast? Most assuredly it feels like love, this pouring of libido upon her child, but every psychologist knows how destructive it may be.

Mothers come off badly these days. They are told they devour their children, poison their lives, cripple their growth; yet in all sincerity the mother thinks that what she gives is love. Can love cripple? Can love poison? I do not believe so. Surely we have made some hideous mistake. We have assumed that giving must be love, and failed to notice that giving what is not needed chokes and hampers; it may even kill.

Woman needs to give. She cannot help herself. Life pours through her and she has no choice but to pass it on, or let it stagnate until it becomes an abscess in her breast. This flow of life is not intended only for her children, but also for her mate. But many a man is too proud to accept her giving, confusing it with the mother's milk he has outgrown, unaware that it is the water of life she offers him. So she, in desperation, pours all her libido upon her sons and daughters not knowing what she does, and wonders why they drown.

Some years ago I heard Michael Fordham[1] give a lecture that I have never forgotten in which he spoke of the reciprocal roles of parents and children. He said that little children, who are beginning to emerge from the sea of the unconscious, need their parents to be strong, firm breakwaters in order to prevent the ever-menacing sea from inundating them again.

And in exchange the child, by his strangely wise words and his unpredictable behaviour, can be a link between his adult parents and the unconscious from which they have themselves broken away; if only they will listen to him and notice what he does. But this denotes a constantly changing situation. As the child grows, linking up the tiny islands of consciousness till finally he is standing on a sizeable piece of land with an ego of his own, the need for his parents' breakwater becomes less and less. So also, as he withdraws himself from the enveloping sea, will his words and actions have less contact with the collective wisdom of the unconscious, and be less in harmony with his own instincts or the psychic situation of his father and mother, and so he will be less and less of a link between the unconscious and his parents. The attitude of parents to children must be changing all the time to meet this fluid situation, if some condition is not to arise which drives love out.

The problem of parents and children, however, is not merely one of reciprocity, but of each generation being in its right place in

[1] Michael Fordham, M.D., B.Ch., M.R.C.P., founder member of the Society of Analytical Psychology.

the chain of posterity. Every individual is so linked with the past through the parents and to the future through the children that it is difficult to remember that it is with our own lives that we are fundamentally concerned. We are very greedy of life and try to live through our children the life we have failed to live ourselves. This puts a terrible burden on the children, making them live out the unused talents or the unconscious desires of their parents. Many a young man finds himself impelled to be an artist or a writer, though he has no great aptitude, and when one looks beneath the surface one finds that a parent or grandparent had repressed real talent thus forcing its outlet upon some unfortunate descendant. In T. S. Eliot's *Family Reunion* the son Harry pushes his wife overboard without really meaning to do so, and only later discovers that he had unwittingly carried out his father's unadmitted desire to get rid of his own wife. All but Harry thought it was an accident.

In actual life one is constantly coming across such things, and it is brought home to me again and again that the sins of the fathers are visited upon the children unto the fourth generation. The real sin is the failure to be conscious where one is capable of being conscious. For it is unconsciousness which gives such libido to the repressed talent or desire that succeeding generations are forced to enact it. Harry would not have had to push his wife into the sea had his father been fully aware of his own desire and then consciously refrained from carrying it out.

This type of burden we put upon the young does not make for love. Neither does the weight of our advice. We forget that, though we have in fact gained a little wisdom from our experience, our children do not start as raw material waiting for us to mould them, but actually build upon the foundations we have laid. They start to a certain extent where we leave off and, from the very fact of being born later, are beyond us. The post-war generation of children are startlingly more conscious than their parents were and the children of parents who have made it their business to be conscious themselves may have been given a start which enables them to leap far ahead beyond those same parents. I am sure we should listen with respect to what the young say, just because they are young, if we would keep love between us.

In our rapidly changing social and psychological patterns, it is difficult to be adaptable enough to make the conditions in which love stays. The young man has always had to struggle away from his mother's influence; but when mothers are as well educated as their sons and turn themselves into the son's intellectual companion, the struggle is even more violent. Mothers are tenacious in a new way. I recall the young man who bitterly complained that although he had left home he could not escape his mother. 'It is terrible, she prays for me every day!' Yet what more natural, or even more laudable, than to pray for one's son? Perhaps the trouble was caused by the way she prayed.

If a woman prays for her son's welfare she may actually divert his fate. Things may even apparently go better with him. He may refrain from marrying the undesirable girl or making some apparently fatal mistake. And yet we know so little of the pattern that belongs to us, or to those for whom we are concerned, that our very intervention, though it be by heartfelt prayer, may be damaging. I suspect that this type of insidious intervention through the unconscious is more potent and far more dangerous than the visible interferences from which one can protect oneself. The good faith in which it is made does not guarantee its freedom from poison. The apparently undesirable girl may be the right one. Some disastrous mistake from which the fond mother tries to save her son may be the very mistake he needs to make.

Parents spend their lives trying to save their children from making mistakes. And yet, when we look back over our own lives, we can all see how fruitful our mistakes have been. The mother who prays daily for her son's welfare is still playing her protective role, still trying to be a breakwater. She is giving in excess of his need and the love between them vanishes. If she could only be content to pray that nothing be allowed to divert him from his true destiny, whatever strange course that might take, then I believe he would be strengthened and not shackled by her prayers, and love might remain between them.

If on the other hand the mother errs in the opposite direction her son may feel cast out and lost, and again love vanishes. Our modern overstress on independence may be one cause of the number of lost young men wandering about today.

To strike the balance and give enough, yet not too much, is immensely difficult. Perhaps trust is all a woman can safely give her children. Trust may be one of the vital conditions wherever we would have love stay.

Look for a moment at the other side of the picture. The parents are growing old and some son or daughter stays at home and cares for them, sacrificing his or her own future marriage or career to do so. Love may be present here, but often it is only duty masquerading in the guise of love, poisoning the atmosphere with repressed and hidden hatred and resentment. The child-parent roles have become reversed without the parents giving up their claim to be masters of the house. Change of attitude has not kept pace with change of need, and love has gone.

It is not easy these days for the aging to keep their right place in the chain. We need the ripe wisdom of the old. That is their culminating contribution. But science will not let them die naturally even when they are ready and longing to depart. This is called respect of life, but I sometimes wonder if it is not, in the words of Buner, 'Man's lust for whittling away the secret of death'. We do not honour death today. So the old are often too long with us, and their cruelly overstretched-out lives become a burden that is insupportable. Love goes, and I wonder if the old, when they have been pushed out from the wholeness of family life, are less able to die because of it. Love and death are strangely kin. To be cared for from duty only sterilizes. We need love to be able to die serenely.

Duty and love are miles apart. I remember the story of a woman who was about to embark on a mountain of family washing, gaily singing to herself the while, when her husband came in and seeing the pile of sheets and pants and socks upbraided her for failure to organize the children to help her more. 'They should all have their duties,' he said. To his surprise his wife burst into tears, abandoned the washing and rushed out of the house. When she returned several hours later, she explained to her bewildered husband that the word duty made her sick. 'Can't you see,' she said, 'that I work for you and the children all day long for love. There are no limits to what I can do for love, but from duty I cannot wash one shirt or cook one meal, and what I cannot do I will never ask my children to do. I do not want their help to be a duty. One day they will help me from love, and then I will accept it.' And one day, a good deal later, unasked, they did so. That woman may have been wrong in her educational methods, but she certainly knew the coldness of duty and the dynamism of love. This dynamic quality is surely one of the hallmarks of love. In the presence of love there are no obstacles man is unable to surmount.

Meeting the other's needs appears to me to be the crux of the matter. Between adults, as between parents and children, it is the same necessary condition for the presence of love. When two people fall in love (whether they be of the same sex or of opposite sexes is irrelevant in this connection) they find that the other somewhere meets their need and together they feel whole. But as each is growing all the time, every day the need is different. Those who are sensitive enough to notice the change of their own and their partner's need can change their attitude along with it. And if both partners are able to do this love may remain between them, or at least visit them very often.

It is those who fail to change with their own and their partner's changing need who fall so desperately out of love. A man may marry a woman younger than himself. To begin with all is well. He is the father on whom she can lean, she the daughter for whom he cares. But if she develops she will no longer tolerate being a daughter-wife nor need a father-husband. If he can sense this change and become the husband-lover, raising her from daughter to be his mistress-wife, then can love still be their constant visitor. Or, if an older wife can see her younger husband growing up and drop the mother role in time, she too may keep love within the marriage.

Please note I have used the word need, not want or desire. We may want things we do not need, and we are often unaware of our deepest needs.

But if either partner becomes possessive or over-zealous, or on the contrary too casual and unthinking, irritation and frustration creep in; the feeling of wholeness is destroyed and the relationship either breaks up, or hangs together merely from force of habit. But the love which was there has left it.

Love and wholeness go inextricably together. One may not be the cause of the other, but they occur together. And before there can be a wholeness there has always been a meeting, always an 'I-Thou' recognition.

I do not wish to give the impression that it is an easy matter to be at the service of another's need. It is difficult enough to know your own need, much more so that of another. The people who are always doing these things because they think it best for someone else generally go wrong, both for the other and themselves.

Paradoxically it is when we are true to our *own deepest* needs (not, I repeat, our immediate desires) that we are most likely to serve the other's need also. The mother who prayed daily for her son was following her desire and longing for his welfare, not her need nor his. Her real need was probably to develop a life of her own and, if she had done so, she would have served his need to be left free at the same time.

The man who stamps out some essential side of himself in order to meet his wife's need for a faithful husband, may cheat her of becoming, through suffering, a more conscious person which she may have needed to become; or he may poison the home atmosphere with his resentment at being warped. It is all heart-breakingly difficult. Mutual service without betraying one's own deepest truth is the paradox at the very centre of the art of living.

Unfortunately only one path to this central point is open to us. No one can know with any certainty the needs of another, but he can, if he will take the trouble, discover his own, and it is a fact that if a man will faithfully follow the path towards greater consciousness of himself, which means greater wholeness within, and at the same time maintain his willingness to serve his partner, he is likely to find he is meeting the need of that one also, and love will be between them. Wholeness is both the goal and the key. Consciousness is the tool.

In my belief it is the same love in every case. Whether we are floodlit or the recipient of only one ray, it is the same love. Love is all one. The difference is, as I have said before, in our capacity, but also in the direction and the emotion felt. Where two people are involved it is as though a spark flashed between their two opposing poles. This is a tension of high emotion, the love is *between* these two and we call it Eros.

But where the individual has found his relative wholeness within himself, the opposites meet *within* him; then there is no external tension and therefore no emotion. He may even be unaware of the love he radiates. This is Agape.

> The great of earth,
> How softly do they live;
> The lesser ones it is are praised,
> Revered;
> Still lesser, feared;
> But these,
> One hardly knows that they are there,
> So gently do they go about their tasks,
> So quietly achieve;

When they have passed,
Their life's work done,
The people look and say:
It happened of itself . . .[2]

To me it is man's task, his greatest task, not to learn to love, but to learn how to create the conditions in which love can alight upon us and can remain with us.

Within the regular patterns of relationship, parents and children, wives and husbands, we have at least precedent and instinct to guide us as to what the necessary conditions may be.

The supreme task comes in those relationships that have no set pattern. Here we have no guide and can only feel our way in each individual case, with unlimited patience and discernment and absence from preconceived ideas. For every relationship between conscious adults is unique, needing freedom to blossom into its own individual flower. We can only tend and cherish the bud with all our care, waiting for the flower to open and declare itself. We must never forget this uniqueness if we are to avoid being led astray by the advice or example of those who have gone before us, or by the teaching of psychologists who can no more know our particular pattern than we do ourselves. The outer form of such a unique relationship tells nothing of its significance. Its value lies in the quality of the meeting.

The tending of an individual flower of relationship may involve much heartbreak and endless sacrifice of personal desire. But even this must not be confused with love itself. Yet the degree of our faithfulness to the needs of a unique relationship, whose ultimate pattern we cannot know, is the degree to which love will shine through it. Even here we have no choice. We are elected into love. Our choice lies in rejecting or taking up the task.

When people speak of healing by love I always feel dubious, for so many things feel like love which may be something quite different. Pouring libido upon a person does not necessarily heal. It may bind with ever stronger silken cords from which there is no escape. I do not call this love.

Giving tenderness and understanding does not always heal. Sometimes it is necessary to have a heart of stone and let the sufferer beat his head against one's lack of comprehension until he has hammered out his own salvation. These things feel very far

[2] Written by Ruth Tenney, based on a poem by Lao Tze.

away from love, and yet the healer may be filling the necessary role so well that healing from within takes place. A wholeness may have been created between the sick man and the healer, or the wholeness may be within the sick man himself. In either case it is love which enters in and heals. For indeed I believe most firmly that the presence of love is the only healer. But let us not flatter ourselves that *we* have healed by love. Healing has happened by a miracle. The miracle is love.

In the analytical situation love is often present. I do not mean only the love of the patient for the analyst, which can so easily turn to hatred, and be just as effective either way. I mean the spark of some divine quality which enters in wherever there is healing, regardless of the specific emotion experienced in the analytical hour.

This is no merit on the part of the analyst. It is his job to keep himself as free as he can from making projections, while accepting the projections of his patient, in order that the channel of healing can remain clear and unobstructed. But when the analyst in rare moments of real healing speaks from the Self, and so speaks more wisdom than he can possibly have had, then love is present. Or when in the silence a flash of illumination suddenly breaks upon the patient, his heightened consciousness allows love to enter in. In either case it is the love which heals.

But it does not stay. There is something terribly hurtful in the word transference. It offends the dignity of the human soul to feel that the immense emotions felt in the analytical hour have been brought about in an artificial context. The transience of the analytical relationship can be wounding to the point of insult.

If we can grasp that love wherever it appears is real love; only that it does not stay when it no longer belongs to the situation, then we need not be hurt at the way love disappears between analyst and patient as strangely as it had come.

Nor should we forget that analysts are helped to stand the strain of their calling by the love which comes to them through the undemanding libido their more mature patients pour upon them. I am convinced that this gives them life and energy, whether they know it or not. This must be equally true of priests and every other kind of healer.

The love betweeen analyst and healed is, moreover, never only one way. A physician once said to me, 'One only loves those whom one serves.' And I am convinced that service, the willingness to serve, is one of the most important criteria for the presence of love.

The analyst certainly does serve. I would go so far as to say that unwillingness to serve is one of the basic causes of neurosis because it shuts love out.

Mutual need and willingness to serve are both inherent in the analytical situation. The patient needs the analyst, but the analyst most assuredly needs his patients, not only for his means of livelihood but also for his need to serve. You might almost say for his need to love, but more accurately for his need to be an instrument whereby love can enter in and heal. This is, I believe, the particular vocation of every healer.

What, I have been asking myself, is the situation in ordinary life where love is not returned? There seems no wholeness there. But if one looks a little closer, one sees that this is not so. Beatrice fulfilled the need of Dante by simply being who she was. He needed her as a focus for his adoration and a mirror for his soul. He adored her from afar and made no demands upon her. During her life he asked no more than a passing smile. And in the unpossessiveness of his giving he did not drive out the love to which he had been elected. I do not doubt that Beatrice was the richer, whether she was aware of it or not. It is our egotistical demands, our petty possessiveness, our stupid jealousies which turn a generous giving (one that makes the giver whole and enriches the recipient) into an irksome burden we try to cast aside. Then there is no love, only an abuse of giving, which is as tiresome as our demands.

Love is unique, and must never be confused with the many qualities which are inherent in a relationship. Tenderness, sympathy, understanding, patience, impatience too and anger, or even jealousy, are essential concomitants of relationship. None of these make love itself, not even all of them put together. A relationship has its own obligations and its legitimate demands, but, as one of my poems expresses it, love claims no rights:

> Let me hold a beacon in my hand
> Shining on your face alone
> My own in shadow
> Passion held in leash with pity.
>
> Let me clear the sanctuary
> Of money-lenders who would seek
> To strike a bargain
> And silence the raucous voice of duty.

> Let me break the chains that bind you
> Every claim the law condones
> Or my devotion warrants
> While giving you the freedom of my City.

We speak loosely of hatred as love's negation, but we all know it is nothing of the kind. Hatred is only the other side of the golden coin of love. One must be very concerned to take the trouble to hate. A novitiate once asked his master how many lives were necessary to reach Nirvana. The master answered, 'For he who loves God seven, but for he who hates God only three.'

That jealousy and love are wholly incompatible seemed to the girl of eighteen axiomatic. If one truly loves, one has no right to resent what gives the other happiness. When I was a child I heard these lines:

> True love in this differs from gold or clay,
> In that to divide is not to take away.

These words fell on my ear like a clarion call and have been a touchstone ever since.

But life has taught me that it is not as simple as that. Jealousy is not necessarily a mere egoistical desire to possess for one's very own, not just a selfish unwillingness to share. It is the anguish of despair; the wholeness one thought one had found with the loved one is shattered. The golden coin of love lies smashed to pieces at one's feet. One is overwhelmed with fear. But this is no cold, dank, cloying fear; it is burning with the intensity of one's desire for wholeness and one's desolation at its betrayal. It burns with a heat which can destroy, which can make Othello strangle his Desdemona. There was no love in that dark moment. Love had been driven out by Othello's blind jealousy.

But if jealousy can be made to see; if a capacity and willingness to understand dwell in the heart at the same time as one is torn to shreds by jealousy, then the agony of despair can be lifted to another plane where its white heat can fuse again the scattered pieces of the golden coin; can make possible the return of love through acceptance of one's desolation and the humility of forgiveness. Wholeness is restored, but this time the wholeness is within the sufferer himself.

Dark jealousy, though often base, must not be despised. Rather let us beware when jealousy is absent. It smacks dangerously of indifference. The man who is so tolerant that he greets his wife's confession of unfaithfulness with, 'All right darling, go ahead,' is likely to be a cold fish who will wreck his marriage through the very coolness of his objectivity. Nothing could be more hurtful than a lover who cannot be fired by jealousy. Understanding needs to be fused with intensity of feeling before any transformation can take place, any forgiveness of betrayal ring true.

Indifference is the poison which seals up every channel of dynamic growth. Indifference, not hate nor anger nor jealousy, but indifference, hiding beneath a cloak of culture and rational behaviour, is the negation of love. It is the rejection and total loss of the golden coin.

Indifference is our failure to meet the other; our failure to meet the situation; or our failure to allow the opposites to meet within us, with all the conflict that entails. Where love is, there has been first a meeting, always a meeting. Without a meeting of opposites there can be no wholeness, and no chance for love to break through.

At eighteen I knew, but could not say, that it was from God that love breaks through. It was a long time before I could bring myself to use the word God. It had been bandied about so lightly and with such dubious assurance by people who, in the eyes of a child, seemed to be very little in touch with God. So I have had to travel a long roundabout way, a voyage of exploration through an inner world of images. And there I have found and brought up to the light of day an image of wholeness where all the opposites meet, even the opposites of our tiny egos and the great unknown.

Jung calls this the transcendent function and names its goal the Self. We do not understand what this means either, but in our need to try to express our fleeting glimpses of wholeness we find, or rediscover, some symbol to denote this moment of transcendence. It may be the Christian symbol, it may be something else. But whatever form it takes, it is the image of totality towards which we aspire; the supreme place of meeting. And it would seem that this essence of wholeness touches us repeatedly throughout our lives, each time to the degree of our capacity, impelling us always towards itself. No matter what we call it, we experience this as love.

I am not equating love with the Self, though I am convinced that wherever there is love the Self, our symbol of totality, is the link which holds the two who meet together. The meeting in every case is in the presence of the Self. When this is not so, what passes for love is something else. It may be lust, it may be duty. It may be greed or a false self-abnegation, but it is not love.

Neither am I trying to equate love with God. I do not know what God is. But I do know, and have always known, with that inner knowing nothing can gainsay, that love is more than the meeting. At the meeting is the presence of the Holy Spirit.

I know no more about love now than I did when I started to write this chapter, but in the course of my musings there have emerged a few of the conditions which, I believe, we must attain if we would have love with us more than as a flitting presence.

IX

The Rainmaker Ideal

IN THE SPRING of 1959 all over the world people were watching and waiting anxiously for news of one man whom most of us knew very little about. Thousands of Chinese troops with massive guns and aided by planes were searching for the Dalai Lama of Tibet who had taken flight. Could he and his small retinue escape? The chances seemed remote. Then the news came through. The Dalai Lama had crossed the frontier into India.

Later an astonishing article appeared in that most respectable paper, *The Times*. The correspondent hesitatingly pointed out that the escape had the semblance of a miracle: the mountains had been unseasonably shrouded in mist during the whole flight, a mist which rolled away the moment the Dalai Lama reached safety. Moreover, the writer had the courage to suggest that this apparent piece of luck may have been due to the person of the Dalai Lama himself. He quoted another instance where an important feast was being held, and told how, as he had looked anxiously at the great menacing clouds overhead, a member of the crowd had come up to him and said, 'There is no need to be so worried, it won't rain till the feast is over, there are several Lamas present.' And in effect it was not until the last richly robed participant had reached his home that the rain drenched down.

I suspect that many a reader of that article will have dismissed it with a shrug and the comment 'That correspondent has been out East too long.' But we can, I think, afford to regard this happening with a more open-minded sense of wonder; and though we do not understand it perhaps we can try very tentatively to grasp its significance.

The Dalai Lama's escape and the reputed influence of Lamas over the weather, bring to mind the traditional Chinese story of the Rainmaker which most of you probably know. In a remote village in China a long drought had parched the fields, the harvest was in danger of being lost and the people were facing starvation in the months to come. The villagers did everything they could. They prayed to their ancestors; their priests took the images from the temples and marched them round the stricken fields. But no ritual and no prayers brought rain.

In despair they sent far afield for a 'Rainmaker'. When the little old man arrived, they asked him what he needed to effect his magic and he replied, 'Nothing, only a quiet place where I can be alone.' They gave him a little house and there he lived quietly doing the things one has to do in life, and on the third day the rain came.

This is to me as profound a story as any parable of Christ and sets an example and an ideal which is a salutary complement to our Western passion for activity.

If only we could be rainmakers! I am of course not thinking literally of rain. I am thinking of those people (and I have met one or two) who go about their ordinary business with no fuss, not ostensibly helping others, not giving advice, not continually and self-consciously praying for guidance or striving for mystical union with God, not even being especially noticeable, yet around whom things happen.

Others seem to live more fully for their presence: possibilities of work appear unexpectedly or people offer their services unsought, houses fall vacant for the homeless, lovers meet. Life blossoms all around them without their lifting a finger and, as likely as not, without anyone attributing to them any credit for the happenings, least of all themselves. Rainmakers are very inconspicuous. It is easier to spot those around whom life withers. We all know the Jonahs in our midst, who, in our smug self-complacency, we cast into the sea.

Indeed, these rare people around whom life blossoms cannot be said to cause the blossoming. The Rainmaker of the story did not cause the rain to fall by the exercise of any supernatural power. Nor I am sure would the Dalai Lama claim that he had caused the shrouding mist to which he owed his escape.

The Rainmaker does not cause, he *allows* the rain to fall. Along with our ever-increasing knowledge by which we wrest from nature the secrets of the physical universe, make the earth more fertile, man more prosperous, and master diseases which attack us; we also erect barriers, block streams and poison wells with the one-sidedness of our understanding and the hardness of our hearts. We may even prevent the rain from falling.

We have forgotten how to allow. The essence of the Rainmaker is that he knows how to allow. The Rainmaker walks in the middle of the road, neither held back by the past nor hurrying towards the future, neither lured to the right nor to the left, but allowing the past and the future, the outer world of the right and the inner images of the left all to play upon him while he attends, no more than attends, to the living moment in which these forces meet.

In those rare moments when all the opposites meet within a man, good and also evil, light and also darkness, spirit and also body, brain and also heart, masculine focused consciousness and at the same time feminine diffuse awareness, wisdom of maturity and childlike wonder; when all are allowed and none displaces any other in the mind of a man, then that man, though he may utter no word, is in an attitude of prayer. Whether he knows it or not his own receptive allowing will affect all those around him; rain will fall on the parched fields, and tears will turn bitter grief to flowering sorrow, while stricken children dry their eyes and laugh.

This attitude of unvoiced prayer which wills nothing and asks nothing, exerts an influence exactly opposite in kind from the deliberate influence beneath the surface which is in constant use today.

There is a vast difference between allowing, and deliberately exerting power. I am not considering the obvious external uses of power, whether of physical force, the weight of general opinion, or the moral canon of the time. I am talking of power effected through the unconscious.

The technique of talking not to a person's conscious mind but direct to the unconscious itself is unquestionably an instrument of power, an instrument used by anyone who throws out an idea and does not follow it up with conscious discussion. The idea is heard and sinks into the unconscious, where, if it happens to fall upon fertile soil, it will take root and flourish and later emerge to the light of day as an idea which the person has thought for himself.

Prophets and teachers from time immemorial have used this method for communication. They have spoken to the multitude, not talked and discussed with conscious minds. The seeds have taken root and flourished. This is how conversions are made, never by argument and rational conviction.

Maybe our churches are so empty today because preachers increasingly talk to the conscious understanding of their hearers, forgetting, in this scientific age, that dynamism comes from emotions and ideas coloured with emotions in the *un*conscious mind.

Speaking to the unconscious is a form of communication against which it is difficult to protect oneself. Advertisers deliberately use this channel to influence and determine what people think and what they think they want. The daily press exploits it to the full in favour of political parties, while dictators and totalitarian governments are past masters of its use.

Speaking directly to the unconscious, bypassing the resistance of the conscious mind, is not necessarily harmful. It is a technique sometimes used deliberately by therapists and by innumerable women who have learned the art of getting their ideas across without arguing. This may be wise and beneficial all round but what a weapon it can become! Like everything else, in its very excellence lies its danger.

Quite apart from its tyrannous employment by dictators and advertisers, we can be unknowingly damaged by its subtle use in our personal relationships. How many men are undermined by the insidious dropping of unsound ideas by wives. In my experience even the most intellectual of men are not immune. How many women are crushed and diverted from their own true path by the insistent assumption of superiority which men let fall without intention.

It is not enough to have good intentions. Without greater consciousness than we normally possess of what we do and say, our good intentions can be the traditional paving stones of hell. But even when we are aware of what we say, the moment we try, through underground methods, to affect other people's thoughts or actions towards definite ends, no matter how alluring or how good the ends may seem, we have inadvertently taken the road that leads away from, not towards, the Rainmaker ideal.

It is for us to choose which way we will go; shall we go towards the exercise of personal power for preconceived ends (not necessarily egoistical ends, for the goal may be the common good); or shall we admit that being only human we do not and cannot know what the ultimate goal should be, and so rest content with working for our own individual poise in the hope that that will be the best way of allowing life to happen around us at its fullest?

Whichever way we choose, we certainly shall not get there by travelling in the opposite direction. If we want to go north we had better avoid the roads which lead south.

It needs a considerable degree of consciousness to avoid turning down the wrong road by mistake. It behoves us to examine the *direction* in which we are travelling: towards power in order to achieve preconceived ends or towards freeing those around us from our dominance in order to allow them to develop along their own lines.

To be a Rainmaker is, except for inspired moments, an ideal that is far beyond us, but ideals are ideals just because they are so nearly unattainable. They serve, not so much as goals to be reached, as lights on the far horizon towards which an occasional sign-post points. If we will follow these pointers I think we can be assured of following a direction which *cannot* lead to illegitimate exercise of power nor to any kind of dictatorship no matter how benevolent.

The remoteness of the ideal is daunting, for how in this complicated world can we influence or interfere with anything at all? Yet if one will only look a little more closely one sees that the outer world unquestionably responds differently according to our own frame of mind.

Take an everyday situation as seen by a shy person who comes to some group meetings. He may hide in a corner or sit in the front row, he will still be almost invisible. The chances are that he will creep away the moment the meeting is over in terror lest someone should speak to him, and still more alarmed at the prospect of no one speaking to him at all. Yet beneath his shyness may be hidden a very positive personality which he has not yet himself encountered. An analysis or some experience of life may bring out the hidden side and the next time he enters this same dreaded room of people he will be amazed to find, not only that his embarrassment has left him, but that the very people who never noticed him before actually speak to him of their own accord. They may even seek him out. Yet the only change in the situation is his own new self-assurance.

Everyone knows those horrible days when everything goes wrong. One just misses the train, one's boss is in a bad temper, the bus conductor is rude and the shop assistants refuse to serve one. If one is capable of being objective at all on such a day, admittedly rather a difficult feat, one knows that at the root of the trouble lies one's own negative mood. Like calls to like.

On the days when everything goes right it is easier to believe that it was entirely due to our own charm, skill, good taste and efficiency. We are apt to take even more to our credit than is our due, just as before we had taken the blame too little. Be that as it may, it is, I think, indisputable that our own inner mood had in both cases affected in some degree the way the outer world had received us.

If we can go as far as this in admitting our own partial responsibility for outer conditions we have already entered that path towards freedom where we need be no longer the blind impotent victims of our environment.

It is a very big step. Big because it is the first one, not because it takes us very far.

Unfortunately we can seldom change our mood by an act of will. But the simple recognition of its existence may enable us to laugh. Kindly laughter at oneself can be like bubbles of oxygen reinvigorating the air of a stuffy room.

In intimate relationships such as marriage it is fundamental to know that it is one's own inner attitude of mind which not only makes the room stuffy but actually influences the reaction of one's partner. For instance, the wife who complains of a bullying husband has generally brought it upon herself by a cringing attitude. In fact her own unconscious tendency to cringe will have caused her to choose a bully for a mate. If she can learn to stand up for herself it is extremely likely that, after the first shock of dismay at being thwarted, the husband's disdain will turn to admiration, even though he may keep his admiration to himself. The bully, whether it be wife or husband, and it is just as likely to be the wife, does not admire but despises the cringing victim.

Similarly the wife who despairs of her husband's inability to understand her, needs to recognize that she has not only failed to tell him what she means, she has probably failed to tell herself. Women's own confusion today about who they are and what they want of life causes a fog around them which confuses everyone. Far more important than an uttered declaration of her meaning is her own inner clarity.

Achieving inner clarity is I believe the prime task of both men and women. I have used the expression inner clarity before,[1] but I should like here to enlarge upon what I mean by it. May I try and explain my own homely imagery.

I like to think of every person's being linked to God from the morning of birth to the night of his death by an invisible thread, a thread which is unique for each one of us, a thread which can never be broken. Never broken or taken away, but a thread which can easily slip from our grasp and, search for it as we may, elude us.

Our bodies are at the lowest point of this thread which runs up through every sphere of heart and head and spiritual attainment. Still on our individual thread but beyond our human reach are, in my imagery, angels or demons which at supreme moments we feel we are able to contact. They are the intermediaries between us and God. To be on our thread is in Jungian language to be in touch with the Self, and the angels and other figures to which I refer are the archetypal images of the Self which all who have had an analysis learn to recognize. I am saying nothing new. I am merely using ordinary language to say the same thing both because I happen to like ordinary language and because it is only when I have put an idea in my own words that I feel I am beginning to understand it.

I am using the expression 'inner clarity' to mean conscious awareness of being on one's thread, knowing what one knows, and having an ability quite simply and without ostentation to stand firm on one's own inner truth.

It is when we are on our vital thread that life happens around us in a way that befits our individual destiny, for we have not interfered. This does not necessarily mean that everything happens as we would like. Misfortunes and mistakes are also part of our pattern. Even illnesses may be necessary from time to time to give us pause or teach us lessons we should not otherwise learn. But everything is meaningful and can be seen sooner or later to fit into the pattern of our lives. It is only when we have lost our thread that life seems purposeless, lacking in significance and unacceptable. I believe it is also an empirical fact that life happens more fully around those who are on their thread. So storms hold off or rain falls as is required. It was not in the destiny of the Dalai Lama to be captured by Chinese troops. He had no need to practise magic.

[1] 'Meeting' — Chapter 1.

It simply happened that the mountains were shrouded in mist until he escaped.

It is all very difficult, for to enter the road of allowing and freedom does not necessarily mean simple acquiescence nor inactivity. The Rainmaker may be an active person and a strong one. But he does not interfere, he does not block the paths. On the contrary, being primarily concerned with his own thread, his activities will be such as to come to him personally and belong to his own pattern. He is not trying to exert influence or to have power over others at all, not even in the unconscious.

His activity, when he is active, will be demanded of him by the dictates of his own inner truth. He only acts when failure to do so would be failure to be true to himself. For instance, a man sitting on the beach engrossed and profoundly concerned with solving an intellectual problem would not forsake his vital thread if he suddenly plunged into the sea to save a stranger from drowning; even though by so doing he lost the mathematical formula or the line of poetry which had been evolving in his head. It is more likely that he would have been untrue to himself had he been deaf to the cries for help. For some, on the other hand, action may be the predominant note of their lives and rightfully so. We cannot judge.

But whichever way it leads us, being true to oneself must never, never be mistaken for egoism. On the contrary the man who succeeds in maintaining contact with his own vital thread holds unceasingly in his heart the words, 'Thy will not mine be done.'

So long as we are in touch with this thread it is as though our individual Guardian Angel hovered above us guiding our steps. The moment we lose it we feel lost, purposeless and unsafe, shorn of the pristine magic which guards every small child. The little child, if he is allowed to follow his instinct, encounters danger again and again and miraculously survives. For the thousand or so children who are killed or maimed on the roads, millions just escape the whizzing wheels.

My heart still thumps when I recall a tiny gipsy boy, dressed in nothing but a shirt which barely reached his waist, walking along the top of a wall which dropped to a mountain gorge hundreds of feet below. Yet I am sure he was quite safe. He walked on the edge of that precipice with the assurance of a cat. I should not have feared that a cat might fall. This child also had not yet forsaken his guiding thread of instinct.

Here in the West we are taught to distrust our instinct from the moment we are first squeezed into conventional patterns of behaviour. On the one hand reason, on the other brute force, usurp the place of the invisible thread. Reason is raised up on a throne from where it issues orders we are expected to obey. It builds an edifice of conformity in which we all must fit. Brute force is extended till it encompasses global wars. And these two false gods of Force and Reason are held together by a colossal will to power.

The sick and disillusioned seek again their thread. It is the task of the analyst to help them find it. But need they ever have lost it? I believe the small child's instinct can merge into the inner voice of the adult without break or interruption if only we will allow it so to do; if only we will trust our children and teach them to trust their own sound sense instead of maintaining our prevalent over-insistence on obedience to outer authority and conformity to the outer pattern.

Obedience to the instinctive demands of the body is the individual's first hold on his thread from God. When I speak of the body I am not referring particularly to sex. I refer to the behaviour of all or any part of our bodies. If we would only pay more attention we should notice that our bodies speak to us continually.

The medical profession[2] is beginning to recognize this. It is well known that stomach ulcers may be symptoms of anxiety and that skin complaints are apt to have a psychological cause. Indeed our bodies literally complain to us when we go astray. Jung has pointed out the need to listen to this 'complaint' of any physical symptom as well as treat it medically. If a man's throat is causing trouble it behoves him to consider if there is some situation or attitude he cannot swallow. If he has indigestion perhaps there is literally something he cannot stomach.

I know one woman who from time to time is awakened in the night by an acute pain in the rectum. Discovering on the first occasion that it did not call for any physical action she took Jung seriously and searched to see if she had swallowed some posionous precept which needed to be eliminated. She was not slow to find it; whereupon the pain immediately disappeared. She has learned

[2] See especially: A. T. W. Simeons, *Man's Presumptuous Brain*, New York, Longmans Green.

from experience that an inadvertent over-glib psychological explanation of a happening is likely to have this painful result which may be eliminated by emphatically throwing out the mistaken idea.

I myself at the beginning of my analysis was worried by a pain in the right hand when I tried to hold anything. First I could not hold a needle, then a pen; but it was not until I could not wield a broom without excruciating pain and I noticed that my hand was actually swollen, that it occurred to me to tell my analyst. 'You can't grasp things,' he suggested. Then after a moment's pause, 'Are you not failing to grasp the problems with your husband?'

I was dumbfounded. But on the way home I determined this could not go on. If my body was refusing to function the matter must be serious indeed. By the time I alighted from the bus the swelling in my hand had gone and when that evening I broached the troublesome matter with my husband I suddenly noticed that, without thinking and without pain, I had picked up a needle and was darning the family's socks. I have never forgotten that lesson.

Sometimes we need to do more than allow our bodies to speak to us, we need to allow them to act. We are taught that the body should be the obedient servant of the mind but there are times when servants know better than their masters. A man immersed in books is not weak-minded because he entrusts the planting or pruning of his roses to his gardener. And a man riding his horse over unknown and difficult ground knows that there are times when his horse will be a better judge than he where to put its feet.

One's body is very like one's horse. There are occasions when one's horse jibs at the jump because instinctively it knows that there is hidden danger on the other side of the fence. We should notice when our bodies jib. We should heed the situations which make us sick in the stomach.

What we do about them is a matter for conscious decision, but the sickness should not be ignored or treated as unimportant. Sometimes it is helpful to notice which way our feet take us if we leave them to choose their own direction. When neither my thinking nor my heart will tell me clearly whether I should go to a certain place of importance, I personally notice whether I am putting on my shoes or hanging my coat in the cupboard.

I am not for one moment suggesting that we should necessarily desist from some undertaking because we feel sick or have swollen feet, nor because obstacles sprout up on every hand. The Kontiki expedition was a marvellous example of determination overcoming every difficulty. But I am suggesting that the sickness or the obstacles should be considered as important factors in the situation and not simply ignored. Physical symptoms may tell us that we are going in the wrong direction or they may be evidence of something in the unconscious which will undermine the whole enterprise unless countered psychologically as well as with aspirin.

None the less it is the conscious mind which must make the final decisions. That is its business. When I follow the way my feet take me because I am not sure which is the right road, I am deliberately and consciously seeking the guidance of a more instinctive level of my being to help me. This is quite different from wandering about without purpose, or superstitiously following every omen.

Some horses no doubt are more reliable than others but perhaps this is because the co-operation and sympathy between rider and horse are greater. So also between a man and his body. This may be largely a question of type, and certainly of individual destiny. It may be the concern of some to dwell habitually higher up their thread than others. A philosopher is unlikely to be as in tune with his own body as a peasant. But to lose touch with it altogether is to be wholly divorced from our basic instincts and to have lost contact with an essential part of the vital thread of which I have spoken.

It is not only our bodies to which we can listen; there are other voices which will speak to us if we will only allow them to do so. We need to listen, listen all the time. Dreams also speak to those who listen with trust, and help to guide them so that they do not lose their thread.

One of the most striking instances I know of trust in the unconscious was that of a woman in England whose son was declared missing in the fighting in Africa during the last war. She was an American citizen about to be officially repatriated, but how could she leave Europe not knowing what had happened to her son? He might be in need of her. She prayed and prayed for guidance. That night she had a dream; *she was wandering uphill and down dale searching vainly for her son when suddenly she noticed that a shadowy figure was standing beside her. Then the figure spoke.*

'*Stop looking for your son,*' it said, '*he is on his way to Germany via Italy.*' She woke with this voice ringing in her ears. It was a voice of such authority that there was no room for doubt. Next day she sailed for America. Her son had in fact been taken prisoner by the Germans and he was actually taken via Italy to a prison camp in Germany, though this did not happen until two years later.

Allow and *trust* are the key words. We need to allow and trust the voices of the unconscious which speak to us in dreams, or through the body, while at the same time using all our faculties of thought and reason and discrimination, all our knowledge, all our strength and delicacy of feeling, all our practical good sense and the fineness of intuition with which we may be gifted. This is the paradoxical meeting of all opposites from which the Rainmaker can emerge.

If only we would learn to listen. For the most part we do not listen, we prefer to talk. We discuss, we argue, we strive to convince or we chatter about nothing at all — anything rather than listen.

I am not decrying the spoken word. Formulation in words is essential for clarity of thought, though the most subtle and the most profound truths can only be expressed indirectly in images and symbols, in poetry, in music or in colour. All art, and art is the search for truth, is the result of listening, even visual art. And truth when voiced in words is no longer talk but speech.

There is a great difference between speech and talk. Anyone can talk. It can be utterly futile or a delightful pastime. We sharpen our wits by talk and occasionally even gain a little understanding. But it is only in those rare moments when we are truly on our thread that we can speak.

Speech in a moment of inner clarity is the language of wisdom. The Rainmaker seldom even speaks. He communicates through the silence without effort and without intention.

We need to listen, and again listen, and only then to speak, or to allow the inner clarity we have attained to penetrate the silence in its own good time.

One of the most striking effects of silence which it has been my fortune to witness was that between a man and his wife.

As a girl the wife had been unusually dumb because, like so many women, she had been quite unable to put into words what she innately knew, and nothing else seemed worth talking about.

As a middle-aged woman she had an analysis and gradually learned to formulate her own inborn wisdom. Very naturally she tried to tell her intellectual husband of the inner world she was discovering, but when she put it into words she lost the essence and only succeeded in exasperating him and driving a wedge between them.

When later he became seriously ill a dream warned her that she must cease to try and get her ideas across to him. She obeyed, and during the last two weeks before he died of cancer she watched a miracle unfold before her eyes. A radiance seemed to emanate from the dying man. The house was filled with it. It affected everyone who entered. Their grown children gravitated to their father's room in a way they had never done before; and often when his wife came near his bed, he would take her hand and kiss it. One day he told her, 'I cannot tell you what you are doing for me. I never knew before all the things that were behind your mind. How should I have known? But now I know.' It was his wife's silence which enabled her to be the mediator to this dying man, not of the things in her mind, but of his own soul.

We shall do no harm, indeed we shall certainly be a force for good, by ourselves being on our own thread, but there are occasions in which we are so near to some problem concerning others that we feel we must participate.

Silence does not always seem the answer. What then can we legitimately do? Advice is generally useless. We know too little. Advice can only be given from the store of general wisdom or from our own personal experience of life.

The store of general wisdom which has crystallized into conventional attitudes frequently fails us because the particular circumstances do not fit. The commandment, 'Thou shalt not commit adultery,' if slavishly adhered to, may make us commit another sin which is, in effect, no less than murder. The moral precept or conventional advice can at times be wholly inadequate.

But neither may our personal experience of relationships and of life be wide enough to form a judgment on which we can give advice in the particular case we are considering. Moreover we do not know the pattern of another's life. Advice, even when sought, is mostly arrogance and a forgetting of the depth of our own ignorance.

Yet I believe we can do something. The first step is to disentangle ourselves and our own personal wishes from the problem and, having done so, become as conscious as possible of where we ourselves stand. Then we may provide a fixed point of reference, a post as it were stuck firmly into the sand around which a rope can be thrown from the little barques being tossed helplessly by waves of emotion. If several friends can offer firm posts, though the posts may stand for different points of view, they may yet provide some strength and stability which will help the storm-tossed people to find their own solution. Not our solution, theirs.

It is neither our advice nor our solution which is needed, but our concern. I use the word concern deliberately but perhaps I should make quite clear what I mean by it. I do not mean planning for another's welfare. I do not mean fussing over him. I do not mean nursing one's natural anxiety. And above all I do not mean exerting power in any sense whatever, physical, mental, moral or spiritual. Power is one of the most suspect of all our motives and one of the most insidious. It is so easy to exert power for someone else's good and thrive on the uplift that it gives us.

If power is the most poisonous of the false attitudes we can adopt, anxiety is the most useless. Our worry never helps anyone. It is a most destructive form of idle fantasy. We surround the person we wish to protect with a mist of anxiety which only befuddles his possibility of clear thinking or clear action. Who knows whether it may not even bring about the disasters we are trying to avoid.

To have a deep concern for anyone is to keep him in one's heart without the interference of wishing, or still worse willing, any particular goal or outcome for him; yet with faith in the purposefulness of life and the belief in the need for that individual to fulfil his own unknown destiny.

Concern is a leaving free with the utmost readiness to help if asked, and in the meantime a knowing that being on one's own thread is true tending of the soil which will provide the surest ground for the right outcome; for it will help to keep clear the channels between what is and what will be, and blow away the confusing mists between our muddled existence and the ultimate purpose of our lives.

This is to be concerned. But to know who or what claims one's concern is no easy matter. Most of us are posed with the problem nearly every day. For those whose eyes are focused on a particular piece of work, the writing of a book, the painting of a picture, the solving of a scientific problem or the attainment of a career, the matter is comparatively simple. Everything else can be swept ruthlessly aside as irrelevant, regardless of the consequent narrowing of their lives.

But those who dwell habitually on the level of diffuse awareness may find great difficulty in restricting at all the sphere of their concern. We all know those kind-hearted women who can never say no, and who dissipate their energy on people who have no real significance for them, to the detriment of those others or those matters really needing their concentration; and all without any compensating benefit to those on whom they squander themselves.

Or, on the other hand, the men who are so busy doing good works or serving a cause that they neglect their own families; and the young women who give sympathy with such warm indiscriminate readiness that they spread havoc and broken marriages around them. These latter are legion. Their intentions are not bad but they have not learned what is, and what is not, their own concern.

We know too those people who are always seeking some new experience or some new philosophy, who wander from lover to lover, or through all the ranges of psychological schools and religious sects. They also have not learned to limit themselves to their own particular concern. They seek but cannot find.

There are those who are so open to what happens around them that the chirp of every sparrow is deemed of personal significance. These are the people who have lost their personal boundaries altogether, though they are not wholly wrong, for who is to say that everything is not connected?

Most of us hover somewhere between these extremes, and every one of us has to learn how to distinguish what is, and what is not, our particular concern. The man who is pin-pointed and ruthlessly throws aside all else may be following his rightful path. Family and friends may have to stand aside while he courses through space alone. Or it may be that he has erroneously taken too narrow a path and is digging for himself a living grave, and relegating to those who love him the role of perpetual mourners.

A great Spanish philosopher[3] used to say to his students, 'Plough your furrow deep but not so deep that you cannot see over

3 Francisco Giner de los Rios.

the top.' For a few even that precept may not be sound. Some may
have to plough so deep that they risk losing not only width of
vision but their very lives. We cannot judge. But for most this
saying seems to be extraordinarily sound. Plough your furrow
deep but not so deep that you lose the vision of the far horizon.

What anyone's concern may be is not a question which can be
answered once for all. It changes every day. Subtly without noticing we are new each day, one day older, one day nearer death.
And if we are wise we shall notice that our concerns change too. As
we advance in years the inner demands which have rightfully lain
dormant during youth, claim our attention more and more. Or
our concern may shift from the welfare of our immediate family to
that of our particular community or group.

When the threads of two people touch, so long as they are
together that relationship is vital, no matter how inconvenient or
unconventional it may be. Threads may intertwine for a lifetime
but they do not always do so. People who cling together in obedience to nothing but convention or the law are likely, both of them,
to lose their hold on their own vital thread and find life deprived
of meaning.

Do not misunderstand me. I am not suggesting that differences
and difficulties between people should be taken as signals for separation. Suffering together may be part of the pattern, linking the
threads more firmly for all their seeming divergence. It may be an
essential prelude to new growth. Women who have had babies
will know that one must go *with* pain, not resist it, or one is torn
asunder and birth retarded. This is equally true of spiritual pain.
People leap apart to avoid their pain far too easily. So nothing
comes of it. Their renewed relationship is never born.

The acceptance of conflict and suffering is an essential part of
being on one's thread, while the deliberate search of happiness for
its own sake is, I should say, one of the best ways of ensuring that
our thread will slip from our grasp.

I have travelled full circle and return to the place from which I
started. To keep in touch with one's own vital thread is to live the
paradox of holding the opposites together, and it is this which
enables us to be concerned with others without crippling involvement, and to influence life around us without exerting power
for preconceived ends.

If we can resist the compulsive pressure of our logical thinking,
without relinquishing our precious heritage of lucid thought; if we

can hold our ground with our own hardly won ego personalities, yet bow our heads and say, 'Thy will not mine be done'; if we will but notice the reactions of our bodies; and heed the behaviour of the world towards us; if we can learn to listen to the voices within and to the whisper in the wind, with trust as well as with discrimination, we may be able to follow the road where the Rainmaker walks.

X

The Older Woman

IT WOULD SEEM easy enough for me to write on 'The Older Woman' since I am one, but perhaps it is for that very reason that I find it difficult. One can really only see situations clearly when one is outside them, not when one is in the middle of living them. However there is no help for it. When I have passed the stage of being an older woman I shall also be beyond writing at all.

It is obvious that there are two distinct classes of older women: the wife and mother on the one hand, and the professional woman on the other, although today these two merge more and more. It is with the former that I am most familiar.

The fundamental truth to remember in thinking of woman, irrespective of the role she plays, is that her life's curve, unlike that of man, is not a slow rising to the zenith of power followed by a gradual decline in the later years. The curve of a woman's life span follows more nearly the pattern of the seasons. She almost literally blossoms in the spring, but the long summer which follows is a very slow ripening with nothing much in the woman herself to show for it. If she lives a traditional family pattern she will be giving all the sap which rose so abundantly earlier to nourish her offspring, materially, emotionally and spiritually.

Then suddenly her children are all grown up, gone on their separate journeys, and she finds herself bereft. The apparent purpose of her life, for which she had strained every nerve, is snatched from her with the attainment of the goal. She feels stranded on the mud flats, while the river races by bearing away each new craft as it embarks, and she no part of the flowing waters. What then? What can happen then, with another thirty or forty years still to run and no one needing her? Even her husband has centred his life on his career and other interests apart from her while she was occupied with the growing family. At the best his need of her is not absorbing enough to assuage her aching emptiness.

What then? This is the crucial moment in the life of any wife and mother. It is then that she may notice, almost by accident, that from where the early blossoms fell fruit is hanging almost ripe. Unsuspected fruit, fruit which has swelled and grown unheeded, is now ready and waiting to be plucked. The autumn of a woman's life is far richer than the spring if only she becomes aware in time, and harvests the ripening fruit before it falls and rots and is trampled underfoot. The winter which follows is not barren if the harvest has been stored, and the withdrawal of sap is only a prelude to a new spring elsewhere.

Conscious modern women of course know these things. They prepare for the autumn before the long dry summer is over. But far too many women still feel that life is finished at fifty and that vibrant loving ends with the menopause. This last bogie should be swept away at the outset. It is utterly untrue.

You may know some version of the famous story of the young man who asked his mother at what age women cease to be interested in sexual intercourse. 'I do not know,' she replied, 'you had better ask your grandmother.' He sought out grandmother and repeated his question. 'How should I know?' she answered gruffly. 'Great Granny may be able to tell you.' This is perhaps not as far-fetched as would appear.

It is true enough that some men cease to be interested sexually in women when their physical fertility is ended, causing their wives, who have a recrudescence of sexual interest at this time, great distress. Such a situation is the survival of an inherent primitive pattern where sexuality was for humanity, as it is for animals, only a matter of procreation.

Since the age of chivalry and the development of romantic love, sex has become very much more than that. And with the discovery and spread of contraceptives sex has entered a new phase. The contraceptive can certainly lead to irresponsibility, licence and a devaluation of sexuality. In fact it often does so. But on the other hand it opens the door to immensely heightened emotional experience where sex ceases to be solely a biological function, and becomes an expression of love in its own right. In this context age with its absence of fertility is irrelevant.

This cultural achievement gives mankind a chance of healing the cleavage between body and spirit which has been fostered for centuries by the Church, and may enable us to weld once more the two together.

In this whole development the older woman is actually at a great advantage. She does not need the contraceptive, and I believe this is one reason why a woman's most profound and meaningful sex life often occurs after fifty when she is no longer caught in the biological net. For the first time she is able to give herself in the sex act completely free from fear of conception, a fear which in countless women does still operate beneath the surface, even when reason and science assure them that they have taken the most complete precautions.

Moreover to a great many women contraceptives, though accepted intellectually, are still unaesthetic, and to a deep basic feminine morality they are wholly unacceptable, all of which inevitably causes inhibitions so long as they have to be used. When once a woman is free to use her body as an expression of deep feeling, without its becoming the impersonal vehicle of nature's insistent demand for life and yet more life, she can transcend her earlier inhibitions and attain physical expression of an emotional relationship beyond anything of which she had ever dreamed.

Do not misunderstand me. It is a grave mistake for a woman to look for some great spiritual experience in sex at any age, or even to assume that she ought to have such a thing. All assumptions about sex are disastrous. They tend to lead to disappointment and recriminations. To my mind most modern books on sex do more harm than good for this very reason: they fill women's heads with assumptions and expectations which actually *prevent* experience at its fullest. It is one's own personal experience that counts and it should not be measured up against any generalization. The statistical so-called normal man or woman does not in fact exist, and it is foolish to weigh our actual living experience against such a mythical figure.

Sex delight is like happiness. It does not come when sought. It is not until a woman ceases to strive for her own sensual satisfaction, but allows the voice of her heart to speak to her man through the medium of her body, that she finds that heart, spirit and body are all one.

Important as the heightening fulfilment of sex may be, it is none the less only a small part of the ripe autumnal fruit to which I have alluded. A woman's liberation from the service of nature's purposes frees an enormous amount of energy for something else. A man at fifty is probably at the height of his intellectual or administrative power. A family woman at the same age may be aware of an entirely new stirring. Latent possibilities dance before her unbelieving eyes.

I recall one such woman seated on the lawn of her house one summer evening holding forth to her family. I say holding forth but she was certainly not laying down the law. It was almost as though a dam had burst and a torrent of ideas came tumbling out to which she herself seemed to be listening with the same astonished amusement as were her hearers. She simply emanated vitality and I remember her ending up with the words: 'I have no idea what is going to happen but I am quite sure something is.' And as I watched and listened so was I. She did in fact become a writer some ten years later.

The expression 'change of life' exactly fits the situation. The menopause does not spell the end of life but a change of direction, not a living death but a change of *life*.

If this were more generally understood I am convinced that women's menopause problems would rapidly diminish. Glandular changes are inevitable but it is woman's own dread of this mysterious change on the whole tenor of her life which, I am sure, brings about the neurotic state she fears. No, change of life means an enormous release of energy for some new venture in a new direction.

The direction in which the newly released energy will flow depends of course entirely on the type of person and the particular gifts with which she has been endowed. Some may develop a latent talent, painting, writing or some such thing. Voluntary societies serving social, political and cultural causes of all kinds abound with such women. But these only cater for the more conscious and extraverted type of woman. There are innumerable others who can find no outlet. They suffer deeply, for energy which finds no channel in which to flow seeps into the ground and makes a marsh where nothing can be planted, where only slime and insects breed.

Women who find they are no longer vitally needed by their families yet have no other place where they can give themselves, sink into lassitude and finally fall ill. The magnates who organize society have hardly begun to notice this happening. The autumnal energy of countless older women escapes silently down the kitchen sink along with their tears.

Not only is the nation poorer for its loss, the wastage is double, for these women who could have been healthily active and useful become a wholly unnecessary burden upon the health services, while as likely as not their frustration poisons the atmosphere of the home. Swamps breed mosquitoes. Uncanalized, wasted energy breeds gloom and nagging.

Part-time work is at least one answer to this problem, but part-time work is not easy to find. Industry seems to frown upon it and our modern passion for degrees and paper diplomas shuts many a door. It is not sufficiently recognized that running a home can afford very valuable experience in organization, and particularly in handling other people with diverse temperaments. The mother of a family is generally an adept at that very difficult accomplishment of attending to half a dozen things all at the same time, an asset by no means to be despised if diverted to other fields.

That society is gravely at fault in not providing outlets for the older woman's energy is unquestionably true. But her real problem is to discover in which direction her newly released libido wants to flow. Libido is like water, it always seeks its proper level. No amount of coercion can make it flow uphill.

So long as a woman is fulfilling her traditional role of bringing up a family, she is carried along by the stream of life. Indeed she has no alternative. She goes with the stream even though cooking and cleaning and changing diapers are not at all her ideal occupations. She has no real choice. But she herself develops as the family grows and she learns to meet the demands as they arise. Changing diapers gives way to helping with obstreperous homework and providing meals for expanding appetites in every field. But when all this is past and the river flows on without her, her own little stream of energy is dammed up. If she is fortunate the waters will rise till they are strong enough to burst out in a channel of their own.

What the channel will be depends on her concern. Even today, when education does its best to divert women's activity into every branch of industry and money-making, there are still older women who slide happily into the estate of grandmother because their children's children do in fact become the centre of their interest and their concern. Dedicated grandmothers who gladly put themselves at the service of the future generation without trying to run the show themselves are a boon to any family, but they are becoming increasingly rare. Like maiden aunts they are dying out, and the services which both maiden aunts and grandmothers used to give as a matter of course and with genuine devotion now frequently have to be bought with money. We all know what a poor substitute that is and how expensive.

The modern trend seems to be in the opposite direction. More and more mothers wait with impatience for their children to be grown and gone. Then at last they feel free to carry on with the career which family demands had forced them to abandon. These women are faced with relatively little conflict. They nearly always succeed in finding an outlet before the problem becomes acute. As the children grow they dovetail the new life into the old so that there is no traumatic moment when they feel deserted.

The ones who cannot look forward to any vibrant future or any sphere of usefulness to which they can give themselves, are those with whom I am particularly concerned here. For them especially is the surprise and delight of discovery. And for them above all is the paramount need to know what is and what is not their true concern.

I spoke about concern in my previous chapter on the Rainmaker. I will not repeat what I said then. But in the case of woman, the outstanding almost invariable object of her concern is, as we all know, the person or persons whom she loves. This is true right through her life. It is, I repeat, the essential ingredient of her nature. When she is true to herself love is her primal driving force. Love and the service of those she loves. I mean a wholly personal love, not the love of causes or of country. I believe this to be true for all the various ranks of women, and it is as true of professional women as of wives and mothers. It is not always apparent that this is so. We are all very good at covering up our mainspring. But I have yet to meet the woman who did not know in her heart that love is her main concern and that the secret of her success in any field was her personal love in the background.

Men really can give themselves to a cause, working wholeheartedly for it and inspired by it. Unless their ingredient of masculinity is very great, women cannot. If one is allowed to penetrate their secrets one finds beneath their apparent impersonal enthusiasms some very personal love, the existence of which makes them feel whole and gives them the energy which enables them to act.

The schoolgirl will work double for a teacher whom she loves. The career woman will either have a person who is the focus of her love at work who provides her dynamism, or some love outside which is her stimulus. It may be a lover in the background or children for whom she needs to earn.

Wherever I look I meet this incontrovertible fact that a woman always needs some person to do things *for*, even though to the outsider there is no apparent connection with the loved person and what she may be doing. We all know how difficult it is for a woman even to cook a meal for herself. She cannot be bothered. A bit of bread and cheese will do. But if there is someone to cook *for* she prepares quite elaborate dishes with delight.

The same prevails throughout. The work of a woman, whether factory hand or professional, will be quite different in quality if in some way she can connect it with her love. I have talked with women artists, painters, singers, actors. They all agree that art in itself is seldom quite enough. Beneath their devotion to their art is some person whom they love and for whom in some mysterious inner way they perfect their art. Even the nun, who is an extreme case of selfless devotion, is contained in and inspired by a very personal love of Christ. I suspect that men are far more single-mindedly purposeful.

The need to have someone to do things for comes out in most curious places. I recall a woman who was threatened with blindness which only an operation could prevent. Operations of any kind had always been anathema to her, and the thought of an eye operation was more than she could face. She raged internally at the meddlesomeness of doctors. Why couldn't she be allowed to go blind in peace? Then suddenly she realized what she might be doing to her children and grandchildren if she went blind. A blind old grandmother was the last thing she wanted to impose on them. Her torment ceased. She entered hospital without a further qualm. She had found someone to have her operation *for*.

This tendency only to be able to do things for someone whom one loves makes it difficult for a woman to know what she herself really wants. She is often accused quite naturally by men of futility or hypocrisy, because when asked what she wants to do, she replies 'Whatever you like.' But it is not hypocrisy. She really means that her desire is to to do what he wants. It has not occurred to her to have any special preference. Even if she knew she wanted to dance it would give her no pleasure to do so if her lover was longing to watch a cricket match. This adaptability is not unselfishness and has no particular merit. It is the way a woman functions. Perhaps I am describing the last generation. I think it possible that the present generation of women not only know themselves better but are far more decisive than the last, thus changing their relationship with men. Whether the change is for the good, or rather a disaster, is still an open question. Perhaps it is both.

However this may be, the older woman's dilemma is precisely here. If no one whom she loves wants her services there is no one to do things for. There is in fact no reason for which to live. She is faced with an entirely new situation in which for the first time maybe she has to discover what are her *own* wishes, her *own* tastes and in which direction her energy, with no love focus to act as magnet, will consent to flow. It is fascinating to notice how a widow will sometimes reverse the habits of a married lifetime after her husband's death. The extent to which she does so is the measure of her earlier adaptability.

In the following poem I have tried to express an old woman's bewilderment. It is called 'The Last Years':

Now that my loves are dead
On what shall my action ride?

I will not make my children
Lovers nor tune my time
By footsteps of the young
To ease my solitude;

But sing of springs, forgotten
In slow summer's tedium,
And autumn ripe with fruit;
Of winter branches, bare

Beneath the storm, bowed
With weight of rain, and after,
Lifting knotted fingers
Towards a translucent sky;

And wrest from the gathered sheaf
Forgiveness, buried in the heart
Of every grain, to knead
My bread for sustenance.

My action, sharing bread,
Love becomes ability
To bless, and be, in blessing,
Blessed.

To go back and collect up one's past as this poem suggests, writing it down in poems or as good prose as one can achieve, has in itself a healing effect. I believe one has to return to one's past, not once but many times, in order to pick up all the threads one has let fall through carelessness or unobservance.

I believe above all one has to return again and again to weep the tears which are still unshed. We cannot feel all the grief of our many losses at the time we suffer them. That would be too crippling. But if we would really gather our whole lives into a single whole, no emotion that belongs to us should be left unfelt.

Moreover, the review of our lives enables us to notice the constant repetition of the same pattern of happening, met by the same pattern of behaviour. Seeing this we cannot help being struck by the apparent purposefulness of every detail of our lives even though we do not like our fate. Those who do in fact gather up and write their story are enormously enriched. And women for whom nothing is worth the effort unless it is for the sake of someone they love, can write their outer or their inner story quite deliberately for their own grandchildren (if they have any) to read when they are grown up. If there are no grandchildren, most women will need to find someone else to write it for.

What fascinating pictures of antiquated ways of living we should have if this were done more often. Every single person has the material for at least one book. It is, I think, important that publication should not be the aim. Too many books are published already. Too many mediocre pictures are put upon the market. No, the aim is creativity for its own sake. The grandchildren or some other persons are merely the excuse which the aging woman needs to enable her to make the effort.

Creativity once begun goes on. Nothing is so satisfying to the human soul as creating something new. If the old can become creative in their own right they are lost no longer. We all long to see our works in print, I know, but this is not the point. It is the act of creation which counts. Every act of creation adds to the creativity in the world, and who knows if it has not some similar effect as the ritual breathing towards the East at dawn of those primitive tribes who believe that their breath helps the sun to rise.

Unless some outer activity claims her, the family woman may make the discovery earlier than either men or professional women that libido changes its direction as old age approaches. It is a change that all must encounter sooner or later: at some time or other outer activities lose their glamour and the inner world demands attention. So strong is this demand that the old who refuse to turn their faces inwards, clinging desperately to outer values even though they watch them daily slipping from their grasp, are frequently made ill. Forced by illness or accident to be inactive, they are given the opportunity which they had been unable to take of their own free will, to ruminate and ponder and put forth new shoots in an unaccustomed inner world.

Illnesses at any time of life should not be merely cured, but utilized for growth in a hitherto unknown field. Particularly does this apply to the aging, whether man or woman.

If the old can become creative in their own right, they are, as I have said, lost no longer, but above all it is imperative that the older person should have a positive attitude towards death. The young can forget death with impunity. The old cannot. They are fortunate indeed who have faith that they will not be extinguished when they die, and can look forward to a new beginning in some other dimension or some other realm. But faith is a gift. Like love it comes by grace. No amount of thought or striving can achieve it; which paradoxically does not mean that there is no need to strive. We get from life in the measure with which we give to it, and our fundamental attitudes demand unceasing strife. But this is only preparing the soil. The actual planting of a spiritual seed like faith is beyond our control. It comes when it will.

To those who have been denied such faith I would ask, is it not a fact that the people who accept death most readily are the ones who have lived most fully? I do not mean necessarily the people who have done the most. Outer visible achievement is no criterion of living fully. The life of a great business magnate whose industry has erected huge buildings, set innumerable wheels whizzing and employs thousands of people, may have been so narrowly focused on the gain of material wealth that the riches of the spirit, art, music, literature and the warmth of human contacts, may have escaped him altogether. This is not full living.

At the opposite extreme I recall Spanish beggars seated on the cathedral steps, idly watching the passers by, receiving as though it were their lawful due occasional gifts of alms with a dignified 'God bless you'. How well the beggar must know those oft recurrent faces, nearly as constant in their daily presence as the stone saints and gargoyles behind him, the hourly chiming of the cathedral bells and the chant from within the church. What a setting in

which to dwell and ponder! Does this man live fully? I do not
know, but Unamuno, one of Spain's greatest writers believed he
did. Unamuno even declared that the most interesting philosopher he had ever met was a beggar, one of a long line of beggars.

I am not advocating beggary, but neither it nor visible achievement is any criterion of the quality of living. There is no yardstick
for the surmounting of obstacles, the wrestling with angels and the
transcending of suffering.

There is no yardstick for the measurement of others, but maybe
for ourselves there is. One's yardstick is one's full capacity to *be* as
complete a person as within one lies, and that includes becoming
as conscious as it is possible for one to be in order to bring out
and develop the buried talents with which one was born, and in
order to realize one's own innate knowledge.

The more diverse the talents of any person, the more difficult
may be the task. We only have a certain amount of psychic energy
and throughout our lives we have to choose the road we will take,
abandoning the fascinating paths in other directions. But the development of an ability to choose, and the consistent following of
the path chosen, may be a large part of becoming as whole a
person as one can be. So also is our flexibility a very real asset. The
man or woman who has chosen the wrong path by mistake, and
we all make mistakes, may need to retrace his steps and start
again. This needs courage and should not be mistaken for the idle
whim of the dilettante. Moreover, many people follow a vital
thread towards a wholly invisible goal. We cannot possibly judge
the value of their achievement.

To be conscious is not in itself a goal. It is possible to be a highly
conscious person without one's character being influenced at all.
Consciousness is not enough in itself. But one cannot develop a gift
if one does not know that it is there, so to be conscious is indispensable. Many of us, through ignorance of our own capacities,
only allow a small part of ourselves to flower. Neither can one lop
off a branch that is marring the beauty of a tree if one has not
noticed its presence and seen that its unbridled growth is spoiling
the harmony of the whole. Or it may have to be sacrificed because
it is impeding the growth of other plants.

Our individual psyche is very like a garden. The kind of garden
will be determined by the nature of the soil, whether it is on a
mountain slope or in a fertile valley. It will depend upon the
climate. Green lawns flourish in England. In parts of Spain to sow

a lawn is to make a present to the wind, for literally the seed is blown away.

Climate and geology are powers beyond our altering. They are the conditions we have been given to make the most of it, and for some the task is immensely harder than it is for others. The slopes of arid hills in Spain are a marvel of man's endeavour. Every inch is terraced with little walls of stones so that not a drop of the rare precious rain shall be lost in tumbling streams but held for the thirsty vines and olive trees. All honour to such gardeners. Some of us dwell in more temperate climes where the task is not so hard, but any gardener will know the unceasing vigilance which is needed to tend a garden, wherever it may be. Weeds are never eradicated once for all.

So, too, our psyches. They also can be invaded by pests from other gardens which have been neglected, making it harder to maintain the health of ours. Indeed, to maintain our psyche or our garden free of pests is a responsibility to our neighbours as well as to ourselves. Some gardens are more formal than others. Some have corners deliberately left wild, but a garden with no form and no order is not a garden at all but a wilderness.

The psyche which is a total wilderness ends in the asylum or burdens its family with unhealthy emanations. The well-tended but over conventional garden, on the other hand, may have no stamp of individuality upon it. It expresses the psyche of the mass man, and suburbia is full of them. The garden which is tended with care yet is not quite like any other garden, for it conveys the atmosphere of its owner, is like the psyche of an individual who has become a mature personality from where the scent of honeysuckle and roses and wild thyme will perfume the air for all around.

But gardens cannot grow without earth, and the loveliest flowers thrive on soil that is well manured and black. Dirt has been defined as matter in the wrong place. Manure is not dirt when dug into the borders. And rich emotional living in the right places is as indispensable for the flowering of wisdom in old age as the purity of the air and the brilliant sunlight of consciousness. No flower and no wisdom was ever reared on a ground of shiny white tiles washed daily with antiseptic.

It is the older person, whether man or woman, who has the need and the obligation to tend the garden of the psyche. The young are generally too immersed in active living; study, work, careers, and bringing up a family absorb all their energies. Indeed, a too early absorption with their own psyche may be an actual poison for the young. It may deprive them of the essential spontaneity which is needed for living. Actual experience can never be replaced by thinking about life or examining inner motives. To be ever conscious of the possible hazards before us snatches away our power to leap. We can only live fully by risking our lives over and over again.

It is in the latter part of life that people need to turn attention inwards. They need to do so because if their garden is as it should be they can die content, feeling that they have fulfilled their task of becoming the person they were born to be. But it is also an obligation to society. What a man or woman is within affects all those around. The old who are frustrated and resentful because they have omitted to become in life the persons they should have been, cause all in their vicinity to suffer.

Being is not the same as doing. Most people have had to sacrifice in some direction their capacity to *do*, but none are exempt from *being* to the full. There can be no limit to one's endeavour to become more and more aware of the depths of one's own psyche, discovering its lights and its shadows, its possibilities of unexpected vision as well as its dark regions.

The old woman, like the old man, needs to turn her natural receptivity towards the inner voices and inner whisperings, pondering on the new ideas which will come to her if she is attuned to her own inner self. Mrs. Moore, in E. M. Forster's *Passage to India*, was doing precisely this in her sudden and unexpected refusal to be drawn into the whirl of outer events. But we should not expect the insights of the *very* old to be revealed to the rest of us. There may be weeks and months or even years of slow, quiet gestation in the minds of quite old people. To speak of half-formed ideas is to destroy their growth as surely as to burn a seedling with the sun's rays shining through a magnifying glass. The very frailty of age guards its secrets.

Indeed, the insights of the very old may never quite reach the level of consciousness where they can be clothed in words. But this does not mean that they are not at work beneath the surface. The conscious mind is only a small part of our total psyche.

The very old, those who have given up all interest in the outer world even to the stage of being withdrawn from any point of contact, may still be receiving and quietly nurturing within themselves new insights which will enable them to meet the unknown future. One wonders sometimes what holds them here. Perhaps they are not ready. They cannot die till they are ready. I have often felt that modern medicine is very cruel to the old for it keeps them here when they are longing to be allowed to go.

But perhaps longing to go is not the same as being ready to meet the other side. I doubt if science could keep anyone alive if in this sense they were truly ready for their death.

It is a fallacy that the old are necessarily lonely when they are alone. Some are. But never those who are quietly pondering, preparing themselves, albeit without deliberate intention, for their coming death. They need long hours of solitude to round out their lives within, as they have earlier done without.

There is a lovely little book *All Passion Spent*, by Victoria Sackville-West. She tells of an old lady after the death of her husband with whom she has shared a long life. Her children hold a family council. What can be done with mother? They plan it all out. She shall stay with them and their growing families in turn so they can share the burden of looking after her and keeping her from feeling lonely.

The plan is unfolded to the old lady who, to the amazement of her children, thanks them politely and declines their offer of hospitality. It transpires that for years she has been longing to have a little house of her own where she could live alone and undisturbed with her thoughts. Miraculously the chance had come and nothing should cheat her of it now.

This old woman had the good fortune to know her own mind, which many of us do not. Many old men and women are cheated of their essential solitude, and kept continually focused on outer things by the mistaken kindness of the young and their own unawareness of their need to be alone. We die alone. It is well to become accustomed to being alone before that moment comes.

Old age is the time of reckoning, our achievements balanced by our needless omissions and our mistakes. Some of our mistakes are hideous, but this is no reason for not facing them. Some we would never know if our children did not tell us the awful things we had done to them without realizing the dire effect of our advice, the example of our behaviour or our condemnation.

The old are generally too much shielded. The next generation fears to hurt them. I say the next generation deliberately for it is seldom the young who overshield the old. The vital calls to live of the young are more likely to make them callous, which is really far more healthy. It is those who are already advanced in middle age, often themselves already older women, who over-protect the very old. Nothing must be told to worry them. They must have every comfort and never be left. Frequently they are so pampered and humoured that they are turned into querulous children.

Indeed, it is more often than not our own dislike of feeling hard, rather than genuine affection, which makes us so falsely kind. Moreover there is no need for us to take upon ourselves the responsibility of sheltering the very old from worry. Griefs do not shatter them as they do the young. They have their own protection from those emotions which are more than they can bear. It is not our task to turn them into breathing fossils.

That is no kindness to the old. Rather it is cruelty because it deprives them of their power still to grow. It is an unpardonable belittling of the role of the aged, for it is they who, whether they can formulate it or not, are in fact the depositories of wisdom. Very often it is they who have lived more than those who shelter them. To the older woman who has the aged in her care I would say: Be careful not to spend more energy upon the very old than you can rightly afford to do. Your own life too makes claims. Deep thought and wise judgment are needed to give them libido where it is really due. If too much is given to the aged at the expense of the giver it will only breed bitterness, and that helps no one.

The care of the very old is a terribly difficult problem and every case has to be dealt with on its own merits. Many family women find an old parent a good substitute for the children who have grown and gone. Many others who have had no children turn the parent unwittingly into the child they have never had. In either case the old person is wrapped in cotton wool which he or she has not the strength to throw aside. They can very easily become victims, rather than grateful recipients, of our over-coddling.

And so they end their days either with a complacency to which they have no right, or in puzzled resentment that the young do not give them the love they thought they had deserved. There are no deserts in love. Greater outspokenness is better for everyone concerned, though the young might certainly temper their frankness with the constant remembrance that the old have done their best. Deliberate malice on the part of parents is, I believe, very rare. The vast majority of parents undoubtedly do the best they know. And as undoubtedly the next generation will have found it wrong, and rightly so. To be a parent is the most difficult task in the world. For a parent not to be understanding enough cripples. To be too understanding imprisons.

I have yet to meet the parents who have not made serious blunders with their children in one direction or the other. The childless in this are fortunate. The false steps they have taken in life are likely to have had less dire consequences on others.

I think it is important that mistakes should be brought out into the light of day, for how otherwise may they be forgiven? Forgiven by those sinned against but also forgiven by the sinner himself. This is something very different from complacency for it implies full consciousness and condemnation of the sin. To forgive oneself is a very difficult thing to do, but perhaps it is the last task demanded of us before we die. For the man or woman who can forgive him- or herself can surely harbour no vestige of rancour against any other.

Impersonal forgiveness is very like love, but love on a higher plane than the personal love which women above all find so necessary. It is Agape as distinct from personal Eros. It is the charity spoken of by St. Paul. It is only possible for those who are completely on their own thread to God. No little isolated ego can forgive itself. In the last verses of the poem quoted the old woman found forgiveness of herself as well as others to be her inspiration and her goal.

And so, in the end, if endeavour is unceasing and the fates are kind, almost without noticing how it happened an old woman may find that love is still, as it always had been, the centre and the mainspring of her being, although, along with her years, the word has grown in meaning.

XI

Soul Images of Woman[1]

I OFFERED TO write this paper in a rash moment. I have found it much more difficult to do than I had anticipated. The occasion which spurred me to make the effort was Dr. R. D. Scott's lecture on schizophrenic women patients, in the course of which he said, 'It is as though they had no anima.' During the discussion it was queried whether women could in fact have an anima, as the concept of anima referred to man's psychology, to which Dr. Scott replied that he had not known what else to call it. I suggested that 'soul' was perhaps the word he was looking for and to this he acquiesced.

There was undoubtedly confusion in all our minds, for as someone said, why not call it animus? I felt the time had come to try to clarify, hence this paper.

It is common knowledge that the unconscious of man is feminine and that the anima in some form or other is its personification. And it is generally accepted that the personification of the unconscious of woman is the animus. So long as the unconscious is considered as a whole that is good enough, but with greater differentiation of the images of the unconscious it becomes clear that the pattern of woman's psyche is not just that of man the other way round. At the very beginning of her life she emerges from a feminine being, like herself, which no man does, and this in itself must make a great difference in attitude.

With analysis man becomes aware of other figures, masculine shadows of all kinds, a wise old man, etc., but the figure of the anima which seems to represent his innermost soul always remains feminine.

This paper is asking a question: As women become aware of the other figures of the unconscious, feminine shadows etc., do their innermost souls continue to be represented by a male figure or not?

[1] This lecture—keystone of the author's thoughts—was found among her papers.

Many women are troubled with the idea that they do and I personally believe that they do not.

I am, however, convinced that a woman cannot find her feminine soul image at all unless she first becomes on very good terms with her animus. It is he in fact who, bearing aloft his torch, leads the way into the innermost recess where the soul image of a woman so successfully hides. As it is he whom a woman meets first he may appear to be himself the soul image she is seeking; but if she ventures with him further into the dark and unknown she may find that he does not himself represent her soul but is rather acting as her guide towards it.

In this context the dreams sometimes speak of the animus as the father of a woman's soul image. Several dreams have come my way which seem to bear out the idea that the animus is not himself the image of a woman's soul, but the father of that image. And though to do so is to forestall my argument I should like to give you one of these dreams straight away in order to make it clearer what I am trying to get at in this talk.

This was the dream of a woman a little over fifty who had had considerable analysis, and who had years earlier recognized and digested the implications of her own incestuous daughter-father relationship in the unconscious. She described this dream as one of the most exciting dreams she had ever had. I will give it to you in her own words: *I was going up the stairs of a humble house accompanied by a little girl aged twelve with loose hair who looked exactly like the early photos of myself. In the top room we knew we should find this child's father. Who could he be? I had no idea. Suspense mounted at every step until we reached the attic door. I knocked and slowly opened it. To my utter astonishment in the middle of a bare room I saw a man kneeling on the floor in an attitude of prayer. He was the well-known inner figure with whom I habitually conversed when doing active imagination, and whom I had come to regard as my own creative animus.*

So here this woman's most advanced, co-operative, creative animus was described as the father of this little pre-adolescent girl. If she had been a small boy I should not have been surprised. It would have seemed natural enough that this animus figure should father a male child, standing perhaps for the whole enterprise of becoming conscious. Yet it was inconceivable that with such a father this particular little girl could be the dreamer's infantility. I am aware that the Self will sometimes appear in the form of a child but I cannot imagine that an animus could ever be styled the father of the Self. What else then could this little girl be but the dreamer's own soul image before it got overlaid with a masculine education and hidden out of sight? And this idea immediately brought numbers of other dreams to mind where this same child had appeared before without adequate explanation. If she were a soul image then they all fitted into a pattern, in particular a very early hitherto inexplicable dream where she had appeared up against the wall some feet from the ground like a shadowy bas-relief with arms outstretched making her falling draperies look like wings.

Once conscious of who she was this figure grew up and now appears an ageless but very feminine woman. She no longer re-sembles the dreamer for she, though not this soul child, has adopted a persona with which to meet the world. But if ever the dreamer deliberately calls her to mind she appears accompanied by another figure who is undoubtedly an image of the Self. If on the other hand in moments of extremity she appeals to the Self, this latter will appear holding the soul image by the hand.

I will presently give you some more dreams, my own and other women's, but if you will allow me I want to go back and consider what we mean by certain psychological concepts which we so blithely bandy about, and try to explain in what sense I am using them. I have to confess that I am not at all clear myself and I am only trying to place before you my own very tentative way of seeing things.

Perhaps you will bear with me if I ask you for a moment to follow the course of my own muddled thinking, not because my particular muddle is valuable but because the elucidation of some-one else's confusion sometimes helps to clarify one's own, and I am sure that many of you are quite as muddled as I am.

The concept of animus was my first big puzzle. I have for a long time been trying to understand it, in fact I once wrote a paper on the animus to rid myself of the uneasy suspicion, shared by many women, that to have an animus problem was a polite way of saying one was smitten by the plague.

At that time it seemed to me that all attempts by a woman to focus or analyse were carried out with the help of her animus. It was her animus which studied or embarked on a career. It was her animus which enabled her to analyse and discriminate, her animus which brought to her notice all the well-worn truths which

culture had formulated. This figure it seemed to me was positive
and helpful so long as the woman took the precaution of inform-
ing him how she, as woman, felt about the matters in hand and
only became negative when she failed to do so. For then, being
deprived of the essential data of her feeling he had no alternative
but to voice the general truths of the day. These, through her own
omission with regard to her feelings, turn out to be no more than
clichés, irrelevant to the actual situation. Irrelevance is, I believe,
as I have said elsewhere, the invariable signature tune of a negative animus statement.

That was how I saw the animus: as the total focusing power of a
woman whether she was focusing on the outer or the inner world.
But on the other hand I realized that women are also driven by an
immensely strong life force, sometimes going with it in accordance
with their nature, but quite often unwilling victims, compelled
along a course or plunged into entanglements which they do not
want but are quite unable to resist.

It was only gradually that I realized that my picture of women
driven by the life force on the one hand, and on the other focusing
and discriminating solely with the good offices of the animus, itself
a collective figure, had left no place for an ego at all.

I got out of my difficulty by deciding that for a woman at least
the ego was only the chooser, that part of her which could say to
the impersonal forces impinging upon her, 'Yes, all right I will go
that way,' or, 'No, no, I refuse to be driven there, or accept this,
that or the other slogan.'

This seemed all right for a while though I still felt that a
woman's ego, according to me, was having a very thin time, which
did not seem to fit at all the young women with whom I talked,
many of whom had no doubt that they were the possessors of
strong, reliable egos of far more substance than my 'chooser'.

It was with something of a shock that I realized one day that the
thing I called 'I' was not by any means the chooser but something
far deeper and more elusive. I saw that I was actually identifying
in my own mind far more with a figure which had already appeared again and again in dreams, the figure of a woman whom I
had learned was never far away from the image of the Self yet
always distinguishable from it, a figure I had learned to think of
as an image of the soul.

Though my animus warned me that to identify with the soul
seemed dangerously like an inflation, the idea refused to leave me.

I began to notice that women really were identified with their souls. The idea was not new. I had heard it before. I recall Philip Metman saying, 'Woman *is* soul.' Mrs. Jung had said it and so had Barbara Hannah, but I was understanding this statement for the first time.

Gradually I realized that there was nothing inflated about it. Everyone is born with a soul. But women, being closely tied to their original instinctive pattern, are less easily separated from their essential soul by the development of intellect and so continue to identify with it. You will remember Eva Metman's contention that little girls remain in contact with the Self in the way that a boy does not. This is another way of saying the same thing. To identify with the Self is an inflation indeed. But to recognize that one is a soul inhabiting a body is to know who one is. And this comes more easily to women than to men.

What my ego could be was still a mystery, but I was convinced that the thing which used my tongue to communicate with the world outside, or the world within, and was continually saying 'I', could with impunity stand up against and refute at any particular moment the dictates of the animus, but it belied the soul at its peril. To do that was an utter betrayal of one's essential being. I was forced to the conclusion that the soul is the essential core and the ego merely its mouthpiece. This does not remove from the ego the role of chooser. It can choose *not* to be the mouthpiece of the soul. It can choose *not* to go with the Self or it can choose consciously to do so of its own freewill.

Still bewildered, Neumann came to the rescue. In his *Origins of Consciousness* he depicts the emergence of the masculine ego from the feminine matrix of the unconscious. And in his essay entitled 'On the Moon and Matriarchal Consciousness' published in *Spring*, 1954,[2] he put forward the idea that the focused consciousness of the ego is always masculine whether in man or woman, but that there is another layer of more diffuse awareness which is feminine in character even when found in man, this awareness not to be confused with the unconscious itself.

I hailed this with relief. In my own thinking I had given far too much to the animus, thus largely denuding woman of a conscious ego. Neumann redressed the situation. His conception of a masculine ego in both sexes conceded to women the ability to analyse and discriminate in their own right without having to call on a

[2] *Spring*, Analytical Psychology Club of New York.

conceptual archetype to help them. In talking to modern women this seems wholly acceptable. My notion that they were only intelligent people by virtue of an animus had grated uneasily.

If Neumann is right that the ego is masculine in women as well as in men, it would not be very surprising to find that the soul appears as a feminine figure not only in men but also in women.

For years I have been collecting dreams which show how women themselves visualize their souls, but first of all, what do I mean by that word 'soul'?

Naturally I turned to Jung. Perhaps English-speaking people who do not know German and are dependent on translations are unduly confused because the English word soul and the German word *seele* do not mean the same thing. Whether anima and soul mean the same thing is continually a puzzle to many people, still worse soul and animus.

In *Psychological Types*, after a long description of the anima, Jung says, 'If, therefore, we speak of the *anima* of a man we must logically speak of the *animus* of a woman, if we are to give the soul of woman its right name.'[3] That was written more than thirty years ago. This sentence has caused great trouble to innumerable women to whom it does not ring true. Mrs. Jung was one of the first to point out that to many women's ears it did not click. I have been at pains to search Dr. Jung's more recent writings to see whether or not he still retains his early definition of a woman's soul. I was relieved to find that neither in *Aion* nor in *The Archetypes and the Collective Unconscious*, nor in the revised edition of *Two Essays on Analytical Psychology* is there a single suggestion that the animus is the equivalent of a woman's soul.

In *Aion* he explicitly states that he is not using the word soul at all but prefers the term anima as indicating something specific. The animus is portrayed as woman's representative of the Eternal Logos. He is the word, the power to formulate, to analyse, to discriminate between the opposites. This is nowhere equated with soul.

The animus is indeed woman's faculty to separate, not unite; which is why, if she is trying to make a relationship as a woman, she had better keep this analytical separating part of her well out of the situation or he will wreck it with his impersonal, collective character.

[3] C. G. Jung, *Collected Works*, Vol. 6, Par. 805, Princeton University Press.

In *Aion* Jung describes the positive aspect of the animus in these words:

> Through the figure of father he expresses not only conven-
> tional opinions but — equally — what we may call 'spirit',
> philosophical or religious ideas in particular, or rather the
> attitude resulting from them. Thus the animus is a psycho-
> pomp, a mediator between the conscious and the unconscious
> and a personification of the latter. Just as the anima becomes,
> through integration, the Eros of consciousness, so the animus
> becomes a Logos; and in the same way that the anima gives
> relationship and relatedness to a man's consciousness, the ani-
> mus gives to woman's consciousness a capacity for reflection,
> deliberation, and self-knowledge.[4]

Here the animus is explicitly described, not as soul but as spirit
or meaning, and I do not think any woman will quarrel with that;
but the question still remains what does she mean by a soul and
what do I mean in this paper? I am certainly not thinking of the
attitude resulting from philosophical or religious ideas, nor the
function of relationships which Jung has elsewhere called the
anima. Nor have I found that Victor White's *Soul and Psyche*
helps me.

It was not until I turned to the language of poets that I was able
to get myself at all clear. The soul has always been referred to as
immortal and poets have invariably spoken of the eyes as the
windows of the soul. The soul looks out through the eyes and we
penetrate their depths in search of another soul.

The eyes of Dr. Scott's schizophrenic patients were vacant. No
soul looked out. These women were alive and functioning more or
less, possessed perhaps by some partial aspect of themselves or at
the mercy of an archetype, but no personal soul looked out of their
eyes for they had lost contact with their souls and were wandering
in chaos.

May I repeat here an image I have used earlier: in my way of
envisaging life I see everyone of us as being linked to God by an
invisible thread. The lowest point is his body and the thread passes
up through heart and head and spiritual aspirations. The angels
or images of the Self which it is vouchsafed to anyone to see are I
believe only those which embrace his particular thread. I mean

[4] *Ibid*, Vol. 9, ii, Par. 33.

embrace for such a figure may embrace or hold more than one person's thread. These are the intermediaries between him and God, and somewhere in their vicinity and yet always inseparable from them dwells I believe the individual's immortal soul which looks out of a man's or woman's eyes in a way with which we are all familiar.

To be on one's thread is to be in touch with the Self so that life has meaning. It is when we lose touch with our vital thread that we feel lost, forsaken, and life purposeless. This can happen to any of us on occasions in varying degrees but the schizophrenic has for the time being let go of his thread altogether. His soul cannot find the windows through which to look out. They are shuttered up or blocked by an invader.

In this talk I am trying to limit the use of the word soul to its popular usage in the English language as the essential and immortal part of any person, from the moment he is born. It is this immortal essence that looks out of a baby's eyes the moment it can see and smile. It movingly greets one from the eyes of any small child before it has learned to conceal itself from the world's intruding gaze. May I, in parenthesis, add that I am begging no question here in taking for granted the immortality of the soul. It is a question I am not asking. Man has always taken it for granted and Jung in his B.B.C. television interview declared, not his belief, but his knowledge that the soul survives; for man, as he said in his closing words, cannot lead a meaningless existence. Moreover, I am not the only person who feels that they know from their own experience that the soul continues after death.

The purpose of this paper is not inquiry into the immortality of the soul but into how women actually envisage their immortal souls in the hierarchy of images with which the unconscious presents them.

As I have already said, at the outset the whole of the unconscious of a man is projected upon a woman, notably his mother, and it is only gradually that he comes to recognize masculine figures whether of the wise old man or devilish shadows. But the image of woman continues to hold for him his own soul qualities in the person of the anima, whether or not he projects the figure on to an actual woman. With a woman on the other hand, though the first total projection of the unconscious may indeed be on to a man, with greater differentiation I hope to show that with some women at least the soul image appears as a feminine figure. I think this may have some bearing on the well-known fact that whereas women generally carry a man's anima projection gladly and without strain, only revolting when the image projected is confused with a lot of extraneous characteristics, such as for instance qualities which belong to the man's mother, men do not seem to carry a woman's animus projection so readily. He is often irked and irritated by it. I find it hard to believe that a man objects to being the bearer of an image of Logos, the giver of meaning. To carry this is his legitimate pride. Experience also seems to show his readiness to play the role of authority and capability. But it occurs to me that the real reason for his exasperation may be that the woman, in addition to projecting her animus on to him where it may legitimately dwell, frequently looks to him also to reflect for her her soul, and this he cannot do for the simple reason that he is not sufficiently identified with his own soul to be able to mirror that of another.

A woman may indeed carry his soul for him until he can take it into himself, for the nebulous immortal quality of the soul is an essential part of *her* nature. But as she is really identified with her soul all the time, her projection of it is mere confusion on her part and does not enter into the mutually projecting bargain of relationship.

It is almost as if a woman were so unconscious of herself that she does not notice that she has breasts so she looks for them on the man and is surprised at his annoyed repudiation. When a man makes love he is, of course, by no means always aware that he is looking for his soul though in fact this probably is so, but for a woman physical union with the soul apparently ignored makes her acutely unhappy. We all know this. But her distress may I believe be mainly due to her own lack of awareness that no man can truly meet her body without also encountering her soul because, as she is identified with soul, her body and her soul are indivisible.

I think it is indisputable that women recognize their own soul quality the moment they think about the matter, but this brings us back to the part of my talk to which I have already alluded: they cannot really focus upon such a thing to the point of being able to see it and realize its meaning without prior development of their masculine side, so that the Logos development of a woman is the essential first step towards her becoming really conscious of her own soul images.

For a woman to be unconsciously identified with her soul may be good enough to enable a man to find his, and for the woman to feel united to her man, but it is a far cry from consciously knowing her own soul quality. For then she looks to the man as the keeper of her soul which only makes him impatiently declare that she is reading more into the relationship than exists (how often we hear that) while she feels sad and belittled. I suggest, however, that the moment a woman recognizes that she does not need to look for her immortal essence in a man, for it is imbedded in and permeates her very body, this mutual exasperation disappears. She may even laugh at herself for having imagined the man was leaving the soul out (just sex as she calls it), while at the same time she frees him from a projection he cannot carry.

In short, whereas man has to find his image of the soul and hold her to him to be complete, it seems that woman has to win by hard work and the prior co-operation of her animus the knowledge that she and her soul are one. May I, before going on, give you another dream showing this father relationship of the animus to the soul: *Here a number of rosy-cheeked children of both sexes joined an obvious animus figure and hailed him as father.* (He had indeed brought these inner figures into being.) *But then running across a field to join him too and calling: 'Father,' the dreamer saw a fey little girl aged seven with a daisy chain on her head who had got left behind.*

This dreamer was a woman of fifty-eight who had had many years of analysis and experience of unconscious imagery, but this fey, ethereal little girl was a very late comer. That she was crowned with the loveliest and earthiest and most child-like of starry flowers seemed a fitting meeting of opposites to depict an image of the soul with its inevitable affinity with the Self.

The meeting of opposites is beautifully portrayed in the painting of a woman of about forty-five. To her own surprise she painted a large winged vase in a luminous cavity beneath the earth. The vase is a typical feminine symbol but this one had no base on which to stand. Its base was a point so it was actually held upright by great spiritual wings. Moreover the luminosity of the spirit is found in the darkness of the earth itself. This woman knew in the dream that this vase was an image of the soul.

Another woman about fifty or so dreamt: *She was travelling on a difficult journey on foot. The path was precipitous and stony and*

*a strong wind was blowing. Sheltered within her two cupped
hands was a white moth. To guard the moth from harm was her
passionate concern. She was beset with anxiety lest she might trip
and bruise its wings or let it fall and be blown away by the wind.*

The dreamer was in Zürich at the time and Toni Wolff un-
hesitatingly declared that the moth represented the woman's soul.
The dreamer had always thought of the moth as she.

Here it seems that the dreamer is warned of the dangers that
beset a woman's soul throughout life and perhaps especially in
analysis. It can be harmed by any false step and actually lost if not
protected from the strong wind of the masculine spirit.

I recall a poem by Edith Sitwell entitled 'The Youth with the
Red-Gold Hair':

> Fear only the red-gold sun with the fleece of a fox
> Who will steal the fluttering bird you hide in your breast.

Are not these lines also a warning that a too bright sun of consciousness is a thief who comes to steal away our treasures, not in
the night but in the day? It is the peril of over-intelectualization to
the soul of man or woman alike — the desperate peril with which
Western man is faced. I often wonder if the dreams of burglars or
frightening men in the basement which are so common to women
may not express woman's fear of the rape of her soul every bit as
much as the fear of the rape of her body.

I think a white moth must be an archetypal image of the soul.
Carla Lanyon has written a poem entitled 'The White Moth'. She
describes a thundery night with windows flung wide to a hot
garden and one lamp burning:

> We talked, a group of friends, young men and women
> Who turned the world with talk to put it right,
> And all the heavens too, because the burden
> Of our argument obliterated God.

Then suddenly she tells how a white moth flew in and settled
above her head, and here is her final verse:

> I saw its furred face, the exact design
> Of three black circles set in a triangle,
> The pure eurythmy of all curve and line;
> A white moth, antennae just a tingle,

Poised like a spirit, consummate, divine.
And I forgot our heady talk and wrangle,
Forgot we had obliterated God.

This I believe is what the poet is never allowed to forget, the existence of the immortal soul.

One woman of about fifty-five dreamt: *She was on a journey alone in some sort of vehicle, travelling across a highish plateau from which she had extensive views. At one point she passed a church on her right hand which she felt she had seen before and which filled her with a warm glow of recognition and delight. It was very old, built of yellow stone. A low squat building with no windows.*

In the distance she saw another church with two very phallic-looking towers which she knew in the dream to be Manchester. It was unfamiliar and far away but she felt that she must visit it sometime. However before doing so she came to another church where she alighted from her vehicle. There were a number of people outside the big open door of the church all talking to one another. These people she knew in the dream were Jungians and she wondered why they talked so much and why they stayed outside the church instead of going in. It was perhaps because they preferred to stay in the sunshine and open air. These people were all very friendly but she decided not to stay with them and continued her journey. She walked through an arched doorway into the hillside and proceeded along many winding corridors and down staircases (always down never up) until she arrived in the large entrance hall of what was obviously a great mansion. It had a big door to the outside which must of course have been on a much lower level than the three churches she had seen earlier, as she had been coming down all the time.

She did not apparently attempt to go out or even look out of the great door for she found herself sitting up in bed in a small waiting room adjoining it. There were two other figures in the room, dark and shadowy. As she sat and wondered who they might be, she glanced through the open door of the waiting room into the entrance hall and there she saw to her astonishment a woman with loose dark springy hair clothed in filmy blue edging her way down the stairs along the blue wall which was exactly the same colour as her dress. She crept as though she were trying to escape detection. Having arrived opposite the door of the waiting room this blue-

clad figure looked around carefully to make sure no one was look-
ing, then dashed across the hall into the waiting room itself and
stood beside the two dark shadowy figures at the foot of the
dreamer's bed, who then awoke.

She did a lot of work on this dream by active imagination and
later she discussed it at length with Mrs. Jung. The old, low,
squat, windowless church with which she had felt so akin seemed
to grow out of the earth and to represent perhaps the spirituality
of the earth itself. The dreamer's own feminine earthiness recognized this church as something to which she belonged. The two-
towered church in the distance clearly represented the spirituality
of Man, for Manchester means the City of Man. This was something about which she knew almost nothing. She had not yet
visited this church. She only saw it in the distance.

The fact that the Jungians stayed outside the next church talking in the sunshine of consciousness expressed no doubt her own
feeling at that time that psychology was not providing her with the
spiritual answer she was seeking. So she did not stay with them but
penetrated the hillside, once more the feminine earth, descending
lower and lower until she found herself in the waiting room within
the great entrance hall of the large mansion.

Active imagination produced the wholly unexpected realization
that the woman in blue, who was so shy of being seen, was a soul
image, and that the two dark shadowy figures whom she joined in
the waiting room were the Emissaries of Death. They appeared as
two, as frequently happens in dreams when something is only
emerging into consciousness and is still too vague for any apprehension of distinct qualities.

She has learned since that the Emissaries of Death and the soul
are never far apart, for the soul being man's immortal essence is at
home with death and never ceases to await death's consummation.
One could also say that in the dream the two dark shadowy Emissaries of Death are the dark, menacing, destructive aspects of the
soul of which the woman in blue is the light aspect, so, as opposites, they are invariably found together.

That the soul can be dark, negative and destructive may seem a
strange idea but it is impossible to imagine that the immortal soul
has human attributes such as kindness, courage or forgiveness.
Those are qualities acquired through being mortal and human.
The soul is not human but our immortal essence and I can imagine that anyone who was completely identified with their

immortal essence might be an insufferable person to live with and destructive in the extreme to the more vulnerable people around them.

In later years the blue-clad woman has appeared again and again and very often accompanied by another figure who is clearly the Self. If this dreamer consciously attempts to conjure up either the blue woman or her image of the Self the other also appears. It was Mrs. Jung who drew the dreamer's attention to the importance of the waiting room. They had often talked together of waiting as an essential positive quality of the feminine. The feminine in every woman is always waiting. She may not know it if she has another more masculine side which is busy with active achievement but I believe that every woman if she looks deep enough will find that the essential core of her is waiting.

As a tiny girl she waits to be grown-up, filling the time with all sorts of occupations and study, which to the essential growing point are quite irrelevant. As time passes most women quite consciously wait for a coming lover or husband no matter how vociferously they declare the contrary. No woman as woman can plan her future. She can plan a career, but as woman she can only wait for the future to unfold itself. Her lover emerges from the mists of time and in his wake so also does the place where she will dwell. Whether it is near her birthplace or on a distant shore will be determined for her by the love to which she has been elected. It could not be foretold or planned. So she needs must wait and the more conscious women know for what they wait.

A woman is always waiting — she may or may not conceive — she can only wait and see. Nine long months she waits, not knowing whether her child will be son or daughter, dark or fair, morose or gay, brilliant or a dunce. This is equally true in realms of the spirit or the intellect in both men and women. Intellectual achievement when it is not merely mechanical always has to wait for inspiration. It is the feminine which waits whether it is in man or woman and it is the masculine which moulds and formulates in either sex.

Waiting is I believe as essential a part of feminine psychology today as it was for Penelope. The picture of Penelope working at her loom every day as she listened to the wooing entreaties of her many suitors, and undoing her weaving at nightfall so that she could await the return of Ulysses, is I believe the picture of any woman who listens to the seductive voices of collective opinion and plans her life accordingly yet in the solitude of her own heart unravels her false weaving every night knowing that it is not planning for the future, but waiting which will bring her future to her.

A woman once talked to Dr. Jung about a number of things and ended by asking him, 'What do I do with all this?' 'Just wait,' he answered, 'and whatever you have to do will come to you.' In a few years it did so. Feminine spirituality I have likened elsewhere to the sacred oil which the wise virgins kept always ready in their lamps waiting, waiting for the coming of the bridegroom.

This is very near the final waiting of the soul for the coming of death, a constant unceasing waiting throughout every moment of the span of life, for the soul belongs to death as much as it belongs to life. I am of course no longer speaking of the soul image but of the soul itself. It is the rest of our personality which fears to die. Our animal instinct clings to life, our minds dread the unknown, and our hearts with good reason tremble lest we may be cut off before we have carried out the tasks which have been set us, tasks at which sometimes we can only guess.

It is certainly those who have lived fully who seem least afraid to die. Perhaps they have left fewer tasks undone. But it is the feminine soul in man or woman which waits ceaselessly without fear and without impatience for the coming of death, the last lover, who will lead to a new unfolding. I am aware that I am going beyond the boundaries of the provable. I am not out to prove anything. I am merely offering you the fruits of my own minute experience, in no attempt to be scientific. If they do not ring a bell or touch a chord of sympathetic knowing from my readers it matters not at all.

The idea that the soul has to be humanized seems to be borne out in the active imagination of a young professional woman named Jane who had come to analysis because she felt dry and stale. The moment her natural capacity to fantasize reasserted itself, she recovered her poise, disentangled herself from the sterile relationships in which she was caught and fell in love with the man she married a little later.

In the particular fantasy I am referring to: *She re-entered a dark room in a large moated country house of which she had dreamt. There was cold moonlight outside and some men,* (presumably animus figures) *were looking for her. There was no light in the room other than a large fire, beside which sat a very old*

woman and a fair-haired little girl. The old woman said to Jane,
'Don't bother about the men who are looking for you. You are
quite safe here within the moat. They can't see anyway even
though there is moonlight. Presently they will fall into the moat
and take their darkness with them. Now you come and play
draughts with me. You take the white and I will be black.' They
sat down and played draughts but the old woman contrived that
Jane should win, seemingly playing the white draughts as well as
her own, though it was Jane's hands which moved them.

While the game was in progress Jane noticed that the child
seated by the fire was getting bigger. Her hair was long and looked
wet as though she had come out of the sea. Suddenly three silver
fish leapt out of her mouth into the fire where they swam around
and turned a rosy gold colour, whereupon the girl reached out,
lifted them from the fire and swallowed them again. One could see
them swimming down her throat turning her hitherto white neck
a rosy colour.

'Don't bother about her,' said the old lady, 'she is growing up
and has to warm bits of herself outside. They'll stay warm once
they are inside her again.' As she spoke the girl got up and moved
round the room, the three fish inside her producing an odd light
which enabled Jane to see that the walls were covered with beautiful and ancient pictures, tapestries and metal engravings. The girl
moved out into the garden and wherever she walked the lawns
and flowers were lit up until the moonlight could no longer be
noticed. She wandered down the garden and dived into the
moat.

I dare say some of you will be able to throw more light on this
fantasy but the main things which impressed me are the following:

Within the moated country house which is presumably a
symbol of the Self is found not a wise old man but a wise old
woman. The game of draughts between the old woman and Jane
seems to express an excellent relationship between the Self and
the ego for the Self contrives that though the ego shall win it is in
obedience to the Self. We must have an ego and at this particular
time in Jane's life it was important that she should free herself
from the animus world in which she had been caught (expressed
by the men who were looking for her) and make her own judgments and decisions. It is this which the wise old woman
ensures.

At the same time Jane finds her own soul image seated close beside the old woman and visibly growing.

The three silver fish puzzled me for a long time but I think they must stand for the innate spiritual quality of the soul which only when it has been transformed in the fire of feeling and passion becomes warm and golden so that it glows from within. The cold, impersonal feminine moonlight disappeared when the fish had been warmed in the fire of passion.

Perhaps when the girl dived into the moat she will have illumined the darkness of the animi who had fallen in and they will all emerge together on better terms, but that is only my guess.

The transformation of the fish and the growing of the child both seem to suggest that the innate soul quality needs to be humanized and grow up, perhaps even be made conscious before it can become the golden light that visibly glows, but I think it is important to emphasize that the silver fish came in the first place from *within* the feminine soul figure and are not something imbibed from without.

May I conclude with a dream of my own: *I was walking arm in arm with Barbara Hannah.* (Miss Hannah is for me the person of all the Jungians who has penetrated most deeply into feminine psychology, as in her memorable and far-reaching lecture on 'Women's Plots' and the light she has thrown on women's creativity in her studies of the Brontë sisters.)[5] *I was walking with her on the hillside when we came to a stairway leading down into the bowels of the earth. We proceeded down this stair together until we reached a long gallery with beds in it looking rather like a hospital ward. In the floor we found a trap-door which we lifted disclosing a still more rugged stone stairway leading yet further down. I descended this stair alone until it ended in a rope ladder hovering above a sea in which strange primitive reptilian beasts were swimming, and among them one woman with long flowing hair in evident great distress. I did not dare swim out to her unaided. But two men came to my rescue, one my former analyst with whom I was still in touch, another a man of actual importance in my life. These fastened two ropes around my waist and each held one, so that I could be held safe and pulled back again. With this assurance I swam out to the woman and the men pulled both of us to safety.*

[5] B. Hannah, *Striving Towards Wholeness*, C. G. Jung Foundation, New York, 1971.

The woman was either too exhausted or too bewildered to walk, but we three dragged her up to the hospital ward and were about to put her to bed when an authoritative voice rang out: 'It is no use leaving her there,' it said, 'she must be taken up into the sunlight.'

With the help of other people who were about we got her up the last lap of stairway. The sun was shining brilliantly and we laid her on the grass.

If it had not been for this dream I doubt if I should be giving this talk today for it put me on the alert. To me the dream is saying that the feminine soul image of a woman is still in great distress because it has remained in the unconscious and it desperately needs to be brought into consciousness.

The hospital ward is, I suggest, the level of the unconscious where healing takes place in analysis. It is the region of deliberate organized healing. It is not enough to bring this distressed figure into the sphere of analysis. She needs to be brought right up into the consciousness of every day.

The role of the two men in the dream is of paramount importance. Taken as inner animus figures they represent the power to focus, make conscious and give meaning to what I saw. But they are also actual men with whom I had a close relationship. They stand for reality and it was, I think, only because I had this double hold on reality, both analytical and personal, that I could risk swimming quite so far out of my depth.

This paper, inadequate as it must inevitably be, is my first attempt to get this distressed feminine figure out into the light of day where she can be acknowledged and accepted. I cannot possibly succeed alone.

My paper, more than anything else, is an appeal to all of those of you who feel the task worthwhile, to help lift this figure, which I believe to be the image of the feminine soul of woman, right up into the sunshine and lag her on the green, growing grass of conscious reality.

Index

Index

Lobsticks and Stone Cairns

Lobsticks and Stone Cairns

Human Landmarks in the Arctic

Richard C. Davis, editor

University of Calgary Press

© Richard C. Davis and The Arctic Institute of North America. All rights reserved

University of Calgary Press
2500 University Drive N.W.
Calgary, Alberta, Canada T2N 1N4

Canadian Cataloguing in Publication Data

Main entry under title:
    Lobsticks and stone cairns

    Includes bibliographical references and index.
    ISBN 1-895176-88-3 (bound)—ISBN 1-895176-69-7 (pbk.)

    1. Arctic regions—Discovery and exploration. 2 Arctic
regions—Biography. I. Davis, Richard Clarke, 1946-

G634.L62 1996   910′.9163′27   C96-910557-6

Illustrations without credit lines are taken from R.M. Ballantyne, *Hudson Bay;
Or, Everyday Life in the Wilds of North America* (London: T. Nelson and Sons,
1896) and Major W.F. Butler, C.B., F.R.G.S., *The Great Lone Land: A Narrative
of Travel and Adventure in the North-West of America* (London: Sampson Low,
Marston, Searle & Rivington, 1878).

COMMITTED TO THE DEVELOPMENT OF CULTURE AND THE ARTS

The profiles included in this volume are based on earlier versions initially
published in the Arctic Profiles series of *Arctic, Journal of the Arctic Institute
of North America*, from June 1982 (*Arctic,* Vol. 35, No. 2) to December
1987 (Arctic, Vol. 40, No. 4). One-time only permission to reprint these
profiles is granted by the copyright holder, The Arctic Institute of North
America.

The purposes of the Arctic Institute are to assist and
cooperate in the orderly development of the North
through the sponsoring of research and the acquisition
and dissemination of information. The Institute, founded and incorporated by an Act of Parliament in 1945, is
a nonprofit, tax-exempt research and educational organization. It has been an institute of the University of Calgary since 1979 and
is governed by a Board of Directors. The U.S. Corporation is headquartered at the University of Alaska, Fairbanks, and is governed by a Board
of Governors. The Arctic Institute's activities embrace all scholarly disciplines. Though mainly concerned with the North, its interests extend
also to Antarctica and to alpine environments. The Arctic Institute pub-
lishes the scholarly journal *Arctic*, North America's premier journal of
northern research. Direct inquiries regarding memberships and sub-
scriptions to: The Arctic Institute of North America, The University of
Calgary, 2500 University Drive N.W., Calgary, Alberta T2N 1N4.
Phone: (403) 220-7515. Fax: (403) 282-4609.

Book design by FEVER communications inc., Calgary, Alberta

Printed and bound in Canada by Hignell Printing Ltd.

∞ This book is printed on acid-free paper.

TABLE OF CONTENTS

Foreword

They were an exceptional group of people who ventured into the High Arctic regions—some vain, some magnanimous, many courageous, a few foolhardy and yet all with a deep and abiding respect for the icy opposites of the Polar cap: breathtaking beauty and yet ultimate terror.

When Professor Richard Davis presented this project to the board of the Frederick A. Cook Society at The Ohio State University in 1993, it seemed an appropriate way to deliver the message of the work and achievements of a largely unrecognized group of explorers and travellers who helped fill in the blank spaces of the vast unchartered map of North America to the magical 90 degrees North where all longitudes come together.

We have been privileged to be a part of the publication of this volume and feel that the generous treatment accorded all nationalities who have penetrated into this part of the world is one of its outstanding features. Canadian writer Frank Rasky observed many years ago that Dr. Cook had "broken through the barriers of Kabloona prejudice [and] prepared the way for explorer-ethnologists Stefannson and Rasmussen. They were to follow his trail, and like him, strive for a genuine human and scientific understanding of the peoples of the north."

Cook's *My Attainment of the Pole* was the first by an explorer which was dedicated to the Arctic's aboriginal pathfinders, the spirit of which continues in this volume:

> *To the Indian who invented pemmican and snowshoes;*
> *To the Eskimo who gave the art of sled traveling;*
> *To this twin family of wild folk who have no flag*
> *Goes the first credit.*

Dr. Frederick A. Cook Society
Warren B. Cook, President
Russell W. Gibbons, Executive Director

Acknowledgements

A book of this scope arises out of the energies of many individuals and offices, and *Lobsticks and Stone Cairns* is no exception. The authors of these one hundred biographical profiles have contributed their expertise freely, wanting to share their considerable knowledge with others. Their generous efforts will be repaid every time this book brings a better understanding of the Arctic to the reader. Other individuals—too numerous to list—have played important back-stage roles, assisting with the preparation of the text, the maps, the illustrations, and the index. Their efforts have made this book possible.

Three substantial grants have also helped make *Lobsticks and Stone Cairns* a reality. They came from the Dr. Frederick A. Cook Society, the McLean Foundation, and the Devonian Foundation. As well as providing financial assistance for the preparation of the maps used here, the Devonian Foundation has also placed a hardcover copy of the book in every senior high school in Alberta, the Yukon, and the Northwest Territories. The University of Calgary's Office of Research Services and the Arctic Institute of North America have also generously contributed to this project.

Finally, I should like to thank the many staff members of the Arctic Institute of North America and University of Calgary Press for their assistance. The editorial staff of *Arctic* gave freely of their time when earlier versions of these profiles appeared in their journal, and the staff at the University of Calgary Press have been unstinting in their efforts to make *Lobsticks and Stone Cairns* the attractive and comprehensive book that it is.

Richard C. Davis

Introduction

Midway through the last century, Henry David Thoreau stood musing at the Citadel of Quebec, speculating on the history of a region that had been so central to the struggles between French, British, American, and aboriginal North American cultures. Yet as his gaze turned to look "beyond the frontiers of civilization," Thoreau felt those powerful historical associations being swept away in the presence of an even greater influence that "flowed from the Arctic fastness and Western forests with irresistible tide over all."

Thoreau was certainly not alone when he sensed the irresistible power of the Arctic. The North has inspired the music of Glenn Gould and Richard Wagner, the paintings of Lawren Harris and the photographs of Fred Bruemmer, the poems of Robert Service and Al Purdy, and the stories of Jack London and Mary Shelley. From remote sections of the globe, it has drawn thousands in the search for adventure, scientific understanding, fame, wealth, and solitude. Over the centuries, it has been a meeting place of many different peoples—American, Inuit, Canadian, British, Chipewyan, French, Norwegian, and others—who have travelled in it, either as visitors or as permanent residents. That "irresistible tide" of the Arctic has indeed left its mark on a broad spectrum of individuals and cultures.

But just as the North has left its mark on humankind, civilization has, in turn, put its stamp on the North. There are, in effect, two Norths. One is a vast piece of physical geography that can be weighed, measured, and quantified. The material features of that North—the cold, the distances, the ice—have shaped the people who have lived there or travelled in it. The other North—elusive, ambivalent, powerful—is a construction of the human imagination, built upon the experiences of humans as they have come into contact with that other and more physical North. One North is a Place, the other an Idea. One North is the geologist's or the topographic surveyor's "land"; the other is the artist's "landscape." This book is an exploration of both those Norths and of the interplay between them.

Lobsticks and Stone Cairns attempts to convey something of the way this "Idea of North"—to borrow Glenn Gould's title—has been created, while simultaneously enhancing the reader's familiarity with the North as Place. From earliest history, humankind has projected our humanity onto the physical realm in which we live. Every time we have named the site of a secure winter encampment or told a story about a desperate journey through inhospitable terrain, we have projected a part of ourselves. Taken collectively, all those names and stories constitute an imaginative construction that both reflects our past response to the land and shapes how we might deal with it in the present and future. The best resource, then, to help us grasp both the human and the geographical aspects of the North is the story of human endeavour in the Arctic. Thus, *Lobsticks and Stone Cairns* offers one hundred sketches of some of the individuals who have constructed our image of the Arctic while they have revealed its physical features. The players are both men and women, indigenous peoples and European visitors, permanent residents and itinerant travellers, Americans and Canadians.

Witness, for instance, the centuries-long search for the Northwest Passage. The quest for that arctic grail was largely a British undertaking but, as this book reveals, one frequently influenced both by aboriginal and fur-trade residents of the North. In 1845, when John Franklin set out with 128 British seamen aboard two of Her Majesty's ships, his voyage was viewed by many as a ceremonial ribbon-cutting ceremony, a final traverse of the Passage that had eluded Europeans for so long. Nonetheless, Franklin's expedition disappeared without a trace for nearly a quarter of a century, and in the years spent probing for signs of its fate, individuals from diverse cultures, nationalities, and backgrounds contributed to the unveiling of arctic geography. Complementing the elaborate Admiralty-mounted rescue expeditions were privately sponsored American searches, French volunteers, and fur-trade contributions. Many of these were made possible through the services of Inuit and Indian interpreters, guides, and hunters. And if the British dominated the search for the Passage, it was a Norwegian who finally navigated it from east to west early in the twentieth century, and still later, a Canadian Mountie who traversed it from west to east.

Just as the search for the Northwest Passage and, subsequently, the missing Franklin expedition spurred much of the charting of the High Arctic, the fur trade played a crucial role in shaping our understanding of subarctic regions. While not without some unfortunate consequences, the trade in furs established a valuable long-term relationship between unique cultures in the North. Trade stimulated relationships that could be mutually beneficial to all parties, and traders and aboriginal peoples learned the art of negotiation

with each other, rather than the patterns of domination that frequently accompany the settlement of agricultural lands.

Thousands of people, of course, have contributed to our understanding of the North, so one might well ask why these one hundred in particular have been selected. Why, for example, are such significant or familiar figures as Roald Amundsen or Henry Hudson not included? Certainly this book is not intended to be used as an encyclopedic "Who's Who in the Arctic." Rather, the purpose of *Lobsticks and Stone Cairns* is to enhance our knowledge of the North. The individuals included here should not be considered benchmarks against which others are to be measured, but as landmarks guiding the reader on this journey to increased familiarity with the North American Arctic. The "Further Readings" section accompanying each sketch offers additional reading for any curiosity piqued by the profile.

In the forested regions of the North, travellers of the past lobbed off all but the topmost branches of prominent spruces or pines to create landmarks for other travellers—hence, the word "lobsticks." Farther north beyond the tree line, piles of stones were gathered into "cairns" to mark the way. The men and women featured here are landmarks, too, on this journey through the human history of the Arctic.

When we think about that Idea of North, a flood of contradictions sweeps across our minds. We see a land of feast or famine, a land where vast herds of caribou once stretched beyond the horizon but where death by starvation has been all too common, a sparsely peopled land but one where countless heroes have been moulded, a land where the sun shines at midnight but where the northern lights dance against what seems an eternal nighttime sky. Increasingly, our Idea of North encompasses a land where aboriginal peoples and long-term residents struggle to balance traditional lifestyles against modern attractions of the Outside, as northerners term everywhere that is not the "North." It is important that this book reflects the sometimes perplexing and contradictory nature of the Arctic.

Accordingly, these sketches often include opposing claims, such as who was the first to reach the North Pole, or differing assessments of someone's contribution. While each piece is factually correct and reflects the knowledge and opinion of the author, as editor, I have not attempted to eliminate differences of opinion among the authors. Similarly, the diversity of voices that grows out of multiple authors—professional writers, family members, academics, friends and admirers—helps convey the confusing and sometimes haphazard ways in which our image of the Arctic has been constructed. The multiple voices and the diverse range of subjects collected here capture, I think, a sense of the formal and highly orchestrated British probings into this foreign realm, as well as something of the more colloquial textures of oral histories that often reveal the contributions of northerners themselves. This multiplicity of voices and cultural backgrounds best reflects our constructed image of the North.

The same principles have governed the organization of this book, which resists the temptation to create order simply for the sake of convenience. A chronological or alphabetical ordering of the sketches would be tidy, but there has been nothing tidy or orderly in the geographical discovery of the Arctic. Nor are the profiles arranged according to nation of origin, gender, cultural background, or primary interests of the subjects. Instead, government geologists and surveyors are placed alongside romantic adventurers, whalers beside anthropologists, English ladies with Inuit guides. This is the

manner in which our image of the North has evolved, and this is the only way it can be reflected.

Books, however, necessarily impose structure, and the inevitable structure here is geographical and spatial. The book is divided into sixteen units, each unit including several sketches and a map. Most of the place names used in the sketches appear on the unit maps, allowing the reader to learn about arctic geography as he or she enjoys these stories of human endeavour and achievement in the North.

Yet even with such spatial ordering, readers must not expect too rigid a structure. The sixteen units described here do not reflect sixteen distinct and autonomous regions of the Arctic, they do not mirror political boundaries, and they do not follow a single scale. Instead, the units are determined solely with the reader's enhanced learning in mind. A map of the Labrador Peninsula, for example, might serve for one unit, while a map of the entire western Arctic might be required for another. The determining principle has been to provide a relatively uncluttered map for each grouping, and while a map of the Labrador conveniently illustrates the tightly focused travels of the Hubbard party and a few others, a much larger map is required to reveal the scope of, say, John Rae's or Henry Larsen's activities. While such an arrangement lacks what might be called classical unity, it accurately reflects the nature of human travel in the North.

Perhaps the only structural element here that could be described as "classical" is the order in which the various units appear. *Lobsticks and Stone Cairns* begins where Horace said all great classical epics should begin—*in medias res*, "in the middle of things." That is, rather than tidily beginning in the east and progressing steadily west, the book begins with a large map of the Arctic in unit 1 and then focuses in on

Hudson Bay in unit 2 and the central region of the Arctic archipelago in unit 3. From there, the focus gradually shifts west, but certainly not in a lock-step fashion. Reaching the westernmost extent of the North American Arctic in unit 11, the focus is brought back to the central Arctic, from where it moves in a more or less easterly direction. *In medias res* is an appropriate way to start this epic story of northern discovery, for such an arrangement introduces the major landforms and maritime features of the central Arctic, and opens the story midway in the search for the elusive Northwest Passage.

It only remains to make a few suggestions about how best to enjoy *Lobsticks and Stone Cairns*. No reader should feel obliged to begin with unit 1 and read steadily through to the final pages. This is a book made for browsing. Pick any one of the profiles and read it, referring frequently to the unit map. Connect the place names in the sketch with those on the map. Then try reading another profile in that same unit, comparing the contributions of the figures and the geographic sphere of their activities. Or perhaps the sketch will mention another name that arouses your curiosity. If an asterisk (*) appears after that name the first time it appears in a profile, that person is the subject of another biographical sketch in this book, although not necessarily in the same unit. Using the table of contents or index, you can locate the sketch and read more about him or her.

This book is intended only as a beginning. The authors have supplied a short list of interesting titles relevant to each sketch, and you are encouraged to put aside *Lobsticks and Stone Cairns* and to read in greater detail about the person, region, or undertaking that has captured your attention. Most recommended titles are readily available and will greatly enhance your understanding of northern history, culture, and geography.

When we read a novel by Charles Dickens, we cannot help but come away with a powerful sense of Victorian England as Place. If *Lobsticks and Stone Cairns* is successful, it will not only leave readers with an improved understanding of the North as Place, but also something of how the North as Idea has been constructed.

Lobsticks and Stone Cairns

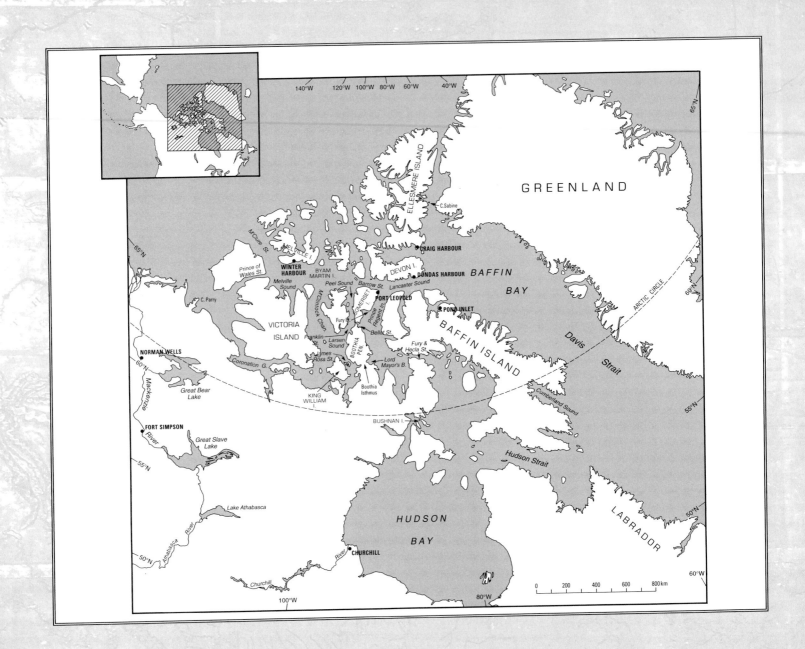

GREENLAND

ELLESMERE ISLAND

C.Sabine

CRAIG HARBOUR

DEVON I.

DUNDAS HARBOUR

BAFFIN

BAY

MELVILLE I.

M'Clure St.

WINTER
HARBOUR

BYAM
MARTIN I.

Prince of
Wales St.

Melville
Sound

Peel Sound

Barrow St.

Lancaster Sound

ARCTIC CIRCLE

PORT LEOPOLD

SOMERSET
I.

POND INLET

65°N

65°N

60°N

C. Parry

M'Clintock Chain

Fury B.

Prince
Regent Inl.

Bellot St.

BAFFIN ISLAND

Davis

Strait

VICTORIA

ISLAND

Franklin
St.

Larsen
Sound

James
Ross St.

BOOTHIA
PEN.

Fury &
Hecla St.

NORMAN WELLS

Coronation G.

Lord
Mayor's B.

Cumberland Sound

Mackenzie

Great Bear
Lake

Boothia
Isthmus

55°N

60°N

KING
WILLIAM
I.

BUSHNAN I.

FORT SIMPSON

River

Great Slave
Lake

Hudson Strait

LABRADOR

55°N

Lake Athabasca

Athabasca

River

HUDSON

50°N

50°N

River

CHURCHILL

BAY

60°W

Churchill

0   200   400   600   800km

80°W

140°W 120°W 100°W 80°W 60°W 40°W

100°W

UNIT
❧ I ❧

John Ross, Edward Sabine, William Edward Parry, James Clark Ross,
Joseph-Elzéar Bernier, Vilhjalmur Stefansson, Henry Larsen

This first unit is designed to provide the reader with a substantial, although not complete, map of the North American Arctic. The individuals grouped together here ranged widely throughout the central and eastern regions of the North, where Parry, Sabine, and the two Rosses were involved in the nineteenth century search for the Northwest Passage. Larsen, in the twentieth century, was able to navigate that elusive Passage from both east and west. Yet even a map sufficiently large to illustrate the Northwest Passage cannot accommodate the full extent of the exploratory investigations of men such as Bernier and Stefansson.

JOHN ROSS (1777–1856)

The space accorded John Ross in the history of the Canadian Arctic is out of proportion to his achievement, circumstances arising from his invincible self-confidence and refusal to admit error. When convicted of blunders—obvious but excusable—he retorted on his critics with a repetitive bitterness that added much to his celebrity, although it did little for his reputation. His first unlucky arctic voyage at least restored the faded character of William Baffin; his second was a miracle of survival. In retrospect, its drama was a little dulled by Ross's tedious and wordy narrative, but it exemplified his leadership and undaunted courage. Ross's combativeness probably helped his popularity, and his futile voyage, at the age of seventy-three, to the rescue of John Franklin* won him admiration and respect.

Portrait of John Ross by J. Green, 1833. By courtesy of the National Portrait Gallery, London, U.K. No. 314

John Ross, the younger son of a good Scottish family, joined the Navy and served in the Revolutionary and Napoleonic wars. After the wars, he was appointed to resurvey Baffin Bay and seek an outlet from that basin to the Pacific. He rounded the bay in 1818, confirmed Baffin's nearly forgotten survey, but erroneously declared that the three possible western outlets were blocked by land. William Edward Parry* and others of his officers disagreed with his opinion. In 1819–20 Parry proved Lancaster Sound an open channel leading into the heart of the Canadian archipelago, but he failed to prove the existence of an outlet to the Pacific—a Northwest Passage. Nonetheless, John Barrow,

Second Secretary to the Admiralty, bitterly censured Ross for his mistake, to which Ross replied angrily.

Ross, though poorly educated, was courageous, enterprising, and inventive. Refused fresh naval employment, he secured the backing of Felix Booth, a wealthy distiller, for the discovery of the Passage. His plan was to take a small ship of light draft, equipped with auxiliary steam power, to the bottom of Prince Regent Inlet, and make his way west along the continental shore.

He set out in 1829, in the little *Victory* with his nephew James Clark Ross* as second-in-command. The ship was fitted with paddle wheels that could be hoisted up to avoid contact with ice, but the experiment was not a success. With great difficulty, Ross penetrated to Lord Mayor's Bay at the bottom of the inlet, where he dismantled his worthless engine and flung it on the beach. The ship was soon frozen in and, after three winters, was finally abandoned by her crew. Such long confinement might have wiped out the entire crew by scurvy, but Ross won the friendship of the local Inuit, who supplied him with enough fresh meat to keep his men in good health. The natives also taught him to use sleds, or sledges as they are known in the British tradition, and although the fifty-two-year-old John Ross was too old for strenuous sledding, his nephew James conducted most of the expedition's geographical work through this newly learned method of travel.

After three winters, the *Victory* was deserted, and the crew, hauling sleds, travelled up the east shores of Boothia Peninsula and Somerset Island to Lancaster Sound, with the hope of being rescued by whalers. In this they were disappointed, and went many miles back to Fury Point on Somerset Island, where Parry, on an earlier expedition, had cached the supplies of his wrecked ship, the *Fury*. In the summer of 1833, they returned to Lancaster Sound, where they were at last picked up by a whaler and carried back to a country that had long given them up for dead.

Ross's dogmatic self-assertiveness had procured him malicious critics, but the country at large could not withhold its admiration for his daring endeavour and his maintenance of the discipline and courage of his crew through four seasons of unforeseen hardship and danger, and, towards the last, of frightful suspense. The Admiralty discharged his indebtedness to his crew, whose period of employment had vastly exceeded the terms of their contract. As well, a committee of the House of Commons, brushing aside hostile criticism, expressed approval of his expedition and awarded him a grant of £5,000 for having so well sustained the national honour. King William IV, ex-officer and ever the sailor's friend, granted him a knighthood. After serving as British consul in Sweden, Ross retired with the rank of rear-admiral.

He still felt a lively interest in the Arctic and, in 1847, was the first to raise the alarm over the prolonged absence in the North of the last Franklin expedition. When the first rescue expeditions failed, the old sea dog, although over seventy years of age, obtained help from private sources and took his own ship into Barrow Strait on an equally fruitless search. He died in 1856.

John Ross was of an original—but in his youth apparently uncultivated—mind. Self-educated and unused to the give-and-take of academic life, he was positive and overbearing, although no more than his chief critic, John Barrow. He was an early advocate of the introduction of steam power, and this antagonized the conservative Navy chiefs. Although bitter in controversy, he was amiable in social intercourse. The American explorer Elisha Kent Kane,* who met him in Barrow Strait in 1850, was charmed with his cordiality; in the same season, Lt. Sherard Osborn made a winter journey of some distance to pay a courtesy visit to the old sailor, his senior by fifty years. Ross's contribution to arctic endeavour was considerable, and his eccentricities helped to keep up public interest in the North.

Further Readings

Kane, Elisha Kent. 1854. *Grinnell Expedition in Search of Sir John Franklin: A Personal Narrative*. London: Sampson Low, Son, and Company.

Neatby, L. H. 1970. *Search for Franklin*. Edmonton: M.G. Hurtig.

Parry, Ann. 1963. *Parry of the Arctic*. London: Chatto and Windus.

Ross, John. 1819. *A Voyage of Discovery*. London: John Murray.

_____. 1835. *Narrative of a Second Voyage in Search of a North-west Passage*. London: A.W. Webster.

Ross, M. J. 1995. *Polar Pioneers: John Ross and James Clark Ross*. London and Montreal: University College London Press and McGill-Queen's Press.

L.H. Neatby

Edward Sabine (1788–1883)

Edward Sabine, soldier, scientist, and arctic explorer, was a forceful and ambitious man, skilled in the politics of science, and very much in control of the enterprises he espoused. He was born in Dublin on 14 October 1788, educated in England, and entered the Royal Military Academy at Woolwich in 1803. His active service was relatively brief and based in Upper and Lower Canada, where in 1813 and 1814 he was engaged in resisting American attacks.

After the Napoleonic wars, he, like many others in the British Army and the Royal Navy, found himself underemployed; he chose to pursue scientific studies, notably in ornithology, astronomy, and magnetism. In 1818, he was elected a Fellow of the Royal Society of London and shortly thereafter found himself appointed astronomer to John Ross's* first expedition in search of the Northwest Passage. Ross sailed in May on HMS *Isabella,* accompanied by William Edward Parry* on HMS *Alexander.*

Sabine was far more than the expedition astronomer. He carried out observations in natural history and anthropology, publishing his biological results and an account of the West Greenland Inuit, including a tribe near Thule previously unknown to Europeans. On 25 July, he discovered a new species of gull, the fork-tailed or Sabine's gull, at its breeding station off the west coast of Greenland. He carried out pendulum experiments, significant for acquiring a detailed understanding of the shape of the earth, and he also carried

Portrait of Edward Sabine. Used by permission of the President and Council of the Royal Society, London, U.K.

out magnetic observations. Once, Ross tied the ships to icebergs while an observatory and tents were set up on shore for Sabine and his companions. On another occasion, the ships were lifted onto ice floes and driven into collision during a storm, which frustrated subsequent attempts to carve out safe docks in the ice field. Sabine and his companions meanwhile landed on Bushnan Island, where they found Inuit remains.

John Ross believed that he had seen a chain of mountains closing the entrance to Lancaster Sound; none of the other officers saw the mountains, or rather what was surely a mirage, and Sabine seems to have led subsequent questioning about the correctness of Ross's decision not to advance farther up the sound. The ensuing controversy was sometimes bitter; John Barrow, Second Secretary to the Admiralty, sided against Ross and suggested that Sabine's scientific observations were the best thing to have come out of the expedition.

In May 1819, Sabine returned to the Arctic, this time under Parry on the Hull-built bomb *Hecla.* The expedition was a young one—Sabine, at thirty, was the oldest member. Sabine again carried out a wide variety of scientific observations, collecting mineral specimens, observing the remains of Inuit houses on Byam Martin Island, compiling geomagnetic data, and carrying out a series of pendulum experiments that were rewarded, in 1821, with the Copley Medal of the Royal Society.

Parry succeeded in following the northern shore of Lancaster Sound until ice blocked farther progress. The ships wintered at Winter Harbour, slightly to the east of Hearne Point or the western enclosure of Winter Harbour. The crew were kept busy and entertained through a winter in which the sun was below the horizon for ninety-six days. Sabine, besides maintaining a program of scientific observation, was also the editor and censor of the expedition's newspaper, the *North Georgia Gazette and Winter Chronicle*, which was published on board the *Hecla* and ran to twenty-one issues.

Sabine could be formidable in his professional capacity, but seems to have been a genial and equable companion; certainly the *North Georgia Gazette*, which was mostly from his pen, displays sustained good humour and occasional whimsy. As for his tabulation of scientific data, this was well received not only by the Royal Society, but also by Parry. Indeed, Sabine was acknowledged as being responsible for almost all the scientific appendix to Parry's account of the expedition.

In 1821, Sabine again set out in pursuit of his geophysical researches, measuring the length of the second pendulum in different latitudes. He was away from the Arctic in HMS *Pheasant* until 1823. Then, from May until December, he was on HMS *Griper,* which had accompanied *Hecla* in 1819–20. Now Sabine visited Greenland and Spitsbergen, where he killed another pair of Sabine's gulls, showing that this species was to be found to the east as well as the west of Greenland.

He was promoted first captain in 1827, and in the following year, after the abolition of the Board of Longitude, was appointed one of three scientific advisers to the Admiralty. His principal scientific activity was in geomagnetism. In 1823, he had been the first to demonstrate the correlation of magnetic variations on a chart. In 1834, he began work on a magnetic survey of Great Britain; his old arctic companion James Clark Ross* joined him in the enterprise. In 1835, he led the British Association for the Advancement of Science in urging the government to sponsor an antarctic expedition in search of the South Magnetic Pole, and further lobbying contributed to the appointment of James Clark Ross, discoverer of the North Magnetic Pole, as commander of the British Antarctic Expedition of 1839–43.

Sabine also became the key figure in the establishment of a chain of colonial magnetic observatories, including the Toronto observatory, from which John Henry Lefroy, on Sabine's orders, undertook his marathon magnetic survey of the Canadian Northwest. Sabine both encouraged and was jealous of Lefroy, whose sweep through Great Slave Lake, Athabasca, and Fort Simpson was on precisely the grand scale that Sabine advocated. Indeed, he wanted nothing less than worldwide data to resolve "the cosmical features of terrestrial magnetism."

Edward Sabine continued to be consulted about arctic matters. He was one of the experts who recommended in February 1847 that there was as yet no need to send out a relief expedition to search for John Franklin.* His career, however, was henceforth in science and in the army, not in the polar regions. He was president of the British Association for the Advancement of Science in 1852, president of the Royal Society from 1861 to 1871, author of more than one hundred scholarly papers, and a general in the Royal Artillery. He died at Richmond on 26 June 1883.

Further Readings

Dodge, Ernest S. 1973. *The Polar Rosses: John and James Clark Ross and their Explorations*. London: Faber and Faber.

Levere, Trevor H. 1993. *Science and the Canadian Arctic: A Century of Exploration 1818–1918*. Cambridge and New York: Cambridge University Press.

Ross, M.J. 1995. *Polar Pioneers: John Ross and James Clark Ross*. London and Montreal: University College London Press and McGill-Queen's Press.

Sabine, Edward 1821. Appendices to *Journal of a Voyage for the Discovery of a North-West Passage, 1819–20*, by W.E. Parry. London: John Murray.

_____. 1824. *A Supplement to the Appendix of Captain Parry's Voyage for the Discovery of a North-West Passage*. London: John Murray.

Trevor H. Levere

WILLIAM EDWARD PARRY
(1790–1855)

Edward Parry, British admiral and arctic explorer, was born on 19 December 1790, the son of a fashionable doctor at Bath. He joined the Navy in 1803, serving at the blockade of Brest and in the American War of 1812. He became an accomplished navigator and surveyor and published a small book on nautical astronomy. He was at home on half-pay when appointed second-in-command of John Ross's* 1818 expedition to Davis Strait: he spent the best part of the next decade in the Arctic.

Through the influence of John Barrow, ships and men left idle by the end of the Napoleonic wars were engaged to seek a commercially viable Northwest Passage—a quest already three hundred years old. This first expedition, in two small ships, HMS *Isabella* and HMS *Alexander,* was disappointing, for Ross returned home to report that Lancaster Sound was landlocked. Some of his officers disagreed, Barrow remained unconvinced, and in the following year Parry, still only a lieutenant, was given command of a further expedition with the same objective.

This expedition of 1819–20 set the pattern for arctic exploration for a generation. Parry, in the sturdy bomb-vessel *Hecla* with the smaller *Griper* as consort, sailed through Lancaster Sound and westward as far as 112°51′W, thus winning the £5,000 prize offered by parliament for the first ship to pass 110°W within the Arctic Circle. He wintered at

Portrait of William Edward Parry engraved by R.J. Lane, after the original portrait by George Richmond, 1842. Courtesy of Ann Parry

Melville Island, hoping to continue westward in the new season, but he was frustrated by pack ice. This was the first time ships of the Royal Navy had wintered in the Arctic, although whalers had sometimes spent the winter trapped in the ice of Davis Strait, and Parry's meticulous care of his men ensured that all came through safely. The expedition returned home with a mass of scientific data and aroused great popular enthusiasm. John Franklin's* first overland expedition was ancillary to Parry's voyage.

In Parry's three major arctic voyages, many problems of northern exploration—health, clothing, boredom in the long winter nights—were mitigated. Among other things, he experimented with tinned food, to which he erroneously attributed antiscorbutic properties, with Mr. Mackintosh's waterproof canvas, and with Mr. Sylvester's patent stove, which warmed the ship throughout by means of flues. He taught the men to read and write, and he put on plays for their entertainment. Several of the midshipmen who sailed with Parry—notably James Clark Ross,* Francis Crozier,* and Edward Bird—later became famous explorers themselves, having learnt their skills in "Parry's School."

His so-called "second voyage" of 1821–23 via Hudson Strait, the most arduous of all, and his "third voyage" of 1824–25, again via Lancaster Sound, added much to the map of the Canadian Arctic, but were less successful in their prime object of "going west." The latter nearly ended in disaster when *Fury* was wrecked in Prince Regent Inlet; both crews immediately returned to England in *Hecla*. Parry's misfortune proved the salvation of John Ross's 1829 expedition, however, for Ross's party lived off the stores of the abandoned *Fury* after Ross had a similar mishap.

In 1827, Parry made one more arctic voyage, over the ice from Spitsbergen in an attempt to reach the North Pole. He failed, of course, but his "farthest north" (82°43′32″N) stood for nearly fifty years.

Incredible as it now seems, Parry had, since 1823, concurrently held the post of hydrographer of the Navy, nominally supervising the preparation of all Admiralty charts. He had been advanced to post captain in 1821, married Isabella Stanley in 1826, and was knighted in 1829. In that year, he accepted an offer to go to Australia as commissioner of the Australian Agricultural Company, a joint stock company holding a million acres of land in New South Wales from the Crown. Setting the company's affairs in order proved an interesting but difficult and thankless task.

After his return from Australia, Parry successively held the posts of comptroller of steam machinery, just at the time the Navy reluctantly turned to steam as an auxiliary source of power; captain superintendent of the naval hospital at Haslar; and, upon getting his flag in 1853, lieutenant governor of Greenwich hospital for naval pensioners. He took a leading part in organizing the search for his old friend John Franklin, a massive search that, years after Parry's death in July 1855, ultimately revealed the pattern of islands in the Canadian Arctic and set at rest forever the question of a viable Northwest Passage. He was survived by his second wife, Catherine Hankinson, and by six of his thirteen children.

Contemporaries speak of Sir William Edward Parry as tall and strikingly handsome. He was a fervent, cheerful, evangelical Christian. Sir Clements Markham, in his book *The Lands of Silence*, called him "the beau ideal of an Arctic officer."

Further Readings

Markham, Clements R. 1921. *The Lands of Silence*. Cambridge: Cambridge University Press.

Parry, Ann. 1963. *Parry of the Arctic*. London: Chatto and Windus.

Parry, William Edward. 1821. *Journal of a Voyage for the Discovery of a North-West Passage, 1819-20*. London: John Murray. [The journals of Parry's subsequent voyages were also published by John Murray].

_____. 1857. *Memoirs of Rear Admiral Sir W. Edward Parry, Kt., F.R.S.* London: Longmans.

Ann Parry

JAMES CLARK ROSS
(1800–1862)

James Clark Ross took part in more arctic voyages than any other officer of the period. He is less celebrated than some, because the only northern expedition he commanded—a fruitless search for John Franklin*—was unjustly damaging to his reputation. He was, nevertheless, a trusted officer on all the William Edward Parry* expeditions to the Arctic. Under John Ross,* he discovered the North Magnetic Pole and helped transform the seagoing polar traveller into an amphibian by using the Inuit sled for long land journeys. He is remembered chiefly for his voyage to the Antarctic (1839–43).

James Ross was the nephew of the explorer John Ross. The younger Ross was enrolled by his uncle in a search for the Northwest Passage with HMS *Isabella* and *Alexander*, the latter commanded by Parry. James Ross had a flair for science and was employed in recording the magnetic observations taken by Captain Edward Sabine.* In this capacity, he was later called upon to testify regarding his uncle's alleged misappropriation of Sabine's findings.

The Admiralty, dissatisfied with John Ross's report on Lancaster Sound, sent Parry to correct it. Parry chose James Ross as one of his officers on this and three successive arctic voyages. On this first (1819–20), Ross accompanied his chief through Lancaster Sound to Melville Island. On the second (1821–23), Parry entered Hudson Strait and discov-

James Clark Ross mezzotint by A. Scott after Stephen Pearce. From the Arctic Institute of North America collection (UC 170137)

ered, but failed to penetrate, the ice-choked Fury and Hecla Strait. Ross and others, however, did learn the art of sled travel from the Inuit. The third voyage (1824–25) failed when HMS *Fury* was wrecked. Parry cached her stores—which would later save the lives of John and James Ross—at Fury Point in Prince Regent Inlet. In 1827, Ross sailed on his fourth voyage with Parry. From Spitsbergen, they made for the North Pole with two boats that were convertible into sleds, but were turned back at 82°45′N.

On all these voyages, Ross proved invaluable in the tasks of scientific research, especially geomagnetism. Hence, in 1829, when John Ross set out on his single-ship search for the passage, he chose his nephew James as second-in-command. Their ship, the *Victory*, was frozen in at the bottom of Prince Regent Inlet, where her crew remained for the years 1829 to 1832.

The important geographical discoveries of that expedition belong to James Ross, who made extensive use of the Inuit sled. In 1830, he crossed Boothia Isthmus and an arm of the sea to discover King William Land. He failed to realize that it was an island, being unable to distinguish between low-lying flat land and snow-covered frozen sea, a failure that may have contributed to the Franklin disaster sixteen years later. Ross continued past the northwestern tip of King William Island and built a cairn to mark his "farthest"; in

1848, Franklin's crews abandoned their ice-bound ships within sight of that point. In 1831, James Ross assured himself of fame by arriving at the North Magnetic Pole, near the west shore of Boothia Peninsula. In the following year, their ship still ice-bound, the men were reduced to the desperate expedient of escaping on foot and by boat. They tramped two hundred miles to Fury Point, repaired the boats found there, and sailed to Lancaster Sound. But the sound was ice-bound, and after a weary vigil, the crew returned to Fury Point for a fourth winter in the Arctic. In the summer of 1833, they were more fortunate and were carried back to England by a whaler.

Between 1839 and 1843, James Ross commanded HMS *Erebus* and *Terror* on a search for the South Magnetic Pole, which proved to be inland and inaccessible. But in the Ross Ice-Sheet, he found a gate of entry into the new continent which would be much used by later discoverers. On their return, the two ships were fitted with auxiliary steam power for an attempt on the Northwest Passage. Ross declined the command, which was given to the aging John Franklin. Three years later, Ross took command of HMS *Enterprise* and *Investigator* to attempt to rescue the lost explorer.

With a touch of inspiration, Ross enlisted as junior lieutenant Francis Leopold McClintock,* nearly thirty years old and without polar experience. The ships were frozen in at Port Leopold on Somerset Island. Ross, in poor health that winter, fell short of Parry in his care for the crew, and when he and McClintock sledded into Peel Sound, the party broke down from insufficient rations. This excursion prompted McClintock to make the improvements in sledding practice that permitted him to make land journeys of unprecedented length. In all, seven members of the expedition died from scurvy and overexertion, and when the ships finally freed themselves from the ice and returned to England, Ross was given a shabby reception, whereas chance and weather were chiefly to blame.

James Clark Ross is less known than some of his polar contemporaries. Five of his six arctic voyages were made in a subordinate rank. His only published book concerns his antarctic journey. Unlike his uncle, Ross was not given to self-advertisement or to wrangling with his critics. His services to Canadian geography are many, however, and not the least is his employment in the arctic service of the man destined to unravel the Franklin mystery, Francis Leopold McClintock.

Further Readings

Parry, William Edward. 1819. *Journal of a Voyage for the Discovery of a North-West passage, 1819-20*. London: John Murray.

Ross, John. 1819. *A Voyage of Discovery*. London: John Murray.

_____. 1835. *Narrative of a Second Voyage in Search of a North-West Passage*. London: A.W. Webster.

Ross, M. J. 1995. *Polar Pioneers: John Ross and James Clark Ross*. London and Montreal: University College London Press and McGill-Queen's Press.

L.H. Neatby

JOSEPH-ELZÉAR BERNIER
(1852–1934)

Born on the first of January 1852 in the town of L'Islet on the south shore of the St. Lawrence River about fifty miles below Quebec City, Joseph-Elzéar Bernier belonged to the fading era of wooden ships and iron men.

His father and grandfather were sea captains and shipbuilders. He attended school in L'Islet until he was fourteen and then went to sea. Three years later, he became master of his vessel. After a hundred voyages to many ports, he came ashore to accept the unlikely position of governor of the Quebec jail.

This fitted into Bernier's scheme, for it gave him time to read and to study. Since 1872, he had been fascinated by arctic exploration, so now he absorbed all of the published accounts of British, American, Danish, and Norwegian expeditions. In 1898, he gave a lecture before the Quebec Geographical Society expounding on both how he might reach the North Pole by ship and dog-team and how he might sail through the Northwest Passage. This created a stir. He resigned from the jail and started campaigning.

In 1902, he called on Prime Minister Wilfrid Laurier and won his support. It would be a great triumph for Canada to have a Canadian be the first to stand at the North Pole and to sail through the Northwest Passage. Laurier asked parliament for an appropriation of $100,000 to build a ship for the task. Meanwhile, Bernier lectured across Canada to gain public support and financial backing.

Photograph of Joseph-Elzéar Bernier, by Roy Tash

What appeared to be a key to the realization of his dreams in 1904 was the availability of a stoutly built 650-ton sailing ship with an auxiliary steam engine. This was the *Gauss,* named for a German astronomer and magnetician, built in Kiel, in 1901, for a two-year antarctic expedition that had been successfully completed. Bernier purchased her for the Canadian government at a bargain price of $75,000 and sailed her to Quebec where she was renamed *Arctic.*

But, alas, the government had surprising and disappointing plans for Bernier. Instead of heading his own expedition to the North Pole, he was to serve only as master of the *Arctic* for a year-long patrol of the North West Mounted Police into Hudson Bay to control foreign traders and whalers. However, this interlude gave Bernier experience in arctic travel and living, standing him in good stead for the future. His ship performed well, so he was now ready for whatever northern responsibilities he could assume.

With abundant self-confidence and, at last, full command of the *Arctic* and his own expeditions, in 1906 he began a series of extensive voyages (1906–07, 1908–09, 1910–11) to various islands in the Canadian eastern Arctic. He found no new land. He simply patrolled islands already charted, at least superficially. He gathered records left by his predecessors of the nineteenth century, depositing new records and setting up cairns and monuments of his own. He raised the flag everywhere, claiming all the islands for Canada. Detractors in those days considered this a work of superergogation, for Great Britain had ceded all of the islands above the mainland to Canada in 1880. But in future years, Bernier's markers may have helped reinforce Canadian sovereignty in the Arctic.

On his 1908–09 expedition, Bernier took the *Arctic* through half the length of M'Clure Strait. It was invitingly open and he might have realized his dream of sailing through the Northwest Passage, which Roald Amundsen had already done with a much smaller vessel by a more southerly route in 1903–06, but Bernier lacked authorization to proceed and reluctantly turned back. On his next voyage, he had the authorization, but this time M'Clure Strait was ice-choked. Then Dr. Frederick A. Cook* and Rear Admiral Robert Edwin Peary* both claimed that they had reached the North Pole in 1908 and 1909 respectively, so the challenge of being the first to reach the Pole was gone for Bernier, although he discounted both claims.

All during her ownership by the Canadian government, the *Arctic* was popularly thought of as Bernier's, but a decade elapsed when he had nothing to do with her. In 1912, when he had left the service of the government to engage in a private gold-hunting and fur-trading venture around Pond Inlet, Baffin Island, with a smaller vessel of his own, the *Arctic* was taken by another master on a four-month government scientific cruise to Hudson Bay. Subsequently, until after World War I, she was unromantically used as a floating lighthouse on the lower reaches of the St. Lawrence River.

In 1922, the *Arctic* was refurbished for the first of a series of annual government expeditions to the eastern Arctic archipelago. Bernier, who had found no Baffin gold and was now seventy years old, was glad to be placed in charge of his old ship again.

The tasks of the expeditions were to maintain sovereignty among the arctic islands (showing the flag, as it were), establish new posts of the Royal Canadian Mounted Police and reprovision and rotate the men at existing ones, see to the health and welfare of the resident Inuit, and conduct scientific investigations.

The ship's loading and departure point was at King's Wharf, Quebec City. Bernier, bald and rosy-cheeked, with a white moustache, was below medium height, broad-shouldered and overweight, but still fit and eager. He stood proudly on the bridge conversing in French or English with well-wishers and giving orders to his French-Canadian officers and men.

The 1922 voyage was highlighted by the establishing of a RCMP detachment at Craig Harbour on the south coast of Ellesmere Island. The 1923 voyage was carried out successfully, but that of 1924 nearly ended in disaster. The *Arctic*, northward bound, was struck by a fierce storm off the coast of Labrador and would have foundered had it not been for the desperate efforts of all hands in jettisoning deck cargo and manning hand pumps and bucket lines. After nearly a week the storm subsided and the battered vessel continued on her way.

A supply depot was placed as far north as Cape Sabine, Ellesmere Island, for the support of patrols from Craig Harbour, 150 miles to the south, and a new police detachment was set up at Dundas Harbour, Devon Island.

On her 1925 voyage, the *Arctic* spent a fortnight trapped in ice off Cumberland Sound, Baffin Island, but managed to get as far north as Cape Sabine to restock the RCMP depot there. Despite repeated mishaps and breakdowns she completed her rounds, with stops at outposts and settlements on Ellesmere, Devon and Baffin islands. After more than three months, bruised and leaking, the *Arctic* docked at Quebec City.

With no regard for her worth as an historical relic, the *Arctic* was condemned and sold for $9,000 to the Hudson's Bay Company, which dismantled her. Her stripped hull, too tough to be broken up, was towed across the river to a sandbar near the Levis shore and abandoned there within sight of Bernier's home, as though to taunt him. Today, all that remains of the *Arctic* is her bell, which is displayed at the Bernier Maritime Museum in L'Islet.

In 1927, Bernier commanded two tugs towing a dredge and steel scow from Halifax to the Hudson Bay port of Churchill. That same year he was granted a government pension of $2,400 annually, plus a medal, rewarding him for what he had done to strengthen Canada's title to arctic islands whose potential value was still beyond anyone's dreams—except perhaps his own.

On 26 December 1934, at the age of eighty-two, Joseph-Elzéar Bernier died. Despite having been thwarted in his early ambition of going to the North Pole or through the Northwest Passage, he had earned a niche in the history of Canadian arctic exploration.

Further Readings

Bernier, Joseph-Elzéar 1939. *Master Mariner and Arctic Explorer*. Ottawa: Le Droit.

Dorion-Robitaille, Yolande. 1978. *Captain J.E. Bernier's Contribution to Canadian Sovereignty in the Arctic*. Ottawa: Indian and Northern Affairs.

Finnie, Richard S. 1974. "Farewell Voyages: Bernier and the *Arctic*." *The Beaver* 305(1): 44–54.

Richard S. Finnie

The CGS *Arctic* in 1924. Photograph by O.S. Finnie

VILHJALMUR STEFANSSON
(1879–1962)

One of the last great arctic explorers of the era of boats, dogs, and sledges, Vilhjalmur Stefansson was also a highly articulate and innovative spokesman for the North. He is best known for his field work in anthropology and for his outspoken defence of the North as a rich and habitable land.

On the third of November, 1879, Stefansson—or "Stef" as he was known to friends—was born in Arnes, Manitoba, to Icelandic parents. They took him in early childhood to North Dakota, where he grew up. Successfully racing through a four-year arts course at the State University of Iowa in a single year, he proceeded to study anthropology and theology at Harvard. There he became a teaching fellow after two summers of field work in Iceland, and left the university in 1906 to engage in arctic exploration. His not waiting to take postgraduate degrees was to militate against him among certain academics, although honourary doctorates were bestowed on him in later years by eight universities.

He turned toward the Canadian Arctic and spent eighteen months with the Inuit of the Mackenzie River delta, learning their language and folkways. From 1908 to 1912, under the auspices of the American Museum of Natural History and the Canadian government, he explored the area from the Colville River in Alaska to Cape Parry, Coronation Gulf, and Victoria Island in Canada's western Arctic, where he observed "blond" types among the Copper Inuit.

His finale as an active arctic explorer was leadership of the Canadian Arctic Expedition of 1913–18 to the Alaskan and Canadian Arctic. It was marred by eleven fatalities

Photograph of Vilhjalmur and Evelyn Stefansson by Richard S. Finnie

when ice crushed its base ship, *Karluk*. Stefansson and others, who had gone ashore to hunt, were unable to help the twenty-five people left on board. With small parties of whites and Inuit, he subsequently ventured over floating ice much farther than anyone before him had deliberately driven dog-teams without ample provisions. He supported himself and his companions by hunting and fishing, exploding the myth of a lifeless polar sea. He filled in coastline gaps and found and mapped the last sizeable unknown islands in the Canadian Arctic.

Having completed his last arctic journey at age thirty-nine, Stefansson entered the second half of his life, that of a researcher and writer, preaching the gospel of the North —its liveability and potentialities. This man of imposing stature and leonine head, who had once out-travelled and out-hunted many of his native companions, now turned to the lecture-tour circuit and the writing of more than two dozen books and innumerable pamphlets and articles. In sharp contrast to the athletic life he had led in the North, his New York life was remarkably sedentary: short walks to and from taxis and subways were the only exercise he took.

He became almost wholly a man of ideas. He promoted a scheme to introduce domestic reindeer to Baffin Island, and although it failed miserably, the mismanagement that brought about the failure was beyond Stefansson's control. He also devised an ambitious scheme to send four white volunteers with an Inuit cook-seamstress to Wrangel Island, off the coast of Siberia. Disregarding the sector principle of Arctic Island ownership, they were to take possession of it for Canada. The volunteers perished. The woman was rescued, and soon the island was permanently occupied by the Soviets. Along with the *Karluk* disaster, these two ill-starred ventures damaged Stefansson's reputation.

But that innovative mind also inspired several far more successful undertakings. Along with Richard Finnie, he was one of the first to suggest a crude-oil pipeline between Norman Wells and a refinery in the Yukon, a project realized years later in the construction of the Canadian Oil Project (Canol) pipeline. Similarly, he was an early proponent of a road to Alaska, an idea that ultimately led to the Alaska Highway of today. Significantly, Stefansson seriously disagreed with the final routes chosen for both pipeline and road, arguing that the highway should follow the Mackenzie River to a point below Norman Wells, before crossing over a relatively low divide to Dawson City and down the Yukon River.

Nevertheless, conflicting opinions were nothing new to Stefansson, who was always too busy writing and lecturing, promulgating his ideas, to be discouraged by scepticism or hostility. In fact, he thrived on opposition. He also practised what he preached, whether it was supporting himself by hunting amid the ice floes of the Arctic Ocean, or being the subject of an experiment to determine the physiological effects of an all-meat diet. The seeming arrogance and aggressiveness of which he was sometimes accused in earlier years–fellow explorer Roald Amundsen denounced him as a charlatan, onetime friend Dr. R. M. Anderson unflatteringly referred to him as "Windjammer"—may have arisen from his being a man with a mission, impatient with the conservatism of politicians, administrators, and scientists with whom he had to deal.

In 1941, at the age of sixty-two, Vilhjalmur Stefansson married Evelyn Baird, a twenty-seven-year-old staff member in charge of his library. Over the next decade, they divided their time between New York and an old farm they had bought near Bethel, Vermont. In 1951, the Stefanssons moved from New York with their immense polar library to Dartmouth College at Hanover, New Hampshire. The explorer and anthropologist was installed there as a living legend-in-residence, as it were, available to students and visitors for consultation, with Evelyn as the first librarian of what became known as the Stefansson Collection. On 26 August 1962, shortly after completing the manuscript of his autobiography, *Discovery,* he died of a stroke.

Further Readings

Diubaldo, Richard J. 1978. *Stefansson and the Canadian Arctic*. Montreal: McGill-Queen's University Press.

Lebourdais, D.M. 1963. *Stefansson: Ambassador of the North*. Montreal: Harvest House.

Stefansson, Vilhjalmur. 1913. *My Life with the Eskimos*. New York: Macmillan.

_____. 1921. *The Friendly Arctic*. New York: Macmillan.

_____. 1922. *The Northward Course of Empire*. London: Harrap.

_____. 1938. *Unsolved Mysteries of the Arctic*. New York: Macmillan.

_____. 1940. *Ultima Thule*. New York: Macmillan.

_____. 1964. *Discovery*. New York: McGraw-Hill.

Richard S. Finnie

HENRY LARSEN (1899-1964)

Henry Astrup Larsen was the first man to traverse the Northwest Passage from the Pacific to the Atlantic, beginning his historic voyage in Vancouver in 1940, and ending it in Halifax in 1942. Within two years of this major success, Larsen navigated the Passage from east to west, thus scoring another "first" by crossing the continent in both directions.

In 1940, desirous of asserting its sovereignty over the Arctic Islands, the Canadian government entrusted the Royal Canadian Mounted Police with the task of patrolling this barren, largely unexplored region of half a million square miles. Corporal Henry Larsen, captain of the RCMP schooner *St. Roch* and a sixteen-year veteran of the Arctic, was chosen as a key figure in this dangerous, ambitious, and politically expedient undertaking.

Born in 1899, in the same coastal district of Norway as Roald Amundsen, Larsen early displayed an interest in the history and geography of the Arctic. He yearned for new lands and wished to follow in the footsteps of the great explorers, especially his boyhood hero, Amundsen. Virtually growing up in boats, Larsen truly began his maritime career at the age of fifteen. Later, en route to Vancouver in 1924, he read of an arctic trader named Klengenberg who wanted a navigator. Henry Larsen applied and was hired on the spot.

Based off Victoria Island, Klengenberg's ship the *Old Maid* plied arctic waters, bringing Larsen into amicable contact with the "Mounties," who often travelled on the *Old*

Photograph of Henry Larsen. Courtesy of the RCMP, Neg. no. 1086-1

Maid on their way to arctic detachments. When the RCMP decided, in 1928, to build their own ship, Henry Larsen sensed that his dream might come true. The policeman given charge of the ship was Larsen's friend, and he wanted Henry aboard. By now a Canadian citizen, Larsen applied to the RCMP and was accepted. In his interview with Superintendent Duffus, Larsen confessed to knowing very little about horses, perhaps a serious shortcoming for a position in the "Mounted Police." But to Henry's surprise, Duffus directed his sergeant-major to "make sure that this man does not get near a horse for a while. He is too valuable to us to become hospitalized now."

The solid, 104-foot *St. Roch*, equipped with a 150-horsepower diesel engine, was one of the last wooden ships to challenge the arctic ice. Her round bottom, designed to escape ice pressure, sent her bucking and heaving in a gale like a bronco, as one constable described it while he was still able to speak. Larsen called her the "Ugly Ducking" and declared her the most uncomfortable ship he had ever travelled in, but he quickly came to love her versatility. The ship's cramped quarters, spartan food, and unseemly behaviour in a rough sea, Larsen asserted with a smile, were no match for the *esprit de corps* of the RCMP.

Larsen's first twelve years aboard the *St. Roch* were a long string of successes. He plied the icy waters with cargo and personnel in the summer; in the winter, he undertook lengthy dogsled journeys, all a part of the RCMPs versatile police work. He became known for his ability to navigate ice-choked and uncharted waters, but the modest Larsen credited his devoted crew for the *St. Roch*'s success. In police work, he showed a remarkable sensitivity to native culture, born of a cruel environment and often colliding with the laws of the white man. He admired the natives' cheerful outlook and undaunted struggle to survive, and accepted their well-intentioned—though frequently unsanitary—hospitality with the gentleness of a saint. Hanorie Umiarpolik ("Henry with the Big Ship") was the true friend of Canada's native people. He was, however, displeased with the effect of the white man's attempts to "civilize" them.

But it is for his navigation of the Northwest Passage in the 1940s that Larsen will be remembered. On his first crossing, ice conditions were at their worst. Enormous ice floes in M'Clintock Channel and Franklin Strait blocked the *St. Roch*'s advance for two consecutive years and upon two occasions nearly crushed the ship. Finally, Larsen managed to reach Bellot Strait and the open waters to the east. On the return trip, in 1944, through Lancaster and Viscount Melville sounds and Prince of Wales Strait, ice conditions were much improved and the entire trip from Halifax to Vancouver was completed in three months.

Larsen's dedication to arctic work was unswerving. Over an eight-year period, he took but one short trip south "to get married and learn to walk again with ordinary shoes." He was promoted to staff sergeant after the first crossing, commissioned with the rank of inspector after the second, and later made a superintendent. He especially

RCMP vessel *St. Roch* under Larsen's command. Courtesy of the RCMP, Neg. no. 1061-1

cherished the Patron's Gold Medal and an Honorary Fellowship bestowed upon him by the Royal Geographical Society of London for his outstanding achievements in the field of exploration. He received the Massey Medal from the Royal Canadian Geographical Society, and his name is immortalized in Larsen Sound, the body of water between James Ross Strait and Franklin Strait, the place where he and his crew miraculously escaped death.

Henry Larsen remained in the RCMP until his retirement in 1961, when he moved with his family to Vancouver. After a brief illness, he died there in 1964. Through his outstanding efforts, the voyages of the *St. Roch* put the final capstone on the centuries-old search for the elusive Northwest Passage.

Further Readings

Basset, John. 1980. *Henry Larsen*. The Canadians Series. Don Mills, Ontario: Fitzhenry and Whiteside.

Larsen, Henry. 1948. *The North-West Passage, 1940-1942 and 1944*. Vancouver: City Archives.

_____, with Sheer, Frank R. and Edvard, Omholt-Jensen. 1967. *The Big Ship: An Autobiography*. Toronto: McClelland and Stewart.

Edvard Omholt-Jensen

Photograph of Henry Larsen. Courtesy of the RCMP, Neg. no. 963

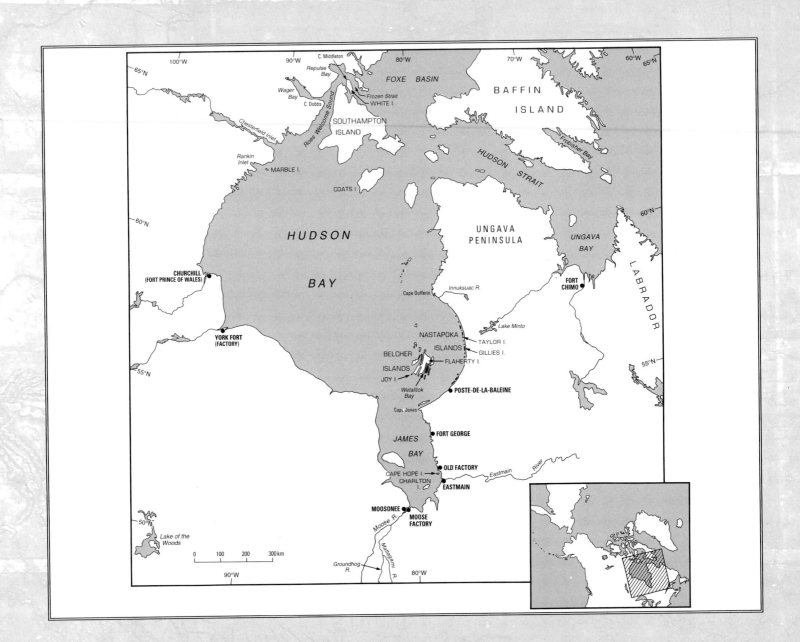

UNIT

❧ 2 ❧

*Jens Munk, Thomas James, Christopher Middleton,
Moses Norton, George Weetaltuk, Robert Flaherty*

The individuals assembled in this second unit generally concentrated their efforts in the region of Hudson Bay and Baffin Island. Their geographical activities stretch from Jens Munk's seventeenth century search for the Northwest Passage to Robert Flaherty's and George Weetaltuk's twentieth century contributions, which were concentrated largely in the James Bay and southern Hudson Bay region. The biographies of at least two of the men in this unit also bring to the surface something of the political intrigue that often surrounded and shaped exploration.

Jens Munk (1579-1628)

On the fourth of June, 1620 Jens Munk must have surveyed a dismal scene surrounding him in Munk's Harbour, a place now more familiar as Churchill. On that day he penned his last will and testament, giving little thought to any idea of ever getting back to Denmark, which, after the grim winter on this forbidden coast, must have seemed far away indeed. A decade earlier, Henry Hudson's mutinous crew had set him adrift in the same bay that now trapped Munk, a bay that received more than Hudson's name. To Munk, this must have seemed his own final voyage as well.

Munk's life can best be described as a long series of determined, but frustrating efforts to gain recognition and a legitimate place in the ranks of the Danish nobility. Born on 3 June 1579 in southern Norway, Jens Munk and his brother Niels were sons of the Danish nobleman Erik Munk and Anna Bartholomaeidatter. If it were not enough that Erik's family tree was already somewhat tainted, the fact that he and Anna were not officially married assured the children much misery and endless frustration, particularly Jens. In the Age of the Reformation, such behaviour was not easily forgiven, and illegitimacy was a cause for shame and ridicule for the two boys.

As a child, Jens Munk spent much of his time near the docks watching the excitement of ships arriving from distant lands. Not surprisingly, he went to sea at the age of thirteen. In 1609, he set sail with his partner Jens Hvid for the ice-filled Barents Sea in search of fox and bear. The trip was a disaster, ending in the wreck of the ship and the near loss of all the men: however, the voyage proved Munk's capacity to survive severe arctic conditions and to conquer seemingly impossible odds.

In 1618, the Danish king, Christian IV, ordered Munk to

Munk's mothership, the *Unicorn,* would have been similar to the heavy three-masted vessel illustrated here. Illustration from *The Way to Hudson Bay: The Life and Times of Jens Munk,* copyright ©1965 by Thorkild Hansen, English translation by James McFarlane and John Lynch copyright ©1970 by Wm. Collins, Sons and Company, and Harcourt Brace and Company, reprinted by permission of Harcourt Brace and Company, and Gyldendolska Boghandel, Denmark

ready a major expedition to embark for East India via Cape Horn. Tirelessly, Munk organized the ships, the men, the provisions, and the thousand details involved in such an undertaking. To his astonishment, however, the command was not to be his: it fell to a man of suitable nobility, Ove Giedde. Munk's setback was compounded by the deaths of his brother Niels and good friend Jorgen Daas. The future was bleak, but Munk was not easily discouraged. He approached the king with a plan to launch another expedition to the Far East, this one to proceed through the assumed Northwest Passage. Perhaps feeling somewhat guilty of his treatment of Munk, the king assented. Munk chose sixty-one men and two vessels, one the heavy mothership the *Unicorn (Enhjoringen)* and the other the light reconnaissance vessel the *Lamprey (Lampren)*.

The ships were towed out of the harbour in a dead calm on Sunday, 9 May 1619. Soon after they were under way, a bizarre suicide by one of the crew cast a shadow over the voyage. Another death followed shortly. Then they were detained in Norway to repair the leaking *Lamprey*. Not until the end of May did they depart from Norway with three new men. They crossed the Atlantic and entered Frobisher Bay by mistake, and when they finally found their way into Hudson Strait, they accidentally sailed deep into Ungava Bay before they got back on the true course. By the time they reached Hudson Bay on 4 September, signs of scurvy were already present in the men.

A savage storm forced Munk to make a spectacular entry with the *Unicorn* into a protected bay on the west coast at the site of present-day Churchill. The *Lamprey* soon followed, and the place was named Nova Dania. A wintering was clearly in store for the expedition, and little time was wasted in getting the ships to safe locations. The sheltered bay was a broad river mouth with extensive tidal flats. The *Lamprey* was hauled out of tidal reach and the *Unicorn* secured and used as winter quarters for both crews. Aware of the dangers of scurvy, Munk encouraged his men to eat berries and roots as long as possible, and the ravages of the dread disease were postponed for a while. Nevertheless, on the twenty-first of November one man died of scurvy, and another death followed soon after.

Christmas was made as festive as possible, and for a few days the reality of the harsh and increasingly cold environment was held at bay. Yet for all but three of the crew, this was to be their last Christmas. With the arrival of the new year—1620—death began to stalk the ship regularly. One by one the men were buried on a nearby hill, but when May arrived no one had the strength to carry the dead off the ship. Only seven men were alive when Jens Munk sat down to write his last will and testament, and a few days later he and the ship's dog were the only living members on board. From the deck he was much surprised to see two crew members on shore and still alive: they had been unable to return to the ship several weeks earlier. Together, the three men began the slow road to recovery as spring prepared the land for summer.

In order to escape, a formidable task awaited them. The *Lamprey* provided the only hope for a return voyage, and it had to be hauled into the sea and rigged for a crew of three instead of sixteen. On 16 July, Munk began another, perhaps the greatest, epic journey. One can only imagine the next sixty-seven days in ice-infested and storm-swept seas, across Hudson Bay, through the Strait, round the southern tip of Greenland, and forever eastward. The master mariner got the ship through it all, and on 20 September, he spotted the distant mountains on the west coast of Norway.

No hero's welcome awaited Jens Munk. One of his men was involved in a tavern brawl, and as the captain responsible for his men, Munk was jailed; the revenge of the nobility was never far away. Apparently, the king was in no hurry to see Munk released, but he finally ordered his release after three months' imprisonment.

The king was not finished with Munk, however, and ordered him to prepare for a second expedition to Nova Dania, this time to colonize the region. The plan came to naught when no volunteers could be found, and Munk was undoubtedly relieved. The expansionist king was not doing well, battles were being lost, and at the battle and defeat at Kiel in the spring of 1628, Jens Munk seems to have been wounded. He returned to Copenhagen, where his new young wife cared for him until his death a few months later.

Jens Munk had lived a remarkable life. In Canada, however, only one small island in Foxe Basin bears his name. Munk himself never saw Jens Munk Island, but members of the Danish Fifth Thule Expedition named it in his memory, considering it appropriate to leave one small reminder of his brief presence in this part of the world that had become— not Nova Dania—but Canada.

Further Readings

Birket-Smith, Kaj. 1929. *Jens Munks Rejse og andre danske Ishavsfarter under Christian IV.* Copenhagen.

Gosch, C. C. A. 1897. *Danish Arctic Expeditions 1605-20.* Vols. 1–2. London: Hakluyt Society.

Hansen, Thorkild. 1966. *Jens Munk.* Copenhagen: Gyldendal.

Knudsen, Johannes. 1902. *Den danske Ishavsfarer Jens Munk.* Copenhagen.

Munk, Jens. 1723. *Navigatio Septentrionalis. Heri: Capitain Jens Munks Livs og Levnets beskrivelse. Til største deels af Hans egenhaendige Journaler og Resten af andre Trovaerdige Documenter uddragen.* Copenhagen.

Peter Schledermann

THOMAS JAMES
(ca. 1593–ca. 1635)

Although his name is emblazoned on the map of Canada and in the annals of his native Bristol, Thomas James remains a shadowy figure. Even the fact that he was born in Bristol has been questioned, as has the date of his birth. But scholars agree—for the present, at least—that he was probably born about 1593, in Bristol, England. It is likely, too, that he came from an eminent family, and was a wealthy barrister. But the records are too scanty to provide any real insight into the man himself, or into the experiences that might have shaped him.

James emerged from the shadows for only one brief period. In 1631, he was selected by some Bristol merchants to see if there was a passage leading from Henry Hudson's newly discovered bay into the fabled Pacific. After an unsuccessful search (for there was no passage), James wintered near the northeast corner of Charlton Island, and returned to Bristol the following summer. In 1633, James published an account of his expedition, *The Strange and Dangerous Voyage of Captain Thomas James.*

This was received with such enthusiasm that James became a popular figure in London's political and social circles. He did not spend much time in the limelight, however, for he was back at sea within a couple of months. On this occasion, he was commander of the *9th Whelp of the Lion*, one of the royal vessels that were patrolling the Bristol Channel and the Irish Sea in an attempt to suppress the pirates infest-

Portrait of Thomas James. National Archives of Canada/C 9529

ing the area. In October of that same year, the Earl of Stafford, Lord Deputy of Ireland, recommended that James be promoted because he was diligent, civil in his conversation, and capable in his profession. But it was not to be. For he died, probably in 1635, while still in his early forties. He was apparently unmarried, because he left all his worldly goods to his sister. And it is probable, though not certain, that he was buried in the Lord Mayor's Chapel in Bristol.

Although James was a popular and respected figure at the time, he is generally held in rather low esteem today. His initial popularity was undoubtedly related to the fact that he wrote a very lucid book on an interesting and fashionable topic. His journal, after all, was the first book in English to describe a wintering in the Arctic, an experience he described in vivid detail.

In addition to this popular acclaim, based largely on the elegance of his prose and the dramatic qualities of his narrative, James was received with signal respect by the merchants of London, as well as Bristol. For example, they accepted without question his conclusion that a Northwest Passage did not exist, except possibly at such a high northern latitude that it would have no commercial value. And this ended the initial phase of arctic exploration in Canada, a phase that started in 1576 when Martin Frobisher* sailed the *Gabriel* into Frobisher Bay.

Although both the merchants and the Admiralty were completely satisfied with his performance, the feeling persists that James was not an experienced mariner. This feeling can be traced back to a comment made by Luke Foxe. Foxe, who was exploring Hudson Bay for a group of London merchants, sighted James's ship, the *Henrietta Maria*, on 29 July 1631. After dining with James the following day, Foxe noted in his journal that "he was no seaman." Foxe also criticized James's vessel as being unsuited to the task at hand. As Foxe offers no evidence in support of his opinion of James, we can probably attribute it to personal or political rivalry. But we cannot be sure.

Our uncertainty derives from the fact that James was—and remains—a shadowy figure. We simply do not have enough information on which to base a balanced opinion of the man. I see no reason, however, to doubt his statement that he did have previous experience in arctic navigation, even though he mentioned it only once, and that in a brief, parenthetic comment. We do know, moreover, that he carried a comprehensive list of navigational instruments, all fashioned to his own exacting specifications. This would suggest most strongly that he was acquainted with the latest developments in the theory and practice of navigation, as would his association with Henry Briggs, the Oxford mathematician.

Thomas James was the fourth explorer to winter in that vast, inland sea; he was preceded by Henry Hudson (1610–11), Thomas Button (1612–13), and Jens Munk* (1619–20). If we compare James with his predecessors, he stands up very well. He explored more miles of coastline than any of the others. And being a thoughtful and experienced leader of men, he did not suffer the dissension that wracked Hudson's crew. Nor did he suffer the frightful mortality that almost wiped out the Button and Munk expeditions. Munk lost sixty-one of the total complement of sixty-four men who sailed with him. James, in contrast, lost only six out of a crew of twenty-two men—two to accident and four to scurvy.

Further Readings

Christy, Miller, ed. 1894. *The Voyages of Captain Luke Foxe and Captain Thomas James*. London: Hakluyt Society.

Kenyon, Walter, ed. 1975. *The Strange and Dangerous Voyage of Captain Thomas James*. Toronto: Royal Ontario Museum.

Walter Kenyon

CHRISTOPHER MIDDLETON
(ca. 1690–1770)

In his will, Christopher Middleton described himself as a master mariner of Norton, County Durham, the same county where he had been born at Newton Bewley, near Billingham. He appears to have gone to sea at quite an early age, his service aboard Hudson's Bay Company ships beginning around 1719, possibly even earlier. Appointed to command the Company's ship *Hannah* in 1725, Middleton rose rapidly to become one of its most experienced and trusted captains. He was twice given command of new vessels on their maiden voyages to Hudson Bay (*Seahorse I* in 1734 and *Hudson's Bay V* in 1737) and for sixteen successive seasons commanded these and other Company ships on their annual voyages to the various posts in the Bay without mishap.

Early in his career, Middleton established his reputation as a meticulous and innovative navigator: In the spring of 1726, he published a paper in the Royal Society's *Philosophical Transactions* on the variation of the magnetic needle in Hudson Bay. The following year, he was elected a Fellow of the Royal Society, a great honour for a ship's captain of only two years' standing.

Shortly afterwards, Middleton's path crossed that of Arthur Dobbs, an influential Anglo-Irish landowner and a hard-line free trader who bitterly resented the Hudson's Bay Company's monopoly. Furthermore, Dobbs was convinced that a practicable Northwest Passage could be found via Hudson Bay, and he decided to pursue its discovery, incidentally hoping to break the Company's monopoly in the process.

Using his considerable influence in London, Dobbs persuaded the Admiralty to mount an expedition to search

The names of Middleton's ships, *Furnace* and *Discovery*, were carved in the rock at Sloop Cove during the wintering in 1741-42. Photograph courtesy of Grant Barr

for the Northwest Passage via Hudson Bay. Further, by arranging a commission for Middleton in the Navy, Dobbs induced him to leave the Company and to command this enterprise. The expedition's ships, the bomb-vessel *Furnace* and the ex-collier *Discovery,* sailed from the Thames in June 1741.

Reaching the vicinity of Coats Island on 1 August, Middleton and his officers decided to winter at Fort Prince of Wales (Churchill). It was a winter marked by oscillating relations between the Navy expedition and the resident Hudson's Bay Company personnel, led by James Isham. While relations were on the whole cordial, Middleton undoubtedly caused serious problems for Isham by his lavish distribution of alcohol, a generosity he extended both to the Company personnel and to the Indians. Worse still, in order to compensate for the men he lost to scurvy, Middleton persuaded five Company men to join the expedition when it sailed in the spring of 1742.

Leaving Churchill on 30 June 1742, Middleton's ships headed north. They discovered and entered Wager Bay, but were then locked in the bay for several weeks by drifting ice. By means of boat journeys, however, Middleton established to his own satisfaction that the Northwest Passage did not lie through Wager Bay. Emerging again into Roes Welcome Sound, he pushed north once more, only to have his hopes dashed on reaching the cul-de-sac of Repulse Bay. Frozen Strait was still ice-covered; hence, there was no chance of pursuing the search into Foxe Basin. Having called at Marble Island for water, Middleton sailed for home, satisfied in his own mind that there was no route to the Pacific through Hudson Bay.

Initially Dobbs accepted this verdict, if reluctantly. But then somehow his suspicions were aroused. He conceived the notion that Middleton had indeed found a route west via Wager Bay but had deliberately falsified his log and journals to conceal the evidence, having been bribed to do so by his former employer, the Hudson's Bay Company. Dobbs even went to the length of persuading various junior officers, including Middleton's mate, Lieutenant John Rankin, to perjure themselves by providing written statements to support his version of the story.

Early in May 1743, Dobbs laid a number of charges along those lines against Middleton with the Admiralty. There followed a protracted pamphlet war between

A

VINDICATION

OF THE

CONDUCT

OF

Captain *Christopher Middleton,*

IN A

Late Voyage on Board His Majesty's Ship the FURNACE,

FOR

Discovering a North-west Passage to the *Western American Ocean.*

IN ANSWER

To certain *Objections* and *Aspersions*

OF

ARTHUR DOBBS, Esq;

WITH AN

A P P E N D I X:

CONTAINING

The Captain's Instructions; Councils held; Reports of the Inferior Officers; Letters between Mr. *Dobbs,* Capt. *Middleton,* &c. Affidavits and other Vouchers refer'd to in the Captain's *Answers,* &c. With as much of the *Log-Journal* as relates to the DISCOVERY.

The Whole as lately deliver'd to the Lords Commissioners of the ADMIRALTY.

To which is Annex'd,

An ACCOUNT of the Extraordinary Degrees and Surprizing Effects of Cold in *Hudson's-Bay,* North America, read before the ROYAL SOCIETY.

By *CHRISTOPHER MIDDLETON,* Late Commander of the FURNACE, and F. R. S.

LONDON:

Printed by the AUTHOR's Appointment; and Sold by *Jacob Robinson,* at the *Golden-Lion* in *Ludgate-Street.* 1743.

The title page from Middleton's effort to clear his name

Dobbs and Middleton and a formal inquiry in which Middleton was entirely cleared of Dobbs's charges.

Despite these findings, despite the country being at war, and despite Middleton's vast experience, he was not immediately given a command; one suspects Dobbs's influence yet again. In May 1745, he was given command of the little sloop *Shark,* but it was only a temporary appointment. In the summer of 1748, Middleton again found himself on the beach, on half-pay of 4s Od per day. He never received another command in the Navy, and not surprisingly, he was never again employed by the Hudson's Bay Company. He died on 12 February 1770 at Norton, County Durham.

To Christopher Middleton we owe the exploration and mapping of Wager Bay, the northern part of Roes Welcome Sound, and Repulse Bay. Such a highly qualified judge as William Edward Parry,* for whom Middleton's discoveries were the starting point of his own expedition, was extremely impressed by the carefulness and accuracy of Middleton's observations and surveying. It is extremely ironic that, while the names of Lt. John Rankin and Arthur Dobbs have been commemorated in the place names of Rankin Inlet and Cape Dobbs for 250 years, Middleton's name did not appear on the map of Hudson Bay until 1982. On 28 October of that year, the Canadian Permanent Committee on Geographical Names bestowed the name "Cape Middleton" on the northernmost cape of White Island, at the entrance to Frozen Strait.

Further Readings

Barr, W. and G. Williams, eds. 1994. *Voyages to Hudson Bay in Search of a Northwest Passage 1741–1747.* Volume 1: *The Voyage of Christopher Middleton, 1741–1742.* London: Hakluyt Society.

Clarke, D. 1958. *Arthur Dobbs Esquire 1689–1765.* London: Bodley Head.

Davies, K.G. and A.M. Johnson, eds. 1965. *Letters from Hudson Bay, 1703–1740.* London: Hudson's Bay Record Society.

Middleton, Christopher. [1743] 1967. *A Vindication of the Conduct of Captain Christopher Middleton.* Reprint New York: Johnson Reprint Corporation.

Rich, E.E. and A.M. Johnson, eds. 1949. *James Isham's Observations on Hudson's Bay, 1743.* Toronto: Champlain Society.

Williams, Glyndwr. 1962. *The British Search for the Northwest Passage in the Eighteenth Century.* London: Longmans.

William Barr

MOSES NORTON
(ca. late *1720–1773*)

It cannot have been easy for the Hudson's Bay Company to find good commanders for that handful of little forts beside Hudson Bay where, until the last quarter of the eighteenth century, all its trading was done. The task was demanding and the field of choice limited. A man could only learn the job by serving in the country. The Company's employees there were few, and of those few many were illiterate labourers. Seniority also had to be considered. These facts help explain why a character such as Moses Norton rose to be commander of Prince of Wales' Fort, at Churchill, from 1762 until his death in 1773.

Norton certainly knew the country. He was born at Churchill, the son of Governor Richard Norton and a Cree woman. Like Henry Kelsey and William Stewart, Richard Norton was one of the Company's pioneer travellers among the Indians, and in the winter of 1717–18 had brought the first Chipewyans to trade at Churchill.

He sent his son to England to be educated. Moses stayed there nine years, and would seem (from his occasional spelling troubles with the letter "H") to have acquired a cockney accent. In May 1744, he was apprenticed to Captain George Spurrell, a seaman who made many voyages to Hudson Bay. In 1753, after this apprenticeship, the Company engaged him as mate of their sloop *Churchill* at the Bay. Moses's father had now long been dead, but this was a good job, with prospects of promotion.

The *Churchill* was employed trading with the Inuit along the west coast of the Bay, and during her voyages Norton doubtless played a part in the efforts the Company was making to establish peace between these Inuit and their hereditary enemies, the Chipewyans. As his father had, Norton did some exploring when his boss, Ferdinand Jacobs, sent him to

Fort Prince of Wales. From J.B. Tyrrell's Champlain Society edition of Herne's *Journey from Prince of Wales Fort* (1911)

Chesterfield Inlet in 1762. He returned to report having reached its very end, without finding the hoped-for Northwest Passage. That autumn, Jacobs went to command York Fort, or York Factory as it was also known, and Norton succeeded him at Churchill. He now had opportunities to display what the late Professor E. E. Rich generously called his "uncommon energy and perception." One may allow the "energy," for Norton was full of ideas, but they were too often impractical for his "perception" to be very impressive.

One was a notion that live moose could usefully be sent to England, and, in 1767, he dispatched a young pair to London. The male died on the voyage, however, and the Company would have been happier if the female had died so too, for, they complained, it cost them £9 10s 11d to feed her from

October 1767 to February 1768, when they at last managed to dispose of her as a gift to King George III. She was then shipped upriver to Richmond Park, and by their next boat the Company ordered Norton to send no more livestock home.

On his northward voyages, Norton had doubtless seen bowhead whales (*Balaena mysticetus*), and in 1765 he persuaded his employers to start a whaling business at Churchill. The result was disastrous. A century later, bowheads were profitably hunted around Southampton Island, but Norton ordered his whalers to stay south of Marble Island. There only four whales were caught in seven years, and in 1772 the Company cancelled this enterprise after losing over £20,000.

Another of Norton's brain waves concerned the copper which had long been known to exist in the North. James Isham had shown there was no way of exploiting this copper profitably, but in 1765 Norton hired two Chipewyans, Idotliazee and Matonabbee,* to find its source. Three years later, when Norton was about to go to England on leave, these Indians reappeared at Churchill, with actual copper samples and a "map" purporting to show where they had been. This map has not the slightest resemblance to the real northern Canada, but nobody then knew any better, so at least it looked impressive. Norton bore it triumphantly off to London and there persuaded his employers to send Samuel Hearne* on his famous journey to the mouth of the Coppermine River in 1769–72.

Of the journey, we can say here only that Norton's crazy planning ensured the failure of the first two attempts (e.g. on each he sent Hearne off with a worthless guide, first a crook, then an ignoramus). By a happy chance, however, Hearne met Matonabbee when returning to Churchill from his second false start, and together these two men planned the third attempt, which was successful, and on which Hearne produced one of the great books about Canada's North. Geographers found their discoveries most interesting, but they brought the Company no new trade to compensate for what had been spent on them, so another Norton scheme was a business failure.

This third and successful attempt also caused a bitter quarrel between Norton and Hearne, for Norton tried to force Hearne to take along some of his Cree relatives. Hearne, who had had enough of Norton's kin on his earlier journeys, refused; and thereafter, he writes, Norton "used every means in his power to treat me ill." It is therefore unfortunate that nobody but Hearne has left any description of Norton's personality; Hearne's picture of him living "in open defiance of every law, human and divine," is so lurid that one would welcome corroboration. That Norton "kept for his own use five or six of the finest Indian girls which he could select" is entirely believable—among his Cree relations polygamy was common and socially acceptable. One can but hope that Hearne's report of his using poison to dispose of Indians who offended him is based on misinformation. Anyway, wherever the truth on that last point lies, Moses Norton's death on 29 December 1773 would hardly seem a great loss to his employers.

Further Readings

Glover, Richard, ed. 1958. *A Journey to the Northern Ocean*. Toronto: Macmillan Canada.

Rich, E.E., ed. 1958–59. *The History of the Hudson's Bay Company, 1670-1870*. London: Hudson's Bay Record Society.

Richard Glover

GEORGE WEETALTUK
(ca. 1862–1956)

The historic Inuit occupation of the James Bay region is largely associated with the name of one man, George Weetaltuk. This Inuit leader was a respected Hudson's Bay Company pilot, boat builder, and artist, as well as patriarch of the Cape Hope Island Inuit community. His reputation and accomplishments are attested to in various written sources, and his many drawings comprise the earliest extensive collection of Canadian Inuit graphic art.

One of the earliest and most widely reproduced of Weetaltuk's sketches is his 1910 map of the Belcher Islands archipelago in Hudson Bay, an archipelago unknown to mapmakers at the time. This remarkable map, drawn about twenty years after Weetaltuk had left the Belcher Islands to live in James Bay, led Robert J. Flaherty* to search for and subsequently to explore the Belcher Islands during the years 1914–16. Indeed, Weetaltuk's map is a more complete and accurate representation of the archipelago than the map Flaherty published in 1918, which is clearly heavily based on Weetaltuk's chart. Both maps have been reproduced in standard cartography and geography texts to illustrate the extraordinary map-making skills of the Inuit.

Such detailed and extensive geographic knowledge (the archipelago is a maze of islands with deeply indented coastlines, covering an area of over three thousand square

George Weetaltuk in 1954, aged 93 years.
Courtesy of Fred Bruemmer, Neg. no. CA4

miles) doubtless served him well during the years when he acted as pilot on the Hudson's Bay Company's ships entering James Bay. This employment resulted in his moving, in 1892, with his family to Charlton Island, at that time the northern terminal for the Company's transatlantic sailing fleet serving the James Bay posts. In 1933, the railway to Moosonee was completed, however, and Charlton Island was no longer the northern terminal and transhipment point for the James Bay fur trade. Weetaltuk then moved his family to Cape Hope Island, and by 1935 a thriving community of eight families was permanently established. A granddaughter, recalling those days, has written:

> On Cape Hope Island he was the leader of his people.... He chose where the seasons would be spent. He performed the church services, did baptisms and burials and divided the animals that were killed. When freeze-up came he was the first to test the ice to see if it was safe to travel. His supply of qallunaat goods—sugar, tea and flour—was always plentiful....His house was the centre of every activity: dances, church and feasting. He lacked no equipment of any sort....

Between 1930 and 1950, Weetaltuk gained fame as a canoe and boat builder. He had constructed a sawmill and a steamer on the island for shaping wood, and there he built the renowned Cape Hope Island canoes, which are still being made today in Poste de la Baleine, Quebec, by his descendants. However, especially noteworthy were the three large, masted boats he built; the largest, the *Carwyn,* was over fifty feet long and was built in 1944 when Weetaltuk was more than eighty years old. The first large boat he built was resold by the Hudson's Bay Company to the Roman Catholic missions, who renamed it *Notre Dame de l'Esperance,* and under that name it sailed the East Main and Labrador coasts for many years. Weetaltuk, though an excellent draughtsman, did not build his boats from plans. He did, however, make a wooden model from which he developed the *Carwyn.* Apparently his model-making skills were well known, for it is reported that he made an exact replica of the Hudson's Bay Company vessel *Discovery* from memory, many years after it had been scrapped.

Weetaltuk's woodworking skills resulted in the arrival of many orders for handmade furniture, from cities and towns all over Canada and the United States. The Anglican churches at Old Factory, Quebec, and Moose Factory, Ontario, commissioned him to carve their ornate bishop's chairs.

The Cape Hope Island community consisted, for the most part, of Weetaltuk's descendants, and was the most southerly Inuit community in Canada until its relocation in 1960. The community enjoyed harmonious relations with adjacent James Bay Cree communities, and all the Inuit spoke Cree (several spoke French and English too).

Mentally active and still spry at the time of his death, Weetaltuk had outlived three wives. There are now about thirty grandchildren and more than sixty great-grandchildren alive, and as befits their adventurous forebear, they have scattered from Resolute Bay and Baffin Island to Yellowknife, and throughout Nouveau-Quebec.

The largest bay in the Belcher Island archipelago, Wetalltok Bay, commemorates George Weetaltuk's role in the early explorations and mapping of this region of Hudson Bay.

Further Readings

Buemmer, Fred. 1955. "George Wetaltuk: Eskimo." *Canadian Geographical Journal* 50: 157-59.

Flaherty, R.J. 1918. "The Belcher Islands of Hudson Bay: Their Discovery and Exploration." *Geographical Review* 5(6): 433–58.

Freeman, Minnie Aodla. 1978. *Life among the Qallunaat.* Edmonton: Hurtig Publishers.

Sources for Weetaltuk's Sketches

Danzker, Jo-Anne Birnie, ed. 1979. *Robert Flaherty, Photographer/Filmmaker: The Inuit 1910-1922.* Vancouver: Vancouver Art Gallery.

Cameron, W.B. 1948. "Runaway ship." *The Beaver,* Outfit 279:5-9.

Flaherty, R.J. 1924. *My Eskimo Friends: Nanook of the North.* New York: Doubleday Page and Company.

Raisz, E. 1948. *General Cartography.* 2nd ed. New York: McGraw-Hill .

Milton M.R. Freeman

Robert Flaherty
(1884–1951)

Robert J. Flaherty is probably best remembered for his first film, *Nanook of the North*. Less well known are his experiences as an arctic prospector-explorer on the Mackenzie expeditions and the exploration of the remote Belcher Islands.

Eldest of the seven children of Robert H. and Susan Kleockner Flaherty, Robert J. was born in Michigan in 1884. He left school at twelve and with his father moved to Rainy Lake. Two years later, the entire family moved to Burleigh Mine in Lake of the Woods. Father and son went on numerous prospecting expeditions throughout northern Ontario. Flaherty attended Upper Canada College in Toronto until 1900, when his father joined U.S. Steel and moved the family to Port Arthur. He then attended the Michigan College of Mines, where he met Frances Hubbard, who, in 1914, was to become his wife and eventually the mother of their three daughters.

Of average stature, with slow, gentle movements, Flaherty nevertheless had a monumental appearance. His body was bulky and strong. He had a broad, rugged face with brilliant blue eyes, ruddy cheeks, expansive mouth, solid chin and jaw, bull neck, and blond hair that turned to silver in later years.

Flaherty possessed a childlike inquisitiveness and was delighted by new discoveries. A fundamentally kind person, he was generous and easy to know, but given to short-lived temper tantrums. He was an accomplished storyteller and violinist. Although remarkably self-reliant, he was at the same time a lonely, sentimental man, seeking the company of others.

His love for a primitive, unsophisticated way of life developed early, and as a young man, Flaherty pursued a career as explorer, prospector, and railroader. He worked in a Michigan copper mine and for the Grand Trunk Pacific Railway, and he prospected for marble on Vancouver Island and for iron ore at

One of the few photographs of Robert Flaherty during his arctic days. Courtesy of The Robert and Frances Flaherty Study Center at The School of Theology at Claremont, California

Lake Huron and the Mattagami River. It was while his father was employed by Mackenzie and Mann in Toronto that Flaherty met Sir William Mackenzie.

Mackenzie was building a railroad across Canada—the Canadian Northern (now the Canadian National Railway)—and looking for iron ore and other mineral deposits. It was Mackenzie's judgement of men and his receptiveness to new ideas that helped start Flaherty on his career as a filmmaker.

Setting out on his first expedition to survey the Nastopone Islands, Flaherty took the railroad to Ground Hog, travelled by canoe down the Ground Hog, Mattagami, and Moose rivers to Moose Factory, sailed to Charlton Island, then went by schooner to Fort George. With a party of Indians, he continued by sled to Cape Jones. From the Great Whale Inuit camp, Flaherty travelled 250 miles by sled through the isolated Subarctic to survey Taylor and Gillies Islands, but he found no important deposits of iron ore. It was from the Inuit that Flaherty learned of the Belcher Islands. Their descriptions led him to believe he would find mineral deposits there. He reported his findings to Mackenzie, who excitedly asked him to make a second expedition.

Flaherty set out on this nineteen-month-long expedition in 1911. His ship was wrecked trying to reach the Belchers, so he instead journeyed by sled with a party of Inuit across the barrens of the Ungava Peninsula, the first to survey it from Fort Chimo to Lake Minto. During the summer of 1912, he made a cross-section of an area of over 11.6 million miles. Upon returning to Lower Canada, he again reported his findings to Mackenzie. Although at the time his survey results were thought to be mineralogically unimportant and economically unfeasible to work, their significance was later realized.

Mackenzie, impressed by the Inuit tales, insisted Flaherty should go to the Belcher Islands by proper ship. He commissioned *The Laddie* and equipped it for an eighteen-month expedition. Before setting sail in August 1913, Flaherty decided to take a movie camera, along with the glass-plate still camera he had taken on previous trips. His only formal training in filmmaking consisted of a three-week course in Rochester. *The Laddie* sailed along the coast of Labrador, through the Hudson Strait to Baffin Island, then put into winter camp for ten months at Adadjual Bay. Early in 1914, Flaherty began filming Inuit women, igloo building, conjuring dances, sledding, and seal hunting.

In the summer of 1914, with the aid of highly accurate Inuit maps, Flaherty mapped the Belcher Islands, but found no ore of high enough quality to warrant mining. He spent the winter of 1914–15 shaping his film, but he thought it crude and uninteresting and vowed to attempt a better one. From his third expedition, Flaherty received two rewards: the Canadian government named the largest Belcher Island for him, and he became interested in the possibility of filmmaking as a career.

A fourth trip to the Inuit was undertaken mainly for filming. With over twenty-two thousand yards of exposed film, Flaherty returned to Toronto and tried to edit his footage, but the resulting film was not what he had hoped for. He was an explorer and mineralogist, not a filmmaker. His aim had been to produce footage that he could incorporate with lantern slides of his photographs into an illustrated lecture.

In 1920, Flaherty met Captain Thierry Mallet, of Revillon Frères, who agreed to finance a filmmaking expedition to the company's subarctic fur trading post, Port Harrison on Cape Dufferin. Departing in August 1920, he travelled up the Innusuk River with a group of Inuit who had agreed to participate in the project. He filmed under the harshest of circumstances for man, camera, and film, journeying as far as six hundred miles to shoot a bear-hunting scene. He returned home in August 1921.

Nanook of the North (1920–21) was the beginning of Flaherty's filmmaking career. His passion to communicate his experiences resulted in other films, all of which contain a recurrent theme: through their struggle with nature, human beings are purified, cleansed, and achieve maturity and dignity. Often made under equally difficult circumstances, his films include *Moana* (1923–25), *The Pottery Maker* (1925), *Twenty-Four Dollar Island* (1927), *Industrial Britain* (1931), *Man of Aran* (1932-34), *Elephant Boy* (1935–37), *The Land* (1939–41), *Louisiana Story* (1946–48), and *Guernica* (unfinished, 1949).

Robert J. Flaherty died at his home, Black Mountain Farm, near Brattleboro, Vermont, in July 1951. His achievements under incredibly severe hardships assure his place not only in the history of Canada, but of the world. As an arctic explorer, Flaherty's contributions were significant. Today, untold wealth is mined in Ungava and the Belchers. As a filmmaker, Flaherty's contributions were monumental, creating a documentary film and tradition that continues to engage audiences and to influence filmmakers.

Further Readings

Danzker, Jo-Anne Birnie, ed. 1979. *Robert J. Flaherty—Photographer/Filmmaker.* Vancouver: Vancouver Art Gallery.

Flaherty, Robert. 1924. *My Eskimo Friends.* With Frances Flaherty. New York: Doubleday.

Griffith, Richard. 1953. *The World of Robert Flaherty.* New York: Duell, Sloan and Pearce.

Murphy, William T. 1978. *Robert Flaherty: A Guide to References and Resources.* Boston: G.K. Hall and Company.

Rotha, Paul. 1983. *Robert J. Flaherty: A Biography*, edited by Jay Ruby. Philadelphia: University of Pennsylvania Press.

Janis Essner and Jay Ruby

Photo of Allakariallak (Nanook) at Port Harrison post, with record player, 1920-21, Inoucdjouac. Courtesy of The Robert and Frances Flaherty Study Center at The School of Theology at Claremont, California

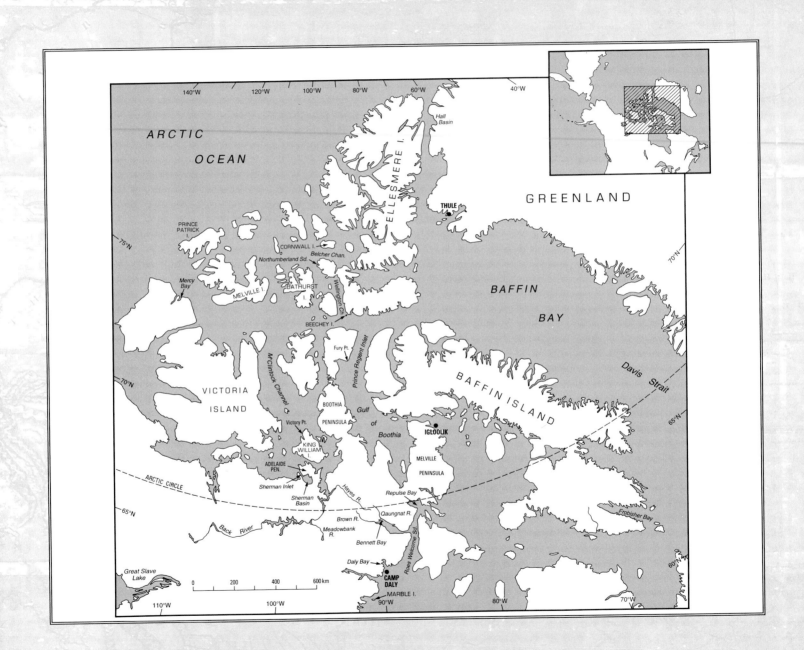

ARCTIC

OCEAN

Hall
Basin

GREENLAND

ELLESMERE I.

THULE

140°W 120°W 100°W 80°W 60°W 40°W

PRINCE
PATRICK
I.

75°N 70°N

CORNWALL I.

Belcher Chan.

Northumberland Sd.

BAFFIN

Mercy
Bay

MELVILLE I.

BATHURST
I.

Wellington Ch.

BAY

BEECHEY I.

M'Clintock Channel

Fury Pt.

Prince Regent Inlet

70°N

VICTORIA

ISLAND

BOOTHIA

PENINSULA

Gulf

of

Boothia

BAFFIN ISLAND

Davis Strait

65°N

Victory Pt.

KING
WILLIAM
I.

IGLOOLIK

ADELAIDE
PEN.

Sherman Inlet

MELVILLE

PENINSULA

ARCTIC CIRCLE

Sherman
Basin

Hayes R.

Repulse Bay

Frobisher Bay

65°N

Back River

Brown R.

Meadowbank
R.

Qaungnat R.

Bennett Bay

Ross Welcome Sd.

60°N

Great Slave
Lake

Daly Bay

CAMP
DALY

0 200 400 600 km

MARBLE I.

110°W 100°W 90°W 80°W 70°W

UNIT
❦ 3 ❧

Jane Franklin, Francis Crozier, Edward Belcher,
Charles Francis Hall, Ebierbing, Frederick Schwatka

This unit focuses on the central region of the Canadian Arctic archipelago. The human landmarks brought together here are linked through their connection to the disappearance of John Franklin's 1845 expedition to navigate the Northwest Passage. From Crozier, who died in the attempt, to Lady Franklin, whose unflagging energies spurred many of the searches for her husband, to Schwatka, who determined no written records of the expedition had survived, these explorations were concentrated to the north and south of Barrow Strait and Lancaster Sound, where Franklin's orders had directed him.

Jane Franklin (1791–1875)

In her biography of Jane Franklin, Frances Woodward notes that one is "tempted to believe that the most interesting thing about [John] Franklin* is his choice of wives." The temptation exists because both of his wives were anything but shadowy presences next to their accomplished husband: both were intelligent, curious, and high-spirited to the point of stubbornness. The first, a London poet, succumbed to tuberculosis after only eighteen months of marriage, but even when one week from death, she encouraged her husband to leave her and proceed with his 1825 arctic overland expedition. The second, Jane, outlived her husband by many years,

Portrait of Jane Franklin. Courtesy of the Scott Polar Research Institute, Cambridge, U.K.

and her indefatigable efforts and "will to believe" led to the recovery of the only document that suggests the fate of the lost Franklin expedition. Her refusal to give up the search inspired many others, and while they searched for Franklin, they laid bare large areas of the Arctic that had hitherto been *terra incognita*.

Jane Griffin was born on 4 December 1791, the daughter of a silk weaver of Huguenot stock. She was educated in a Chelsea boarding school. She possessed an active intelligence and a certain "unfeminine" curiosity that took her, at the age of seventeen, into the hold of a prison ship stationed in the Tamar near Plymouth, as it would later take her into prisons in Van Diemen's Land and into regions where no European woman had ever before ventured.

A compulsive journal keeper and traveller, Jane displayed a corresponding interest in reading and study. As a young woman, she drew up a formidable plan calling for daily study of the gospels and epistles, history and logic, languages, mathematics, conversation and music. The saving feature of the plan is the rueful "Alas! Alas!" written at its end.

The first "Arctic" reference in Jane's journals is a note about the Buchan/Franklin expedition of 1818. But she had not yet met John Franklin, and, until her early thirties, her romantic concerns were polarized between Adolphe Butini, a doctor-to-be, and Dr. Roget, future author of the *Thesaurus*.

She was soon to be introduced to Franklin, however, as her close friend Eleanor Porden married him in 1823. A child was born the following year, and in the year after that, Eleanor Franklin died of tuberculosis. On 5 November 1828, Franklin married Jane Griffin.

In the early 1830s, in the troubled aftermath of the Greek struggle for independence, Franklin was stationed in the Mediterranean. Jane visited him at Corfu. She also travelled into Spain, Greece, North Africa, Syria, and Crete. She writes of fending off, undaunted, "bugs, cockroaches, ants, fleas, spiders, and rats."

In 1836, Jane accompanied her husband to Van Diemen's Land (Tasmania), where he served a troubled term as lieutenant-governor of the penal colony until his ignominious recall in 1843. During Franklin's tenure, Jane's zeal for travel and social reform blossomed: she became the first woman to climb Mount Wellington and the first woman to travel overland from Melbourne to Sydney. She established an agricultural settlement on the Huon River to encourage free immigration, and she sought to improve the lot of female convicts.

After his recall from Van Diemen's Land, Franklin welcomed the prospect of a renewed search for the Northwest Passage, for success here would restore his somewhat tarnished reputation. After HMS *Erebus* and *Terror* set sail for the Arctic, Lady Franklin busied herself with travel to the West Indies and the United States. And no doubt because it was there, she climbed Mount Washington. By September 1847, some uneasiness concerning the fate of the Franklin expedition began to be voiced, and in the next two years, the Admiralty sent out several relief expeditions.

Lady Franklin proved tireless in her support of the search. She offered £3,000 of her own money to supplement the £20,000 Admiralty reward to ships of any flag that helped the lost expedition. With the assistance of friends, she purchased and equipped the 90-ton *Prince Albert*, which sailed into the Arctic twice, under different commands, to search for her husband. She purchased another vessel, the steam yacht *Isabel*, which soon joined the many vessels scouring the Arctic in the early 1850s. Due to her behind-the-scenes efforts, her choice of commander, a whaler (not a Royal Navy officer), was put in charge of two government search vessels, *Lady Franklin* and *Sophia*. She inspired Henry Grinnell, an American philanthropist, to purchase two ships, *Advance* and *Rescue*, which sailed under the command of American naval officers. She visited the Orkneys and Shetlands to interview whaling parties returning from the Arctic, and she appealed to the czar of Russia for assistance north of Siberia.

When John Rae* reported, in the autumn of 1854, that Inuit had seen white men dying on King William Island four years previously, Lady Franklin concentrated her energies on winning for her husband the distinction of having discovered the Northwest Passage, for by this time Robert J.L. McClure* had returned from the Arctic to claim that honour. But she still wished to determine the circumstances of the disaster and to rescue any survivors. All her hopes were now placed on Francis Leopold McClintock* in command of the *Fox,* a yacht purchased and refitted for work in the ice at Lady Franklin's expense. This seemed her final chance, for the British public was now distracted by the Crimean War. McClintock returned on 20 September 1859 with relics and a single document that told part of the story. For her perseverance, Lady Franklin was awarded the Founder's Gold Medal of the Royal Geographical Society, conferred for the first time upon a woman.

The energy and determination that had thus far sustained Jane Franklin, and won for her husband a triumph even in his death, continued unabated in her later years. She did not retire into a reclusive widowhood but continued to travel extensively, visiting the United States, South America, Hawaii, Japan, China, India, and Africa. She died on 18 July 1875 at the age of eighty-three.

Further Readings

Berton, Pierre. 1988. *The Arctic Grail.* New York: Viking Penguin.

Fitzpatrick, Kathleen. 1949. *Sir John Franklin in Tasmania, 1837–1843.* Melbourne: Melbourne University Press.

Rawnsley, Willingham Franklin, ed. 1923. *The Life, Diaries, and Correspondence of Jane Lady Franklin, 1792–1875.* London: Erskine MacDonald.

Korn, Alfons L. 1958. *The Victorian Visitors: An Account of the Hawaiian Kingdom, 1861–1866.* Honolulu: University of Hawaii Press.

Smith, Dorothy Blakey, ed. 1974. *Lady Franklin Visits the Pacific Northwest.* Victoria: Provincial Archives of British Columbia.

Woodward, Frances J. 1951. *Portrait of Jane: A Life of Lady Franklin.* London: Hodder and Stoughton.

Geraldine Ruszala

FRANCIS CROZIER
(1796–ca. 1848)

It is possible that John Franklin* died a happy man on 11 June 1847. Both HMS *Erebus* and *Terror* had been beset off King William Island since 12 September 1846, but some of his men had travelled to the southwestern part of the island, and they may have returned to the ships in time to report to the dying captain that a Northwest Passage did in fact exist and that they were very close to negotiating it. But the icy grip was not released that summer or autumn, and twenty officers and men died by the end of the following winter. On 22 April 1848, the *Erebus* and *Terror* were abandoned and captains Francis R.M. Crozier and James Fitzjames led the survivors down the west coast of King William Island in a desperate bid to reach the North American mainland. The rest is tragic history. Crozier's "failure," if indeed the failure is his, must be understood in the light of his past successes: because he was not inexperienced in polar matters, the reasons for the Franklin tragedy are even more mysterious and perplexing.

Francis Rawdon Moira Crozier was born in September 1796, at Banbridge, Ireland. He entered the Navy on 12 June 1810, as a first-class volunteer on board the *Hamadryad*. Two years later he was posted as midshipman to the *Briton* and ordered to Valparaiso to arrest the U.S. frigate *Essex*, which was interfering with British whale fisheries. On her return voyage, the *Briton* became the second ship, after the

Portrait of Francis R.M. Crozier. Courtesy of the National Maritime Museum

American sealing vessel *Topaz*, to visit Pitcairn Island. At that time, only one of the original HMS *Bounty* mutineers, John Adams, was alive. On his return to England, Crozier spent nearly two years on the Thames guardship *Meander* and the Portsmouth flagship *Queen Charlotte*. In 1818 he was appointed mate to the *Doterel*.

Crozier then accompanied William Edward Parry* in two successive expeditions in search of a Northwest Passage, in 1821 and again in 1824. An important member of both expeditions was James Clark Ross*; and, in the years to come, the destinies of Crozier and Ross would become inextricably, and sometimes ironically, linked. The first expedition spent two winters in the Arctic, and during the second, which was particularly severe, one of Crozier's duties was to transport invalided Inuit to the *Fury* and *Hecla* sick bays. What did he learn, or fail to learn, of Inuit survival strategy during this time? During the second expedition, the *Fury* was wrecked and unloaded at Fury Beach, on the west side of Prince Regent Inlet. If Crozier had led his men to these stores in the spring of 1848, it is possible that some members of the Franklin expedition might have survived, for the stores were intact and his good friend and would-be rescuer, James Ross, was on his way to that area in the summer of 1848.

On 2 March 1826, Crozier received his lieutenant's commission and rejoined *Hecla* under Captain Parry. Crozier watched over the ship anchored in Treurenburg Bay, Spitsbergen, while Parry, Ross, and two others attempted to reach the North Pole over ice. The inventive and enterprising Parry even tried to use caribou to pull the sleds. Though they failed in their main objective, the men travelled farther north than any white men had previously.

In April 1831, Crozier was appointed to the *Stag,* stationed off the coasts of Spain and Portugal. In December 1835, he was appointed first lieutenant and second-in-command to James Ross, HMS *Cove,* which was sent on a humanitarian mission to bring relief to eleven whaling ships beset in Davis Strait.

Between 1839 and 1841, Ross and Crozier commanded three highly successful expeditions in the Antarctic. Their ships were the same ones that were later used in the last Franklin expedition, the *Erebus* and *Terror,* and a legacy of their passage may be traced upon maps of the Antarctic in the naming of Mount Erebus, Mount Terror, Ross Ice Sheet, and Cape Crozier. The ships were repaired and resupplied at Hobart, Tasmania (then called Van Diemen's Land), where John Franklin was lieutenant-governor. At Hobart, also, Crozier fell hopelessly in love with Franklin's niece, Sophia Cracroft, whereas she, in turn, seemed infatuated with James Ross, who was already engaged. Although she refused Crozier's marriage proposal, made, it is speculated, just before he left for the Arctic for the last time, Sophia Cracroft spent the rest of her life singlemindedly helping Lady Jane Franklin* pressure the British government to try to determine the exact fate of the lost expedition.

On 30 May 1830, James Ross stood at Point Victory on the northeastern corner of King William Island and described the great masses of pack ice coming down M'Clintock Channel—ice that would later entrap the *Erebus* and *Terror* and his friends and fellow explorers, John Franklin and Francis Crozier—as "the heaviest masses I have ever seen...." If Ross, the discoverer of King William "Land," had recognized that it was really an island, and not connected to Boothia, then the *Erebus* and *Terror* might have sailed to the east of that island and successfully negotiated the Northwest Passage.

Further Readings

Beattie, Owen and John Geiger. 1987. *Frozen in Time: Unlocking the Secrets of the Franklin Expedition.* Saskatoon: Western Producer Books.

Cooper, Paul Fenimore. 1961. *Island of the Lost.* New York: G.P. Putnam's Sons.

Cyriax, R.J. 1939. *Sir John Franklin's Last Arctic Expedition.* London: Methuen.

Fluhmann, May. 1976. *Second in Command: A Biography of Captain Francis Crozier, R.N., F.R.S., F.R.A.S.* Yellowknife: Government of the Northwest Territories.

Ross, James Clark. 1969. *A Voyage of Discovery and Research In The Southern And Antarctic Regions, 1838–43.* New York: Augustus M. Kelley.

Vollman, William T. 1994. *The Rifles.* Vol. 6 of *Seven Dreams: A Book of North American Landscapes.* New York: Viking Penguin.

Geraldine Ruszala

EDWARD BELCHER (1799–1877)

Prominent in the important but routine survey work undertaken by the British Navy around the globe after the Napoleonic wars, a spectacular failure as an arctic explorer, and most unpopular officer in the fleet, Sir Edward Belcher remains today in relative, perhaps deserved, obscurity.

Descended from a prominent New England family, Belcher was born in Nova Scotia in 1799, entered the Royal Navy in 1812, and after service in the Mediterranean was made lieutenant in 1818. From 1826 to 1828, he was assistant surveyor under Captain Frederick William Beechey* on the voyage of HMS *Blossom* to Bering Strait, with the aim, nearly achieved, of connecting with John Franklin's* explorations.

Made commander in 1829, Belcher was employed on the west and north coasts of Africa, and then on the home survey, principally in the Irish Sea. His *Treatise on Nautical Surveying* (1835) was a standard reference for many years.

In February 1837, he replaced the ailing Captain Beechey on a survey of the Pacific coast. Taking command at Panama of HMS *Sulphur* and *Starling*, he sailed to the Sandwich (Hawaiian) Islands, thence to Prince William Sound and along the south coasts of Russian America (Alaska), and from there south to San Francisco and again to waters off Central America. In 1839, he retraced the same route. During the two voyages he surveyed many ports and islands, fixed the position of

Portrait of Edward Belcher by Stephen Pearce. By courtesy of the National Portrait Gallery, London, U.K.

Mount St. Elias, and made the first scientific survey of Nootka Sound, settling questions outstanding since the voyages of James Cook and George Vancouver. However, these achievements were marred by Belcher's consistent "bad temper, caprice, and malice," which made him detested by his officers and men. Ordered home by way of the Far East, Belcher returned to England in July 1842, where he was knighted and published his *Narrative of a Voyage Round the World*.

In 1852, in spite of his poor reputation as a commander and his lack of experience handling vessels in ice, Belcher was placed in charge of the largest in the series of expeditions which the British government sent out to seek John Franklin. Five ships were given him for the task: HMS *Assistance* (Belcher, and Cmdr. G. H. Richards), the steam tender HMS *Pioneer* (Sherard Osborn), HMS *Resolute* (Henry Kellett*), HMS *Intrepid* (Francis Leopold McClintock*), and HMS *North Star* (W.J.S. Pullen*).

Leaving the *North Star* at Beechey Island as a base, Belcher sent the *Resolute* and the *Intrepid* westward to Melville Island, while he took the *Assistance* and *Pioneer* northward up to Wellington Channel. As it turned out, they were too far north to find traces of Franklin, but Belcher and Osborn discovered Belcher Channel, explored the north coast of Bathurst Island, and Belcher himself discovered and visited Cornwall Island. Belcher and Osborn spent the winter of 1852–53 in

Northumberland Sound, while the *Resolute* and the *Intrepid*, under Kellett, wintered at Melville Island. In the course of long sledge expeditions, Kellett and his men completed the exploration of Melville and Prince Patrick islands, and found and rescued the men of a previous expedition on the *Investigator* (Robert McClure*), locked in the ice of Mercy Bay.

In the summer of 1853, both divisions failed to extricate themselves, and had to spend a second winter in the ice. By the summer of 1854, Belcher had had enough. Convinced of the impossibility of getting free, unwilling to risk yet a third winter, he disregarded the protests of his subordinates, and ordered the four ships to be abandoned. He and his men made it to the base vessel *North Star*, and in August set out on the return voyage to England.

Court-martialled, Belcher was able to prove that he had acted within his orders. Eager though his men were to chance getting out some of the ships, there was no certainty that this would have occurred. The party would have been threatened by food shortage during another winter, and the Admiralty might have had to organize yet another rescue operation. His name was cleared, but his sword was handed back to him in silence. Although he hastened into print with a new book, *The Last of the Arctic Voyages* (1855), largely an attempt to justify his decision, he was thereafter looked upon throughout the Navy as incompetent, "the very worst man who could have been chosen for the task."

There was a unique postscript to the affair, justifying Belcher's detractors. The *Resolute* started to move. Carried southward by the ice, she broke free and drifted 1,200 miles out to Davis Strait, where she was picked up, unscathed, in September 1855 by Captain Buddington of the American whaler *George Henry*. On the prompting of American friends of Lady Jane Franklin,* Congress voted $40,000 for purchase of the vessel, reequipped her for arctic service, and offered her to the British Admiralty as a gift, in the hope that she would be sent out in a final search for Franklin. The vessel was accepted, but was never recommissioned.

Edward Belcher was never employed again, although through seniority he rose in rank until he was made admiral, in 1872. He passed his remaining years in literary and scientific amusements, and died on 18 March 1877.

Further Readings

Belcher, Edward. 1843. *Narrative of a Voyage Round the World*. London: H. Colburn.

_____. 1848. *Narrative of the Voyage of H.M.S. Samarang*. London: Reeve, Benham, and Reeve.

_____. 1855. *The Last of the Arctic Voyages*. London: L. Reeve.

_____. 1856. *Horatio Howard Brenton, a Naval Novel*. London: Hurst and Blackett.

_____. 1871. *The Great Equatorial Current, Misnamed "The Gulf Stream"*. Woolwich.

Osborn, Sherard, ed. 1865. *The Discovery of the North-West Passage by HMS "Investigator" from the Logs and Journals of Capt. R. LeMesuier MacClure* [sic]. London: W. Blackwood.

Pierce, Richard A. and John H. Winslow, eds. 1979. *H.M.S. Sulphur on the Northwest and California Coasts, 1837 and 1839. The Accounts of Captain Edward Belcher and Midshipman Francis Guillemard Simpkinson*. Kingston: Limestone Press.

Wright, Noel. 1959. *Quest for Franklin*. London: Heinemann.

Richard A. Pierce

CHARLES FRANCIS HALL
(1821–1871)

Marking Charles Francis Hall's desolate grave in northwest Greenland is a bronze plaque set up by the British Arctic Expedition of 1875, four years after his death. It reads in part:

> Sacred to the Memory of Captain
> Charles Francis Hall of the U.S.
> ship Polaris Who Sacrificed his
> Life in the Advancement of Science
> of NOVBR 3rd 1871.

In proper naval fashion, the English gave Hall his titular rank of "Captain," but truth is that the title was only a token of his temporary leadership of a disastrous expedition. Essentially the man had been a loner, a pioneer in arctic travel without the naval protocol and cumbersome paraphernalia so common in nineteen century exploration of the distant North.

Portrait of Charles Francis Hall, from C.H. Davis's *Narrative of the North Polar Expedition* (1876)

Hall came to arctic exploration relatively late in life. Born in New England in 1821, as a youth he went west to settle not on the frontier, but in the booming city of Cincinnati, Ohio. For ten years, as a businessman there, he seemed well pleased with urban life. He was in his late thirties when he began to show an interest in the Arctic, probably stimulated by continued international excitement about the disappearance of John Franklin's* expedition in the late 1840s. In 1859, although many search expeditions had sailed during the preceding decade, Hall suddenly decided he would mount one of his own, arguing to potential backers that Franklin survivors might still be living

with the Inuit. Hall was energetic, determined, and pious enough to believe that God had destined him to succeed where professional naval officers and explorers had failed.

He received some small financial backing from merchants and, in 1860, sailed to Baffin Island aboard a whaling vessel. Put ashore at the mouth of what was then called Frobisher Strait (now Frobisher Bay), he was fortunate to encounter an English-speaking Inuit couple. Ebierbing ("Joe")* and Tookoolito ("Hannah") had been brought to England by a whaler several years before; they became Hall's tutors in arctic survival and remained his loyal companions for the rest of his life. Hall hoped to travel through the "strait" to the area of King William Island, where relics of the Franklin expedition had been found. He soon discovered that the strait was in fact a bay. His first expedition was a failure in that he never even left the area of Frobisher Bay, but he did learn the art of living in the Arctic and he made one remarkable find. Some Inuit, who talked to him about the sixteenth century Martin Frobisher* expeditions as if they were recent events, took him to a place where he found foundations of a building and other relics of Frobisher's activities in the 1580s.

After two years in Frobisher Bay, Hall returned home with Joe and Hannah to find his country embroiled in civil war. He was determined to go north again, nonetheless, and continue his search for Franklin survivors. He virtually ignored the war and set about gathering funds, writing a book about his experiences—*Arctic Researches and Life Among the Esquimaux (1865)*—and giving many lectures. He was able to gather only small sums of money, however, and when he returned to the Arctic in 1865, he again travelled by whaling vessel with minimal equipment.

This time he was put ashore at Roe's Welcome Sound in northern Hudson Bay. In the four arduous years that followed, he made repeated attempts to reach King William Island, but was constantly frustrated by Inuit who refused to cooperate. Finally, in the spring of 1869, he reached the island, but he found only a few more relics of the Franklin expedition, including some skeletons. At this point, even Hall gave up the idea of survivors.

But he was not through with the Arctic. He determined to return, this time to the North Pole. When he reached the United States in 1869, the war was over. President Ulysses S. Grant heard him lecture in Washington, and soon Hall had what he had always wanted: a full-scale expedition. Congress voted funds, and he was supplied with a ship, a crew, and even a scientific staff.

The *Polaris* sailed north in 1871, making for the gap between Ellesmere Island and Greenland. Aboard there were strains, particularly between Hall and Dr. Emil Bessels, the German head of the scientific staff. After the *Polaris* was set for the winter in what is now called Hall Basin, Hall made a brief sled journey northward, returned to the ship, then became violently ill after drinking a cup of coffee. He died in two weeks, during his illness often accusing Dr. Bessels and others of murdering him. He was buried ashore. In the spring, the demoralized expedition headed southward, but the *Polaris,* badly damaged by ice, had to be run aground near present-day Thule.

Tookoolito, Hall, and Ebierbing. Courtesy of the author

After all the crew were rescued, a naval Board of Inquiry was convened. Among its conclusions: Charles Francis Hall had died of what Dr. Bessels called "apoplectical insult"—a stroke.

In 1968, Hall's biographer, Chauncey Loomis, exhumed his body and Dr. Franklin Paddock performed an autopsy. Later tests proved that Hall had received large doses of arsenic during the last two weeks of his life. Arsenic was commonly used as a medicine in the nineteenth century, and the question of whether Hall was murdered remains unanswered. Bessels could have intentionally or unintentionally overdosed him. (It should be noted, however, that Bessels did not tell the board that he had administered any arsenic.) On the other hand, Hall, who hated Bessels and who for a period refused treatment by him, might have overdosed himself. In either case, there is some irony implicit in the statement made on the plaque that still stands at the foot of Hall's grave—the statement that he "sacrificed his life in the advancement of science."

Further Readings

Davis, C.H., ed. 1876. *Narrative of the North Polar Expedition: U.S. Ship Polaris*. Washington: Government Printing Office. (Based in part on Hall's papers from his third expedition.)

Hall, Charles Francis. 1865. *Arctic Researches and Life Among the Esquimaux*. New York: Harper and Brothers.

Loomis, C.C. 1971. *Weird and Tragic Shores*. New York: Alfred A. Knopf.

Nourse, J.E., ed. 1879. *Narrative of the Second Arctic Expedition Made by Charles F. Hall, 1864–69*. Washington: Government Printing Office.

Chauncey Loomis

EBIERBING
(ca. 1837–1881)

Ebierbing, called "Joe" by the many whaling men and explorers who knew him, was a small and diffident man, but in the course of a hard life he consistently displayed remarkable strength, courage, and fortitude, as well as unswerving loyalty to those non-Inuit "kabloonas" who came to depend upon him.

Foremost among those who benefited from Ebierbing's loyalty was the American explorer Charles Francis Hall.* Hall first met Ebierbing and his wife Tookoolito, known as "Hannah," at the mouth of Frobisher Bay in the autumn of 1860. Some years earlier, Ebierbing and Tookoolito had been taken to England by a whaling captain. There they had learned some English and had converted to Christianity; there also they had enjoyed brief celebrity, even meeting Queen Victoria and Prince Albert at Buckingham Palace. ("A fine place, I assure you sir," Tookoolito told Hall.) For Hall, a neophyte explorer on his first venture into the Arctic, they were God sent.

Photograph of Ebierbing, from *Narrative of the Second Arctic Expedition Made by Charles F. Hall, 1864-69,* J.E. Nourse, ed., Washington, D.C. (1879)

In the two years that followed, they introduced him to the ways of the Inuit and taught him how to survive in the Far North.

Hall was a touchy and profoundly suspicious man who made many friends, but kept few. Ebierbing and Tookoolito were to remain loyal to him for the rest of his life, although he often strained that loyalty. They accompanied him when he returned to the United States after two years in Frobisher Bay. The country was torn by the Civil War, but Hall ignored it to gather funds for the next expedition, and he used the Inuit couple to his advantage. They and their infant son, who had been born just before they left Baffin Island, often appeared on the lecture platform with him, and he even arranged for their appearance at Barnum's Museum in New York. Both Tookoolito and her infant became ill, and in the spring of 1863 the baby died. Tookoolito was to lose another baby during Hall's second expedition, and finally she and Ebierbing adopted a child, but that child also died in infancy.

When they were not on the road with the remorse-lessly energetic Hall, they were able to find peace and quiet at the home of whaling captain Sidney Buddington and his wife at Groton, Connecticut. They came to consider Groton their home, in fact, and when they returned with Hall from his second expedition, Ebierbing bought a house and land there.

Hall's second expedition, like his first, was a futile search for supposed survivors of John Franklin's* expedition almost twenty years after it had disappeared. In five arduous years of roaming in the areas of Roe's Welcome Sound, Repulse Bay, Iglooik, and King William Island, he accomplished little but his own survival, and in that accomplishment Ebierbing and Tookoolito again were his mainstay. Rightly or wrongly, he often felt betrayed by other Inuit and by the whaling men whom he hired to assist him, but he could always depend on Joe and Hannah.

Once more they accompanied him when he returned to the United States in 1869. This time, while he gathered funds from the U.S. government to support his projected attempt at the North Pole, they were able to live quietly in Groton. But they willingly left their new little house to join him on his last, fatal venture.

The *Polaris* expedition was a disaster. Hall died early on, possibly murdered by its chief scientist, and with his death the morale of the expedition collapsed. In the spring of 1873 the ship's captain, Buddington, headed the *Polaris* southward. Caught in ice during a storm, he ordered abandonment of the ship. Nineteen members of the expedition, including Ebierbing, Tookoolito, and their adopted child, found themselves marooned on a floe when the partly unloaded ship suddenly drifted away. According to George Tyson, the ranking officer in the marooned party, in the incredible six-month drift on the ice that followed, everyone depended on Ebierbing. "We survive through God's mercy and Joe's ability as a hunter," he wrote in his journal.

At the official investigation of the expedition, held after both Tyson's party and the men aboard the *Polaris* had been rescued, Ebierbing and Tookoolito were questioned, and in the verbatim transcript of that interrogation we can, if we use our imaginations, almost hear their voices—Tookoolito speaking English with more confidence than Ebierbing, but both of them understated, shy, and sub-dued. And during his interrogation Joe revealed the depth of his feeling about Hall, saying at the end: "Captain Hall good man. Very worry when he die. No get north after that. Don't know nothing more."

But he did go north again—twice more in fact. While Tookoolito remained in Groton grieving the loss of their adopt-ed child, Ebierbing sailed with Captain Allen Young on the *Pandora* in 1876, a British expedition in search of the Northwest Passage. The journalist J.A. MacGahan, who wrote about the expedition, devoted a chapter of his book *Under Northern Lights* (1876) to "Eskimo Joe," and in it we learn a few things about Ebierbing. He did not speak English well—he was small and self-effacing, but he had "a quiet dignity and gravity about him"—he was a heavy smoker—he had not been fully paid for his services on the *Polaris* expedition—he liked Buddington partly because he was so kind to Tookoolito, but he virtually worshipped Hall.

Ebierbing returned from the *Pandora* expedition to dis-cover that his beloved Tookoolito had died. He remained in Groton briefly, then set out north again, this time with

Lt. Frederick Schwatka* in his search for records of the Franklin expedition. He guided Schwatka's small expedition overland from Repulse Bay to King William Island, doing for them what he had done for Hall—teaching them the Inuit ways of surviving in the Arctic. He was aging and infirm, however, and he did not join them in their exploration of King William Island.

When Schwatka returned to the United States, Ebierbing stayed in the North. Tookoolito had been buried in Groton. The stone on her grave is marked: "Hannah Eberbing [sic], wife of Joseph. Died 31 December 1876 age 38." Also on the stone, above Hannah's name, is Ebierbing's; obviously it was assumed, probably by the Buddingtons, that he would be buried beside her, but he is not. He died somewhere in the Arctic soon after the conclusion of the Schwatka expedition.

Ebierbing and Tookoolito were known by many people and even became moderately famous in their time. But they lived in a limbo between their own culture and language and the culture and language of another world that they only partly adopted. Although they sometimes were quoted in writing by men who knew them, they are quoted only in their groping English rather than in their native language. For us, and perhaps even for those who knew them, they remain distant and blurred. We can only speculate about what went on in their minds, but we know their strength, decency, and loyalty because they constantly displayed them—and we can at least sense their mute suffering and stoic courage in the face of the adversity that was their lives.

Further Readings

Blake, E. Vale. 1874. *Arctic Experiences: Containing Capt. George Tyson's Wonderful Drift on the Ice-Floe*. London: Sampson Low, Marston, Low, and Searle.

Gilder, W.H. 1881. *Schwatka's Search*. New York: Scribners.

Loomis, C.C. 1971. *Weird and Tragic Shores: The Story of Charles Francis Hall, Explorer*. New York: Knopf.

MacGahan, Januarius A. 1876. *Under Northern Lights*. London: Low, Marston, Searle, and Rivington.

Chauncey Loomis

FREDERICK SCHWATKA
(1849–1892)

In this age of specialization, to conceive of one man achieving professional status in law, medicine, and the military is difficult. Yet in spite of having gained recognition as a certified barrister, a trained medical doctor, and a fighting cavalry officer, Frederick Schwatka will best be remembered as a superlative arctic traveller who brought the thirty-year-long search for John Franklin's* missing expedition to a close. He not only made the longest sled journey on record at the time, but in gathering his nearly conclusive evidence that none of Franklin's official or scientific papers had survived, Schwatka made clear that white men could travel extensively in the Arctic without serious injury or illness if they adopted native methods, a "discovery" often attributed to Vilhjalmur Stefansson* some three decades later.

Like so many other men of achievement, Schwatka rose from modest origins. Born the son of a cooper on 29 September 1849 in Galena, Illinois, the young Schwatka spent his first ten years in the American midwest. In 1859, his family moved west to Salem, Oregon. Even though he was apprenticed to a printer for several years, his diligent study at Willamette University earned him an appointment at West Point, the U.S. military academy in Virginia. Upon graduation in 1871, Schwatka was commissioned as second lieutenant in the Third Cavalry. Over the next six or seven years, which included Custer's defeat at the Little Big Horn

Portrait of Frederick Schwatka, from Gilder's *Schwatka's Search* (1881)

and Chief Crazy Horse's surrender, Schwatka served as a fighting officer at several prairie and desert postings in the American West. Amazingly, Schwatka not only served during this turbulent period in the West, but he also managed to study both law and medicine. Admitted to the Nebraska bar in 1875, he received his medical degree from the prestigious Bellevue Hospital Medical College in New York City the following year.

Schwatka's arctic interests were sparked in the 1860s, when newspapers reported Charles Francis Hall's* searches for Franklin's missing ships and crew. A decade later, whaling captain Thomas Barry returned from the Arctic with a silver spoon bearing the Franklin crest and a report that documents of the lost expedition lay in a cairn on an island in the Gulf of Boothia. The recovery of such papers would be invaluable, not only for answers they might provide about Franklin's fate, but for the scientific information they contained. None of the official papers had ever been recovered, with the single exception of Francis Crozier's* notice, discovered in 1859, that the ships had been abandoned. A search, sponsored by the American Geographical Society and financed by private backers, began to take shape, and Schwatka volunteered to lead it. In spite of his lack of arctic experience, he was given command.

On 19 June 1878 the schooner *Eothen,* supplied by an American whaling firm, sailed from New York. The party comprised five men, including William Henry Gilder, scientific reporter for the New York *Herald,* and "Eskimo Joe" Ebierbing,* an Inuk who had served as guide and interpreter for a number of Franklin searches. They set up a winter base camp near Daly Bay before Schwatka reconnoitred an overland route to the Wager River, which he accomplished in the heart of winter. Early the following spring, accompanied by about twelve Inuit, the men began the 3,250 miles sled journey—at the time the longest on record—that took them to King William Island, along its west coast, and back to explore the Adelaide Peninsula before turning up the Back and Meadowbank rivers and returning to Camp Daly on 4 March 1880. They had been gone from the base camp for eleven months and twenty days. When they returned, they discovered that the *Eothen* had neither waited for them nor left supplies, so Schwatka's party continued to Marble Island, where the whaling vessel *George and Mary* gave them passage back to New Bedford.

Captain Barry's rumour of the cache of papers proved unfounded. Schwatka located a single document—a copy of the Crozier notice found by Lt. William Robert Hobson* in 1859. Furthermore, the Inuit assured Schwatka that all other papers had been destroyed. To be sure, Schwatka did find numerous relics of the missing expedition, including part of one of the ship's boats, a miscellaneous collection of buttons and remnants of cloth, and several graves and corpses. He gave decent burial to all mortal remains and positively identified the grave of Lt. John Irving, third officer of the HMS *Terror.* As well, he made a number of minor geographical discoveries, including a branch of the Back River, which Schwatka

named after President Rutherford Hayes, and Sherman Inlet and Basin on the Adelaide Peninsula.

Yet the genuine significance of "Schwatka's search"—as this exhaustive investigation of the region came to be popularly termed—is that it laid to rest any hope that the records of the Franklin party would ever be retrieved. Schwatka's incredible year-long sled journey had closed off the Franklin search, while it simultaneously opened new possibilities in arctic travel if scientific and exploratory parties would adopt native methods.

Schwatka returned to the North in 1883, when the U.S. Army sent him on a reconnaissance of the Yukon River. With a small party, he built a raft and descended the river from head to mouth, a raft journey of over 1,300 miles and, again, a record. Shortly after his return, he resigned from the Army, but continued exploring and writing of his travels. He returned to Alaska in 1886, leading the *New York Times*'s Alaska Exploring Expedition, and again in 1891. In 1889 and 1890, he made three trips into northwestern Mexico, following them with books and lectures on his experiences.

Charles Francis Hall first stirred Frederick Schwatka's northern interests. Both men were U.S. citizens searching for signs of a lost British expedition in what is today the Canadian Arctic. Neither had arctic experience when he began his search. While Hall's efforts suggested that no human survivors remained, Schwatka's made clear that no written records had survived. These men shared one final similarity—they both died of drug overdoses. An autopsy of Hall's remains showed the presence of lethal amounts of arsenic. On 2 November 1892, in Portland, Oregon, Schwatka died of a self-administered overdose of laudanum, an analgesic he used regularly to combat a painful stomach disorder. By most accounts, the overdose was entirely accidental, but such accidents must be rare among members of the medical profession.

Further Readings

Gilder, William H. 1881. *Schwatka's Search: Sledging in the Arctic in Quest of the Franklin Records.* New York: Charles Scribner's Sons.

Schwatka, Frederick. 1883. *Along Alaska's Great River: A Popular Account of the Travels of an Alaska Exploring Expedition along the Great Yukon River.* New York: Cassell and Co.

_____. 1885. *Nimrod in the North.* New York: Cassell and Co.

Stackpole, Edouard A., ed. 1977. *The Long Arctic Search: The Narrative of Lieutenant Frederick Schwatka, U.S.A.* Chester, Connecticut: Pequot Press.

Richard C. Davis

Lieutenant Schwatka showing the Inuit *The Illustrated London News.* From *The Search for Franklin,* author anonymous (1882)

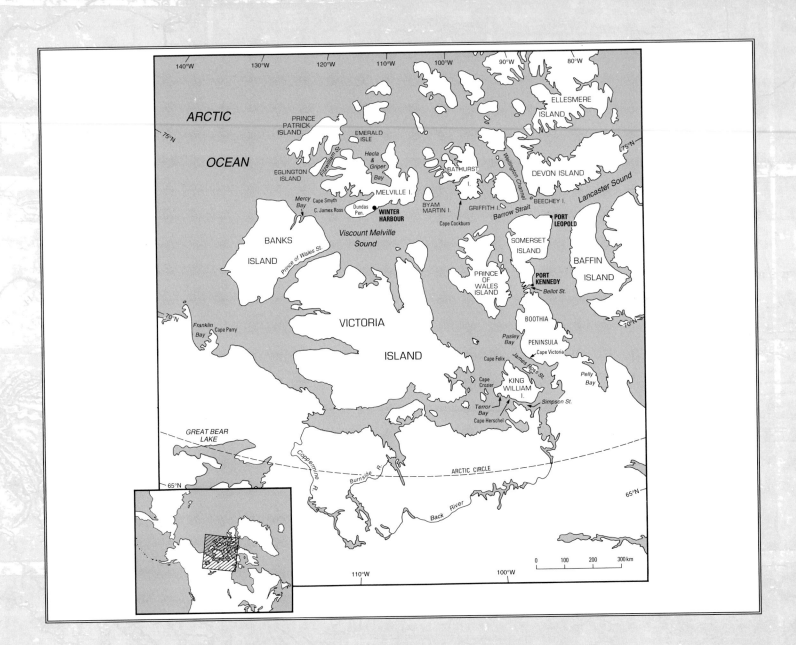

ARCTIC

OCEAN

75°N

PRINCE
PATRICK
ISLAND

EMERALD
ISLE

Hecla
&
Griper
Bay

EGLINGTON
ISLAND

Franklin St.

BATHURST
I.

ELLESMERE
ISLAND

Wellington Channel

DEVON ISLAND

Lancaster Sound

75°N

MELVILLE I.

Mercy
Bay

Cape Smyth
C. James Ross

Dundas
Pen.

WINTER
HARBOUR

BYAM
MARTIN I.

GRIFFITH I.

Cape Cockburn

Barrow Strait

BEECHEY I.

PORT
LEOPOLD

BANKS

ISLAND

Prince of Wales St.

Viscount Melville
Sound

SOMERSET
ISLAND

BAFFIN

ISLAND

70°N

Franklin
Bay

Cape Parry

VICTORIA

ISLAND

PRINCE
OF
WALES
ISLAND

PORT
KENNEDY

Bellot St.

BOOTHIA

PENINSULA

Pasley
Bay

Cape Victoria

70°N

Cape Felix

James Ross St.

Pelly
Bay

Cape
Crozier

KING
WILLIAM
I.

Terror
Bay

Cape Herschel

Simpson St.

GREAT BEAR
LAKE

Coppermine R.

Burnside R.

ARCTIC CIRCLE

65°N

Back River

65°N

110°W

100°W

0   100   200   300 km

UNIT
&4&

Henry Kellett, Robert J.L. McClure, Johann August Miertsching, Francis Leopold McClintock, Samuel Gurney Cresswell, William Robert Hobson

The sphere of activity in this fourth unit overlaps with that of the previous unit, although the focus shifts to the west. All these figures were directly connected either with the nineteenth century British search for the Northwest Passage or with the search for John Franklin's missing expedition. In spite of such connections, however, these profiles reveal the diverse backgrounds and interests of arctic explorers, from the spiritual passions of the German Miertsching to the paintings of Cresswell and the dark ambitions of the Anglo-Irish McClure.

HENRY KELLETT (1806–1875)

Henry Kellett was born in West Ireland and joined the Navy too late to share in the Napoleonic wars, but he found employment in the coastal surveys, which were an important part of the Navy's duties in the peaceful years of the nineteenth century. He served in the China War and was promoted post-captain.

When the search for the crews of John Franklin's* missing expedition began, Kellett was in command of the frigate HMS *Herald,* charting the Pacific coast of lower California; his new orders directed him to spend the summer carrying supplies to the lookout ship HMS *Plover* in Kotzebue Sound, Alaska, and to make excursions into the western Canadian Arctic. Both Kellett and the commander of the *Plover* were in the sound when HMS *Investigator,* under Robert McClure,* arrived. Instead of awaiting the arrival of his commanding officer, McClure plunged ahead with the *Investigator* and began an independent search, a course he justified by pretending that Captain Richard Collinson, of HMS *Enterprise,* had slipped through Bering Strait unobserved and was still ahead of him. Neither Kellett nor the *Plover's* captain would countenance this pretence; Kellett, however, had scruples about meddling with the urgent search for Franklin's expedition, and although he was

HMS *Resolute* and *Intrepid* passing an iceberg in Baffin Bay, July 1852. From McDougall's *Voyage of HMS Resolute* (1852)

the senior officer, he permitted McClure to sail into the Arctic, where he vanished for almost three years.

Shortly afterwards, Kellett was recalled to England and given command of HMS *Resolute,* a part of the search fleet under Sir Edward Belcher.* After passing through Lancaster Sound, Belcher left HMS *North Star* as depot ship at Beechey Island, while he took HMS *Assistance* and *Pioneer* up Wellington Channel. He directed HMS *Resolute* and the tender HMS *Intrepid* to proceed west to Melville Island and, if need arose, to afford help to Collinson or McClure. Finding William Edward Parry's* Winter Harbour blocked by ice, Kellett secured winter protection between the Melville Island coast and little Dealy Island. From there, an officer tramped to Winter Harbour and found McClure's journal of proceedings in a cache, from which it was learned that the *Investigator* had discovered the Northwest Passage, and that McClure's ship had lain and might still be lying at Mercy Bay on the north shore of Banks Island.

Winter, however, was too far advanced by that time for Kellett to attempt a crossing of crossing of Viscount Melville Sound. But there was reason to fear that McClure's supplies were running low and that his men might be driven to make a trek for the continental mainland. Lt. Bedford Pim finally eased his captain's anxiety by volunteering to cross the sound, but not until the cold of early March. Travelling by dogsled, Pim narrowly arrived in time to avert any such hopeless land journey by McClure.

McClure sent his invalids, his interpreter Johann Miertsching,* and Lt. S.G. Cresswell* back to join the *Resolute;* he still hoped to extricate his ship from the ice of Mercy Bay. But Kellett, shocked at the haggard aspect of the half-starved invalids, ordered McClure to abandon his ship and to bring his entire crew to join the *Resolute.* The *Resolute* and *Intrepid* then sailed east, but were frozen in at Barrow Strait, and the hapless crew that had manned the *Investigator* had to spend a fourth winter in the ice. Edward Belcher, unjustifiably in Kellett's opinion, ordered four of the ships under his command abandoned; crews were ordered to tramp to Beechey Island for the transport home on summer supply ships. By producing their superiors' orders, Kellett and McClure were promptly acquitted for the loss of their ships. After a rough passage through court-martial, Belcher, too, was granted a grudging acquittal.

It was resolved to make a handsome grant to the discoverers of the Northwest Passage, and a House of Commons committee sat to apportion shares to the crews of Collinson, McClure, and Kellett. Collinson withdrew all claim and magnanimously refrained from complaining of McClure's desertion. Kellett's position was strong, as but for him the *Investigator* and the record of its exploit might have disappeared as Franklin had done. But McClure smoothly explained that he had not required the *Resolute's* aid. Without it, he might have got his men to the whalers in Baffin Bay with only four casualties. This was contrary to the opinion of the surgeon, Alexander Armstrong, and in flat contradiction to the German Miertsching's assertion that "had not our gracious and merciful Lord and Saviour intervened, and by bringing these ships [the *Resolute* and the *Intrepid*] at the right time, cancelled our intended long journey at the last moment, we must all have perished miserably on the frozen sea." The gross ingratitude of McClure's impudent assertion seems not to have deceived the committee; nonetheless, it awarded the entire grant of £10,000 to the officers and men of the *Investigator,* dismissing Kellett with a few words of commendation, more galling than any insult. This decision may be ascribed to the wish to exalt as much as possible British prestige, which had suffered much from the mismanagement of the Crimean War.

Henry Kellett later commanded the British squadron on the China station, where he won the praise of that tempestuous critic of naval administration, the future Admiral Lord Fisher. Although he hardly rates as an explorer, Kellett rendered a most valuable service to polar history by rescuing the *Investigator* and so preserving the record of her sensational and often perilous voyage.

Further Readings

McDougall, G.F.M. 1852. *The Eventful Voyage of H.M. Discovery Ship "Resolute" to the Arctic Regions, in Search of Sir John Franklin and the Missing Crews of H.M. Discovery Ships "Erebus" and "Terror," 1852–54.* London: Longman, Brown, Green, Longmans, and Roberts.

Neatby, L.H. 1970. *The Search for Franklin.* Edmonton: Hurtig Publishers.

Wright, Noel. 1959. *Quest for Franklin.* Toronto: Heinemann.

L.H. Neatby

The five ships under Edward Belcher's command, Baffin Bay, June 1852. HMS *Intrepid* is on the far left, HMS *Resolute* in centre. From McDougall's *Voyage of H.M.S. Resolute* (1852)

ROBERT J.L. MCCLURE
(1807-1873)

Robert John LeMesurier McClure was born of Anglo-Irish gentry in 1807. He joined the Navy at the advanced age of sixteen and for many years missed promotion. In 1836–37 he was mate on George Back's* HMS *Terror* cruise in Hudson Bay and came back well initiated in the dangers of pack ice. He was immediately promoted lieutenant and given service on the Canadian Great Lakes at that time of political disturbance. After years of obscurity, he was made first lieutenant of HMS *Enterprise,* in which James Clark Ross* was leading the first John Franklin* rescue expedition. McClure gained no credit on this almost abortive cruise, as ill health barred him from major sled journeys, and when Ross was disabled, 2nd Lt. Francis Leopold McClintock* was given temporary charge of the ship. These frustrations are some excuse for the unscrupulous greed with which he was later to grasp at a monopoly of honour and success. On his return to England, McClure was made commander and appointed to HMS *Investigator,* which was to second Captain Richard Collinson of the *Enterprise* in a voyage by way of South America and Bering Strait to search the western Arctic.

The two ships sailed 20 January 1850, and at once encountered foul weather and loss of time in keeping company. Collinson gave orders to sail independently to a rendezvous off Alaska. McClure became obsessed with the fear that, in his speedier vessel, his chief would arrive first at the rendezvous, take the lookout ship stationed there with him into the ice, and leave his junior to

Portrait of Robert J.L. McClure. By courtesy of the National Portrait Gallery, London, U.K.

a passive role in Bering Strait. In fact, Collinson waited and saw his consort tugged through Magellan Strait. In the storms of the South Pacific, the ships parted for the last time. McClure arrived in Honolulu on 1 July to find that the *Enterprise* had taken supplies and sailed the previous day.

Collinson had intended to reach the Arctic by making a wide sweep around the Aleutians; McClure now resolved to halve the distance by striking straight through the uncharted and fog-bound island chain. He surmounted the dangers—found to be real enough—and contacted the lookout HMS *Plover* weeks ahead of his commodore's ship. For a moment he was his own master, for in giving him orders Collinson had not contemplated this early arrival of the sluggish *Investigator.* Disregarding the advice of Capt. Henry Kellett,* his superior, McClure plunged straightaway into the Arctic. He saw the opportunity of being beforehand in the rescue and, not improbably, of completing the still undiscovered Northwest Passage. By good fortune he carried with him two industrious diarists—his surgeon, Alexander Armstrong, and Johann August Miertsching,* a Moravian missionary enlisted as Inuit interpreter—as well as the gifted watercolour artist Lt. S.G. Cresswell.*

Confined near the shore by the pack and calling at Inuit camps, McClure sailed past the Mackenzie River hundreds of miles to the east until at Cape Parry he was shouldered north by ice and made the lucky discovery of Prince of Wales Strait, separating Victoria and Banks islands and the last link in the

Passage sought. Ascending this almost to its outlet, he was caught by gale and tide and swept back to the narrows of the strait, where the ship was almost wrecked in the churning pack. When it froze solid, McClure took a sledge crew to its northern outlet on William Edward Parry's Viscount Melville Sound and linked their joint discoveries into one continuous Northwest Passage.

In the spring, sledge parties mapped much of the shore of Banks and Victoria islands without finding a trace of Franklin's lost crews. Weeks failed to get the ship into the dense pack of Viscount Melville Sound. The proper course was then to return with his valuable report by the way he had come, but McClure, obsessed with the glory of navigating the Passage, attempted the circuit of Banks Island to enter the sound from the west. Off the island's northwest angle, a coast "without parallel for the dangers of its navigation," the ship was pinned to the shore by ice for three weeks and almost hurled on the beach by a gale that left her crew speechless and trembling. Released, she made an adventurous run down the northeast shore, was almost wrecked on a sandbar, and took refuge in the Bay of God's Mercy (Mercy Bay) on 24 September 1851. In the spring, McClure crossed the sound and cached his report on the Melville Island shore.

That report was instrumental to their survival. After caching the message, they were ice-imprisoned in the same bay for a second winter. Supplies were nearing exhaustion; on half-rations for more than a year, many men grew shrunken, haggard, and tottering. McClure's desperate scheme of detaching them for a foot journey to the continent was averted by the arrival of Lt. Bedford Pim with word that two rescue vessels awaited them on Melville Island. Their commander, Captain Kellett, ordered the *Investigator* to be abandoned. Her men trekked across the sound, some carried on sledges, all enfeebled. Early on the return voyage, the luckless fellows were frozen in at Barrow Strait for a fourth winter and reached England on 1 October 1854, after an absence of four years and nine months, having traversed the passage on three different ships, with two intermediate tramps over frozen seas.

Despite an unofficial statement that the Admiralty were displeased at the irresponsibility that had almost caused a second Franklin disaster, McClure was knighted and a House of Commons committee convened to consider a generous reward for the discovery of the Passage and the propriety of granting a portion of the bounty to the rescue ships of Kellett. With ingratitude and gross lack of candour, McClure testified that he could have saved his crew without Kellett's aid and secured the entire bounty of £10,000 for his own ship. He was later employed on the China station and died in 1873 a vice-admiral.

An estimate of Robert John LeMesurier McClure may be formed from his own conduct and the statements of Armstrong and Miertsching. Of his courage, overabundant enterprise, and fortitude in crisis there is no doubt. He was selfish, greedy of fame, and reserved and aloof with naval subordinates, but the civilian Miertsching found him hospitable and sympathetic. Apart from merit, his amazing cruise makes him absolutely unique. He has added an imperishable chapter to the history of arctic exploration, and in varied adventure and intensity of frequent peril, McClure has matched the fabled voyagers of antiquity.

Further Readings

Armstrong, Alexander, 1857. *A Personal Narrative of the Discovery of the North-West Passage.* London: Hurst and Blackett.

Neatby, L.H., trans. 1967. *Frozen Ships: The Arctic Diary of Johann Miertsching, 1850–1854.* Toronto: Macmillan Canada. (English translation from the German.)

_____. 1970. *The Search for Franklin.* Edmonton: M.G. Hurtig.

L.H. Neatby

Johann August Miertsching
(1817–1877)

The German Moravian missionary Johann Miertsching holds a unique position among the historiographers of the Canadian Arctic. He is less inhibited and stereotyped than the naval officers whose journals are the chief primary sources for the great period of polar discovery, 1818–59. He did not belong to the naval club; he was a civilian, writing in a foreign tongue and acutely sensitive to a novel environment, and despite his obvious good nature and his sentimental attachment to the captain under whom he served, he inserted much that a naval officer would have suppressed for the credit of the service and that a sailor would have omitted simply because he took it for granted.

Miertsching was born in Saxony, Germany, in 1817, and trained as a missionary of the Moravian Church. In this capacity he served for some years on the Labrador station of Ogkak and mastered Inuktitut, the Inuit language. He was home on furlough when directed by the rulers of his order to report to the British Admiralty for service on an arctic discovery ship.

As part of the search for the missing ships of John Franklin,* the Admiralty proposed to send two ships by way of Cape Horn and Bering Strait to the western American Arctic. Captain Richard Collinson was assigned to the command; Miertsching was to serve as interpreter for the interrogation of the natives of the arctic shoreline. In the hurry of

Photograph of Johann A. Miertsching. Courtesy of Niels W. Jannasch, Tantallon, Nova Scotia

departure he was temporarily berthed on the second ship, HMS *Investigator,* under Comdr. Robert J.L. McClure.* It so happened that he was never transferred, but remained with McClure for the five years of his all-but-disastrous cruise. If Collinson had had the young German aboard, he would have given him a safer and duller time and, with the means of questioning the natives of Victoria Island, would in all probability have discovered Franklin's fate. Nonetheless, it was good fortune which reserved the voluble and impressible German to be McClure's shipmate throughout, and in his memoir to give permanence to the fantastic misadventures of the *Investigator.*

The two ships under Collinson's command sailed from Plymouth in January 1850, but were soon parted in foul weather. The first to arrive at Bering Strait, McClure's *Investigator* turned her bows into the arctic ice alone. Through Miertsching, McClure questioned aboriginal peoples scattered along the Alaskan and Canadian north shores. He encountered frightful dangers in exploring the last link in the Northwest Passage, Prince of Wales Strait, but found its northern outlet blocked by ice. In the summer of 1851, he rounded Banks Island and saw his ship almost crushed against the rocks of its northwest shore by a massive gale-driven pack. For the winter he berthed his ship in Mercy Bay on the Banks Island north shore, where she was permanently frozen in and her crew reduced to extremity by cold and hunger. They were barely saved by a rescue squadron, and the party returned to England in October 1854, after an absence of almost five years.

When the ship was abandoned at Mercy Bay, McClure, perhaps fearing that revelation of the frightful danger and suffering which his headlong tactics had inflicted on his crew would dim his glory as discoverer of the Passage, collected his officers' journals and conveniently mislaid them. The surgeon Alexander Armstrong contrived to preserve his diary; the resolute Miertsching rewrote his. He was intimate with his captain, but not uncritical, and seems to give a fair portrait of that brave, worthy, but not unflawed discoverer. His great service to the expedition was as its historian. He made a good reproduction of the lost portion of his journal largely from memory and pencilled notes. Armstrong's record is the more exactly factual and reliable, but Miertsching achieves the "truth of poetry" by a convincing representation of the atmosphere of the voyage in its varied phases and of the emotions of the participants. His lurid portrayal of danger at the narrows of Prince of Wales Strait and off the northwest coast of Banks Island, and the ship's passage through a narrow gorge hemmed in on both sides by walls of ice are, in substance, confirmed by the grave, unemotional Armstrong. The emotions he expresses when, after four years in the barren wilderness, he passed up the Thames amid the sights, sounds, and animation of civilized life deserves to be a polar classic. Dramatic too is his description of the grief of women and children who met the returning crew on the dock to greet the father—who "had not come back." Armstrong neither suppresses nor stresses the misery of the starving crew at Mercy Bay. Miertsching depicts it without restraint.

The excellent training of a Moravian missionary enabled him to serve the crew as tinsmith, carpenter, and shoe-repair man. As a teacher of the gospel, he was restricted by his rank as officer, but he gave advice freely to those who asked for it, and no one can read of his dealings with the bereaved Inuit mother and the dying Marine without perceiving his humanity and the depth of his religious conviction. After the voyage, he published a German account of it, dealing lightly with its grimmest aspects. His original journal first appeared in English in 1967.

After Johann August Miertsching had enjoyed a period of rest in Germany, his directors, out of regard for his health, assigned him to a mission in South Africa. But he never ceased to regret his Inuit and the harsh invigorating Labrador climate. Eventually he retired to Germany, where he died worn out before the age of sixty.

Further Readings

Armstrong, Alexander, 1857. *A Personal Narrative of the Discovery of the North-West Passage*. London: Hurst & Blackett.

Jannasch, H.W. 1953. "Grossvater Miertsching." In *Herrnhuter Miniaturen*. Lüneburg, Germany: Heliand Verlag.

Neatby, L.H., trans. 1967. *Frozen Ships: The Arctic Diary of Johann Miertsching, 1850-1854*. Toronto: Macmillan Canada. (English translation from the German).

L.H. Neatby

FRANCIS LEOPOLD McCLINTOCK
(1819–1907)

The Royal Navy's tradition of arctic exploration by means of man-hauled sledges, initiated by William Edward Parry* during his 1827 attempt to reach the North Pole and climaxed in Robert Scott's astounding display of masochism during his journey to the South Pole in 1911–12, is a remarkable example of what the military mind can achieve despite itself. Even such hardened naval officers as Henry Kellett* and Erasmus Ommanney were stunned at the brutal effort involved on their first encounters with this excruciatingly slow method of travel. What makes the stubborn retention of the technique so baffling is that such naval explorers as Parry and even James Clark Ross,* who introduced man-hauling as an integral part of the search for John Franklin,* had frequently observed the superior speed and ease of travel by Inuit dogsled. Both officers, in fact, had extensively used dogsleds themselves. Yet, in spite of this inexplicable resistance to adopt superior methods, the enormous distances logged by man-hauled sledge parties during the Franklin search and the vast area of the Canadian Arctic archipelago that was first mapped using this brutal technique are impressive. And if anyone raised sledge hauling to its peak of efficiency, Francis Leopold McClintock was that man.

Born in County Louth, Ireland, on 8 July 1819, the son of the head of the customs office at Dundalk, Leopold McClintock first went to sea aboard HMS *Samarang* as a first-

Portrait of Captain McClintock, 1856. Courtesy of the Scott Polar Research Institute, Cambridge, U.K.

class volunteer at the age of twelve. Over the next fourteen years, he slowly made his way up through the system, seeing service in such diverse places as the Gulf of California, Brazil, the Irish Sea, the Channel, the Caribbean, Newfoundland, Bermuda, and the Rio de la Plata. He was made lieutenant on 29 July 1845.

In 1847, McClintock was recommended to James Clark Ross, who was fitting out HMS *Investigator* and *Enterprise* for the first of the Navy's seaborne searches for the missing Franklin expedition. McClintock was appointed second lieutenant aboard *Enterprise* under Ross's command. The two ships wintered at Port Leopold on northeastern Somerset Island, and from there in the spring of 1849, Ross and McClintock made the expedition's major sledging trip. Travelling west along the north coast of Somerset Island, they searched the west coast as far south as 72°38′N; the round trip of some five hundred miles took forty days.

The summer of 1850 found McClintock back in the Arctic again as first lieutenant aboard HMS *Assistance* under Captain Erasmus Ommanney, this ship being one of Captain Horatio Austin's four-ship squadron that wintered in the strait between Griffith and Cornwallis islands. In the spring of 1851, McClintock led one of the many sledge parties that fanned out from the ships. Leaving the ships on 15 April, he headed west along the south coasts of Cornwallis, Bathurst, Byam Martin, and Melville islands and reached Cape James

Ross, situated on the southwest tip of Melville Island. Rounding the shores of Dundas Peninsula, he then cut back across that peninsula to the south coast before he headed for home, reaching the ships on 4 July. He had covered a distance of 770 miles in eighty days.

Largely as a result of this achievement, McClintock was given his first command during the following Franklin search expedition, that was led by Capt. Edward Belcher* in 1852-54. McClintock commanded the steam tender *Intrepid,* which was to support HMS *Resolute,* under Capt. Henry Kellett. The two ships wintered at Dealy Island, off the south coast of Melville Island. In the spring of 1853, McClintock led a party that achieved the distinction of making one of the two longest man-hauled sledge trips accomplished in the North American Arctic. McClintock crossed the "waist" of Melville Island to Hecla and Griper Bay, then coasted west to the island's northwest tip. Crossing Fitzwilliam Strait, he discovered and explored Prince Patrick Island, as well as the north coasts of Eglington Island and the west and south coasts of Emerald Isle. In total he covered 1,317 miles in 105 days. This record would be surpassed only by Lt. George Mecham's journey of 1,325 miles in 84 days in the spring of 1854.

Subsequently, after a second wintering in the pack off Cape Cockburn, Kellett and McClintock, on direct orders from Belcher, were forced reluctantly to abandon their ships, which were still in excellent condition. McClintock was fully exonerated by the inevitable court martial on their return to England, and, indeed, on 11 October 1854, he was promoted to the rank of post-captain.

In the spring of 1857, Jane Franklin* was fitting out a private expedition to investigate the stories that John Rae* had recently heard from the Pelly Bay Inuit of white men having been seen on King William Island. She chose Capt. Francis Leopold McClintock to command the yacht *Fox,* which sailed from Aberdeen that summer. Beset in the ice of Melville Bay, the *Fox* drifted south for the full length of Baffin Bay and Davis Strait over the winter of 1857–58. Once his ship was freed, McClintock headed north once again and entered Lancaster Sound; the expedition spent its second winter at the east end of Bellot Strait.

During a sled journey in February 1859, McClintock met a group of Inuit at Cape Victoria on the west coast of Boothia Peninsula who possessed a variety of silverware and other relics from the missing ships. They reported that one ship had been crushed by the ice to the west of King William Island. McClintock planned his spring sledge trips on the basis of this report. On 2 April, he and his second-in-command, Lt. William Robert Hobson,* set off westward, each with a man-hauled sledge and a dog-sledge. Meeting the same group of Inuit, they now learned that two ships had been seen west of King William Island.

On reaching Cape Victoria, McClintock and Hobson separated. In what was clearly a magnanimous gesture to his junior officer in view of the Inuit reports, Hobson was ordered to search the west coast of King William Island. McClintock's party, meantime, was to proceed clockwise around the coast of King William Island. At two Inuit camps on the east coast of the island, McClintock recovered silverware that clearly had come from HMS *Erebus* and *Terror,* as well as various articles made from wood salvaged from the missing ships. On the south coast, he found a skeleton later identified as that of Harry Peglar, captain of the foretop aboard *Terror.*

A short distance west of Cape Herschel, McClintock found a message left by Hobson in a cairn six days earlier with the exciting news that in a cairn at Point Victory he had found a record left by Lt. Graham Gore on 25 April 1848, outlining in frustratingly meagre detail the final outcome of the Franklin expedition, including the information that Franklin had died on 11 June 1847 and concluding with the stunning information that the officers and men of *Erebus* and *Terror* had abandoned their ships and were about to start south by sledge and boat via the Back River.

Encouraged by this message, McClintock continued his search. On 29 May, he reached the western tip of King William Island, which he named Cape Crozier. On 30 May, he discovered a ship's boat mounted on a heavy sledge (earlier found by Hobson on his way back north); it contained two skeletons as well as a strange assortment of abandoned equipment and clothing.

By 19 June, McClintock was back at Bellot Strait, and *Fox* reached London on 23 September 1859. For having led the expedition that solved the baffling mystery of Franklin's fate, McClintock was knighted, granted the freedom of the City of London, awarded honourary degrees by the universities of Oxford, Glasgow, and Dublin, and elected a Fellow of the Royal Geographical Society and the Royal Society.

Sir Francis Leopold McClintock's later career was very distinguished. He reached the rank of admiral in 1884, just before retirement, and was created Knight Commander of the Bath (KCB) in 1891. During his retirement, he took a keen interest in Antarctic exploration and was a leading member of the committee responsible for the design of Scott's ship *Discovery,* used on his National Antarctic Expedition of 1901–1904. Leopold McClintock died on 17

Portrait of Admiral McClintock in later life. Courtesy of the Scott Polar Research Institute, Cambridge, U.K.

November 1907 at the age of eighty-eight and is buried in Kensington Cemetery, Hanwell. He will be remembered by history as the man who refined the technique of arctic exploration by man-hauling to an amazingly high degree, despite the staggering inherent limitations of the technique, and as the man who solved—as far as it ever has been—the mystery of the fate of the Franklin expedition.

Further Readings

De Bray, E.F. 1992. *A Frenchman in Search of Franklin: De Bray's Arctic Journal 1852–1854.* Translated and edited by W. Barr. Toronto: University of Toronto Press.

Markham, C. 1909. *Life of Admiral Sir Leopold McClintock.* London: John Murray.

McClintock, F.L. 1859. *The Voyage of the "Fox" in the Arctic Seas: A Narrative of the Discovery of the Fate of Sir John Franklin and his Companions.* London: John Murray.

McDougall, G.F. 1857. *The Eventful Voyage of H.M. Discovery Ship "Resolute."* London: Longman, Brown, Green, Longmans, and Roberts.

William Barr

SAMUEL GURNEY CRESSWELL (1827-1867)

The family of Samuel Gurney Cresswell lived in or near Lynn, Norfolk, England, enjoying connections with the well-known Quaker family of the Gurneys and an acquaintance with William Edward Parry,* the arctic explorer. Samuel Cresswell was born in 1827, joined the Navy in 1842, and served in the China seas, where he was twice gazetted for service against the pirates of Borneo. On his return to England he was—perhaps through Parry's influence—appointed to the 1848–49 John Franklin* rescue expedition led by James Clark Ross.* On Ross's return from his fruitless mission, his ships were refitted to make the voyage to the western Arctic by way of Cape Horn and Bering Strait. Capt. Richard Collinson took command on HMS *Enterprise*; Cresswell became second lieutenant on HMS *Investigator* under Robert McClure.* With his commanding officer still en route to Kotzebue Sound from Honolulu, the unscrupulous McClure availed himself of a defect in his orders to slip away on an unaccompanied search. The *Investigator* passed through Bering Strait and coasted along the American north shore. Cresswell commanded the whaleboat in which the ship's surgeon Alexander Armstrong and the Inuit interpreter Johann August Miertsching* studied the "smoking cliffs" of Franklin Bay. In late autumn, McClure discovered Prince of Wales Strait and won for officer and crew the honour of completing the Northwest Passage. They wintered in the frozen strait.

In April 1851, McClure sent out travelling sledge parties to search for traces of Franklin. In discharge of his duty, Cresswell explored 170 miles of the east and northeast Banks Island shore, at which time some of his crew

"Sledging Over Hummocky Ice, April, 1853", by S. G. Cresswell. Courtesy of Niels W. Jannasch, Tantallon, Nova Scotia

were disabled by frostbite. A second excursion took him to the south end of the strait.

In the summer, the ship rounded Banks Island by its west shore, a voyage of frightful peril, and her throes in the gale-driven pack have been illustrated by Cresswell in a well-known painting. She took refuge in Mercy Bay on the northeast shore of Banks Island and was permanently locked in the ice from 25 September 1851 until the spring of 1853, her crew being reduced to the verge of starvation.

What would probably have turned out to have been a suicidal dash on foot for the continent was averted on 7 April 1853 by the arrival of Lt. Bedford Pim, with a dog-team, bearing the intelligence that two ships under Capt. Henry Kellett* were berthed at the small Dealy Island off the shore of Melville Island. McClure would not consent to the immediate desertion of his imprisoned ship, but he put Cresswell and Miertsching in charge of a sledge party to conduct six helpless invalids 160 miles over shattered ice-fields to the comfort and security of the rescue vessels. Cresswell carried out this trying and laborious duty with efficiency and no loss of life. Kellett soon despatched Cresswell with more of the sick farther east to Beechey Island; when the ice broke up, he boarded the supply vessel for home. On his arrival in late autumn, Cresswell enjoyed a temporary celebrity as bearer of the news that the long-sought Northwest Passage had been discovered, and he was fêted by the townspeople of King's Lynn.

In 1854, Cresswell served at the rank of commander with the Baltic fleet in the war against Russia. Three years later, he sailed to China with a detachment of gunboats, served in the Chinese war on the Peiho River, and then went on a cruise

"Critical Position of HMS *Investigator* on the North Coast of Baring Island," by S.G. Cresswell. Courtesy of Niels W. Jannasch, Tantallon, Nova Scotia

against pirates. According to the unofficial testimony of his home-town newspaper, he took or destroyed twenty-six junks. He was promoted to full captain in September 1859, but after some years of unemployment, Cresswell was obliged to decline an appointment owing to ill health caused by "fatigue and starvation"—doubtless the deferred effect of many months of toil and hunger in the Arctic. He did not survive long: his funeral is reported in the *Lynn Advertiser* as taking place on 22 August 1867.

Despite his record of service, Samuel Gurney Cresswell seems to have been an officer of not more than routine competence. The diarists of HMS *Investigator*, Armstrong and Miertsching, do not name him as one of the hunters of caribou and hare whose exertions staved off complete catastrophe at Mercy Bay—in fact, they barely mention him at all. He is best remembered as the artist of the cruise. His paintings of the ship in the grip of the ice and almost flung over on her side, and of his Dealy Island party, painfully dragging a loaded sledge up a ramp of ice-rubble, do more than the liveliest prose to bring home to us what was endured by the stalwarts of the British Navy in the mapping of Canada's northern archipelago with wind-jammers and man-hauled sledges.

Further Readings

Armstrong, Alexander, 1857. *A Personal Narrative of the Discovery of the North-West Passage.* London: Hurst and Blackett.

Neatby, L.H., trans. 1967. *Frozen Ships: The Arctic Diary of Johann Miertsching, 1850-1854.* Toronto: Macmillan Canada. (English translation from the German.)

L.H. Neatby

WILLIAM ROBERT HOBSON
(1831–1880)

In April 1854, Dr. John Rae* heard from Inuit at Pelly Bay an account of the last fateful days of John Franklin's* expedition, missing somewhere to the west for a number of years. He also purchased relics from the Inuit that could only have belonged to members of Franklin's party. When his report of this discovery reached England, Lady Jane Franklin* mounted a private expedition, in part financed by public subscription, to search for relics of the expedition on the site. Commander of the expedition was Capt. Francis Leopold McClintock,* who had already participated in three arctic search expeditions, had wintered in the Arctic four times, and had made some of the longest man-hauled arctic sledge journeys to date.

McClintock chose Lt. William Robert Hobson as his second-in-command. Second son of a naval officer of Irish birth, Hobson had been born at Nassau in the Bahamas in 1831. A few years later, when his father—William Hobson, Sr.—was serving as the first governor of New Zealand, the Hobsons were hosts of Lady Franklin, whose husband was then governor of Tasmania. On that occasion Lady Jane took a great interest in their young son, William.

William joined the Navy in 1845 and was promoted to mate in 1852, in the interim serving aboard a number of ships on fairly routine duties. Early in 1853, he was appointed mate aboard HMS *Rattlesnake*, which had been ordered to take supplies to HMS *Plover*, waiting at Point Barrow, Alaska, in support

Portrait of William Robert Hobson. Courtesy of the Scott Polar Research Institute, Cambridge, U.K.

of Robert McClure's* HMS *Investigator* and Richard Collinson's HMS *Enterprise*. These latter ships had entered the Arctic via Bering Strait in 1850 and 1851 to search for the Franklin expedition from the west.

Sailing from England in February 1853, *Rattlesnake* entered the Pacific via the Strait of Magellan and reached Port Clarence, Alaska, just east of Nome, in August 1853. After her rendezvous with *Plover*, *Rattlesnake* settled there for the winter.

In February, Hobson, with two seamen and nine dogs, set off on a sledge journey northward across the Seward Peninsula to Chamisso Island. This had been set as the rendezvous for Frederick William Beechey* in HMS *Blossom* and John Franklin during the latter's second land expedition in 1825–27, and hence it was thought that Franklin might have headed here again. Hobson's task was to check for signs of Franklin at Chamisso Island.

He returned to *Rattlesnake* on 28 March, having reached his goal and having found no sign of Franklin. He and his men had covered 560 miles in forty-seven days despite difficulties that included the loss of his dogs by disease, the theft of provisions by the local Inuit, and an extremely ugly incident with a group of belligerent Inuit from which Hobson successfully extricated his party without bloodshed.

In mid-July, *Rattlesnake* put to sea and cruised north as far as Cape Smyth: by 11 August she was back at Port Clarence to find *Plover* waiting for her. At this point, Lt. Hobson transferred to *Plover*: after a short voyage northward, *Plover* met up with Collinson's *Enterprise,* and both ships started back south. *Plover* reached San Francisco on 28 October, where it was condemned, and Capt. Maguire, Lt. Hobson, and the rest of her crew took over the prize ship *Sitka,* captured during the siege of Petropavlovsk, and sailed her back to England.

On the basis of this arctic experience, McClintock chose Hobson as his second-in-command for his search expedition aboard *Fox.* Sailing from Aberdeen on 2 July 1857, *Fox* made her way north to Melville Bay, where she was caught in the pack ice and drifted for eight months before she could break free. The *Fox* found more secure winter quarters the next year at Port Kennedy, near the east end of Bellot Strait, and Hobson led several depot-laying trips to the west side of Boothia Peninsula.

On a reconnaissance sledge journey that winter, McClintock and his men heard Inuit reports that at least one of Franklin's ships had been crushed in the ice to the west of King William Island. The Inuit, who also possessed relics from the missing ships, were visited again early in April by McClintock and Hobson, each leading a party that included one man-hauled sledge and one dog-sledge. This time, the Inuit spoke of two ships that they had seen off King William Island.

McClintock and Hobson sledged as far as Cape Victoria together, at which point they separated. Hobson, clearly the junior officer, was ordered to search the west coast of King William Island, which was where the Inuit had reported seeing the ships. The generous McClintock, who gave Hobson his orders, proceeded down the island's east side. Significantly, when the parties separated, Hobson was already complaining of stiffness and pains in his legs.

Heading west across Ross Strait, Hobson and his men reached the coast of King William Island. Near Cape Felix they found a cairn and the remains of a camp; by the clothing and equipment scattered around, Hobson deduced it had been a hunting or observatory camp occupied for quite some time by a party from HMS *Erebus* and *Terror.* Three days later they found another cairn, originally built by James Clark Ross,* and inside it, in a cylinder, the only record that has ever been found describing, in but a few words, the fate of the crews of the *Erebus* and *Terror.* Franklin had died, and the men were about to abandon the ships and march to the mainland. Nearby lay an extraordinary heap of discarded clothing and equipment.

Hobson and his men continued south on 7 May. For nearly two weeks they struggled south along the barren west coast of King William Island despite almost constant blizzards. Having left most of his men at a snow-house camp in Terror Bay, Hobson reached Thomas Simpson's* cairn at Cape Herschel on 19 May. Next, he crossed Simpson Strait to the mainland and continued some distance farther east, finally turning back on the twenty-first. On returning to the camp in Terror Bay, he left a cairn and message for McClintock, detailing his finds thus far. From McClintock's account, it is clear that the commanding officer thought Terror Bay had been the southern limit of Hobson's journey.

By this time, Hobson's incipient scurvy had forced him to ride on the sledge; by the time he got back to the ship he could not stand without assistance. On the way back north, the party discovered more evidence of the Franklin disaster, including two skeletons in a life boat and another message, this one signed by Lt. Graham Gore well before the ships were abandoned, and hence with no further details of the final fate of the expedition. Hobson and his men returned to *Fox* on 14 June, after an absence of seventy-four days. McClintock returned soon after, having found nothing of significance not already discovered by Hobson.

Fox reached London on 23 September 1859, where Hobson was soon promoted to commander. Subsequent commands included the sloop HMS *Pantaloon* on the Cape of Good Hope station and HMS *Vigilant* on the East Indies station. Hobson was promoted to captain in 1866 and retired in 1872. He died at Pitminster, Somerset, on 11 October 1880.

Even allowing for McClintock's generosity in permitting William Robert Hobson to search the coast that promised clues to the fate of *Erebus* and *Terror,* Hobson has been largely eclipsed by his superior officer. Hobson was the first to find the important sites and relics on King William Island as well as the only two messages relating to the final phase of the expedition. For his achievements on King William Island, made in the face of vile weather and despite a progressively incapacitating attack of scurvy, Hobson deserves better than the passing recognition that has been accorded to him.

Further Readings

McClintock, F.L. 1859. *The Voyage of the "Fox" in the Arctic Seas. A Narrative of the Discovery of the Fate of Sir John Franklin and his Companions.* London: John Murray.

Jones, A.G.E. 1979. "Captain W. R. Hobson, R.N. (ret.)." *The Mariner's Mirror* 65(2): 168.

William Barr

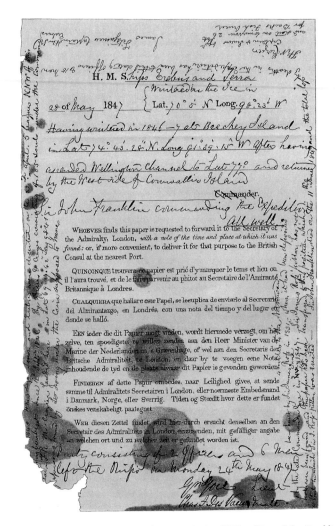

Document found by Lieutenant Hobson on 6 May 1859, telling of the Franklin expedition's fate

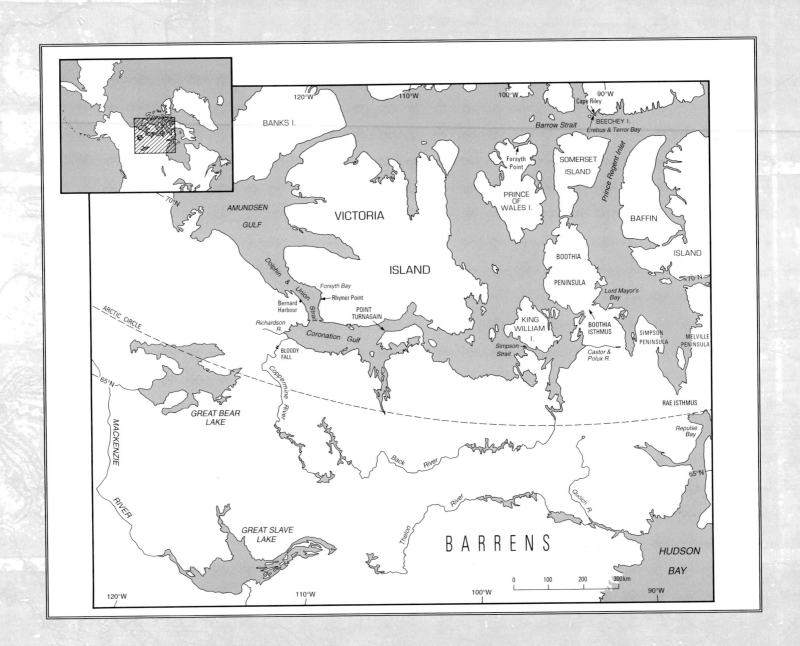

BANKS I.

120°W   110°W   100°W   90°W

Cape Riley
Barrow Strait   BEECHEY I.
Erebus & Terror Bay

Forsyth
Point

SOMERSET
ISLAND

PRINCE
OF
WALES I.

AMUNDSEN
GULF

VICTORIA

BAFFIN

ISLAND

BOOTHIA

PENINSULA

70°N

Dolphin & Union Strait

Forsyth Bay
Rhymer Point
Bernard
Harbour
POINT
TURNAGAIN
Richardson
R.

ARCTIC CIRCLE

KING
WILLIAM
I.

Lord Mayor's
Bay

BOOTHIA
ISTHMUS

SIMPSON
PENINSULA

MELVILLE
PENINSULA

BLOODY
FALL

Coronation   Gulf

Simpson
Strait

Castor &
Polux R.

65°N

Coppermine   River

RAE ISTHMUS

GREAT BEAR
LAKE

MACKENZIE

Back   River

Repulse
Bay

65°N

RIVER

River

Quoich R.

GREAT SLAVE
LAKE

Thelon

BARRENS

HUDSON
BAY

0   100   200   300 km

120°W   110°W   100°W   90°W

278

UNIT
❧5❧

**John Richardson, Thomas Simpson, Charles Codrington Forsyth,
John Rae, Diamond Jenness, Ikey Angotisiak Bolt**

This unit focuses on the region bordered on the east by Baffin Island and on the west by the maze-like delta of the Mackenzie River, which has been the scene of diverse human activity. It includes the extensive explorations along the northern continental coast by Richardson, Rae, and Thomas Simpson and the important cultural contributions of Bolt and Jenness. As well, the map for unit 5 includes the place where Rae first collected stories and artifacts from the Franklin expedition, missing since 1845, although when he brought home evidence of cannibalism among surviving crew members, the British public seemed less eager to learn of the expedition's fate.

JOHN RICHARDSON
(1787–1865)

John Richardson first achieved fame as a surgeon and naturalist with the two arctic land expeditions led by John Franklin* in 1819–22 and 1825–27. A true generalist, Richardson was competent in geology, mammalogy, ichthyology, and botany—including the difficult field of lichenology—and soon became knowledgeable in ornithology, although his artist, William Swainson, usurped much of the credit that was his due. Richardson wrote three of the four volumes of *Fauna Boreali-Americana*, contributed most of the plants for Hooker's *Flora Boreali-Americana*, and edited zoological appendices for the voyages of William Edward Parry,* James Clark Ross,* George Back,* Frederick William Beechey,* Henry Kellett,* and Edward Belcher.* A formidable ichthyologist who described forty-three still-accepted genera and over two hundred new species of fish, he was also a key member of the Strickland Committee, which set the rules of zoological nomenclature.

The oldest of twelve children of Gabriel Richardson and his wife Anne, née Mundell, John was born in Dumfries, Scotland, on 5 November 1787. His father was a brewer and, for a time, provost of Dumfries. A precocious boy, John learned to read at four years of age and was apprenticed to his surgeon uncle at thirteen. During the winters he attended classes in Edinburgh, obtaining his licence from the Royal College of Surgeons in 1807. He then served seven years in

Portrait of John Richardson in 1822, by Thomas Phillips. Courtesy of the author

the Royal Navy, throughout much of the Napoleonic wars, and spent five months with the Royal Marines in Halifax, Montreal, and the Richelieu Valley during the War of 1812.

Richardson returned to Edinburgh for another winter of study, wrote a thesis on yellow fever (in Latin), and obtained his medical degree in 1816. He began medical practice in Leith, the port of Edinburgh, but his ability as a naturalist soon gained him an appointment with John Franklin's expedition. His previously unpublished journal, more direct and more succinct than Franklin's, describes the ordeal of arctic exploration in birchbark canoes and the harrowing return trek across the Barrens, on which eleven of twenty members of the party perished. Richardson details events on fifty-one days not covered by Franklin's public narrative. He frankly reports some items that Franklin omitted—for example, how the starving men, reduced to eating year-old caribou robes from the refuse of the previous winter's camp, found warble-fly larvae a delicacy.

During the second Franklin expedition, Richardson, by canoe and ice sledge, mapped most of the shoreline of Great Bear Lake, the fourth largest lake in North America. In the following summer, after parting with Franklin at the mouth of the Mackenzie, Richardson's party turned east to explore and map 863 miles of unknown coastline as far as the Coppermine River, thus linking up with the coastal survey conducted to the east of that river during the first Franklin expedition. He then made one of the most remarkable journeys of any bird-watcher before or since: in order to join his assistant naturalist, Thomas Drummond, in time to study the spring bird migration on the Saskatchewan River, Richardson left Great Slave Lake on Christmas Day and walked over 900 miles through the snow, to arrive at Carlton on 12 February 1827.

When the return of John Franklin's third and final attempt to find the Northwest Passage—this time by ship— was overdue, Richardson and fellow doctor John Rae,* in 1848, made the fastest canoe trip on record, leaving Sault Ste. Marie on 3 May and arriving at the mouth of the Mackenzie on 3 August. After a month of futile searching along the familiar arctic shore, Richardson, then sixty years old, kept up with the younger men on the fifteen-day overland march back to Great Bear Lake.

In his medical career, Richardson became the chief medical officer at Haslar Hospital, Gosport, at the time the largest hospital in the world and the largest brick building in the British Empire. He consulted with Florence Nightingale, raised the quality of nursing care in the Navy, improved the treatment of mental disease in sailors, and introduced general anaesthesia into naval surgery.

Sir John Richardson was knighted in 1846 and was made Companion of the Bath in 1850, received the Royal Medal of the Royal Society of London in 1856, and was granted the degree of LL.D. from Trinity College, Dublin, in 1857. He died near Grasmere on 5 June 1865 and is buried near William Wordsworth. His name is perpetuated by numerous plants, fish, birds, and mammals (including Richardson's ground squirrel), and by such geographical features as the Richardson Mountains and Richardson River. As David A.

Stewart has said:

> He had in his life many of the conventional honours and some special marks of distinction as well. His was perhaps a life of industry more than a life of genius, but it was a full, good life, and in many ways a great life. It is not every day that we meet in one person— surgeon, physician, sailor, soldier, administrator, explorer, naturalist, author, and scholar, who has been eminent in some roles and commendable in all.

Further Readings

Hooker, William Jackson. 1840. *Flora Boreali-Americana, or the Botany of the Northern Parts of British America.* London: Henry G. Bohn.

Houston, C. Stuart, ed. 1984. *Arctic Ordeal: The Journal of John Richardson, Surgeon-Naturalist with Franklin.* Montreal: McGill-Queen's University Press.

_____. 1988. "John Richardson, Deserving of Greater Recognition." *Canadian Field Naturalist* 102: 558–63.

Johnson, Robert E. 1976. *Sir John Richardson, Arctic Explorer, Natural Historian, Naval Surgeon.* London: Taylor and Francis.

Richardson, John. 1829, 1831, 1836. *Fauna Boreali-Americana, or the Zoology of the Northern Parts of British America.* Part First, *the Mammals.* Part Second, *The Birds* (with William Swainson). London: John Murray. Part Third, *The Fish.* London: Richard Bentley.

Stewart, David A. 1931. "Sir John Richardson: Surgeon, Physician, Sailor, Explorer, Naturalist, Scholar." *British Medical Journal* 1: 110–12.

C. Stuart Houston

THOMAS SIMPSON (1808–1840)

Thomas Simpson was born in the north of Scotland and graduated from the University of Aberdeen with more than mere competence. He was enrolled in the service of the Hudson's Bay Company, and in the New World he exemplified the popular conception of the clever academic launched into society. He expressed the utmost contempt for his colleagues and, in a letter, assured his brother Alexander that his talents would secure him speedy advancement. This arrogance made him most unpopular in the service and caused George Simpson,* in doubt of his kinsman's fitness to command, to appoint Chief Factor Peter Warren Dease to lead the expedition that he was planning to extend the northern coastal survey earlier initiated by John Franklin* and John Richardson.* Although the leadership escaped him, Thomas Simpson was made responsible for the actual survey work, an arrangement that worked admirably. Dease and Simpson's first task was to fill the gap between Franklin's Return Reef and Point Barrow, Alaska. Simpson proved his zeal and adaptability on this 1837 assignment. When the boats were blocked by ice, he took to the shore to do the work on foot; on seeing that the ice had receded, he finished the work in a borrowed *umiak,* a skin boat used by Eskimo and Inuit women. No one applauded his success more than himself: "Mine alone is the victory," he wrote. "Dease is an unworthy, indolent, illiterate soul."

Portrait of Thomas Simpson. Courtesy of the Hudson's Bay Company Archives, Provincial Archives of Manitoba

In the next season, 1838, when an eastward thrust from Point Turnagain was halted by ice, Simpson landed and added one hundred miles to the map on foot. The summer of 1839 proved more friendly. Simpson and Dease sailed through Simpson Strait, which divides King William Island from the continent, passed the estuary of Back's Fish River (now Back River)—to become grimly memorable 15 years later—and reached Boothia Isthmus at the mouth of the Castor and Pollux River. The ruthless Simpson still did not spare the boat crews; overruling the kindly Dease, he slowed the return voyage to map parts of the south shores of King William and Victoria islands, forcing the crews to ascend the Mackenzie River in subzero weather with ice masses already floating downstream.

Dease now took the European leave to which both explorers were entitled. Simpson made application for the sole command of an expedition to complete the outline of the north shore. But the governor still mistrusted his cousin's fitness for command, so Thomas Simpson transferred his request to the directors in London. Word of its acceptance was slow in arriving, and consequently the impatient young man—overwrought, frustrated, and fearing that Dease would reap the honour for work already done—also applied for leave. With an escort of four mixed-bloods, he set out for St. Paul, en route to New York. On the American prairie, Simpson met a violent death that has never been fully explained.

Alexander Simpson vowed that his brother had fallen a victim to the "long-treasured animosity" of the mixed-bloods. The mixed-bloods who survived the fatal brawl made a report that was plausible and contained a most convincing portrayal of Simpson's profound despondency. They were crossing the prairie in some fear of hostile Indians when Simpson was seized with the conviction that his escorts were plotting to murder him, and he ordered a return to Red River, alleging ill health as the reason. Told that a doctor could be had in a settlement nearby, he replied that "no doctor could do him any good. He did not need one."

Asked one evening whether they should encamp, he answered moodily that "that was just as the others chose." They were pitching the tent when Simpson shot two of them with his double-barrelled gun. He came forward declaring that he had done no wrong, that they had plotted to murder him. The two who remained mounted their horses and galloped off to join a wagon train that was not far behind. The next day, one of them returned with four men who testified that they found two bodies lying in the open, while Simpson was stretched in his tent with the top of his head blown off.

Depositions were taken in Iowa and at Red River, but the matter ended there. The Company had no jurisdiction over the conduct of its servants in foreign territory, and the Iowa justice of the peace on the rude, unpoliced frontier was doubtless willing to accept a report that was quite probable and that spared him the labour of further investigation.

It occurred, however, that Thomas Simpson's death was a twofold tragedy. Had he lived to continue the survey of King William Island, he might have saved over one hundred lives by averting the HMS *Erebus* and *Terror* catastrophe.

Further Readings

Simpson, Alexander. 1845. *The Life and Travels of Thomas Simpson, the Arctic Discoverer.* London: Richard Bentley.

Simpson, Thomas. 1843. *Narrative of the Discoveries on the North Coast of America; Effected by the Officers of the Hudson's Bay Company during the Years 1836–39.* London: Richard Bentley.

L.H. Neatby

CHARLES CODRINGTON FORSYTH
(ca. 1810–1873)

Charles Codrington Forsyth's career in the Arctic was very brief. He was the commander of the first, and least successful, of Lady Jane Franklin's* private expeditions in search of her husband, John, and the crews of HMS *Erebus* and *Terror,* missing since 1845. The expedition, based upon the schooner *Prince Albert*, 89 3/4 tons, "merely made the voyage to the Polar Sea and back," in the words of Richard King.* It achieved nothing, although it was the means by which news of the discovery of Franklin's wintering site on Beechey Island was brought back to Britain.

The circumstances of the expedition are, however, of interest. It was so badly organized and had such a heterogeneous collection of participants that its commander would have had to be a genius to make it succeed. Forsyth was certainly no genius, but he was a conspicuously meritorious naval officer, and his exploits both before and after the expedition were such as would lead one to suppose that he was an ideal candidate for such an appointment. Undoubtedly, had he been fortunate enough to find himself on the quarterdeck of one of the naval vessels that sailed north instead of on a civilian ship with a difficult—not to say mutinous—

"Dangerous Position of the Prince Albert." From W.P. Snow's *Voyage of the 'Prince Albert'* (1851)

crew, his name would have a prominent place in the polar hagiography of the period instead of being virtually forgotten.

Forsyth entered the Navy on 28 December 1826. His early service was spent on antislavery operations on the African coast. Moving to the South Atlantic station, he was posted to the famous HMS *Beagle* under Capt. R. Fitzroy. While belonging to that vessel, he was active in surveying operations and had much detached duty. He passed the lieutenant's examination on 25 November 1836, but such was the promotion blockage that he was not actually promoted until 1843, by which time he had been employed on operations in Burma and on surveying duties in Australia, where he met the Franklins, Sir John being governor of Van Diemen's Land (Tasmania). As lieutenant, he participated in further antislavery operations and in active service in support of the army on the South African coast. He was promoted commander in 1849, a mere six years after being made lieutenant, and this clearly indicates the high opinion of him held in the Admiralty.

When the first mention of a private expedition in search of Franklin was bruited, Forsyth volunteered his services to Lady Franklin, who accepted him with alacrity, appointing him to the command. He had obtained permission from the Admiralty by 27 April 1850 and was the recipient of advice from a number of prominent arctic figures, among them Frederick William Beechey,* Francis McClintock,* and William Edward Parry.* However, even though Forsyth was to command the expedition, he had nothing to do with the appointment of the mates of the ship or its crew, who were whalers selected by William Hogarth, a confidant of Lady Franklin at Aberdeen, or of the "chief officer" of the expedition, William Parker Snow, who was selected by Lady Franklin herself. Nor was Forsyth involved in the choice of vessel.

The expedition left Aberdeen on 5 June 1850. It was a disaster. Forsyth was completely out of his depth and could not cope with the novel situation on board. The "culture shock" of a civilian vessel was too much. The mates were incompetent, the crew independent-minded, and Snow was insufferable. "I had not a soul that I could associate with without my condescension being imposed upon, nor could I leave anyone in charge of the vessel." During the 1850 season, there were many naval ships in Barrow Strait, and Forsyth never lost an opportunity to consort with their officers.

The instructions of the expedition were for the vessel to penetrate Prince Regent Inlet, to establish winter quarters, and then for two travelling parties to examine the western coast of Boothia. Clearly, this was the very area that required searching, and one of the great unknowns of polar history revolves around the question of whether the *Prince Albert* parties would have been able to obtain early information concerning the fate of Franklin. The ship duly entered the inlet, but Forsyth, after seeking the opinion of the mates, of the crew, and of Snow, decided on 22 August 1850 that the ice could not be penetrated and retraced his path. Passing near Cape Riley, Snow went ashore and obtained news of the relics that had been found by one of the other expeditions, relics indicating that Franklin had wintered nearby. It seems clear, in retrospect, that this was a godsend to Forsyth, who now had a splendid excuse for abandoning the expedition and for returning to Britain. This he determined to do. He was careful to ensure that, on meeting HMS *North Star*, a vessel also returning home but a faster sailer than *Prince Albert*, he did not give news of the discovery of the wintering site to Mr. Saunders, her commander. Forsyth did not wish Saunders to steal his thunder.

In any event, the reception accorded Forsyth was all that he could have desired, although the Franklin *ménage* was furious at his early return. Barrow considered that he had accomplished "one of the most extraordinary voyages ever performed in the polar seas," while Forsyth commented that he had received letters that showed the return had "given fresh hopes to many an aching heart." There was also much favourable comment in the press.

The aftermath of the voyage is also of interest. Forsyth was not involved in the future planning, but Snow certainly was. He published his journals as *Voyage of the 'Prince Albert' in Search of Sir John Franklin* (1851), and the book was intended to serve Lady Franklin's aim of raising fresh funds for a further expedition and, for its author, as a means of securing his promotion. With the arrival of William Kennedy from Canada, however, Snow's place in Lady Franklin's estimation rapidly declined, and he never again went to the Arctic. The second *Prince Albert* expedition is history.

Forsyth returned, with, we imagine, a sigh of relief, to an orthodox naval career. After having been inspecting-commander of the Coast Guard at Berwick-on-Tweed and Brighton, he was appointed to the command of HMS *Hornet,* a steam vessel. This was the high spot for Forsyth, since he found himself engaged in two wars, both in the Far East theatre. These were hostilities against the Russians on the Siberian coast between 1854 and 1855 as part of the Crimean War, and against the Chinese in 1856 and 1857. Forsyth conducted himself with distinction, especially in the latter operations, and *Hornet* was engaged in several battles. In one, she fought no fewer than 150 "war junks" and defeated them. He was promoted captain on 10 August 1857, and received the command of HMS *Valorous* at the Cape and then of coastguard vessels on the Humber. He retired in April 1870 and died in 1873.

Despite the brevity and lack of distinction of his arctic career, Charles Codrington Forsyth's name endures on the map of northern Canada. Two localities are named after him: Forsyth Bay and Forsyth Point on Prince of Wales Island.

Further Readings

Snow, William Parker. 1851. *Voyage of the 'Prince Albert' in Search of Sir John Franklin: A Narrative of Every-Day Life in the Arctic Seas.* London: Longman.

Stone, Ian Rodney. 1978. "Profile: William Parker Snow, 1817–1895." *Polar Record* 19: 163–65.

_____. 1993. "An Episode in the Franklin Search: The *Prince Albert* Expedition, 1850." Parts 1 and 2. *Polar Record* 29: 127–42 and 197–208.

Ian R. Stone

JOHN RAE (1813–1893)

Dr. John Rae, who spent twenty-two years in British North America, accurately mapped more miles of North America's unknown northern coastline—excluding Hudson Bay—than did any other explorer. Rae was a frugal Orkney Islander, and his explorations were the most thrifty ever undertaken. Unusually adaptable and a crack shot, he learned native methods of living off the land. Remarkably fit, he set records that have never been surpassed for speed and endurance on snowshoes.

John Rae was born on 30 September 1813 in the Hall of Clestrain, near Stromness in the Orkney Islands. At age sixteen, he went to Edinburgh to study medicine and qualified as licentiate of the Royal College of Surgeons of Edinburgh in 1833.

His first medical job was as a surgeon on the *Prince of Wales*, the Hudson's Bay Company supply ship. A sailing ship of 400 tons, it carried thirty-one Orkneymen bound for employment at distant fur-trading posts. After loading the season's furs at Moose Factory, the *Prince of Wales* was turned back by heavy ice in Hudson Strait and was forced to winter at Charlton Island in James Bay. There, Rae successfully treated his scurvy-afflicted men with cranberries and tender sprouts of the wild pea.

Instead of returning to England, Rae accepted an offer from the Hudson's Bay Company of five years' employment as "clerk and surgeon." House calls were often ardu-

Dr. John Rae. Photograph courtesy of the Hudson's Bay Company Archives, Provincial Archives of Manitoba

ous; on one occasion he walked nearly 25 miles to reach a patient. Another time he walked 105 miles to Fort Albany, covering 31 miles the first day and 74 miles the second. He later commented that "a long day's march on snowshoes is about the finest exercise a man can take."

In 1844, Hudson's Bay Company Governor George Simpson* proposed that Rae complete the survey of the northern coastline of North America. After studying surveying in Toronto, Rae left York Factory in June 1846 with ten men and two twenty-two foot boats. In April 1847, the expedition crossed Rae Isthmus to reach Lord Mayor's Bay, mapping the shore of Simpson Peninsula on the return journey. They then explored the west coast of Melville Peninsula, the two legs adding up to 650 miles of new coastline mapped. For the most part they lived off the land; Rae shot nearly as much game as the other twelve men together.

Soon after Rae's return, Dr. John Richardson* offered him the position of second-in-command on the first search expedition for the missing John Franklin.* They left Sault Ste. Marie on 4 May 1848, and in the fastest canoe travel in history they reached the mouth of the Mackenzie River on 3 August. Turning east, Richardson and Rae searched the coast as far as the mouth of the Coppermine River, 850 miles of coast first explored by Richardson in 1826. They found no trace of Franklin.

Richardson returned home, but Rae attempted another summer of search. Unfortunately, ice conditions prevented him from crossing to Victoria Island. Rae's Inuit interpreter drowned at Bloody Fall on the Coppermine River that summer, the only fatality in any of his expeditions.

In 1851, Rae set out on his third expedition with two men, two sledges, and five dogs. After crossing Dolphin and Union Strait, they explored 190 miles of Victoria Island coastline on foot. They next used two boats to complete the 460 miles of exploration of the southern and eastern shorelines of Victoria Island. When Rae turned back, Franklin's ships HMS *Erebus* and *Terror* were trapped in the ice only about 50 miles to the east, although he did not know it. On the return journey, Rae found two pieces of wood that had been parts of a ship, almost certainly one of Franklin's. Continuing on his way home, Rae walked from Fort Chipewyan to Crow Wing, Minnesota—1,720 miles in 54 days.

Rae's fourth and final expedition in 1853 was designed to complete the survey of the continental coastline for the Hudson's Bay Company. He explored the Quoich River for over 200 miles, wintered at Repulse Bay, and set out in March 1854. At Pelly Bay, the Inuit gave him second-hand news of the fate of the Franklin expedition—other Inuit had seen dead and dying men about four years earlier. Rae mapped 266 miles of coastline along the west side of Boothia Peninsula, leaving 150 miles south of Bellot Strait unexplored. He proved that King William Island was indeed an island, separated from Boothia Peninsula by what is now called Rae Strait.

Back at Repulse Bay, Inuit brought him a silver plate, a medal, and several forks and spoons with names or initials of Franklin and his officers. Rae did not risk his men in searching further for the bodies of Franklin's men, but instead rushed back to England to recall the other search parties, which were widely scattered in the wrong areas of the Arctic.

When Rae presented his report and his Franklin relics to the Admiralty on 22 October 1854, he forthrightly told of the Inuit account of cannibalism practised by the British sailors. In spite of strong opposition from Lady Franklin,* who was displeased with Rae for passing on what she considered an outrageous account, Rae and his men received the £10,000 reward for ascertaining the fate of Franklin's party.

In 1857, Rae moved to Hamilton, Ontario, where he practised as a surgeon. Two years later, he accompanied James Carnegie, Earl of Southesk, to Fort Garry, helping him to make preparations for his prairie hunting trip. Rae married Kate Thompson in Toronto, in January 1860, and then returned to England. That year he surveyed for the Atlantic Telegraph Survey, via the Faroe Islands, Iceland, and Greenland. In 1861, he guided two wealthy English sportsmen, Henry Chaplin and Sir Frederic Johnstone, on a hunting trip in what is now southern Saskatchewan. His final Canadian expedition, in 1864, for the Canadian Telegraph Survey, explored the Carlton Trail, the Yellowhead Pass, and the Fraser River.

After two years in his native Orkney Islands, he and his wife retired to London. He wrote one book, twenty papers, and published forty-five letters in *Nature,* but his arctic correspondence, edited by E.E. Rich, was not published until 1953. He received an honorary LL.D. degree from Edinburgh University.

Rae died at his home in London on 22 July 1893, not quite eighty years old. He was interred in the churchyard of

St. Magnus Cathedral, Kirkwall, Orkney Islands, where a fine memorial was later erected by public subscription. His wife, childless, lived until 1919.

What were the outstanding characteristics of John Rae? Perhaps one is impressed first by his great physical strength and remarkable powers of endurance. He walked 6,504 miles during four exploring expeditions, and he travelled another 6,634 miles in small boats. He surveyed and mapped 1,751 miles of previously unexplored territory, including 1,538 miles of northern coastline. He was intelligent, an accurate observer, a competent writer, and an accomplished doctor. He was pleasant, cheerful, generous, and sensitive. He was frugal, conducting his surveys more economically than anyone before or since. He was sympathetic to the natives and willing to learn their methods of travel, hunting, and building snow houses. And he was candidly honest to the point of forfeiting the knighthood he so richly deserved.

Further Readings

Bunyan, Ian et al. 1993. *No Ordinary Journey: John Rae, Arctic Explorer, 1813–1893*. Montreal: McGill-Queen's University Press.

Rae, J. 1850. *Narrative of an Expedition to the Shores of the Arctic Sea in 1846 and 1847*. London: T. and W. Boon.

Rich, E.E., ed. 1953. *John Rae's Correspondence with the Hudson's Bay Company on Arctic Exploration, 1844-1855*. London: Hudson's Bay Record Society.

Richards, R.L. 1985. *Dr. John Rae*. Whitby: Caedmon of Whitby.

C. Stuart Houston

Portrait of John Rae. Courtesy of the Hudson's Bay Company Archives, Provincial Archives of Manitoba

DIAMOND JENNESS
(1886–1969)

In the spring of 1913, Diamond Jenness, a young New Zealand-born anthropologist, was invited to participate in a four-year scientific expedition to the Canadian Arctic. He accepted, and so began an illustrious sixty-five-year career devoted to the study of Canada's native peoples. Diamond Jenness—ethnologist, linguist, archaeologist, musicologist, and physical anthropologist—ranks among the prominent Canadian social scientists of this century.

Born on 10 February 1886 in Wellington, Jenness attended local schools and colleges, graduating from the University of Wellington in 1908 with First Class Honours in Classics. Upon graduation, he entered Balliol College, Oxford, where he planned to continue reading in Classics. However, a friendship struck with Marius Barbeau (later to become a celebrated Canadian folklorist) sparked Jenness's interest in anthropology, an interest that ultimately led to a Diploma in Anthropology in 1911, and an Oxford Master of Arts five years later.

Jenness quickly found his curiosity about anthropology blossoming into a vocation. In 1911, he was appointed Oxford Scholar to Papua, New Guinea, where he spent twelve months studying the Northern Entrecasteaux. Upon his return to New Zealand, he was asked to join the Canadian Arctic Expedition, an ambitious government-funded scientific enterprise under the direction of the well-known arctic explorers Vilhjalmur Stefansson* and R.M. Anderson. In June 1913, Jenness found himself aboard the refitted whaling vessel *Karluk* steaming north-

Photograph of Diamond Jenness. Courtesy of Canadian Museum of Civilization, #67220

ward to the Bering Strait and beyond to the Beaufort Sea.

The voyage of the *Karluk* was destined to be a tragic one. In the autumn of 1913, the small vessel became locked in the sea ice off the northern coast of Alaska. Unable to free itself, the ship drifted helplessly westward towards the Siberian Sea, where it was finally crushed in the ice off Wrangel Island. Eight men perished in their bid to reach the mainland. By a stroke of fortune, Jenness was not aboard the *Karluk* when she drifted off; he, Stefansson, and several others had left the ship earlier on a routine hunting trip. Abandoning the hopeless task of searching for the *Karluk*, which was lost to sight when they returned, the hunting party headed for Barrow, Alaska, to rendezvous with the remaining two vessels of the expedition, the *Alaska* and the *Mary Sachs*.

Jenness spent his first arctic winter at Harrison Bay, Alaska, where he learned to speak Inuktitut, gathered information about Western Eskimo customs and folklore, and experienced at first-hand the precarious existence of the northern hunter. In the spring of 1914, he set out along the coast to the expedition's base camp at Bernard Harbour in the Coronation Gulf region. Here he engaged in one of the most important goals of the Canadian Arctic Expedition—the study of the Copper Inuit of Victoria Island, a people first brought to the attention of the "civilized" world by Stefansson only four years earlier.

When Jenness arrived in the Coronation Gulf region, only a handful of Europeans had visited the land of the Copper Inuit.

Merchants had only just begun to ply their trade in the area, and the missionaries and North West Mounted Police were yet to arrive. As a consequence, the Copper Inuit remained largely unaffected by contact with the outside world. Jenness, therefore, was charged with recording a virtually pristine aboriginal way of life that would change radically within a generation.

Jenness spent two years with these Central Inuit people, living for one year as the adopted son of the hunter Ikpukhuak and his shaman wife Higalik. During that time, he hunted and travelled with his "family," sharing both their festivities and their famine. The monographs and publications that resulted from this field work have been recognized by scholars as "the most comprehensive description of a single Eskimo tribe ever written."

After serving with the Canadian Expeditionary Force in France during World War I, Jenness returned to Canada to marry Frances Ellen Bleakney and to take up a position with the National Museum of Canada. He continued to write up his research from the Canadian Arctic Expedition and also conducted several "salvage ethnology" programs among the Sarcee, Carrier, Sekani, Ojibway, and Coast Salish Indians—groups thought at the time to be doomed to cultural extinction. *The Indians of Canada* (1932), the partial fruit of this labour, is still considered the definitive work on the aboriginal peoples of Canada.

During his tenure with the National Museum, Jenness published two seminal articles on northern archaeology. The first paper identified a new prehistoric culture in the eastern Arctic—the Dorset culture—which Jenness believed to have preceded the Thule culture (the ancestors of the contemporary Inuit) by a millennium or more. The second paper hypothesized the Old Bering Sea culture of the Bering Strait area, a complex which Jenness believed not only preceded the Thule culture in the western Arctic but which was ancestral to it. Considered radical at the time of their publication, these theories are now widely accepted, having been vindicated by carbon-14 dating and subsequent field research.

Jenness's interest in the Arctic never waned. As late as 1968, he was still articulating his concern for the Inuit struggle to survive. Among his last works was a series of five volumes published by The Arctic Institute of North America that reviewed government policies toward the Inuit of Alaska, Canada, and Greenland.

Numerous universities awarded Diamond Jenness honorary doctorate degrees during his lifetime. He was also named a Fellow of such societies as the Royal Society of Canada, the Royal Danish Geographical Society, and The Arctic Institute of North America. In 1962, the Royal Canadian Geographical Society awarded him its highest accolade, the Massey Medal. His most prestigious laurels, however, were granted posthumously, four months after his death: In March 1970, Diamond Jenness's adopted country presented his widow with the Companion of the Order of Canada Medallion.

Further Readings

Collins, Henry B. and W.E. Taylor Jr. 1970. "Diamond Jenness (1886–1969)." *Arctic* 23: 71–91.

Jenness, Diamond. 1955. *The Indians of Canada*. Revised edition Ottawa: National Museum of Canada Bulletin No. 65.

Jenness, Stuart E. 1991. *The Diary of Diamond Jenness 1913–1916: Ethnologist with the Canadian Arctic Expedition in Northern Alaska and Canada*. Hull: Canadian Museum of Civilization.

Kulchisky, Peter. 1993. "Anthropology in the Service of the State: Diamond Jenness and Canadian Indian Policy." *Journal of Canadian Studies* 28(2): 21–50.

Richling, Barnett. 1989. "An Anthropologist's Apprenticeship: Diamond Jenness' Papuan and Arctic Fieldwork." *Culture*: 9(1): 71–86.

James Helmer

IKEY ANGOTISIAK BOLT
(1894–1981)

The arrival of the Canadian Arctic Expedition (1913–18) was of profound influence in exposing the Copper Inuit of Coronation Gulf and Victoria Island to the culture, lifestyle, and technology of White North America. And Ikey Angotisiak Bolt was one of the most outstanding members of that party. He was an Alaskan Eskimo who, far from his native land, made his home among these people and built a reputation for integrity and community service that will not easily be forgotten.

Ikey Bolt was born in Point Hope, Alaska, on 19 January 1894, in a whale-hunting culture that provided him with stories of the hunt with which he would regale his listeners all his life. Recruited in his late teens as an interpreter for the Canadian Arctic Expedition, he made his initial trip to Canada. Although he was principally assigned to assist Dr. R.M. Anderson, he was quite familiar with other expedition members.

A contemporary saga of those years was the trading ventures of Charlie Klengenberg, a Danish entrepreneur who was the first white trader in the Coronation Gulf-Victoria Island region. His report on the native people of the area, in fact, initiated Vilhjalmur Stefansson's* interests. With his Alaskan wife, Unalena, Klengenberg raised a large family, of which Etna was the eldest daughter. Years after the conclusion of the Canadian Arctic Expedition in 1924, Etna Klengenberg married Ikey Bolt at Herschel Island.

Photo courtesy of Mrs. Etna Bolt, Coppermine, Northwest Territories

Serving as traders in the so-called Klengenberg empire of small posts, Ikey and Etna settled at Rymer Point on southwest Victoria Island. A lifelong member of the Anglican Church, Ikey was invited by Bishop Stringer to assist the newly arrived Anglican missionary, the Reverend J. Harold Webster. With this appointment began a long ministry as catechist in the Anglican Church and regular church services in more remote settlements, as well as in the Coppermine area, where Ikey Bolt spent his later years.

During his life, he served as an ice-pilot for supply ships, first serving the Canalaska Trading Company and then the Hudson's Bay Company. While serving as interpreter with the Canadian Arctic Expedition, Ikey Bolt began to lose the sight of one eye, which he blamed on an accidental spotting of the sun through a telescope. Yet he put his handicap into healthy perspective: with only one eye functioning, he believed that he was forever immune to seasickness. Accordingly, he saw himself as a "natural" for this work as an ice-pilot.

By the late 1940s, the Bolts had moved to Coppermine, where Ikey trapped in winter and worked the ships during summer. But as the government of Canada increased its interest and investment in the North—initially through schools and nursing stations—bilingual native people were in special demand. Accordingly, Ikey was employed as care-taker and interpreter for the first federal school at Coppermine, a task which included operating a highly unpredictable diesel plant. Recognition for his services culminated in his being awarded the Coronation Medal in 1953, which he proudly wore in the following year as he acted as interpreter for Prince Philip, the Duke of Edinburgh, on his royal visit.

Ikey and Etna Bolt had one daughter of their own, but she died early in life. They did, however, raise an adopted family who are today raising their own families; the name of Bolt is numbered among the leading families in Coppermine.

The best appreciation of Ikey Angotisiak Bolt's contribution to the region can only be understood in the context of the times. Here is a native Alaskan whose people had been long exposed to the influence of southerners in the traumatic whaling era, a period of mixed blessings if ever there was one. In joining the Canadian Arctic Expedition, he made contact with a people who were literally just emerging from the Stone Age, a people who had no steady contact with explorers until the expedition arrived. They hunted with harpoons and with bows and arrows, and they had no recourse to any products of southern technology except for bits of iron traded with distant neighbours who had obtained them from abandoned ships. The introduction of a different way of life—new methods of trapping animals to be exchanged for trade goods—had all the potential for cultural devastation and the erosion of even the best of their indigenous philosophy. But the presence and influence of natives who had themselves survived similar upheavals and yet maintained a strong sense of spiritual and cultural values made a profound difference. The people of the Arctic today owe an immense debt to all the Ikey Bolts of the North, and especially to the man who inspired this profile.

John R. Sperry

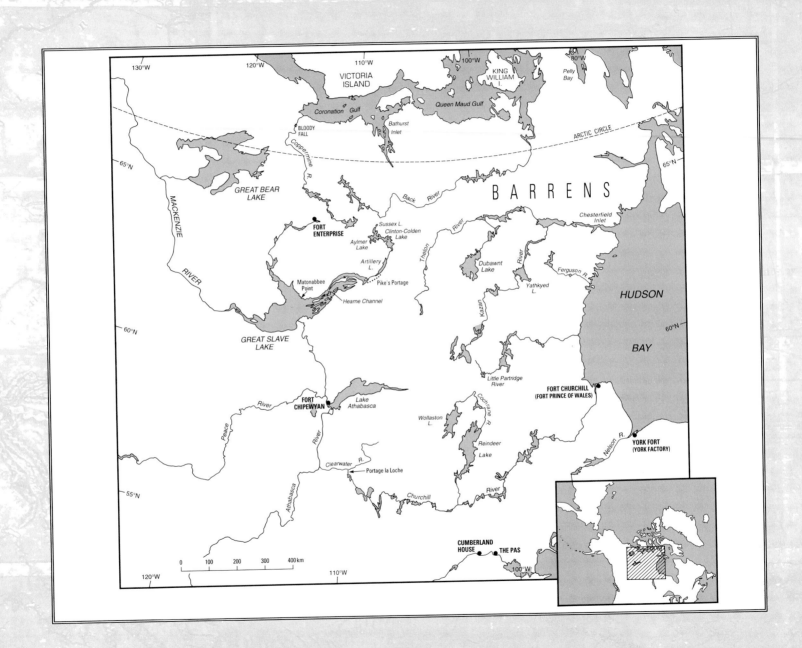

UNIT
❧ 6 ❧

Thanadelther, Matonabbee, Samuel Hearne, George Back,
Richard King, Joseph Burr Tyrrell, Ernest Thompson Seton, John Hornby

This sixth unit encompasses the huge subarctic land-mass sweeping between Hudson Bay and the Mackenzie River. This region is known variously as the Barrens, the barrenlands, or the Barren Grounds, and is as rich in mystique as it is barren of trees. This most inhospitable and highly romanticized part of the Arctic stretches in a great arc north of the tree line from Hudson Bay to the eastern reaches of Great Slave and Great Bear lakes. The contributions of aboriginal peoples, such as Matonabbee and Thanadelther, become increasingly important in this land, which differs so remarkably from the more familiar forested realms of continental North America. Tyrrell identified much of its mineral wealth, while Seton and Hornby clearly felt the mystical and romantic allure of the Barrens.

THANADELTHER
(ca. 1700–1717)

The Thanadelther of Chipewyan legend was one of the most important and enduring figures of northwestern Canada and perhaps the only woman to play a truly significant part in its early history. Her importance extends far beyond her own culture. The journals of York Fort celebrate a woman they refer to as the Slave Woman, and although they never record her Indian name, which means "marten shake," Thanadelther and the Slave Woman are one and the same. Serving as guide and interpreter, she led employees of the Hudson's Bay Company to their first meeting with the Chipewyan in the Indians' home territory. As well, she was instrumental in establishing peace between the Cree and their traditional enemies, the Chipewyan, an absolute requisite before the Chipewyan could be brought into the trade with the Company. At the time of her early death, Capt. James Knight, governor-in-chief in Hudson Bay for the HBC, had selected the Slave Woman as his agent for making peace with all the other Northern Athapaskan-speaking Indians of Rupert's Land.

Thanadelther's story, as it is still recited by Chipewyan elders, is remarkably similar to that recorded by Capt. Knight in the daily post journal of York Fort in the period 1715–17. The legend holds that, when still a girl or very young woman, Thanadelther was captured and enslaved by the Cree. Some time after, the Cree were encamped near York Fort, where they traded furs for goods of European manufacture, items that were strange, beautiful, and wondrous to the Slave Woman. Thanadelther managed to escape her captors, but when her attempt to return to her own people proved impossible, she fled to the security of the English traders. When she arrived at York Fort, she amazed and delighted the

"Ambassadress of Peace: A Chipewyan Woman Makes Peace with the Crees, 1715," by Franklin Arbuckle. Courtesy of the Hudson's Bay Company Archives, Provincial Archives of Manitoba

English with her beauty and intelligence, for the Cree had told them that the Northern Indians—as the Chipewyan were known —were subhuman and had pointed tails like animals. Their understanding of Northern Indians now dramatically altered by their meeting with the Slave Woman, the English determined to send a mission to the Chipewyan, to provide gifts, to make peace between them and the Cree, and to bring them to trade. All these goals were realized through the service of Thanadelther as guide and ambassador. The

Company men distributed gifts—including axes, awls, knives, and muskets—and more gifts were promised if the Chipewyan brought furs to a new fort to be established for them at the mouth of the Churchill River. But first, the Northern Indians had to be trained in the use of the musket, and Thanadelther taught them to prepare the pelts of fur-bearing animals. Some Chipewyan men accompanied Thanadelther and her party back to York Fort, and beginning the next year (after Thanadelther's return, or 1717), when the new fort was built, the Northern Indians came annually to trade at Fort Churchill or the "great Stone House." To this day, the Chipewyan term for the English or English-Canadian is *theye-hotine* or "stone house dwellers."

The Hudson's Bay Company Archives provide a parallel but more detailed account of this embassy of peace and trade. Soon after the Treaty of Utrecht restored the Hudson's Bay Company's territories and forts to them in 1713, Capt. Knight assumed command at York Fort, replacing N. Jérémie, the French commandant. Knight discussed with Jérémie the prospects of establishing peace between Chipewyan and Cree, but the latter laughed at the proposal, for he had been unsuccessful at this effort for many years. Nevertheless, Knight wrote in the post journal that "I am Endeavouring to make a peace in the whole Country Round from N to SWt for a 1000 Miles."

He had placed his hope in the ability of a Chipewyan boy to be the guide and interpreter, and on the boy's death, Knight was near despair. Then in the autumn of 1714, the Slave Woman—who had just escaped her Cree captors—met English goose hunters at Ten Shilling Creek. "Almost Starv'd," she was taken to York Fort on 24 November 1714, where she strongly impressed Knight with her forcefulness and intelligence. Knight's former despair turned to hope, for the Slave Woman spoke the language, knew at least some Cree, was learning English, and knew the territory.

On 7 June 1715, Thanadelther left York to guide William Stewart and a party of about 150 Cree as the peace delegation. This group moved into the barrenlands along the edge of the woods, experiencing many hardships and much hunger. Indeed, big game was so rare that the Cree were forced to split into many smaller parties, some of which took the opportunity to return to York. The Slave Woman, Stewart, and about a dozen Cree, however, went on. But sometime in midwinter, their spirits faltering, they were unable to continue. Thanadelther asked them to remain for ten days while she went ahead to find the Chipewyan and return. They agreed, and she left alone. On the morning of the tenth day, as Stewart and the Cree were contemplating returning to York in failure, Thanadelther arrived with a band of four hundred Chipewyan. But the four hundred Northern Indians were only a part of the population that the Slave Woman had found, for there were "above a 100 Tents of her Country Men … and that abundance more would have gon wth her to See the English Man… but she would not let them come for fear of Mischief that they should do by quarrelling but they lay'd a little ways of ready to come if any Difference had happened."

After a return journey of sixty days, the Slave Woman, Stewart, ten Chipewyan, and the dozen Cree arrived at York Fort, on 7 May 1716. They had been gone nearly a year. The following seven months Thanadelther spent instructing her Chipewyan companions about desirable pelts and the proper methods of preparation. Her knowledge of the Cree language developed from indifferent to fluent, and she learned

English. She was probably married to one of her companions. She was Knight's constant advisor concerning his plans for exploration of the northwest. He planned that she and William Norton, an apprentice later to become a governor, were to leave with the Chipewyan in the spring of 1717 to contact other northern Athapaskan nations, but she fell ill, and in spite of all efforts to save her, the Slave Woman died on 5 February 1717.

In a society in which the status of women was extraordinarily low, Thanadelther was the leader and the strength of the journey across the Barrens, the forceful orator, the one of indomitable courage. Both Knight and Stewart recognized that the success of the mission was due to her as "the Chief promoter and Acter of it." On the day of her death, Knight wrote: "She was one of a Very high Spirit and of the Firmest Resolution that ever I see any Body in my Days and of great Courage & forecast."

Acknowledgements

I am indebted to the elders of the Northlands Band for the legendary material, and to Shirlee Ann Smith, Archivist of the Hudson's Bay Company Archives. All quotations are published with permission of the Hudson's Bay Company.

Further Readings

Davies, K.G., ed. 1965. *Letters from Hudson's Bay 1703–40*. London: Hudson's Bay Record Society.

Hudson's Bay Company Archives. *1714—1717 York Fort Post Journals*. HBCA B.239/a/1-3. (On deposit in the Public Archives of Manitoba, Winnipeg.)

Johnson, Alice M. 1952. "Ambassadress of Peace." *The Beaver* 283(4): 42–46.

Van Kirk, Sylvia. 1974. "Thanadelthur." *The Beaver* 304(4): 40–45.

James G.E. Smith

MATONABBEE (ca. 1736-1782)

Ask the man in the street who was the most outstanding Indian leader of the past, and he is likely to say "Sitting Bull," unless, of course, he comes from Ontario, and then he may say "Tecumseh." Yet one may doubt whether either of these was more able than the Chipewyan diplomat, trader, and explorer Matonabbee—Samuel Hearne's* guide on his final, and successful, attempt to reach the Coppermine River.

Long before white men started importing Africans to their settlements in eastern America, slavery was well known among the Indians, and Matonabbee's mother was a "slave woman" who had been traded to the Hudson's Bay Company at Fort Prince of Wales at Churchill. There Richard Norton, the fort's governor (1731–41), gave her the Chipewyan man who became Matonabbee's father.

Nearly all we know about him comes from Hearne, who was so long employed at that post. Matonabbee was early orphaned, and for a while Governor Norton adopted him. He rejoined his Chipewyan relatives after Norton retired in 1741, but he returned to Fort Prince of Wales in 1752, when Ferdinand Jacobs was appointed governor and "employed [him] in the hunting service"—i.e. supplying the fort's larder with game.

At Churchill, Matonabbee learned much. He became a "perfect master" of the Cree language, as well as his native Chipewyan; he "made some progress in English" too. Hearne records the interesting fact that Matonabbee could "tell a better story of our Saviour's birth and life than one half of those who call themselves Christians," but he never believed it! However, adds Hearne, no man could "have been more punctual in the performance of a promise" and his "adherence to truth" was "scrupulous." Physically, he

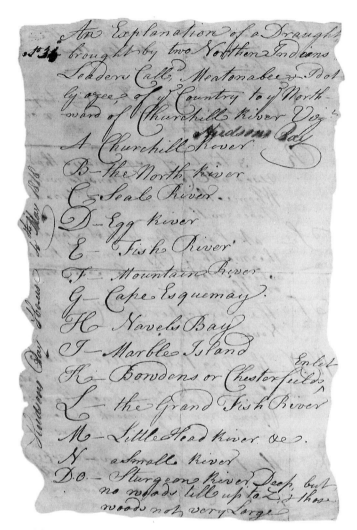

Part of the key or legend to a map drawn by Moses Norton, based on Matonabbee's and Idotli-azee's "rude sketch" of the country between Churchill and the Coppermine River. The map itself is too faint to reproduce. Courtesy of the Hudson's Bay Company Archives, Provincial Archives of Manitoba, G.2/27

grew to be "nearly six feet high," and he was "one of the finest and best proportioned men" that Hearne ever saw. He certainly did not lack courage.

In view of these qualities, Ferdinand Jacobs made a good choice in selecting Matonabbee "when but a youth as an Ambassador" to make peace between the Chipewyans and the far western Crees of Athabasca. This task was dangerous and slow, because the tribal feud was old and deep-seated. But Matonabbee was alert enough to baffle all Cree plots, and brave and patient enough to repeat his visits to them "for several years successively; and at length, by a uniform display of his pacific disposition and by rendering a long train of good offices to those Indians, in return for their treachery and perfidy," he succeeded "in not only bringing about a lasting peace, but also of establishing a trade and reciprocal interest between the two nations."

It was doubtless during these early peace-making journeys that Matonabbee took up the career of being one of those Leading Indians who were so important in the fur trade. These were men who, regularly and literally, "led" to trade other Indians, many of whom might not visit a fort twice in a lifetime. The Chipewyans, who had no convenient waterway to Churchill, commonly came there in winter, when snow provided easy hauling and rivers were bridged with ice. Their only draft animals were dogs, and they always employed their wives, as early African explorers employed professional native porters, to carry their goods and camp kit; however unchivalrous this latter practice may seem, it was simple common sense in a society that lived by hunting and fishing. For hunting was the men's job, and as Matonabbee said, they could not do it when "heavy laden." Naturally, wives were most important to the men who had most goods to transport, namely, the Leading Indians, and Matonabbee accumulated no fewer than eight of them—all fine, strong women, chosen for work, not beauty. When they reached a trading post, Leading Indians exchanged the furs they had brought for European goods, with which they would buy from Indians far up-country the furs they would carry back on their next trip to the trading post. In this role Matonabbee rendered "great services to the [Hudson's Bay] Company … by bringing a greater quantity of furs to … Churchill River than any other Indian ever did or ever will do." Yet he was still ready to do business with that pioneer of the fur traders from Montreal to the Far North, Peter Pond (as the latter told William Walker, of the Hudson's Bay Company, at Cumberland House on 15 June 1779).

It was presumably at this meeting with Matonabbee that Pond first learned of Hearne's explorations. He could hardly have had a better informant, for Matonabbee had contributed so much to them. One may perhaps date his contribution as starting in 1765. In that year Moses Norton*—Richard's mixed-blood son who now commanded at Churchill—sent him with an older Indian, Idot-li-azee, to find the route to the long-famous "coppermine." Three years later they returned, bringing copper samples and "a rude sketch, drawn with charcoal on a deer skin," of the country. With this evidence, Norton persuaded the Company's directors to send Hearne on his explorations.

It is well known that Norton's misguided planning ensured the failure of the explorer's first two attempts, and after the failure of the second, when the guide Norton had chosen had lost all interest in him, Hearne very probably owed his life to a chance encounter with Matonabbee. For the latter gave him a suit of fur clothing, which, in

September, was already becoming indispensable on the Barrens, and directed him to woods where he could make sleds and snowshoes. The two men, English and Indian, also agreed to make yet a third trip to the Coppermine, which, with Matonabbee as the real planner and effective leader, was to succeed.

Matonabbee, however, can hardly be blamed for the unhappy climax of that journey—the murder of the Inuit at Bloody Fall on 17 July 1771. That tragedy was due to the evil intentions of a crowd of Indians who attached themselves to him specifically for that purpose. Many of the Indians believed that the Inuit were "magicians" whose "incantations" caused "all the evils they experience." Matonabbee himself was free from this superstition, so much so that he and Idot-li-azee had traded to the Coppermine Inuit on his earlier journey, and he was to do so again (probably in 1773). For it could only have been from them that he received the first skin to reach Europe of the then-unknown deer that we call the Arctic Island caribou, *Rangifer tarandus pearyi*.

Matonabbee's death was a surprising one—suicide. Being an old trader at Churchill, he found news of the French destruction of the fort there in 1782 an unbearable humiliation and hanged himself, with the tragic result that "six of his wives and four children all … starved to death" in the following winter.

Further Readings

Glover, Richard, ed. 1958. *A Journey to the Northern Ocean*, by Samuel Hearne (1795). Toronto: Macmillan Canada.

Pennant, Thomas. 1784–85. *Arctic Zoology*. London: H. Hughs.

Rich E.E., ed. 1951–52. *Cumberland and Hudson House Journals*. London: Hudson's Bay Record Society.

Richard Glover

SAMUEL HEARNE (1745–1792)

Samuel Hearne was a contradictory and controversial character. He was a gentle man who avoided violence when he could, but lashed out when it was necessary to achieve his goal; he loved good clothes and food, but could go long periods without either; he drank almost no alcohol, but on his retirement joined the exclusive Bucks Club in London whose sole purpose was to get roaring drunk and go rampaging through night-time streets. As an historical figure, commentators then, and historians now, have never agreed on what manner of man he was or on the significance of his work. To one school, he was an arrant coward, too unimportant to warrant a biography and too inept to deserve respect. The opposite evaluation places him high on the roster of giants who made the Age of Discovery the most adventuresome era in history.

Hearne was born in 1745 in London. He was an indifferent schoolboy and by the age of eleven was in the Royal Navy, under the command of Adm. Samuel Hood. He saw action during the Seven Years War but left the Navy and, in 1766, became an employee of the Hudson's Bay Company, which sent him to Fort Prince of Wales at the mouth of the Churchill River.

The charter of the Hudson's Bay Company gave it virtual sovereignty over all the lands draining into the west shores of Hudson Bay, but it provided also that the Company explore, establish posts in the interior, and search for the

Portrait of Samuel Hearne. National Archives of Canada/C-020053

Northwest Passage, or Strait of Anian as it was generally termed on non-English charts. No one knows how the concept of a waterway through North America came to be, but from Juan de la Cosa, 1500, to Jonathan Carver, 1788, cartographers depicted it on their maps. The nation that discovered and controlled it would break the Spanish hold on Pacific-Orient trade and open a shorter and more profitable route to the Far East. Jacques Cartier, Martin Frobisher,* Humphrey Gilbert, John Davis,* Henry Hudson, Jens Munk,* and many others had sought it. But it was left for Samuel Hearne to prove their labours had been in vain.

During its first century, the Company had made no determined attempt to penetrate the interior and only the most half-hearted excursions were sent to seek Anian. By the 1730s, however, significant opposition to Company sovereignty and its implementation of its charter obligations had arisen in both England and America. Arthur Dobbs, surveyor-general of Ireland, initiated a twenty-year struggle to force the Company to meet its charter terms. His challenges generated enough interest to induce the House of Parliament to offer a prize of £20,000 for the discovery of a strait.

By 1769, it had been demonstrated that no such passage existed between the Churchill River and the Gulf of Mexico, and by then, too, Samuel Hearne had become dissatisfied. He disliked routine Company work. He detested Moses

Norton,* chief factor at Fort Prince of Wales, and as yet there had been no opportunity to "make a name" for himself, as he phrased it.

Rumours of extensive inland copper deposits had often come to the HBC fort at the mouth of the Churchill, but nothing had been done about them. Hearne saw his chance. He applied for and was granted permission to lead an expedition into the North, accompanied by two white men and certain Indians, to "promote ... our trade, as well as for the discovery of a North West passage, Copper Mines etc...." The attempt was a humiliating failure. Two hundred miles northwest of the fort the Indians robbed the white men and left them to reach safety as best they could.

Hearne began again in February 1770, with only native companions. He got three hundred miles inland and four hundred miles north of the Churchill before he was robbed. He turned toward home. Nevertheless, it was the farthest north any European had yet explored inland North America.

On the return to the Churchill, Hearne met Matonabbee,* an important Chipewyan leader, who offered to guide a third attempt toward the Arctic. Norton agreed, and between December 1770 and June 1772, Hearne—again the only white man—headed an expedition across the Barrens. In our day of elaborate preparations for even a minor venture, it is difficult to appreciate Hearne's courage. He proposed to, and did, walk overland to the North without any civilized supplies beyond the first few miles. Starvation and death in arctic storms were constant attendants, but, in the end, he was at the mouth of the Coppermine River on Coronation Gulf. He made only the most cursory search for copper, although he did carry home a lump of the ore which can still be seen in the British Museum, London.

The Company mounted no follow-up on this sample. Summing up his work, Hearne wrote "... my discoveries are not likely to prove of any material advantage to the Nation ... or ... to the Hudson's Bay Company, yet I have the pleasure to think that I have ... complied with [my] ... orders, and it has put a final end to all disputes concerning a North West Passage through Hudson's Bay."

But he had paid a price. He had watched the butchery of Inuit at Bloody Fall on the Coppermine River and seen starvation decimate his companions. And he was to see his work sneered at by the scientific and military worlds. Among other criticisms, they said there could be no plant life where he reported because there was none on Greenland in that latitude; the sun could never be visible for twenty-four hours as he said; and the Indians could not possibly roam over such vast areas as he claimed. Eighteen years later, Alexander Mackenzie* brazenly took credit for being the first European to reach the Arctic by land and disprove the myth of Anian. Nevertheless, between 1819 and 1822 John Franklin* covered much of Hearne's route and verified his reports.

When competition from interlopers reduced profits, the Company sent Hearne to establish the successful Cumberland House, not far from The Pas, after which he was recalled to be chief factor at Fort Prince of Wales. Profits still fluctuated, Hearne was blamed, and when the Frenchman La Perouse challenged the fort in 1782, Hearne surrendered it—an act for which he was branded a coward by his critics. But La Perouse had three ships, 146 guns, and 400 men. Hearne had no ships, 40 guns, and 39 untrained personnel. When La Perouse released his prisoner, the Company sent him back to the Churchill as chief factor. Hearne retired to London in 1787 and died there in 1792.

Samuel Hearne was the first European to cross the barrenlands to the Arctic and thus prove there is no waterway through our continent. He discovered and charted many major lakes, including Great Slave Lake, where Matonabbee Point and Hearne Channel credit his work. His record of natural history of the Barrens and the peoples who roamed over them stands unchallenged, and the establishment of Cumberland House saved the great Company from failure and set it on its way to its present eminence as the longest lived commercial venture of all time.

Further Readings

Glover, Richard, ed. 1958. *A Journey to the Northern Ocean*, by Samuel Hearne (1795). Toronto: Macmillan Canada.

Laut, Agnes Christina. 1904. *Pathfinders of the West*. Toronto: Ryerson.

Speck, Gordon. 1963. *Samuel Hearne and the Northwest Passage*. Caldwell, Idaho: Caxton Printers.

Tyrrell, Joseph Burr, ed. 1934. *Journals of Samuel Hearne and Philip Turnor*. Toronto: Champlain Society.

Gordon Speck

GEORGE BACK (1796–1878)

George Back, British admiral and arctic explorer, was born in 1796 and joined the Navy in 1808. At the age of thirteen he was wounded, made a prisoner of war, and lodged in the French fortress of Verdun. He passed several years of captivity by devoting himself to the study of drawing and mathematics.

Returning to the Navy in 1818, Back sailed as mate in HMS *Trent,* under Lt. John Franklin,* on an abortive voyage into the Spitsbergen ice. In the following year, his qualifications as artist procured him an appointment on Franklin's first overland expedition to the polar sea (1819-22).

Portrait of George Beck, from John Franklin's
Journey to the Shores of the Polar Sea (1829)

Franklin's party, consisting of five naval personnel and a contingent of Indian hunters and voyageurs from the fur posts, set up base at Fort Enterprise in the wilderness north of Great Slave Lake. Back made a tour of trading stations, canvassing for supplies, but he almost wrecked the expedition by a squalid quarrel with his fellow midshipman Robert Hood* over a Yellowknife woman. In July and August, 1821, with twenty men in two large canoes, they defied ice-pack and gale to map the arctic coast from the mouth of the Coppermine River through and beyond Bathurst Inlet. They started back to their base camp at Fort Enterprise, an overland march made hideous by cold, famine, and suspicions of murder and cannibalism. Hood and more than half the voyageur escort perished;

Franklin, with most of the remainder of the party, lay down starving and helpless at Fort Enterprise. With the strongest men, Back went forward to seek help from the roving Indians. In spite of weakness and hunger, he did not lose heart. Keeping the lagging voyageurs on the march, Back chanced upon Indians who hastened to rescue his comrades. The courage and endurance displayed by Back at that time was a greater service to discovery than any of the later expeditions made under his own command: he saved the lives of Franklin and his surgeon-naturalist John Richardson* and so preserved much of the priceless geographical and scientific data gathered by the expedition.

Between 1825 and 1827, Back was second-in-command of Franklin's second overland expedition. The lessons of the costly previous journey had been well learned; with minimum hardships and casualties, the map of the North American Arctic was vastly extended. Nearly half of a previously unknown shoreline was laid down by the two expeditions.

Back took command of a government-aided private expedition in 1833. Its mission was to find the source of the Great Fish (now Back) River, which lay to the north of Great Slave Lake, but was known only by Indian report. Back was to descend the river to the sea and bring aid to the John Ross* expedition, thought to be lost in or near the Gulf of Boothia. When the Ross party unexpectedly returned to England before the relief party's departure, Back was directed to explore the coast westward from the river's mouth. By patient groping through rock and bush, he found the source of the river in tiny Sussex Lake, and in a boat fashioned by ship's carpenters from the primaeval forest, Back, accompanied by Dr. Richard King* and Scottish servants of the Hudson's Bay Company, overcame the obstacles of partially frozen lakes and chafing rapids to explore the long and turbulent watercourse to its mouth. There he was forced by pack ice to end his journey. Except in a crisis, Back was prone to be slack and self-indulgent, and on his return home he was publicly censured by Dr. King for sloth, poor discipline, and lack of enterprise.

In the years 1836–37, Back commanded HMS *Terror* on a cruise into northern Hudson Bay. The ship was beset and drifted for months in bitter cold, heaved upon a mound of ice. When this frozen platform collapsed, the ship was nearly capsized into the waters of the bay, but she escaped with numerous leaks and a badly wrenched keel to reach a home port. On this cruise, the captain seems to have depended on his competent first lieutenant, as he had formerly depended on the industrious Dr. King. The fiasco was no fault of Back's, but his health was broken, and although he remained on the active list and attained the rank of admiral, he was never again employed afloat. He served on the Arctic Council, which directed the Franklin search, and in extreme old age was appointed to unveil the Franklin monument in Westminster Abbey.

In George Back, the "gentleman" predominated over the "officer." He managed his Fish River boat crew with tact, but he exasperated the factors of the fur trade—who professed to be his equals and whom he ought to have made a point of conciliating—by his conceit and patronizing airs. On the other hand, his aptitude for dialects permitted him to fraternize with Metis, Indian, and Inuit. He relished posing as a "great chief," but he was not a "great captain." His qualities of courage, of endurance, and of resource in calamity were best displayed in a subordinate capacity under Franklin. Nevertheless, he gave "colour" to his sphere of life by his numerous adventures and by his manner of recording them. He shows humour and good-fellowship in recounting his tippling bout with Indians and how his guide wormed brandy out of him as medicine. He had the artist's eye for scenery; his descriptions of the panorama at Portage la Loche, of the fire-scarred landscape at Artillery Lake, and of the descent of boiling rapids on the Great Fish River have an instant appeal to those who know the North. In natural and effortless prose, he depicts the crew's breathless suspense when the *Terror* listed till her lee boats touched the water and she "trembled on the brink of eternity." He has a special claim on the regard of Canadians as a pioneer of the North and as a prose artist who has described its landscapes and peoples with love and understanding.

Further Readings

Back, George. 1838. *Narrative of an Expedition in HMS Terror, 1836–37*. London: John Murray.

_____. [1836] 1970. *Narrative of the Arctic Land Expedition*. Reprint. Edmonton: M.G. Hurtig.

Franklin, John. [1828] 1971. *Narrative of a Second Expedition to the Polar Sea in the Years 1825, 1826 and 1827*. Reprint. Edmonton: M.G. Hurtig.

_____. [1823] 1969. *Narrative of a Journey to the Shores of the Polar Sea in the Years 1819, 20, 21 and 22*. Reprint. Edmonton: M.G. Hurtig.

Houston, C. Stuart, ed. 1994. *Arctic Artist: The Journal and Paintings of George Back, Midshipman with Franklin, 1819–1822*. Commentary by I.S. MacLaren. Montreal: McGill-Queen's University Press.

Neatby, L.H. 1970. *Search for Franklin*. Edmonton: M.G. Hurtig.

_____. 1958. *In Quest of the Northwest Passage*. Toronto: Longmans, Green.

Wiebe, Rudy. 1994. *A Discovery of Strangers*. Toronto: Alfred A. Knopf Canada.

L.H. Neatby

RICHARD KING (1810–1876)

Dr. Richard King was an explorer, geographer, and ethnologist who commented discerningly upon much that happened in arctic exploration in the period 1833–69. The Cassandra of this period, he accurately prophesied a good deal of the arctic map and of arctic happenings without, however, gaining public acceptance for his predictions.

Born sometime in the period between January and May 1810, King was educated at St. Paul's School, the Apothecaries Society, and Guy's and St. Thomas Hospital, all in London. Recently qualified with the Royal College of Surgeons, he joined the expedition of George Back,* down the Back River in 1833–35, as naturalist, medical officer, and second-in-command. On that trip, he differed with his commander on the nature of Boothia and upon style and method in arctic exploration. Back's method was to travel "heavy," with a primarily naval and military party that favoured equipment from home; King's was to travel "light," with a small party and fur-trade equipment, methods, and personnel.

On his return to England, King published his own account of Back's expedition and speculated (correctly) that Boothia was peninsular. Back's River was the most suitable means, he said, to delineate Boothia and so complete a Northwest Passage by a land approach. He warned against Back's 1836 sea expedition through Foxe Basin, but could find no sponsor for his own alternative plan. A difficult man, he had alienated the Navy, the Hudson's Bay Company, the Royal Geographical Society, and Back himself.

Frustrated in exploration, King became eminent in his profession. An obstetrician, he helped, in practice and writing, in the remarkable nineteenth century lowering of infant mortality. He was, for a time, editor of the *Medical Times* and was a pioneer in the use of statistics in medical research. He was on the councils of the Statistical Society and the British Association for the Advancement of Science. He also showed an interest in Amerindians and the Inuit and contributed in this regard to the *Ethnological Journal*. He was a founding member of the British Ethnological Society and, later, of the Anthropological Institute of Great Britain and Ireland.

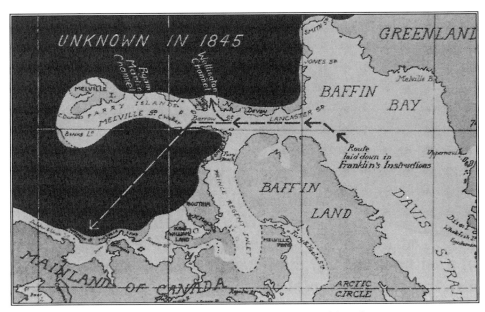

The Admiralty's view of the Arctic, 1845. Courtesy of the author

In 1845, the Board of Admiralty felt that discovery of a Northwest Passage westward from Baffin Bay and eastward from Bering Strait was all but completed. All that remained was to "cross the threshold." It sent out the vessels HMS *Erebus* and *Terror* through Baffin Bay under John Franklin* to finish the job. King felt that discovery of a passage would be completed to the west of Boothia, but he continued to stress inland and civilian means to do this; he warned that Franklin was being sent out "to become the nucleus of an iceberg." Using a combination of geographical data (some of his own discernment) and anthropological and other reasoning, King produced a remarkable sketch map of the Arctic as he saw it, which had a number of correct and newly visualized features,

and which contrasted sharply with the Navy's current view of the Arctic. For example, just as he had once trusted direct information from the Inuit themselves (when he was with Back) in order to perceive a coastal Northwest Passage, so King now used his observations of the Inuit cultures and their distribution in order to recognize a more northerly passage. In our own day, some of King's views have been borne out by archaeological findings on Greenland and Ellesmere Island. King had also suggested, in writing, the existence of Prince of Wales Strait and had realized, ahead of others, the large size of Victoria Island. Indeed, the obvious implication of King's map was that Franklin's party had been ordered to sail across impervious land where, as we know today, Victoria Island is situated.

Richard King's view of the Arctic, 1845. Courtesy of the author

Franklin's party might become embayed in ice, King said, leading not to discovery of a passage, but instead to a perhaps lengthy hiatus in the quest for one.

In fact, Franklin's party did become embayed in ice. It sought safety by making toward the Back River, but by 1848 or 1849, all the party had perished. At home, King had predicted in June 1847 that scurvy and starvation would threaten "the lives of 126 [actually 129] of our fellow creatures … whose miseries above most men I can comprehend." Strongly motivated by his medical training, he specified an area to the west of Boothia and toward the mouth of the Back

River where, he wrote, the Franklin party might be found. He asked once again for support to go down the Back River, a project he tried again to initiate in succeeding letters to officialdom in 1848 and 1850. Had such a trip been made, it would likely have directed the search for Franklin to the right quarter at an early stage. But the answer was always "no," and the search by numerous expeditions under the Navy, the HBC, and private sponsors became diverted far to the north and west of the correct location. Ironically, Lady Jane Franklin* had a strong and accurate feeling that one should search the Boothia area; nevertheless, she stressed reaching this area by sea, not by the inland means of the Back River, which King favoured. Partly for this reason, King was as alienated from her as he was from almost all the other "Arctics" of the period. Indeed, an irony is that dislike of King probably helped divert the search away from that same Boothia area that he rightly advocated.

Indisputable concrete news of the lost party came in 1854. In that year Dr. John Rae* of the HBC, who had already proved that (as King had predicted) Boothia is peninsular, now met Pelly Bay Inuit when he was attempting to complete exploration of the northern coast of North America. These Inuit had Franklin party artifacts, and they also carried news, gathered from other Inuit, of a party perishing at a great river in the west. James Anderson's* HBC expedition of 1855 and Capt. Francis Leopold McClintock's* 1857–59 expedition aboard the *Fox* amplified upon this evidence, thus confirming much that King had predicted. Indeed, the *Fox* expedition found the only written document we have of the Franklin party's progress after it entered upon exploration, and that document closes with the words, "and start on to-morrow … for Back's

Fish River." It was McClintock's expedition that had also completed discovery of Boothia and final knowledge of a coastal or "Franklin's" Northwest Passage, which King had also to a large extent predicted. A great deal had happened according to the views and predictions of the discerning but unfortunate surgeon.

Richard King tried again in 1856, after John Rae's initial discovery of Franklin's fate, to go down the Back River in search of the Franklin party or signs of it, but again he was unsuccessful in securing sponsorship. In 1855, he published his correspondence with the Admiralty and other writings regarding the Arctic under the title *The Franklin Expedition from First to Last* (1855). In January 1856, he became a vocal claimant for the Admiralty's award of £10,000 for initial news of the lost Franklin party. Admiralty files suggest to us today that in adjudication for the award—given to John Rae—King may have been runner-up.

By 1855, King had won a measure of sympathy from the public in regard to his arctic activities. This was counterbalanced, nevertheless, by King's own eccentricities. He lived some twenty years more, dying in relative obscurity on 4 February 1876. It was the very year when, in sending out George Nares's* arctic expedition, the Royal Navy was again making (from King's point of view) many of the same mistakes as made by the lost Franklin expedition.

It is typical of Richard King's role in the arctic story that there is no known portrait of him. Faceless himself in the extant records so far as we know them, he had delineated or anticipated much of the topography of the Canadian Arctic. He had gone to that region only once, and yet had perceived and forecast much that was accurate in regard to its map and to events in the unrolling of it. His work on the Arctic still helps us to understand what other explorers had done—and failed to do—in discovery of the region. Indeed, had King not existed, perhaps "someone would have had to invent him," so as to shed light upon certain arctic realities of which King had been very aware and of which most of his contemporaries had not been. He had predicted the existence of Queen Maud Gulf, the peninsularity of Boothia, the insularity of King William Island, both a coastal and a more northern Northwest Passage, and a superiority of the latter over the former as a navigable channel. He had warned against Franklin's disastrous expedition of 1845; he had also predicted (perhaps his most famous forecast) where the lost Franklin expedition would be found and what the causes of its loss might be. King was the Cassandra of arctic exploration in its greatest era: his fate had been to know and prophesy future arctic events and future knowledge of the Arctic without, however, the public believing his prophesies until much later, when there was a tendency to forget that it was he who had made them in the first place.

Further Readings

King, Richard. 1855. *The Franklin Expedition from First to Last*. London: J. Churchill.

Neatby, L.H. 1970. *The Search for Franklin*. Edmonton: M.G. Hurtig.

Wallace, Hugh N. 1980. *The Navy, the Company, and Richard King*. Montreal: McGill-Queen's University Press.

Hugh N. Wallace

Joseph Burr Tyrrell
(1858–1957)

Great explorers are like great poets and great athletes. They often possess a kind of brilliance and genius that manifests itself early in life. Although Joseph Burr Tyrrell lived for almost a century, he had completed his famous discoveries by the age of thirty-six. In this respect, he is similar to earlier Canadian explorers with whom he should be ranked—Samuel Hearne,* Alexander Mackenzie,* Simon Fraser, and David Thompson.* There is only a relatively short period of one's life when knowledge, judgment, the peak of physical abilities and endurance, and historical circumstance may all combine to create a truly great achievement. J.B. Tyrrell had such a period in his life.

The rural environment of southern Ontario, where he was born in 1858, gave Joe Tyrrell an early intimacy with the natural world, which he was to study from a number of perspectives for the rest of his life. Education at Upper Canada College was followed by biological studies at the University of Toronto. In 1881, at the age of twenty-three, Tyrrell was fortunate to secure, through family political connections, a position with the Geological Survey of Canada (GSC), a wonderful institution for an eager young scientist to join. Tyrrell arrived at the GSC in its most glorious era. Between 1880 and 1910, the men of the Survey, who surprisingly numbered only about twenty, travelled to almost every part of Canada, mapping geographical and geological features, surveying potential mineral deposits, and making exhaustive

Portrait of Joseph Burr Tyrrell. National Archives of Canada/C 81838

botanical and zoological collections. The accomplishments of this small group are outstanding, especially when one realizes most of the work was done on horseback, on foot, or by canoe. Not only were their observations astonishingly accurate, but reading between the lines of their voluminous reports, it is obvious they were exceptionally capable wilderness travellers.

Tyrrell's first field seasons with the GSC were spent in western Alberta. In one amazing week in June 1884, he discovered both the major coal deposits around Drumheller and the famous dinosaur remains. Every summer for a decade Tyrrell travelled the west, eventually working his way northward to Athabasca country in 1892. That year he heard tales of routes leading father north onto the barrenlands.

In 1893, Tyrrell, his brother, and six canoemen struck north from Lake Athabasca in three canoes, into an area known only to a small number of aboriginal people. Prior to 1893 there had been forays by traders and missionaries onto the fringes of the Barrens. Samuel Hearne had traversed the Barrens from Churchill to the mouth of the Coppermine in 1770–72. However, other official knowledge of the landscape and the main routes through the interior was virtually nonexistent. For much of the 1893 trip, the Tyrrell brothers literally felt their way through true *terra incognita*, paddling the shores of the lakes looking for the outlets of rivers, poking through thin leads of open water along the shore of ice-filled Dubawnt Lake, and following the northward flow of the great river, always hoping but never certain that they would not end up on the arctic coast. Seriously short of food and soaked by autumn storms, they emerged on the west shore of Hudson Bay at Chesterfield Inlet in mid-September. Although the object of their expedition had been achieved, and although there was no uncertainty as to where the route back to civilization lay, the problems of paddling Hudson Bay in open canoes in late fall were awesome. For five weeks, Tyrrell's party fought high winds, storms, snow, and freezing temperatures, finally reaching Churchill on 19 October. Amazingly, just two and one-half weeks later they set off by snowshoe and dog-team for the railway, arriving in Winnipeg two months later at New Year's.

A scant five months after that, Tyrrell, now married, was back in northern Manitoba commencing his second passage through the Barrens, this time via the Cochrane and Little Partridge rivers, Kasba Lake, and on to the main corridor, the Kazan River. His party encountered "The People"—the Inland or Caribou Inuit—at many locations along the Kazan, and with their guid-

Tyrrell, ready for the trail

ance, left the main river just north of Yathkyed Lake and travelled east on what Tyrrell named the Ferguson River in honour of his travelling companion. This put the party on the shore of Hudson Bay well south of Chesterfield Inlet and about one week ahead of the 1893 schedule. With the extra time and good weather, they experienced a much less difficult trip down the Bay to Churchill than in 1893.

The early years in the GSC had given Tyrrell a rigorous training in the skills of exploration which were so necessary to the successful completion of these epic journeys of 1893 and 1894. Such feats require enormous personal drive and leadership ability, vast reserves of physical strength, and a measure of good fortune. It was a period of intensity and accomplishment impossible to sustain for very long. Tyrrell's next several years at the GSC were not particularly happy ones for him, and he finally left his $1800 per annum position in 1889 at the age of forty.

Once again the North lured Tyrrell, this time in the form of gold. Six years in the Klondike brought Tyrrell an income and capital base which had been impossible to achieve as a civil servant. The Klondike years also developed the business acumen and mining expertise which were to be at the centre of Tyrrell's activities for the next thirty years as mining consultant, promoter, shareholder, and company director.

Although not as well known as his explorations, Tyrrell's scholarly pursuits are impressive. In addition to his impeccably thorough technical reports for the GSC, in 1897 he made a major contribution to the study of glaciation in North America. In works prepared for the Champlain Society he brought to the attention of a wide audience the works of Samuel Hearne and the man whom he considered "the greatest practical land geographer who ever lived," David Thompson.

Joseph Burr Tyrrell was a large man, well over six feet with a robust physique which, despite the ravages of scarlet fever in childhood and a severe heart attack at seventy, was to last for ninety-nine years. He was one of the last explorers to record the extent and nature of the Canadian landscape in the old style. He grasped the significance of the achievements of Hearne and Thompson because he travelled and worked as they had. Before Tyrrell's own life was out in 1957, the kind of exploratory work he had accomplished was being done by large parties supported by bush planes, helicopters, radio communications, airphotos, and sophisticated sensing and surveying equipment. The circumstances necessary for the flowering of the kind of exploratory genius possessed by J.B. Tyrrell no longer exist.

Further Readings

Inglis, Alex. 1978. *Northern Vagabond*. Toronto: McClelland and Stewart.

Tyrrell, James Williams. [1898] 1973. *Across the Sub-Arctics of Canada*. Reprint. Toronto: Coles.

Tyrrell, Joseph Burr. 1898. *Report of the Doobaunt, Kazan and Ferguson Rivers*. Annual Report of Geological Survey of Canada 1896. Report F. Ottawa.

_____, ed. 1916. *David Thompson's Narrative of his Explorations in Western North America, 1784-1812*. Toronto: Champlain Society.

_____, ed. 1934. *Journals of Samuel Hearne and Philip Turnor*. Toronto: Champlain Society.

Hugh Stewart

Ernest Thompson Seton
(1860-1946)

The decades immediately previous to World War I witnessed a marked shift in popular attitudes toward the North. The imperialistic ethos that had driven such conquests as Caspar Whitney's assault on the Barrens in 1894–95 or Leonidas Hubbard Jr.'s* expedition into Labrador in 1903–04 gave way to a new impulse, one shaped by a desire to celebrate and to conserve the beauty of a bountiful natural environment that was seen as a significant alternative to the artifice of civilization. Vilhjalmur Stefansson* loudly voiced his notion of "the friendly Arctic." Ernest Thompson Seton played what was perhaps an even more fundamental role in bringing about this widespread change of attitude.

Self-portrait of Ernest Thompson Seton in 1879. Courtesy of Dee Seton Barber, Seton Village, Santa Fe, New Mexico

naturalist. But soon after being admitted to the prestigious Painting School of the Royal Academy, Seton abandoned formal training in art and returned to Canada, where he would be closer to the natural world that fascinated him. His strong interest in natural history drew him to Manitoba, where two of his brothers were homesteading. His brother Albert complained that Seton spent all his time collecting and identifying specimens of wildlife instead of pulling his weight on the farm.

In the fall of 1883, he travelled to New York to work as an illustrator, and it was in the city that Seton's reputation for his pictures of wildlife began to grow. As well, he wrote "Benny and the Fox" that winter, the first of many realistic animal stories that would bring him fame as an author, but that would virtually destroy any chance he had to be recognized as a credible naturalist. The next spring saw Seton's return to the Manitoba homestead, establishing a pattern of oscillation between bush and urban centre that characterized much of his life. The natural world of forest and prairie vitalized him, but only the city could give him the recognition he craved. Such oscillation between extremes of residence is perhaps parallelled by the numerous names Seton used before he legally changed his name in 1901. The many and extreme changes of residence and the evident dissatisfaction with the name given him at birth point to a man with a troubled sense of identity.

Born Ernest Evan Thompson in 1860 at South Shields, a village in northern England, Seton was one of eleven children —ten boys and one girl—in a large Victorian family. When he was five years old, his family emigrated to a farm in Ontario, where his father, Joseph Thompson, hoped to mend the meagre family fortune. Those years spent at the edge of the wilderness were formative; Seton would bear their mark throughout his life, even though his family soon moved to Toronto. Short and skinny as an adolescent, Seton proved a bright student, but an uncooperative and selfish individual. After demonstrating considerable skill at painting while in Toronto, the youth embarked for England to continue his studies in art, although his true ambition was to become a

His 1907 canoe trip to the northeast of Great Slave Lake sharply focuses the impact Seton had on how we view the northern wilderness. Along with two guides and Edward Preble of the United States Biological Survey, Seton carried over Pike's Portage and canoed the lengths of Artillery, Clinton-Colden, and Aylmer lakes in search of *la foule,* the nearly legendary herds of migrating caribou. Seton was struck not only by the bounty of thousands of caribou, but also by the unlimited range of colour in the late summer vegetation and by the lushness of the ground-cover stretching as far as the eye could see. Yet ironically, this region was called the barrenlands; previous travellers— among them John Franklin,* Joseph Burr Tyrrell,* and Warburton Pike*—had branded the land as empty, sterile, and forbidding. Seton, however, dubbed them "the arctic prairies," a name he considered apt for a locale in which, he observed, the herbage vastly surpassed many agricultural regions of Texas and Wyoming. The Barrens, Seton asserted, was a thoroughly libelous name, and he popularized this new vision by publishing *The Arctic Prairies* (1911), Seton's account of that journey.

Yet Seton's influence on the new response to the North was far more deep-seated than this single trip. He was in the advance guard of a new era of wildlife conservation, having sensed that a way of life fundamental to all mankind was rapidly growing extinct in the face of modern technology and communications. Unlike many outdoorsmen of his time and certainly unlike those of past generations, Seton saw the wilderness as a place that needed to be preserved, rather than conquered. He published over forty books on the natural world. He undertook extensive lecture tours. He began "The League of the Woodcraft Indians," a youth organization that encouraged conservation and understanding of the natural world. When Robert Baden-Powell added a strong militaristic dimension to Seton's organization, the Boy Scouts came into being, and Seton, wholly dissatisfied, withdrew.

When he died at famous Seton Village in Santa Fe, New Mexico, Ernest Thompson Seton was eighty-six years old. His life had stretched from the very heart of the Victorian era into the middle of this century. He was, in many respects, only a product of these remarkably changed times, but in the philosophy he developed toward untamed nature, he blazed a path leading directly to the conservationist attitudes of today.

Further Readings

Keller, Betty. 1984. *Black Wolf: The Life of Ernest Thompson Seton.* Vancouver: Douglas and McIntyre.

Redekop, Magdalene. 1979. *Ernest Thompson Seton.* Don Mills: Fitzhenry and Whiteside.

Seton, Ernest Thompson. 1898. *Wild Animals I Have Known.* New York: Charles Scribner's Sons.

_____. 1900. *The Biography of a Grizzly.* New York: The Century Company.

_____. 1911. *The Arctic Prairies.* New York: Charles Scribner's Sons.

_____. 1940. *Trail of an Artist-naturalist: The Autobiography of Ernest Thompson Seton.* New York: Charles Scribner's Sons.

Richard C. Davis

JOHN HORNBY (1880-1927)

At first glance, John Hornby's life would not appear to have the ingredients of a legend. Unlike most important northern travellers, Hornby did not distinguish himself in the realm of exploration, in a natural science, or in any other discipline. His only accounts of two decades of subarctic travel were his "Caribou Notes," a few incomplete diaries, and notes for a projected book, *The Land of Feast and Famine*. Nor would Hornby's personality seem likely to make his name endure. A very enigmatic and eccentric person, he was evasive and misleading even to good friends, and frequently inconsistent and irresponsible as a leader of men. Yet he had an endearing nature and was hard to dislike intensely. Peers and travelling companions frequently spoke of him with respect and affection. Ultimately, it is this curious personality rather than accomplishment on which Hornby's fame rests.

By birth the member of an affluent textile family, the son of an outstanding cricketer and rugby player, and by education an Harrovian, John Hornby was twenty-three years old when he came to Canada from England, in 1904. From then until his death twenty-two years later, he pursued a lifestyle uncomplicated by long-range goals and plans. After spending four years just north of Edmonton homesteading, trapping, hunting, and packing, Hornby went north to the Great Bear Lake region with Cosmo Melville on a trading expedition in 1908. Fascination for the country was immediate, intense,

John Hornby at Fort Norman, summer 1919. Photograph reprinted with permission from George Whalley's *The Legend of John Hornby*, London: John Murray (1962)

and so strong that except for occasional trips to Edmonton, England, and service in World War I, he was to spend the rest of his life in the barrenlands and the adjacent "land of the little sticks."

Travelling sometimes with Indians, sometimes with whites, and frequently alone, Hornby's practice of living off the land with an absolute minimum of food staples and equipment was irrevocably confirmed over the next few years. The season of 1911–12 was spent in the company of the George Mellis Douglas* expedition, which was undertaking a mineralogical survey in the Coppermine River area. In retrospect, this season can be seen as a critical time in Hornby's life. Douglas became a lifelong friend and possibly Hornby's only true confidant. But the peace and contentment of these first years in the North were not to last. Never again did Douglas and Hornby travel together, although Hornby wrote Douglas many times broaching the possibility expectantly. Never again were the relations with neighbouring trappers and Indians as good, and never again was the game quite as plentiful. Two unhappy years later, Hornby departed for the war in Europe, and although he won a commission and a Military Cross, he was profoundly disturbed by what the civilized world had come to, and, in 1916, he returned North.

For the next decade, Hornby wandered at the edge of the barrenlands, shifting to the area east of Great Slave Lake in 1919. His reluctance to plan ahead and his improvident ways led to some very difficult times. Having left Edmonton too late in the season, he was obliged to pass the winter of 1918–19 in an enlarged wolf den near Fort Chipewyan. During the next two winters at the east end of Great Slave Lake, starvation was exceedingly close.

By the early 1920s, one suspects Hornby felt vaguely compelled to legitimize his years of travelling and wandering. He mentioned his proposed book, *The Land of Feast and Famine*, more frequently. Such compulsion also may have been the motivation for his unsuccessful attempt to secure federal government funding for his second-last trip in 1924. This was an expedition with James Critchell-Bullock, whose purpose was to travel to the Barrens to film caribou and musk-oxen. However, because Hornby's temperament inclined him toward the unstructured and fortuitous life of a trapper and hunter, it was difficult for him to consistently direct his energies to the specific objective of the expedition. Hornby was sometimes with Bullock and sometimes not, giving advice and help at one time and obstructing progress at another. Although there was not any loss of life, the venture was a semidisaster. A miserable winter was passed in a hastily constructed cave in an esker near Artillery Lake, little film was shot, and their $14,000

Hornby with Punch and Harry, upper Coppermine River, May 1912. Photograph reprinted with permission from George Whalley's *The Legend of John Hornby*, London: John Murray (1962)

worth of white fox fur was rotten by the time they reached "the Outside," after an arduous trip down the Thelon River to Chesterfield Inlet.

On the fatal foray onto the barrenlands in 1926 with two inexperienced companions—his eighteen-year-old cousin Edgar Christian and Harold Adlard—Hornby's ability to survive with a rifle, a bare minimum of food, and some good luck was not sufficient. In distinctively Hornby style, the party dallied high up on the Thelon for no explicable reason in the late summer, and missed the caribou migration southward. Consequently, they wintered without adequate food, and, in the spring of 1927, all three

Hornby calls Potash to be harnessed at Hodgson's Point. Photograph reprinted with permission from George Whalley's *The Legend of John Hornby*, London: John Murray (1962)

John Hornby did not find new fur country or mineral deposits or otherwise enhance the riches of the civilized world. He was fascinated by the Barrens and saw the life of the wilds as morally superior to that of civilized society. In this sense, he was typical of many who travel the North half a century later. The land is attractive for the moral alternative it offers, and that alone is sufficient justification to travel it. Hornby is a popular legend because his story sparks the imagination of wilderness travellers of the late twentieth century. With him they have a natural empathy and affinity.

succumbed to starvation in their cabin midway down the Thelon.

Most likely, had the manner of Hornby's passing and the final depletion of strength and energy not been so dramatically and poignantly chronicled in Edgar Christian's diary, Hornby would only be a minor footnote in the history of subarctic travel. Yet, today, his status must surely approach that of a folk hero. He has been the subject of a number of books and articles, dramatic productions, and radio programs, and countless pilgrimages have been made to the site of his last cabin.

Further Readings

Christian, Edgar. [1937]1980. *Death in the Barren Ground*. Ottawa: Oberon. Introduction by George Whalley. (Originally published in 1937 under the title *Unflinching*).

Waldron, Malcolm. 1931. *Snowman*. Boston: Houghton Mifflin Company.

Whalley, George. 1962. *The Legend of John Hornby*. London: John Murray.

_____. 1969. "Notes on a Legend." *Queen's Quarterly* 76(4): 613.

Hugh Stewart

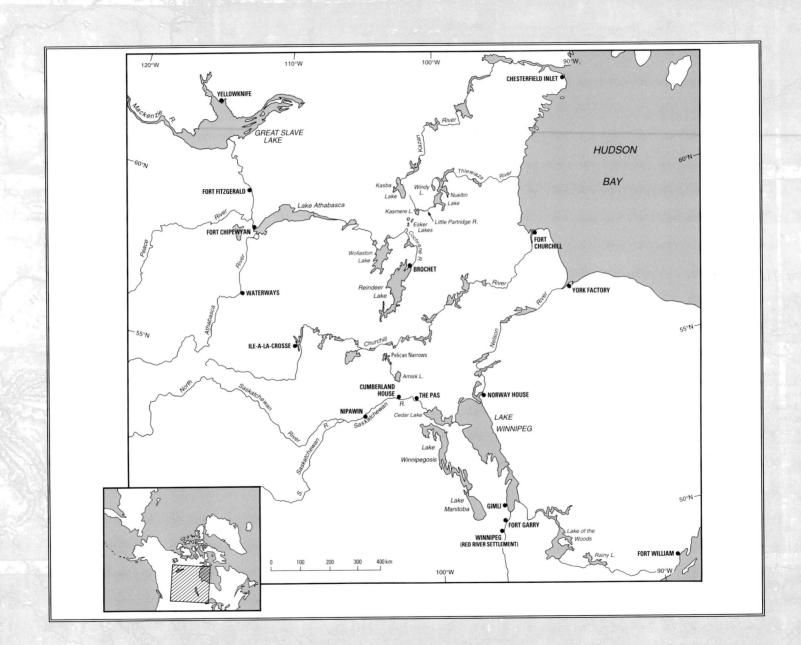

YELLOWKNIFE

Mackenzie R.

GREAT SLAVE
LAKE

120°W   110°W   100°W   90°W

CHESTERFIELD INLET

HUDSON

BAY

60°N

FORT FITZGERALD

River

Lake Athabasca

FORT CHIPEWYAN

Kazan

Thlewiaza   *River*

River

Kasba
Lake

Windy
L.

Nueltin
Lake

Kasmere L.

Little Partridge R.

Esker
Lakes

FORT
CHURCHILL

Peace

River

Wollaston
Lake

Cochrane R.

BROCHET

WATERWAYS

Athabasca

Reindeer
Lake

River

YORK FACTORY

55°N

ILE-A-LA-CROSSE

Churchill

Nelson

River

Pelican Narrows

North

Saskatchewan

River

Amisk L.

CUMBERLAND
HOUSE

THE PAS

NORWAY HOUSE

NIPAWIN

R.

Saskatchewan

R.

Cedar Lake

LAKE
WINNIPEG

S.

Lake
Winnipegosis

Lake
Manitoba

GIMLI

FORT GARRY

WINNIPEG
(RED RIVER SETTLEMENT)

Lake of the
Woods

Rainy L.

FORT WILLIAM

60°N

55°N

50°N

0   100   200   300   400 km

100°W   90°W

UNIT

❧7❧

**David Thompson, Alexander Kennedy Isbister,
R.M. Ballantyne, Ernest C. Oberholtzer, Prentice G. Downes**

The more southerly region between Hudson Bay and the Mackenzie/Athabasca watershed includes the Churchill River, which was a main artery for the fur trade as it pushed west of Hudson Bay and into the Athabasca district. It comprises a large section of Laurentian Shield country and is bordered on the north by the treeless Barrens. It has been the place of major discovery work by Thompson, has provided Ballantyne with a setting for much of his fiction, and has given Downes and Oberholtzer a point of entry into the "old North." It remains the home of many aboriginal and mixed-blood peoples today.

DAVID THOMPSON (1770–1857)

David Thompson's cartographic achievement is still one of Canada's best-kept secrets, even though the maps by this patient and determined explorer are the first surveyed representations of much of the country. That Thompson's work should have been ignored so long would appear to be due to the circumstances of its first reception—circumstances intimately bound up with the politics and fortunes of the early-nineteenth-century fur trade.

Born of Welsh parents, Thompson attended a London charity school where he was prepared for a career in the Royal Navy. After the peace of Versailles, he was apprenticed instead to the Hudson's Bay Company. In the summer of 1784, he arrived at Churchill, then under Samuel Hearne's* command, instructed to serve in the warehouse, keep accounts, and be "employed in ... occasionally making Observations." But the boy found that apprentices were generally used as simple labourers; he complained to Hearne that he was actually losing the skills he had learned at school. Any further training would have to depend on his own initiative.

His big chance came in 1789. A broken leg stranded him at Cumberland House on Cedar Lake: there he spent the winter with Philip Turnor and a fellow apprentice, Peter Fidler. Turnor had participated in the worldwide observation of the transit of Venus in 1769, and had charted the region north of Lake Winnipeg for the HBC London Committee. Turnor could not have found more diligent students for his lessons in "practical Astronomy." In all their subsequent survey work in the western interior, Thompson and Fidler used

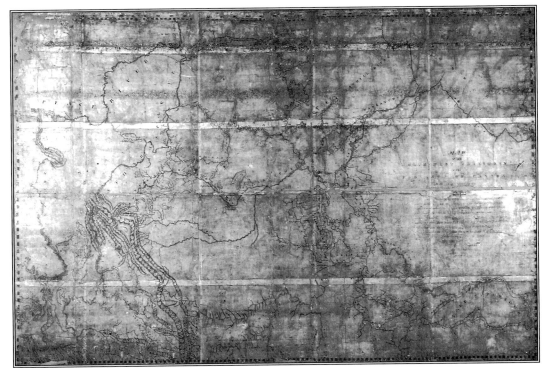

David Thompson's "Map of the North-West Territory of the Province of Canada, 1813." Courtesy of the Archives of Ontario

the techniques of observation and the conventions of carto-graphic drawing that are recorded in Turnor's journals and maps. This "route traverse" method, practised by most colonial surveyors in the eighteenth and early nineteenth centuries, was reliable for all practical purposes. It required a succession of compass bearings with estimates of the distances between them, adjusted by frequent observations. Only the routes thus surveyed were charted; large spaces were left blank while lakes and rivers were drawn in amazing detail. Thompson's maps even show the sand bars of large rivers such as the Columbia.

For the next seven years, Thompson traded and surveyed in the Churchill and Nelson watersheds, going west to Nipawin and north as far as Wollaston Lake. He wintered at Reindeer Lake in 1796–97 and then, in a surprise move, set out from the Hudson Bay Company post in a May snowstorm, bound for the nearest "Canadian" or North West Company fort. Thompson gave no reason for his shift of allegiance; his journal simply records the fact of his departure and adds, "May God Almighty prosper me." But the reasons are not hard to find. Hudson Bay Company posts were chronically short of trade goods, conservative in their relationships with natives, and overly cautious about advancing into new territory. For a young man of Thompson's ambition, the Bay was a backwater. Once more he saw his chance: since the loose association of merchants from Montreal had engaged him as an "Astronomer," he could hope to accomplish more than Fidler, or even Turnor.

Thompson immediately set out on two expeditions of pure explorative survey. First he visited the country of the Mandans south of Lake of the Woods, then followed Peter Pond's old Athabasca route to the rich fur region west of Fort Chipewyan. Thompson was greatly impressed by Alexander Mackenzie's* daring voyages beyond this point to the Arctic and Pacific oceans; he also admired George Vancouver's scrupulous coastal surveys, and he resolved to fill in the blank interior that stretched from Lake Winnipeg to the Pacific. Unfortunately, even in the North West Company, trade took precedence over exploration. More than ten years were to pass before Thompson reached the mouth of the Columbia River, in July 1811. Meanwhile the Lewis and Clark expedition had established an American claim to the region, and John Jacob Astor's Pacific Fur Company was actively trading with coastal native groups. But during his four years west of the continental divide, Thompson managed to solve the puzzle of the Columbia's winding course from source to mouth—a puzzle that had defeated both Mackenzie and Simon Fraser. Thompson then left the West to settle in Montreal and map the country he had explored.

The subsequent fortunes of the North West Company directly affected Thompson's reputation and influence as a cartographer. After a desperate, often vicious period of rivalry with the Hudson's Bay Company, the two companies merged in 1821. Records at Fort William were lost or destroyed, and George Simpson,* the new Company governor, forwarded details of Thompson's discoveries to the HBC London Committee, "who may perhaps allow Arrowsmith [the leading British cartographer] to correct his map [of North America] thereby which in its present state is very erroneous." The bankruptcy of a North West Company agent deprived Thompson of his fur trade income: instead of retiring, he served on the International Boundary Commission under the Treaty of Ghent. From Lake of the Woods to the Eastern Townships of Quebec, the Canadian-American border is in large part the work of David Thompson.

What still most interested Thompson, however, was the West and especially his Columbia department. Negotiations with a view to establishing the international boundary west to the Pacific meant a division of the territory explored as much by Thompson as by Lewis and Clark. Thompson patriotically offered the information he had to the British side. He sent a set of maps to the Foreign Office in 1826, and a second set in 1843; they met with the same complete indifference. By this time, Thompson was desperately poor, so he petitioned the Earl of Aberdeen, the Foreign Secretary, for an income as well as recognition. On the advice of Arrowsmith, Lord Aberdeen refused him all but a token remuneration. Thompson could not forebear replying, "I have several times been obliged to point out the errors on [Arrowsmith's] Maps of North America. He has had his revenge on me." Thompson then turned to writing a narrative of his years in the fur trade. It is for this narrative, rather than his maps, that he is best known.

Historians' subsequent neglect of David Thompson's cartographic work may well originate in the concerted disregard of Simpson, Arrowsmith and Lord Aberdeen. Official channels were closed to Thompson, both in the fur trade and in government. Since maps are produced and given authority only with institutional support, Thompson's career as a cartographer was limited to what he could accomplish while active as a trader and as a boundary commission surveyor. Certainly there is irony in the fact that Thompson the storyteller is more esteemed than Thompson the cartographer. He himself feared neglect of his life work, and wrote of "the mass of scientific materials in my hands, of surveys, of astronomical observations, drawings of the countries, sketches and measurements of the Mountains, &c &c &c, all soon to perish in oblivion." Fortunately, however, this "mass of scientific materials" has not perished. It is merely in eclipse, waiting in various archives for interest in Thompson to bring it to light.

Further Readings

Belyea, Barbara, ed. 1994. *David Thompson: Columbia Journals*. Montreal and Kingston: McGill-Queen's University Press.

Glover, Richard, ed. 1962. *David Thompson's Narrative*. Toronto: Champlain Society.

Hopwood, Victor, ed. 1971. *David Thompson: Travels in Western North America, 1784–1812*. Toronto: Macmillan Canada.

Nisbet, Jack. 1994. *Sources of the River*. Seattle: Sasquatch Books.

Tyrrell, Joseph Burr, ed. 1916. *David Thompson's Narrative of his Explorations in Western America, 1784–1812*. Toronto: Champlain Society.

Barbara Belyea

ALEXANDER KENNEDY ISBISTER
(1822-1883)

As a committed and effective spokesman in London, England, for the poor indigenous people of mid-nineteenth century Rupert's Land—that is how Alexander Kennedy Isbister should be remembered by all Canadians and revered by those who were his people. Only one portrait of Alexander Isbister is known to exist, the photograph shown here. A few brief obituaries, magazine articles, and historical papers comprised the printed record until the publication of his biography by Barry Cooper in 1988. A short street in Winnipeg and a classroom building at the University of Manitoba are named after him. So are the Isbister Scholarships, although the money disbursed is no longer the return on Isbister's generous bequest to the university. This gift disappeared through embezzlement in 1914. The tangible record that remains, then, is slim, surprisingly so for a man who in his time was regarded as a great figure by the people of Red River.

Church records list Alexander Kennedy Isbister's grandmother on his mother's side as Agatha, an "Indian woman." His grandfather, Alexander Kennedy, hailed from the Orkneys and worked for the Hudson's Bay Company, as did Thomas Isbister, his father. Alexander was born in Cumberland House as his mother had been, in June 1822, forty-eight years after this first HBC inland post was established by Samuel Hearne* and in the same year that John

Photograph of Alexander K. Isbister. Courtesy of the Provincial Archives of Manitoba: Isbister, A.K. 1(N16210)

Franklin* and John Richardson* visited the trading house on the return from their first land expedition to the Arctic.

As was done with many other offspring of the Company's personnel, young Alexander was sent away for his education: first, at age ten to the Orkneys for a year or so of schooling and then, in 1833, to the Red River settlement for more of the same. He finished school at sixteen and entered the service of the Hudson's Bay Company. Although he held his position as apprentice postmaster for only two years, these were to be the most formative years of his life.

For the Company, Isbister travelled through the lower part of the Mackenzie Basin. When he left British North America in 1842, barely twenty years old and never to return, he had acquired some valuable firsthand knowledge of the West and the North. More importantly, he had developed both an intense interest in the geology and geography of the land and a consuming compassion for its people.

In England, where Isbister established himself as a teacher, a writer of school textbooks, and later as a barrister, he made good use of the knowledge he had of what was then a still unknown country inhabited by largely forgotten Indians, Métis, mixed-bloods, fur traders, and missionaries.

Two scientific papers, published in 1845 and 1855, form a solid base on which rests the reputation of Isbister as a pioneer geologist of northwestern Canada. In these treatises, he summarized all previous geological observations, added his own, and, in 1855, provided a geological map on which the distribution of stratigraphic units is shown in much greater detail than on other contemporaneous maps, such as the one by John Richardson, published in 1851. He also recognized the importance of fossils or organic remains in the rocks "by which alone their relative ages and their true characters can be determined."

The native people of the West and Northwest do not owe their debt to Alexander Isbister merely for calling the attention of the British or even the international scientific community to the physical characteristics of their country. That debt is owed mainly because young Alexander became an educated man—attending King's College, Aberdeen, obtaining a Master of Arts degree from the University of London—and yet proudly maintained his ties with those he left behind. He was successful in what he undertook; he became a man of means. He provided an example of what others could aspire to, even though they would never come close to his achievements.

If not for himself, then for his people, Alexander Kennedy Isbister earned his crown by his persistent battle against the injustices he saw being perpetrated by the Company. The battle began when, at age twenty-five, he became the trusted representative of petitioners who charged "that the Company impoverished the natives for their own profit." He never came to a halt. In 1871, as a shareholder, Isbister took up a claim of the chief traders and chief factors at the general court of the Hudson's Bay Company. By then he had become the leading authority on all matters affecting British North America. This distinction was not only well earned but also well deserved.

Further Readings

Cooper, Barry. 1988. *Alexander Kennedy Isbister: A Respectable Critic of the Honourable Company.* Ottawa: Carleton University Press.

Know, H.C. 1957. "Alexander Kennedy Isbister." Papers read before the Historical and Scientific Society of Manitoba. Series 3, no. 12: 17–28.

Kupsch, W.O. 1977. "Métis and Proud." *Geoscience Canada* 4(3): 147–48.

Walter O. Kupsch

R. M. BALLANTYNE
(1825–1894)

During my school days in the early years of the present century, the fur trade stories of R.M. Ballantyne, an ex-HBC clerk, were at the height of their popularity…. Certainly I read them avidly, for who could fail to be thrilled with the romance of the fur trade? I was thus in a receptive mood to the merest suggestion that I should become a fur trader.

J.W. Anderson, *Fur Trader's Story* (1961)

More than a few northern men of the late nineteenth and early twentieth centuries—particularly those raised in Scotland and England—have attested in their memoirs to the seductive tug they felt as boys when reading Robert Michael Ballantyne's books about the Canadian North. It is something of a happy irony, given his own uneasy and brief period of service with the Hudson's Bay Company, that Ballantyne's boys' novels *The Young Fur Traders* (1855) and *Ungava* (1857) and, more especially, his personal account of that service, *Hudson's Bay: or Every-Day Life in the Wilds of North America* (1848), recruited so many able young men for both the HBC and Revillon Frères. As Ballantyne's six years in Rupert's Land and the King's Posts, and his narrative of that experience, are the cynosure of this profile, the balance of his life must be dealt with summarily.

Photograph of Robert M. Ballantyne. From Eric Quayle's *Ballantyne the Brave* (1967)

A nonentity when he returned home from Canada in 1847, Ballantyne was famous a decade later, for he made his name as a story teller with the two northern novels and *Coral Island* (1857). He went on to publish another hundred or so boys' books on such varied subjects as the lighthouse and lifeboat services, gorilla hunting, the London Fire Brigade, Algerian pirates, and the like. The latter half of the Victorian century, the high noon of the British Empire, was, concomitantly, the heyday of the boys' adventure story, and Ballantyne's popularity was as strong as that enjoyed by Charles Kingsley, G.A. Henty, Rider Haggard, and Robert Louis Stevenson. His exciting tales were characterized by unchaperoned boy heroes (an innovation), factual accuracy, and pietistic moralizing and conveyed the sensibility of their time. When he met his death in February 1894, thousands of schoolboys raised money to commemorate him.

R.M. Ballantyne was born in Edinburgh in 1825 into a publishing family damaged by Sir Walter Scott's financial ruin. His formal education consisted of two years at Edinburgh Academy. In May 1841, spurred by his father's romantic notions of arctic exploration, he apprenticed himself to the Hudson's Bay Company, and sailed in the sixth *Prince Rupert* to a way of life that, incongruously enough, was to determine his eventual career. He spent his first winter at Fort Garry, being "broken in to the desk," as he put it, and was present when the corpse of the great Thomas Simpson*—murdered? a suicide?—was brought in to Red River. That spring he went to Norway House, where he stayed for a year. Here he was a spectator of the swirling drama of the outbound spring brigades from the northwest with their crews of "wild and uncouth" voyageurs. In June 1843, he was posted to York Factory—"a monstrous blot on a swampy spot, with a partial view of the frozen sea." But he himself was by now regarded as a blot of sorts by his superiors, for his clerkly application was less than outstanding: it would have been a better idea, wrote William Mactavish to James Hargrave, to have sent him a pair of trousers stuffed with straw rather than Ballantyne. We, however, have reason to be grateful for his sojourn on the Bay, for he recalled it vividly in his descriptions of Bachelors' Hall and HBC Christmas celebrations. In 1845, under orders for Lachine and Tadoussac, Ballantyne travelled to Norway House and then on by express canoe to Fort William. On this leg of his journey he met the brilliant Dr. John Rae,* bound for Repulse. Ballantyne astutely noted and approved what Vilhjalmur Stefansson* would one day call the Rae Method—Rae's determination, thought bizarre then, to travel light and to live off the land. From Fort William, Ballantyne voyaged in a *canot de maître* (the large thirty-six foot canoes used by the fur trade between Montreal and the head of Lake Superior) to Lachine, where, under the god-like eye of George Simpson,* he worked (no doubt more conscientiously) until January 1846. Then, by sleigh and on snowshoes, he made his way to the King's Posts of Tadoussac and Isle Jeremie before taking charge at Seven Islands that April. It was there, in that desolate and static post, that he began to compose the story of his service in the Company. He wrote simply for want of anything better to do. "I had no books, no game to shoot, no boat … and no prospect of seeing anyone to speak to for weeks, if not months, to come. But I had pen and ink, and, by great fortune, was in possession of a blank paper book, fully an inch thick. These, then, were the circumstances in which I began my first book." In May 1847, fed up and homesick, and his term of apprenticeship having expired, he returned to Scotland.

It is for *Hudson's Bay* that we still remember Ballantyne. Detailed and valuably informative, the account is enlivened by youthful intensity. As well as describing fur trade operations, it contains powerful evocations of terrain, waterways, and weather, and shrewd sketches of an assortment of personalities. Furthermore, the accompanying illustrations (which suffered at the hands of the wood engraver) are Ballantyne's own: although he lacked the facility of Paul Kane or Alexander Hunter Murray, his pictorial talent was considerable. What most enhances the book, however, is its personal flavour. Unlike earlier (and too many later) accounts of far northern life and exploration, which were written in a detached, laconic manner, *Hudson's Bay* projects the personality of its author, conveys his spirits, alert curiosity, and mental growth. Still, few books on the North win favourable reactions from old northern hands, and there were those in the Company who snorted disdainfully at *Hudson's Bay*, among them chief factor Donald Ross, who in 1850 wrote to a colleague: "I have just finished Ballantyne's book. It is the work, apparently, of an amiable young man with a strong perception of the ridiculous … but void of originality and vigour in a rather remarkable degree. His everyday life in

Hudson Bay was easy enough. I wish he had seen some of my everyday life for many years." But such opinions were in a minority. Let the last judgment rest with another prominent Company man of that long lost world: "Of the many books of adventure by different writers on life in the wilds, those of R.M. Ballantyne can be placed in the front rank for faithfulness of detail and correctness of observation. His descriptions of conditions are nearly perfect."

Further Readings

Ballantyne, Robert M. [1848] 1972. *Hudson's Bay: or Every-Day Life in the Wilds of North America*. Reprint. Edmonton: M.G. Hurtig.

Parnell, C. 1941. "Ballantyne the Brave." *The Beaver* 272 (December): 4–6.

Quayle, Eric. 1967. *Ballantyne the Brave: A Victorian Writer and His Family*. London: Rupert Hart-Davis.

R.H. Cockburn

ERNEST C. OBERHOLTZER
(1844–1977)

It was a hazardous undertaking for you to go
through that northern country with one Indian who
knew of nothing of it ... and I heartily congratulate
you on having made a good adventurous journey
which will add materially to our knowledge of that
portion of Northern Canada.

(J.B. Tyrrell to E.C. Oberholtzer, 16 November 1912)

In 1912, Ernest C. Oberholtzer and Titapeshwewitan, an
Ontario Ojibwa better known among white men as Billy
Magee, made a canoe voyage of some two thousand miles,
during which they explored Nueltin Lake and the Thlewiaza
River, Northwest Territories. This epic journey, more arduous
and commendable than certain of the acclaimed explorations
that preceded it, has remained all but unrecorded to the present day.

Oberholtzer was born in Davenport, Iowa, on 6 February
1884. At seventeen, he contracted rheumatic fever and was
instructed by doctors to never indulge in any activity involving
strain. He attended Harvard, taking his Bachelor of Arts degree
in 1907 and returning for a year's study of landscape architec-
ture under Frederick Law Olmsted. But his one insatiable
yearning was for the north woods, and he spent the summers
1908–09 along the then still largely pristine Minnesota-Ontario
border, traversing, with local Indians, "all the main canoe routes
in the Rainy Lake watershed." It was there that he first canoed
prodigiously and began a lifelong friendship with "the most
wonderful Ojibway or any Indian I have ever known," Billy
Magee, whose tribal name meant "Far-distant echo."

The year 1910 found Oberholtzer visiting Europe and
England. He had worked briefly as a newspaperman in Iowa

Ernest Oberholtzer (right) and Billy Magee in the 1920s. Courtesy of Ernest C.
Oberholtzer Foundation

and also had spent the summer of 1907 composing a pamphlet
on wilderness travel for the Canadian Northern Railway. The
official who had given him that job now encouraged him to stay
on in England to write and lecture on the Indians and wildlife
of the southern Laurentian Shield. Oberholtzer did so; on one
memorable occasion, as a last-minute substitute for the celebrated central Asia explorer Sven Hedin, he recounted tales told
him by Billy, illustrating his talk with lantern-slides of moose
and the boundary waters canoe country. During that winter in
London, he read everything he could find about far northern
exploration and "came across the works of J.B. Tyrrell,* who
was by all odds the greatest of all modern geographers." There
and then, Oberholtzer decided to follow Tyrrell's 1894 route
across the Barrens: "And my imagination was at work. I

Oberholtzer at Mallard Island, Rainy Lake, late 1930s. Courtesy of Ernest C. Oberholtzer Foundation

thought, well, there are probably other groups of those Eskimos [the Caribou Inuit of the Kazan River] up in there. What that would mean, what a delight to be the first one ever to find them!" After serving as American vice-consul at Hanover, Germany, in 1911, he translated his dreams into action.

On 26 June 1912, Oberholtzer and Magee left The Pas, Manitoba, in an eighteen-foot Chestnut Guide Special. Their destination was Chesterfield Inlet, by way of the Kazan. Neither man had ever canoed north of Rainy Lake, and from the first Billy was unsettled by the prospect of strange Indians, far stranger Inuit, and the treeless regions for which they were bound. He was fifty-one years old. Oberholtzer, twenty-eight, stood 5′6″ and weighed 135 pounds. A month out from The

Pas they reached Lac du Brochet, the remote HBC post and Oblate mission at the northern end of Reindeer Lake. There, as at Cumberland House and Pelican Narrows, they were warned against attempting so audacious a venture, especially since no guides were to be had. Undeterred, and with Tyrrell's map to steer by, they pushed up the Cochrane, then followed what Oberholtzer called the Esker Lakes to "Theitaga" Lake, today known as Kasmere Lake, just south of the sixtieth parallel. From here Tyrrell had gone northwest, to Kasba Lake and the Kazan. But it was now the eighth of August. Knowing of the hardships and perils Tyrrell and his men had experienced in navigating the coastline of Hudson Bay in open canoes late in the season, and realizing that he and Magee could not possibly reach Chesterfield Inlet in time to get out, Oberholtzer chose instead to strike northeast, toward the Chipewyans' mysterious "Nu-thel-tin-tu-eh," or Sleeping Island Lake, where he hoped to find the vaguely charted Thlewiaza River and thereby make the Bay soon enough to get out ahead of winter weather. He and Magee now entered completely unknown territory, and Oberholtzer commenced time-and-compass mapping of their route. Following the river known today as the Kasmere, they entered Nueltin on 14 August. No white man had seen this enormous lake since Samuel Hearne* crossed it in the winter of 1770–71.

Nueltin's shoreline is indented with deep arms, tortuous inlets, and hundreds of blind bays; its surface, in places a maze of islands, elsewhere presents a canoeman with windswept traverses on which land drops from sight. Not until 28 August did Oberholtzer locate, at the lake's northeastern tip, the outlet of the Thlewiaza; there he also found freshwater seals and deteriorating weather. Beset by high winds, cold, and hunger, it took the Rainy Lake men—who had not seen another human being since leaving Kasmere Lake—two weeks to follow the rapids-choked and desolate Thlewiaza to saltwater. There, at the river's mouth, they providentially met a family of Padlemuits, with whom they sailed—not uneventfully—to Churchill. A hazard-ridden passage by canoe to York Factory followed. Then came the stiff journey upriver on the Hayes to Norway House, which they reached on 19 October. Having missed the last lake steamer of the season, they had no choice but to turn south and battle wind, waves, and snow the length of Lake Winnipeg until they arrived at Gimli, where they took out on 5 November.

In our time, perhaps only the tradition-minded canoeist, one paddling and portaging a wooden canoe, sleeping under canvas, carrying the old staples of flour, black tea, and bacon, and packing his loads by tumpline, can come close to grasping the feel and achievement of an undertaking like Oberholtzer's. Yet even such a traveller will be armed with accurate maps, is bound to find evidence of modern intrusions on the most remote of routes, and will become the target of an aerial search should he be much overdue at his destination. That Oberholtzer and Magee, complete strangers to the Far North, canoed such a distance without mishap, and that the

Oberholtzer, circa 1918. Courtesy of Ernest C. Oberholtzer Foundation

exploratory reaches of their journey were traversed without native guides, attests not only to their skills, fitness, and tenacity, but, above all, to the firmness of their friendship.

An unassuming man, Oberholtzer never published a word about his odyssey. So Tyrrell's expectation that the American's findings would "add materially to our knowledge of that portion of Northern Canada" came to nothing. The eloquent journal kept during the trip was lost for many years: found in an attic on Rainy Lake in 1983, it is now being prepared for publication by the present writer.

Ernest Oberholtzer devoted the rest of his life to the cause of conservation, indefatigably leading a decades-long campaign to preserve the Quetico-Superior country as an international wilderness. Concomitantly, he pursued his profound interest in the culture of the Ojibwas. Billy, for whom the Nueltin Lake voyage had been as much a spiritual as a physical journey, died in 1938. In 1963, Oberholtzer, still robust, returned to Nueltin by air and borrowed a boat: "With my own map made 51 years before, we had not the slightest difficult finding our way....We located the cairn and the very same tin container in which I left a note all that time ago."

When he was a young man, keen to know their lore, Ojibwas had named Ernest C. Oberholtzer "Atisokan," meaning "legend." Following his death in 1977, the children and grandchildren of those Indians gathered at his island home on Rainy Lake, made medicine, and placed the island under a protective and reverential spell.

Acknowledgements

The Ernest C. Oberholtzer Foundation; Minnesota Historical Society; Hudson's Bay Company Archives.

Further Readings

Cockburn, R.H. 1986. "Voyage to Netheltin." *The Beaver* 66:1 (Jan. Feb.): 4–27.

_____. 1988. "After-Images of Rupert's Land." In *Rupert's Land: A Cultural Tapestry,* edited by R.C. Davis. Waterloo: Wilfrid Laurier University Press.

Oberholtzer, E.C. 1929. The Lakes of Verendrye: A University of the Wilderness, American Forests and Forest Life.

Searle, R. Newell. 1977. *Saving Quetico-Superior, a Land Set Apart.* St. Paul: Minnesota Historical Society Press.

R.H. Cockburn

PRENTICE G. DOWNES
(1909–1959)

Prentice G. Downes was one of the most singular men to travel in the North in the last years before World War II. An able man in the wilderness and a gifted cartographer, ethnologist, and naturalist, he is best remembered as the author of *Sleeping Island: The Story of One Man's Travels in the Great Barren Lands of the Canadian North* (1943), a classic of northern canoe travel.

"Spike" Downes, as he was known to friends, was born in New Haven, Connecticut, in 1909. He attended the Kent School, and then Harvard, where he majored in psychology and indulged an appetite for amateur boxing. In 1933, he began a fruitful career at Belmont Hill School near Boston, where he taught Latin and geography, coached football and hockey, and became head of the history department: he was a talented, idiosyncratic, and much-beloved teacher. Short, powerfully built, and spectacled, he combined a passion for physical action with an uncommon intellectual curiosity, traits that were to invigorate his Canadian explorations.

In a letter to George Mellis Douglas* in 1943, Downes remarked that his having read Napoleon Comeau's *Life and Sport on the North Shore of the St. Lawrence* "had a great deal to do with my ever going north, as I was so interested that I set off for the North Shore to find the old gentleman." Comeau had died, but thus in 1935 Downes commenced

Prentice G. Downes with deer meat on Sandy Hill at Kasmere Lake, 1940. Courtesy of Mrs. E. G. Downes

his northern travels. In 1936, he took passage aboard Royal Mail Steamer (RMS) *Nascopie* from Montreal to Churchill, during which trip he made copious notes on climate, geography, wildlife, Ungava Inuit vocabulary, and northern society. From Churchill he went to Pelican Narrows and, with an Indian companion, canoed to Reindeer Lake and back again. In 1937, the New England Museum of Natural History sponsored a solo trip by Downes to study the Inuit of the Boothia Peninsula, before which he made his way to Brochet at the north end of Reindeer Lake and investigated the histories, languages, and ways of the Crees and the Chipewyans. This fascination with northern Indians, and above all with the significance of dreams in their culture, was central to Downes's travels. The Crees named him "The-man-who-talks-about-dreams." Two of Downes's unpublished writings are a Cree-Chipewyan dictionary and a volume titled "The Spirit World of the Northern Cree: Contributions to Cree Ethnology."

The first of Downes's major canoe trips, in 1938, found him paddling with Indians from Ile-à-la-Crosse to Waterways, then on alone, in a 13´4″ canoe, to Fort Fitzgerald; continuing by boat to Eldorado on Great Slave Lake, he eventually flew to the raw boom town of Yellowknife before returning south. It was on this journey that he met Douglas, who introduced him to Charles

Camsell* with these words: "Dr. Camsell, I wish to introduce Mr. Downes; he knows more of the history of this north country than J.B. himself"—meaning Joseph Burr Tyrrell.* The *Sleeping Island* trip of 1939, from Brochet to Nueltin Lake, which inspired Downes's trenchant book, was followed by another, less triumphant, venture into that region in 1940. Despondent as he was at his failure to reach Kasba Lake by way of the Little Partridge River, Downes could still confide in his journal: "Three important routes and one previously unknown river have been worked out. Kasmere Lake is now plotted, both north and east arm. Actually, far more was accomplished than a successful trip through to Kasba would have afforded." Much of the North was as yet imperfectly mapped then, and one of Downes's primary achievements was his meticulous mapping of every obscure route he followed. It was on this trip that he met Charles Planinshek, "Eskimo Charlie," who won northern immortality by canoeing, with his Cree wife and children, from Windy Lake to the Gulf of Mexico and on to New York and Montreal. Among his friends, Downes counted Douglas Leechman, Del Simons, Paddy Gibson, Richard Finnie, George Douglas, and numerous Hudson's Bay Company men, Indians, white trappers, Mounted Policemen, and missionaries; by 1940, his name was a familiar one from the eastern Arctic to

At Fort Smith, 1938. Courtesy of Mrs. E. G. Downes

Great Slave. His was a winning, unforgettable personality.

From 1942 to 1945, Downes served as chief of the Target Research Department of the U.S. Army Map Service, was seconded to Air Force Intelligence, and was appointed to the National Research Council, Division of Cartographic Techniques. At war's end, he lived for six months on a Vermont mountainside where he dined on porcupines and "became a medical curiosity, a modern day scurvy case." He then worked at Harvard for the great cartographer Dr. Erwin Raisz before resuming his teaching position at Belmont Hill in 1947. That summer he made his last canoe trip, "a sort of dream trip, alone, just visiting Indians," from Amisk Lake to Lac la Ronge. In the years that followed, he added to his stature as a teacher, wrote articles and stories, and researched the life of the "White Indian" John Tanner. Downes's journals of his northern trips, valuably detailed, intimate, and compelling, have been edited and published in recent years by the present writer. Prentice Downes died, much too soon, in 1959: he is survived by his wife and their two children.

Early in that final year of his life, Prentice G. Downes was asked to contribute autobiographical notes for a school reunion, and wrote of his travels into the Far North:

I liked that life and I liked the people there. I saw a lot of it just as the old north was vanishing; the north of no time, of game, of Indians, Eskimos, of unlimited space and freedom....I remember one time after a dreadful trip, camping on the edge of the tree line, again it was one of those indescribable smoky, bright-hazy days one sometimes gets in the high latitudes. I had hit the caribou migration and there was lots of meat; it was a curious spot, for all the horizon seemed to fall away from where I squatted, and I said to myself: Well, I suppose I shall never be so happy again.

Further Readings

Cockburn, Robert H. 1988. "After-Images of Rupert's Land." In *Rupert's Land: A Cultural Tapestry,* edited by R.C. Davis. Waterloo: Wilfrid Laurier University Press.

Downes, Prentice G. 1943. *Sleeping Island.* New York: Coward-McCann.

_____. 1954. "First Comers." In *North of 55,* edited by C. Wilson. Toronto: Ryerson Press.

_____. 1988. *Sleeping Island,* edited by R.H. Cockburn. Saskatoon: Western Producer Prairie Books.

R.H. Cockburn

Prentice Downes aboard RMS *Nascopie,* 1937. Photograph by Richard S. Finnie, courtesy of Mrs. E.G. Downes

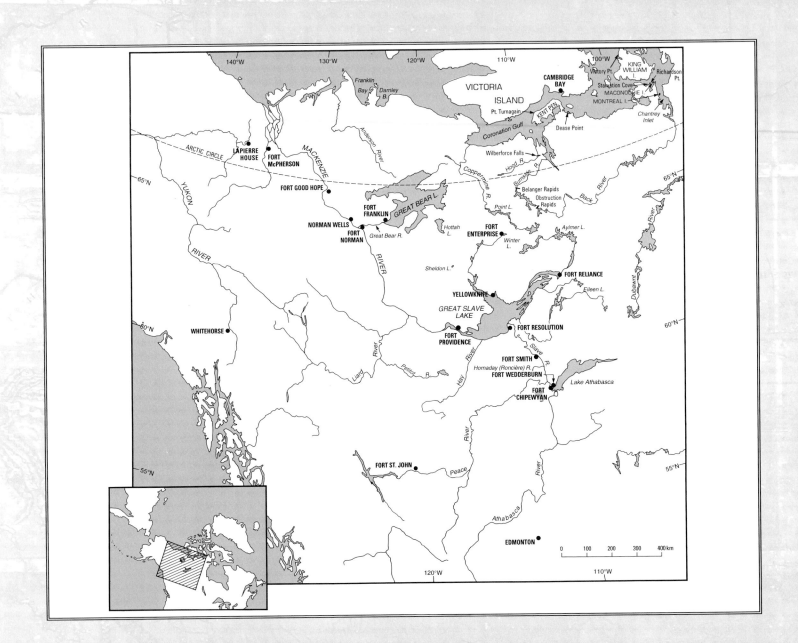

UNIT
❧ 8 ❧

**John Franklin, Akaitcho, Pierre St. Germain, Robert Hood,
James Anderson, Emile Petitot, Charles Jesse Jones, Guy Blanchet**

The individuals in this unit reflect a broad mix of backgrounds and objectives. Four of them were crucial fi-
ures on John Franklin's preliminary survey of the arctic coast
in the early nineteenth century, a geographical undertaking
on which over half the party's lives were lost. Others, such as
Petitot and Blanchet, continued the quest for knowledge of
northern geography well into the twentieth century. The por-
traits of Jones and Anderson reveal still more diverse attractions to the Arctic, while simultaneously capturing two very
different embodiments of a powerful cultural icon in North
America—the Frontiersman.

JOHN FRANKLIN (1786–1847)

One of the ironies accompanying fame is that the solid merits of celebrated men are often obscured by events of no real significance. Perhaps no reputation has suffered this irony more than John Franklin's. The man who charted nearly 1,850 miles of the coastline of North America is best remembered as the leader of an expedition that cost the British Admiralty two ships and the lives of 129 men and that made no direct contribution to the geographical unfolding of the Canadian Arctic.

John Franklin was born on 16 April 1786, one of twelve children in a family of waning fortune. In the fourteenth and fifteenth centuries, the word "franklin" marked a landowner of free, but not of noble, birth; however, by the time of John's birth in Spilsby, Lincolnshire, the family had long been involved in trade to meet economic realities. Franklin's biographers disagree about what Willingham Franklin thought of his son going to sea at age thirteen aboard a merchant vessel, but the young Franklin at least was eager. Family connections soon got him into the Royal Navy, first aboard HMS *Polyphemus,* later aboard HMS *Investigator.* Engaged in a coastal survey of Australian waters, the *Investigator* provided an excellent opportunity to learn about navigation and geographical work. Franklin was an apt student and subsequently became signals midshipman aboard the HMS *Bellerophon:* he was aboard that ship in 1805 when it squared off against *L'Aigle,* one of Napoleon's fleet, in the Battle of Trafalgar. Casualties

Portrait of John Franklin. Courtesy of the Scott Polar Research Institute, Cambridge, U.K.

were heavy, and although Franklin was not wounded, his hearing was permanently damaged by the guns' roar.

After Trafalgar, Franklin gained steady promotion and by 1815 was a first lieutenant. But that same year marked Napoleon's defeat at Waterloo, and in the ensuing peace, advancement in the Royal Navy all but ceased. Franklin endured an enforced idleness for three years before he was put in command of the brig HMS *Trent,* which was to accompany HMS *Dorothea* under David Buchan up the east coast of Greenland and, it was hoped, over the Pole to the Orient. The voyage came to naught, the ships being turned back by heavy ice near Spitsbergen.

In the same year, 1818, John Ross* had been sent on an ancillary expedition to look for an opening leading out of Baffin Bay. When Ross returned to England to report that Baffin Bay offered no westward egress, Second Secretary to the Admiralty John Barrow refused to believe him.

Hence, in 1819, the Admiralty dispatched William Edward Parry to search Baffin Bay again, while Franklin went across the mainland to explore the northern coast east of the Coppermine River's mouth. He built his base camp—Fort Enterprise—northeast of present-day Yellowknife, and, in the summer of 1821, his small party crossed overland to the Coppermine, descended it, and surveyed eastward along the coast. The advanced season and a reluctant crew forced him back at Point Turnagain on Kent Peninsula. To avoid the treacherous return along the coast in the much-weakened bark canoes, Franklin decided upon a 300 mile overland crossing by compass-bearing to Fort Enterprise, a journey that took them across the Barrens and that witnessed the deaths by starvation and exposure of nearly half the party of twenty, in addition to at least one murder, an execution without trial, and suspected cannibalism. Franklin and two of his three officers survived; the voyageurs paid the heaviest toll, only two out of eleven returning.

Franklin sailed back to England, where he married Eleanor Anne Porden, but when he was ordered to return to North America in 1825, he left his ailing young wife on her death bed and sailed for New York. With a well-disciplined crew of twenty-seven, comprising mostly British seamen and marines and including Dr. John Richardson* and George Back,* survivors of the 1819–22 expedition, Franklin set off for Great Bear Lake. There the party built Fort Franklin, a winter residence near the Great Bear River, which drains the lake into the Mackenzie River. After wintering at Fort Franklin, they descended the Mackenzie in the summer of 1826, using four sturdy boats rowed by seamen in place of the frail bark canoes manned by voyageurs of the previous expedition. At the delta, Dr. Richardson and E.N. Kendall turned east with two boats and about half the men, surveying the coast as far as the mouth of the Coppermine, where the eastward survey had begun on the first Arctic Land Expedition.

Franklin and George Back took the remaining men and boats and headed west. They hoped to meet Capt. Frederick William Beechey,* who had sailed around Cape Horn and through the Bering Sea as an ancillary to Franklin's overland journey. But poor weather and ice conditions made travel along the coast slow, even in the wooden boats, and Franklin did not want to repeat the experience of five years previous. Thus, at Return Reef, far short of Icy Cape, the intended rendezvous with Beechey, Franklin turned the party back, and everyone reached Fort Franklin safely. Franklin would later learn that he had come within 150 miles of a boat sent out from Beechey's ship.

Under John Franklin's command, then, two small parties of about two dozen men each put over 1,700 miles of previously unknown coastline on the map. The 1819–22 expedition had charted the shore almost 560 miles east of the Coppermine, the 1825–27 party had explored just short of 1,200 miles of coast to the Coppermine's west. The north shore of mainland North America stretches some 76° of longitude between the Alaska/Yukon border and the northern tip of Labrador; the coastline mapped under Franklin extends 40° of that longitude. Such is the accomplishment that earns John Franklin his greatness.

Notwithstanding this major achievement, Franklin is more often known by his final expedition of 1845. Shortly after the 1825–27 expedition, Franklin remarried, this time to Jane Griffin, who became the well-known Lady Franklin,* and the Franklins spent most of the next two decades in the Mediterranean and in Van Diemen's Land (modern Tasmania), where Franklin was governor. By the 1840s, a passage through the Arctic had been explored from the east and the west; it remained for someone to make the short connection around King William Land (at the time, not known to be an island) and to navigate the Northwest Passage from east to west. The Admiralty's choice of Franklin, already fifty-nine years old, to command the expedition suggests that they saw the voyage as a ribbon-cutting ceremony presenting little hazard. It was to be a ceremonial culmination of the centuries-old search for a passage to the Orient. John Franklin's ships HMS *Erebus* and *Terror* were last sighted by whalers in Baffin Bay in July 1845, two months after they hailed from London. Not a single crew man ever returned.

The many searches for the missing ships and men led to the mapping of much of Canada's Arctic, but the Franklin expedition itself added nothing to that discovery. The mysterious fate of the 1845 expedition, nevertheless, almost totally obscures the geographical triumphs Franklin made in the 1820s when he—to use L.H. Neatby's phrase—"put a roof on the map of Canada."

Further Readings

Davis, Richard C., ed. 1995. *Sir John Franklin's Journals and Correspondence: The First Arctic Land Expedition, 1819–1822.* Toronto: Champlain Society.

Franklin, John. [1823] 1969. *Narrative of a Journey to the Shores of the Polar Sea in the Years 1819, 20, 21 and 22.* Reprint. Edmonton: M.G. Hurtig.

_____. [1828] 1971. *Narrative of a Second Expedition to the Shores of the Polar Sea in the Years 1825, 1826, and 1827.* Reprint. Edmonton: M.G. Hurtig.

Neatby, L.H. 1970. *The Search for Franklin.* Edmonton: M.G. Hurtig.

Owen, Roderic. 1978. *The Fate of Franklin.* London: Hutchinson.

Richard C. Davis

AKAITCHO (ca. 1786–1838)

The Yellowknife Indian leader Akaitcho stepped upon the stage of Canadian history in the afternoon of 30 July 1820 when he met Capt. John Franklin* and affirmed his willingness to guide and provision Franklin's expedition of exploration "to the shores of the polar sea." A year later, almost to the day, Akaitcho and his band delivered Franklin and his complement to a point on the lower Coppermine River within five hours of the ocean. The drama of the succour of the starving survivors by Akaitcho and his followers in the following November assured Akaitcho's place in history.

Known in Franklin's time as Copper Indians, the Yellowknives were the northwesternmost division of the widespread Chipewyan peoples. Speaking a somewhat distinctive dialect of Chipewyan, they were a small "tribe" of about 190 souls in 1820. Akaitcho, "Big Foot," was the paramount leader. His band included about 40 men and boys. The Hook and Long Legs, who were also involved in the Franklin expedition, headed smaller groups.

Ranging broadly in the caribou lands from the East Arm of Great Slave Lake to the Coppermine River, Akaitcho and the Yellowknives traded as meat provisioners into the North West Company post of Fort Providence on the North Arm of Great Slave Lake. For at least a decade, the Yellowknives had pillaged furs, stolen women, and occasionally killed Dogrib and Hare Indians, their neighbours to the west and northwest. Dogribs were forced to avoid parts of their traditional hunting range during Akaitcho's years of aggressive leadership.

Akaitcho's ferocity is featured in Dogrib lore to the present day. Franklin and his officers experienced Akaitcho's character in more diverse aspects. At their first meeting in 1820, at Fort Providence, Akaitcho was at pains to impress

Akaitcho and his son, drawn by Robert Hood. From John Franklin's *Narrative of a Journey to the Shores of the Polar Sea* (1823)

Franklin with his dignity and importance. Franklin was to discover that Akaitcho did not easily yield in matters regarding his own judgment or self-interest. After the expedition was under way, Akaitcho resolutely balked at attempting the journey to the arctic coast in one season, pointing out that when he had agreed to do so he had no idea of the "slow mode of travelling" of Franklin's party. In consequence, the expedition established winter quarters at Fort Enterprise on Winter Lake. The following spring, Akaitcho had a try at demanding immediate distribution of promised trade goods before he would undertake the summer's expedition to the coast. When other Yellowknives did not support his allegations of bad faith, Akaitcho backed down, offering as justification that "as the leader of his party, he had to beg for them all."

When, after the terrible overland return from the arctic coast, the starving remnants of the Franklin expedition were rescued by Yellowknives, Akaitcho revealed another facet of his character. Treated with the "utmost Tenderness" by their rescuers, Franklin and his party from Fort Enterprise were conveyed to the camp of "our chief and companion Akaitcho." There, in Franklin's words, Akaitcho "shewd us the most friendly hospitality and all sorts of personal attention, even to cooking for us with his own hands, an office he never performs for himself." To survivor George Back,* Akaitcho was "generous and humane."

By 1825, when Franklin arrived at Fort Resolution on the south shore of Great Slave Lake to launch his second overland expedition, Akaitcho and the Yellowknives had suffered a change of fortune. In consequence of the merger of the North West Company and the Hudson's Bay Company in 1821, the post of Fort Providence had closed in 1823. Akaitcho and the Yellowknives now perforce had

to direct their trade into Fort Resolution in company with Chipewyans already attached to that post. (Their intermarriage and absorption into that population brought the eventual disappearance of the Yellowknives as a distinct people.) Driven by vengeance or desperation over killings perpetrated by Yellowknives earlier in the year, in October of 1823 Dogribs attacked the Yellowknife Long Legs and his band, who were encamped in the area between Hottah Lake and Great Bear Lake. Thirty-four Yellowknives perished—four men, thirteen women, and seventeen children. This was a bitter reversal. Akaitcho refused to join Franklin's expedition to Great Bear Lake, sending word that he and his hunters would not go into the lands where their kinsmen had died, "lest we should attempt to renew the war." "Peace" took the form of mutual avoidance between Dogribs and Akaitcho's band. In 1829 a tense encounter, apparently the first since the destruction of Long Legs's band, was resolved without bloodshed.

Akaitcho reemerged in the history of northern exploration in the winter of 1833–34 during an "appalling period of suffering and calamity" at Fort Reliance, the base that Back had established for the overland search for John Ross,* believed lost in the polar region. Akaitcho's energy and resolve in the hunt and the example of psychological fortitude he set in that time of famine commanded Back's admiration. Yet later in his journal, Back remarked that Akaitcho, who was then about fifty years of age and in poor health, had lost much of his authority over the Yellowknives.

In 1838, word came to the trader at Fort Resolution that Akaitcho had died that spring. Dogrib tradition has it that Akaitcho is buried on an island in Yellowknife Bay.

Further Readings

Back, George. [1835] 1970. *Narrative of the Arctic Land Expedition*. Reprint. Edmonton: M.G. Hurtig.

Davis, Richard C., ed. 1995. *Sir John Franklin's Journals and Correspondence: The First Arctic Land Expedition, 1819–1822*. Toronto: Champlain Society.

Franklin, John. [1823] 1969. *Narrative of a Journey to the Shores of the Polar Sea in the Years 1819, 20, 21 and 22*. Reprint. Edmonton: M.G. Hurtig.

Gillespie, Beryl C. 1981. "Yellowknife." In *Subarctic, Handbook of North American Indians*, Vol. 6, edited by J. Helm. Washington: Smithsonian Institution.

Helm, June and Beryl C. Gillespie 1981. "Dogrib Oral Tradition as History: War and Peace in the 1820s." *Journal of Anthropological Research* 37: 8–27.

June Helm and Beryl C. Gillespie

PIERRE ST. GERMAIN
(1790–ca. 1870)

Of the fifteen hired men on John Franklin's* first land expedition, Pierre St. Germain has been the most underrated. Although a rogue, a rebel, and a troublemaker, he was the strongest, most resourceful, and most versatile man on the expedition. The journals of John Richardson* and George Back,* as well as the Red River records and Robert McVicar's unpublished Fort Resolution journals, shed considerable new light on the character of this hunter and interpreter.

St. Germain, part French and part Indian, served in the Athabasca district for the North West Company from 1812 to 1818. In 1819, he joined the Hudson's Bay Company at a wage of 2,000 Montreal *livres* (£100) per annum and served as an interpreter at Fort Resolution, Great Slave Lake. His previous service with the larger, rival North West Company was referred to by Governor George Simpson* in his letter of 26 January 1821 to McVicar: "St. Germain is out of a bad nest and I trust we shall soon be able to shake off this Fraternity. I expect a few attached English half-breeds into the country next season and then we shall be more independent of N.W. renegadoes."

On 5 June 1820, Colin Robertson wrote McVicar, giving permission for St. Germain to join the arctic land expedition under the command of Lt. John Franklin. On 25 July 1820, St. Germain entered into an agreement with Franklin for wages of "3000 Livres per annum until his return to Ft. Wedderburn." This £150 was two-and-a-half times the amount Franklin offered a French Canadian voyageur.

St. Germain's employers recognized his ability, but also his independent ways. Robertson described St. Germain as "an intelligent young man" and on 5 June 1820 wrote "I have given up an excellent Chippeyan [sic] interpreter, St.

Joseph and Mary Ann (née Plamandon) St. Germain, around 1890. Joseph was the second-oldest son of Pierre St. Germain. Photograph courtesy of the Washington State Historical Society, Tacoma

Germain." McVicar considered him indispensable, mentioning how he could travel without either a blanket or provisions, but also noting his liking for alcohol. When St. Germain delayed his departure from Fort Wedderburn, opposite Fort Chipewyan on Lake Athabasca, until after the New Year's celebrations of 1820, McVicar remarked that "his long stay shews a complete contempt for the interests of the concern." Later, McVicar wrote of "that scoundrel's machinations ... a dangerous man." McVicar noted on 2 July 1820 that "St. Germent has joined the service of the Expedition and has taken up his quarters in the N.Wt. Fort."

Richardson considered St. Germain to be one of the most reliable men on the expedition and the one with the most influence on the accompanying Copper (Yellowknife) Indians. St. Germain was intelligent, determined, and, when reasonably fed, indefatigable. He made the preliminary trip to Point Lake with Back and Robert Hood* in the autumn of 1820. During the winter of 1820–21, he snowshoed 273 miles from Fort Enterprise to Fort Resolution, bringing back the two Inuit, Augustus and Junius. Strong, resourceful, practical, a man of great stamina, St. Germain was also exceedingly dexterous, evidenced by his use of a made-down canoe to cross the Burnside River on 9 September and, five days later, to ferry Franklin across Belanger Rapids. St. Germain alone had the ability to improvise that allowed him single-handedly to convert the fragments of "painted canvas" or "oil-cloth" into a cockleshell that would finally transport everyone across Obstruction Rapids on 4 October, after nine days of crucial delay.

One can sense the varying degrees of Richardson's regard for St. Germain as he refers to him in his journal as "Pierre," "Pierez," "Perez," and "Pierish." He even uses the affectionate diminutive "Pierrot" after St. Germain had been particularly helpful. This use of "Pierrot" confused Franklin greatly; working from Richardson's journal after losing his own in the rapids, Franklin twice in his published narrative ascribed actions to the voyageur Ignace Perrault that Richardson's journal credits to St. Germain. One of these was the sharing of an extra portion of meat with the officers on 14 September, an act of generosity singled out for special mention in Louis Melzack's introduction to M.G. Hurtig's 1969 reprint of Franklin's narrative. The second was the crucial killing of a fine caribou on 15 September, when they were starving.

As a troublemaker, St. Germain gained the enmity of both Franklin and Back. As early as 23 March 1821, St.

Germain expressed his concern about the dangers involved in the proposed arctic explorations and shared his views with Akaitcho's* Copper Indians. Because of this indiscretion, Franklin that day described him as "an artful man" and said he was "perfectly satisfied of his baseness."

Franklin suspected St. Germain and the Indian hunters of lessening their efforts, hoping that poor hunting would prevent the expedition from getting under way, and Franklin threatened to "convey him to England for a trial if the Expedition should be stopped through his fault." At the mouth of the Coppermine on 19 July, the two native interpreters, Jean Baptiste Adam and St. Germain, "made many urgent requests to be allowed to return with Mr. Wentzel." Franklin denied them because the two interpreters had already proved to be the party's only skilled hunters. To prevent their "plan for eloping," they were in fact conscripted: "Lest they should leave us by stealth, their motions were strictly watched…. The rest of the men knowing that their own safety would be compromised had they succeeded, kept a watchful eye over them." George Back's recently published journal tells of St. Germain's attempt to persuade him to act as navigator and to press ahead of the straggling party on their tragic return trip across the Barrens.

By September 1822—the Franklin expedition over—HBC chief trader Alexander Roderick McLeod engaged St. Germain at Lake Athabasca to serve in the capacity of interpreter. According to "A List of people having Families Supported at the Company's Establishments in Mckenzies River District," St. Germain resided at Fort Perseverance (Fort Norman) in 1823–24. In the Northern Department Abstracts of Servants' Accounts for 1825–26, he was listed as being thirty-five years of age. He continued to serve the Company as an interpreter in the Mackenzie River District until 12 September 1834.

St. Germain then retired to the Red River Settlement, where he purchased fifty acres of land on 13 April 1835. The Red River census returns dated 31 May 1835 list him as a Roman Catholic, with two acres of land under cultivation. Living with him were his wife, one son above the age of sixteen, one son below the age of sixteen, and two daughters below the age of fifteen. The 31 March 1840 census listed a third daughter and gave his age as forty years, though more likely he was fifty.

In 1841, taking his wife and five youngest children with him, including a year-old son, his was one of sixteen families who trekked across the Rocky Mountains with James Sinclair to the Oregon Territory, now Lewis County, Washington. His oldest son, Pierre, already married, remained in the Red River colony. Our hero is presumed to have died in Washington about 1870; the family claimed he was 105 years of age. Although too independent to fit easily into naval discipline, Pierre St. Germain was an indispensable man. Without his hunting and craft skills, Franklin, Richardson, Back, and John Hepburn would have perished. Without him, Franklin's first arctic land expedition, like the 1845 disaster, would have had no surviving officers and no published accounts. It was a close call indeed.

Acknowledgements

I wish to thank Shirlee Anne Smith and Judith Hudson Beattie, Hudson's Bay Company Archives, Provincial Archives of Manitoba, for assistance far beyond the call of duty. John C. Jackson and Mary Black-Rogers have helped in tracing some of the many St. Germains in the Northwest, Red River, and Oregon.

Further Readings

Franklin, John. [1823] 1969. *Narrative of a Journey to the Shores of the Polar Sea in the Years 1819, 20, 21 and 22.* Reprint. Edmonton: M.G. Hurtig.

Houston, C. Stuart, ed. 1994. *Arctic Artist: The Journal and Paintings of George Back, Midshipman with Franklin, 18191822.* Commentary by I.S. MacLaren. Montreal: McGill-Queen's University Press.

_____, ed. 1984. *Arctic Ordeal: The Journal of John Richardson, Surgeon-Naturalist with Franklin, 1820–1822.* Montreal: McGill-Queen's University Press.

C. Stuart Houston

ROBERT HOOD (*1797–1821*)

Robert Hood was a junior officer with the badly timed, inadequately supplied first Arctic Land Expedition led by John Franklin* in 1819–22. Hood made a major contribution to the expedition's incredibly accurate mapping of over 600 miles of arctic coastline. He was the first to prove the action of the aurora borealis on the compass needle and to show that the aurora was an electrical phenomenon. He also made important contributions to our knowledge of terrestrial magnetism, climatology, anthropology, and natural history. Hood's journal, a less formal and more sprightly account of the journey than Franklin's published narrative, was published with many of his watercolour paintings 153 years after his tragic death on the barrenlands.

Robert Hood, the second son of the Reverend Richard Hood, LL.D., was born in 1797 and educated in Bury, Lancashire, eight miles north of Manchester. At fourteen, he became a midshipman and continued his education on board ship.

The Franklin expedition, with John Richardson* as surgeon-naturalist, sailed from Gravesend in May 1819 in a Hudson's Bay Company supply vessel. Before the advent of photography, one or more illustrators were customarily attached to such an expedition; the Admiralty chose Robert Hood and George Back* as midshipmen because of their artistic abilities and their scientific proficiencies. Richardson and Hood spent the first winter at Cumberland House, where

This silhouette of Robert Hood is the only surviving image of him

Hood painted Indians, animals, and birds, including five bird forms not yet described to science.

Throughout the journey, Hood was the primary surveyor and draughtsman. Whether on foot or in a canoe, Hood plotted accurately as many as thirty-three changes of course in a single day. His sketches and paintings, executed twenty-seven years before those of Paul Kane, were done under trying circumstances; sometimes his brush would freeze to the paper.

It is a miracle that Hood's exquisite watercolours from Cumberland House arrived at York Factory in such good condition. No doubt they were well wrapped in beaver skins and well protected from the spray during the negotiation of numerous rapids. The paintings were conveyed by Gov. William Williams of the Hudson's Bay Company, who that year took the longer, more difficult Minago route to avoid capture by rival North West Company men who were lying in wait for him at Grand Rapids.

Some of Hood's scenes were used to illustrate Franklin's 1823 public narrative. Comparison with the original paintings, however, shows that the engravers took considerable liberties. Hood realistically portrayed the men in their soiled and somewhat ragged garb, whereas the engravers depicted them in clean and tidy uniforms. These paintings and Hood's original journal were found, well protected from light, in the attic of a coach house in Tipperary, Ireland, when Hood's sister's granddaughter died there in 1933.

At Fort Enterprise, their winter quarters in 1820–21, Hood and Back were rivals for the favour of an attractive sixteen year-old Copper Indian (Yellowknife) girl, called Greenstockings by the officers. This rivalry, which led to the two midshipmen planning a duel, may have contributed to Franklin's decision to send Back on a remarkable 1,100-mile snowshoe trip to and from Fort Chipewyan in midwinter. In any event, Hood won the maiden's approval, and some time after his death, Greenstockings bore an infant daughter, later listed in the official census as "orphaned daughter of Robert Hood, R.N."

The last entry in Hood's extant journal is for 15 September 1820. The extant journal of John Richardson begins at nearly the same time, with only eight days of overlap. Collectively, the journals of the officers, which have all now been published, offer a vivid portrayal of the fatigue and starvation suffered on the tragic return trek overland across the Barrens, after a successful summer of arctic exploration. Eleven of the twenty members of the party perished. Hood was within a few days of death from starvation when on 20 October 1821, less than thirty miles from Fort Enterprise, his end was hastened by a bullet through the head fired by Michel Teroahaut, one of the voyageurs. Richardson and John Hepburn, his two remaining companions in the straggling rearward group, owed their survival in part to eating, knowingly or unknowingly, some human flesh and Hood's buffalo robe.

Robert Hood contributed in full measure to the success of the first expedition before he paid the supreme sacrifice, and his journals and paintings remain one of the earliest and most vivid records of life in the Canadian North. Although his promising career was terminated prematurely, his memory is perpetuated by a flower, the moss phlox, *Phlox hoodii*; a sedge, *Carex hoodii*; and by the mighty Hood River that plunges over Wilberforce Falls before entering the Arctic Ocean.

Further Readings

Franklin, John. 1823. *Narrative of a Journey to the Shores of the Polar Sea in the Years 1819, 20, 21 and 22*. London: John Murray.

Houston, C. Stuart, ed. 1974. *To the Arctic by Canoe, 1819–1821: The Journal and Paintings of Robert Hood, Midshipman with Franklin*. Montreal: McGill-Queen's University Press.

_____, ed. 1984. *Arctic Ordeal: The Journal of John Richardson, Surgeon-Naturalist with Franklin*. Montreal: McGill-Queen's University Press.

_____, ed. 1994. *Arctic Artist: The Journal and Paintings of George Back, Midshipman with Franklin, 1819–1822*. Commentary by I.S. MacLaren. Montreal: McGill-Queen's University Press.

Wiebe, Rudy. 1994. *A Discovery of Strangers*. Toronto: Alfred A. Knopf Canada.

C. Stuart Houston

JAMES ANDERSON (1812–1867)

Canada's northern frontier, far from being a "wild west," was a region where Indians and the Hudson's Bay Company dealt with each other to their mutual advantage. James Anderson, better known as an arctic explorer, was one of the men who made the orderly system work.

A career on the frontier of the British Empire came naturally to a young man with his family connections. General Outram was a famous warrior in India. Another cousin stood his battalion at attention on the sinking *Birkenhead* so that women and children could be saved. In 1831, James left Britain as an apprentice with the Hudson's Bay Company. For

Photograph of James Anderson. Courtesy of Mrs. Goodfellow, a descendant

twenty years he served with energy, judgment, and business acumen in the James Bay, Lake Superior, and Athabasca areas. George Simpson,* HBC governor at the time, entrusted him with the remote and valuable Mackenzie District. He improved profits by better book-keeping and retrenchment on the upper Yukon basin. His preference was to open trade directly with the Inuit via the Anderson River north of Fort Good Hope.

Suddenly, in 1855, he was ordered to take part in the search for John Franklin's* expedition. The Admiralty had wearied of the expensive probing of the arctic islands, but Dr. John Rae* of the Hudson's Bay Company had reported finding relics while surveying Boothia Peninsula. Inuit had told him of white men perishing on an island west of a great river.

This was obviously the river down which George Back* and Richard King* had taken a York boat in 1834. Now, the British government asked the Company to use the same route to check out Rae's report. Simpson had confidence that Anderson would see the matter through without creating new disasters.

Anderson's second-in-command, James Green Stewart,* despite his Yukon reputation, proved to be of little use on the expedition. For instance, he allowed inferior bark to be used in the construction of the special, shortened North Canoes. However, the actual crews that Simpson had ordered to assemble at Fort Resolution were the pick of the service and included three Caughnawaga steersmen. Unfortunately, Rae's Inuit interpreter could not be found in time.

Because he could not carry enough supplies to overwinter, Anderson had to accomplish his mission in the short interval between break-up and the onset of the next winter. On Indian advice to bypass frozen lakes, he chose a new, more direct mountain portage route from Great Slave Lake. Solid ice on Lake Aylmer put him twelve days behind the schedule of Back, whose carefully mapped route he joined at that point. The Back River lies wholly beyond the tree line and has eighty-three rapids. At the last rapids, Anderson interviewed Inuit fishermen. Two of the crew understood some Inuktitut, but the lack of a real interpreter was vexing. The Inuit had hearsay evidence of the Franklin disaster and were using some European materials. On 31 July, only two days later than Back, Anderson entered Chantrey Inlet. It was choked with wind-driven floes, and the fragile canoes could not operate as icebreakers. When the men managed to reach Montreal Island, they began finding wood and metal fragments along the shore and in Inuit caches. One chip bore the name "Mr. Stanley" of HMS *Erebus*.

Using an inflatable rubber raft, three men pushed on to Maconochie Island. Many years later, one voyageur claimed he had sighted the masts of a ship stuck in the ice far to the north, but had said nothing because he had feared any further delay in returning to the safety of the tree line. Probably he had not really seen a ship, but there was another tantalizing might-have-been. Anderson, with a true instinct, wanted to search Cape Richardson but was prevented by a "millstream" of jagged ice. Had he done so, he would have encountered, a scant five miles to the west in a *cul-de-sac* later known as Starvation Cove, the last encampment of the Franklin expedition. Instead, he packed up the raft in the canoes, which had been repaired and regummed, and gave the order to return.

Not until 1962 was the whole Back River canoed and kayaked again. Many regard it as an ultimate challenge due to its remoteness and exposed terrain. At a mid-August date when modern canoeists are anxiously scanning the skies for their pick-up plane, Anderson's men had to paddle, line, and portage their way up the Back, across the height of land, and through windy lakes, over 930 miles to Fort Resolution. In the weakened canoes, they risked death in the icy waters.

Anderson's official report was brief and restrained. He had found no papers or bodies and could merely confirm Rae's statement that the disaster had occurred somewhere northwest of the Back. Nonetheless, Simpson warmly thanked him, his fellow officers gave him a silver cup, and the British government awarded him the Polar Medal and £400. Dr. King, however, was upset that Anderson had not specifically checked his 1834 cache on Montreal Island. Lady Jane Franklin* financed another sea-and-sledging expedition under Francis Leopold McClintock,* which found the message at Point Victory. But this was far beyond the range of canoes in 1855.

Anderson's health had been undermined by the trip. After three more years as chief factor in the Mackenzie District, he asked to be transferred. At Mingan on the St. Lawrence, he straightened out the account books and entertained the governor-general with salmon fishing. He finally retired, as a country squire, to Ontario, where his children were entering the professions.

James Anderson's service to the Company was exemplary, and he narrowly missed fame at Starvation Cove. Altogether, he was a fine frontiersman—Canadian style.

Further Readings

Clarke, C.H.D., ed. 1940–41. "Chief Factor James Anderson's Back River Journal of 1855." *Canadian Field-Naturalist* 54 and 55.

Cundy, Robert. 1970. *Beacon Six.* London: Eyre and Spottiswoode.

C. Stuart Mackinnon

EMILE PETITOT (*1838–1916*)

Emile Petitot was not the only Oblate missionary in the Canadian Northwest to distinguish himself outside his professional sphere, but the primacy of his contribution to northern geography and ethnology sets him apart from others of his order.

Born the son of a watchmaker on 3 December 1838, at Grancey-le-Château, France, Emile Fortuné Stanislas Joseph Petitot entered the Congregation of the Oblate Missionaries of Mary-Immaculate in 1860. Fourteen days after his ordination, Petitot left France for the Mackenzie River, where he lived for the next twelve years, based at missions in Fort Providence, Fort Resolution, and principally Fort Good Hope.

His accomplishments during his stay were remarkable. He collected material for his *Dictionnaire de la langue Dénédindjié*, a dictionary of the major Athapaskan languages; Petitot's work still remains the best available in the field. *Les Traditions indiennes du Canada Nord-ouest* (1888) records extensive legends from the Hare, Chipewyan, Loucheux, Dogrib, Cree, and Blackfoot cultures, all gathered during this period. Rarely at the missions, he travelled widely with native companions, often into territory completely unknown to both Petitot and his guides. In *Les Grands-Esquimaux* (1887), he tells of his visit to the Tchiglit Inuit, where, in March 1865, he met Noulloumallok-Innonarana, "chief" of the Tchiglit, on the Anderson River *en route* to the Arctic Ocean. Noulloumallok's immense respect for the missionary—characteristic of the general response of native peoples to him—is evident in the name the

Emile Petitot. Courtesy of the Northwest Territories Archives.

Inuk bestowed on Petitot: "Mitchi Pitchitork Tchikraynarm iyoyé" (Mr. Petitot, son of the Sun). Attending to the physical, as well as spiritual, well-being of the Indians, Petitot nursed them when they were sick, and supplied them with necessary food and clothing. Although suffering from an abdominal rupture, he designed, decorated, and helped build the Good Hope chapel, declared an official historic site in 1981.

In June 1870, he journeyed from Fort McPherson to Lapierre House in the face of strong resistance from the Protestants, who considered that territory as inviolably theirs. His maps of the vicinity of Great Slave Lake, of the Anderson River, and of the western branches of the Yukon are remarkably accurate. Travelling between the Mackenzie and Liard rivers, he charted the Petitot River, named in his honour. He corrected and completed the maps of his precursors, notably John Franklin.* The Rivière La Roncière-Le Noury, which Petitot discovered in 1868 and placed on the map in 1875, was later denied any existence. Over thirty years after Petitot's discovery, the mouth of a large river (the Hornaday) was found to empty into Darnley Bay east of the supposed mouth of Petitot's Roncière, although the river's course was not extensively surveyed beyond its mouth. Later explorers—Vilhjalmur Stefansson* in particular—concluded that, since no river entered Franklin Bay as described on Petitot's map, the Roncière River, 190 miles in length, did not exist! But aerial photography has proven—some eighty years after its discovery—that

Petitot's Roncière River indeed exists: it is one and the same as the Hornaday. After exploring nearly the entire length of the river, Petitot left its course shortly before it drained into Darnley Bay; thus, he only misjudged the exact point at which it meets the sea. Other aerial surveys done after WW II have corroborated the general accuracy of Petitot's maps of the Northwest.

The pace of Petitot's northern life could not continue indefinitely. Exhausted after twelve years in the North, he returned to France in 1874, where he arranged for the publication of his dictionaries and numerous other works. At the International Congress of Americanists, held in Nancy the year after his arrival in France, Petitot spoke out in strong support of the Asiatic origin of Inuit and Indians of North America. He also received at this time a silver medal from the Société de Géographie de Paris for his map of arctic regions.

On 24 March 1876, Petitot again embarked for the North. But his health was broken, and his great period of geographical discovery had come to a close. After spending most of this second trip helping and studying the Indians in the Great Slave Lake vicinity, ill health ultimately demanded that he give up missionary work entirely. He returned to France in 1883. Upon his return, he was awarded the George Back* prize by the Royal Geographic Society of London in recognition of his scientific contributions. He joined the secular clergy and, on 1 October 1886, became parish priest at Mareuil-lès-Meaux, France, where he spent the remaining thirty years of his life ministering to his parish and publishing books and articles on northern Canada. His death came on 13 May 1916.

The geography of the country and the ethnology of its people were Petitot's primary northern interests, but he also made substantial contributions to our knowledge of the geology, paleontology, zoology, and botany of the region. As one reads through the massive volume of his manuscripts, publications, and personal letters, one can see that he was a keen and astute observer; he had a subtle and inquisitive mind and an encyclopedic knowledge. Canada formally recognized Petitot's accomplishments on 22 September 1975, when the Honourable Judd Buchanan, then minster of Indian and Northern Affairs, unveiled at Mareuil-lès-Meaux, a plaque commemorating the scientific contribution of Emile Petitot to the Canadian North. In October 1980, the new minister, the Honourable John Munro, donated a copy of Petitot's works, originally published in France, to the Institute for Northern Studies at the University of Saskatchewan.

Further Readings

Northern Research Division, ed. 1980. *Amerindian Territorial Occupation of the Canadian Northwest in the 19th Century, as recorded by Emile Petitot.* Ottawa: Department of Indian and Northern Affairs.

Petitot, Emile. 1887. *Les Grands-Esquimaux.* Paris: E. Plon, Nourrit et Cie.

_____. 1888. *En Route pour la Mer Glaciale.* Paris: Letouzey et Ané éditeurs.

_____. 1888. *Traditions Indiennes du Canada Nord-Ouest.* Alençon: E. Renaut- de-Broise.

_____. 1889. *Quinze Ans sous le Cercle Polaire.* Vol. 1. Mackenzie, Anderson et Youkon. Paris: E. Dentu.

_____. 1891. *Autour du Grand lac des Esclaves.* Paris: Nouvelle Librairie Parisienne, Albert Savine éditeur.

_____. 1893. *Exploration de la région du Grand Lac des Ours.* Paris: Téqui Libraire-éditeur.

Savoie, Donat, ed. 1970. *The Amerindians of the Canadian Northwest in the 19th Century, as Seen by Emile Petitot.* 2 vol.. Ottawa: Department of Indian and Northern Affairs.

Donat Savoie

CHARLES JESSE JONES
(1844–1919)

On 12 June 1897, fifty-three-year-old Charles Jesse ("Buffalo") Jones left Garden City, Kansas, for the Far North to do what nobody had done: capture a musk-ox and bring it back alive to "civilization." Jones was already internationally famous as "The Saviour of the American Bison." A former buffalo hunter, he experienced remorse when he saw overkill pushing the species toward extinction. He began lassoing calves from wild herds, rearing them on his Kansas ranch, then crossbreeding them with cattle to create hybrids he called "cattalo." He hoped these would prove more practical for western and northern ranges than cattle or buffalo.

In 1889, he caused an international incident by purchasing nearly all the buffalo left in Canada, Major Bedson's noted Manitoba herd, for an estimated $50,000 for eighty-three head—over the protest of the Dominion government. In 1891, Jones created a further sensation by taking a shipment of buffalo to England for sale to breeders and zoos. Buffalo Bill's Wild West Show had acquainted England with live buffalo, but never with anything like this lanky frontiersman-entrepreneur who resembled a cartoonist's Uncle Sam. Jones was invited to Buckingham Palace to visit the Prince of Wales.

He then went to Edmonton where he bought a ton of supplies, including a rubber life preserver for strapping around himself while floating northward down rivers that led

"Buffalo" Jones, original photograph by Cherry Kearton, first published in 1911. This was probably at the time of Jones's journey to Africa. Courtesy of R. Easton and M. Brown

to the musk-ox range. Jones was driven by a passion to capture and tame wild animals. Perhaps it stemmed from the words of Genesis read aloud by his father in their Illinois cabin: "replenish the earth … have dominion over … every living thing." To Jones, it seemed God had commanded him to go forth and subdue all animals in His name.

At Fort Smith on the Slave River he was invited by Indians to a council. "The musk-ox is sacred to us," they warned. "If you take musk-ox away, it will offend the Great Spirit. All our game will leave!"

Jones replied he'd come not to destroy, but to preserve an animal they killed for food. He wanted musk-oxen for study and use as well as display. He might even hybridize them with cattle. He advised the Indians to domesticate and propagate musk-ox as ordained by the Great Spirit in the White Man's bible; then they would never starve. The Chipewyans, Crees, and Slaves who comprised the council left, planning how to thwart Jones.

In company with a brawny Scot named Rea, Jones built a winter cabin on Great Slave Lake. In February 1898, he and Rea started for the musk-ox range. After harrowing adventures they discovered a herd in the snowy wasteland north of the Dubawnt River. The musk-oxen split into two groups as they approached. In one were five calves. Jones's famous lasso came into play. When the five were captured, they were fitted with hackamores and tethered at intervals to a long rope.

But as the men travelled south with their prizes, the Indians struck. While Jones and Rea slept in their tent, each calf's throat was cut in what appears to have been a ritual killing. In the snow nearby Jones found a bloody knife, its blade fastened to a caribou rib, apparently left behind deliberately. Thus ended Jones's dream of capturing a musk-ox. Others, marching to the words of another god, had thwarted him. Undismayed, he returned home via the Mackenzie River and Yukon gold camps, inspecting an island in the Bering Sea with a view to establishing a breeding farm for silver foxes.

Jones was part hero, part entrepreneur, part promoter, always indomitable. He had a vision of mankind and wild animals living together in mutually beneficial fashion. Today's hybridizing and captive breeding programs continue his dream.

In 1902, President Theodore Roosevelt named him first game warden of the newly created Yellowstone Park. Poachers were decimating the park's wildlife. Roosevelt wanted someone who could stop them. Jones did. Soon he introduced Zane Grey to the West by taking him on a trip to lasso lions in Arizona. Grey, impressed, decided to make the West the subject of his writing and to pattern his heroes on Jones. Grey's book about their hunting trip and Jones's life, *The Last of the Plainsmen* (1908), appeared just in time for Jones's next adventure.

In 1910, Jones was off to lasso bigger lions, those in Africa. He brought one back to the Bronx Zoo. This led to his next, and greatest challenge. The gorilla, publicized as the "missing link" between man and ape, had never been brought into captivity and survived. At age seventy-five Jones went to West Africa and lassoed one. But it was so strong it broke even his famous lasso. Before he could catch another, the outbreak of World War I forced the abandonment of his plans.

Typically, death found Charles Jesse Jones writing a book about his experiences and promoting a centrifugal siphon pump he'd invented, while dreaming of hybridizing domestic sheep with Rocky Mountain bighorns. The *New York Times* for 2 October 1919 said: "Charles Jesse Jones, known throughout America as 'Buffalo Jones,' famous cowboy and big game hunter and friend of the late former president Theodore Roosevelt, died today." The lengthy obituary failed to say that Jones was the first, great, and highly original preserver-user of North America's wildlife.

Further Readings

Easton, Robert and MacKenzie Brown. [1961] 1970. *Lord of Beasts—The Saga of Buffalo Jones*. Lincoln: University of Nebraska Press.

Grey, Zane. 1908. *The Last of the Plainsmen*. New York: Outing Publishing Company.

Jones, Charles Jesse and Henry Inman. 1899. *Buffalo Jones' Forty Years of Adventure*. Topeka: Kansas Publishing Company.

Robert Easton and Mackenzie Brown

GUY BLANCHET (1884–1966)

Season after seasons, college students and others returning from part-time jobs with survey parties in northern Alberta, Saskatchewan, and Manitoba would tell how their leader, though older and half their size, would consistently outwalk, outpack, and outpaddle any of them. It was hard work for them just to tag along behind him, and he was a hard if amiable taskmaster. His name was Guy Houghton Blanchet, and he kept up his pace across the Canadian Arctic and Subarctic and elsewhere for nearly a half century. As a surveyor, engineer, and explorer, he became a legend in his own time.

Blanchet, of remote French ancestry, was born in Ottawa, on 12 February 1884. He attended local schools and McGill University, Montreal, where he received a Bachelor of Science degree in mining engineering in 1905. After two years of work among the coal deposits of Crows Nest, British Columbia, he qualified as Dominion Land Surveyor, entitling him to put the letters D.L.S. after his name. That was comparable to a doctorate, requiring proficiency in astronomy, spherical trigonometry, and land laws, with strenuous examinations and extended apprenticeship in the field.

In 1910, he joined the Topographical Survey of Canada and laid out base lines in the northerly reaches of the prairie provinces, mostly Alberta, during the next few years. In those years he gained his reputation as a tough, tireless worker and traveller.

From 1921 to 1925, he carried out exploratory surveys in the Mackenzie and Keewatin districts of the Northwest Territories. His work was centred in the Great Slave Lake area and northward, which he traversed by canoe and on foot, encompassing over 115,000 square miles from Hay River on the west to the Dubawnt River on

Guy Blanchet on the first reconnaissance flight from Norman Wells to Whitehorse, 12 June 1942. Photo by Richard S. Finnie

the east, the sixtieth parallel on the south to the Coppermine River on the north. Until then, the easterly shoreline of Great Slave Lake had appeared on maps much as George Back* had placed it in the early nineteen century. Blanchet's printed report described his journeys and summarized the history, geology, and typography of the country, plus sections on settlements, transportation, climate, vegetation, and wildlife.

Through an eighteen-month period in 1928–29, Blanchet represented the federal government and led a mineral exploration expedition of Dominion Explorers, Ltd., a private company. This geological survey was set up to investigate huge areas along the western side of Hudson Bay between Churchill and Chesterfield Inlet, and inland to

Great Slave Lake and northward as far as Coronation Gulf, with scattered bases. The expedition pioneered large-scale use of aircraft in northern Canada. However, geological work of the field parties became subordinate to the task of keeping airplanes in operable condition and finding lost people.

When an aerial inspection group headed by Col. C.D.H. MacAlpine, a Toronto promoter and president of the company, disappeared in the Arctic, Blanchet took charge of the search. After six weeks' effort, the search ended successfully as winter set in. The MacAlpine group had been forced down at Dease Point on the arctic coast and taken by Inuit with dog teams across the ice to the settlement of Cambridge Bay, Victoria Island. MacAlpine and his companions were soon picked up and flown south, little the worse for wear.

In 1930, after another season in the Mackenzie District, Blanchet retired from government service. He became an independent engineer and geologist, doing work in Labrador and the Northwest Territories. In the late 1930s, with his wife Eileen (after whom he had named a lake southeast of Fort Reliance) he moved permanently from Ottawa to Victoria and spent two years at the Astro Physical Observatory. Next, he was off to New Zealand and Fiji.

Following Canada's entry into World War II in 1939, Blanchet, although then fifty-five, volunteered for active military service overseas. Claiming to be forty-five, he passed a physical examination and was accepted. He survived strenuous training exercises in Canada and got as far as England. There, however, he was hospitalized and his true age was disclosed. He was shipped home with a medical discharge.

In Victoria, on 1 June 1942, he received a message from Edmonton: Would he join a small group making an aerial reconnaissance across the Mackenzie-Yukon divide to find a route for an emergency pipeline to carry crude oil from Norman Wells to Whitehorse? He was in Edmonton within a couple of days. Thus began the field work for the Canol (Canadian oil) Project, designed by the U.S. Army to help fuel the new Alaska Highway and its airfields from an inland source relatively safe from Japanese attack.

The first direct flight from Norman Wells to Whitehorse was made on 12 June, with one stop at Sheldon Lake, the approximate halfway point, west of the Mackenzie-Yukon divide. Blanchet observed the terrain with a practised eye and traced out what he believed would be a feasible route for a service road and pipeline. The most difficult parts would be among the little-known mountains east of the divide, which he wanted to examine on the ground himself. So, between late October and late November 1942, with Indians and dog-teams from Fort Norman, he cut inland from a campsite along the Mackenzie River opposite Norman Wells and trudged about 280 miles to Sheldon Lake. He did this when he was nearly fifty-nine years old and despite a painful foot injury, adverse weather, and a dangerous shortage of food.

As chief of surveys for the project, he investigated other routes by air and on foot, but the original route was finally chosen. When detailed ground work replaced general reconnaissance, with more and more engineering and construction men in the field and personnel and red tape in the offices, Blanchet became impatient. A few months before the project wound up in the spring of 1944, he quietly withdrew. Subsequently, he did engineering work for the federal government in the Mackenzie District and around Vancouver Island and in the Yukon for private companies.

In 1951, he was called out of retirement to be chief surveyor of the right-of-way for the Trans-Mountain oil pipeline from Edmonton to Vancouver. Even then, in his late sixties, he could walk long distances and work long hours, to the wonderment of younger colleagues and helpers.

Besides official reports prepared during his career, Blanchet occasionally contributed to several Canadian periodicals. In his last years, referring to his diaries and note-books, he set down reminiscences of his work and travel. Out of these, in 1960, came an entertaining and historically valuable book: *Search in the North*, chronicling the Dominion Explorers expedition. His story of the Canol adventure appeared posthumously in *North/Nord* magazine, but his autobiography as a whole remains unpublished.

Guy Houghton Blanchet had no children. Eileen and his sister Helen were with him at home in Victoria when he died of a heart attack, 17 August 1966.

Further Readings

Blanchet, Guy H. 1926. *Great Slave Lake Area, Northwest Territories*. Ottawa: Department of the Interior.

_____. 1930. *Aerial Mineral Exploration of Northern Canada*. Ottawa: Department of the Interior.

_____. 1960. *Search in the North*. Toronto: Macmillan Canada.

_____. 1970. "Oil over the Mountains: Canol, the First Oil Pipeline in the Canadian North," edited by Don W. Thomson. *North/Nord* (March–April, May–June).

Richard S. Finnie

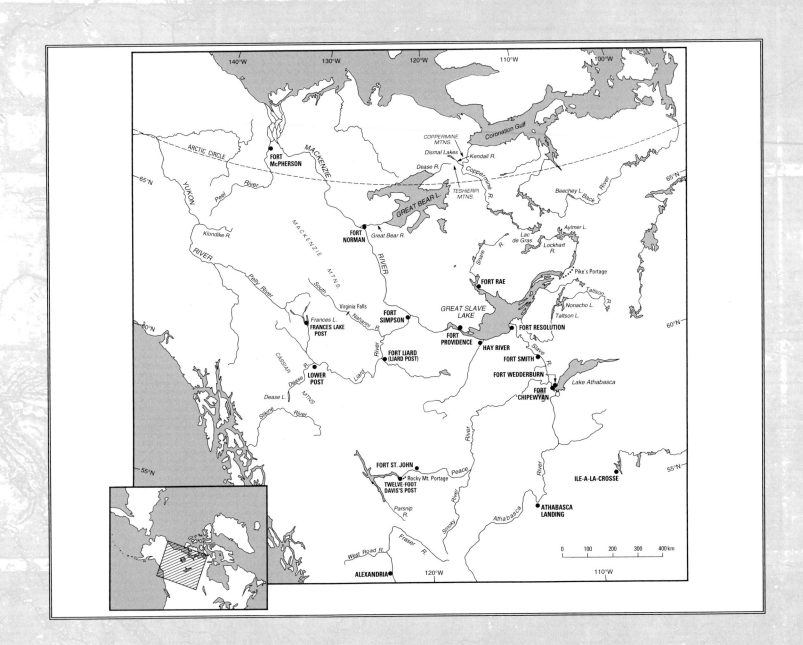

140°W　　　130°W　　　120°W　　　110°W　　　100°W

Coronation Gulf

ARCTIC CIRCLE

MACKENZIE

COPPERMINE MTNS.

Dismal Lakes • Kendall R.

Dease R.

FORT McPHERSON

65°N

YUKON

Peel R.

River

Coppermine R.

Beechey L. Back R.

65°N

GREAT BEAR L.

TESHIERPI MTNS.

Klondike R.

MACKENZIE

FORT NORMAN

Great Bear R.

Lac de Gras

Aylmer L.

Lockhart R.

MTNS

RIVER

Snare R.

Pike's Portage

FORT RAE

Taltson R.

Pelly River

South

Nahanni R.

Virginia Falls

FORT SIMPSON

GREAT SLAVE LAKE

Nonacho L.

Taltson L.

60°N

Frances L.

FRANCES LAKE POST

FORT LIARD (LIARD POST)

FORT PROVIDENCE

FORT RESOLUTION

60°N

CASSIAR

Dease R.

River

Liard

HAY RIVER

Slave R.

FORT SMITH

LOWER POST

Dease L.

MTNS

FORT WEDDERBURN

Lake Athabasca

Stikine River

FORT CHIPEWYAN

River

55°N

FORT ST. JOHN

Peace

River

55°N

TWELVE-FOOT DAVIS'S POST

• *Rocky Mt. Portage*

River

ILE-A-LA-CROSSE

Parsnip R.

Smoky River

Athabasca

ATHABASCA LANDING

Fraser R.

West Road R.

0 100 200 300 400 km

ALEXANDRIA •

120°W

110°W

UNIT
❧9❧

Alexander Mackenzie, George Simpson, Warburton Pike,
George Mellis Douglas, Charles Camsell, Albert Faille, Frank Conibear

The map for unit 9, which shows the lands draining into the Beaufort Sea via the Mackenzie watershed, pulls together a diverse collection of individuals. This unit includes not only the fur trade's most powerful governor and the first European to "discover" North America's second longest river, but it includes as well the less familiar, but no less important, personalities of Conibear, Faille, Pike, Douglas, and Camsell. Each one has played a significant role in our understanding and construction of the North, regardless of whether his contribution has the solidity of rocks and minerals or the intangible nature of compassion and perseverance.

ALEXANDER MACKENZIE
(1764–1820)

Lionized for his speed and efficiency in penetrating new lands as he sought a route to the Pacific, condemned and celebrated for the way he drove men as he pursued his goals, the powerfully built Alexander Mackenzie had no illusions about why he was drawn to the unexplored tracts of Rupert's Land. Soon after completing his second historic journey, he candidly expressed his feelings toward the Athabasca District in a personal letter: "I think it unpardonable in any man to remain in this country who can afford to leave it." Before he turned thirty years old, Mackenzie could afford to leave.

He was born at Stornoway, on the Isle of Lewis, Scotland, in 1765. His mother died early in his life. When Alexander was about ten years old, his father moved the family to New York. But only months after they arrived, the American War of Independence broke out, and Mackenzie's father was called away to fight for the king. The young Mackenzie resided with two aunts in the Mohawk Valley until his safety demanded that he be sent to Montreal. After only a year in school, Mackenzie took employment with a small firm engaged in the fur trade; it was a timely move, because his father died suddenly in the next year. This initial situation led to a series of positions in the fur industry that ultimately produced a substantial fortune for Mackenzie.

Through a number of expansions and mergers that proved advantageous to the ambitious and clever young man, Mackenzie found himself in charge of the North West Company post at Ile-

Portrait of Alexander Mackenzie. Thomas Lawrence, artist/National Archives of Canada/C-002146

à-la-Crosse between 1785 and 1787. During the winter of 1787–88, he worked under Peter Pond in the Athabasca District. Pond speculated that a river, which Indians said flowed out of the west end of Great Slave Lake, was the same that Capt. James Cook had reported emptying into the Pacific. Such a river—if it were to exist—would provide a navigable water link between the Atlantic and Pacific oceans. But the tempestuous Pond was sent home from the Athabasca in 1788; it was left to Mackenzie to test Pond's hypothesis. In 1789, accompanied by four voyageurs, a young German, a Chipewyan guide called the "English Chief," and an assortment of Indian wives and retainers, Mackenzie put his North Canoe (designed especially for northern travel) into Lake Athabasca at Fort Chipewyan, descended the Slave River, skirted the shores of Great Slave Lake, and travelled down the unknown river until he perceived the rise and fall of the tide in the fog-bound delta. Although he is celebrated today for having discovered this major North America watercourse and for having made the return trip of 3,100 miles in a phenomenal 102 days, Mackenzie considered his expedition a failure. The river, after all, had not led to the Pacific. According to one popular, but unfounded account, Mackenzie used the name "the River Disappointment" when he wrote of the river that today bears his name and guarantees his immortality.

After two years spent managing the Athabasca District and a winter in England making preparations for a second expedition, Mackenzie again set off in search of a navigable passage to the

Pacific. 1793 saw him paddling up the Parsnip River, after having wintered at the forks of the Peace and Smoky rivers. He made a difficult carry over the height-of-land into the Fraser River (which he mistook for the Columbia) and descended it until Indians living near modern Alexandria, British Columbia, advised him not to follow the Fraser down to the ocean, but to go back upriver to where the West Road River flows into it. At that juncture, they cached canoe and supplies and trekked overland to reach the Pacific at the mouth of the Bella Coola River. There, on a rock facing the ocean, Mackenzie wrote the now famous words with a mixture of vermilion and melted grease: "Alexander Mackenzie, from Canada by land, the twenty-second of July, one thousand seven hundred and ninety-three." Had he arrived six weeks earlier, he would likely have met Capt. George Vancouver, who had sailed up the coast and visited the Bella Bella Indians. Possibly as a consequence of Vancouver's visit, the tribe was decidedly unfriendly toward the small overland party, but Mackenzie managed affairs well, and no one was hurt. Again, although recognized as the first man to cross the breadth of this continent north of Mexico—a feat he achieved more than a decade before the widely extolled Lewis and Clark expedition even set out—Mackenzie considered the expedition a failure, as the strenuous passage he had made was not suitable for trade.

By his thirtieth birthday, Mackenzie's geographical conquests were behind him. A highly nervous and restless Mackenzie returned to Canada, where he spent much of his energy arguing for a reorganization of the fur trade, an idea that involved bringing together the North West Company, the Hudson's Bay Company, and the East India Company. He published the narrative of his two expeditions in 1801; *Voyages from Montreal* contains a lengthy "General History of the Fur Trade" (possibly written by his cousin Roderick Mackenzie) that espouses reorganization. Knighted in 1802, he held enough shares in the new North West Company, later known as the XY Company, that it was sometimes called Sir Alexander Mackenzie and Company. But when the older North West Company merged with the new North West Company, Mackenzie, who had come to be considered a troublemaker, was denied a role in the new management.

Frustrated, Alexander Mackenzie returned to Britain for good in 1810, having already spent much of the past five years there. He was briefly involved with Lord Selkirk's scheme to colonize part of the HBC's holdings, but when he realized the scope of Selkirk's plan, Mackenzie became an outspoken critic of the Red River Colony. In 1812, he married Geddes Mackenzie and retired at her family's estate at Avoch, which he purchased for £20,000. He was forty-eight; she was fourteen. His health began to fail around 1818, and on 12 March 1820, he died while resting at an inn on his way home from London, where he had gone in search of medical advice. He was laid to rest far from the country in which he had secured his fortune and which had made him into one of those "who can afford to leave it."

Further Readings

Daniells, Roy. 1969. *Alexander Mackenzie and the North West.* London: Faber and Faber.

Lamb, W. Kaye, ed. 1970. *The Journals and Letters of Alexander Mackenzie.* Cambridge: Hakluyt Society.

Mackenzie, Alexander. [1801] 1971. *Voyages from Montreal through the Continent of North America to the Frozen and Pacific Oceans in 1789 and 1793.* Reprint. Edmonton: M.G. Hurtig.

Smith, James K. 1973. *Alexander Mackenzie, Explorer: The Hero Who Failed.* Toronto: McGraw-Hill Ryerson.

Richard C. Davis

GEORGE SIMPSON
(ca. 1787–1860)

George Simpson, overseas governor-in-chief of the Hudson's Bay Company, is remembered chiefly for his success in integrating the field operations of the rival Hudson's Bay and North West companies after their union in 1821. No explorer himself, he assisted, albeit reluctantly, John Franklin's* first land sortie into the Arctic and, more willingly, subsequent Admiralty expeditions. He was also responsible for organizing Company-mounted explorations and searches in the North.

Simpson was born about 1787 in Loch Broom Parish, Scotland, of unmarried parents. Little is known of his early life, but by 1800 or soon after, he was employed in the London firm of his uncle, Geddes Simpson, engaged in the sugar trade.

The little red-headed Scot was physically unimpressive, but grew up with a vast thirst for success and renown, perhaps in reaction to his small stature and illegitimate birth. Ruthless and insensitive in business, he made many enemies, but through his unswerving loyalty to his friends he gained some equally firm admirers. He became as notorious for his amorous exploits as he was famous for his commercial achievements. After ten years with and children by a "country wife," he married his cousin Frances Simpson and sired another family. In addition, he begat an indefinite number of off-the-record progeny. Today his direct descendants can be found in many parts of Canada.

Photograph of George Simpson. Courtesy of Hudson's Bay Company Archives, Provincial Archives of Manitoba

Although Simpson himself was completely ignorant of the fur trade, the Honorable Company, in which his uncle's partner Andrew Wedderburn had an interest, sent him to North America. He was to serve as replacement for Gov. William Williams, whose imminent arrest by the Nor'Westers—as the rival North West Company employees were called—was anticipated. When Williams escaped apprehension, the Company sent Simpson to Fort Wedderburn, on Lake Athabasca, to take charge of the Athabasca Department. So successful was he during 1820–21 in confronting the aggressive, even violent opposition headquartered in nearby Fort Chipewyan, that when the two companies were amalgamated in 1821, Simpson was appointed governor of the Hudson's Bay Company's Northern Department.

It was while he was at Fort Wedderburn that Simpson had his first, albeit indirect, contact with the Arctic, for during his tenure there, John Franklin passed that way on his first arctic land expedition. His party seemed inordinately intimate with the Nor'Westers—yet made what Simpson regarded as unreasonable and excessive demands on the resources of the older company.

Simpson had spent the winter of 1820–21 in the North, although as governor of the Northern and soon of the Southern Department and, from 1827, as governor-in-chief of the HBC, his principal residence was briefly at Upper or

Lower Fort Garry, later at Lachine. But almost every year until his death he journeyed to the distant reaches of the Company's realms. In 1822, 1823, and 1824 he returned to Lake Athabasca, sometimes even reaching Great Slave Lake.

Simpson's concern with the Arctic was that of his employers; they regarded it primarily as a source of furs—and profits. Yet in the early 1800s, the Company's very existence was endangered through attacks on its splendid charter by which Charles II had granted it possession of a quarter of North America and exclusive trading rights therein. In return, the Company was to promote settlement, civilization, and exploration in its territory, obligations which it was slow to meet. True, it had mounted a few exploring expeditions, abortive and sometimes fatal, in Hudson Bay, but they were long ago. To meet persistent criticism, in 1838, the governor sent young Thomas Simpson* and experienced Peter Warren Dease to complete the mapping of the arctic coast. Their three-year odyssey resulted in surveys of hundreds of miles of coastline, and a knighthood for Governor Simpson. A planned second expedition under Thomas Simpson was prevented by the young man's untimely and violent death.

In 1844, Simpson chose a Company clerk, Dr. John Rae,* to head another sortie to the "Frozen" Ocean. In 1846, Rae led a small party to brilliant exploring success in the northeast corner of the continent. In an 1854 HBC-organized foray, Rae discovered the first relics of John Franklin's lost expedition.

Throughout the long search for Franklin, the Company—under Simpson's direction—assisted such Admiralty expeditions as Dr. John Richardson's* with material and personnel, and mounted its own searches, such as James Anderson's* 1855 journey. All, of course, were futile. Not until 1859 did Francis Leopold McClintock* discover definitive evidence of Franklin's fate. George Simpson died in Montreal a few days after hosting an elaborate reception at Lachine for the visiting Prince of Wales.

Further Readings

Galbraith, John S. 1976. *The Little Emperor: Governor Simpson of the Hudson's Bay Company*. Toronto: Macmillan.

Merk, F., ed. [1931] 1968. *Fur Trade and Empire: George Simpson's Journal 1924–25.* Cambridge, Mass: Harvard University Press.

Morton, A.S. 1944. *Sir George Simpson: Overseas Governor in the Hudson's Bay Company*. Toronto: J.M. Dent.

Rich, E.E., ed. 1938. *Simpson's Athabasca Journal.* Toronto: Champlain Society.

_____, ed. 1947. *Simpson's 1828 Journey to the Columbia.* Toronto: Champlain Society.

Williams, Glyndwr, ed. 1975. "Simpson's Character Book." In *Hudson's Bay Miscellany 1670–1870*. Winnipeg: Hudson's Bay Record Society.

John W. Chalmers

WARBURTON PIKE (1861–1915)

British Columbia has lost her foremost sportsman, and the Dominion is the poorer by an author who had achieved considerable note, by the death of Mr. Warburton Pike. News of the demise of the well-known hunter was received in a cable from London, but the manner of his death is unknown.

(*Daily Colonist*, 30 October 1915)

Warburton Pike was born into an old Westcountry family near Wareham, Dorset, in 1861. He was educated at Rugby School in an atmosphere of muscular Christianity, the physical emphasis of which was not lost on him. From Rugby he went up to Brasenose College, Oxford, where he became a close friend of Douglas Haig, the future field marshal. Like many another young Englishman of his time and class, Pike was attracted to outdoor life and distant lands. In 1884, drawn by the raw emptiness of British Columbia, he purchased ground on Saturna Island, where he thereafter resided periodically, between bouts of wanderlust. For the next several years he toughened himself and honed his skills as a wilderness traveller on hunting trips to the British Columbia interior and other parts of the North.

August 1889 found Pike embarking by canoe from Fort Resolution on what he called "an ordinary shooting expedition" north of Great Slave Lake, where he hoped to "penetrate this unknown land, to see the musk-ox, and find out as much

Photograph of Warburton Pike. Courtesy of Provincial Archives of British Columbia No. 4510

as I could about their habits, and the habits of the Indians who go in pursuit of them every year." Thus commenced the fourteen months of hard travel, privation, and adventure described so vividly in Pike's classic book *The Barren Ground of Northern Canada* (1892).

For five months he explored and hunted with the Beaulieu clan—"the biggest scoundrels I ever had to travel with"—and Yellowknives (Copper Indians) as far as the Coppermine country north of Lac de Gras. The trip was replete with austere satisfactions of the sort valued by this hardbitten Englishman: brutal weather, near starvation, and the company of mixed-bloods and Indians whose improvidence and untrustworthiness he despised, but whose skills and powers of endurance moved him to admiration; he also relished competing with these men. On this, as on every trip he took, he travelled light and lived off the land, for he held well-provided expeditions in contempt.

Pike wintered—not at all passively—at Fort Resolution; then, on 7 May, bound for Back's Great Fish River, he started north again. Only George Back* and Richard King* (1833–35) and James Anderson* and James Green Stewart* (1855) had been there before him. He was accompanied on this stiff canoe journey by James Mackinlay, the Hudson's Bay Company factor at Fort Resolution, Murdo Mackay, a Company servant, and a mixed crew of natives. Mackinlay seems to have hoped to find a site for a trading outpost in Inuit territory, but nothing came of this possibility. After reaching Aylmer Lake, they descended the Back River as far as Beechey Lake; finding no Inuit there, and given Pike's plans to head "outside" to British Columbia, they turned south on 25 July, returning by way of the Lockhart River and Pike's Portage. They took out at Resolution on 24 August. Two impatient days later, Pike departed for Quesnel, British Columbia, some 1,675 miles away. Mackay went with him. Having ascended the Peace River and crossed the Rocky Mountain Portage to Twelve-Foot Davis's trading post, they were waylaid by snow and advised to wait for freeze-up before going farther. A few days passed, and a warm chinook wind came through. Then, as R.M. Patterson has remarked, Pike's "demon took possession of him." Ignoring warnings, he set off upriver on the Parsnip in a dugout canoe, bound for Fort McLeod. With him were Mackay, two guides, and an old-country deadbeat, the latter three of whom claimed to know the route. But winter arrived with a vengeance, they got lost below McLeod Lake, and the useless canoe was abandoned. Fiercely driven by Pike, retreating desperately, frostbitten, starving, feeding on their moccasins, they struggled back down the Parsnip. On 27 December, near death, they "crawled up the steep bank" to Davis's cabin and salvation.

The Barren Ground of Northern Canada, substantial, candid, compelling, was popular for many years among men who themselves lived and travelled north of the fifty-fifth parallel. Two such men, however, George M. Douglas,* the author of *Lands Forlorn* (1914), and Guy Blanchet,* the peerless Topographical Survey of Canada explorer and surveyor, believed that Pike plagiarized from Mackinlay's journal when writing the book. But scrutiny of the two works proves this charge to be groundless.

Pike's next major outing, which he recounted in *Through the Subarctic Forest* (1896), began in July 1892. With a Canadian and an Englishman, in an eighteen-foot spruce canoe painted light blue, Pike farewelled Fort Wrangle, Alaska, pushed up the Stikine River to Dease Lake in the Cassiar Mountains, ran down the Dease River to the Liard River, and spent the winter near Lower Post. There he built a cabin, indulged his liking for cold-weather tripping, and was bitten by the gold bug. In the spring of 1893, having hauled his outfit some 204 miles to Frances Lake, Yukon Territory, he and the men he had now enticed into joining him, three HBC mixed-bloods from Manitoba, explored a new route across the height of land to a tributary of the Pelly River. Paddling through unexplored country until they linked with G.M. Dawson's route of 1887, they then followed the Pelly to the Yukon and ran down it to Russian Mission. From there, they portaged to the Kuskovim, which took them to the Bering Sea. "In rags and poverty," Pike and his crew then navigated 300 miles of hazardous, weather-swept coastline to Nushugak, where they took out on 18 September. The canoe had been holed once on this journey of some 3,475 miles.

In the years remaining to him, Pike continued to wander restlessly, often alone or with Indians, testing himself to his limits. He became obsessed with prospecting and engaged in mining ventures in the Dease Lake region, but none of them flourished. Throughout this period he was renowned as much for his generosity to the down-and-out as for his feats of travel and endurance. When in civilization, he dressed meticulously for dinner in the English tradition and was sought after socially. One year, he served as British Columbia's commissioner at an international game exhibition in Vienna. But like others of his ilk who ventured to the wildest ends of the earth, he welcomed the shedding of formal conventions, and it was for the best of reasons that those who knew him in the bush and the mountains nicknamed him "Dirty Pike" or "One-Shirt Pike." High in the Cassiars, a pair of reeking companions at his side, gnawing caribou meat in the firelit snow, he must, one imagines, have sometimes remembered *fondues* at Brasenose and the serene watermeadows of the Frome near Wareham.

The type of man Pike was now seems as extinct as the British Empire itself, with its host of far-eyed, ofttimes eccentric, travellers and explorers. His unquestioning self-confidence, his paternalistic fondness for native peoples, his passion for white blanks on maps, his code of self-effacing, stoical masculinity, and his inviolable principles of perseverance, *noblesse oblige*, and duty bespeak an ethos which, though susceptible to derision now, was honoured in its time.

In 1915, Warburton Pike sailed for England, anxious to serve his king and the empire. On October 20, in Bournemouth, a few miles from his birthplace, he was turned down. He was fifty-four. He walked out of the recruiting office and down to the shore; then, striding into the sea until he was nearly submerged, he stopped, opened his clasp-knife, felt for the spot he wanted, and drove the blade up into his heart.

Acknowledgement

The Stefansson Collection, Dartmouth College Library.

Further Readings

MacKinlay, James. 1958. "Journal Fish River Exploring Party." *The Arctic Circular* 10(3): 32–50, 10(4): 51–69.

Patterson, R.M. 1968. *Finlay's River.* Toronto: Macmillan Canada.

Pike, Warburton. 1892. *The Barren Ground of Northern Canada.* London: Macmillan.

_____. [1896] 1967. *Through the Subarctic Forest.* Reprint. New York: Arno press.

R.H. Cockburn

GEORGE MELLIS DOUGLAS
(1875-1963)

George Mellis Douglas was one of the most efficient and well-informed explorers of the Mackenzie district, particularly the northerly reaches of Great Bear Lake and the Coppermine River as far as the arctic coast, during the early years of the twentieth century. A lean, muscular six-footer, he was a pioneer who opened up new vistas for mineral investigation and development. Yet he is chiefly known for his only book, *Lands Forlorn*, which, published in 1914, is noteworthy for its accuracy, attention to detail, and superb photographs. It stands as one of the classics of northern literature.

Douglas was born in Halifax, Nova Scotia, in 1875, the son of a distinguished Canadian medical doctor. He was educated at the Grove School, Lakefield, Ontario; Trinity College School, Port Hope, Ontario; the University of Toronto; and Rutherford College, Newcastle-on-Tyne, and was apprenticed as an engineer with the Armstrong and Leslie Works from 1894 to 1897. He went to sea as a marine engineer between 1897 and 1900 and then began a career in Mexico and Arizona as an engineer, later as a consulting engineer, until 1940.

His work in the southwest was interrupted by the first of his northern explorations. This was for a 1911–12 expedition to Great Bear Lake, the Dismal Lakes, and the lower Coppermine River to search for copper deposits. It was sponsored and financed by Dr. James Douglas, a wealthy cousin after whom the mining town of Douglas, Arizona, was named. The three-man

Photograph of George Mellis Douglas, by Richard S. Finnie

party, headed by George Douglas, included his brother, Lionel, a master mariner, and Dr. August Sandburg, a geologist.

They travelled with the Hudson's Bay Company transport as far as Fort Norman on the Mackenzie River. Among their companions to that point chanced to be Robert Service, the already renowned Yukon bard, on his way back to Dawson City alone in a canoe from Fort McPherson.

The Douglas party tracked up the swift-flowing Great Bear River with a York boat to Great Bear Lake, towing a canoe. They sailed across the lake to the northeasterly corner at the mouth of the Dease River, where Lionel Douglas built a substantial cabin for the winter. Meanwhile, George Douglas and August Sandburg canoed up the Dease to the Dismal Lakes and thence to the Kendall River and the Coppermine. They explored the Coppermine Mountains during the first season before returning to the cabin.

Part of the time they were joined by John Hornby,* a diminutive, eccentric Englishman who was as inefficient as the others were efficient. His mission, if any, was to hunt and trap and to trade with the Inuit of Coronation Gulf. Despite his untidiness and aimlessness, he was befriended by George Douglas through ensuing years until he starved to death with two other men on the fringe of the Barrens northeast of Great Slave Lake in 1927.

In the spring of 1912, the Douglas party returned to the Coppermine and found the extent of the mineralized area to be much greater than had been supposed, the width of the belt being about fifteen miles. It was deemed significant enough to justify more extensive prospecting, but the effects of World War I and the copper industry discouraged it.

The party ranged as far as Coronation Gulf, meeting some of the Copper Inuit but missing Vilhjalmur Stefansson,* who had visited the Dismal Lakes only a few months prior to their arrival. (Douglas and Stefansson eventually became life-long friends.) The entire expedition was noteworthy for its meticulous planning and successful execution, with no serious mishaps.

In 1928, Douglas carried out a summer journey with two canoes along the southeastern shores of Great Slave Lake for the United Verde Copper Company. Four years later he investigated coal deposits on the western shore of Great Bear Lake, and, in 1935, he conducted mineral exploration around Lake Athabasca and the country between it and Great Slave Lake, as well as on Great Bear Lake. He resumed his mineral exploration in 1938 along the Snare River and between Great Slave Lake and Taltson Lake, including Nonacho Lake.

The Douglas expedition York boat *Jupiter* on Great Bear Lake. July 1911. Photograph by George M. Douglas

He wrote well and kept journals of all his journeys, profusely illustrated with his photographs of consistently professional quality, yet he published only one book and a couple of articles for technical magazines. There were conspicuous reasons for this. Finally retiring as an engineer and explorer, he became increasingly preoccupied with chores around his properties near Lakefield, Ontario, where he and his young wife, Kay, lived almost primitively. They moved from their main house, owned originally by his father, into one or another of several cabins and a houseboat, according to whim or season. In summer he did much canoeing and sailing on nearby lakes. He also spent a great deal of time corresponding with acquaintances in different parts of the world, and each of his letters was a gem of fact and philosophy.

Several years before his death, he was repeatedly interviewed by George Whalley, professor of English at Queen's University, Kingston, who was compiling a definitive biography of John Hornby, about whom Douglas was the foremost living authority. Douglas felt that Hornby did not deserve another book, two having already been published, but he gave freely of his time and became Whalley's principal source of information.

Whalley seemingly failed fully to realize that the man he was interviewing and who would soon be gone had spent an infinitely more interesting and productive life than the ill-fated Hornby and that he—not Hornby—was a far better subject for a biography. Whalley published his Hornby book, a fascinating piece of research, but died before he could give Douglas his due, although there is much about him in the Hornby book.

George Mellis Douglas was a life member of the Explorers Club, a fellow of the Arctic Institute of North America and the American Geographical Society, and a member of the American Society of Mechanical Engineers, the Canadian Institute of Mining and Metallurgy, and the Toronto Arts and Letters Club.

After his death in June 1963, Mrs. Douglas sold their properties and settled into a cottage near the Grove School in Lakefield, where she could enjoy the modern comforts and facilities to which he had been indifferent. She sorted and distributed to appropriate archives his papers, photographs, large library, and many canoes.

Further Readings

Douglas, George M. 1914. *Lands Forlorn: A Story of an Expedition to Hearne's Coppermine River.* New York: G.P. Putnam's Sons.

_____. 1924. *Copper Deposits of Arctic Canada.* Engineering and Mining Journal Press.

_____. 1928. *A Summer Journey Along the Southeastern Shores of Great Slave Lake.* Canadian Mining and Metallurgical Bulletin.

Whalley, George. 1962. *The Legend of John Hornby.* London: John Murray.

Richard S. Finnie

CHARLES CAMSELL (1876-1958)

Born at Fort Liard, North West Territories, in 1876, Charles Camsell was one of the post manager's eleven children. After attending school and university in Winnipeg, he went home to Fort Simpson, where his father had been promoted to chief factor of the entire Mackenzie River district. The eighteen-year-old Camsell had no definite plans. All he knew was that he wanted to stay in the North.

Unable to find permanent work, he spent the next five years doing odd jobs —working on the river, building cabins at Hay River, teaching at Fort Norman, fishing, and trapping. When word came of a gold strike in the Klondike, Camsell and his brother Fred set out with four other men. After struggling for seven months over rough and unexplored country in bitter weather, they decided that to continue was futile, for they were still far from their destination. As quickly as it had come, the dream of sudden wealth evaporated.

A trip to Fort Providence in 1900 was the turning point in Camsell's life. He met James MacIntosh Bell of the Geological Survey of Canada, who was on his way to explore around Great Bear Lake and south to Great Slave Lake. When Bell learned that Camsell knew the region and could speak the Indian languages, he asked him to join the party, and thus began Camsell's career as a geologist.

The party consisted of Bell, Camsell, two white assistants, and Sanderson, an Indian who had travelled with

Charles Camsell in 1932. Courtesy of the Geological Survey of Canada (photo no. GSC 91823)

Camsell. They steamed down the Mackenzie River to Fort Norman, where they purchased limited supplies, including only two rifles and a fishnet. Plunging into the bush in mid-June, 1900, they reached Great Bear Lake when it was still covered with thick ice. While they waited for the ice to break up, Bell arranged for a group of Indians encamped nearby to meet the geologists on 15 August at the southeastern corner of Great Bear Lake. When conditions allowed, Bell's party surveyed along the north shore of the lake and travelled down the Dease River to the Teshierpi Mountains. By the time they were in the barrenlands, the food supply had grown short. Most of the party was sent back to Great Bear Lake, and with little food and no rifle, Camsell and Bell continued prospecting. When a heavy snowstorm hit on 5 August, they turned back. That same afternoon, they sighted an Inuit camp, but the natives fled upon their approach, leaving behind a supply of caribou meat. Bell and Camsell gorged themselves, and left two steel needles and a tin plate as a goodwill offering.

When they finally reached the southeast corner of the lake, it was 27 August, nearly two weeks later than the rendezvous established with the Indians who were to guide them south to Great Slave Lake. The Indians had not waited. The geological party, now reduced to four, headed south on their own, often breaking the newly formed ice to allow canoe passage. Fortunately, they met friendly Dogribs who supplied them with food and moccasins, and guided them to Fort Rae on Great Slave Lake. The rest of the journey to Edmonton by canoe, dogsled, and horse and sleigh was relatively easy. They arrived in December 1900.

During the next two years, Camsell continued prospecting, usually with Bell. He explored the James Bay region for iron, prospected for gypsum in Manitoba, and found quartz with a gold-coloured vein in northern Ontario. Four gold mines—Dome, McIntyre, Porcupine, and Hollinger—are now located near Camsell's discovery in that latter region.

Early in June 1904, Camsell was appointed to the Geological Survey of Canada, and a career of over forty years in the civil service began. Early surveys included the Severn River area of Ontario and the Peel River, the latter involving 2,500 miles of river travel in the Yukon and Northwest Territories. Then, for two years, he conducted geological work in British Columbia, a welcome change from the Arctic.

On 1 January 1914, Camsell was given a new appointment: geologist in charge of explorations, with the task of exploring all unsurveyed parts of Canada, an area of 900,000 square miles! By the time he had completed his first exploration, World War I had broken out. He enlisted in the engineers, but was soon removed from the army to search for minerals vital to the war effort—tungsten, mercury, potash, manganese, chromite, and magnesite.

In 1920, Charles Camsell was promoted to deputy minister of mines and later, when several departments were merged, deputy minister of mines and resources. His experience and practical knowledge gave him a clear understanding of the needs of the GSC and the test laboratories, and he was able to make changes that rendered them more effective.

He was also appointed to the National Research Council, the International Niagara Board, and later to the post of commissioner of the Northwest Territories. He made many trips to the North, visiting in a few hours by plane areas it had taken him months to cover by dogteam and canoe. He retired in 1945 and died in Ottawa in 1958.

Further Readings

Camsell, Charles. 1954. *Son of the North*. Toronto: Ryerson Press.

Shaw, Margaret Mason. 1958. *Geologists and Prospectors*. Toronto: Clarke, Irwin.

Margaret Mason Shaw

ALBERT FAILLE (1887–1973)

Albert Faille's life in the Canadian North was exceptional. Had his early years in Minnesota given him greater access to a formal education, he might well have achieved great fame even earlier in life. With the firsthand experience he gained in the then-uncharted wilderness of the Mackenzie Mountains, Faille might have been a member of the Explorers Club and might have attained public notice through writing and lecturing on northern Canadian land exploration.

Born in Duluth, Minnesota, Faille spent his early years working in lumber camps, guiding tourists on canoe trips in the lake district, and trapping fur-bearing animals in the winter months. After serving in the armed forces in World War I, he immigrated to Canada in 1927, coming directly to the South Nahanni River via the Mackenzie waterway and Fort Simpson.

Albert Faille was a simple man with no pretensions, a scanty formal education, and little knowledge of the academic world. But he was an excellent woodsman, and having spent much of his life on inland waters, he grew remarkable in his ability to navigate fast-flowing mountain streams. An inveterate "loner" without being eccentric or irascible, he had an unerring sense of direction and would often spend the summer months exploring mountain passes and valleys.

In winter, he trapped fur-bearing animals in order to pay for his supplies and equipment. Each summer in June, he came down the rivers to Fort Simpson, which at that time

Photograph of Albert Faille. Courtesy of the Northwest Territories Archives

was an isolated trading post at the junction of the Liard and Mackenzie rivers. He travelled by dog-team in winter; in summer, he walked overland with a pack on his back or canoed on the navigable streams. These explorations took him into areas where few, if any, white men had walked before.

Beginning in the 1950s, he appeared in three different television documentaries wherein it was suggested that his obsession was to find a lost placer gold deposit. He did indeed spend much time in that fruitless search, but those who knew him well realized that it was a deep love for the woods, the wilderness, and the fast-moving mountain streams that amounted to an obsession, rather than the search for gold itself.

Men who knew him, and who lived the same kind of life Albert Faille lived, were impressed with the quality of his character, his temperament, and his abilities. While he was neither a saint nor an exceptionally wise man, he was quietly self-assured, never allowing himself to panic and always cool in the face of danger, even in the most hazardous situations. He came near to death many times. In his later years, he sometimes used outboard motors on his travels. His mechanical aptitude in servicing these machines was amazing; he seemed, for instance, to have an intuitive understanding of magnetos.

Faille's temperament was equally impressive. He was invariably optimistic and always cheerful, a disposition that became manifest after he had spent extended periods of up to a full year totally alone in the bush. When he encountered his fellow man after these periods of isolation, his mental equilibrium, good humour, and downright sanity were noted. His faults and shortcomings were few. He was perhaps overly sensitive to criticism, and he had an assiduous respect for those with authority, power, or great wealth. Quite understandably, he enjoyed the degree of fame that came to him in his declining years.

In retrospect, it can be seen that the contribution Albert Faille made to Canada's North was twofold. Largely as a result of press publicity he generated, public attention was drawn to the remarkably scenic areas of the South Nahanni River and its Virginia Falls. Canadian federal authorities took note, and following then-Prime Minster Pierre Trudeau's trip into the region by airplane and river boat, the present Nahanni National Park was created.

The second part of his contribution was inadvertent and less obvious, but just as real and perhaps of a more profound importance: interest in Albert Faille and his life as a trapper, prospector, and explorer inspired several writers to record his exploits in the North. Both adults and children now know of Faille at firsthand through these accounts. The writings in turn have led to a more extensive and accurate picture of the life of a northern pioneer and have laid to rest some of the misconceptions of early life in the Canadian North.

At the age of seventy, Albert Faille still plied the waters of the South Nahanni River with his little wooden boat. He passed away quietly early in 1973 at the age of eighty-six.

Further Readings

Farrow, Moira. 1975. *Nobody Here But Us: Pioneers of the North.* Vancouver: J.J. Douglas

Patterson, Raymond M. 1954. *The Dangerous River.* New York: William Sloane Associates

Turner, Dick. 1975. *Nahanni.* Saanichton, British Columbia: Hancock House.

Dick Turner

FRANK CONIBEAR *(1896–1988)*

"I have a dream—a dream that someday my trap will become the SPCA of the forests," said Frank Conibear, longtime trapper and inventor of the humane trap for fur-bearing animals.

Frank Conibear was only three years old in 1899 when his family left their home in Plymouth, England, to settle in Orville, Ontario. Twelve years later, the Catholic mission in Fort Resolution, Northwest Territories, required an engineer for their boats, and Frank's father, Lewis Conibear, was sent to fill the position by the shipbuilding firm that employed him. The following year, in early spring, Mrs. Ada Conibear singlehandedly shepherded her family of three sons and two daughters across Canada. After a tiresome four-day train ride from Ontario, they mounted the stage coach on its final run out of Edmonton. Boarding a scow at Athabasca Landing, they descended the Athabasca and Slave rivers to Fort Resolution on Great Slave Lake to become the first independent white family to settle in the Northwest Territories.

Frank, age sixteen upon his arrival, quickly realized that trapping was the way of life in the North. He accompanied a seasoned Métis trapper, Frank Heron, and from him learned how to set traps, travel by dog-team, and survive in the bush. By 1916, the Conibear family had built a house in Fort Smith and relocated. Frank established his own trapline on the Taltson River, a line he gradually extended nearly 200 miles into the Barrens. His harvests were abundant, and as he visited the traps on his long line during thirty-two years as a trapper, he walked and paddled roughly the equivalent of four times around the world. During that time, he

Frank Conibear at about thirty-eight, fleshing a beaver pelt. The pelts hanging behind him are fox. Photograph courtesy of the author

176

had ample opportunity to observe the habits of wild animals and to improve his trapping techniques. Conscientious at his craft, he also kept accurate records and made notes on his observations.

His summer activities were varied. He guided mineral and survey crews farther north, largely into the Great Bear Lake region. At the age of twenty, he joined one of the first group of Fire Rangers for the whole of the Northwest Territories and was appointed captain of their steamer, *The Hope*. And he became a river man and boat pilot as well, engaged in portaging, loading, and transporting goods to the Far North while the rivers were navigable.

In 1923, he travelled to Rochester, Minnesota, for treatment of hearing problems. There he met and married Cecelia Powell and returned with her to Fort Smith to continue trapping. The Conibears had acquired property, and on it Frank built a hotel with a pool room and café, which he and Cecelia operated for over ten years.

Winters were still spent trapping, however, and as the price of mink pelts rose to a high of $40 in 1928, Frank found that the loss of animals escaping from the leg-hold trap not only had drastic financial implications, but also was inhumane and disturbing, especially when he discovered in some of his traps, a claw or leg that an animal had chewed off to escape a slow and agonizing death.

What was needed was an improved trap, a humane one, that killed instantly. The trap had to be practical—easy to carry, light, compact, and inexpensive. After much thought, Conibear came up with an idea derived from the kitchen egg beater. "If a mink stepped into an egg beater and the handle was turned, it would be there to stay."

The first model, handmade by him in 1929, was cumbersome, although it showed promising results. This trap, designed to snap across the animal's chest and crush it, was not yet sufficiently powerful nor practical. The next model had a stronger spring, but still needed improvement.

By 1935, the Conibears had five children. Fort Smith had no school, so Frank Conibear moved his family to Victoria, British Columbia, but he returned north to trap in the winters. Summers he spent working in Fort Smith or Victoria. In 1942, he sustained a severe back injury while on his trapline, and after treatment at the Mayo Clinic, he was forbidden to work. He left the North in 1944 and rejoined his family, where he began writing pamphlets and books based on his keen observations of forest animals. *Devil Dog* was modelled after one of his lead dogs. His best-known book is *The Wise One*, a story about the adventurous life of a black beaver, coauthored with J. L. Blundell and published in 1949. An abridged edition newly adapted and particularly suitable for young readers has recently been on the market.

Although he had turned author, Conibear had not forgotten his trap. After ten years, he came up with an outstanding improvement, based on a pair of his mother's embroidery hoops. The model was square, constructed with spring-powered steel jaws that snapped with tremendous force over the neck or chest of the animal as it passed through the square hoops, resulting in instant death.

The Association for the Protection of Fur Bearing Animals financed the manufacture of fifty traps, and Eric Collier, president of the Trappers' Association of British Columbia, both supported their field testing and advocated them in *Outdoor Life*. Success at last—a trap that was light, could be built in various sizes, and could be set on land or in water. Frank Conibear contacted the Woodstream Corporation of Pennsylvania, and within a year the Victor-Conibear trap was on the market. To introduce this product, the Canadian Association of Humane Trapping, working with the Canadian Provincial Wild Life Services, encouraged trappers to exchange their leg-hold traps for the conibears—free.

The trap became popular and recognition followed. In 1961, Frank Conibear was presented the first Certificate of Merit by the American Humane Association, acknowledging his achievement. In 1981, he shared a first prize of $24,000 with two others for his ideas submitted to the Humane Trapping Committee, an award made by the British Columbia government for "outstanding creativity in the development of more humane animal traps."

In 1970, during Queen Elizabeth II's tour of the North, Frank Conibear was invited back to Fort Smith to meet Her Majesty in recognition of his outstanding contributions. Conibear Park, located in the center of Fort Smith, was created on land donated by the Conibears. It provides a pleasant, relaxing spot for travellers and local residents, and a large plaque honours the donor.

In the final years of his life, Frank Ralph Conibear was a lean, distinguished-looking gentleman. He resided in Victoria, where, though widowed, he had the joy of his sons and daughters and their families to fill his life. He continued to write about his experiences and to ponder improvements on his trap, particularly to

Photograph courtesy of *Slave River Journal*, Fort Smith. Northwest Territories

think about designing one suitable for humane trapping of larger animals. Only his death on 22 March 1988 brought to a close this inspired man's dream of eliminating cruelty from the centuries-old occupation of fur harvesting.

Further Readings

Bateman, James. *Animal Traps and Trapping*. Harrisburg, Penn: Stackpole Books.

Gilsvik, Bob. 1976. *The Complete Book of Trapping*. Radnor, Penn: Chilton Book Company.

Angie [Angeline] Bevington

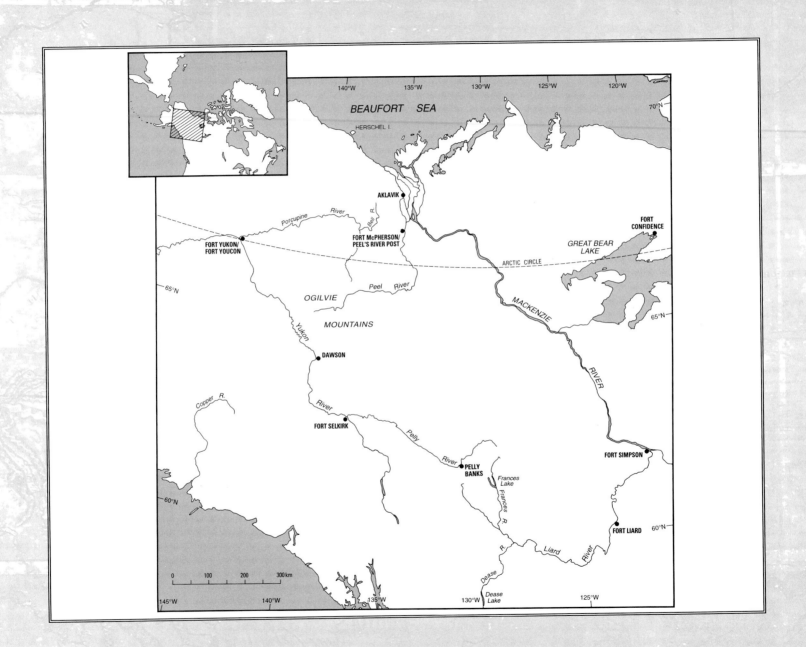

BEAUFORT SEA

HERSCHEL I.

AKLAVIK

FORT CONFIDENCE

Porcupine River

Bell R.

FORT McPHERSON/
PEEL'S RIVER POST

FORT YUKON/
FORT YOUCON

GREAT BEAR
LAKE

ARCTIC CIRCLE

Peel River

OGILVIE

MACKENZIE

MOUNTAINS

Yukon

DAWSON

RIVER

Copper R.

River

FORT SELKIRK

Pelly

FORT SIMPSON

River

PELLY
BANKS

Frances
Lake

Frances R.

FORT LIARD

R.

Liard

River

Dease

Dease
Lake

0   100   200   300 km

UNIT

❧ 10 ❧

John Bell, Robert Campbell, James Stewart, F.J. Fitzgerald,
W.J.D. Dempster, Catharine McClellan

As much as any of the units in this book can be said to echo political boundaries, this geographic region of Unit 10 roughly encompasses the modern Yukon Territory. Even so, it also encompasses some of the upper Mackenzie River. Here is the stage where Stewart, Bell, and Campbell played out their roles in the fur trade, where policemen Fitzgerald and Dempster established a route between Dawson and Fort McPherson, and where McClellan focussed her work as an anthropologist.

John Bell (1796–1868)

John Bell, discoverer of the Yukon River and associate of Drs. John Richardson* and John Rae* in the John Franklin* search expedition of 1847–49, represented the classic blend of fur trader and explorer. His contributions to the expansion of the Hudson's Bay Company's trade in the far northwest and to the cause of arctic exploration have gone largely unnoticed, due in some measure to his unassuming and modest character.

Bell was born on the Isle of Mull in 1796. Like many young men from Scotland, he was attracted by the North America fur trade, joining the North West Company as a clerk in 1818. His northern career began in 1824 when, as an officer of the reorganized Hudson's Bay Company, he was transferred to the Mackenzie District. In 1837, Thomas Simpson* and Peter Warren Dease had discovered the Colville River on the arctic coast. Anxious to exploit this find, Gov. George Simpson* ordered that John Bell, by now an experienced northern trader, attempt to locate an overland route joining the Mackenzie and the Colville.

In 1839, Bell travelled along the lower reaches of the Peel River, looking for a breach in the mountains that would take him west. Though he did not immediately succeed, his reports of the excellent prospects for trade encouraged the

A summer Indian encampment on the Yukon River. John Bell's explorations west of the Mackenzie and into the Yukon watershed brought such bands within the Hudson's Bay Company's trading network. From Frederick Whymper's *Travel and Adventure in the Territory of Alaska* (1868)

Company to establish a trading post. Bell opened Peel's River Post, later renamed Fort McPherson, in 1840. On Gov. Simpson's directions, he also continued his explorations of the lands west of the Mackenzie.

The task proved more difficult than expected, largely because the local Indians, anxious to protect their monopoly over the Peel River trade, offered little help in the push to the west. Several times, Bell had to cancel or abort expeditions when the natives hired to guide the Company's men across

The Hudson's Bay Company post Fort Youcon opened in 1847, two years after John Bell's exploration of the region. From Frederick Whymper's *Travel and Adventure in the Territory of Alaska* (1868)

Hunter Murray opened Fort Youcon.

Bell's work on exploration was not done. The HBC took an active part in the attempt to locate the lost Franklin expedition. In 1847, Gov. Simpson assigned John Bell to assist with an expedition, led by John Richardson and John Rae, that searched the coast between the Mackenzie and Coppermine rivers. Bell's primary responsibility was to provide logistic support for the venture; during 1848, for example, Bell built Fort Confidence on Great Bear Lake as a wintering station for the expedition. At the completion of Richardson and Rae's journey, Bell returned to his fur trade duties and was assigned to Fort Liard.

Bell's name has not taken a prominent place in the annals of northern exploration. Many northern explorers rushed descriptions of their travels into print, anxious to share news of their discoveries and to bask in the fame due a northern explorer. Bell did not, offering lengthy accounts in his letters to HBC officers, but making little effort to spread his story further. He tackled these duties without the enthusiasm and sense of destiny that inspired other Company explorers. He was, in fact, a fur trader rather than an explorer, both in talent and temperament. Throughout his northern career, he placed primary importance on the organization and management of

the divide refused to continue. Bell crossed the mountain range in 1842 and descended some distance down the Bell River. He was convinced, however, that the route was not feasible for trading and turned back. The HBC was determined to press its advantage in the area, however, and Bell was ordered to extend his explorations. He did so in the summer of 1845, when he reached the junction of the Porcupine and Youcon (later Yukon) rivers. Plans were immediately set in motion for a new trading post on the new river, and, in 1847, Alexander

the trading posts he commanded, and although he accepted the exploration assignments with few complaints, he preferred the life of a fur trader.

He was less pleased with the northern postings he received through much of his career. Although he was hesitant to complain too loudly, he did make known his displeasure with being sent to "this dismal and secluded part of the country." Bell often despaired at his isolated location, the lack of companionship, and the unattractiveness of the northern environment. As he wrote at one point, "I am as usually the case with me in this miserable and distant part of the country, a bankrupt for news of any kind. Where my friend shall I glean any? from the Indians, animals or Fowls of the air." He longed for transfer to a more salubrious climate, but because of his talent and experience, the Company was loath to move him south.

Bell did not have the commanding presence of other major northern explorers. He was a quiet man, well liked by his colleagues in the fur trade, and noted for his abilities as a manager of men. His skills were those of the fur trade officer; he took orders well, demonstrated notable loyalty to the Company, was a fair and consistent commander, and sought corporate approval rather than public fame during his years in the North. From the Hudson Bay Company's perspective, Bell was one of their most useful officers—accounting for his long and often miserable tenure in the North—because of his professionalism, flexibility, and dedication to the interests of the fur trade.

John Bell remained in the North until 1851, when he was transferred to the Cumberland District. He later moved to Sept Iles (Seven Islands), near Quebec City, where he stayed until he retired. He left the Company's service in 1860 and moved to Saugeen, Ontario, where he died in 1868.

Further Readings

Karamanski, Theodore. 1983. *Fur Trade and Exploration: Opening the Far Northwest, 1821–1852*. Vancouver: University of British Columbia Press.

Richardson, John. 1851. *Arctic Searching Expedition: A Journal of a Boat-Voyage through Rupert's Land and the Arctic Sea, in Search of the Discovery Ships Under Command of Sir John Franklin*. London: Longman, Brown, Green, and Longmans.

Wright, Allen. 1976. *Prelude to Bonanza: The Discovery and Exploration of the Yukon*. Sidney, B.C.: Gray's Publishing.

Ken Coates

Robert Campbell
(1808–1894)

Known as "Campbell of the Yukon," a sobriquet that commemorates his years as an explorer and fur trader in the southern Yukon, Robert Campbell was born in 1808, in Perthshire, Scotland. Stories told by his cousin, chief factor James McMillan of the Hudson's Bay Company, sparked an intense interest in the North American frontier. In 1830, at the age of twenty-two he was hired to work on the Company's experimental farm at Red River. The work proved less exciting than he expected, and, after four years, he requested a transfer to the fur trade.

Campbell spent two unproductive years in the Dease Lake area, trying to break the Russian American Fur Company's hold on the interior fur trade. An agreement between the HBC and its Russian competitor in 1839 freed Campbell to turn his attentions northward. Thomas Simpson* and Peter Warren Dease had, in 1837, crossed a major new river, which they named Colville, during their excursion along the arctic coast. Campbell, who had learned from the natives of the "Toutcho" or "Great Water" to the north, was directed to push in that direction in search of the headwaters of this new river. He completed the exploration in two stages, reaching the Pelly River in 1840 and descending that stream to its junction with the Lewes (Yukon) River three years later.

Gov. George Simpson* ordered Campbell to establish a trading post at the promising "Forks," but poor trading and

Photograph of Robert Campbell. Courtesy of the Hudson's Bay Company Archives, Provincial Archives of Manitoba

provisioning conditions at Frances Lake and Pelly Banks and Campbell's own hesitations stalled the expansion until 1848. These were hard times for Campbell and his men, as starvation threatened almost every year. Finally established at Fort Selkirk, he was directed to explore the remaining distance between that post and Fort Yukon. His 1851 voyage proved that both posts were on the Yukon River and completed Campbell's contributions to the exploration of the North.

With the years of hardship behind him, Campbell expected that his district would now bring handsome returns. Those hopes were soon dashed. The strong opposition of the coastal Tlingit (Chilcat) Indians to the Company's presence culminated in an attack on Fort Selkirk in 1852 that left the post a charred ruin. Campbell, who James Anderson* said "is mad when he touches on the prospects of Selkirk," was determined to reestablish the fort. He travelled to Fort Simpson, but Anderson, his immediate superior, would not grant him permission to return. Campbell refused to see his years of suffering in the North go for naught, so he set out on a three-thousand-mile march on snowshoes from Fort Simpson to Minnesota. From there he continued on to Lachine, near Montreal, where he pleaded his case before Gov. Simpson. The governor would countenance no further expense on the unproductive field and sent Campbell on a long-overdue furlough to England. The trip provided him an opportunity to circulate news of his discoveries. In particular, he helped the Arrowsmiths, famous map makers, add the Pelly, Lewes, and Yukon rivers to the map of the far northwest. His accomplishments had been duly noted.

Although these exploits demonstrate his contribution to northern exploration, Campbell remains an enigmatic personality. He was a tall, powerful man, possessed of great strength and a tenacious approach that often bordered on obsession. His contemporaries spoke favourably of his compassion, his devout Christian faith, and his courage in the face of personal danger. Those who earned his ire, and there were a number, discovered Campbell's other side. His correspondence reveals a dour, unforgiving man given to extreme and unreasonable criticism of Company officers he felt were not assisting his efforts as an explorer with sufficient zeal. Campbell's constant complaints, repeated threats to retire (all recanted), and his tendency to overrate his importance to the HBC angered many of his fellow officers.

Robert Campbell dearly sought the fame he felt would accompany geographic discoveries in the Far North, but he lacked the flair and originality of other northern explorers. Campbell advanced northward in a tentative fashion, stopping short of the bold exploratory thrust that would have solidified his claim to being a great explorer. He developed a myopic view of the Company's affairs in the far northwest, incorrectly believing that Gov. Simpson assigned Campbell's own explorations top priority and had given him *carte blanche* to requisition supplies and men for his work. Gov. Simpson disabused him of this, and he ordered Campbell to pay greater attention to his trading responsibilities. Campbell's determination to place his name among the great explorers often blinded him to the Company's interests and made the

task of establishing a fur trade in his inhospitable district even more difficult. Still, his efforts helped bring the Hudson's Bay Company into the Yukon River valley and helped fill in one of the last remaining gaps on the map of North America. That alone was an appropriate legacy for a man driven to be a northern explorer.

Robert Campbell's Yukon career ended with the debacle at Fort Selkirk. He returned to Fort Liard in 1854, and from there was reassigned to the Athabasca District. He eventually achieved the rank of chief factor, but resigned his commission in 1871 under unfortunate circumstances. He retired to a ranch in Manitoba, where he died in 1894 at the age of eighty-six.

Further Readings

Coates, Kenneth S. 1991. *Best Left as Indians: Native-White Relations in the Yukon Territory, 1840–1973.* Montreal: McGill-Queen's University Press.

Karamanski, Theodore. 1983. *Fur Trade and Exploration: Opening the Far Northwest, 1821–1852.* Vancouver: University of British Columbia Press.

Wilson, Clifford, 1970. *Campbell of the Yukon.* Toronto: Macmillan Canada.

Ken Coates

JAMES GREEN STEWART
(1825–1881)

James Green Stewart, a classic example of the often-neglected second rank of the northern exploratory corps, made a noteworthy contribution to the opening of the far northwest. Although his part in northern exploration has been obscured by the more dynamic and public careers of his superior officers, most notably Robert Campbell,* Stewart played a vital role in the Hudson's Bay Company's efforts to expand into the Yukon River valley.

Born in 1825, in Quebec City, James Stewart joined the HBC in 1844 as an apprentice clerk. He was soon sent to the

Ruins of old Fort Selkirk. From Frederick Schwatka's A *Summer in Alaska* (1892)

northwest, where he was assigned to assist Robert Campbell. Campbell had been active in the Liard and Pelly river regions for almost a decade and had just opened Fort Selkirk at the junction of the Pelly and Lewes (Yukon) rivers when Stewart joined him in 1848. As Campbell's assistant, Stewart faced the onerous task of helping to make this isolated fur post a viable enterprise.

The challenge proved difficult and, ultimately, unsuccessful. Fort Selkirk was poorly positioned, for it thrust the Company's trade into the midst of trading networks maintained by the coastal Tlingit (Chilcat) Indians, who, ironical-

ly, exchanged their furs at coastal points with other HBC traders. The post suffered as well from its isolated position. Supplies had to be brought in along the Liard River, a violent and dangerous stream that claimed the lives of many Company tripmen.

In 1849, while Campbell remained at Fort Selkirk to supervise the trade, Stewart was sent to Pelly Banks to pick up supplies cached there the previous year. Having sent the trade goods on to Fort Selkirk, Stewart and Andrew Flett remained behind to wait for the annual supply boat from Fort Simpson. The wait was in vain, and Stewart and Flett were forced to retreat to Fort Selkirk. Sorely missing the expected shipment of supplies, the fort was in desperate straits, having no goods for trade and barely able to support its inhabitants. Stewart, who Campbell said was "always ready for any enterprise," was dispatched in April 1850 to Fort Simpson on the Mackenzie River. Campbell was ready to abandon Fort Selkirk if Stewart's journey was unsuccessful. The trip was long—1,085 miles, in fact—and arduous, but the urgency spurred Stewart on. Stewart secured some supplies at Fort Simpson, then set out immediately on his return journey. Stewart's remarkable expedition preserved, at least for a time, the HBC post at Fort Selkirk.

Two years later, in 1852, Campbell and Stewart were forced to abandon the post they had fought so hard to sustain, when Tlingit Indians, long-time rivals of the HBC traders at Fort Selkirk, attacked it. Stewart was away when the place was ransacked, but he returned in time to help salvage what was left of the supplies. Campbell's attempts to secure the Company's permission to reopen the post at Fort Selkirk failed, and both men were reassigned.

Because he spent his Yukon career in a subordinate role, Stewart has seldom received proper credit for his

contributions. There is no doubt that Robert Campbell, himself plagued by doubts as to the viability of the Yukon trade, relied heavily on James Stewart. Although second in command, Stewart provided much strength and commitment, at a time when Campbell's resolve was dwindling rapidly. His fellow officers spoke highly of his physical prowess and his willingness to accept tasks that others avoided. He seemed, from Campbell's journals, to have also been a very personable colleague.

Campbell's comments for those times when Stewart was away reflect the musings of a lonely man, isolated from "civilization" in a land he found unappealing. When Campbell

Indians from the vicinity of Fort Selkirk. From Frederick Schwatka's A *Summer in Alaska* (1892)

and Stewart were together at Fort Selkirk, however, an infectious, spritely tone dominates the post commander's writing, reflecting Stewart's optimism and the deep friendship of the two men. During his time in the Yukon, Stewart was the quintessential second-in-command, willing to follow orders, provide advice, assume a leadership role when conditions warranted, and carry out difficult tasks under very trying circumstances. Gov. George Simpson* valued Stewart's advice greatly, corresponding with him directly on matters connected to the future of the Yukon trade. The governor seemingly put greater stock in Stewart's comments than he did in those from the post commander, Robert Campbell.

For both Stewart and Campbell, the debacle at Fort Selkirk marked the end of their Yukon careers. Stewart, however, continued to serve in the North. He was stationed for short periods at Fort McPherson, Fort Carlton, and Fort Resolution. In 1855, Stewart was assigned to assist James Anderson's* Back River expedition, sent to confirm reported sightings of the lost crew of John Franklin.*

The journey was racked by discord between the two principal men. Anderson repeatedly overruled Stewart, challenging his selection of guides and route. Bad luck and poor planning plagued the trip throughout. Anderson claimed that Stewart had used poor judgment in securing bark for the canoes, which proved incapable of handling the rough waters of the Back River and the heavy ice conditions along the coast. The troubles continued at the end of the expedition, when Stewart was accused of lacking initiative and chastized for not following orders. As Gov. Simpson noted, "Stewart has unfortunate failings for which he received from myself, at the request of the Council, a severe reprimand this season." It was an ironic twist in Stewart's career, which hith-

erto had been characterized by the laudatory comments of his superior officers. The experience severely damaged Stewart's reputation, which clearly had peaked during his Yukon career.

Stewart remained with the Company, rising to the rank of chief factor in 1869. He served at Cumberland House, Oxford House, and Norway House before being dropped from the Hudson's Bay Company's list of officers in the deed poll of 1871. James Green Stewart died ten years later, at the age of fifty-five.

Further Readings

Holmgren, E.J. 1980. "The Diary of J.G. Stewart, 1855, Describing his Overland Journey in Search of the Franklin Expedition." *The Beaver* 310(4): 12–17.

Karamanski, Theodore. 1983. *Fur Trade and Exploration: Opening the Far Northwest, 1821–1852.* Vancouver: University of British Columbia Press.

Wilson, Clifford. 1970. *Campbell of the Yukon.* Toronto: Macmillan Canada.

Ken Coates

F.J. FITZGERALD (1869-1911)

Francis Joseph Fitzgerald, veteran of fourteen years' northern service with the North-West (later the Royal North-West) Mounted Police (NWMP), and commander of the famous "Lost Patrol" of 1911, was born in Halifax on 12 April 1869. In November 1888, he enlisted in the NWMP. Except for a year's service in the Boer War as a sergeant with the Canadian Mounted Rifles, he spent the rest of his life with the Mounted Police, eventually rising to the rank of inspector. He served in the Yukon during the gold rush and was a member of the expedition of 1897–98 that blazed an overland trail to the Yukon from Edmonton via Fort St. John, British Columbia, a journey that put Fitzgerald at the forefront of the force's most experienced men in northern patrolling.

In 1903, Fitzgerald, then a sergeant, was picked as second-in-command of the government expedition sent to the western Arctic to demonstrate Canadian sovereignty and halt the alleged mistreatment of the Inuit there by American whaling crews wintering at Herschel Island. In the late summer of that year, he left his detachment at Fort McPherson and, accompanied by one constable and an interpreter, set out in an open whaleboat through the Mackenzie Delta and west along the coast of the Beaufort Sea on the 250-mile trip to Herschel Island. Once there, he established a detachment, collected customs duties, and warned the crews against abusing the Inuit (though he reported that the stories of

Photograph of F.J. Fitzgerald. Courtesy of the RCMP. Photo no. 2394

debauchery were much exaggerated). Although his detachment was woefully undersupplied because of government parsimony, he managed by a combination of tact and firmness to enforce what Canadian laws were applicable in such a remote region.

After several years in the North, Fitzgerald took an Inuit wife, Unalina, "after the fashion of the country." He wished to marry her, but his superior refused permission. Their daughter, Annie, crippled as a child, died in her teens at the mission school at Hay River.

What brought Fitzgerald to the attention of the world was an episode arising out of his service in the western Arctic. Beginning in 1904, a midwinter patrol was sent from Dawson to Fort McPherson and return, a distance of about 500 miles each way over a variety of routes long used by the Kutchin Indians, to carry mail and show the flag in the region. It was no light duty; the trail followed a complex of rivers and creeks and went over some mountainous terrain. There was little game in the mountains, and in the flat, wide, treeless valleys, deeply covered in snow, it was easy for a novice to turn up a wrong creek: thus, the patrol always took along an Indian guide. In 1905, Fitzgerald was a member of the patrol on the Dawson-Fort McPherson leg, but he had never been over the route the other way.

In 1910, in recognition of his northern service, he was selected as a member of the police contingent to attend the coronation of George V in London, and he was given the command of the patrol, which for that one time only was to leave from the Fort McPherson end. In December 1910, he came from his post at Herschel Island to Fort McPherson, and, on the twenty-first, he and three other men left for Dawson. None of the men had ever been over the trail in that direction; the guide, ex-Constable Carter, had, like Fitzgerald, been over it only from Dawson.

The police recorded the number of days the patrols took and published the figures in their annual reports. Although the Mounted Police were later at pains to deny it, it seems evident that Fitzgerald was aiming at a new speed record for the patrol. It was possible to make the trip one way in as little as fourteen days, and Fitzgerald took enough supplies for thirty days. On the other hand, it had once taken fifty-six days, and, since the time depended a good deal on the weather, Fitzgerald was leaving himself no margin for error or misfortune. Unfortunately for him and his men, he was dogged with both.

From the beginning the weather was bad. The snow was unusually heavy, making trail breaking difficult. Within a week, the men were lost and found the trail only because they fell in with some Kutchin families, who set them right. Fitzgerald could have hired one of the Kutchin men as a guide, but did not—perhaps he did not want to admit he needed one.

By 2 January, they had gone a third of the way and eaten nearly half their food. Then the weather got even worse; between the third and the ninth of January the temperature averaged –50°F in strong wind. On the twelfth, they realized they were badly lost; Carter, the guide, could not find the landmarks. They had nine days' food left, and with luck could have made it to Dawson, fallen in with some Indians, or gone back to Fort McPherson. But Fitzgerald would not admit defeat, and spent seven more days looking for the trail. It was not until 18 January, with their food almost gone, that they started back to McPherson. The weather continued foul. Snowstorms had covered their tracks, and on 23 January, the thermometer touched –63°F on a windy day. By 1 February, they had killed and eaten eight of their fifteen dogs. The last entry in Fitzgerald's diary was dated 5 February; on that day they were 71 miles from Fort McPherson, but they had only five dogs left and were making only a few miles a day. The four men struggled on for another week. Between 12 and 18 February 1911, all four died, three of starvation and one of suicide. On Fitzgerald's body was his will, scratched on paper with a piece of charcoal; it read: "All money in dispatch bag and bank, clothes, etc., I leave to my dearly beloved mother, Mrs. John Fitzgerald, Halifax. God bless all. F.J. Fitzgerald, RNWMP."

Though the Mounted Police were the targets of criticism when news of the tragedy became public, especially from the explorer Vilhjalmur Stefansson,* who said that if the patrol had followed his method of travelling light and living off the land the men would not have come to grief, the evidence shows that Francis Joseph Fitzgerald succumbed to misfortune and bad judgment—a fatal combination in the North.

Further Readings

Morrison, William R. 1985. *Showing the Flag: The Mounted Police and Canadian Sovereignty in the North, 1894–1925*. Vancouver: University of British Columbia Press.

North, Dick. 1978. *The Lost Patrol*. Anchorage, Alaska: Northwest Publishing.

William R. Morrison

W.J.D. DEMPSTER (1876–1964)

William John Duncan Dempster, veteran of thirty-seven years' northern service with the Royal Canadian Mounted Police, was born in Wales on 21 October 1876. Emigrating to Canada as a young man, he joined the North-West Mounted Police in 1897, and the next year was posted to the Yukon, where he spent the rest of his career.

Between 1898 and 1934, Dempster served in a dozen different Yukon communities, but his name received national attention in connection with the famous "Lost Patrol" of 1910–11 (mentioned in the previous biographical sketch F.J. Fitzgerald*). The 500-mile route used by the midwinter patrol was a most arduous one, following a complicated series of rivers and creeks and flat, treeless valleys, as well as some mountainous terrain. Dempster joined these patrols in 1907-08.

When members of the patrol of 1910–11, of which Dempster was not a member, did not arrive at Dawson as expected, Dempster, then a corporal, was sent out with two other members of the force and an Indian guide to find and rescue the patrol. In viciously cold weather (the wind chill factor falling on occasion to –85°F) he headed toward Fort McPherson. When he set out, he believed that nothing serious could have happened to a man as experienced in northern work as Fitzgerald was, but as he covered the trail he began to discover ominous signs of trouble—old campsites that indicated that Fitzgerald had lost his way, an abandoned

Photograph of Inspector W.J.D. Dempster. Courtesy of the RCMP. Photo no. 4313

dog harness and other gear, and "the paws of a dog cut off at the knee joint, also a shoulder blade which had been cooked and the flesh evidently eaten." On 21 and 22 March, he discovered the bodies.

After this disaster, Dempster was ordered to make the route safe for future patrols, and thus he spent much of the winter of 1912–13 establishing supply caches, building shelter cabins, and blazing the trail by making "lobsticks"—trees stripped bare except for their top branches and two branches sticking out lower down, to make them evident as trail markers—something that might have saved Fitzgerald's life had it been done earlier.

It was ironic that Fitzgerald's name became better known in southern Canada than Dempster's, for it was Dempster who set the record for fastest patrol over the route—nineteen days in connection with the Lost Patrol, and later, in 1920, fourteen days over the same ground. But unlike Fitzgerald, Dempster avoided the publicity associated with disasters, for he did not take unnecessary chances in an attempt to set records, and he was not too proud to employ Indian guides or admit the fact on the rare occasions when he lost his way.

A less well-known, but equally important patrol carried out by Dempster was in connection with the Canadian government's wish to locate a route from the Porcupine River to Dawson that did not go through the United States. In 1917 he

Corporal Dempster, centre. Courtesy of the RCMP. Photo no. 4314

ease with which Dempster accomplished this mission, the difficulty of the terrain precluded the trail's further use, and no more patrols were sent in that direction.

In 1926, W.J.D. Dempster married Catherine Smith of Sydney, Nova Scotia, and the couple had a son and a daughter. When he retired in 1934 with the rank of inspector, he was the most widely known and respected Mounted Policeman in the North and was generally held to be the best trail man in the Yukon. Before he died on 25 October 1964, at the age of eighty-eight, he had the satisfaction of knowing that the new road from Dawson to Aklavik was to be named, in his honour, the Dempster Highway.

was ordered to find such a route. Travelling through the heart of the formidable Ogilvie Mountain range, a region that had been little explored, he made the trip in less than three weeks. Indians his party met along the route expressed surprise upon hearing that a route existed, claiming that "this trail has never been travelled over by white men or Indians, although different parts are travelled by different Indians." But despite the relative

Further Readings

Morrison, W.R. 1985. *Showing the Flag: The Mounted Police and Canadian Sovereignty in the North, 1894–1925.* Vancouver: University of British Columbia Press.

North, Dick. 1978. *The Lost Patrol.* Anchorage, Alaska: Northwest Publishing.

William R. Morrison

Dempster's Patrol preparing to leave Dawson in search of the Lost Patrol, 27 February 1911. J. Doody, photographer/ National Archives of Canada/C 3070

Royal North West Mounted Police Patrol of 1909-1910. National Archives of Canada/PA 29622

CATHARINE MCCLELLAN
(1921–)

Anthropological research by Catharine McClellan has received two markedly different kinds of recognition in two very different worlds. In North American anthropology, her clear detailed descriptions of western subarctic Tlingit and Athapaskan culture and her insights into social organization, myth and folklore, and fur-trade history have earned her international stature. In Yukon native communities, her openness, her wit, and her intelligent appreciation of everything she has been taught have earned her a place in the kinship network.

Kitty, as she is known by both her academic colleagues and her friends in the Yukon, has spent thirty-five years applying her remarkable energies and research abilities to integrating those two worlds. Whether she is writing an academic paper or taking her turn telling a story in a cabin on a winter's evening, her contributions to documentation and analysis of northern intellectual history have been outstanding.

Like many others who have become northern scholars, Catharine McClellan began her life with interests far removed from the North. She was born in a rural Pennsylvania Dutch community, Spring Grove, and her childhood was spent exploring the countryside and developing an interest in the different languages and cultures in her community. An avid reader, her interests began to focus more and more on classical archaeology, which she went on to study as an undergraduate at Bryn Mawr college. U.S. Navy service during World War II interrupted her studies, but in 1946, she returned to university at Berkeley, California. Attracted by the anthropological concept of culture, she shifted from classical studies to anthropology.

In the summer of 1947 she helped Douglas Leechman and Frederica de Laguna with an archaeological survey preliminary to the building of the Saint Lawrence Seaway. The next summer

Catharine McClellan with Mrs. Angela Sidney, a Tagish Indian storyteller. Whitehorse, Yukon, circa 1970. Photograph courtesy of Catharine McClellan

brought an opportunity to do an ethnographic survey in the Yukon Territory, shortly after the Alaska Highway opened the area to easy access for scientists. Research stipulations were rather different for female anthropologists even as recently as the 1940s, and McClellan was informed by the funding agency, the National Museum of Canada, that a woman researcher could not go to the Yukon "alone." After unsuccessful efforts to locate a scientific party going to the Yukon with other interests but willing to take along a graduate student in anthropology, she and a fellow student, Dorothy Rainier (Libby), persuaded the museum to give them a small stipend and let them proceed on their own.

That summer, friendships and research interests developed that have grown and flourished during the intervening years.

Catharine McClellan completed her doctoral dissertation "Culture Change and Native Trade in the Southern Yukon Territory," for the University of California in 1950. Over the years she has continued her studies in the Yukon Territory and northern British Columbia on Tlingit, Tagish, and Southern Tutchone culture history. She has worked extensively, too, in Alaska with Dr. Frederica de Laguna on archaeological and ethnological problems in coastal Tlingit settlements, and in Ahtna communities on the Copper River. In 1956, she did field work in western Alaska Eskimo communities for the Arctic Health Research Center.

McClellan's fascination with the North has led her to investigate a broad range of questions. Her writings provide us with detailed descriptions of Athapaskan ethnography, particularly for the southern Yukon. She has followed up specific questions about shamanism, sib and clan organization, oral narrative, and culture contacts. Her publications have become documents that a generation of anthropology students and young native people now use in the Yukon to reconstruct patterns of land use, social change, and prehistory. In fact, her work is so firmly established as the baseline for present research that the debit often goes unacknowledged.

Included in her writings are a two-volume ethnography, a monograph on oral narrative, and articles in the *Handbook of North American Indians, Vol. 6* and the *Canadian Encyclopedia* as well as other articles and book reviews. She was the editor of *Arctic Anthropology* from 1974–82 and is a past president of the American Ethnological Society.

She has taught at the University of Missouri, at the University of Washington, at Barnard College, and at Columbia University. In 1983, she retired as Bascom Professor of Anthropology at the University of Wisconsin where she began teaching in 1961. She has also held visiting positions at Bryn Mawr College, and at the University of Alaska, Fairbanks, in 1973.

Catharine McClellan's position in North American anthropology is important, but equally important is her recognition in the Yukon. For her academic work she has received distinction; in the Yukon, she has become part of the folklore. Not infrequently, anthropologists refer to "informants" as "my people" and speak of "trips to the field." A generation of Yukon Indians ranging from elderly people to adults who were toddlers when she first arrived refer to Catharine McClellan as "our Kitty" and see her primary residence as the Yukon with periodic "field trips" back to her university. They welcome her visits as those of a returning family member and regret her departures as temporary absences.

Catharine McClellan is currently writing a book on Yukon native history for the Council for Yukon Indians. She plans to write up more of her accumulated years of field research and to spend time, as she has for almost four decades, visiting her friends in the Yukon.

Further Readings

McClellan, Catharine. 1971. *The Girl Who Married the Bear.* Publications in Ethnology No. 2. Ottawa: National Museum of Canada.

_____. 1975. *My Old People Say: An Ethnographic Survey of Southern Yukon Territory.* 2 vol. Publications in Ethnology No. 6. Ottawa: National Museum of Man.

_____ (with L. Birckel, R. Bringhurst, J. Fall, C. McCarthy, and J. Sheppard). 1987. *Part of the Land, Part of the Water: A History of the Yukon Indians.* Vancouver: Douglas and McIntyre.

Julie Cruikshank

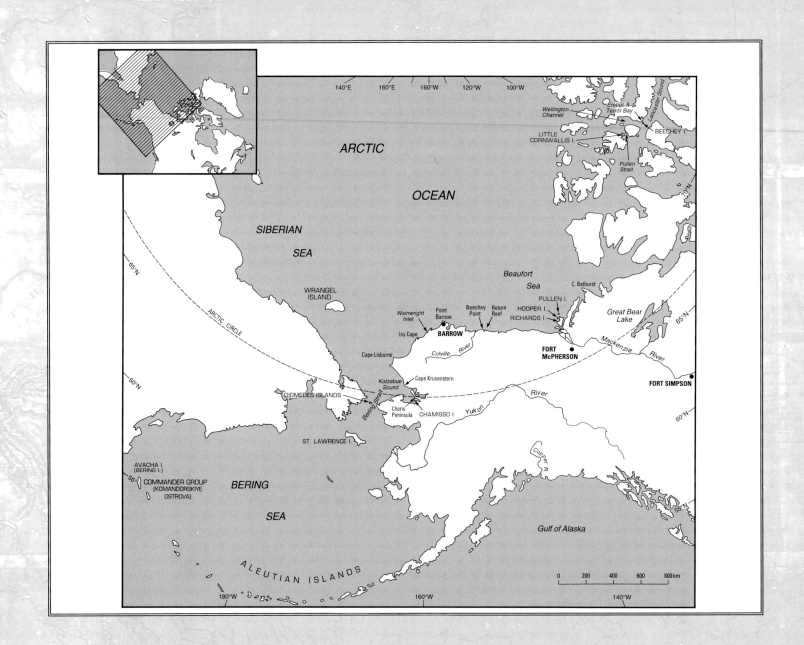

ARCTIC

OCEAN

SIBERIAN

SEA

WRANGEL
ISLAND

Beaufort
Sea

C. Bathurst

PULLEN I.

Wainwright
Inlet

Point
Barrow

Beechey
Point

Return
Reef

HOOPER I.

RICHARDS I.

Great Bear
Lake

Icy Cape

BARROW

Cape Lisburne

Colville   River

FORT
McPHERSON

Mackenzie   River

Cape Krusenstern

Kotzebue
Sound

FORT SIMPSON

DIOMEDES ISLANDS

River

Choris
Peninsula

CHAMISSO I.

Yukon

ST. LAWRENCE I.

Copper   R.

AVACHA I.
(BERING I.)

COMMANDER GROUP
(KOMANDORSKIYE
OSTROVA)

BERING

SEA

Gulf of Alaska

ALEUTIAN   ISLANDS

180°W

160°W

140°W

140°E   160°E   160°W   120°W   100°W

Wellington
Channel

Erebus &
Terror Bay

LITTLE
CORNWALLIS I.

BEECHEY I.

Lancaster Sound

Pullen
Strait

65°N

ARCTIC CIRCLE

60°N

55°N

65°N

60°N

Bering Strait

0   200   400   600   800 km

198

UNIT

❧ I I ❧

Vitus Bering, Frederick William Beechey, W.J.S. Pullen

Two especially important factors motivated geographical exploration at the far western extremity of the North American Arctic: the region's proximity to Russia and its potential as a western access to the Northwest Passage. The former led to Russian fur interests in North America and to Russian control of the modern state of Alaska, the latter to numerous expeditions designed to support mariners seeking a way through the Passage from the east. Less well known that the eastern Arctic, where gradual exploration and expansion from a familiar European base have shaped our conception of the region, the western access to the Arctic still retains a stamp of "foreignness," much like the different culture that lies beyond the Bering Sea.

VITUS BERING (1681–1741)

The navigator and explorer Capt. Comdr. Vitus Jonassen (in Russian, Ivan Ivanovich) Bering was one of many foreign specialists brought to Russia by Tsar Peter the Great in order to help modernize the growing, but lagging empire. He is principally known for his two voyages of exploration and discovery in the second quarter of the eighteenth century, the first to Bering Strait —which he did not personally discover —and the other to the Gulf of Alaska.

Bering was a native of Denmark, where he was born on 12 August 1681, in the Jutland seaport of Horsens. Very little is known of his upbringing or personality. He was fairly well educated, and well mannered and devout. As a commander, he was cautious and unhurried, and he seems to have been liked for his gentleness and humility.

By the time Bering was invited by Admiral Cruys in 1703 to join the fledgling Russian Navy as a sublieutenant, he had already voyaged to the East Indies. Apparently he acquitted himself quite satisfactorily in Russia's naval campaigns in the Baltic, Black, and White seas, as he was promoted to lieutenant in 1707, captain lieutenant in 1710, and captain (second class) in 1720. In 1723, he requested promotion to captain (first class) but was refused, and he resigned to live on an estate at Vyborg.

Meanwhile, the thoroughgoing and draconian transformation of Muscovy by Peter the Great along Western lines included not only the creation of a respectable navy, but the

Portrait of Vitus Bering, from Golder's *Bering's Voyages* (1822-25)

extension of Russian geographical knowledge and political dominion. The lands and waters of the far North Pacific —still unexplored and unsettled by European powers—had long interested the inquisitive and versatile tsar, who now decided to satisfy his scientific curiosity and imperial appetite with a secret expedition. Bering's lengthy naval experience was brought to Peter's attention by Admiral Apraskin, who persuaded the retired veteran to reenlist in 1724 at the rank of captain (first class) and take charge of the one hundred man First Kamchatka Expedition, 1725–30.

The tsar's personal instructions, penned only two days before his death, were not handed to Bering until the very day of his departure from St. Petersburg. This was done deliberately in order to minimize publicity, for xenophobic Russia with its national inferiority complex feared that its western European imperial rivals might beat it to the *terra incognita* of northwestern America. Bering was directed to build one or two ships in Kamchatka, sail northwards through the Otter (Bering) Sea, determine whether Asia and America were separated, go ashore and make a firsthand report and a map, and contact any European settlement or ship to learn the name of the locale. The third point was a ruse to mask the expedition's real purpose, namely, to probe the American coast; Peter the Great had known since the end of the previous century that Semyon Dezhnev had sailed between the two continents in

1648. But Bering followed his instructions and navigated Anian (Bering) Strait as far north as 67°18′ in 1728, discovering St. Lawrence Island and the two Diomedes. The next year he sailed eastwards from Kamchatka for three days but found no land. Upon his return to the imperial capital he was promoted to captain commander and awarded 1,000 silver rubles.

Neither Bering nor the government was satisfied with the results of the expedition, the latter because it had not reached America and the former because he was aware of how much exploration remained undone. So, at Bering's suggestion, the Second Kamchatka Expedition, 1733–42, was mounted, again under his command. It was one of three components of the grandiose Great Northern Expedition, one of the most ambitious and expensive undertakings in the history of exploration and discovery. Charged with surveying the northern and eastern coasts of Siberia from the Northern Dvina to the Amur and probing Japan and America, it comprised thirteen ships and some three thousand men, including many savants from the infant Academy of Sciences (notably Germans like Gerhard Müller, Georg Steller, and Johann Gmelin). This second expedition was even more onerous and protracted than the first. Bering left St. Petersburg at the beginning of 1733, but did not embark from Okhotsk, Siberia's chief Pacific port, until September of 1740, because of the enormous distance and staggering difficulties of transport, the obstacles to shipbuilding at Okhotsk, bureaucratic delays, personality clashes, and jurisdictional disputes. Finally, the springboard of Kamchatka was reached and a new base, Petropavlovsk, named after the expedition's two packetboats, the *St. Peter* and *St. Paul*, was founded on superb Avacha Bay.

The two vessels sailed in June 1741, heading southeastwards at first in order to locate the imaginary De Gama Land. After two weeks, they were permanently separated by a storm, but both continued eastwards and made landfalls on the Gulf of Alaska coast in July (fifteen well-armed men from the *St. Paul,* under Capt. Aleksey Chirikov, went ashore and never returned). On the return passage, some of the Aleutian and other islands were discovered. The rickety *St. Peter* with its scorbutic crew was wrecked on Avacha (Bering) Island in the Commander Group (Komandorskiye Ostrova). There the survivors wintered, but several, including the elderly Bering on 6 December, died of scurvy and hypothermia. The following summer the stragglers fashioned a vessel from the remains of the *St. Peter* and made their way to Petropavlovsk to rejoin Chirikov, who had returned safely the previous fall.

At last, Vitus Jonassen Bering had accomplished his mission, albeit at the cost of his own life. He had sighted and reconnoitred the "big land," and thereby laid the basis for a Russian claim and paved the way for further Russian exploration and settlement. He also introduced a source for future profits in the two thousand sea otter pelts brought back by his expedition. They triggered a fur rush down the Kuriles and across the Aleutians to Alaska and the northwest coast, eventually culminating in the establishment of Russian America and the Russian-American Company, in 1799. Thus was realized Peter the Great's original plan of extending his country's eastward drive for new fur sources as the sables and foxes of Siberia were depleted. The treasury's share of income from this lucrative industry in the form of taxes and tribute was essential to help finance the tsar's costly foreign campaigns and domestic reforms.

Further Readings

Fisher, Raymond H. 1977. *Bering's Voyages: Whither and Why.* Seattle: University of Washington Press.

Frost, O.W., ed. 1992. *Bering and Chirikov: The American Voyages and Their Impact.* Anchorage: Alaska Historical Society.

Golder, Frank A. 1922–25. *Bering's Voyages.* 2 vols. New York: American Geographical Society.

Kushnarev, Evgenii G. 1990. *Bering's Search for the Strait: The First Kamchatka Expedition 1725–1730,* translated by E.A.P. Crownhart-Vaughan. Portland: Oregon Historical Society Press.

Müller, Gerhard Friedrich. 1986. *Bering's Voyages: The Reports from Russia,* translated by Carol Urness. Fairbanks: University of Alaska Press.

Polevoy, B.P. 1982. "The 300th Anniversary of the Birth of Vitus Bering," translated by James R. Gibson. *Polar Geography and Geology* 6:294–303.

[Georg Wilhelm Steller]. 1988. *Journal of a Voyage with Bering, 1741–1742,* translated by Margritt A. Engel and O.W. Frost. Stanford: Stanford University Press.

Urness, Carol. 1987. *Bering's First Expedition: A Re-examination Based on Eighteenth-Century Books, Maps, and Manuscuipts.* New York: Garland Publishing.

Waxell, Sven. 1962. *The Russian Expedition to Americ*, translated by M.A. Michael. New York: Collier Books.

James R. Gibson

FREDERICK WILLIAM BEECHEY
(1796–1856)

Frederick William Beechey, named after his godfather William IV, was born in London, England, on 17 February 1796, the second son of the eminent portrait artist Sir William Beechey, R.A. He served both the Royal Navy and geographical science with distinction, authored books on arctic discovery, and at the time of his death, 29 November 1856, was vice president of the Royal Society and president of the Royal Geographical Society.

Beechey went to sea in 1806, at the early age of ten, attaining midshipman's rank the following year. After nearly twelve years of active service, he began his career as arctic voyager and geographer. In 1818, he joined the *Trent*, a hired brig commanded by John Franklin,* which was ordered to accompany HMS *Dorothea,* under Capt. David Buchan's command, on an attempted voyage across the Polar Sea. The next year, he was appointed to the *Hecla,* Capt. William Edward Parry,* and made the remarkable voyage to "Parry's West," sharing the parliamentary reward of £5,000. Upon his return, Beechey was appointed to the sloop *Adventure* from which he was dispatched with his brother Henry W. Beechey to conduct an overland survey of the northern coast of Africa. During this service he was promoted to the rank of commander. At the end of the voyage, he seems to have been unemployed, perhaps for reasons of health after his physical exertions in the Arctic and in the

Portrait of Frederick William Beechey.
Courtesy of the National Maritime Museum
London

desert country of Barca and Syrt. His next appointment was to the sloop HMS *Blossom* on 12 January 1825.

The *Blossom's* object was to meet with Franklin's second overland expedition. She reached Kotzebue Sound, via the Pacific, on 22 July 1826, and arrived at Chamisso Island on the twenty-fifth. Beechey was only five days late for his intended rendezvous with Franklin. A general reconnaissance of the surrounding country revealed it to be impenetrable, uninhabitable, and infested with mosquitoes. Consequently, Beechey decided not to send a party overland to the northern coast of America. He left provisions for Franklin at Chamisso and then took the *Blossom* northward in the hope of meeting him, charting the coastline as he proceeded. The *Blossom's* course was within sight of the shore, the barge skirting along as close as possible with her crew periodically erecting cairns and leaving bottles with messages for Franklin. Beechey's party had traced the coast to within twenty miles of Icy Cape when heavy weather set in, forcing the *Blossom* from shore and into ice floes. She was later able to return to the coast and rejoin the barge, which was then sent along the coast to find Franklin, who was expected daily. The *Blossom* herself returned to Chamisso to take on wood and water, strong westerly winds preventing her further use along the northern coast. On 23 August, the barge reached its farthest east, 156°21′ W longitude, at Point Barrow, named after Sir John

Barrow, the architect of the venture. Pack ice, moving sea ice astern, and warlike Inuit forced even the barge to turn back at that point, but not before Beechey's party had added 126 miles of new coastline to the chart.

Franklin, meanwhile, had been making his way westward, surveying the coast to Beechey Point, 149°37′ W longitude. He decided to go no farther than what he called Return Reef. This place, Franklin's farthest west, was reached on 18 August, five days before the barge, under Thomas Elson, made Point Barrow, only 146 miles to the west. It would have been an historic meeting at that end of the earth. There is no doubt, however, that Elson and Franklin acted wisely in not pressing on in the face of early winter conditions. Neither knew of the other's position; in any case, had Franklin continued, he might not have been able to overtake the barge. Franklin was now forced to retrace his steps to Great Bear Lake, his object having again eluded him. It remained for two Hudson's Bay Company servants, Peter Warren Dease and Thomas Simpson,* to complete the exploration of the western Arctic between Point Barrow and Return Reef some ten years later, thus completing the outline of the shores of the polar sea.

While Franklin retraced his steps, the barge made a difficult retreat to the west and south. The ice was so close to the shore that the barge had to be tracked by rope, the crew scurrying along precipitous banks. The Inuit were a further concern. The barge was reunited with the *Blossom* in Kotzebue Sound on 9 September, and even at that late date, Franklin might still be expected to arrive at the intended rendezvous. Beechey now had to decide how long he should wait. His vessel was not reinforced against the pressures of pack ice, and he had insufficient supplies to winter in the North, although his orders suggested that he should stay at the rendezvous until the end of October. Nevertheless, with a sudden deterioration of the weather, Beechey and his officers agreed they must leave the sound and proceed southward for provisions, which they did on 14 October. As late as the sixteenth, Beechey was hoping for a change of wind that would allow him to return to Cape Krusenstern "in order to give Captain Franklin the last chance."

Beechey's second summer on the coast was equally disappointing, with even worse weather conditions than in the previous season. The barge was driven on shore during tempestuous weather in early September on the Choris Peninsula, Kotzebue Sound. She was wrecked and three of her crew drowned. It was also disappointing to Beechey that Franklin did not appear. Nor was there any news of him.

Frederick William Beechey never returned to the Arctic, but the rest of his life was full of naval service and scientific inquiry. He surveyed South American waters and the coasts of Ireland, advancing to the rank of rear-admiral,in 1854. The following year, Beechey was elected president of the Royal Geographical Society, and in his last annual address in that capacity he summed up the scientific aims of his life. He told his audience that after forty years, "the major problem," the Northwest Passage, had been solved "and Science at least had reaped her harvest." Arctic discovery had shown what men could endure with little loss of life, Sir John Franklin and his men notwithstanding. "They have, in short," he correctly concluded, "expunged the blot of obscurity which would otherwise have hung over and disfigured the history of this enlightened age."

Further Readings

Beechey, F.W. 1831. *Narrative of a Voyage to the Pacific and Bering's Strait in His Majesty's Ship Blossom, 1825–1828.* London: H. Colburn and R. Bentley.

_____. 1843. *Voyage of Discovery towards the North Pole, 1818.* London: R. Bentley.

Gough, Barry M., ed. 1973. *To the Pacific and Arctic with Beechey: The Journal of Lieutenant George Peard of HMS Blossom 1825-28.* London: Hakluyt Society.

Barry M. Gough

W.J.S. PULLEN (1818–1887)

Like many of his Victorian contemporaries, William John Samuel Pullen left his mark on the Canadian Arctic during the extensive searches for John Franklin's* missing ships and crew. His name is perpetuated by Pullen Island in the Mackenzie River estuary and by Pullen Strait to the east of Little Cornwallis Island. Pullen himself added the island to naval charts; the strait was named in his honour.

Born on 4 December 1813, at Devonport, England, Pullen was the eldest son in a naval family. It was no surprise, then, that he joined the Royal Navy as a First Class Volunteer before his fifteenth birthday. While serving in the Mediterranean fleet, he passed the provisional examination for second master and was appointed to HMS *Alban* in 1835. On her return to England, the *Alban* carried several passengers, one of them a Col. William Light, newly appointed surveyor general of the new colony of South Australia. During the voyage, Light persuaded Pullen to leave the Navy and to join him as assistant surveyor, which he did until 1841. The next year, 1842, Pullen returned to England and rejoined the Royal Navy as a mate, being appointed to HMS *Columbia*, engaged in surveying the Saint John River and the Bay of Fundy until 1848. At that time, he was appointed as first lieutenant of HMS *Plover*, a depot ship for one of the first three searches for Franklin. But it was not until the summer of 1849 that Pullen met up with the *Plover*, which was already in the Pacific when Pullen's appointment was made.

W.J.S. Pullen wearing his Baltic and Arctic discovery medals. Photograph courtesy of Capt. T.C. Pullen

Shortly after joining the *Plover* off Chamisso Island, he was sent with two boats to find a suitable berth for the ship near Cape Lisburne. Finding none, he returned, and the *Plover*, accompanied by HMS *Herald* and the yacht *Nancy Dawson*, proceeded along the coast to Wainwright Inlet. From there, Pullen again set out along the coast in boats, this time to search for signs of Franklin as far east as the Mackenzie River. On passing Point Barrow he found ice conditions so severe that he sent the two larger boats back, continuing himself with one officer and fourteen men in two twenty-seven-foot gig whale boats and an *umiak* purchased from the Inuit. The route to the Mackenzie, lying some five hundred miles eastward, was shallow and relatively unknown, while to seaward lay the polar pack. Nevertheless, in spite of bad weather and hostile Inuit, the small party gained the Mackenzie on 2 September, and arrived at Fort McPherson four days later. Some of the men were posted at McPherson for the winter; others wintered upriver on Great Slave Lake. Pullen and two men remained at Fort Simpson, where Dr. John Rae* was in charge.

The following summer Rae, Pullen, and his party left Fort Simpson, bound for York Factory and England. On Great Slave Lake, however, they met two Indians in a canoe, "bearers of an extra ordinary despatch from England which contained my commission as Commander ... and also the sanction of the Admiralty for renewed prosecution of the search for John Franklin and his party on the coast, but eastward of the River Mackenzie if Captain Pullen should consider it practicable." Accordingly, Pullen and his men returned to Fort Simpson, where they outfitted themselves and headed down to the Beaufort Sea. They turned east when they met the saltwater, but could reach no farther than Cape Bathurst before an impassable mass of broken, jumbled ice stopped them. After waiting a week for the ice to clear, Pullen turned back to the river. It was on his return that he observed and named Pullen and Hooper islands, lying to the north and west of Richards Island. They spent a second winter up the Mackenzie before returning to England in 1850.

Less than two years later, Pullen made a second arctic journey. Commanding HMS *North Star,* store-ship for Sir Edward Belcher's* 1852–54 expedition, Pullen spent two winters in Erebus and Terror Bay, Beechey Island, and during his stay he made several reconnaissances across Lancaster Sound and up the Wellington Channel. Of the five ships that left England on Belcher's search expedition, only the *North Star,* under Pullen's command, returned. Belcher had ordered the others—HMS *Resolute, Assistance, Intrepid,* and *Pioneer*—abandoned, an act for which he was subsequently court-martialled.

Pullen's later career saw the command of HMS *Falcon* against the Russians in 1855, and his promotion to captain in the next year. He commanded HMS *Cyclops,* involved in surveying for the submarine telegraph from Suez to Aden and, later, along the coast of Ceylon. After four years in charge of the Bermuda Survey, Pullen was placed on the retired list in April 1870. His promotions to rear-admiral and vice-admiral followed in 1874 and 1879.

William John Samuel Pullen married Abigal Louisa Berton in Saint John, New Brunswick, on 25 August 1845, the same year HMS *Erebus* and *Terror* sailed for northern waters. Their union produced four sons and one daughter. A typical Victorian naval officer, Pullen was both a deeply religious man and a first-class seaman and navigator. When he died at Torquay, Devonshire, England, on 11 January 1887, a life full of naval service ended. No single event in Pullen's contribution to the Arctic was remarkable: his geographical discoveries were clearly minor; his journeys, although strenuous and difficult, were restricted by his good judgment; and the Franklin searches in which he participated were completely fruitless. Yet without the honest dedication to the task of British officers of Pullen's calibre, the more celebrated, but no more important accomplishments could never have been realized.

Further Readings

Hooper, W.H. 1853. *Ten Months among the Tents of the Tuski.* London: John Murray.

Rich, E.E., ed. 1953. *John Rae's Arctic Correspondence with the Hudson's Bay Company on Arctic Exploration. 1844–55.* London: Hudson's Bay Record Society.

Pullen, H.F., ed. 1979. *The Pullen Expedition.* Toronto: Arctic History Press.

Pullen, W.J.S. 1947. "Pullen in Search of Franklin." *The Beaver* (March & June).

H.F. Pullen

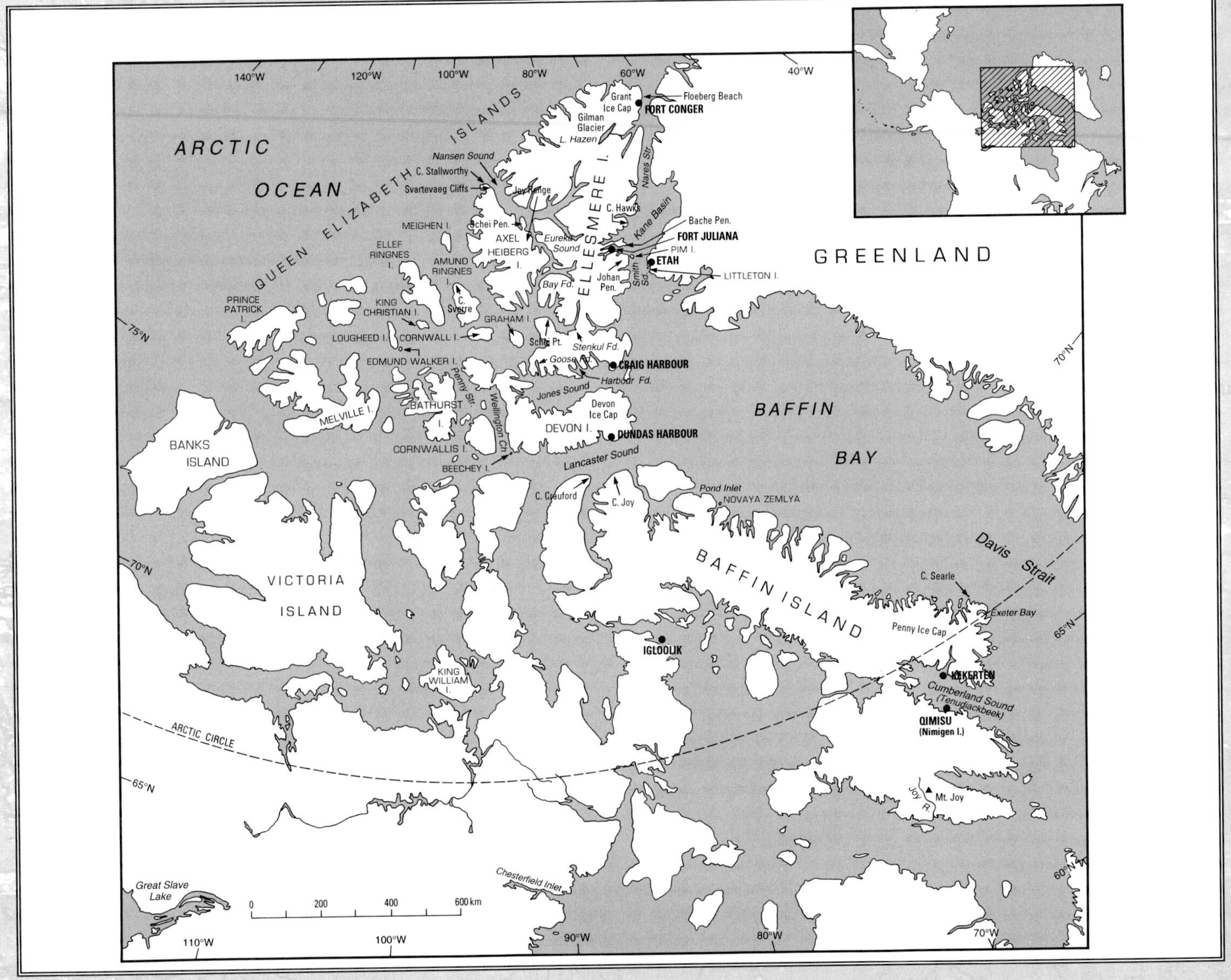

140°W
120°W
100°W
80°W
60°W
40°W
ARCTIC
OCEAN
QUEEN ELIZABETH ISLANDS
Grant Ice Cap
Floeberg Beach
FORT CONGER
Gilman Glacier
L. Hazen
Nares Str.
Nansen Sound
C. Stallworthy
Svartevaeg Cliffs
Joy Range
ELLESMERE I.
C. Hawks
Kane Basin
Bache Pen.
FORT JULIANA
PIM I.
ETAH
LITTLETON I.
MEIGHEN I.
Schei Pen.
AXEL HEIBERG I.
Eureka Sound
ELLEF RINGNES I.
AMUND RINGNES I.
Johan Pen.
Smith Sd.
GREENLAND
Bay Fd.
PRINCE PATRICK I.
KING CHRISTIAN I.
C. Sverre
GRAHAM I.
LOUGHEED I.
CORNWALL I.
Schei Pt.
Stenkul Fd.
75°N
EDMUND WALKER I.
Goose Fd.
CRAIG HARBOUR
Harbour Fd.
70°N
Penny Str.
Jones Sound
BATHURST I.
Wellington Ch.
Devon Ice Cap
BAFFIN
MELVILLE I.
DEVON I.
DUNDAS HARBOUR
BANKS ISLAND
CORNWALLIS I.
BAY
BEECHEY I.
Lancaster Sound
C. Crauford
C. Joy
Pond Inlet
NOVAYA ZEMLYA
Davis Strait
BAFFIN ISLAND
70°N
VICTORIA ISLAND
C. Searle
Exeter Bay
Penny Ice Cap
65°N
IGLOOLIK
KING WILLIAM I.
KEKERTEN
Cumberland Sound (Tenudiackbeek)
QIMISU (Nimigen I.)
ARCTIC CIRCLE
65°N
Joy R.
Mt. Joy
Chesterfield Inlet
60°N
Great Slave Lake
0
200
400
600 km
110°W
100°W
90°W
80°W
70°W

UNIT
❦ 12 ❦

William Penny, Eenoolooapik, George Strong Nares, Otto Sverdrup, Per Schei, A.H. Joy, H.W. Stallworthy

The map for this twelfth unit shifts back to the central regions of the Arctic. The individuals collected here came from diverse origins—Norwegian geologists, Canadian policemen, British mariners, and a well-travelled Baffin Island Inuk. Under some of the most rigorous conditions, these men identified many of the islands in the vast Canadian Arctic archipelago. Police efforts to "show the flag" were especially important to Canada in those remote areas that, even today, remain populated largely by only a few scattered temporary or seasonal communities.

WILLIAM PENNY
(ca. 1809–1892)

> I am perfectly acquainted with the arctic regions, my knowledge having been acquired by thirty-three voyages to these regions, and by spending three winters there. I have become intimately associated with the Esquimaux and their habits and manners.

So wrote William Penny, arctic whaling master, in 1856 at the age of forty-seven. Three years later, he declared that he had sailed ten times to the East Greenland Sea and "twenty-five times or upwards" to the Davis Strait whaling grounds west of Greenland. In the dangerous business of pursuing Greenland (bowhead) whales in wooden sailing ships among pack ice and icebergs, all the while coping with the hazards of cold, snow, fog, and uncharted reefs, Penny must be considered successful. The ships that he commanded from 1835 to 1864—including the *Bon Accord, Saint Andrew*, and *Lady Franklin* of Aberdeen, the *Advice* and *Polynia* of Dundee, and the *Queen* of Peterhead—brought into Scottish ports approximately 1,470 tons of whale oil and 90 tons of baleen from 162 whales. He never lost a ship, although wrecks were all too common in arctic whaling.

William Penny was born in Peterhead, Scotland, in 1808 or 1809, and followed his father (William Penny, Sr.) into the whaling trade at the age of twelve. He became a mate before he was twenty-one and a master before twenty-seven. From

Portrait of William Penny. Courtesy of the Scott Polar Research Institute, Cambridge, U.K.

1821 until 1864, he sailed almost annually—and sometimes twice in one year—to arctic whaling and sealing grounds, interrupting the whaling by a few mercantile voyages from 1841 to 1843 and a John Franklin* search expedition in 1850–51. Penny was not content merely to follow established routines in familiar places. With the help of Eenoolooapik,* an Inuk who had accompanied him to Scotland in 1839, he expanded the limits of the Davis Strait whaling ground in 1840 by leading other vessels into Cumberland Sound—the first European visitors there since John Davis* in 1585. He introduced the technique of wintering on board ship in 1853–54, and helped develop the practice of floe whaling. He was a strong proponent of shore whaling bases and, with other members of the Aberdeen Arctic Company, designed an ambitious scheme for arctic whaling between Novaya Zemlya and Baffin Island, involving steam whalers, permanent settlements, and subsidiary mining of plumbago. But because Penny's application to the British Colonial Office for a large grant of land on Baffin Island was opposed by rival whaling interests and rejected by the government, his grand scheme was never realized. Nevertheless, he established small, temporary shore bases during his whaling voyages and wintered in Cumberland Sound on four occasions.

To William Penny belongs the distinction of undertaking the first maritime search for the ships of John Franklin. In

1847, during a whaling voyage on the *Saint Andrew*, he penetrated Lancaster Sound to 78°W but failed to find traces of HMS *Erebus* and *Terror*. In 1849, while in command of the whaler *Advice,* he again attempted to search Lancaster Sound, in company with the *Truelove* under Captain Parker, but ice barred their progress. Penny then offered his services to the Admiralty and, with the support of Lady Jane Franklin,* obtained leadership of an expedition. With HMS *Lady Franklin* and *Sophia* he entered Lancaster Sound in 1850, helped discover Franklin's 1845–46 winter quarters on Beechey Island, wintered near Cornwallis Island, explored Wellington Channel, and laid down some place names. But Penny was rankled by the superior bearing and adverse public comments of Capt. Horatio Austin and other naval officers, by the suggestion at home that he and Austin had not done enough in the time available, by what he considered unfair treatment by the Arctic Committee reviewing the work of the two expeditions, and by the Admiralty's unwillingness to offer him another opportunity to search for Franklin in 1852. He dropped out of the Franklin search in frustration and anger, turning his considerable energies toward the development of whaling and the establishment of a mission in Cumberland Sound.

The extension of whaling to the coast of Baffin Island about 1820 had initiated a period of rapid cultural and economic change among the Inuit. Contact between natives and whalemen intensified after wintering was introduced to Cumberland Sound in the 1850s. Penny was astute enough to realize that some aspects of whaling, particularly the introduction of alien modes of behaviour and unfamiliar diseases, had proved harmful to the native inhabitants, and he was determined to soften the blow of whaling by introducing

Christian teaching. When he sailed to Cumberland Sound in 1857, he was accompanied not only by his wife, Margaret, and their son, William, but also by the Moravian missionary Mathias Warmow, who preached to the Inuit at Kekerten and other places during the winter. To the great disappointment of Penny and Warmow, however, the Moravian church later decided that it would not be feasible to establish a permanent mission in the region.

One of Penny's concerns was that the arctic regions north of Canada, which were ostensibly British on the basis of many discovery expeditions since Martin Frobisher's* in 1576, might fall to the United States if Britain failed to exert her authority there. When he applied for a land grant in 1852, he emphasized that a permanent British presence would forestall the plans of American whaling interests to establish bases on Baffin Island. The point aroused considerable discussion in the Colonial Office, Foreign Office, and Admiralty, and although the government in the end refused to sanction Penny's scheme, it did instruct its ambassador in Washington to notify the American Secretary of State that Cumberland Island (Baffin Island) was British territory and that American whalemen should not trespass there. That gesture marked a step in the evolution of British attitudes towards the North American Arctic, a step that led to the transfer of the Arctic Islands to Canada in 1880, shaping the destiny of the Canadian North.

By expanding the frontier of the Davis Strait whale fishery, by developing the technique of wintering on board whaleships, by pointing the way into Lancaster Sound for subsequent Franklin searches, and by initiating the first missionary presence on Baffin Island, William Penny influenced the course of Euro-American activity in the eastern Arctic during the nineteenth century. Among all those who sailed along the barren coasts or travelled across the tundra spaces, Penny stands out for the breadth of his experience, for his skill in navigation, and above all for his concern for the native people. His vision extended far beyond the normal requirements of the whaling profession, and if his goals were not always attained, it was not because of a lack of ability or determination, but probably because he found it difficult to exercise tact, persuasion, and patience when faced by less competent and less decisive men. An ice cap, a highland, and a strait in arctic Canada now bear the name of this extraordinary Scottish whaling captain.

Further Readings

Allen, Greg. 1982–83. "Our Silver Penny." *Leopard Magazine* (Aberdeen), (November 1982):12–14; (December/January 1982–83):14–16; (February 1983):21–22.

Holland, Clive A. 1970. "William Penny, 1809-92; Arctic Whaling Master." *Polar Record* 15(94): 25-43.

M'Donald, Alexander. 1841. *A Narrative of Some Passages in the History of Eenoolooapik, a Young Eskimaux, Who was Brought to Britain in 1839, in the Ship 'Neptune' of Aberdeen.* Edinburgh: Fraser and J. Hogg.

Stevenson, Alex. 1966. "Penny's Polar Probe, 1850-51." *North* 13(6): 31–37.

Tillotson, John. 1869. *Adventures in the Ice ... Including Experiences of Captain Penny, the Veteran Whaler.* London: James Hogg.

Woodward, F.J. 1953. "William Penny, 1809–92." *Polar Record* 6(46): 809–11.

W. Gillies Ross

EENOOLOOAPIK (ca. 1820–1847)

In 1840, life for the Cumberland Sound Inuit was much the same as it had been for many years. Although they knew of the whalers, the British Navy, and the Hudson's Bay Company, these Inuit had felt but little influence from such strangers. Within twenty years, however, their way of life was changed profoundly, and although he probably did not realize it, Eenoolooapik was the harbinger of that change.

Eenoolooapik was born around 1820 at Qimisu, on the west coast of Cumberland Sound. While still young, he travelled with his family on an unusual voyage by *umiak*, skirting the coastline of Cumberland Sound until they reached Davis Strait. The boy closely observed the outline of the coast as they paddled slowly past. They met a group of whalers and decided to continue their voyage to Cape Searle, a location frequented by the whalers, where they settled. Contact with these strangers fired Eenoolooapik's curiosity about their land, and a desire grew in him to visit their homeland. Twice he made plans to depart, but each time the pleas of his mother kept him at home.

At about this same time, unpredictable catches in Davis Strait and worsening ice conditions had the fishery concerned. At least one widely publicized article appeared in Britain suggesting that only diversification into trade and the establishment of permanent whaling stations could save the fishery. In 1833, William Penny,* mate on the *Traveller,* was sent to investigate Inuit reports of a large bay full of whales to the south of Exeter Bay. Penny's

Portrait of Eenoolooapik from Alexander M'Donald's *A Narrative of Some Passages in the History of Eenoolooapik, a Young Esquimaux* (1841)

trip failed, but he tried again in 1839, when he discovered that Eenoolooapik was a native of Tenudiackbeek (Cumberland Sound) and could map its entire coastline.

Here, the desires of both Penny and Eenoolooapik merged. Penny wanted to take the Inuk to Britain because he felt Eenoolooapik's information could convince the Navy to sponsor an expedition to Tenudiackbeek, and perhaps keep the fishery alive. Eenoolooapik, for his part, still harboured a desire to visit the land of these strangers, and so, after Penny gave presents to Eenoolooapik's family, the Inuk boarded ship and departed for Scotland, even amid continued entreaties from his mother.

Who was more surprised by their encounter, Eenoolooapik or the natives of Aberdeen? Eenoolooapik must have been overwhelmed by all he experienced, but other than his expression of wonder and delight at what he saw, he gave every evidence of being in complete control. The skills so necessary to life in the Arctic were turned to the task of blending into Scottish society. His powers of observation, memory, and mimicry were so great that, while the Scots were delighted by his kayaking and bird hunting demonstrations, they were especially impressed by his ability to mimic correct manners and to act the gentleman on all occasions.

Unfortunately, as with many indigenous people removed from their native clime and subjected to that of Britain, Eenoolooapik soon became sick and spent much of his time in

Aberdeen deathly ill with pneumonia. The newspapers regularly reported on his condition, and when he was fully recovered, he was shown the town. He almost certainly witnessed the wedding of his friend Penny; coming from a culture where little ritual surrounded marriage, Eenoolooapik must have been struck by this elaborate ceremony. Even more strange were the elegant balls he attended in honour of Queen Victoria's marriage to Albert; one can only imagine Eenoolooapik's astonishment when he learned that all this extravagant entertainment—a full orchestra, military band, speeches, and much toasting—was in honour of the chief of the Britons, who was not even present. Such balls, his theatre attendance, his visit to a new department store where he was given a china tea cup and saucer for his "mamma," and his sense of humour were common features in the local papers.

For Penny, his part in the experiment was not such an immediate success. Despite an excellent map Eenoolooapik prepared of Tenudiackbeek, the Navy was unwilling to back an expedition. Without government support, Penny was forced to catch whales first, and only then, if time permitted, to explore. As well, Penny's plan to educate Eenoolooapik in boat building and other skills came to naught because of the Inuk's poor health.

Although Eenoolooapik had made many friends in Aberdeen, he eventually grew homesick, sailing for the Arctic on 1 April 1840. On 2 August, the *Bon Accord*, along with three other ships, entered Tenudiackbeek, and three weeks later Eenoolooapik rejoined his mother and siblings who had travelled overland from Cape Searle to meet him. His biographer, Alexander M'Donald, notes that he did not seem at all unhappy when he left the whaler.

Back home, he resumed a normal life and does not appear to have tried to impress people unduly with his tales or possessions. He married Amitak shortly after leaving Penny, and by 1844, when Penny once again returned to Cumberland Sound, Eenoolooapik had a son called Angalook. Three years later, in the summer of 1847, Eenoolooapik died of consumption, and after his death his name—according to custom—was given to a newborn nephew.

Certainly Eenoolooapikk's family were great travellers, even more so than the average Inuit family. Both Eenoolooapik and his brother Totocatpik were well known as great voyagers and intelligent men. A sister, Kur-king, migrated to Igloolik, and another sister, Tookoolito or Hannah, travelled to England in 1853 and later accompanied Charles Francis Hall* to the United States, to Hudson Bay, to King William Island, and to Greenland.

Every year after Eenoolooapik's return, whalers visited Cumberland Sound. In 1851–52 Sidney Buddington led the first intentional wintering by a whaling crew, and two years later Penny conducted the first wintering with ship. Penny's endeavour was so successful that wintering over and the maintenance of permanent whaling stations became common practices until the end of commercial whaling in the eastern Arctic. Several stations were established both in and around Cumberland Sound. This constant presence of the whalers and their requirements for both whaling crews and for hunters led to a profound change in the local Inuit's lives.

Further Readings

M'Donald, Alexander. 1841. *A Narrative of Some Passages in the History of Eenoolooapik, a Young Eskimaux, Who was Brought to Britain in 1839, in the Ship 'Neptune' of Aberdeen*. Edinburgh: Fraser and J. Hogg.

Ross, W. Gillies. 1985. *Arctic Whalers, Icy Seas*. Toronto: Irwin Publishing.

Susan Rowley

GEORGE STRONG NARES
(1831–1915)

George Strong Nares, born in 1831, was the son of a naval officer and followed his father into the Royal Navy at the age of fourteen. From 1848 to 1851, he sailed in HMS *Havannah* in Australian waters. On his return, while waiting at the Admiralty in the hope of employment, he met G.H. Richards, who had been with them on the homeward voyage after taking part in the *Acheron*'s survey of New Zealand. Richards promised to recommend him for the forthcoming expedition to search for John Franklin* and his men. In 1852, Nares sailed for the Arctic in HMS *Resolute,* under Capt. Henry Kellett.*

HMS *Resolute* and *Intrepid* wintered off Melville Island, and Nares took part in sledge journeys searching unavailingly for traces of the missing ships. Instead they found a message that led to the rescue of Robert J.L. McClure* and the crew of HMS *Investigator,* frozen in off Banks Island after passing through the Bering Strait.

Back at home, having been promoted to lieutenant, Nares went on a gunnery course prior to sailing for the Crimea. He was still hoping that the Admiralty would send out another Franklin search expedition so that he could return to the North, not, however, because of the lure of the Arctic, which he described as a "wretched place," but because in a generally peaceful age it offered a chance for promotion. Instead, he was selected to assist in setting up training ships for boys and, in 1863, took command of the *Boscawen*. His textbook, *Seamanship,* was reprinted many times.

Photograph of George Strong Nares. Courtesy of the National Maritime Museum London

The turning point in Nares's career came in 1865 when he was given command of HMS *Salamander* on the coast of Queensland, work which involved surveying reef-infested waters. This led, in 1868, to the command of the survey ship *Newport* in the Mediterranean. Nares was promoted to captain for work in conjunction with the opening of the Suez Canal and, in 1871, commissioned to HMS *Shearwater* for service in the Red Sea.

On the outward voyage they carried out studies of water movements in the Strait of Gibraltar for W.B. Carpenter, an eminent biologist, who believed that density differences between water masses played an important part in generating ocean currents. His ideas led to the voyage of HMS *Challenger,* 1872–76, the first major expedition for the scientific study of the deep oceans. Nares was appointed to command it, but after only two years he was recalled to lead a new arctic expedition.

The British Arctic Expedition of 1875–76, in HMS *Alert* and *Discovery,* was inspired by the recurring myth of an open polar sea. They attempted to reach the North Pole by sailing into the Arctic Ocean via Smith Sound, separating Greenland from Ellesmere Island. This proved impossible, but the *Alert* succeeded in reaching Floeberg Beach, in 82°N, on the northeast tip of Ellesmere Island. The following spring, sledging parties set out to explore the nearby lands and to attempt to reach the North Pole over the ice. Disaster struck when an outbreak of scurvy led to several deaths. Scurvy's cause was still not understood, but it had ceased to be a serious problem in the Royal Navy following the introduction of lemon juice as a preventive in the early 1800s. Unfortunately, less effective lime juice had later been substituted, and, in arctic conditions, with little fresh food available, this did not provide sufficient vitamin C. The expedition was forced to withdraw, having achieved a farthest north of 83°20′N.

In the enquiry that followed, Nares was blamed for the outbreak through not ensuring that lime ice was carried on the sledges. It had sometimes been omitted because of the difficulties in storing and administering it at subzero temperatures. Some people thought that this was unfair, for scurvy had also broken out in the ships, where some of the victims had never stopped taking lime juice. It was unfortunate for Nares, as the Arctic had appeared healthy compared with the diseases awaiting mariners elsewhere. In the 1850s, he had foreseen how future expeditions could be made less arduous by using dogs to replace backpacking or man-hauled sledges, but the snow and ice conditions encountered by the 1875–76 expedition were very different from those experienced farther south in the Canadian Arctic archipelago. Their old-fashioned heavy equipment did not help, and dogs were of little use. However, their achievement and the seamanship on which it relied were recognized when Nares was given a knighthood on his return.

Nares spent a further season surveying with the *Alert* in the Magellan Strait, before moving to a post in the harbour department at the Board of Trade. He retired in 1896 and died in 1915. He had been elected a Fellow of the Royal Society in 1875. His wife, Mary Grant, whom he had married in 1858, died in 1905. Two sons entered the Navy, and one, John Dodd Nares, became assistant hydrographer.

George Strong Nares was the antithesis of the romantic explorer. He did not seek adventure for its own sake, either for himself or for those under him. Exploration for him was a job, which he performed meticulously, but he perhaps suffered from belonging to an organization that by its nature was poorly fitted to respond to the peculiar challenges of travel in an arctic environment and was trapped by a lack of imaginative comprehension that he partly shared.

Further Readings

Carpenter, K.J. 1986. *The History of Scurvy and Vitamin C.* Cambridge: Cambridge University Press.

Deacon, Margaret. 1971. *Scientists and the Sea, 1650–1900: A Study of Marine Science.* London: Academic Press.

_____ and Ann Savours. 1976. "Sir George Strong Nares (1831–1915)." *Polar Record* 18: 127–41.

Hattersley-Smith, Geoffrey. 1976. "The British Arctic Expedition, 1875–76." *Polar Record* 18: 117–26.

Nares, G.S. 1878. *Narrative of a Voyage to the Polar Sea during 1875–76.* London: Sampson Low.

Watt, James, E.J. Freeman, and W.F. Bynum, eds. 1981. *Starving Sailors: The Influence of Nutrition upon Naval and Maritime History.* London: National Maritime Museum.

Margaret Deacon

OTTO SVERDRUP (1854–1930)

Born on his father's farm, Haarstad, in the Helgeland area of Norway on 31 October 1854, Otto Sverdrup spent his childhood among the fiords, forests, and mountains. From an early age, he was an excellent skier and could handle rifle or small boat with equal skill. He went to sea at the age of seventeen, sailing aboard both Norwegian and American vessels, and obtained his mate's ticket in 1878 and his master's certificate in the early 1880s. After a few more years at sea, from 1885 he stayed ashore for a number of years helping his father, who, in the interim, had moved south to the farm of Trana, near Steinkjer.

There he became a close friend of a young lawyer, Alexander Nansen, and when the latter's brother Fridtjof was looking for volunteers to attempt the first crossing of the Greenland Ice Cap on skis, Sverdrup volunteered and was accepted. The plan was that they would be landed from the sealer *Jason* on the east coast of Greenland in July 1888, but ice prevented the ship from reaching shore, and hence the six-man party left the ship in two boats. It took them ten days to reach land, having been carried well south of their starting point by the ice drift, and a further two weeks to retrace their steps north along the coast to where the ski journey was to begin. After forty days on the ice cap, they safely reached the first rocks and tundra on the west side. Since it was now late in the season, the party was obliged to winter at Godthab and did not finally return to Norway until May 1889.

Portrait of Otto Sverdrup, from the German edition of Sverdrup's book *Neves Land: Viere Jahre in Arktischen Gebeiten*, Leipzig: Brockhaus, Vol. 1 (1904)

Almost immediately Nansen began planning for an even greater expedition. In 1884, various items indisputably from the wreck of De Long's *Jeannette*, which had been crushed in June 1881 north of the Novosibirskiye Ostrova, had been found on an ice floe off the coast of southwest Greenland. Clearly they must have been carried by ice drift across the Arctic Basin and south via the East Greenland Current. On this basis, Nansen conceived the idea of deliberately placing a specially built ship in the ice near where *Jeannette* had been crushed and allowing the ice drift to carry the ship along her presumed transarctic drift route; scientific observations would be made throughout the drift. Right from the start, Otto Sverdrup offered his services as captain of the expedition vessel, and for three years (1890–93) his attention was almost wholly devoted to the building of the ship. This remarkable vessel, named *Fram*, was designed and built by Colin Archer, but every stage of her construction was personally supervised by Sverdrup.

Having taken *Fram* eastward through the Northern Sea Route, Nansen and Sverdrup deliberately allowed her to become beset northwest of the Novosibirskiye Ostrova in September 1893, and there her slow westward drift began. By November 1894, it was clear that *Fram*'s drift course was not going to take her as far north as Nansen had calculated, and hence, in late February 1895, Nansen and Johansen set off with two dog-teams to get as far north as was possible, and then to make their own way south to Zemlya Frantsa Iosifa and home. This meant that from that date until mid-August 1896, when *Fram* emerged safely from the ice northwest of Svalbard, Sverdrup was in sole command of the ship. He was entirely responsible for the ship, its crew, and the scientific program for more than half of the total duration of the famous ice drift.

Soon after *Fram's* return to Norway, at Nansen's suggestion, Sverdrup began planning for another arctic expedition aboard *Fram*, but this time he would be in sole command. The plan was to head north via Smith Sound and Kane Basin, then east along the north coast of Greenland to some suitable wintering site. From there, sled journeys would be made to the northernmost point of Greenland and south along its unknown northeast coast. There was no intention of making an attempt at the Pole. With a well-knit team of sixteen men, *Fram* sailed from Norway on 24 June 1898. But in Smith Sound, impassable ice stretching from Littleton Island to Pim Island blocked further progress northwards; after a prolonged wait and vain attempts to push north, Sverdrup snugged his ship down for the winter in a secure bay, named Fram Haven, at the north end of Rice Strait between Pim Island and Johan Peninsula on Ellesmere Island. The autumn was spent hunting walrus and musk-oxen for dog food, and while thus engaged at his main camp at Fort Juliana on Hayes Fiord the inlet between Johan Peninsula and Fort Juliana, Sverdrup was visited by Robert Edwin Peary,* whose ship *Hope* was wintering near Cape Hawkes. Peary immediately saw in Sverdrup a rival in the race for the Pole and, in an unforgivable breach of arctic manners, refused Sverdrup's hospitable offer of a cup of coffee.

During their hunting trips, Sverdrup and his men explored most of the Bache Peninsula area, discovering, incidentally, that it was a peninsula and not an island. Then, in the spring of 1899, two sledge expeditions made major thrusts westward across Ellesmere Island, one of them reaching the sea at the head of Bay Fiord.

That summer, Smith Sound and Kane Basin were again solidly packed with ice, and Sverdrup was forced to abandon his original plan for northern Greenland. Well aware of the vast unknown lacuna that lay west of Ellesmere Island and north of Jones Sound, he decided to make it the alternate focus of his expedition. With this intention, he took *Fram* south, then west, into Jones Sound and settled down for a second wintering in Harbour Fiord on the south coast of Ellesmere.

From there and from Goose Fiord, to which *Fram* moved in the summer of 1900, in a truly remarkable series of sledging expeditions over the next three summers, Sverdrup and his finely tuned, well-coordinated team explored the entire west coast of Ellesmere Island north to beyond the mouth of Nansen Sound, the entire coastline of Axel Heiberg Island, Amund and Ellef Ringnes islands, King Christian, Cornwall and Graham islands, as well as much of the north coast of Devon Island. In total, this represented one of the most impressive feats of polar exploration ever achieved, effected in an extremely workmanlike fashion with a minimum of fuss or fanfare.

In the closing lines of his account of the expedition, Otto Sverdrup makes the unequivocal statement that he had taken possession of the lands he had discovered for the Norwegian king, and he so informed King Oscar on his return to Norway in the autumn of 1902. Thus arose the dispute that was to cloud Norwegian/Canadian relations for the next quarter-century.

It is not generally known that Sverdrup was involved in three further expeditions to the Arctic. In 1914, he was invited by the imperial Russian government to take command of the whaling ship *Eclipse* and search the Kara Sea for traces of the missing Rusanov and Brusilov expeditions; he found no sign of them, but during the wintering on the Taymyr coast, he played a major role in a precautionary overland evacuation of half of the crews of the Russian icebreakers *Taymyr* and *Vaygach,* which had also been forced to winter in the ice of the Kara Sea. Then in the spring of 1920, this time at the request of the Soviet government, Sverdrup took command of the icebreaker *Svyatogor* and rescued the icebreaker *Solovey Budimirovich,* beset and drifting in the ice of the Kara Sea, her coal and food supplies almost exhausted. Finally, in 1921, aboard the icebreaker *Lenin,* Sverdrup escorted a convoy of freighters to the mouth of the Yenisey, thus contributing to the early stages of the build-up of the Soviet Union's important Kara Sea shipping operation.

Throughout this period and until the end of his life, Sverdrup continued to pursue two goals: one was to save his fine old ship, *Fram;* the other was to bring to fruition his claim that the lands he had discovered west of Ellesmere Island were Norwegian territory. The former fight Sverdrup won. Through his efforts at fund-raising, by the spring of 1930 *Fram* had been completely restored. And in the summer of 1936, the *Fram* Museum, which still houses the old ship in Oslo, was opened by King Haakon.

The other fight the tenacious old patriot lost, although it was a dignified defeat. The dispute over sovereignty of the Sverdrup Islands, by which name the islands he discovered are still known, was settled between Norway and Canada in a gentlemanly fashion that salved national pride. On 11 November 1930, the Norwegian government formally recognized Canada's title to the lands Sverdrup had explored. And in a related gesture, which was covered in the same article in many Canadian newspapers, the Canadian government paid Sverdrup $67,000 for his original maps, diaries, and documents relating to his expedition in 1898–1902. Before the month was out, Sverdrup was dead.

Were he still alive, however, Otto Sverdrup would undoubtedly have been raising a storm in the Norwegian press and in the Storting during the past few decades. Intense exploration in the early 1970s revealed that the Sverdrup Basin, which in part underlies the islands he and his men had discovered, contains proven reserves of 10 trillion cubic feet of gas and 100 million barrels of oil. Probably reserves are vastly greater. One doubts if such a doughty old fighter as Sverdrup could have remained silent on finding that his hunch to hang on to these islands had so dramatically been proved right.

Further Readings

Fairlye, T.C., ed. 1959. *Sverdrup's Arctic Adventures.* London: Longmans.

Kokk, D. 1934. *Otto Sverdrups liv.* Oslo: Jacob Dybwad.

Nansen, F. 1890. *The First Crossing of Greenland.* London: Constable and Company.

_____. 1897. *"Farthest North," Being the Record of a Voyage of Exploration of the Ship Fram 1893-96 and of a Fifteen Months' Sleigh Journey by Dr. Nansen and Lieut. Johansen with an Appendix by Otto Sverdrup, Captain of the Fram.* London: Constable and Company.

Sverdrup, Otto. 1904. *New Land: Four Years in the Arctic Regions.* London: Longmans, Green and Company.

_____. 1928. *Under Russisk Flag.* Oslo: H. Aschehoug and Company.

William Barr

PER SCHEI (1875-1905)

Per Schei, Norwegian geologist and explorer, died a young man. From 1898 to 1902, as a member of Capt. Otto Sverdrup's* second expedition in the *Fram*, Schei made his mark on the geological understanding of a vast region of the eastern Canadian High Arctic. Schei died before he could write a detailed report for publication, but by the time of his death, his status as a talented scientist and outstanding expedition man was established.

Peder Elisaeus (Per) Schei was born on 16 February 1875 in Snåsa, a part of the Trondheim district. The son of a farmer, he spent many of his childhood years in the family of his uncle, a parish vicar. Schei attended high school in Copenhagen, and, in 1892, he passed his final examination with distinction. Schei showed an early enthusiasm for the natural sciences, and after schooling in Denmark he returned to Norway to study geology at the University of Kristiania (now Oslo). He graduated in mineralogy and geology early in 1898 with first class honours.

Two noteworthy events occurred prior to graduation: Schei's promising ability, recognized by his tutors, earned him a position as university amanuensis (lecturer) in the metallurgical laboratory; and, in 1897, he married Inga Jorgine Ulve, the daughter of a ship's captain, and they had a son. However, Schei also met his portion of misfortune: an illness left him with a stiff knee—hardly an attribute for a future arctic explorer.

Photograph of Per Schei. Courtesy of Jacob Schei and family, Trondheim, Norway

In 1897–98, Otto Sverdrup was organizing a scientific corps for the second expedition in Fridtjof Nansen's polar ship, the *Fram*. Schei applied for the post of geologist and, despite his slight physical disabilities (he was also short-sighted), impressed Sverdrup so much that he was taken on. The choice was a shrewd one; in all respects Schei proved his full worth to the expedition, not only for the successful execution of his scientific responsibilities, but also for his participation in the long sledge journeys that led to the expedition's spectacular geographic discoveries.

In collaboration with Nansen, Sverdrup had decided to explore northernmost Greenland, and possibly to circumnavigate the subcontinent. Using the so-called Smith Sound route, Sverdrup was to direct *Fram* up the narrow channels separating Greenland and Ellesmere Island and winter in Greenland as far north as possible. These channels, now known as Nares Strait, had been explored by British and American expeditions since the 1850s. Sledge parties from *Fram* were to delimit the northern part of Greenland and to reach as far south down the east coast as possible. There was to be, as Sverdrup remarked, "no question of trying to reach the Pole."

However, the Norwegian thrust north in the summer of 1898 was stopped by unfavourable ice conditions in Kane Basin. *Fram* had to winter off the Ellesmere Island coast south of 79°N, some 430 miles from unexplored parts of the Greenland coast and, as it happened, only a short distance south of Robert Edwin Peary's* winter quarters in the *Windward*. Peary was also enroute to the North. Another attempt the following summer to negotiate Kane Basin was thwarted by ice, and following this Sverdrup sailed *Fram* southward and westward into Jones Sound to spend the next three winters in southern Ellesmere Island. This was a fortunate decision: it led to the discovery and charting of "New Land" west of Ellesmere Island. Up north, it was left to Peary to prove the insularity of Greenland, in 1900. Actually, not until the summer of 1900 did Sverdrup give up the plan of following Nares Strait, and when he did, the main consideration was the fervent interest generated during the first two years by the geographical and geological discoveries. Sverdrup concluded that his duty was "to go through with what he had begun"; there would be no forfeiting a thorough exploration of "New Land" for another summer in the tormenting ice of Kane Basin.

Schei took to expedition life quickly, but not without mishap. After an episode of frostbite during early sledging on Bache Peninsula, which necessitated amputation of several toes on each foot, Schei developed into one of the most skillful dogsled handlers and hunters on the expedition. His courage and dedication could not be overwhelmed by such small disabilities as a stiff leg, lost toes, and short-sightedness. Sverdrup liked him as a travel companion, with perhaps one misgiving—Schei did not smoke!

Sverdrup's well-organized and coordinated team work produced results unsurpassed in arctic exploration, and Schei was an important member of that team. He participated in some of the longest and most arduous sled jouneys leading to the discovery of the numerous and substantial Sverdrup Islands—Axel Heiberg, Ellef and Amund Ringnes,

King Christian, and smaller islands—and the mapping of the entire west coast of Ellesmere Island and much of northern Devon Island. He was with Sverdrup during the final sled campaign of 1902, northward up Nansen Sound to reach the Arctic Ocean and the northwestern tip of Ellesmere Island. They discovered coal measures at Stenkul Fiord (Ellesmere Island) and determined that Axel Heiberg is an island. Schei identified the volcanic rocks at Sorte Vaeg (Svartevaeg on the expedition charts; both names meaning "black wall". The dark cliffs have been named Svartevaeg Cliffs on Canadian maps.) Sverdrup and Schei returned to the ship on 16 June 1902, only weeks before *Fram* was finally released from her winter berth, ready for the voyage home.

The geographic and scientific advances achieved by Sverdrup's expedition rank it as one of the most successful in the history of arctic exploration, and Schei returned with a rich geological and paleontological collection from a hitherto unknown region. In 1902, the expedition committee elected him as chief scientific editor for the proposed official reports, and, in 1903, he took up a coveted amanuensis appointment at the University of Kristiania's mineralogical institute. The government, in recognition of his contribution to the scientific program of the expedition, awarded Schei an extra gratuity of 4,000 kr.

In May 1903, Sverdrup and Schei were honoured at a meeting of the Royal Geographical Society in London. Schei's summary geological account was read to the society, as was Sverdrup's address, by the president, Sir Clements Markham.

Schei's preliminary accounts appeared in 1903 in several languages, and these papers, although only a few pages each, were regarded by his contemporaries as forming some of the most important contributions ever made to arctic geology. Aware of the mammoth task of dealing with the extensive collections, Schei induced a number of specialists in Europe to identify and systematically describe the fossil assemblages. Only one treatise appeared in Schei's lifetime, but, by 1917, ten geological reports had been completed, and Professor Olav Holtedahl concluded the four-volume work with a summary report based on Schei's diaries. One can only wonder how much greater Schei's contribution to arctic geology would have been had he lived.

Professor W.C. Brøgger noted Schei's decline in health early in 1905. Later that year, Brøgger wrote that "he was seized with a severe illness and after a long suffering the promising career of this amiable and talented scientist came [to] a close on 1st November, 1905." Schei died of dropsy, a result of kidney malfunction that was thought at the time to be related to the four strenuous years in the Far North.

Schei's name is firmly established in the literature and legend of the Canadian High Arctic: Schei Peninsula (Axel Heiberg Island), Schei Point (Ellesmere Island), the Schei Point group (shale, siltstone and sandstone beds of Triassic age), and the Schei syncline (a large fold structure of southern Ellesmere Island). Schei can be credited with making the most impressive contribution by a single person to the geological understanding of the Arctic Islands prior to the advent of aircraft.

Further Readings

Brøgger, W.C., et al. 1904–1917. *Report of the Second Norwegian Arctic Expedition in the 'Fram' 1898–1902.* 4 vols. Kristiania: Videnskabs-Selskabet

Fairly, T.C., ed. 1959. *Sverdrup's Arctic Adventures.* London: Longmans.

Sverdrup, O. 1903. "The Second Norwegian Polar Expedition in the 'Fram', 1898–1902." *Geographical Journal* 2: 56-65. (Summary of geological results by P. Schei).

_____. 1904. *New Land: Four years in the Arctic Regions.* 2 vols. London: Longmans, Green and Co. (Appendix by P. Schei, vol. 2: 455–66.)

Peter R. Dawes and Robert L. Christie

A.H. Joy (1887–1932)

Inspector Alfred Herbert Joy of the Royal Canadian Mounted Police (RCMP) is best known for a remarkable 1800-mile patrol by dogsled across the heart of the Queen Elizabeth Islands in 1929. He had a keen interest in and extensive knowledge of the Arctic, its wildlife and people, and was dedicated to upholding the law and jurisdiction of Canada in isolated arctic regions.

A.H. Joy was born in Maulden, eight miles south of Bedford, England, on 26 June 1887, where he attended school, leaving the classroom in 1899 for work as a farm labourer. He then travelled to Canada, enlisting in the Royal North-West Mounted Police on 19 June 1909, after a short period of homesteading on the prairies. He rose rapidly through the ranks: corporal in 1912, sergeant in 1916, staff-sergeant in 1921, and inspector in 1927. He thrived on the challenge of life on the northern frontiers of Canada—from 1914 to 1931, he had never spent a summer in "civilization."

After gaining valuable experience in the Mackenzie and Liard river regions, in 1920 he accompanied Inspector J.W. Phillips on a patrol by canoe, sailboat, and motor launch to investigate a complex murder case on the Belcher Islands. In 1921, following Canada's decision to extend jurisdiction into the Arctic Islands, Joy was selected to represent the government at Pond Inlet, northern Baffin Island. Soon after his

Sergeant A. H. Joy with Inuit, 1920. Photograph courtesy of the RCMP. Photo no. 4237

arrival, he undertook investigation of the Janes murder case. Joy travelled to Cape Crauford in December, where he found and exhumed Janes's body and conducted an autopsy. Later, in his capacity as coroner, he held an inquest and gathered a jury, the accused, and witnesses from as far away as Igloolik, in addition to presiding as justice of the peace at the trial. Following the trial, he received a notable tribute from Mr. Justice Rivet for his outstanding work on this case—particularly for his thoroughness and fairness. He had enforced the law in the Arctic Islands for the first time.

In 1924, Joy made a hair-raising attempt to cross Lancaster Sound by dogsled from northern Baffin Island to test the practicability of communicating with the RCMP detachment on Ellesmere Island. Wide leads, fast-moving ice, buckling pressure ice, and polar bears were among the hazards Joy and his two native assistants encountered. With characteristic determination and understatement, Joy concluded that the trip to Ellesmere Island could be made in any kind of winter season—providing a return trip was not necessary!

After 1925, when Joy took over detachments on eastern Ellesmere Island (Craig Harbour, Bache Peninsula) and Devon Island (Dundas Harbour), he began a series of long exploratory patrols across the Queen Elizabeth Islands which would do credit to any great polar explorer. During these trips, he was able to correct errors on maps, explore new sled routes, make notes on wildlife, vegetation, coal outcrops, archaeological sites, sites of historic interest, weather, and sea-ice conditions. His detailed remarks on the numbers and migration of Peary caribou among the Queen Elizabeth Islands and the long distances arctic hares can travel on their hind legs are of great biological interest. He also foresaw new ways of patrolling the High Arctic, stating: "It would be possible, if necessary, I believe, to carry on an extensive survey of the islands west of Eureka Sound by aeroplane." He made important biological and archaeological collections for Canada's national museums. His collection of seven hundred specimens from a Palaeo-Eskimo site was acknowledged by the chief of the division of anthropology to be "one of the most valuable accessions that the Division has received since I took charge of it in 1910."

In 1926, Joy travelled with his assistant, Nookapingwa, some 975 miles from Craig Harbour via Jones Sound to Axel Heiberg Islan, in forty days. As a preliminary to this trip, Joy,

Constable Dersch, and Nookapingwa explored a new, and at times dangerous, route from Craig Harbour to Dundas Harbour and back, across the Devon Island Ice Cap. In 1927, Joy, Nookapingwa, and Ahkeeoo made a 1,300-mile, fifty-four day patrol from Bache Peninsula to King Christian Island and back. Once they travelled steadily for twenty-nine hours. Joy's longest and most famous patrol involved a circuit of approximately 1,800 miles in eighty-one days from Dundas Harbour on Devon Island to Bache Peninsula by way of the following islands: Cornwallis, Bathurst, Melville, Edmund Walker, Lougheed, King Christian, Ellef Ringnes, Amund Ringnes, Cornwall, and Axel Heiberg. He was accompanied by Constable Taggart and the ever-reliable Nookapingwa. The first part of this journey along the southern coast of Devon Island was extremely difficult.

Joy was a big, well-built man, who towered over his Inuit comrades. He was quiet and self-contained with a gift for making friends and commanding the respect of his fellows. He led by example, and was careful in giving proper credit to those who had helped him. In addition to his skill as a horseman, marksman, and boxer, Joy was fond of the dogs that aided him on his epic trips, and he was an accomplished dogsled driver.

Several geographical features have been named after Inspector Joy: Cape Joy, Mount Joy, and the Joy River, all on Baffin Island; Joy Island among the Belcher Islands; and Joy Range on Axel Heiberg Island.

A.H. Joy's end was tragic. He died at the age of forty-three, apparently of a stroke, on the morning of the day he was to be married in Ottawa. Maj.-Gen. J.H. MacBrien, commissioner of the RCMP, wrote his epitaph: "Inspector Joy was a particularly fine officer, a magnificent Arctic traveller and his death was greatly regretted."

Acknowledgements

I thank Supt. J.R. Bentham, S.W. Horral, H. Kerfoot, H. Margetts, Col. L.H. Nicholson, A.F. Cirket, Mrs. E. Herman, and L. Adamson.

Further Readings

Fetherstonhaugh, R.C. 1938. *The Royal Canadian Mounted Police.* New York: Carrick and Evans.

Royal Canadian Mounted Police. *Commissioner's Reports of the Royal Canadian Mounted Police* (particularly the "blue books" for the years 1921-1931).

Steele, Harwood 1936. *Policing the Arctic.* London: Jarrold's.

Taylor, Andrew. 1955. "Geographical Discovery and Exploration in the Queen Elizabeth Islands." *Geographical Branch Memoir 3.* Ottawa.

C.R. Harington

H.W. STALLWORTHY (1895-1976)

Sgt. Maj. Henry Webb Stallworthy of the Royal Canadian Mounted Police (RCMP) came to prominence following an arduous 1,400-mile dogsled journey in search of the German explorer Dr. H.K.E. Krueger in 1932, during which he circumnavigated Axel Heiberg Island. Much of Stallworthy's thirty-one years with the RCMP was spent in isolated parts of northern Canada. He was tough, energetic, unassuming, devoted to duty, and expert at arctic travelling—qualities that led to his secondment to the 1934–35 Oxford University Ellesmere Land Expedition.

H.W. Stallworthy ("Stall" to his friends) was born in Winson, Gloucestershire, on 20 January 1895. After schooling at Cirencester Grammar School, he came to Canada in 1913 to visit his brother, who had taken a homestead south of Calgary. Joining the Royal North-West Mounted Police (RNWMP) the next year, he trained in Regina before being posted to Calgary, and later, to Dawson and Vancouver. He served overseas with the NWMP contingent of the Canadian Expeditionary Force from May 1918 to March 1919, and after leaving the RCMP in 1921, he rejoined two years later. His subsequent postings included Chesterfield Inlet, Jasper, Bache Peninsula, and Fort Smith, as well as other locations, and he steadily advanced to the rank of sergeant-major in 1943.

Acting Sergeant H.W. Stallworthy (extreme right) with four members of the Oxford University Ellesmere Land Expedition in 1934 (left to right: A.W. Moore, E. Shackleton, R. Bentham, Dr. G.N. Humphreys). Photograph courtesy of the Scott Polar Research Institute, Cambridge, U.K.

His career in the North was outstanding. He volunteered for the famous winter mail patrol between Dawson, Yukon Territory, and Fort McPherson, Northwest Territories, under the stern leadership of Sergeant Dempster* in 1921—a severe initiation into northern dogsled travel. In 1923, he went to Chesterfield Inlet, where, under the tutelage of Nowya, his Inuit travelling companion, he learned to drive dogs in the "fan hitch," cook on the trail, and hunt large marine mammals for dog food. In his second year at Chesterfield, a tragic event occurred that left a permanent mark on his nature. Maggie Clay, young wife of the staff sergeant in charge of the detachment, was attacked by dogs while walking on the beach. The flesh was stripped from her lower leg, and she was bleeding profusely. Stallworthy, Father Duplain, and Norman Snow of the Hudson's Bay Company were forced to operate, removing her leg at the knee. Although she survived for three days, severe loss of blood and lack of proper facilities resulted in her death. During this incident, Stallworthy proved his coolness in adversity and showed great inner strength.

In 1930, he was posted to Bache Peninsula, Ellesmere Island, the most northerly detachment in Canada. Nothing could have suited him better. He was in the land of such famous explorers as Frederick A. Cook,* Robert Edwin Peary,* and Donald MacMillan.* With him were Inuit who had travelled with these men, and those same Inuit would become his friends and companions on long, hazardous patrols. After his first winter, Stallworthy made a gruelling trip over tough sea ice to Craig Harbour on southeastern Ellesmere Island, only to find that the German explorer Dr. H.K.E. Krueger, for whom he was searching, had not passed that way. While hunting a polar bear on the return trip, he fell into a snow-covered crevasse, becoming wedged in about twenty-three feet below the surface. He was extricated by his Inuit companions, who dropped him a harpoon line.

The highlight of his career came in 1932 during his continued search for the Krueger expedition. Following Insp.

A.H. Joy's* search plan, Stallworthy and Const. R.W. Hamilton left Bache Peninsula on 20 March 1932, with seven Greenland Inuit, eight sleds, and 125 dogs. Hamilton's party returned on 7 May, after a 900-mile trip to Amund Ringnes and Cornwall islands. Stallworthy, with three Inuit, travelled along Eureka Sound to the northern tip of Axel Heiberg Island, where he found a record indicating that Krueger was heading for Cape Sverre on the northern tip of Amund Ringnes Island. Except for a record found on Meighen Island in 1957, no further trace of the Krueger expedition has been found. Although Stallworthy was unable to reach Meighen Island (where he suspected Krueger had gone), because of poor ice conditions and a shortage of food, he completed his journey around Axel Heiberg Island and returned to Bache Peninsula on 23 May—an epic sixty-five-day trip of 1,400 miles. During the journey, he confirmed that Schei "Island" was a peninsula, and was told by his chief hunter, Etookashoo, that Dr. Frederick A. Cook, who claimed to have reached the North Pole in 1908, had actually taken his photographs of the "Pole" within sight of northern Axel Heiberg Island at about 82°N. Stallworthy's party faced starvation on this journey and had to kill some sled dogs to survive. As Ernest Shackleton later commented, Stallworthy "would be the first to admit, if it had not been for the skill of his Eskimos, he might never have returned."

In 1933, he married Hilda, a schoolteacher, and after a brief honeymoon in England was seconded by the RCMP as a technical advisor to the Oxford University Ellesmere Land Expedition (1934–35). Between 3 April and 26 May 1935, Stallworthy, A.W. Moore, Nookapingwa, and Inutuk penetrated Grant Land (the main goal of the expedition) via Fort Conger and Lake Hazen, from their base in Etah, Greenland.

Stallworthy's unfailing energy, enthusiasm, and willingness to sacrifice were demonstrated when he agreed to remain at Lake Hazen to fish for critically needed dog food, while Nookapingwa and Moore explored inland via the Gilman Glacier, reaching 82°25′N. Stopping at Fort Conger on the return trip, Stallworthy left a record of this most northerly sled journey ever made by an officer of the RCMP.

Following his retirement from the force in 1946, Stallworthy was called on to act as supervisor of security for the Distant Early Warning (DEW) Line—a string of radar stations crossing northern North America. Eventually, he and Hilda moved to Vancouver Island, where they built with their own hands "Timberlane," an exclusive resort on Saratoga Beach, and ran it for twenty-one years. Stallworthy died at Comox, British Columbia, on 25 December 1976.

For outstanding service to his country, H.W. Stallworthy was made an Officer of the Order of Canada in 1973. Other honours included election as a Fellow of the Royal Geographical Society in 1935 for his contribution to the success of the Oxford University Ellesmere Land Expedition, and the naming of Cape Stallworthy—the northernmost tip of Axel Heiberg Island—after him.

Acknowledgements

I thank Supt. J.R. Bentham, S.W. Horrall, Lord Shackleton, J. Fossum, D.J. Viner, Dr. T. Armstrong, and above all Mrs. Hilda Stallworthy.

Further Readings

Featherstonhaugh, R.C. 1938. *The Royal Canadian Mounted Police*. New York: Carrick and Evans.

Fossum, Jack. 1981. *Cop in the Closet*. North Vancouver: Hancock House.

Royal Canadian Mounted Police. *Commissioner's Reports of the Royal Canadian Mounted Police* (particularly the "blue books" for the years 1930–36.)

Shackleton, Edward. 1936. *Arctic Journeys: The Story of the Oxford University Ellesmere Land Expedition, 1934-35*. London: Hodder and Stoughton.

Stallworthy, H.W. 1934. "Winter Patrols in the Arctic" *Royal Canadian Mounted Police Quarterly* 2(2): 17–25.

Steele, Harwood. 1936. *Policing the Arctic*. London: Jarrold's.

Taylor, Andrew. 1955. "Geographical Discovery and Exploration in the Queen Elizabeth Islands." *Geographical Branch Memoir 3*. Ottawa

C.R. Harington

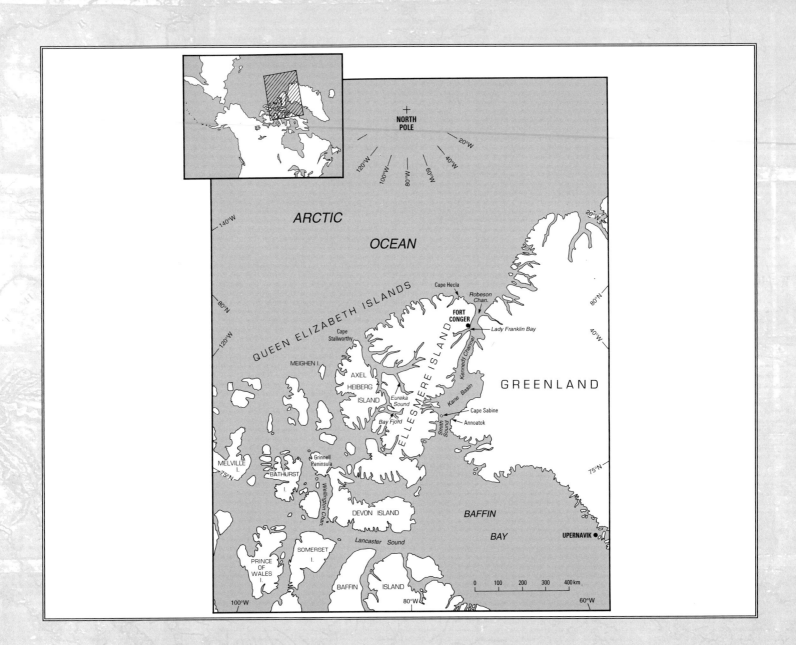

UNIT
❧ 13 ❧

Elisha Kent Kane, A.W. Greely, Robert Edwin Peary, Frederick A. Cook, Matthew Henson, Donald B. MacMillan, Robert Bartlett

This most northerly region, stretching from Lancaster Sound to the North Pole, has been the scene of both great adventure and great controversy. Whether searching for the "Open Polar Sea" or striving to be the first person to stand at the North Pole, these men contributed to the understanding of High Arctic geography. Perhaps of greater importance, their experiences did much to create for North Americans their image of the Arctic, an image perhaps appropriate to this High Arctic region, but that is often wrongly extended to embrace a vision of the entire Arctic.

ELISHA KENT KANE
(1820–1857)

The first American arctic explorer of note, Elisha Kent Kane was a man of broad interests and varied talents. Although he died when he was only thirty-seven years old, he distinguished himself as a career naval officer, medical doctor, scientist, author, and artist, and his death inspired a funeral procession by train from New Orleans to the home of his birth in Philadelphia. Eulogies hailed Kane as America's "Arctic Columbus."

Well-travelled prior to his midcentury arctic voyages, Kane had journeyed through South America, Africa, Europe, and the Far East. Small of stature and physically frail as a result of a rheumatic heart, the naval doctor nevertheless sought challenges of physical endurance, which led to his volunteering for the arduous U.S. Polar Expedition in 1850 as ship's surgeon and again in 1853 as leader.

American whalers had long navigated arctic waters, but the serious search for a Northwest Passage had been a predominantly British enterprise. Not until President Zachary Taylor and Henry Grinnell, the wealthy New York shipbuilder, responded to Lady Jane Franklin's* appeal for aid in finding her missing husband and his crew did the United States officially enter into the exploration of the Arctic.

The fate of HMS *Erebus* and *Terror* had captured the American imagination. Motivated by humanitarian interests, Congress and Grinnell cosponsored two searches. Politically, the undertaking allowed the United States to participate with Britain in exploration within the territory of North America. There was a further justification as well. U.S. Navy oceanographers were intrigued with the theory of an open polar sea, and although Britain's experience in the ice-choked Arctic had dampened her enthusiasm for such a theory, the fresher and more idealistic Americans—including the scientifically trained Kane—justified

Portrait of Elisha Kent Kane, M.D., by Thomas Hicks, 1858. Collection of The New-York Historical Society

the extravagant and risky search expeditions as an altruistic quest for geographical knowledge.

The first voyage gave no evidence of an open polar sea. Kane, undaunted, sought command of another. He accomplished this by lecturing and publishing his analysis of the open polar sea theory for the American Geographical Society, and by energetically preparing a popular account of the *Rescue* and *Advance's* 1850 voyage. Published in 1854, his *U.S. Grinnell Expedition in Search of Sir John Franklin, 1850-'51* was enhanced by steel engravings based on Kane's own skilled drawings and watercolours.

The first voyage had attempted a passage through Lancaster Sound and north into Wellington Channel. The second, under Kane's leadership and including only one ship, the *Advance*, sailed due north up the west coast of Greenland to latitude 78°N, where the ship was icebound and never released. Two of Kane's crew continued by sled and on foot to 81°22′N, "the northernmost land ever trodden by a white man," where they saw "open water stretching to the northern horizon. The unending shore line was washed by shining waters without a sign of ice." Kane, believing this to be the scientific culmination of their journey, declared: "The great North Sea, the Polynia has been reached."

By the spring of 1855, after three summers and two winters that proved far harsher and more impoverished than the men's most pessimistic fears, Kane and his crew faced imminent starvation. Consequent unrest and disloyalty, coupled with the belief that they had met their scientific objective of sighting the open polar sea, led Kane to abandon the search for John Franklin;* he began planning the dangerous escape by small boat and sled. Brilliant organization and meticulous rationing of their remaining supplies proved Kane a leader of great resource, and he led his men to safety and rescue at Upernavik, 1,300 miles to the south.

Kane returned a hero and was soon preparing his second popular account of the Arctic. More ambitious than the first, *Arctic Explorations: The Second Grinnell Expedition in Search of Sir John Franklin, 1853, '54, '55* (1856) was extremely successful, selling 65,000 copies the first year and 145,000 copies by the third year. More elaborate in every way, the book described the adventure in vivid prose and visually illustrated the enterprise with 21 full-page steel engravings and 256 woodcuts of high aesthtic quality. Kane's health, however, had been broken by the deprivations of the expedition and by his exertions on the account, and he exclaimed that "This book has been my coffin." He died soon after, while trying to regain his strength in the warmth of Havana.

Kane never found Franklin or the open polar sea, but the Grinnell expeditions had made important advances. The first voyage discovered "Grinnell Land" [Grinnell Peninsula] in Wellington Channel, and the second had mapped the narrow passage between Ellesmere Island and the west coast of Greenland to 78°N. During the lengthy second journey, Kane and his crew learned much about survival from the Inuit, and their contact established good relations that would benefit such later explorers as Isaac Hayes and Charles Francis Hall.*

Still, it was Elisha Kent Kane's literary talent that was the cornerstone of his reputation. Through the poetic flare of his popular narratives, in which he minimized his own fragile health and the considerable trials of wintering in the North, Kane inspired Pierre Berton to celebrate him as "the outstanding polar idol of mid-century."

Further Readings

Corner, George. 1972. *Doctor Kane of the Arctic Seas*. Philadelphia: Temple University Press.

Kane, Elisha Kent. 1853. "Access to an Open Polar Sea." In *American Geographical and Statistical Society*. New York: Baker, Godwin and Company

_____. 1854. *U.S. Grinnell Expedition in Search of Sir John Franklin, 1850–'51*. New York: Harper Bros.

_____. 1856. *Arctic Explorations: Second Grinnell Expedition in Search of Sir John Franklin, 1853, '54, '55*. Philadelphia: Childs and Peterson.

Martin, Constance. 1983. *James Hamilton Arctic Watercolours*. Calgary: Glenbow Museum Exhibition Catalogue.

_____. 1985. "'Toward No Earthly Pole': The Search for Franklin in Nineteenth Century Art." *In The Franklin Era in Canadian Arctic History 1845-1859*, edited by Patricia D. Sutherland. Ottawa: National Museum of Man, Mercury Series, No. 131.

Constance Martin

A.W. GREELY (1844–1935)

A.W. Greely became a world celebrity almost overnight in 1884, when the six survivors of the Lady Franklin Bay Expedition under his leadership were rescued from starvation in the Arctic. Yet he was far more than the central figure of one tragic expedition. Explorer, soldier, scientist, and author, Greely was respected as an international authority on polar science from the 1880s until his death fifty years later.

Born in Newburyport, Massachusetts, in 1844, Adolphus Washington Greely volunteered for Civil War service in the Union Army before he was eighteen. He was grievously wounded at Antietam in 1862, but returned to active duty the following spring as an officer of the U.S. Colored Infantry, made up of free black soldiers. When the war ended, he held the brevet rank of captain of volunteers and decided on service in the regular army as his career. By the time he retired as a major general in 1908, he had set a record as the first soldier to enter the U.S. Army as a private and achieve a general's rank.

What distinguished Greely from his earliest days was his serious application to everything in which he took an interest and that he saw as his duty. While fellow-officers would devote their evenings to card games and other amusements, Dolph (as his friends called him) would be deep in a book. He respected knowledge of all kinds, and lacking any more than a high-school education, he set about to teach himself.

A.W. Greely circa 1880. Photograph courtesy of John C. Greely, grandson of General A.W. Greely

And although he appreciated all forms of literature, especially poetry, he dwelt most heavily on the physics, earth sciences, chemistry, mathematics, and other branches of learning that he considered "practical" for his professional development.

Greely's particular interest early on lay in telegraphic signaling, which had proved itself during the war, and the use of meterological reports sent by telegraph to predict changes in weather. By 1869 he was detailed to Washington as a signal officer. Here he fell under the spell of Capt. Henry W. Howgate, a Signal Service officer who was an enthusiast for arctic exploration and who opened his extensive library of arctic literature to the younger officer. It was through this chain of events that Greely was inspired to a deep interest in leading an arctic expedition. He had several motives: to visit a strange and romantic part of the world, to study the physical conditions of the Far North, to conduct signaling experiments under severe weather conditions, and also, perhaps, to make a name for himself that would help his promotion.

In October 1879, an International Polar Conference held in Hamburg agreed on a common program of meterological and other physical observations by expeditions supported by a dozen countries, all to be placed as far toward the top of the known world as possible. This was to be the first International Polar Year, set for 1882–83, to last from summer to summer. Greely was chosen to head one of two U.S.

expeditions. His observation post, named Fort Conger, was at Lady Franklin Bay on the east coast of Ellesmere Island, a few miles across Robeson Channel from the Greenland coast.

The plan was for Greely's party to spend two years at Lady Franklin Bay—from summer 1881 to summer 1883—exploring the coasts, documenting the wildlife, and carrying out other observations going beyond the program of the Hamburg conference. A supply ship was scheduled to bring mail and relief personnel in summer 1882 and to return in 1883 to bring the party home with its scientific findings.

By August, the expedition of twenty-five men was comfortably installed in a large wooden building assembled from lumber brought on shipboard. A plentiful supply of fresh musk-ox meat was on hand, thanks to the expedition hunters, and there was adequate coal hacked from an outcropping a few miles to the east that had been found by George Nares's* expedition in 1875. During the following twenty-four months, the expedition carried out the prepared program of scientific observations and measurements in relative comfort. These included hourly recordings of temperature, tidal levels, barometric pressure, precipitation (there was little), wind velocity and direction, and other phenomena.

In addition, several exploration trips by dog sledge and on foot led to detailed mapping of much of Ellesmere Island

A.W. Greely after being rescued, 1884. Photograph courtesy of John C. Greely, grandson of General A.W. Greely

and the nearby Greenland coast and the naming of newly found mountains, lakes, streams, fiords, and capes. One three-man party led by Lt. James B. Lockwood set a record for the farthest north yet attained, exceeding the previous record set by Lieutenant Beaumont of the Nares expedition by some four miles. Contrary to some later uninformed reports, however, there was no attempt "to reach the North Pole." Greely, armed with his high-school Latin and several reference books, documented many of the Ellesmere Island plants, lichens, and grasses and observed several species of birds. All these findings and observations were meticulously recorded in the official logs of the party. Greely had insisted that, as a condition of joining the expedition, every man keep a diary, and in these various accounts, the personal observations from different viewpoints added human detail to the scientific record.

In summer 1882, the supply ship was forced to turn back without reaching Lady Franklin Bay because of heavy ice. Again, in summer 1883, the supply ship *Proteus* ran into heavy ice in the Kane Basin, was crushed, and sank. Not aware of this, the Greely party, as previously arranged, moved south in August in three small boats (one of them steam-powered) through Kennedy Channel and Kane Basin toward an agreed-on rendezvous point at the entry of Smith Sound. After weeks of struggle, they came ashore on 29 September to find a meagre cache of supplies from the *Proteus* wreck, along with a message telling of the disaster to the ship and hope that the survivors could send help soon. At this point, Greely knew they were doomed to spend a winter in the Arctic with no prepared shelter, inadequate food, and virtually no fuel.

From October until the following June, Greely's command withstood the ravages of hunger and cold as best they could on Cape Sabine in a shelter built of small stones piled into a low wall to break the wind and covered by the overturned boat and a few tarpaulins. Rations were about one-fifth the normal military ration, until even that was exhausted. Then the men lived on stew made from lichen scraped from the rocks and tiny shrimp netted at the shore. When an occasional bird was shot, it provided about an ounce per man, eaten raw. A U.S. Navy relief ship finally reached the Greely camp on 22 June 1884 to find that Greely and only six others were still alive. Most of the others had died of starvation or exposure. One man died aboard ship on the return journey.

Greely's story as it unfolded was an epic of heroism and self-sacrifice. Although there were individual incidents of some men behaving selfishly, the common characteristic throughout the ordeal was a concern for all. In the years that followed, Greely always spoke in the most respectful terms of the behaviour of his command throughout their long winter of trial. His official report, published in 1888 in two massive volumes, combined both the scientific findings of the two years at Fort Conger on Lady Franklin Bay and the struggle for survival of the third year at Cape Sabine. The report became a standard reference work for arctic studies over the next several decades.

A.W. Greely was named chief signal officer of the U.S. Army in 1887, being promoted in one jump from captain to brigadier general. Under his leadership over the next nineteen years, the Signal Service acquired the first motorized vehicles for the Army, promoted the development of the "flying machine," and assisted Marconi in the development of the radio. Always a pragmatist, Greely encouraged every innovation that would bring the military service into the mechanized, electrified twentieth century. He visited Alaska and described its potential in prophetic terms in his *Handbook of Alaska*. He was active in patriotic societies, in historical and biographical research, and in the Literary Society of Washington. He was a founder of the National Geographic Society, a prolific writer for its magazine, and also served as the first president of the Explorers Club in New York. In 1935, on his ninety-first birthday, he was awarded the Medal of Honor by the United States government for his lifetime of service to his country.

Further Readings

Brainard, David L. 1940. *Six Came Back*. Indianapolis, New York: Bobbs-Merrill.

Greely, Adolphus W. 1927. *Reminiscences of Adventure and Service*. New York: C. Scribner's Sons.

_____. 1886. *Three Years of Arctic Service*. 2 vols. New York: Charles Scribner's Sons.

Todd, A.L. 1961. *Abandoned: The Story of the Greely Arctic Expedition 1881–1884*. New York: McGraw-Hill.

Alden Todd

ROBERT EDWIN PEARY
(1856–1920)

Robert Edwin Peary could be called a self-made man in the truest sense. Within three years of his birth on 6 May 1856, at Cresson, Pennsylvania, his father died. His mother packed family possessions and took her "Bertie" and Charles Peary's body back to her native Maine. There she buried her husband, established residence, and devoted herself to bringing up "Bertie"—almost as a girl. Mary Wiley Peary taught him the handiwork practiced by genteel young ladies of that period and sent him out to play wearing a bonnet to protect his fair skin. Nearly as dismaying to this sensitive boy was the fact that he and his mother (who never remarried) were considered poor relations by the family. All this propelled him at an early age to prove himself. Significantly his youthful companions soon used "Bert" as his nickname.

"I *must* have fame," young Peary told his mother more than once. In the dwindling nineteenth century, large areas of the planet still had not been visited by man. After much deliberation, Peary made his choice: he would become an arctic explorer,

Photograph of Robert Edwin Peary in furs. Courtesy of the Library of Congress

would be the first man to reach the North Pole.

Peary graduated from Portland High School, earned a degree from Bowdoin College, then took a naval commission in the U.S. Civil Engineer Corps with the thought that work on a proposed Nicaraguan canal might win him fame such as had come to the Frenchman De Lesseps for the Suez Canal. Nicaraguan plans collapsed, but Peary stayed in the Navy.

About 1885, Peary's interest in the North was rekindled. He began poring over voluminous reports of arctic explorers during his free hours. On 13 October of that year, he wrote himself a memorandum (which I found in 1962 in his own voluminous papers) that the time had come "for an entire change in the expeditionary organization of Arctic research." Instead of utilizing large parties and several ships, he wrote, he would have a small group relying on Inuit assistance. He had not been to the Arctic then, but the method he outlined would eventually bring him success.

From 1886 to 1909, Peary devoted himself to planning and leading eight arctic expeditions—

one of them of four years' duration. With increasing difficulty, he obtained leaves of absence from the Navy, raised his own money, recruited his own men, made his own rules, and expected strict compliance.

During one expedition he froze his feet and lost most of his toes to amputation, then suffered hellish agony when frequent bumps against jagged ice left the stumps bloody and aching. Nevertheless, arctic exploration continued to come before all else: health, the Navy, finances, and family (he married Josephine Diebitsch in 1888; they had two children).

The early desire for fame became an obsession to reach a goal. During years of exploration Peary mapped unknown lands and showed Greenland to be an island, but he did not get to the North Pole. To him this meant failure.

Finally, he succeeded, at the age of fifty-two—a wiry, auburn-haired, mustached man who could still hold his six-foot frame erect, but whose drawn, ruddy face and squinting eyes indicated hard experience. On 1 April 1909, he said good-bye to the last of four compact supporting parties that had accompanied him across the treacherous, ever-shifting ice of the Arctic Ocean. Then, with his African-American assistant Matthew Henson,* four Inuit, five sleds, and forty dogs, he struggled across more floating ice and reached the Pole five days later, according to his navigation, only to return to civilization and learn that Dr. Frederick A. Cook,* a former Peary expedition member, was claiming to have arrived first. Virtually all scientific and geographical organizations eventually credited Peary with the achievement and discredited Cook, but controversy still flares occasionally.

After 1911, Peary retired as a rear admiral, voted the "Thanks of Congress." For nearly a decade he and his

Photograph of Peary, from the author's collection. Courtesy of Marie Peary Stafford

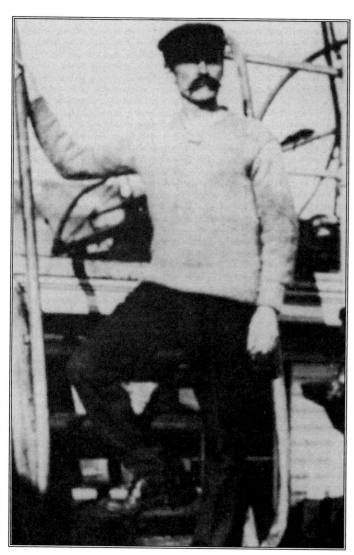

Photograph of Peary, from the author's collection. Courtesy of Marie Peary Stafford

family enjoyed normal life, although the Cook dispute cast a pall. On 20 February 1920, Peary died from pernicious anaemia.

Letters of condolence and tribute came from presidents, kings, geographers, and explorers. It was Robert Edwin Peary himself, however, who had expressed the most appropriate tribute, years earlier. After the polar attainment, a college classmate recalled that Peary had an affinity for quoting some poignant lines written by another Bowdoin man, Henry Wadsworth Longfellow:

"A boy's will is the wind's will,
And the thoughts of youth are long, long thoughts."

Further Readings

Hobbs, William Herbert. 1936. *Peary.* New York: Macmillan Company.

Holland, Clive. 1994. *Farthest North: The Quest for the North Pole.* Toronto: McClelland and Stewart; New York: Carrell and Graf.

Peary, Robert Edwin. 1898. *Northward over the "Great Ice."* 2 vols. New York: F.A. Stokes.

_____. 1907. *Nearest the Pole.* London: Hutchinson.

_____. 1910. *The North Pole.* New York: F.A. Stokes.

_____. 1917. *Secrets of Polar Travel.* New York: Century Company.

Weems, John Edward. 1967. *Peary: The Explorer and the Man.* Boston: Houghton Mifflin; London: Eyre Spottiswoode.

_____. 1960. *Race for the Pole.* London: Heinemann; New York: Holt.

John Edward Weems

FREDERICK A. COOK
(1865–1940)

In the earlier years of what is called "the Great Polar Controversy," Gen. A.W. Greely,* leader of the ill-fated Lady Franklin Bay Expedition, gave this ringing testimony to other explorations that, like his own, would invoke bitter passion: "Rarely, if ever, would they be equalled and never surpassed for their extent, duration and experience." Greely was alluding to the achievements of the Cook North Polar Expedition of 1908–09. Its commander, Dr. Frederick Albert Cook, nevertheless spent almost half of his life surrounded by such controversy that his real field work has been largely overlooked. While self-serving, Cook's own words, written in the twilight of an amazing career, may best express the depth of his personal torment: "Few men in all history ... have ever been made to suffer so bitterly and so inexpressibly as I because of the assertion of my achievement."

Cook caught the polar wanderlust only a year after his graduation from the College of Physicians and Surgeons at New York University, in 1890, perhaps influenced by the death of his first wife in childbirth. Hardened by a youth spent in the Catskill Mountains (he was born in Hortonville, New York, to an immigrant German physician), and later supporting his widowed mother in Brooklyn while securing his education, Cook had ambition and enormous energy. Over the next two decades, he earned a reputation as a doctor afield, interrupting a sporadic medical practice to offer

Photograph of Dr. Cook in 1936. Courtesy of the author

himself as surgeon or leader of eight expeditions "Poleward," a term he often used.

First going north with the young naval civil engineer Robert Edwin Peary* on his North Greenland Expedition in 1891, Cook earned Peary's praise for "unruffled patience and coolness in an emergency." After returning to an erratic general practice, Cook went north again in two arctic commands on the *Zita* (1893) and the *Miranda* (1894). When near-disaster struck the *Miranda,* the twenty-nine-year-old Cook navigated an open boat across 90 miles of polar sea to obtain rescue. The Arctic Club of America was born out of this voyage, and Cook became its first president. He would later preside over the prestigious Explorers Club as well.

After a four-year stint of medical practice and lecturing, the polar quest drew him again, this time to the Belgian Antarctic Expedition. The party became locked in the ice of the Bellingshausen Sea, and its survival was largely attributed to Cook. Roald Amundsen, the first mate, credited Cook with "unfailing hope and unfaltering courage" in his scheme to free the ship.

Peary's 1902 attempt to reach the Pole from Cape Hecla on northern Ellesmere Island was forced back at 84°17′N: Cook had been with him as the expedition's doctor. The trip convinced Cook that the so-called American route through Kane Basin was unsatisfactory, and that, in any event, he would never again serve under Peary. Soon, Cook mounted expeditions to Alaska's Mount McKinley, being the first to circumnavigate it in 1903 and making the first claimed ascent of North America's highest peak in 1906. At a dinner sponsored by the National Geographic Society—with a seething Peary in attendance—President Theodore Roosevelt hailed Cook as the conqueror of McKinley and the first American to explore both polar regions. In 1994, an expedition to McKinley on Ruth Glacier determined that Cook had reached a point at eleven thousand feet approaching the top of the mountain.

None of Cook's first seven expeditions ventured into the Queen Elizabeth Islands. But his eighth—his longest, most celebrated, and most controversial—took him into that region for two years. He sailed north on the schooner *John R. Bradley* in 1907. Leaving his base camp at Annoatuk in February 1908 with Rudolph Francke, his German assistant, 10 Inuit, 11 sleds, and 105 dogs, he followed Otto Sverdrup's* game lands through Ellesmere and Axel Heiberg islands, reached Cape Stallworthy, and went over the sea due north. His last supporting party turned back after three days' march, and with two Inuit companions, Cook fought pressure ridges and ice floes to reach what he determined to be the geographical North Pole on 21 April 1908. "We were the only pulsating creatures in a dead world of ice," he wrote in his diary.

The return journey was an epic in sled travel—in terms of pure survival, a classic experience. After living in an ancient Inuit cave on Devon Island through the polar night of 1908–09, Cook and his party returned to Greenland, whence he sailed to the adulation of the world, first in Copenhagen, and later in New York. Cook's wire that he

Photograph of Frederick Cook in furs. Courtesy of the author

had reached the Pole was sent on 1 September 1909: Peary's announcement followed five days later. The great controversy that began then is still simmering today.

Cook disappeared from public view after a bitter media campaign that did little for the reputation of either antagonist and even less for historical geography. Until he died in 1940, still maintaining his achievements, Cook was championed more in Europe than in North America. Since 1960, a revival of literature on the question has favoured Cook. Such arctic experts as Jean Malaurie, Silvio Zavatti, and A.F. Treshekenov have elevated Cook's claims to "probable and possible" attainment. Many of the international presenters at a symposium on Cook at the Byrd Polar Research Centre in 1993 agreed that he was a serious claimant.

Frederick A. Cook's unquestioned prior physical description of conditions at the Pole and his apparent descriptions of then-unknown ice islands weigh in his favour, and his non-discovery of Meighen Island (Stefansson* found this "impossible to explain") gives credence to his reporting a westward drift of the polar ice. A troubled later life (imprisonment for promoting Texas oil lands which subsequently produced the largest pool of oil in the United States) did not contribute to any public vindication for the explorer, termed "the American Dreyfus of the North." Ultimate rehabilitation may yet come as the claims of the once-discredited Cook are given a more dispassionate examination.

Further Readings

Cook, Frederick A. 1910. *My Attainment of the Pole*. New York: Mitchel Kennerley.

_____. 1951. *Return from the Pole*. New York: Pellegrini and Cudahy.

Freeman, Andrew. 1961. *The Case for Dr. Cook*. New York: Coward-McCann.

Hall, Thomas F. 1917. *Has the North Pole Been Discovered?* Boston: Badger.

Holland, Clive. 1994. *Farthest North: The Quest for the North Pole*. Toronto: McClelland and Stewart; New York: Carrell and Graf.

Horwood, Harold. 1977. *Bob Bartlett: The Great Canadian Explorer*. Garden City, New York: Doubleday and Co.

Malaurie, Jean. 1989. *Ultima Thule: The Quest for the North Pole*. Paris: Bordas.

Wright, Theon. 1969. *The Big Nail*. New York: John Day.

Russell W. Gibbons

MATTHEW HENSON
(1866–1955)

The only famous African-American polar explorer was the co-author of the major geographical quest of the century—the search for the North Pole. For Matthew Alexander Henson, descended from former slaves, the road from Charles County, Maryland, to the Arctic was long and arduous. He was born into dismal, hopeless poverty on 8 August 1866. At the age of twelve he escaped a loveless home—he never knew his mother, who died when he was two—and found his way to Baltimore and the benign Capt. Childs, master of the ship *Katie Hines*. Befriending the frail, hungry, frightened boy, Capt. Childs bent the rules in signing Matt on as cabin boy: he recorded Henson's age as fifteen rather than the illegal age of twelve. In the five years that Matt sailed on the *Katie Hines*, Childs taught him reading, writing, mathematics, navigation, and general proficiency at the sailor's varied trade. These skills would ultimately prove indispensable in Henson's travels with Robert Edwin Peary.*

The two men who were to find fame in the Arctic twenty-two years later first met in 1887 in a haberdashery in Washington, D.C., where Matt was a stockboy. Peary, then a lieutenant in the United States Navy Corps of Civil Engineers, had recently returned from his first of many attempts to gain the summit of Greenland's ice cap in search of a way to the North Pole. He had just been assigned to the survey team on the Nicaragua Ship Canal project, and

Photograph of Matthew Henson. Courtesy of the author

though reluctant to postpone another assault on Greenland, Peary accepted the assignment provided he could hire his own orderly. The day of the chance meeting, Henson was hired.

After proving his value to Peary during a year in the Nicaraguan jungle, Henson worked alongside him in a Philadelphia shipyard until Peary took another leave of absence to return to Greenland in 1891. Henson joined the party. His ochre-coloured skin, far from an asset in the racist United States, helped him in the Arctic. To the Inuit, Henson was not a white man, but a prodigal brother who had forgotten his native tongue and the ways of survival in the harsh northern environment. In successive expeditions, his rapidly growing skills in speaking Inuktitut, driving dogsleds, hunting, and trading for dogs and furs proved invaluable. In a short time "Miy Paluk," as the Inuit called him, was to become hero and legend. He was the most important member of the seven subsequent Peary expeditions spread over a period of eighteen years. One expedition alone lasted four years, during which Matt's courage, sacrifice, and physical strength saved Peary's life and the lives of others more than once.

Still convinced that Greenland was a continent leading to the Pole, Peary and Henson made several futile and dangerous attempts before abandoning the route. On the last Greenland effort, both men nearly perished. Caught by blizzards and having exhausted their food supplies, they ate their dogs. Suffering from frostbite, scurvy, and exhaustion, the two men stepped into the dog traces and dragged the sled, on which a sick companion lay, over the ice cap and down the steep, treacherous glacier back to camp. Many times, Matt was to witness the sight of strong men beaten by the elements. He was to see robust, athletic men turn into weak, whimpering, helpless children. He was himself to feel the crippling exhaustion, the fierce slashing cold, the madness of near-starvation, and to come out the stronger for it. While Henson suffered no permanent damage from his long years in the Arctic, Peary was not so fortunate—he was crippled for life.

Between expeditions, Henson worked in varied jobs. He assisted taxidermists and artists of the Museum of Natural History in New York in mounting displays of the skins he and Peary brought back from the North. On one occasion, he accompanied Peary on a fund-raising tour; sweltering in furs, he demonstrated the handling of a dog team and sled, while Peary introduced him as "my assistant, Matthew Henson."

In 1898 the U.S. Navy granted Peary a four-year leave of absence to search for the Pole once more. Peary planned to approach his goal this time via the frozen arctic sea. Threatened by rumours that a competing explorer, the Norwegian Otto Sverdrup,* was also planning a polar expedition, Peary and Henson immediately sailed north.

A completely new strategy was worked out for this expedition. They would sail as far north as the ice would allow in the frozen strait between Greenland and Ellesmere Island, and then travel by sledge to Fort Conger. Unused for fifteen years, Fort Conger had been the headquarters for the A.W. Greely* Geological Expedition, and would make an ideal winter outpost.

Henson selected the field teams, choosing the best and strongest Inuit hunters, skilled sled builders, and dog han-dlers. The Inuit were loyal to Matt, who now spoke their language fluently. They would follow him anywhere, for "Miy" was already a legend; several of the men he picked had been mere boys when he first arrived in their land.

The plan to use Fort Conger had tragic results. While still aboard ship, Peary's party was visited by Sverdrup, who admitted he too was aiming for Fort Conger. It was the dead of winter, the worst possible time to travel the 250 miles to the fort. Matt argued that Sverdrup could not possibly reach his objective before spring. Peary stubbornly refused to listen; reluctantly, Matt organized four teams and they set out for Fort Conger.

The march nearly cost the lives of the entire party. Arriving at the fort, Henson discovered that Peary had badly frozen his feet. Removing his companion's sealskin boots, he found both legs a bloodless white to the knees. When Matt gently removed the rabbit-skin inner boots, two or three toes from each foot clung to the hide and snapped off at the first joint. He nursed Peary through the next two months, fighting a desperate battle against gangrene, knowing that amputation was urgently required. By February the weather improved, and with Peary lashed to the sledge, Henson led the party south on the eleven-day trek to the ship. The surgeon aboard the *Windward* immediately amputated all of Peary's toes. Tragic as it was, this blow did not diminish Peary's burning ambition to discover the Pole.

Matthew Henson now became more indispensable than ever. His strength, courage, and field experience suited him to the role of leader, and there was no other man Peary could trust as he could Matt. But a new method of travel for Peary had to be worked out. No longer able to walk behind a sled, he would have to ride, which had never been allowed. To preserve his pride and dignity, Peary would be the first man out of camp, shuffling slowly, and when the others had passed, he would climb aboard the last sledge.

On the next-to-last march of the successful expedition, Henson knew at the outset how far the last day's journey would be, and his experience told him how many hours it would take to travel that distance. The sun was his clock. Sighting the position of the sun as he started that final advance on 6 April 1909, Matt knew where it would be when he had reached the Pole. Thus it was that he arrived forty-five minutes before Peary, who, after taking an instrument sighting, said "This is it, the Pole at last."

Upon their return to the United States, in the public controversy brought on by Dr. Frederick A. Cook's* claim to have beaten Peary to the Pole, the question was raised of why Henson, an African-American, had accompanied Peary on his final march. Donald MacMillan,* a member of the successful expedition and of several others, understood Peary's total dependence on Matt. "He never would have reached the Pole without Henson," he later wrote. "Matt was of more real value than the combined services of all of us. With years of experience, an expert dog driver, a master mechanic, physically strong, most popular with the Eskimos, talking the language like a native, clean, full of grit, he went to the pole because Peary couldn't get along without him."

Back in the States, Matt drifted into semi-obscurity. In 1913, President William Howard Taft appointed him to a civil service job as a messenger boy at the New York Customs House. Over the ensuing years, as many as six bills were introduced in Congress to retire Matt with honour and a pension, but all failed.

On 9 March 1955, Matthew A. Henson died at eighty-eight. He died proud of his humble collection of awards, many given to him over the years by African-American societies—two gold watches, a lacquered steel medal, a silver-plated loving cup from the Bronx Chamber of Commerce, a Navy medal given belatedly in 1946, and a medal bestowed by President Dwight D. Eisenhower in 1953. Two African-American universities presented him with Masters of Science degrees. In Charles County, Maryland, a new public school was named after him. Capt. Childs would have been ecstatic to know that his twelve-year-old urchin pupil had raised himself, literally, to the top of the world.

Further Readings

Henson, Matthew A. 1912. *A Negro Explorer at the North Pole*. New York: Frederick A. Stokes.

Robinson, Bradley. 1947. *Dark Companion*. New York: R.M. McBride; London: Hodder and Stoughton (1948).

Bradley Robinson

Donald B. MacMillan
(1874–1970)

Donald B. MacMillan—"Dan" to his family; "Cap'n Mac" to the crew of his beloved schooner *Bowdoin;* rear admiral, United States Naval Reserve, to those whose paths crossed his later in his life—was one of this century's pioneers of arctic exploration. He viewed himself, however, as a learner and teacher. When asked why he continued to journey north, he always replied, "to learn."

Hundreds of young men, as well as the distinguished scientists, engineers, and university professors who served with him aboard the *Bowdoin,* attest to his ability to encourage their learning—through example, through his insatiable curiosity about the world around him, through his quiet, but steady encouragement, and through his profound belief in the capacity of the individual to develop himself to his highest potential.

There were many shaping influences in Mac's life. His family were legatees of a long seafaring tradition in Canada and in New England, producing a love of the sea in Mac that seemed almost inborn. His high school principal in Freeport, Maine, encouraged the penniless young Mac to attend Bowdoin College in nearby Brunswick, and his experiences at the college were formative. Then came a serendipitous meeting with Robert Edwin Peary,* who learned of Mac's rescue of nine people in a boating accident off an island in Casco Bay. This chance encounter later induced Peary to ask the young MacMillan to serve on the expedition that led to the discovery of the North Pole in 1909. (Mac took charge of the support group on that expedition and did not accompany Peary to the Pole.)

He was born in Provincetown, Massachusetts, in 1874, the son of Capt. Neil MacMillan, an intrepid skipper of sail-

Donald B. and Miriam MacMillan aboard the *Bowdoin.* Mrs. MacMillan served alongside her husband as chief supplier and ship's photographer for over fifteen years. Photograph courtesy of the Peary-MacMillan Arctic Museum, Bowdoin College

ing vessels, and of Sarah Gardner MacMillan, a shipbuilder's daughter. Capt. Neil MacMillan and his crew were lost at sea, in 1883, when the schooner *Abbie Brown* sank during treacherous gales off the west coast of Newfoundland. Gallant, but her health frail, Mrs. MacMillan was not equal to the demands of supporting and caring for a family of five children. She died in 1886. After several years in Provincetown as the "adopted son" of another sea captain's family, Dan moved to Freeport to live with an older sister.

Donald B. MacMillan was never overpowered by adversity. To help with meagre family finances after his father's death, Dan, at age nine, peddled cranberries at a penny a quart, sold lemonade, skinned dogfish, and dove for pennies thrown by passengers on excursion boats in Provincetown. Later, to meet expenses at Bowdoin, from which he graduated in 1898, he served as janitor in the Freeport High School, pumped the organ in a local church, cut linings in a shoe factory, sold books door-to-door, drove a milk wagon very early in the morning, and took time off from college to earn money by teaching school. Upon graduation, all his bills had been paid through his own efforts; he was in debt to no one.

After teaching for ten years, MacMillan joined Peary's polar expedition in 1908. His life was centred on the Arctic for the next forty-six years, most of which he spent aboard the *Bowdoin*. In fact, Mac's last trip north aboard the *Bowdoin* came in 1954, when he was eighty years old. His wife, Miriam, accompanied him on six expeditions as a participating member of the crew.

Between 1913 and 1917, while in northern Greenland, Mac drew on his experience and observation to conceive the design for the eighty-eight-foot *Bowdoin,* a wooden schooner of incredible strength that took its name from Mac's alma mater. The *Bowdoin* is a story in herself. During twenty-six voyages between 1921 and 1954, MacMillan sailed her to and explored parts of northern Greenland, Ellesmere Island, Bay Fjord, Eureka Sound, Labrador, Baffin Island, Iceland, and the east and west coasts of Greenland. Over the years, he mapped many previously uncharted northern waters. Owing to his unique and extensive knowledge of those areas, MacMillan was recalled to active duty by the U.S. Navy during World War II. He served in Washington while his schooner, commissioned the USS *Bowdoin,* served the Navy in her "home" waters. Now fully restored, the schooner *Bowdoin* is the official state sailing vessel and is owned and operated as a training vessel by the Maine Maritime Academy. She has made two return voyages to Greenland in recent years.

The contributions made by MacMillan and his crews to the knowledge and understanding of the North are too numerous to elaborate. They include studies in the botany, ornithology, meteorology, oceanography, archaeology, glaciology, and anthropology of the regions explored. As well, Mac and his crews demonstrated that airplanes could be used effectively above the Arctic Circle and that short-wave radio could provide instant communication with the rest of the world.

Those scientific and technical accomplishments—"firsts" in their time—were paralleled by Mac's interest in and love for the native people with whom he often lived, whose languages he mastered, and by whom he was deeply revered. He provided lumber and materials for the building of the MacMillan-Moravian Mission School for Inuit children in Nain, Labrador, for many years providing books, food, and clothing for the students, equipment for the school, including an electric generator that also lighted the mission house and church, and even false teeth for the adults in the community. He compiled a 154-page book, *Eskimo Place Names and Aid to Conversation*, for the armed forces during WW II.

Donald B. MacMillan—learner, teacher, leader, explorer—was a very modest man. He wore lightly the honours bestowed on him during his lifetime. Perhaps the one that tickled his fancy the most was the following telegram from Alan Shepard on behalf of the astronauts in NASA, sent on the occasion when, at age ninety-three, Mac was awarded the Bradford Washburn special medal from the Boston Museum of Science: "Hearty congratulations. Sorry we could not have helped you at the Pole. Have space for a trip to the moon ... are you available?" Dan, who very seldom swore, turned to me and said, "Damn sure I am."

Further Readings

Allen, Everett S. 1962. *Arctic Odyssey: The Life of Rear Admiral Donald B. MacMillan.* New York: Dodd, Mead and Company.

MacMillan, Donald B. 1927. *Etah and Beyond: Life within Twelve Degrees of the Pole.* Boston: Houghton Mifflin.

_____. [1918, 1925] 1933. *Four Years in the White North.* Boston; Hale, Cushman, and Flint.

_____. 1943. *Eskimo Place Names and Aid to Conservation.* Washington, D.C.: The Hydrographic Office, U.S. Navy.

MacMillan, Miriam. 1948. *Green Seas and White Ice.* New York: Dodd, Mead and Company

Miriam MacMillan

ROBERT BARTLETT (1875–1946)

Although he was indisputably one of the world's greatest arctic mariners, Capt. Robert A. Bartlett's name and accomplishments are relatively obscure. As a sealer, arctic explorer, ice captain, and scientist, Bartlett made over forty voyages in more than half a century at sea. He was decorated by the American Congress, the Explorers Club, and geographical societies on two continents. He survived two shipwrecks and, thanks to his skill and perseverance, prevented a number of others, and he saved the lives of many shipmates. An eccentric who could play Chopin records as his ship was about to sink below the arctic ice, a man frequently inconsistent in accounts of his own voyages, a man blessed with incredible good luck when at sea, a known drinker who professed to be a teetotaller, Bartlett was, nevertheless, an exceptional leader of men.

Photograph of Robert A. Bartlett. National Archives of Canada/C 25962

Bob Bartlett was reared in Brigus, Newfoundland, a community with a strong seafaring tradition. Born in 1875 into a family of eminent captains and ice navigators, he never really seriously considered any other occupation. Bartlett's nautical apprenticeship was served primarily on sealing and trading ships. While his skills as an ice navigator were developing, the actual sealing was never very successful for Bartlett. He returned to it frequently over the years, but his real love and accomplishments lay in voyages farther north.

From the perspective of the late twentieth century, three periods loom preeminent in Bartlett's life. The first was the decade between 1898 and 1908, during which he accompanied Robert Edwin Peary* on three separate attempts to reach the North Pole, the second was his captaincy of the *Karluk* on the Canadian Arctic Expedition in 1913 and 1914, and the third, his scientific voyages on the *Morrissey* from 1925 to 1945.

Robert Peary encountered Bartlett in 1898 when Bartlett was the first mate on the *Windward*, the flagship of Peary's first unsuccessful journey to the North Pole. On Peary's subsequent expeditions Bartlett played critical roles. On the 1906 trip—Peary's second attempt —Bartlett literally chopped ice and broke trail over pressure ridges and contorted ice formations to allow Peary to try for the Pole. Although the attempt was unsuccessful, without Bartlett, Peary would have been too distant to make any attempt at all. The arduous six-month voyage south from the north end of Ellesmere Island was a series of disasters, with the *Roosevelt* being constantly battered by heavy ice and storms. Only countless ingenious temporary repairs by Bartlett prevented complete catastrophe. On Peary's third attempt in the winter of 1908–09, Bartlett, again breaking trail for the sled-ridden Peary, reached latitude 87°40′N, about 150 miles from the Pole—at that time the highest confirmed latitude reached by anyone. Yet Peary denied Bartlett a part in the final dash for the Pole and reserved this privilege for himself. Peary purported to have attained the Pole on about 6

April 1909. Soon after began the famous controversy between Peary and Dr. Frederick A. Cook,* who claimed to have reached the Pole a year before in 1908. The controversy is well known, but without the efforts of Bob Bartlett, Peary would not have been a party to the debate.

The *Karluk*, under Bartlett's captaincy, was to be the main vessel in the Canadian Arctic Expedition of 1913. The expedition to the western Arctic is famous for the anthropological and geographical work conducted by Vilhjalmur Stefansson* and Diamond Jenness;* however, the real hero of the venture surely has to be Robert Bartlett. When Stefansson left the *Karluk* in September 1913, ostensibly for a brief hunting foray on the mainland, she had been held fast in the ice for a number of weeks northeast of Point Barrow. But soon after Stefansson's departure, a gale carried the *Karluk* far to the west, still firmly fixed in the ice, and upon returning, Stefansson gave the ship and crew up for lost. Eventually, in January of the next year, the ship succumbed to ice pressure and sank about 250 miles from the Siberian coast.

Under Bartlett's leadership, the crew passed the next few months in an ice camp before the captain led the remnants of his party to Wrangel Island. From there, Bartlett and an Inuit companion travelled through incredible ice fields 200 miles to Siberia, and a further 400 miles to the Bering Strait and thence over to Alaska. By virtue of Bartlett's exertions, the survivors were picked up on Wrangel Island nearly a year after the *Karluk* had become entrapped in the ice. Bartlett's journey through incomparably tough ice conditions to save his crew is an event of epic dimensions, similar to Sir Ernest Henry Shackleton's heroic journey from Elephant Island to South Georgia in his small boat. Such raw courage and deter-mination to discharge responsibility in the toughest of physical circumstances is rarely witnessed now. Modern communications have made unnecessary such feats of leadership, strength, and endurance in remote situations.

In 1925, Bartlett purchased the *Morrissey*, which he was to captain for the next twenty years. In these two decades, Bartlett explored both northeast and northwest Greenland and various remote parts of the Canadian Arctic. He gathered botanical specimens and Inuit relics for many museums and societies and brought back numerous live arctic mammals for zoos. It was a phenomenal achievement for a man with little formal scientific training. Not only did he make a sizable contribution to scientific and geographic knowledge, but he piloted the *Morrissey* through countless storms, adventures, and close calls in what was by now vintage Bartlett style—a unique mixture of determination, bravado, skill, leadership, and luck. In twenty voyages on the *Morrissey*, not a single man was lost. One of his most ambitious projects, a three-year drift across the Arctic Ocean while locked in the ice, was never undertaken. Yet the scope of his proposal and the understanding of the information that could potentially be gathered reveal a keen scientific mind thirsting for knowledge and capable of correlating and synthesizing it.

The exigencies of remote northern travel and exploration prior to World War II demanded a range of skills, knowledge, and leadership that, in today's era of specialization, are rarely demanded of one person. In this sense, Bartlett was a product of the time in which he lived. He was the complete explorer: navigator, adventurer, scientist, and leader of men. It does not seem just that men whose ships Bartlett captained, such as Peary and Stefansson, and whose expeditions Bartlett personally saved have received so much more historical and popular attention than has Bartlett.

Although he was first and foremost a Newfoundlander, after World War I, Robert A. Bartlett spent most of the time when he was not at sea in New York City. Much of the financial backing for his voyages over the years had come from American sources, and he received far more recognition in the United States than in Canada. It was in New York, a stark and cosmopolitan contrast to his beloved Arctic, that Bob Bartlett died in April 1946, just five months after his last voyage on the *Morrissey*.

Further Readings

Bartlett, Robert. 1928. *The Log of Bob Bartlett*. New York: Putnam.

_____. 1934. *Sails Over Ice*. New York: C. Scribner's Sons.

_____ and Ralph T. Hale. 1916. *The Last Voyage of the Karluk*. Boston: Small, Maynard and Company.

Horwood, Harold. 1977. *Bartlett, The Great Canadian Explorer*. Toronto: Doubleday.

Hugh Stewart

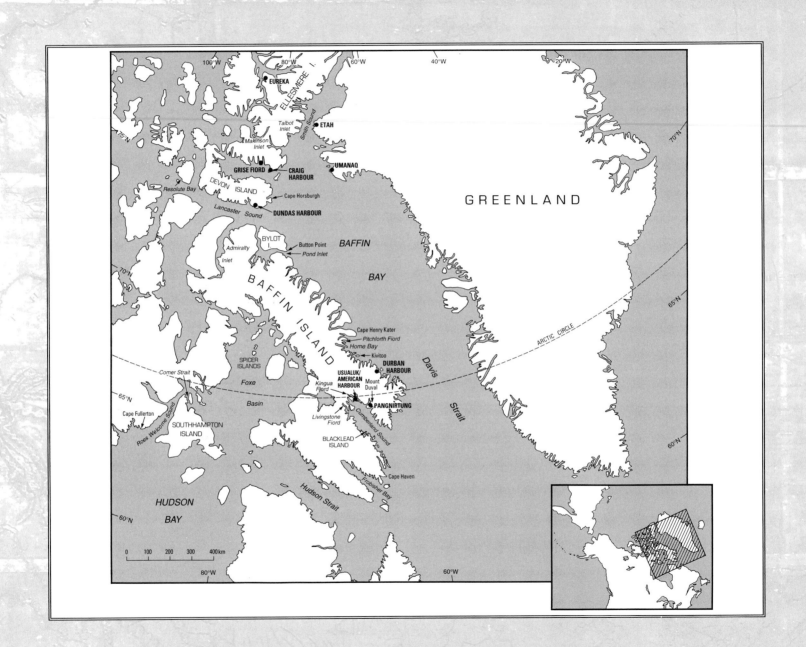

EUREKA

ELLESMERE I.

Talbot Inlet

Smith Sound

ETAH

Makinson Inlet

GRISE FIORD — CRAIG HARBOUR

UMANAQ

Resolute Bay

DEVON ISLAND

Cape Horsburgh

Lancaster Sound

DUNDAS HARBOUR

GREENLAND

BAFFIN

BYLOT I.

Button Point

Admiralty Inlet

Pond Inlet

BAY

BAFFIN ISLAND

Cape Henry Kater

Pitchlorth Fiord

Home Bay

Kivitoo

DURBAN HARBOUR

SPICER ISLANDS

Comer Strait

Foxe

USUALUK/ AMERICAN HARBOUR

Kingua Fiord

Mount Duval

Davis

PANGNIRTUNG

ARCTIC CIRCLE

Basin

Cape Fullerton

Livingstone Fiord

Cumberland Sound

Strait

Roes Welcome Sound

SOUTHHAMPTON ISLAND

BLACKLEAD ISLAND

Frobisher Bay

Cape Haven

Hudson Strait

HUDSON BAY

0 100 200 300 400 km

100°W 80°W 60°W 40°W 20°W

75°N

70°N

65°N

70°N

65°N

60°N

60°N

80°W 60°W

UNIT
₰ 14 ₰

Merqusâq, Franz Boas, George Comer, William Duval,
Henry Toke Munn, Hector Pitchforth, Lazaroosie Kyak

Shifting to the south and east, the far more populated region of Baffin Island and southern Greenland comes into focus. The myriad bays and inlets of Baffin Island provide both shelter and access to many northern communities. It is a place where Europeans and aboriginal peoples came into contact largely through the whaling industry, much as the fur industry stimulated most primary contacts in continental North America. As these profiles demonstrate, that marriage of cultures has brought substantial changes to the inhabitants, while it has stimulated efforts to preserve a record of traditional Inuit practices.

MERQUSÂQ (ca. 1850–1916)

In 1903, when Knud Rasmussen, a member of Mylius-Erichsen's Danish Literary Expedition, visited the Polar Inuit for the first time, he interviewed a man called Merqusâq, one of the last of a group of Baffin Island Inuit who had migrated north and crossed to Greenland half a century previously.

Merqusâq was born during a winter journey, probably in Admiralty Inlet or Pond Inlet. His parents were Uqqumiut people who had come from the region of Cumberland Sound around 1840, along with several other families escaping a blood feud. After their enemies pursued them to Pond Inlet, these people decided to move even farther north, crossing Lancaster Sound probably in 1851. Still in his infancy, Merqusâq would later recall little of his home on Baffin Island.

The migrants, numbering more than forty, were led by two men: Qitlaq, who was Merqusâq's uncle, and Uqi. Settling amidst plentiful game on the southeast coast of Devon Island, they were visited at Dundas Harbour in 1853 by the explorer Edward A. Inglefield.* Inglefield told them of the Inuit he had seen on the Greenland shore and probably showed them his map of the region.

Merqusâq told Rasmussen that after hearing of Inuit on the other side of the sea, Qitlaq "could never settle down to anything again." He finally decided to search for the new people, and his drive and prestige as shaman were so strong that the migrants chose to follow him. In 1858, Francis Leopold McClintock* met the old leader and some of his followers near Cape Horsburgh on Devon Island's east coast.

The journey was long and difficult. They spent the darkest part of the winters in stone-and-turf houses, leav-

Watercolour of Merqusâq, by Harold Moltke. Used by permission of the National Museum of Denmark, Department of Ethnography, and Rose Moltke Schou and Alette Ahlefeldt

ing only when the sun returned. Yet part of the summer had to be spent encamped, to allow them to stockpile food for the next winter. They had to pass over rough ice and cross dangerous glaciers. Near Talbot Inlet, most of the original migrants, having tired of following Qitlaq without ever seeing the promised land, lost faith in the old man. Led by Uqi, they turned back to the south, where most were to die of starvation several years later.

Merqusâq was barely adolescent when he crossed Smith Sound to Greenland. The group settled near Etah, and, in the following year, they finally met the long-sought Polar Inuit, with whom they lived for several years. Merqusâq's people introduced several cultural elements— notably the kayak and the bow—which had been forgotten by these northernmost inhabitants of Greenland.

Not too many years passed before Qitlaq, who had just killed a local shaman, became sick. Wishing to see his homeland once more before dying, he decided to return to Baffin Island, and most of the migrants followed him. The followers included Merqusâq, his wife Agpaliapik (Uqi's daughter), his parents, his elder brother Qumangâpik, and the latter's family.

Qitlaq died soon after crossing Smith Sound. Although his people continued southward, they had lost their charismatic leader and ill fortune dogged them. By the second year they reached the head of Makinson Inlet, but game and fish were extremely scarce, leaving them in dire straits. The dogs had already been eaten, and the older people began to die. Two men, Minik and Maktaq, grew dangerous. Not only did they eat the victims of starvation, but they resorted to murder to get more food. One day, while Merqusâq fished alone through the ice, Minik, his brother-in-law, flung himself on him with a knife and succeeded in gouging out his right eye and seriously wounding him in the throat before Qumangâpik could come to his rescue. Later, recuperating from his wounds, Merqusâq watched as Minik and Maktaq stole the corpse of his father.

As soon as Merqusâq was able to walk, the two families hurriedly left. Still fearing the murderous Minik and Maktaq, they travelled for several days on the ice of Makinson Inlet, where Qumangâpik managed to catch several seals. After Merqusâq recovered some of his strength, and the party supplied itself with seal meat, the two families began the long journey back to Greenland, reaching the small island off Talbot Inlet where they had wintered the previous year. Refitting the kayaks they had abandoned there, they hunted seal and walrus that summer, and managed to catch a polar bear in a stone trap, which enabled them to spend that winter in relative comfort. In the following spring, they finally reached the Greenland shore.

Of the twenty or so people who had crossed Smith Sound westward a few years before, only five returned. Neither Merqusâq nor his brother ever tried again to return to Baffin Island; they settled permanently among the Polar Inuit, where their sister Aqiggiarjuk had found a husband.

It is not known in what circumstances Merqusâq lost his wife, Agpaliapik (who had given him three children), to another man. Kavssâluk, the only female offspring of their union, later bore a daughter, Navarana, who married Peter Freuchen and died in 1921, just as she was about to join the Fifth Thule Expedition with her husband. But perhaps the best known of Merqusâq's relatives is his grand-nephew Ôdaq (Ûtaq), who accompanied Robert Edwin Peary* on his quest of the North Pole in 1909.

Of Merqusâq, Rasmussen wrote in 1904: "He was born on a journey and all his life has been spent journeying. Although old now and somewhat bowed from rheumatism, he continues his journeys of several hundred miles a year on arduous fishing and hunting expeditions." He was famous as a polar bear hunter and could say to Rasmussen: "Look at my body: it is covered with deep scars; those are the marks of bears' claws. Death has been near me many times … but as long as I can hold a walrus and kill a bear, I shall still be glad to live."

Still suffering at times from the throat wound inflicted by Minik, Merqusâq spent the final years of his life in the house of his granddaughter and Peter Freuchen. He died in 1916.

Further Readings

Mary-Rousselière, Guy. 1980. *Qitdlarssuaq: L'histoire d'une migration polaire.* Montréal: Les Presses de l'Université de Montréal.

McClintock, F.L. 1859. *The Voyage of the Fox in the Arctic Seas: A Narrative of the Discovery of the Fate of Sir John Franklin and his Companions.* London: John Murray.

Rasmussen, Knud. [1908] 1976. *The People of the Polar North,* edited by G. Herring. Reprint. New York: AMS Press Inc.

Uvdloriâq, Inûterssuaq. 1976. *Qitdlarssuakkunnik Oqalualaq. Kalâtdlit nunâne naqiterisitsissarfik.* Det Grønlandske Forlag.

Guy Mary-Rousselière, O.M.I.

FRANZ BOAS (1858–1942)

A desire to delve into "the simple relationships between man and land" among the Inuit of Qikirtaaluk (Baffin Island) was the ambitious goal of a twenty-five-year-old German scientist who left Hamburg aboard the *Germania* on 20 June 1883. The schooner was bound for Kingua (clearwater) fiord Fjord in Tinixdjuarbing (Cumberland Sound), where the young German would stay with his assistant, Wilhelm Weike, for a year, the *Germania* herself returning home with the German scientific team of the First International Polar Year 1882–83. That voyage—more than one hundred years ago—marked the beginning of intensive and innovative field work on Inuit geographical perception, social and economic organization, and

Franz Boas about 1880-81. Courtesy of the American Philosophical Society

religious beliefs. In retrospect, this research was also the pivot of an extraordinary scientific career of an influential and far-sighted man who shaped modern anthropology in North America—Franz Boas. All his life, Boas encouraged rigorous scientific work and international cooperation; moreover, as a conscientious citizen and scientist, he energetically fought cultural and racial prejudices, the implications of which he was keenly aware, having been exposed to them as a Jew in his German homeland. His arctic endeavours, although only a small part of his scientific work, not only advanced the discipline of anthropology in general, but contributed immensely to our knowledge of human-land relations and Inuit culture in the Canadian North.

Born and raised in Minden, Westfalen, Germany, Franz Boas studied natural sciences and philosophy in Heidelberg, Bonn, and Kiel, where he took his doctorate in physics in 1881, writing on the perception of the colour of the water in the Bay of Kiel. His studies clearly reflected his interests in geography and philosophy, disciplines in which he took minors. His curiosity about the Inuit and their arctic environment grew out of the question of how environmental influences on human behaviour affect spatial distribution. The favourable atmosphere of international research cooperation, which began in Germany and other European countries in the 1860s, and culminated in the International Polar Year 1882-83, encouraged his plans for field work that was to move away from simple geographical exploration of uncharted lands and toward an integrated study of both physical and cultural systems in a particular area.

The German Polar Commission helped Boas reach Baffin Island in September 1883, but for the next year he relied on Inuit, on whalers, on his assistant, and on himself, expediently organizing his geographical and anthropological work. Covering nearly 2,500 miles on foot, by sled, and by boat, Boas showed no signs of physical fatigue, always pushing himself to the very limit. He vigorously pursued his scientific goals, but never neglected to ask for local advice and to adjust to unforeseen circumstances, such as when canine disease left him without dogs for long stretches. With simple instruments, he charted the configurations of Tinixdjuarbing (Cumberland Sound) and the east coast of Qikirtaaluk (Baffin Island), producing a map that served as a reference far into the twentieth century.

His relationship with the Inuit was based on mutual respect and appreciation, evident in his sole use of aboriginal place names and in his criticism of explorers and whalers who arrogantly and whimsically assigned European names, thus creating a never-ending confusion. His dedication to the people and their culture was dictated not by a romantic perception of the "native," but rather by the urgent feeling that as much as possible of the cultural tradition of the Inuit must be preserved, an approach he followed in his later work among the Northwest Coast Indians, and instilled in his students. The enormous body of information on Inuit culture, so valuable to today's Inuit, found its way into two major English publications that still retain their immediacy and are accepted source books—*The Central Eskimo* (1888) and *The Eskimo of Baffin Island and Hudson Bay* (1901 and 1907).

After his field work on Baffin Island, Boas returned to Berlin University, where he qualified as *Privatdozent,* to become university professor in geography in 1886 by writing a treatise on his Baffin Island work. His urge to continue field research among the aboriginal peoples of North America led him to the Northwest Coast, his area of study for the rest of his life. His own research interests, the academic quarrels and antisemitism in Germany, and personal ties in the United States strengthened his conviction to seek a career in the United States. After holding various positions (e.g. Clark University, Chicago World Exhibit, and American Museum of Natural History), he found his academic home at Columbia University in 1896, where he remained until his

Boas in a posed photograph done in a German studio. Courtesy of the American Philosophical Society

retirement in 1936. Here he institutionalized and promoted anthropology as an accepted scholarly field of inquiry. He became a leader in the study of race, culture, and language and stimulated new research frontiers in physical anthropology, linguistics, and folklore. Very quickly rising to prominence, Boas established numerous anthropological associations, journals, and congresses.

Even though his achievements were not always accepted uncritically, Franz Boas has remained one of the great anthropologists of our time. The centennial of his arctic year presented an opportunity to review the achievements of an exceptional man who preserved invaluable parts of Inuit culture that would have been lost without his perseverance.

Further Readings

Boas, Franz. [1888] 1964. *The Central Eskimo*. Reprint. Lincoln: University of Nebraska Press.

_____. 1901 and 1907. *The Eskimo of Baffin Island and Hudson Bay*. Bulletin of the American Museum of Natural History. No. 15, Parts 1 and 2. New York.

_____. [1940] 1966. *Race, Language and Culture*. Reprint. New York: The Free Press.

Cole, Douglas and Ludger Müller-Wille. 1984. "Franz Boas' Expedition to Baffin Island, 1883-1883." *Études/Inuit/Studies* 8(1): 37–63.

Goldschmidt, Walter, ed. 1959. *The Anthropology of Franz Boas: Essays on the Centennial of His Birth*. Memoirs of the American Anthropological Association No. 89. Menasha, Wis.

Herskovits, Melville J. 1953. *Franz Boas: The Science of Man in the Making*. New York: Charles Scribner's Sons.

Stocking, George W., Jr., ed. 1974. *The Shaping of American Anthropology. 1883–1911: A Franz Boas Reader*. New York: Basic Books.

Ludger Müller-Wille

George Comer (1858–1937)

While explorers from several nations were seeking sea routes to the Indies around the polar margins of Eurasia and North America, thereby constructing a geographical picture of the Arctic, whalemen were busily exploiting the marine resources of the circumpolar North, in particular the Greenland or bowhead whale. Arctic whaling began around Spitsbergen shortly after 1600, spread to western Greenland before 1700, reached the coast of Baffin Island by 1820, and penetrated into Hudson Bay in 1860. In the Pacific sector, it expanded through Bering Strait in 1848 and extended to the Canadian waters of the Beaufort Sea in 1889. Yet by World War I, the arctic whaling industry had all but faded away.

George Comer was a professional whaleman whose career spanned the final decades of whaling in Hudson Bay. He was extremely successful in whaling, but Comer's achievements went far beyond the sufficiently challenging tasks of pursuing whales, navigating small sailing vessels among pack ice, and wintering in the Arctic. He was a friend to the Inuit and a dedicated student of their culture, an amateur archaeologist, a scientific collector in the fields of ethnography and natural history, and a recognized arctic authority to whom a number of prominent scientists and writers owed much.

Born in Quebec, of an English father and an Irish mother, George Comer soon moved with his mother to

George Comer, from a newspaper clipping in the author's possession

Connecticut. At seventeen, he responded to the lure of the sea and shipped out on the New London whaler *Nile* for Cumberland Sound, Baffin Island. This initiation into the excitements and rigours of arctic whaling was followed by some voyages in the American coastal trade and a series of Antarctic sealing voyages. From 1889 to 1891, he served as mate of the schooner *Era* on three cruises to southeastern Baffin Island, and his introduction to Hudson Bay came in 1893–94 during a wintering voyage of almost fifteen months' duration on board the *Canton*.

On the six Hudson Bay whaling voyages that Comer made between 1895 and 1912, he sailed as master of the *Era* and later of the *A. T. Gifford*. The first of these cruises included a winter spent frozen into harbour ice near the whaling ground of Roes Welcome Sound, and on each of the subsequent five voyages, he and his crew remained two successive winters in Hudson Bay.

Wintering was a common practice in Hudson Bay. Ships and whaleboats could cruise late in the autumn and take up whaling again early in the spring, thus significantly extending the whaling season and vastly improving the chances of securing whales. The disadvantage was that wintering often imposed severe hardship on the crews. Cold and scurvy were formidable adversaries. Comer's men, in contrast to many, usually wintered in relative security and good health (although it would be an exaggeration to say comfort), owing partly to his experience and leadership, but largely to the close association that he maintained with the Inuit. Comer provided trade goods and provisions to many men and women of the Aivilingmiut, Netsilingmiut, and Qaernermiut in return for their services. The native men assisted in whaling and provided a steady supply of fresh caribou meat to combat scurvy, and the women made the fur clothing so vital for outdoor activities in winter. To alleviate boredom during the long ten-month period of immobilization in the winter harbour, Comer arranged dances, concerts, dinners, and sports events for the amusement of sailors and natives alike. During his spare time, he systematically recorded details of Inuit life and collected samples of their material culture. Much of his information was used by the anthropologist Franz Boas* in his well-known book *The Central Eskimo* (1888) and in two subsequent reports on the Inuit of Baffin Island and Hudson Bay; Comer's collections of clothing, implements, and weapons found their way into museums in the United States and Germany. With equipment provided by the American Museum of Natural History, Comer photographed the Inuit, made hundreds of plaster casts of their faces and hands, and took sound recordings of their dances, songs, and stories. The wax cylinders he made during the voyage of the *Era* in 1903–05 were the first ever made among Canadian Inuit.

Comer's journals reveal that he felt genuine affection and concern for the Inuit—comforting a widow in mourning, respectfully placing objects on a grave, making heroic attempts after departing from Hudson Bay to fulfil an oral agreement to deliver a whaleboat to an Inuk, sympathizing with their harsh way of life, helping them out in times of hunger or sickness, pondering the possibilities of govern-ment establishment of scattered relief food caches for times of famine, and protecting them against the boorish behaviour of his own crew. His attitude was by no means typical of his fellow whaling captains, some of whom considered him "native crazy."

As a navigator, George Comer was conscious of deficiencies in the published charts of Hudson Bay. In two papers published in the prestigious *Bulletin of the American Geographical Society of New York*, he presented an improved map of Southampton Island and vicinity, showing the narrow strait at its northern extremity that now bears his name. He also published information on the Inuit of northwestern Hudson Bay, including the isolated inhabitants of Southampton Island, the Sadlermiut, who were doomed to extinction in 1902.

Comer's arctic contributions were not solely in the whaling trade. In 1915, he served as ice master of the *George B. Cluett*, a ship chartered by the American Museum of Natural History to collect the men of Donald B. MacMillan's* Crocker Land Expedition in northwestern Greenland. When the relief vessel was itself trapped in the ice for two years, Comer carried out valuable archaeological excavations at Umanaq, unearthing evidence of what we now know as the Thule Eskimo culture. Another expedition secured his services in 1919, but with less fortunate results. Comer sailed as master of the *Finback,* a yacht chartered by an ethnographer, Christian Leden, to carry out trade and scientific work among the Inuit of western Hudson Bay. The *Finback* went aground in Fullerton Harbour, Hudson Bay, where Comer had often wintered, and was lost.

During the last years of World War I, George Comer served as a lieutenant in the U.S. Navy. He later retired to

East Hadam, Connecticut, and kept active in community and state affairs until his death in 1937 at age seventy-nine. Here was a man skilful and successful in his own profession, but capable of rising above it to make significant contributions in other fields, a man who ran a tight ship but preserved a tolerant, friendly, and cheerful attitude towards his fellow men both at home and in the Arctic.

Further Readings

Calabretta, Fred. 1984. "Captain George Comer and the Arctic." *Log of Mystic Seaport* 35(4): 118–31.

Comer, George. 1906. "Whaling in Hudson Bay, with Notes on Southampton Island." In *Boas Anniversary Volume: Anthropological Papers Written in Honor of Franz Boas*, edited by B. Laufer. New York: Stechert.

_____. 1910. "A Geographical Description of Southampton Island." *Bulletin of the American Geographical Society of New York* 42: 84–90.

_____. 1913. "Additions to Captain Comer's Map of Southampton Island." *Bulletin of the American Geographical Society of New York* 45: 516–18.

_____. 1921. "Notes by G. Comer on the Natives of the Northwestern Coast of Hudson Bay." *American Anthropologist*, n.s. 23: 243–44.

Eber, Dorothy Harley. 1989. *When the Whalers Were up North: Inuit Memories from the Eastern Arctic*. Montreal: McGill-Queen's University Press.

Ross, W. Gillies, ed. 1984. *An Arctic Whaling Diary: The Journal of Captain George Comer in Hudson Bay 1903–1905*. Toronto: University of Toronto Press.

_____. 1984. "George Comer, Franz Boas, and the American Museum of Natural History." *Etudes Inuit Studies* 8(1): 145–64.

_____. 1984. "The Earliest Sound Recordings Among North American Inuit." *Arctic* 37: 291–92.

_____. 1990. "The Use and Misuse of Historical Photographs: A Case Study from Hudson Bay, Canada." *Arctic Anthropology* 27: 93–112.

W. Gillies Ross

Photograph of George Comer. Courtesy of Comer's grandson, George Comer, East Haddam, Connecticut

WILLIAM DUVAL (1858–1931)

A legend has grown up around the circumstances of the arrival of William (Wilhem) Duval, a young whaler, in the North American Arctic over one hundred years ago. The story has it that, as a young man, Duval, son of a well-to-do family in New York, had become engaged to be married, but wanted a year of adventure before settling down. He shipped out on a New England whaler to spend a winter in the Arctic. The following summer, he returned to the United States to find that his fiancee had married a clergyman in his absence. Despondent, he returned to the Arctic and vowed to remain there.

The facts are only somewhat less romantic. Duval had been born Wilhelm Duvel in Germany in 1858. Two years later his parents emigrated with their young family to New York City. At the age of twenty-one, William Duval shipped aboard a whaler for the Arctic; he arrived in Cumberland Sound in the summer of 1879 and remained there for the next four years. He was usually employed as second helmsman aboard the *Lizzie P. Simmonds*, a whaler owned by an American firm, Williams and Company. In 1883, he returned to the United States for a year.

His activities over the next twenty years are little known. In 1884, when he returned north, it was to Williams's whaling station at Spicer Island in Hudson Strait, and, the following year, he ran Williams's station at Cape Haven. Two years later, he was back in Cumberland Sound. When

Photograph of William Duval, from the Kenn Harper Collection

Williams sold out to his rival, Crawford Noble of Aberdeen, Duval went to work for the Scottish concern.

In the Arctic, Duval lived a life not unlike that of the Inuit whom he came to know so intimately. He learned to speak their language fluently, and they gave him an Inuktitut name— "Sivutiksaq," the harpooner. He married a native woman, Aullaqiaq. They had at least four children. A daughter, Towkie, was born in 1900 at Blacklead Island and another daughter, Alookie, was born there two years later. Two sons died in childhood.

In 1903, Duval and his family, with other Cumberland Sound Inuit, accompanied the Scottish whaler James Mutch to Pond Inlet to establish the first shore station there for Robert Kinnes's Dundee-based whaling and trading firm. Duval remained in northern Baffin Island until 1907, when he returned to the United States for a winter. The following year, he went out again and for the next eight years ran a post for Kinnes at Durban Harbour on the Baffin coast of Davis Strait. In 1916, he joined Henry Toke Munn's* Arctic Gold Exploration Syndicate, which was, despite its name, a fur-trading company; he and his family accompanied Munn to Southampton Island, where they traded for two years. Duval returned to Cumberland Sound in 1918, and established a post for Munn at Usualuk, the American Harbour of the whalers. He remained there until 1922; in that year, he returned to the United States again and spent the winter with relatives in New Jersey.

The following year, the Canadian government employed Duval as interpreter for the trial at Pond Inlet of the Inuit charged with the murder of the trader Robert Janes, the first trial in the High Arctic. In interpreting the words of the judge and the verdict of the jury against the three Inuit accused, Duval, a man who had long straddled two immensely different cultures, felt an empathy for the Inuit who could not possibly, he thought, understand the implications of the proceedings of which they were a part.

Back in Cumberland Sound, Duval rejoined his family. That same year he applied for naturalization as a British subject. The year held many changes for Duval and for the Inuit of Cumberland Sound. In that year, Munn sold his syndicate to the Hudson's Bay Company, which now had a monopoly on trade in the sound. As a condition of its agreement with Munn, the Company gave employment to Duval as manager of the outpost it opened at Usualuk. In 1924, he established a new outpost for the Company at Livingstone Fiord, but it was unsuccessful and closed the following year. Duval's health was poor—he was by then sixty-seven years old—and he returned to New Jersey for another year after the post's closure.

In the latter half of the 1920s, Pangnirtung served as a base for official government scientific activity in southern Baffin Island. Geologists, naturalists, and map makers explored Cumberland Sound and beyond. Some of them met the old man of Usualuk, whom they rightly recognized as a living store of knowledge on the Inuit and their land. Maurice Haycock, a geologist, was made welcome in the Duval home, as was Dewey Soper, who had first met Duval aboard the CGS *Arctic* in 1923. The Duval home was laid out in the traditional manner of an Inuit dwelling so that Aullaqiaq, by then totally blind, could more easily perform household duties. Duval, pleased to have the company of English-speaking visitors, would open his home to these guests and chat long into the night on those rare occasions when scientists like Haycock or Soper stopped by. In failing health, he was, nonetheless, a man content, devoted to his wife and family, and expressing no regrets about the unusual life he had chosen to live.

William Duval died at Usualuk on 8 June 1931. The Royal Canadian Mounted Police went there to take his body to Pangnirtung for burial, but Duval's son-in-law, Akpalialuk, objected: it had been the old man's wish to be buried in the shadow of the mountain at Usualuk, and Akpalialuk buried him there. Another mountain, however, bears his name. Mount Duval, rising 1,700 feet behind the community of Pangnirtung, had already, during his lifetime, been named in his honour by his naturalist friend Dewey Soper.

William Duval chose to make the Arctic his home. A man living in two realities, he helped those of both his native and his chosen cultures to understand each other's worlds. Recorded history has had little to say about William Duval, but elderly Inuit of Baffin Island, especially those of Pangnirtung, where many of his descendants live today, remember Sivutiksaq with warmth and admiration.

Kenn Harper

HENRY TOKE MUNN
(1864–1952)

Henry Toke Munn was very much the English gentleman. Born in 1864, he came to Canada at the age of twenty-two and was nearly killed in a shoot-up in the streets of Montreal on the very day of his landing. He became a farmer and then a horse-breeder in Manitoba, and, by 1894, he was hunting musk-oxen and wood buffalo in the far northwest. He subsequently prospected around Kootenay, joined the Yukon gold rush as a storekeeper, and acquired the title of "Captain" while serving in the South African War. While prospecting for gold in northern Ontario, he met George Bartlett, a Newfoundlander who possessed a map that had belonged to the dying cooper of a Dundee whaler, who had found "gold" on Baffin Island. In 1912, Munn and Bartlett chartered the former gunboat *Algerine* to seek the gold: they found none and had their ship crushed by ice for their trouble. The next year, Munn formed the Arctic Gold Exploration Syndicate, whose shareholders were mainly English gentry, led by Lord Lascelles. They purchased the ketch *Albert,* built in 1889 as a hospital ship for the North Sea fishery and since engaged in whaling ventures off Baffin Island under various owners. In 1914, *Albert* dropped off Munn and another man to trade and to search for gold just north of Baffin: that year was enough to convince Munn that there was no gold.

Photograph of Henry Toke Munn. Courtesy of the Scott Polar Research Institute, Cambridge, U.K.

Munn shifted his energies to trade. In 1916, he was left for a two-year stay on Southampton Island with six Inuit families. In 1919, he visited his agents at several arctic posts, but did not stay himself; and he spent the winter of 1920–21 at Button Point, his original station north of Baffin Island. At the end of that stay, he found the Hudson's Bay Company moving north from Hudson Strait in such force that he could not compete, and Munn's backers soon convinced him to sell out, adding the humiliating provison that he should never trade in the Arctic again. In the summer of 1923, he sailed in the Hudson's Bay Company steamer to turn his syndicate's assets over to its new owners, and a series of incidents intensified his long-standing dislike of the Company to a deep resentment, mixed with remorse at having to commit "his" Inuit to the mercy of those he could not trust.

Captain Munn lived in both Canada and England for the next ten years, but arthritis caused him to move to the Seychelles Islands in the Indian Ocean, where he died in 1952. His body was committed to the sea, drifted ashore, and had to be committed again.

In the early years of his retirement, Munn not only encouraged others to break the monopoly of the Hudson's Bay Company, but he waged a constant propaganda war against it. In newspapers, magazines, and books he described the Inuit as "a hunter by task and heredity"—a notion few would hold today—and he claimed that the Hudson's Bay Company created previously unknown wants, thereby depleting wildlife and forcing the Inuit to grow dependent on trapping. He was milder against missionaries, who made the Inuit "soft": here, he expressed a crude form of social Darwinism. Of course, Munn distinguished between his own trading and that of the Hudson's Bay Company; he argued that his own low overheads meant that he did not give credit, or could not give credit, and that he avoided "spoiling," by which he meant changing the only way of life for which he believed Inuit to be genetically suited. He claimed that his party had left Southampton Island because he discovered that they were depleting caribou herds there.

Of Captain Munn's three books, the most interesting is the novel *Home Is the Hunter* (1930), which is largely wish-fulfillment. The hero is a half-Inuit reared in Scotland (as one of Munn's colleagues was said to have been) who, after besting several rivals (as Munn in real life did not), settles down to live the life of an Inuit because his heredity fits him for that life (as Munn's did not). Modern thought would utterly reject such hereditary direction, but Munn did not know that. It is astonishing that despite his many years spent among Inuit, he never learned much of their language: perhaps he felt he was genetically constrained not to learn it.

One of Henry Toke Munn's lesser complaints against the Hudson's Bay Company was that when it acquired his beloved ketch *Albert,* she ran on the rocks off the Scottish coast, and he apparently thought that was the end of her. In fact, she was repaired and sold to the Faroes to begin a new career as mother-ship to fishing vessels off Greenland. After many adventures, including attack by German aircraft in World War II, she was finally abandoned after being damaged by ice in Baffin Bay as late as 1968. The ketch had outlived Munn.

Further Readings

Munn, Henry Toke. 1932. *Prairie Trails and Arctic By-Ways.* London: Hurst and Blackett.

_____ and Elizabeth Sprigge. 1930. *Home Is the Hunter.* London: John Lane the Bodley Head.

White, G. 1977. "Scottish Traders to Baffin Island 1910–1930." *Maritime History* 5(1): 34–50.

Gavin White

HECTOR PITCHFORTH
(1886–1927)

Hector Pitchforth was born in India in 1886, and was brought up mainly in Leeds. Although deaf from a very early age, he qualified as an engineer and, in World War I, served with the fishing fleet. In 1918, he sailed for Baffin Island in the auxiliary schooner *Erme* for the Sabellum Trading Company, which was quite the most irresponsible of the various concerns trading between the end of whaling and the entry to the farther North of the Hudson's Bay Company. John Pearson was the captain, though the legendary James Mutch was in over-all command, but the voyage ended abruptly when the German submarine *U-53* boarded *Erme* and set her afire. All survived, and Pitchforth returned to the fishing fleet. In 1919, he became engineer on *Erme*'s replacement, a former racing yacht built in 1876 and named for a succession of damsels, the last being *Vera*. She was frozen in for a month, but visited all trading posts and returned safely to Scotland. In 1920, she deposited Pitchforth at Cape Henry Kater on the east Baffin coast as a trader.

Pitchforth traded through the winter of 1920–21 and, unusually for a trader, made a number of sledge journeys, naming one fiord after himself. He was removed by *Vera* in 1921, but, in 1922, the vessel was crushed by ice and, more disastrously, James Mutch retired. He had been the only man who really knew the trade, and, in 1922, the Inuit agents were not supplied with goods and their furs were not collected.

Photograph of Hector Pitchforth. Courtesy of the late Ronald Pitchforth and the Scott Polar Research Institute, Cambridge, U.K.

Furthermore, the agent at Kivitoo went mad and had two people killed before being killed himself. And it was at Kivitoo that Pitchforth was settled by Sabellum's new vessel, *Rosie,* in 1923. Early in 1924, he journeyed by sledge to Kater and also south to Cumberland Sound, where the Hudson's Bay Company and the Mounted Police were now to be found.

Meanwhile, the London manager of Sabellum recruited an eighteen-year-old clerk named Wigglesworth, who was sent out on *Rosie* to join Pitchforth at Kivitoo in 1924. But, as Pitchforth wrote that summer, Kivitoo was a poor place for trade, and he was moving back to Cape Henry Kater. Since the house at Kater was only eleven by six feet, there was no room for Wigglesworth, who was sent back to Britain, together with Nauyapik, an Inuk sent to select trade goods, concerning whom Pitchforth wrote, "take him around Harrod's and Whiteley's," elegant department stores. But evidently Capt. Pearson regarded himself as Mutch's successor and on those grounds refused to move the main house from Kivitoo, though he did move Pitchforth, however reluctantly.

By this time, Pitchforth was not only deaf, but suffering from snow-blindness, though, according to impartial witnesses, otherwise fit and competent for his work. But when the Canadian government offered to have him removed by their ship in 1925, the London manager of Sabellum said Pitchforth was "endeavouring to magnify some hardship he has voluntarily undertaken."

At that point, they might have expected *Rosie* to remove Pitchforth, but she met heavy ice in 1925, Pearson fell ill, and he landed stores for Pitchforth 300 miles to the south, together with the unfortunate Nauyapik, who was also ill. Sabellum was virtually without any revenue for that year, and the London manager was reduced to assuring Pitchforth's brother that supplies had been left at an alternative point on the coast and that Pitchforth would have moved there, although he had no way of knowing what had been done and no way of getting there in any case. The manager did arrange for the Hudson's Bay Company ship to collect Pitchforth and his furs from Kivitoo in 1927, but the plans fell through, and Pitchforth was at Kater anyway.

Hector Pitchforth spent an active winter through 1924–25, though his survival was threatened by dog disease that prevented hunting for fresh meat. After that first year, he had nothing to trade and few visitors, and apparently he suffered from scurvy. He also injured his leg. On Christmas Day 1926, he wrote in his diary: "Sky a bit clearer to the Southward, a beautiful ruddy flash tinted the ice and snow most beautifully. Not in the least like Xmas to myself and I feel so ill as to be nearly helpless." A few weeks later, a traveller noted snow drifted over his doorway, and in due course the Mounted Police investigated and took his body to Pond Inlet for burial.

Astonishingly, Hector Pitchforth's death made the headlines when a ship reached Pond Inlet in the following summer: "World's Loneliest Man" and "Alone in the Arctic: Fate of a Gallant Englishman; Deserted and Starved in a Far Northern Island; Hector Pitchforth in War and Peace." Meanwhile, Sabellum refused to pay Pitchforth's wages to his heirs until they gave up his diary, which it was hoped would tell where his furs were stored. It did not, and Sabellum collapsed. In fact, the publicity was so unfavourable that this was the end of almost all the small trading concerns of that period. Pitchforth might have revived Sabellum had he lived, but in dying he destroyed it and changed the pattern of arctic trade for a generation.

Further Readings

Pitchforth, H. 1924. Personal letter to Sabellum Trading Company, 21 August 1924, Baker Library, Dartmouth College, Hanover, New Hampshire.

_____. Diary, Library of the Royal Geographical Society, London.

White, G. 1977. "Scottish Traders to Baffin Island 1910–1930." *Maritime History* 5(1): 34-50.

Gavin White

LAZAROOSIE KYAK
(1919–1976)

At age twenty-four, when Lazaroosie Kyak moved from the nomadic lifestyle of the Inuit into the regimented life of an Royal Canadian Mounted Police special constable, little did he realize that he had the innate character of a great Canadian. Kyak was born in a small Inuit hunting camp near Button Point on Bylot Island, at a time when events in history would have a profound effect on the lives and culture of his people. During his era, gold was thought to exist in the Pond Inlet region. A southern-based Arctic Gold Exploration Syndicate was established, but no gold was found; however, it was soon discovered that the real wealth of the area lay in the furs obtained from Inuit trappers. News travelled fast, and Robert Janes, a free trader from Newfoundland, arrived on the scene. A disruptive two years of questionable trading ensued, eventually resulting in a shooting incident and the death of Robert Janes. Sgt. A.H. Joy* of the Royal Canadian Mounted Police investigated the murder in 1921; his arrival in Pond Inlet coincided with that of the Hudson's Bay

Special Constable Kyak seen through window of wheelhouse, 22 May 1969. RCMP photo 69-112-C

Company, the Roman Catholic Church, and the Church of England. Clearly, the next two decades would introduce dramatic changes in the Inuit way of life; Kyak matured during this period of influence and change.

Married in 1936, Kyak and his wife, Letia, raised a large family. Other members of Kyak's family were destined to play a role in another chapter of arctic history. In 1944, the RCMP motor schooner *St. Roch*, under the command of Sgt. Henry Larsen,* arrived at Pond Inlet on its east-west voyage through the Northwest Passage. Kyak's daughter, brother, and mother, along with several others from the Pond Inlet area, were added to the passenger manifest. Their purpose was to assist with hunting and with the preparation of winter clothing for the crew. However, the *St. Roch* completed the passage in one season, and the Inuit were sent back to Pond Inlet from Herschel Island by dogsled—a remarkable journey which took several years.

Kyak was engaged by the RCMP to assist many patrols out of Pond Inlet during the early 1940s. Members of the RCMP who had the good fortune to travel with Kyak recognized his sense of justice and protection. His dedication to duty eventually led to his engagement as a special constable in September 1943. Being an ardent seaman, he patrolled hundreds of miles of Baffin and Ellesmere islands' coastline. Kyak realized the potential of the site for the existing community of Grise Fiord and was instrumental in its selection. Few can boast of putting in as many miles by dog-team and boat patrol. Originating out of Grise Fiord, Pond Inlet, and Craig Harbour, Kyak's sledge patrols encompassed an area from Eureka on Ellesmere Island east to Greenland, and as far south as Foxe Basin and Home Bay. One must bear in mind that the average dog-team trip from Craig Harbour to Eureka could easily extend over several months, depending on weather and ice conditions.

In recognition of his outstanding service to the RCMP and Canada, Kyak was awarded the Order of Canada in

Lazaroosie Kyak and his wife, on the occasion of his receiving the Order of Canada award, 1970

1970, the first member of the force to receive such an honour. Later that same year, he found himself meeting and conversing with Her Majesty Queen Elizabeth II at Resolute Bay.

Kyak retired from active service with the RCMP in 1971, to return to the life of hunting and trapping he had relinquished twenty-eight years earlier. Unfortunately, the long and arduous patrols had taken their toll, and, when still a relatively young man, he died suddenly in 1976 while visiting his daughter in Frobisher Bay.

Unwritten stories about the adventures and achievements of this exceptional man abound. He will be long remembered by those members of the RCMP who served with him. Officers and constables always said that "on patrol Kyak was in complete command," and no one ever doubted the truth of that statement.

The best appreciation of Lazaroosie Kyak's contribution to his people has to be understood in the context of the traumatic era in which he grew up. He emerged from a primitive lifestyle to a completely new way of life, and he did so without losing a strong sense of his own cultural values. His one desire, as a member of the RCMP, was to provide a bridge between the old and the new. Many in today's Arctic owe a debt of gratitude for his patience and quiet understanding.

R.S. Pilot

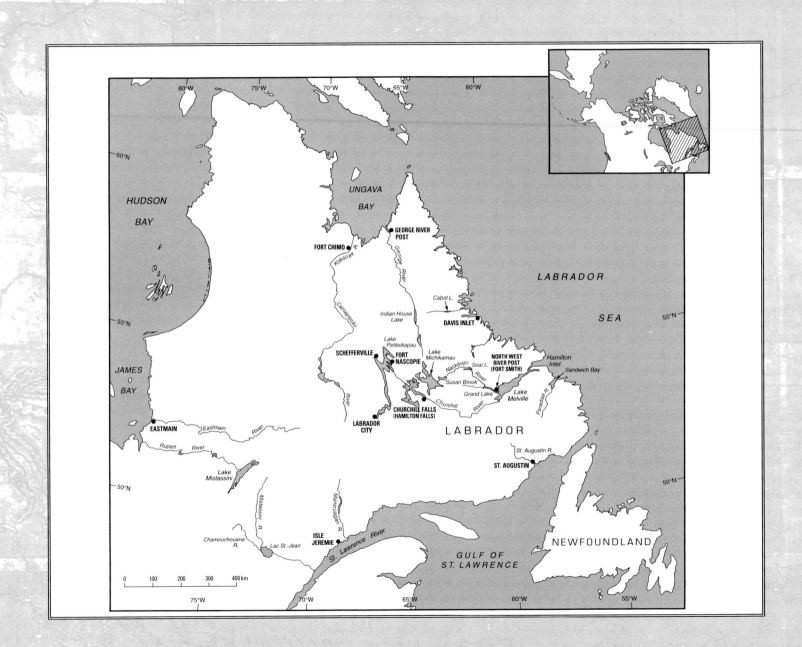

HUDSON
BAY

JAMES
O
BAY

UNGAVA
BAY

GEORGE RIVER
POST

FORT CHIMO

Koksoak R.

Caniapiscau

George River

Cabot L.

Indian House Lake

LABRADOR

SEA

DAVIS INLET

Lake Petitsikapau

SCHEFFERVILLE

FORT NASCOPIE

Lake Michikamau

Naskaupi

Seal L.

River

NORTH WEST RIVER POST (FORT SMITH)

Hamilton Inlet

Sandwich Bay

Susan Brook

Churchill

Grand Lake

River

Lake Melville

Paradise R.

CHURCHILL FALLS
(HAMILTON FALLS)

LABRADOR CITY

River

Eastmain

EASTMAIN

Eastmain

River

LABRADOR

Rupert

River

St. Augustin R.

Lake Mistassini

ST. AUGUSTIN

Mistassini R.

Manicuagan R.

Chamouchouane R.

Lac St.-Jean

ISLE JEREMIE

St. Lawrence River

NEWFOUNDLAND

GULF OF
ST. LAWRENCE

0   100   200   300   400 km

UNIT
❧15❧

John McLean, William Brooks Cabot, A.P. Low,
Leonidas Hubbard, Jr., Mina Benson Hubbard, George Elson

Like the Barrens, this extreme northeast section of the continent has evolved an enchanted character of its own. Encompassing the peninsula between the Atlantic Ocean and Hudson Bay, "The Labrador"—as it is often termed—was seen as the final vestige of true wilderness left in North America at the beginning of the twentieth century. Several of the profiles in this unit are of men and women who responded to what seemed a final opportunity to open up true *terra incognita* and to make a name for themselves. Others show the lives and efforts of men whose motives may have been commercial, but who must have felt that same attraction that lured young Hubbard to his death.

JOHN MCLEAN (ca. 1798–1890)

We tend to picture the nineteenth century Hudson's Bay Company as a vast, impersonal monopoly extending its trade routes and power throughout Canada. If we associate any particular name with the Company, it is probably that of Sir George Simpson,* the tightfisted and wily Scot whose iron rule as governor brought him the title of the "Little Emperor." Yet the Company's wealth was founded, in large part, on the industry and skill of its traders in the field—common men, too often forgotten, such as John McLean, another Scot, who fortunately provided the means for rescuing his name from oblivion in his book, *Notes of a Twenty-five years' Service in the Hudson's Bay Territory*.

McLean was born on the Isle of Mull, Scotland, in 1798 or 1800. It is apparent from his book that he was middle class in origin and well educated. After initial brief employment by the North West Company, he entered the service of the Hudson's Bay Company following the union of the two companies in 1821, and, until 1833, worked as a fur trader in the Ottawa Valley. In his account of those years, we note McLean's cunning in dealing with competitors and Indians, the risks he took to advance the Company's interests, and the sacrifice he made in withdrawing from society to the loneliness of life in the bush. We sense too his physical toughness, daring, and drive to succeed. There was also a testy and sardonic element in him that bespeaks pride. Yet for all this, he could admit to shedding "tears of joy" over a narrow escape from danger, and we see other evidence, occasionally in his treatment of native peoples,

Portrait of John McLean. National Archives of Canada/C-009474

that he was a man of some feeling. McLean was a complex and gifted man.

In 1833, he was transferred to the Company's western department, and his book describes his trek overland to the North Pacific slope of the Rockies (New Caledonia), the difficulties of travel being, as usual, understated. He was struck by the beauty of this territory, which reminded him of "his own poor, yet beloved native land." It was McLean's destiny to cross on foot and by boat and canoe virtually the whole of what is now Canada.

In 1837, he began the greatest adventure of his life, when he was appointed by Simpson to take charge of what was termed the "Ungava venture," i.e., the quixotic attempt to open up a fur trade in the interior of the Labrador peninsula. McLean arrived at the recently built Fort Chimo on the Koksoak River late in 1837, and proceeded with the effort to establish an overland supply and trading route between Ungava Bay and Lake Melville. Simpson's scheme was to provision Fort Chimo through some kind of inland navigation from Fort Smith (North West River post). McLean gamely undertook this virtually impossible task, and what is remarkable is how much he accomplished in obedience to Simpson's instructions. In the first three months of 1838, for example, he trekked back and forth between Fort Chimo and Fort Smith—a feat that had, however, been accomplished earlier, in 1834, by Erland Erlandson, another HBC employee and McLean's coworker. It was apparent that the interior could not be supplied in winter owing to deep, soft snowdrifts: the only way was by canoe. In the summer of 1839, with Erlandson dispatched to Lake Petitsikapau on the plateau of Labrador to build Fort Nascopie, McLean led a party of men along the coastline of Ungava Bay to the mouth of the George River, and headed upstream by canoe. In August, after prolonged torture by mosquitoes and bitter labour, "half starved, half naked, and half devoured," he arrived at Lake Petitsikapau. After a day's rest, he, Erlandson, and two others set out for the Labrador coast. They reached Lake Michikamau, found its outlet, and headed downriver. Before long, their progress was stopped by rapids, and a day later they saw "one of the greatest spectacles in the world," the "stupendous" Grand (now Churchill) Falls. McLean was the first European to describe the falls. No way around the cataract could be found, and the party, "with heavy hearts and weary limbs," returned to Fort Nascopie, and thence to Ungava Bay.

In 1841, McLean did find a navigable route around the falls through a string of small lakes. In effect, he showed that the practical way to approach the interior of Labrador was upstream from Lake Melville rather than from Ungava Bay. To him, this discovery made Fort Chimo unnecessary, and McLean recommended that it be abandoned. He was, in fact, disenchanted with the whole Ungava enterprise and with Simpson's leadership of the Company. In 1842, he was authorized to withdraw from Fort Chimo and, the following year, the post was closed down.

A scholar has recently argued that McLean's recommendation to close the fort was "wrong," that it was abandoned just as it was starting to make money. He suggests as well that McLean's antipathy to Simpson may have been a factor in leading him to make his recommendation. (Fort Chimo was in fact reestablished in 1866.) But whatever McLean may have failed to do in his years in Labrador, his brilliant expeditions were landmarks in the story of northern exploration. His qualities were undeniable.

After his return in 1843 from a furlough in Britain, McLean was posted to Fort Simpson on the Mackenzie River, but on seeing evidence of a "cold and callous heart" in Simpson's treatment of him, in 1846 he resigned from the Company. His life thereafter was obscure. He spent nearly a decade as manager of a bank in Guelph, Ontario, and for twenty-five years thereafter served as clerk of the division court in nearby Elora. His last seven years were spent with his daughter in Victoria, British Columbia. He died in 1890.

John McLean in middle life was described as "a tall, straight, thin man, about six feet tall, and active in all his ways. He had a strong, rugged face and prominent nose, and was clean-shaven, except for side whiskers."

Further Readings

Cooke, Alan. 1969. *The Ungava Venture of the Hudson's Bay Company 1830–1843.* Ph.D. thesis, Cambridge University.

Davies, K.G., ed. 1963. *Northern Quebec and Labrador Journals and Correspondence 1819–35.* London: Hudson's Bay Record Society.

McLean, John. 1849. *Notes of a Twenty-five Years' Service in the Hudson's Bay Territory.* London: R. Bentley.

Wallace, W.S. 1932. "Biographical Introduction." In *Notes of a Twenty-five Years' Service in the Hudson's Bay Territory* by John McLean. Reprint. Toronto: Champlain Society.

Patrick O'Flaherty

WILLIAM BROOKS CABOT (1858–1949)

Between 1899 and 1924, Indian hunters in the Quebec-Labrador peninsula regularly encountered a tattered gentleman from Boston, Massachusetts, wandering about their country. A preeminent engineer of his day, William Brooks Cabot built aqueducts in New York, bridges across the Connecticut and the Charles rivers, and subway tunnels under New York City, but, for more than twenty years, his passion for northern travel could not be assuaged, and he made annual pilgrimages into the remote regions of the far northeast.

Cabot grew up in the central Connecticut River valley, having been born into a prosperous banking family in Brattleboro, Vermont. It was on the Connecticut that Cabot honed his camping skills and wilderness appetite; it pulled his imagination north toward Canada and led him, as a young man, to explore the lakes at its source.

The beginning of what Cabot called his travels in the "Indian North" came during the winter of 1899, when he made a long overland trek from Lac Saint-Jean to the Hudson's Bay Company post at Mistassini. He was accompanied on the journey by two Indian companions, one of whom—John Bastian—had previously crisscrossed the Labrador peninsula in the service of A.P. Low,* of the Geological Survey of Canada.

It was from Bastian that Cabot heard at first hand tales of the Labrador Plateau: a land of immense lakes and uncharted rivers, where vast herds of caribou roamed and where a shadowy, little-known group of Indians still lived for the most part beyond the ken of European eyes. Cabot's life-long fascination with wilderness travel and with Indians, which had smoldered while he erected his professional career, was reignited. With the avowed goal of learning the

William Brooks Cabot, wearing a pointed Naskapi (Innu) caribou-skin coat, Labrador, 1903. From the William Brooks Cabot collection, National Anthropological Archives, Smithsonian Institution, Washington, D.C.

language and the way of life of the region's small bands of Indian hunters, he spent eight summers (1903–10) in northern Labrador among the Naskapi (or, as they prefer to be called, the Innu), five summers (1913, 1915–17, 1920) along the Quebec North Shore with Indians who traded out of the St. Augustin post, three summers (1921, 1923, 1924) with Indian families who traded at North West River post on Lake Melville, and winter cross-country trips in the Chamouchouane and Mistassini rivers region in 1899, 1902, 1905, 1909, 1910, and 1913.

In 1903, Cabot travelled to Labrador with the intention of intercepting the Naskapi Indians when they came out to trade at the Hudson's Bay Company post at Davis Inlet. Cabot shared the voyage north from Newfoundland with Leonidas Hubbard Jr.,* who was planning to explore the interior of Labrador and descend the George River to Ungava Bay. Hoping to benefit from the older man's experiences, Hubbard urged Cabot to join his party. Intrigued by the offer, Cabot nevertheless declined, having set his sights on finding the Naskapi on the coast. Unprepared and overbold, Hubbard's party plunged into the Labrador wilderness, where they went astray and where Hubbard eventually succumbed to starvation and exposure.

Cabot's own trip was far more propitious. He was successful in meeting with the Naskapi hunters at Davis Inlet, and, although unable to accompany them back into the interior, the visit provided the foundation for subsequent encounters. In 1904 and 1905, Cabot renewed his contact with the Naskapi, who encouraged him to come inland with them. In 1906, having worked out a river and portage route onto the Labrador Plateau, Cabot reached Lake Mistinibi, where he met with a small Naskapi band camped at a caribou crossing. During the preceding two weeks, the hunters had speared almost fifteen hundred caribou as they swam across the narrows.

Cabot's last trip to northern Labrador was in 1910. Breaking from his tradition of travelling alone, or with a single companion, Cabot brought a party of four men across the Labrador Plateau to the large Naskapi camp at Tshinutivish on Indian House Lake. The Naskapi were disturbed with this sudden invasion; nonetheless, the party was housed for the night and fed. On the return journey to the coast, Cabot found that a cache he had established on his way inland had been burned by a party of Indians. This was a crushing and unexpected rebuttal from the people Cabot had worked hard to befriend. The Naskapi motives for destroying Cabot's cache are not clear, but it is apparent that they never completely understood his reasons for coming into their country or the sudden expansion in the size of his party.

The events of the 1910 trip marked an end to Cabot's excursions in the caribou country of northern Labrador, but his interest in northeastern Indians was unabated. After a hiatus of several years, Cabot shifted his attention to the southeastern corner of the Quebec-Labrador peninsula, where, as was his pattern, he persuaded Indian families to let him accompany them on their summer hunts. Cabot's reputation had preceded him, and he took pleasure in a growing familiarity with the language and customs of his Indian hosts.

During a trip in 1920, from St. Augustin overland to Sandwich Bay on the Labrador coast, he cut his leg severely while chopping wood. After years of "knocking about" in the subarctic wilderness, the accident on the headwaters of the Paradise River, with his life dependent on the resources of his Indian companions, must have figured significantly in his decision to finally curtail his wilderness journeys. There had been a brief sortie in 1918 to Pelican Narrows in northern Saskatchewan, and there were subsequent trips to North West River post on Lake Melville, but these lacked the rigour of his earlier travels.

Cabot had long sustained an interest in Algonquian languages, manifest both by his publication of Father G. Lemoine's *Dictionnaire Français-Montagnais* (1901), and by a study of New England Indian place names.

Cabot died quietly at his home in Boston a few days short of his ninety-first birthday. During the course of his life, he had seen the last of the empty spaces on the maps of the Quebec-Labrador peninsula filled in. His own geographical contributions were relatively minor ones, based in part on the maps he had had his Indian companions draw for him. One of these maps—the original had been over seventy feet long, drawn in the sand of a riverbank by an old Naskapi (Innu) hunter—was part of the evidence presented in the Labrador boundary dispute.

In recognition of his accomplishments, William Brooks

Ostinitsu, a Naskapi (Innu) leader, stirring a broth of crushed caribou bones, Mistinibi, 1906. From the William Brooks Cabot collection, National Anthropological Archives, Smithsonian Institution, Washington, D.C.

Cabot's name was given to the prominent lake along the Indian route from the George River to the Labrador coast, as well as to the subspecies of caribou from northern Labrador. Cabot was neither geographer, explorer, nor scientist, although he made contributions in all three arenas; rather, he preferred to think of himself as "a minor wanderer," a man with the means to pursue his own intensely personal quest in the North.

Further Readings

Cabot, William Brooks. 1912. *In Northern Labrador*. Boston: Gorham Press.

_____. 1913. "The Indians." In *Labrador*, edited by Wilfred T. Grenfell. New York: Macmillan.

_____. 1920. *Labrador*. Boston: Small and Maynard.

_____. 1870–1949. Journals, manuscripts, letters: William Brooks Cabot collection. National Anthropological Archives, Smithsonian Institution, Washington, D.C.

Stephen Loring

A.P. Low (1861–1942)

The perimeters of the Quebec-Labrador peninsula were well known to European explorers, traders, and missionaries by the very early nineteenth century. Except for the indigenous peoples, however, no one knew very much about the interior and its resources. The only notable accounts before the 1890s were John McLean's *Twenty-Five Years Service in the Hudson Bay Territory* (1849) and Hind's *The Labrador Peninsula* (1863). The man who first gave the public any extensive account of the interior travel routes and the geological, forest, and hydrological resources was A.P. Low. Low's written reports of twenty-three seasons in northern Canada constitute one of the most significant substantiated achievements in Canadian exploration. Many of these seasons were spent on the Quebec-Labrador peninsula.

Albert Peter Low was born in Montreal in 1861 into a Loyalist family that had left the United States in 1783. Immediately after graduating in applied science from McGill University in 1882, Low began his association with the Geological Survey of Canada (GSC). The three decades from 1880 to 1910 were particularly heady and exciting years for the GSC. Between Confederation in 1867 and 1880, Canada's size had increased significantly with the addition of Manitoba, British Columbia, and all the lands of the Hudson's Bay Company. Yet written scientific descriptions of the actual topography and the forest and geological resources of many areas did not exist. The map of Canada was filled in during

A. P. Low

these decades by a small, but exceptionally adventurous and capable group of geologists. They included some of the most significant names in Canadian exploration: Alfred Selwyn, G.M. Dawson, R.G. McConnell, J.B. Tyrrell,* Robert Bell, Charles Camsell,* and Low.

On his first trip into the Quebec-Labrador region in 1884–85, at the age of twenty-four, Low became a central figure in "the Lake Mistassini incident." The expedition, a joint effort of the GSC, the Quebec government, and the Quebec Geographic Society, was led by John Bignell, a veteran surveyor aged sixty-seven. Travelling northward from the St. Lawrence, the party eventually set up a winter base at the HBC post on Lake Mistassini after several days of extremely cold travel on minimal rations. Disagreement with Bignell had apparently been festering for some time, and Low took action toward a resolution. He left Mistassini on 2 February, travelling by snowshoe and dog-team to Quebec City and thence by train westward, arriving in Ottawa on 2 March. Here he was given command of the expedition, and by 29 April he was back at Mistassini—a phenomenal feat illustrating the initiative and physical strength that was to sustain Low through many more seasons on the trail. In the spring, Low finished the work on Lake Mistassini, determining it to be about 100 miles long and 15 miles wide, not the immense interior sea that Indian tales had suggested. The party left the region via the Rupert River in the fall of 1885.

Over the next few seasons, Low continued work in the Hudson Bay watershed, surveying the islands in James Bay and exploring the large area on the east coast of Hudson Bay, then known as "the Eastmain." The three years 1889–91 found Low doing geological mapping in the more well-known and settled regions of Champlain, Portneuf, Quebec, and Montmorency counties.

The travels of the succeeding four years were chronicled in Low's "Report on Exploration in the Labrador Peninsula along the Eastmain, Koksoak, Hamilton, Manicuagan and Portions of Other Rivers in 1892–93–94–95." Low traversed and crisscrossed the peninsula using a variety of routes. On the 1893–94 trip, during which the party wintered over at North West River post, Low covered over 4,700 miles—2,900 by canoe, 1,000 by ship, 500 by dog team, and 1,000 on foot. Not only were the technical aspects of the main travel routes detailed, but his report included extensive historical, geological, botanical, meteorological, entomological, ornithological, and ethnographic information that, to this day, constitutes a standard reference on the region. Its accuracy is remarkable when we realize the

Crew of the *Neptune* in winter dress, 1903-1904, Commander A.P. Low standing fifth from the right. J. D. Moodie, photographer/National Archives of Canada/PA-53567.

report was compiled without aerial photography or sophisticated measuring and sensing equipment. In addition, Low was continually dealing with the exigencies of northern wilderness travel: extreme cold, insufferable insects, exhausting physical labour, and the frequent need to hunt and fish.

Low's visual estimate of the volume of water at Hamilton Falls on the Churchill River demonstrates the quality of his field work. Judged by Low to be, on average, 50,000 cubic feet per second, the flow was calculated at 49,000 cubic feet per second by Brinco Limited in the 1960s, when hydro development was taking place. Low was the first to identify the extensive iron deposits around Schefferville and Labrador City. He was also the first man to realize that the centre of the Labrador Plateau had been the pivot for a continental ice sheet and was, in fact, part of the Laurentian Shield. On journeys from 1896 through 1899, the work on the interior was complemented by extensive mapping and surveying of the Hudson Bay and Ungava coasts. After a brief period in private business, Low assumed command of the *Neptune* for its 1903–04 voyage to the eastern Arctic, which resulted in Canada officially claiming the Arctic archipelago.

In 1906, at the age of forty-five, Albert Peter Low retired from active field work to become the director of the Geological Survey of Canada. Although his tenure was only eighteen months, he oversaw the transfer of the GSC from the Interior department to the new Mines department. In 1907, Low became the first deputy minister of the department of Mines, but, within a few months, he was stricken by what is thought to have been a cerebral hemorrhage and, soon after that, by spinal meningitis. He never fully recovered and eventually retired in 1913 under a cloud of controversy over his physical inability to carry out his work. Amazingly, the strength and endurance of his youth did not totally fail Low, for he lived out a long, apparently quiet, retirement in Ottawa, ultimately dying in virtual obscurity in 1942 at the age of eighty-one.

Further Readings

Alcock, Frederick J. 1944. "Memorial of Albert Peter Low." *Proceedings of the Geological Society of America*, annual report for 1943.

Caron, Fabien. 1965. "Albert Peter Low et L'Exploration du Québec-Labrador." *Cahiers de Géographie de Québec* 18 (av-sept): 169–82.

Low, Albert Peter. 1895. *Report on Exploration in the Labrador Peninsula along the East Main, Koksoak, Hamilton, Manicuagan and Portions of Other Rivers in 1892–93–94–95*. Ottawa: Geological Survey of Canada. Annual report, vol. 8, Part L.

Hugh Stewart

LEONIDAS HUBBARD, JR.
(1872–1903)

As the twentieth century dawned, North America was no longer *terra incognita*. Frontiers had been pushed back, much of the Great Plains and primaeval forests had been tamed by agriculture, and society was becoming settled and urban. Yet the pioneer spirit lingered on in such adventurers as Robert Edwin Peary,* Norman Duncan, Wilfred Grenfell, and others, whose imaginations, fired by nineteenth-century aspiration, drove them to the northern fringes of the continent in pursuit of discovery and inspiration. One such man born out of his time was the explorer Leonidas Hubbard Jr.

Hubbard was born in Michigan in 1872, the son of a restless pioneer father and a loving mother. His childhood was apparently one of parental indulgence, outdoor pleasure, and literary romanticizing. Tales of frontier life and the Indians stirred him deeply. Most men outgrow their boyish fantasies. Despite an education at the University of Michigan (1893–97), subsequent labour in the hard field of journalism, and even marriage to a woman two years his senior (in 1901), Hubbard persisted in his dreams of glory. His was a simple, dogged, idealistic nature. Lack of confidence was something he did not experience; his faith in his saviour was complete. A small man physically, he was determined to do a "big thing" and make his reputation. In 1901, he told his friend Dillon Wallace, a New York lawyer, of his intention to enter the Labrador interior, and two years later, on 15 July 1903, after elaborate preparations, Hubbard, Wallace, and a James Bay Indian of mixed blood named George Elson* set out by canoe from the North West River post of the Hudson's Bay Company into Grand Lake, the northwest extension of Lake Melville.

Leonidas Hubbard, Jr., at the outset. From Dillon Wallace's *The Lure of the Labrador Wild* (1905)

Hubbard's plan was to proceed up the Naskaupi River to Lake Michikamau (now incorporated in the Smallwood Reservoir) on the interior plateau. He would then observe both the annual migration of the caribou herds across the George River and the hunting habits of the Naskapi-Montagnais Indians (Innu), all of which would provide material for articles in the magazine employing him, *Outing*. The George River would take him to Ungava Bay. Thus, his was to be a canoe trip across one of the earth's most forbidding landscapes. He had chosen the more northerly route into the wilderness deliberately. A way to Lake Michikamau by the Hamilton (now Churchill) River had been explored previously, and A.P. Low,* of the Geological Survey of Canada, had published an elaborate map of the region in 1896. Lake Michikamau itself had also been explored and described by Low. But Hubbard wished to plunge into "a region where no footsteps would be found to guide him," and over which "still brooded the fascinating twilight of the mysterious unknown."

In his 1896 map, Low had tentatively sketched, from hearsay, an inaccurate outline of Grand Lake, at the northwestern end of which was a single river. Some miles inland, the map showed this stream dividing into "North West River," which led westward to Lake Michikamau, and the "Nascaupee River," which flowed from Seal Lake in the north. It was this speculative rendering of the geography of Grand Lake that guided the Hubbard expedition. In the early afternoon of 16 July, the men reached what they thought was the mouth of the river depicted on Low's map, and headed inland. This was the error that led to disaster. What they had found was not the Naskaupi but the much smaller, unnavigable Susan Brook.

Hubbard, "ragged and almost barefooted." From Dillon Wallace's *The Lure of the Labrador Wild* (1905)

For two weeks the men dragged, pushed, and carried their canoe and equipment up the narrow, deep valley of the Susan, wading and tumbling in the water, scraping through thick brush, portaging around shoals, beating off the dreadful Labrador mosquitoes, and enduring the heat of late July. When they emerged from this "cursed" valley, more long portages and disappointments stretched ahead. In the evenings, Hubbard read Kipling and the bible to cheer himself and his companions, but they bitterly knew the drudgery of the coming day. On they went, sprinkling the plateau of Labrador with the toponymy of failure. As they plodded on, the days grew shorter, the nights colder, the weather stormier, and food scarcer. Hubbard and Wallace had taken with them only one pair of moccasins each, and, after two weeks, these were wearing through; before long they were practically barefoot. This was but one in a catalogue of blunders. Their more serious mistake was planning to live mostly off the fish and game of the wilderness. In effect, after a month of grinding work, still less than halfway to Michikamau, they were starving. By September, as Wallace later reported, "our bones were sticking through the skin."

The desperate journey back to safety started, too late, on 21 September. They ate the garbage discarded on the way inland, but game eluded them. Winter relentlessly closed in on them. Hubbard gave up the struggle and was left behind in his tent in the valley of the Susan Brook, where he perished. The two others foundered on toward Grand Lake, and were rescued.

Hubbard did not reach Lake Michikamau; but he did see it, from a distance, on 9 September, and recorded in his diary that the sight of the lake "made it a BIG DAY." Thus his boyishness continued, though we note in him as

he proceeded with the journey signs of growing maturity. "What does glory and all that amount to, after all?" he once said to Wallace, adding, "I've let my work and my ambition bother me too much." A quality of innocence and generosity stayed with him to the end.

Perhaps the most telling comment on the ill-fated expedition was made by Wallace in a letter to his sister on 3 December 1903, from North West River post. "I will merely say," he wrote, "that we plunged madly into the interior of an unknown country, into regions never before trod by white men, with almost no provisions." Wallace, and Hubbard's formidable Canadian wife, Mina Benson Hubbard,* undertook separate journeys up the Naskaupi in 1905, in order to accomplish what Leonidas Hubbard Jr. had set out to do. Both expeditions successfully reached Ungava Bay.

Further Readings

Anon. 1904. "Hubbard's terrible death in Labrador." *New York Times.* March 24: 1–2.

Berton, Pierre. 1978. *The Wild Frontier.* Toronto: McClelland and Stewart.

Hubbard, Mina Benson. 1908. *A Woman's Way Through Unknown Labrador.* London: John Murray.

Wallace, Dillon. 1905. *The Lure of the Labrador Wild.* New York: Fleming H. Revell.

_____. 1907. *The Long Labrador Trail.* Toronto: Fleming H. Revell.

Patrick O'Flaherty

MINA BENSON HUBBARD
(1870–1956)

In July, 1905, a young widow, Mina Hubbard, embarked upon a 576-mile journey through a relatively unexplored region of central Labrador. This trip was to complete the work left unfinished by her late husband, Leonidas Hubbard, Jr.* He had conceived the idea of finding and mapping a navigable water route from North West River post on Lake Melville to the George River post. Essentially this route traced the length of the Naskaupi River to its headwaters, crossed the height of land to the George River, and followed its waters down to Ungava Bay. Mr. Hubbard had set out in 1903, but his party was underequipped and misled by primitive maps. The venture cost him his life.

Mina Benson Hubbard became the first white woman to travel over the territory: she was preceded by only two white men. In 1838 John McLean,* a Hudson's Bay Company employee, had passed through much of the region, and, in 1875–76, Père Lacasse, a Roman Catholic missionary, travelled over the area. Mina, however, produced the first reliable maps of the Naskaupi and George river watersheds. Her book *A Woman's Way Through Unknown Labrador* and her diaries provide descriptions of her encounters with the Naskapi and Montagnais Indians (Innu), and of the last great herds of Labrador's barrenland caribou. She was one of the last people to view the life of central Labrador in its pristine state.

Controversy now surrounds Mr. Hubbard's initial trip and the two contemporary, but mutually unacknowledged journeys

Portrait of Mina Hubbard. Reprinted with permission from M.B. Hubbard's *A Woman's Way Through Unknown Labrador*, London: John Murray (1908)

of his widow and of his friend Dillon Wallace. Some believe Mrs. Hubbard's journey to have been motivated by a desire for revenge upon Wallace, whom she held responsible for her husband's death; others see her as a gloryseeker, determined to keep the Hubbard name in the spotlight. Whatever the case may be, her story provides a fascinating glimpse into Labrador history.

Mina Benson was born in April, 1870, the sixth of eight children. She grew up on a one hundred acre farm near Bewdley, Ontario, where she was taught respect for a strict code of Christian ethics and for the value of hard work. The Benson family highly valued a conscientious and philanthropic way of life, and Mina, who entered the nursing profession, was no exception. In the spring of 1899, this spirited, resolute woman completed her nursing degree. Her first patient was an aspiring young journalist named Leonidas Hubbard, who was suffering from typhoid fever. A lasting friendship developed, out of which grew a worshipful love and dedication. Married on 31 January 1901, they spent their five-month honeymoon in the Great Smoky Mountains. Soon afterwards, Leonidas's position as assistant editor of *Outing* magazine required numerous wilderness trips, and Mina sometimes accompanied him, thereby acquainting herself with backwoods travel.

After less than three years of marriage, she saw her husband off on his fateful expedition. She never saw him again; in January 1904, a telegram notified her of his death. The news dealt Mina a severe blow, for her already reverent love had become magnified by her husband's absence. In her diary, Mina dwells on the personality of her "lost Laddie," whom she saw as a hero willing to sacrifice himself for a valiant cause. She describes him as strong and brave, kind and generous, a man who fervently believed in the power of faith, hope, and charity—three words that resounded throughout his own diary. He was a man "who liked to test his own fitness. It meant risk, but he knew his own capabilities and believed in his own resourcefulness." In light of her husband's death, this statement takes on an unintended ironic quality, but Mina's praise was wholly sincere. She herself tried to emulate those virtues she perceived in Leonidas.

Unlike her husband, who was lured to Labrador by romantic notions of adventure, Mina Hubbard was drawn by a desire to clear her husband's name, which she believed had been seriously blemished by Wallace's account of the original Hubbard expedition. In fact, Mina had requested that Wallace write the narrative, and she was prepared to pay handsomely. With a ghost writer, Wallace completed the manuscript of *The Lure of the Labrador Wild* in January 1905. Meanwhile, Mrs. Hubbard found consolation in the letters Leonidas had written before his death, which "took from the hearts of those who loved him best the intolerable bitterness, because [they] told that he had not only dreamed his dream—he had attained his Vision." But this peaceful acceptance disappeared after reading Wallace's manuscript. Mina was appalled by the author's apparent lack of respect for her late husband's reputation. The book renewed her grief, which manifested itself as hostility toward Wallace. She believed that he was trying to reap acclaim by undermining Hubbard's leadership. According to Mina, Wallace depicted Hubbard as all too human, unashamedly revealing the mental and physical weaknesses that she chose to delete from her edition of the diaries. To Mina's thinking, Wallace's offence was great, and she set about to rectify the situation.

Her choice of Wallace as the scapegoat was no coincidence; it was born out of a deep-seated jealousy. Wallace and Hubbard had grown increasingly close on their disastrous journey, and an undeniable "bond of affection and love" developed between the two men. No doubt, both Wallace and Mrs. Hubbard wanted to share the last available part of the young explorer's life—Wallace to tell the story of their trip as he had promised Leonidas he would, Mina to pass on the message "that should inspire his fellow men to encounter the battle of life without flinching." Both Wallace and Mrs. Hubbard believed their own work to be sanctioned by God, and saw each other's as exploitative.

As her resentment grew, she began to suspect Wallace of more than simply taking advantage of her husband's memory. Her distrust centred on Wallace's failure to reach Hubbard's tent with leftover flour retrieved from a cache. Mina dwelt on this, blowing it out of proportion. (She quoted Leonidas as having once said that "real friends [are those] who may be trusted to a finish, who are not quitters.") She firmly denied Wallace's story that he did not see Hubbard's tent (or could not, since he was afflicted with smoke blindness) and that he suffered greatly from frostbite and exposure. George Elson,* guide of both Hubbard expeditions, recounted to Mrs. Hubbard what he had been told by Allen Goudie about Wallace's rescue. In her diary she quoted Elson:

> He had … a good fire and a good bed of boughs, and was quite able to walk. They also tracked him to within 200 yards of the tent. There was no trace of his having wandered about looking.…He simply turned around and went back.…Allen said he and Donald said to each other … that it just looked as if he did not want to get to the tent. He still had some of the flour.

Whatever the reasons for her trip to Labrador, she effectively accomplished what few women would have attempted. Her expedition was efficient, well-organized, and completed on schedule. She was genuinely surprised at how easily she slipped into the routine of wilderness travel. Despite various luxuries (including an air mattress, a feather pillow, and a hot-water bottle) and the fact that she left paddling to the men of her party, the trip was not without hardships. Moreover, she felt the burden of responsibility for the venture.

After the trip, Mina basked in the warmth of public attention. She wrote her story for *Harper's* and set off on a lecture tour in England. In 1908, she met and married Harold Ellis, a British member of parliament. Together they had three children, but were divorced in the 1920s. In 1936, at the age of sixty-six, she returned to Canada and the wilderness once more, accompanying her old friend George Elson on a canoe trip down the Moose River in northern Ontario. At the age of eighty-six, Mina Benson Hubbard died when, in a state of confusion, she walked into the path of a speeding train.

Further Readings

Berton, Pierre. 1978. *The Wild Frontier.* Toronto: McClelland and Stewart.

Cooke, Alan. 1960. "A Woman's Way." *The Beaver* (Summer). 40–45.

Hubbard, Mina Benson. 1908. *A Woman's Way Through Unknown Labrador.* London: John Murray.

Mauro, R.G. 1975. "Dillon Wallace of Labrador." *The Beaver* (Summer). 50–57.

Wallace, Dillon. 1905. *The Lure of the Labrador Wild.* New York: Fleming H. Revell.

Stephanie Hunt

Photograph of Mina Hubbard. Reprinted with permission from M.B. Hubbard's *A Woman's Way Through Unknown Labrador,* London: John Murray (1908)

GEORGE ELSON (ca. *1876–1954*)

Each of us, in our more reflective moments, has speculated on the way a small turn of fate has transformed one's life, making it impossible ever to return completely to the old ways. George Elson, who grew up around Rupert's House on James Bay, must often have felt that way about his adventures with the Hubbard Labrador expeditions in 1903 and 1905.

We know little of Elson's childhood. His father, Charles, worked for the Hudson's Bay Company and married Abigail Ottereyes, a Cree. He had two bothers, James and John, as well as a sister, Emily. From his family, George learned the ways of the woods and the trap line; he also received some education from the Anglican residential school in Moose Factory. In short, he grew up nurtured by both Indian and white cultures. In his midtwenties, having worked for a survey crew of the Grand Trunk Railroad, he found himself in Missanabie, Ontario, when fate struck. A journalist from New York by the name of Leonidas Hubbard, Jr.,* had written the Hudson's Bay Company post, seeking a reliable outdoorsman for an expedition to Labrador on behalf of *Outing* magazine. When two other candidates did not pan out, Elson was chosen.

Hubbard proved to be friendly and generous—full of an almost boyish enthusiasm. But he had never travelled the bush for an extended period, nor had his companion, Dillon Wallace, a New York attorney. Elson felt at home in the woods, but could not help wondering about the expedition's outfit. It included two rifles and pistols, but no shotgun, which would make winging birds much more difficult. Nor was Hubbard able to purchase a gill net in Labrador, as he had hoped.

On 15 July 1903, the trio set off down Grand Lake from North West River post, seeking to ascend the Naskaupi River into central Labrador and witness the autumn caribou hunt of the Naskapi Indians(Innu). Anxious to make up for lost time,

George Elson in Labrador, 1905. From *A Woman's Way Through Unknown Labrador* (1908). Courtesy of James West Davidson

Hubbard missed the Naskaupi River and instead headed up the tiny Susan Brook, which soon dwindled into a rock-filled obstacle course.

As conditions worsened, Elson saw the threat of starvation looming. However, he worked on uncomplainingly, for Hubbard wanted so much to bring back a "bully story" for *Outing*. By 15 September, the expedition was halfway across Labrador, nearly out of food, and pinned down by storms. Elson's indirect, but diplomatic tales of Indian starvation made clear to Hubbard what he must have already sensed deep down: they must turn back if they hoped to escape with their lives.

For the next month the men retraced their steps in raw weather. Elson, with remarkable skill, bagged an occasional goose, but with no shotgun and no gill net, the expedition's plight was desperate. Finally Hubbard collapsed, unable to proceed. Making him as comfortable as possible in a tent, Wallace and Elson continued down Susan Brook on 18 October; three days later they parted in the midst of the season's first blizzard, Wallace to return to Hubbard with some moldy flour they had retrieved (left behind earlier in the expedition), Elson to go for help on Grand Lake.

For five days, he stumbled through snowdrifts, his trousers in tatters, his feet wrapped in scraps of blanket. But upon reaching Grand Lake, another river blocked the way. Somehow, Elson cobbled together a driftwood raft and pushed off. As his own account noted, "the strong current, and the tide and the ice

Leonidas Hubbard, Jr., about to embark. From Dillon Wallace's *The Lure of the Labrador Wild* (1905)

overcame me, and took me out to the lake, then the wind caught me and carried me....got down on my knees and tried to keep the pieces [of the raft] together, and the sea would just cover me. For about two hours I stayed on the raft, and sure it was my finish." The current washed him onto an island, and he doggedly built a new raft, ignoring the icy weather. "Oh! but I was proud of that raft, and talking to myself all the time, and telling myself what a fine raft it was, and I was so proud of my raft. I got across safe and without much trouble at all." Oh, no trouble at all! Not for the likes of Elson, anyway.

Reaching a trapper's cabin, he sped rescuers upstream, but Hubbard was beyond help. He had died the day of the parting. Wallace was only barely alive—a hardly recognizable skeleton. Over that winter, he and Elson recovered at North West River post and returned home in May 1904.

There the story might have ended, but for a grieving widow. Devastated by the loss of her husband, Mina Benson Hubbard* turned from grief to anger. Why had her husband perished, when the other men had not? She summoned Elson, in December 1904, to answer questions. As a mixed-blood, he had already worried what whites might think if he alone had survived; now his worst nightmares were fulfilled. Mina Hubbard, however, absolved him of blame; it was Dillon Wallace she felt had failed her husband. When Wallace, still loyal to the memory of his friend, announced he was returning to Labrador to finish Hubbard's work, Mina secretly organized an expedition of her own.

Elson refused to blame Wallace, yet he was attracted by Mina Hubbard's determination and charm. His primary loyalty lay with Hubbard, he felt, and when Hubbard's widow asked him to take charge of her expedition, he agreed, recruiting two other friends from James Bay. Thus, when Wallace headed north in June 1905, he was surprised to find a female rival determined to upstage him—with an able woodsman in charge of the task.

Under Elson's leadership, Mina Hubbard completed her expedition nearly flawlessly. The party visited the Naskapi

Dillon Wallace and George Elson (right) talking at Susan Brook, 1903. From *Great Heart: The History of a Labrador Adventure*. Courtesy of James West Davidson

(Innu), witnessed the caribou migration, and arrived at George River post in Ungava Bay on 29 August. Wallace, who became lost pioneering an alternate route, did not arrive until mid-October. But the most poignant aspect of the tale was that Elson, struck by Mina Hubbard's kindness and spirited humour, seems to have fallen in love. He knew that, because he was of mixed-blood, the barriers of caste made marriage unlikely, but he could not help confessing to his journal, indirectly, that he hoped to find "a white girl that would marry me and especially if she was well learnt." Mina Hubbard seems to have remained oblivious almost to the end, and Elson, who had rescued the first expedition from total disaster and masterfully led the second, returned home with his bittersweet triumph.

In 1906, he guided Mr. and Mrs. Stephen Tasker on a canoe trip up the Clearwater River in Quebec and on to Ungava Bay. He married Ellen Miller in 1912, and worked for many years for the Revillon Frères fur company and, after 1936, again for the Hudson's Bay Company. He settled at Moose Factory. Only once, in 1936, did he see Mina Hubbard again, when she visited him in her sixties. But the events of 1903 and 1905 remained indelibly in George Elson's mind. And he secured a place in the literature of exploration as the pivotal figure in both Hubbard expeditions.

Mina Benson Hubbard on her 1905 Labrador expedition. From *A Woman's Way Through Unknown Labrador* (1908). Courtesy of James West Davidson

Further Readings

Davidson, James West, and John Rugge. 1988. *Great Heart: The History of a Labrador Adventure*. New York: Viking/Penguin.

Hubbard, Mina Benson. 1908. *A Woman's Way Through Unknown Labrador*. Toronto: William Briggs. (Contains Elson's account of the 1903 expedition).

Klein, Clayton 1988. *Challenge the Wilderness: The Legend of George Elson*. Fowlerville, Mich: Wilderness Adventure Books. (A semifictional account including some valuable biographical facts that are unfortunately indistinguishable from the frequent fictional constructions).

Wallace, Dillon. 1905. *The Lure of the Labrador Wild*. New York: Fleming H. Revell.

_____. 1907. *The Long Labrador Trail*. New York: Outing Publishing.

James West Davidson and John Rugge

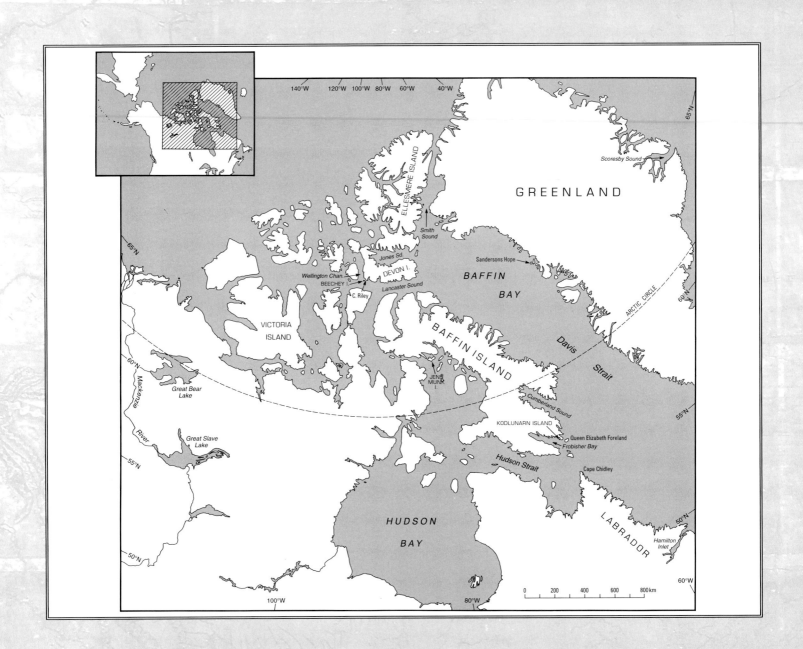

UNIT
❦ 16 ❧

Martin Frobisher, John Davis, William Scoresby, Sr.,
William Scoresby, Jr., Edward Augustus Inglefield

As this book began, it now closes with an expansive map of the central and eastern Arctic. This final unit embraces the early sixteenth century probing into the North American Arctic by Renaissance mariners Frobisher and Davis, and moves forward up to Inglefield's lessor role in the search for John Franklin. It includes, as well, the contributions of two remarkable whaling men, one of whom inadvertently stimulated decades of British activity in the Arctic during the nineteenth century. It is fitting that this final unit includes sketches of men engaged in both the search for the Northwest Passage and for the missing Franklin expedition, because both events dominated how much of the Arctic came to be explored and, thus, known to us.

Martin Frobisher
(ca. 1540–1594)

The Portuguese navigators, who are believed to have been the first to sail up the Labrador coast and to penetrate into Hudson Strait in the early sixteenth century, mistrusted their competitors to such an extent that they hid their operations behind a veil of secrecy that shrouds them to this day. In consequence, the Englishman Martin Frobisher is the first accredited pioneer of northern Canadian exploration. He made known to the world the dangers of navigation in the icy seas, the forbidding terrain of Baffin Island, the type of its inhabitants, and the existence of Hudson Strait. Like the Portuguese, he dimmed his credit by failing to fix his discoveries with precision, by diverting his search—perhaps contrary to his own choice—from exploration to a futile gold hunt, and by failing to emphasize the significance of Hudson Strait. Although his successors in the field—John Davis,* Henry Hudson, and William Baffin—have taken legitimate possession of the honours he neglected, Frobisher's courage and enterprise are indisputable; his original achievements were all in Canadian waters; and he may justly be recognized as the first Anglo-Canadian.

Frobisher was born around 1540, in Yorkshire, England, of Welsh descent. As far as the record discloses, he was engaged in the African trade in defiance of a theoretical Portuguese monopoly. The Privy Council of Queen Elizabeth once called him to question over an alleged act of piracy, but such charges were not always pressed unless the victim was a fellow-coun-

Portrait of Martin Frobisher. Courtesy of the National Maritime Museum London

tryman. He never became a skilled navigator, but was an experienced practical officer—masterful, resolute, and bold.

At that time, Spain and Portugal laid claim to all the Americas and barred foreigners from the lucrative Spice Islands trade by prohibitions, which, though not always enforceable, added to the risks of the traffic. In 1576, Frobisher sailed with three ships, backed by London merchants, to find an unpoliced route to the East—the Northwest Passage.

Off Greenland they encountered storm and ice. One ship foundered with all hands; another stole away home. Frobisher held right on, assuring his frightened crew that "the sea must needs at last have an ending." Approaching Baffin Island, he passed to the north of Queen Elizabeth's Foreland and sailed more than a hundred miles up Frobisher Bay, which he took to be a strait with America on the left and Asia on the right. He returned to England with samples of ore that were supposed to contain gold. He made another voyage in 1577, and returned with a quantity of ore on which analysts gave a noncommittal but optimistic report.

The precious metals found by the Spanish in Mexico and Peru encouraged the hope that such deposits could be found in the Far North. In 1578, Frobisher was sent out with an armada of fifteen sail, not for exploration but for a gold hunt. The fleet was detained off the Baffin Island shore for two weeks by ice and fog, and Frobisher himself sailed many miles up the north shore of Hudson Strait; he afterwards claimed that he could have won through to the Pacific, had he not been detained by his responsibility as captain of the fleet.

The fleet meantime had suffered much discomfort and danger, bewildered in "such a fog and hideous mist" and "so troubled and tossed about in the ice that it would make the strongest heart to relent." The convoy was kept together by the continual sounding of drums and trumpets. When the bark *Dionyse* foundered, the rest manfully took to their boats and rescued her entire crew before the vessel sank. They saved other ships by cutting up their cables and hanging out the fragments to deaden the impact of the ice. Eventually they struggled past Queen Elizabeth's Foreland and anchored in Frobisher Bay with snow a foot deep on their decks.

While the crews were busy in gathering and loading ore, Frobisher and his officers made excursions inland in search of fresh deposits. They failed to establish friendly relations with the local Inuit.

The plan of leaving a party to winter in "Meta Incognita" was abandoned, but a house built of stone and lime was set up on Kodlunarn Island to test the durability of those materials in an arctic climate. On the way home the fleet was scattered by an "outrageous tempest," but all reached port safely. Considering that the voyage had been undertaken in the irresponsible hurry and enthusiasm of a gold rush, this fortunate deliverance may be credited to the Elizabethan seamen, and not least to the "general" who commanded them.

In consequence of the quickly proved worthlessness of the ore, Frobisher fell into disfavour with the government and the financiers—unjustly, for the gold hunt appears not to have originated with him. He reappeared as senior officer in the war against Spain, went on a marauding expedition under Sir Francis Drake to the West Indies, and held a command in the fight against the Spanish Armada. He won his knighthood in this operation—and, characteristically, quarrelled with and vehemently abused his superior, Vice-Admiral Drake. He remained in the naval service and was mortally wounded in a petty operation against the Spaniards on the French coast.

Frobisher seems to have been a gentleman by birth, but was poorly educated, rough in manner, often violent, and an indifferent navigator. He did not "fix" his discoveries. For a long time, it was supposed that Frobisher Bay was on the east shore of Greenland. John Davis visited the bay without recognizing its identity. The sailor-historian Luke Foxe credits Davis, not Frobisher, with "lighting Hudson into his Strait." The identity of Frobisher Bay was only fully confirmed three hundred years later, when the American Charles Francis Hall* found the ruins of Frobisher's house on Kodlunarn Island, and found that the Inuit had preserved an accurate oral record of the voyages made by Frobisher centuries before.

Though not a scientific geographer, Martin Frobisher was the pioneer of the Canadian Arctic. His ignorance permitted him to defy dangers from which better-informed ship masters might have shrunk. Others followed where he had blazed the trail. He pierced the barrier of the realms of frost and opened a breach for more skilled navigators to exploit.

Further Readings

Collinson, Richard, ed. [1867] n.d. *The Three Voyages of Martin Frobisher in Search of a Passage to Cathaia and India by the North-West, A.D. 1576-8.* Reprint. New York: Burt Franklin.

Stefansson, Vilhjalmur, ed. 1938. *The Three Voyages of Martin Frobisher. From the Original 1578 Text by George Best. Together with Numerous Other Versions, Additions, Etc.* London: Argonaut Press.

L.H. Neatby

JOHN DAVIS (ca. 1550–1605)

John Davis, "The Navigator," is deservedly the favourite of historian and biographer among the early English sailors in Arctic waters. He was dedicated to his work and lacked the greed for money and fame that marked many of his contemporaries; he was of kindly disposition and exerted himself to win the confidence of pilfering Greenland Inuit. Unlike Martin Frobisher,* he was a scientific seaman and, along with Jacques Cartier, may be said to have rough-charted the eastern Canadian seaboard from the Gulf of St. Lawrence to Cumberland Sound on Baffin Island. He "fixed" the entrance to Hudson Strait, discovered Cumberland Sound—later the resort of whalers—and sailed far up Baffin Bay. His career had little drama, but he was fortunate in having aboard John James, the nephew of his merchant-patron William Sanderson, who is vivid in both his narrative and descriptive passages.

Born in Devon, England, about 1550, John Davis associated in his youth with sons of the local gentry, which may account for his good education and proficiency in mathematics. He took to the sea early and was a skilled navigator when, in 1585, he was authorized by Queen Elizabeth to search for "the Northwest Passage to China" with the backing of the Queen's minister, Sir Francis Walsingham, and the merchant William Sanderson. He ran up the west Greenland shore, where he showed his good nature in trying to win the friendship of the local Inuit in spite of their differing notions about private ownership. Crossing the strait that bears his name, he went forty leagues (120 miles) up Cumberland Sound, hoping that it might be the desired passage, but was driven home by foul weather. He complained of the mosquitos of Baffin Island: "They did bite grievously."

In 1586, he entered his strait with two ships, encountering weather so cold that his men grew rebellious. He sent the

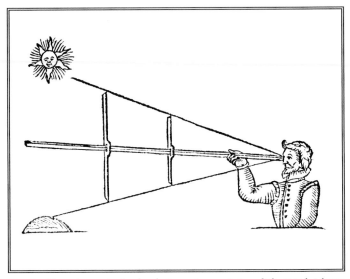

Drawing illustrating navigational techniques. By permission of The British Library. First published in *The Voyages and Works of John Davis, the Navigator, including The Seamens Secrets* (1607), ed. Albert Hastings Markham, for the Hakluyt Society, London (1880)

more mutinous home on one ship, and with the other, *Moonshine,* he coasted down the Baffin and Labrador shores. Owing perhaps to fog, he missed the entrance to Hudson Strait, but far to the south found a gap in the mountainous coast: "A mighty great sea between two lands" (Hamilton Inlet?). Hostile natives attacked his landing party and killed two men. Then, a furious gale nearly tore the ship from her anchorage and threatened to cast her ashore, a prey to the "Canibals." Davis lost no time in escaping from this dangerous coast. He had come south to 54°30′N, within two hundred miles of Belle Isle Strait.

On his third voyage (1587), his two larger ships deserted him, leaving him in the 20-ton *Helen*. He made his highest north in Baffin Bay at 72°12′ N and saw ahead "a great sea, free, large, and very salty and of unsearchable depth." A towering cliff on the Greenland shore he named Sandersons Hope. Being unprovided for a longer voyage, he put about and pried again into Cumberland Sound. He sighted Frobisher Bay without identifying it, owing no doubt to its discoverer's inaccurate "fix." Later in the day, he became aware that he was passing "the entrance or mouth of a great inlet or passage, being 20 leagues broad and situated between 62 & 63 degrees." As he neared Cape Chidley, the flood tide of the Atlantic was moving in, and he "saw the sea falling down into the gulf with a mighty overfall, and the roaring, and with diverse circular motions like whirlpools, in such sort as forcible streams pass through the arches of bridges." He had rediscovered—and "fixed"—the mouth of Hudson Strait.

For the next four years, Davis's services were claimed by the war against Spain. In the interval, interest in the Arctic faded. Walsingham was no more, "and when his honour died the voyage was friendless, and men's minds alienated from adventuring therein." Davis joined the buccaneer Thomas Cavendish in a plan for harrying Spanish shipping on the west coast of South America, after which the explorer intended to attempt the Northwest Passage in reverse. The expedition broke down: Davis alone pushed up the coast of Chile until forced to turn back by failing supplies. His ship was almost driven ashore by a gale, and his mate, John Pery, cried that they could not clear the cape ahead. Davis replied, "You see that there is no remedy; either we must double it, or before noon we must die; therefore loose your sails, and let

us put it to God's mercy." The faith of the dauntless discoverer was justified; a lull in the wind and Pery's and Davis's skilful handling permitted them to weather the point. "I conclude," wrote the captain's friend, John James, "that the world hath not any so skilful pilots for that place as they are." The stubborn captain had exhausted his supplies in the dash up the Chilean coast; he put his men ashore on the mudflats of Patagonia, where they killed barely enough wildfowl to sustain them for the homeward voyage.

The aging and impoverished Davis now betook himself to the theory of navigation and published a "Treatise" in which he restated, with his own additions, the arguments for the existence of a Northwest Passage. But it was granted to few adventurers of that epoch to die in their beds. The author was invited to act as chief pilot, first for the Dutch and then for the English East India fleet. On his third voyage to the Far East, he was killed in an affray with Japanese pirates near the site of the present city of Singapore. In his death, he symbolized the vast range of Elizabethan maritime enterprise. His bones rest among the Spice Islands, as far as the extent of the globe permits from the rocky shores of Greenland and Labrador, which it had been his life's work to trace.

John Davis was not typical of the seagoing adventurers of his age, whether Spanish or English. He indulged in none of their quarrelsome rivalries, and had none of their ravenous greed for wealth and glory. His writing is without the bombast to which some of his contemporaries were addicted. He made no startling original discovery: his work was to extend, clarify, and give shape to Frobisher's casual and incoherent observations. The well-informed Luke Foxe credits Davis, not Frobisher, with "lighting Hudson into his strait." His survey of the Labrador from the north nearly overlapped that of Jacques

Cartier from the south; in truth, the two of them—oddly, both probably of Welsh descent— had roughly laid down the Canadian seaboard from the Arctic Circle to Gaspé Peninsula and furnished a recognizable outline of our eastern shore.

Further Readings

Hakluyt, Richard. [1589] 1965. *The Principal Navigations Voiages & Discoveries of the English Nation.* Facsimile reprint. Cambridge: The Hakluyt Society.

Markham, Clements. 1889. *A Life of John Davis, the Navigator.* London: George Philip and Son.

Neatby, L.H. 1958. *In Quest of the North-West Passage.* Toronto: Longmans, Green.

L.H. Neatby

WILLIAM SCORESBY, SR.
(1760–1829)

Not least among William Scoresby, Sr.'s achievements was being the father of William Scoresby, Jr.* But one is led to wonder what he himself might have accomplished had he been given the opportunities he later gave to his son.

He was of an original and inventive turn of mind, and the "crow's nest," which provided shelter to the mast-head lookout, was his creation. Before this semibarrel was hoisted aloft, with shelf and seat and windproof hood, the lookout man—often the captain him-self— had to be content with an inad-equate piece of canvas for shelter. In storm-tossed, ice-capped waters, the man on the mast sometimes had spells of eight hours and more perched aloft, and he would have good reason to thank Scoresby for his invention. Other of Scoresby's inventions, such as the ice drill, rendered arctic navigation and exploration a far more certain task than it had been previously.

Born near Whitby, England, into a farming community, he ended his formal schooling around the age of nine. Being dissatisfied with an agricultural life, he determined to go to sea, and set himself the task of learning navigation and astronomy. His early voyages as an apprentice to the captain of a ship trading from Whitby to the Baltic took him to places as far away as St. Petersburg. He was captured and made a prisoner in Spain until he managed to escape. After a brief return to farming, and marriage to Lady Mary Smith ("Lady

Portrait of William Scoresby, Sr. Courtesy of Caedman of Whitby Press

Mary" was her Christian name, not a title), he joined a Whitby whaling vessel at the age of twenty-five, and from then on he found ample opportunity for developing his skills.

Scoresby was a powerfully built man, and one of keen intelligence. Studying each job to be done, he soon worked out the quickest and most effi-cient way of doing it. One example involved the flensing (stripping the blubber) of whales. Not long after he had been given command of a whaler, he challenged four men busy at the job, saying he could do it single-handedly in half the time. They were crestfallen when he accomplished it in one-third of the time. In ice navigation, he pos-sessed that extra sense also attributed to Capt. James Cook. It seemed as if he knew what was over the horizon, and he safely led every ship under his command into calm waters heavily populated with whales. In the Greenland whale fish-ery, his reputation was legendary.

But hunting whales was not the sum total of his sailing life. He had an inquiring mind and was early led to report on arctic winds, currents, and ice conditions to Joseph Banks, who voyaged with Capt. Cook. In 1806 he forced his ship, the *Resolution,* through the Spitsbergen ice barrier into open water in the Far North. They reached an estimated 81°30' N latitude, and could have sailed even farther had it not been for the commercial design of the voyage and the scarcity of whales. Even so, the Scoresbys (his son was with him as mate) held the record for sailing farthest north for nearly a century, if one discounts sled journeys.

Those who did not know Captain Scoresby well thought him eccentric, but his son tells us it was actually his actions, based on reflective, philosophical consideration, that made him appear so. Take, for example, his method of freeing the ship from ice-bound conditions by "sallying." He directed the whole crew to run alternately from side to side of the ship, causing it to rock gently and thus loosen its position, enabling it to be eventually freed. He was a fearless man and did not hesitate to risk even his young son's life by sending him over very thin ice, which would not bear a grown man's weight, to harpoon a whale. According to legend, he could subdue a polar bear by merely looking it in the eye. This characteristic bit of folklore derived from the fact that Scoresby had brought the bear to Whitby as a cub, and in later years, he would amuse friends and spectators by putting his hand between the bars and stroking the fully grown animal.

In these conservation-conscious days, it might be thought out of place to say that Captain Scoresby brought more whales back to Whitby than did any other skipper. Yet it is well to remember that the entire British Empire was greatly dependent on whale products for many things, not the least of which was lighting, because gas, like Michael Faraday, was still in its infancy.

The achievements of William Scoresby, Sr. constitute an important chapter in the history of the Arctic. Although lacking formal education and sophistication, he was an original and forceful character who saw in the Arctic opportunities for exploration and investigation far exceeding the commercial endeavours that were his main object. His son brilliantly continued and greatly enlarged his father's early ambition. That the father's example and training won his son for arctic science cannot be doubted.

Further Readings

Scoresby, William, Sr. [ca. 1806] 1981. *The 1806 Log Book of William Scoresby*. Facsimile reprint. Whitby: Caedmon of Whitby Press.

_____. 1917. *Seven Log-Books Concerning the Arctic Voyages of Captain William Scoresby, Senior*. Facsimile reprint. New York: The Explorers Club.

Scoresby, William, Jr. [1851] 1978. *My Father*. Reprint. Whitby: Caedmon of Whitby Press.

Tom and Cordelia Stamp

WILLIAM SCORESBY, JR.
(1789–1857)

To the arctic enthusiast the name of William Scoresby, F.R.S., (Fellow of the Royal Society) needs no introduction. The author of *An Account of the Arctic Regions* (1820), this whaling captain, who turned both scientist and clergyman, is closely associated with pioneer arctic research. Indeed, the activities and achievements of this remarkable man place him in a class apart from almost all who have journeyed and researched in polar regions.

Carrying on with great success the most demanding and arduous of all maritime activities—the hunting and capture of whales—he yet collected, over a period of some fifteen years, data on sea currents and temperatures, ice formation and movement, wind directions and velocities, magnetic variations, marine organisms, biology of whales, structure of snow crystals and much besides, gathering all this original work together in his two-volume *An Account of the Arctic Regions and Northern Whale Fishery*. The publication of this work in 1820, after four years of writing, marks the beginning of the scientific study of the polar regions. Scoresby's next book, *Journal of a Voyage to the Northern Whale Fishery and Discoveries on the East Coast of Greenland* (1823), was a significant addition to the literature of the sea in its accounts of whaling adventures and the dangers and thrills of the chase, which compares favourably with those of the great maritime novelists.

William Scoresby, Jr., at age thirty. Courtesy of Caedmon of Whitby Press

Scoresby was esteemed by the leading men of his time—Alexander von Humboldt, Leopold von Buch, and Sir Joseph Banks (fellow-voyager with Capt. James Cook, yet another Whitby man of the sea), to name but a few. Even men whose interests lay outside the main field of his endeavour were aware of the originality of his arctic work. Writing to Scoresby on his return from the notable 1822 voyage, Humphry Davy showed a keen appreciation and full understanding of the nature of Scoresby's exploratory and descriptive conquests in the North:

I congratulate you on your safe return and on the success that has attended your researches. Your spirit of enterprise and your devotion to the cause of science amidst pursuits of so different a character entitle you to the warmest thanks of all those who are interested in the progress of natural knowledge and do honour to your country.

(H. Davy, October 1822)

The results of Scoresby's scientific work in the Arctic have long been part of the fabric of our polar knowledge, and in his published works he left us first-hand accounts of his voyages in Greenland waters.

In some respects, Scoresby's most important voyage was that of 1822. The uncharted coastline of east

Greenland became clear of ice around 1820, and, in 1822, Scoresby, in the midst of an arduous whaling voyage, sailed along some four hundred miles of this unknown shore, charting it, and naming points as he went in honour of scientific and other friends, chief of which was Scoresby Sound, named for his father William Scoresby, Sr.* Almost all his place names survive today (they have been listed by A.K. Higgins of the Greenland Geological Survey).

But in other respects, his 1817 voyage to the Arctic had far greater geographical impact. He found a vast two thousands square leagues (approximately eighteen thousand square miles) of Greenland Sea free from ice in the winter of 1817–18. Joseph Banks heard of this unusual discovery and wrote to Scoresby; Banks then sought out the Admiralty, and the next year, Britain began a vigorous phase of arctic exploration that lasted from John Ross's* and David Buchan's 1818 searches for the Northwest Passage, through John Franklin's* mid-1840s disappearance, and up to Francis Leopold McClintock's* and William Robert Hobson's* 1859 discovery that HMS *Erebus* and *Terror* had been abandoned. Because Scoresby reported those ice-free conditions in 1817, a chain of events transpired over the next forty-one years that led to the charting of immense regions of the North American Arctic.

Born at Cropton, near Whitby, on the northeast coast of Britain, on 5 October 1789, the young William had his first taste of an arctic whaling voyage at the early age of ten, when he stowed away on his father's ship. Later, winters spent at Edinburgh University sharpened the acute observational and descriptive powers manifested during his summer whaling voyages; these talents ultimately led to the publication of Scoresby's many works.

He left active sea life in his thirties and entered the Church, where, despite a busy life, he continued to work for science with his pen, sending many papers to the Royal Society and the British Association, of which he was a founding member. Scoresby visited America and Canada twice in the 1840s, lecturing to support his many social endeavours in the industrial parish where he pioneered five schools for the illiterate mill-working children of Bradford.

He married three times, but none of his children survived him. He was a gentle man and greatly loved by all who knew him. He remained studious to the end of his life, and all his papers, log books, magnetic instruments, and botanical and geological specimens were left to the Whitby Museum, in whose care they remain.

William Scoresby's life was crowned by his final act of undertaking a voyage to Australia in order to verify his theories of compass behaviour in iron ships; the simple outcome of this was the conclusion that the only reliable place for the ship's compass was aloft. He died at Torquay in 1857.

While researching his records in preparation for his biography, our respect and admiration for William Scoresby, Jr. grew apace, and we marvelled at what manner of man he was who could combine such activities with rigorous descriptive exactitude in the search for new knowledge. Well might Davy have commented on such a phenomenon.

Further Readings

Ross, M.J. 1995. *Polar Pioneers: John Ross and James Clark Ross.* London and Montreal: University College London Press and McGill-Queen's Press.

Scoresby, William, Jr. [1820] 1969. *An Account of the Arctic Regions with a History and Description of the Northern Whale-Fishery.* Reprint. New York: Augustus M. Kelley.

_____. [1815 and 1828] 1980. *The Polar Ice and The North Pole.* Reprint. Whitby: Caedmon of Whitby Press.

_____. [1823] 1980. *Journal of a Voyage to the Northern Whale-Fishery.* Reprint. Whitby: Caedmon of Whitby Press.

Stamp, Tom and Cordelia. 1976. *William Scoresby, Arctic Scientist.* Whitby: Caedmon of Whitby Press.

_____. 1982. *Greenland Voyager.* Whitby: Caedmon of Whitby Press.

Tom and Cordelia Stamp

EDWARD AUGUSTUS INGLEFIELD
(1820–1894)

Edward Inglefield was one of the large number of Royal Naval officers whose careers were advanced by participation in the search for John Franklin*. This was a highly satisfactory time for such men, as it provided ample opportunity for employment in a rigorous environment and in a cause in which there was a gratifyingly high level of public interest. The North was certainly much healthier than the other contemporary area in which naval initiative could be displayed—off the African coast in the suppression of the slave trade. In the Franklin search, Inglefield did not, however, achieve the highest distinction. He visited the Arctic three times, but his second and third voyages were simply means of communication with Edward Belcher's* 1852–54 expedition. His first voyage, on the other hand, did have one solid achievement that greatly redounded to Inglefield's credit, and this is sufficient reason for devoting attention to him.

Born into a naval family and educated at the Royal Naval College in Portsmouth, Edward Augustus Inglefield entered the service in 1832 and immediately saw action in the eastern Mediterranean in operations off the Lebanese coast. Inglefield then served in HMS *Samarang*, engaged in surveying various coasts of the Pacific Ocean, and he was on board that vessel when she sank. After further service in Latin American waters, he was promoted commander on 18 November 1845.

Portrait of Edward Augustus Inglefield, by Stephen Pearce. By courtesy of the National Portrait Gallery, London, U.K. No. 1223

When the Franklin search got under way, Inglefield, frustrated in his efforts to obtain a naval appointment, volunteered his services to Lady Jane Franklin.* He was, in 1852, appointed to the command of *Isabel,* a small vessel of 149 tons that had an auxiliary steam engine. Inglefield was one of Lady Franklin's happier appointments. The expedition differed from the other expeditions in which she was active in that Inglefield was, himself, to "provide a crew, and what other fitments the vessel needed" for the voyage, on return from which the ship was to become his own property.

The voyage, which lasted from 10 July to 4 November 1852, was uneventful. Inglefield had chosen a good, competent crew, and, in this respect, an interesting comparison is afforded with the *Prince Albert* expedition of 1850 in which the commander, Charles Codrington Forsyth,* had no hand in personnel selection and had great difficulties with his men. The plan was to search Jones Sound and the west coast of Baffin Bay for traces of Franklin. The west coast of Greenland was examined on the outward voyage, and new discoveries of geographical features were made. Smith Sound was penetrated to a latitude of 78°28′21″N, "therefore placing the Isabel about 140 miles further than had been reached by any previous navigator, of whom we have any records." Inglefield was determined to land in order to erect a notice "that the British Flag had been first carried into this unknown sea," and, indeed, he believed that he had entered the open polar basin so much sought by previous mariners. Worsening weather prevented him from landing, and following a narrow escape from the lee pack, he headed southward. Jones Sound was investigated as far as 84°10′W, and then a visit was made to Beechey Island in Lancaster Sound, where communication was established with HMS *North Star*, the depot ship of Belcher's expedition. Inglefield "pressed upon Captain W.J.S. Pullen* the acceptance of all my surplus stores and provisions," but this offer was declined as Pullen was "prohibited by his commanding officer from in any way to interfere with a private vessel." Despite this, Inglefield made various presents to the officers' mess, including "preserved beef and ox cheek," and after exchanging letters, *Isabel* set sail. The eastern coast of Baffin Island was then examined, before the approach of winter forced the expedition home.

Inglefield's book *A Summer Search for Sir John Franklin; with a Peep into the Polar Basin*, published in 1853, is one of the more interesting of the genre. Inglefield's account itself only covers 128 pages. The remainder of the short volume comprises observations on the natural history of the area visited, notably 48 turgid pages on the physical geography by Dr. P.C. Sutherland, surgeon to the expedition. The portion by Inglefield is clearly written and provides a matter-of-fact account of the expedition's activities. He felt, however, the need to instruct as well as to inform his readers, especially about such arcane matters as the details of *Isabel's* steam machinery. One wonders quite how much, if anything, was made of such passages in Victorian drawing rooms. The illustrations, which were by Inglefield, are more competently executed than are those of some contemporary works.

Inglefield was well received at home and was awarded honours and medals. In the following year, the Admiralty appointed him to command a voyage by HMS *Phoenix* and *Breadalbane* to take supplies to Belcher's*expedition. Also participating in the voyage was Joseph René Bellot, the French officer who had obtained fame during the *Prince Albert* expedition of 1851–52. From the tone of the instructions issued to Inglefield, one gets the impression that the Admiralty was tiring of the Franklin search, particularly of its cost. Inglefield was told in no uncertain terms that the voyage had a transport function only. His "most essential duty" was to clear the stores, after which he was, "without a moment's delay," to return. His "most especial duty" was to carry out these orders, and "it is our most positive direction that you are on no account whatever" to run the risk of the ships' being detained. The vessels arrived at Beechey Island on 8 August 1853, and Inglefield was immediately made aware of the difficult situation of the Belcher expedition, arising from the character of its commander. He received orders from Belcher, his superior officer, that directly contradicted those he had had from the Admiralty. After consulting Captain Pullen of *North Star*, he prudently decided to comply with the latter. Two unfortunate incidents occurred during this voyage: *Breadalbane* was lost off Cape Riley on 21 August, and Bellot, while carrying despatches up Wellington Channel, was drowned.

Inglefield returned to England with the news that the crew of HMS *Investigator,* which had attempted to penetrate the Canadian Arctic archipelago from the west, was safe and that the Northwest Passage had finally been discovered. He transported home Samuel Gurney Cresswell,* of the *Investigator,* and Cresswell thus became the first person to travel through the Passage from end to end.

Despite the loss of *Breadalbane*, Inglefield received the plaudits of the Admiralty and was appointed to conduct a similar voyage the following year. This time his instructions were much less peremptory: "You are now so well acquainted with the navigation of those seas, and have so successfully performed your previous service, that we do not consider it necessary to bind you with any specific directions." Upon arrival at Beechey Island, Inglefield discovered that all four of Belcher's ships and *Investigator* had been abandoned and that their crews were assembled on board *North Star*, the only remaining vessel. Most of the men were transported home in Inglefield's ships.

This ended Edward Augustus Inglefield's arctic service. He participated in the Crimean War and was present at the fall of Sebastapol and the blockade of Odessa. His later career was one of great success. He held such varied appointments as naval attaché, Washington, and as admiral superintendent of the Malta dockyard. One of his main interests was the mechanical development of the Navy. He invented a new anchor and hydraulic steering apparatus and published several technical works. He retired in March 1885 in enjoyment of a flag officer's good service pension, and died in September 1894.

Further Readings

Inglefield, Edward Augustus. 1853. *A Summer Search for Sir John Franklin: with a Peep into the Polar Basin.* London: Thomas Harrison.

Ian R. Stone

"Isabel Entering the Polar Sea Through Smith's Sound, Midnight." From E.A. Inglefield's *A Summer Search for Sir John Franklin*

Index

About the Editor

Richard Davis grew up in the American Midwest, and attended Indiana University before coming to Canada. Prior to moving to Calgary in the late 1970s, he alternated between an academic life in Fredericton, where he completed graduate studies at the University of New Brunswick, and a more Thoreauvian life on Vancouver Island. He has taught Canadian literature at the University of Calgary since 1979. His special interests include the writing of early explorers and travellers in Canada, and he has published John Franklin's journals and correspondence from his first land expedition to northern North America, as well as a collection of essays about early responses to Canada before Confederation. He is currently at work on documents arising from Franklin's second land expedition. His scholarly interests also include first contacts between Europeans and aboriginal peoples, as well as nineteenth-century cultural attitudes toward Australia.

He and his wife, Michele Phillips, enjoy their own travels, as well as those of others. They have spent many enjoyable days paddling or portaging their sixteen-foot Chestnut canoe, although they are more likely to be found these days cycling in Ireland or on British Columbia's Gulf Islands.